Christian Home Library

Youth's Instructor Part 2

Original Edition

Ellen G. White

Copyright ©2023

LS COMPANY

ISBN: 978-1-0882-5001-3

October 5, 1899—"We Have Seen His Star"—Part 1 187

October 12, 1899—"We Have Seen His Star"—Part 2 190

October 19, 1899—"We Have Seen His Star"—Part 3 192

October 26, 1899—Against Principalities and Powers 195

November 2, 1899—The Joy that is Set Before Us—Part 1 198

November 9, 1899—The Joy That is Set Before Us—Part 2 200

November 23, 1899—The Parable of the Talents—Part 1 202

November 30, 1899—The Parable of the Talents—Part 2 205

December 7, 1899—"Lord, Teach Us to Pray" 208

December 21, 1899—"Tempted in All Points Like as We Are"—Part 1 211

December 28, 1899—"Tempted in All Points Like As We Are"—Part 2 214

January 4, 1900—"Tempted in All Points Like as We Are"—Part 3 217

January 11, 1900—"Tempted in All Points Like as We Are"—Part 4 218

February 1, 1900—Christ Before Pilate 220

February 8, 1900—Christ Before Herod 223

February 15, 1900—"If Any of You Lack Wisdom, Let Him Ask of God" 225

February 22, 1900—The Saviour's Mission 228

March 1, 1900—Justification by Faith—Part 1 230

March 8, 1900—Justification by Faith—Part 2 232

March 22, 1900—Knowing God 234

March 29, 1900—John the Beloved—Part 1 236

April 20, 1899—The Resurrection of Lazarus—Part 4 133

April 27, 1899—The Resurrection of Lazarus—Part 5 135

May 4, 1899—The Resurrection of Lazarus—Part 6 137

May 11, 1899—The Resurrection of Lazarus—Part 7 140

May 18, 1899—The Resurrection of Lazarus—Part 8 143

May 25, 1899—The Resurrection of Lazarus—Part 9 145

June 8, 1899—Doers of the Word—Part 1 148

June 15, 1899—Doers of the Word—Part 2 150

June 22, 1899—God's Purpose Concerning the Youth of Today—Part 1 153

June 29, 1899—God's Purpose Concerning the Youth of Today—Part 2 155

July 13, 1899—"Give Us This Day Our Daily Bread" 157

July 20, 1899—"Sacrificed For Us" 160

July 27, 1899—The Character that God Approves—Part 1 163

August 3, 1899—The Character that God Approves—Part 2 165

August 10, 1899—Marriages, Wise and Unwise 167

August 17, 1899—Self-culture 171

August 24, 1899—"The Will of God Concerning You" 174

August 31, 1899—True Education 177

September 14, 1899—Teaching from Nature 180

September 21, 1899—An All-Powerful Saviour—Part 1 183

September 28, 1899—An All-Powerful Saviour—Part 2 185

August 25, 1898—A Peculiar People 71

September 1, 1898—Take Heed How You Hear 73

September 8, 1898—"And the Grace of God Was Upon Him" 76

September 15, 1898—Prayer Our Stronghold 80

September 22, 1898—"That I Should Bear Witness Unto the Truth" 83

October 13, 1898—"Search the Scriptures"—No. 1 86

October 20, 1898—"Search the Scriptures"—No. 2 89

October 27, 1898—"Search the Scriptures"—No. 3 92

November 3, 1898—Thy Father Which Seeth in Secret Shall Reward Thee Openly 95

November 10, 1898—The First King of Israel—No. 1 99

November 17, 1898—The First King of Israel—No. 2—The Presumption of Saul 102

November 24, 1898—The First King of Israel—No. 3 105

December 1, 1898—The First King of Israel—No. 4—The Final Test 108

December 8, 1898—The Higher Education 111

December 15, 1898—Peter's Fall and Restoration—No. 1 115

December 22, 1898—Peter's Fall and Restoration—No. 2 118

December 29, 1898—One That Is Mighty 121

March 30, 1899—The Resurrection of Lazarus—Part 1 124

April 6, 1899—The Resurrection of Lazarus—Part 2 127

April 13, 1899—The Resurrection of Lazarus—Part 3 130

Content

March 24, 1898—Lessons From God's Handiwork 15

March 31, 1898—The True Object of Education—No. 1 18

April 7, 1898—The True Object of Education—No. 2 21

April 14, 1898—The Little Things—No. 1 24

April 21, 1898—The Little Things—No. 2 27

April 28, 1898—The Little Things—No. 3 30

May 5, 1898—Timothy 34

May 12, 1898—The Fight of Faith 38

May 19, 1898—The Unseen Watcher—No. 1 41

May 26, 1898—The Unseen Watcher—No. 2 44

June 2, 1898—The Second Adam 47

June 30, 1898—God's Word Our Study Book—No. 1 49

July 7, 1898—God's Word Our Study Book—No. 2 51

July 14, 1898—Be Ye Holy 53

July 21, 1898—The Risen Saviour 56

July 28, 1898—The Risen Saviour—Part 2 60

August 4, 1898—The Risen Saviour—Part 3 62

August 11, 1898—The Risen Saviour—Part 4 65

August 18, 1898—Prayer Our Stronghold 68

April 5, 1900—John the Beloved—Part 2 238

April 12, 1900—"A New Commandment" 241

April 26, 1900—"Go Work Today in My Vineyard" 244

May 3, 1900—The Student's Privileges and Responsibilities—Part 1 247

May 10, 1900—The Student's Privileges and Responsibilities—Part 2 249

May 17, 1900—"The Violent Take it by Force"—Part 1 251

May 24, 1900—"The Violent Take It by Force"—Part 2 253

May 31, 1900—The Price of Our Redemption—Part 1 255

June 7, 1900—The Price of Our Redemption—Part 2 257

June 14, 1900—The Price of Our Redemption—Part 3 260

June 21, 1900—The Price of Our Redemption—Part 4 262

June 28, 1900—The Price of Our Redemption—Part 5 264

July 12, 1900—Mary's Offering—Part 1 266

July 19, 1900—Mary's Offering—Part 2 270

July 26, 1900—Our Words 273

August 2, 1900—Our Influence 276

August 16, 1900—Seed-sowing 278

September 6, 1900—A Lesson From Daniel's Experience 281

September 13, 1900—A Sin-pardoning Saviour—Part 1 284

September 20, 1900—A Sin-pardoning Saviour—Part 2 286

September 27, 1900—We Are His Witnesses—Part 1 288

October 4, 1900—We Are His Witnesses—Part 2 290

October 11, 1900—We Are His Witnesses—Part 3 292

October 18, 1900—Love Not the World..295

October 25, 1900—Words to the Youth 298

November 1, 1900—God's Care for His Children..301

November 8, 1900—Ye Are Not Your Own..305

November 15, 1900—From Persecutor to Disciple—Part 1 307

November 22, 1900—From Persecutor to Disciple—Part 2 310

December 6, 1900—In Meekness and Lowliness of Heart..313

December 13, 1900—The Burning Bush 316

December 20, 1900—Christ's Humiliation 319

December 27, 1900—Rejoice in the Lord 322

January 3, 1901—Tempted in All Points 324

January 10, 1901—Rejoice in the Lord Alway 327

January 17, 1901—Faithful in That Which Is Least...329

January 24, 1901—The Christian Pathway..331

January 31, 1901—Idleness Is Sin—Part 1 333

February 7, 1901—Idleness Is Sin—Part 2...336

February 14, 1901—Ministering Spirits 338

February 21, 1901—Christ's Entry Into Jerusalem—Part 1 341

February 28, 1901 Christ's Entry Into Jerusalem—Part 2...343

March 21, 1901—"Show Us a Sign From Heaven" 345

April 4, 1901—How to Meet Criticism 348

April 11, 1901—In Gethsemane 350

April 25, 1901—After the Crucifixion 353

May 2, 1901—The Lord Is Risen 356

May 9, 1901—Sowing and Reaping 359

May 16, 1901—Character-Building 361

June 6, 1901—Unquestioning Obedience 363

June 13, 1901—Joshua's Last Words—Part 1 366

June 20, 1901—Joshua's Last Words—Part 2 368

July 18, 1901—In the Wilderness With God 371

July 25, 1901—With Power and Great Glory 374

August 22, 1901—A Perfect Ideal 376

September 12, 1901—Conquering Temptation 378

September 26, 1901—"A New Heart Also Will I Give You" 380

October 3, 1901—The True Shepherd 383

November 21, 1901—Apostasy 386

December 5, 1901—The Reward of Faithful Toil 389

January 16, 1902—A Call to Labor 391

January 23, 1902—The Fair Flowers of Promise 393

February 6, 1902—Faithfulness in Service 395

February 13, 1902—God's Purpose for the Youth 396

February 27, 1902—The Blessing of Labor 398

March 6, 1902—What Shall It Profit? 400

March 20, 1902—Living for Christ 402

April 17, 1902—"How Much Owest Thou?" 404

May 1, 1902—The Hand That Never Lets Go 406

June 5, 1902—The Danger of Self-confidence 408

June 12, 1902—In Service for Christ 410

June 26, 1902—Onward and Upward 412

July 3, 1902—A Faithful Witness—Part 1 415

July 10, 1902—A Faithful Witness—Part 2 418

July 24, 1902—Search the Scriptures 420

July 31, 1902—Found Wanting 423

August 21, 1902—Liberty in Christ 425

September 11, 1902—Living Water 427

October 2, 1902—"It Is My Way" 429

October 9, 1902—What Shall We Read? 431

October 23, 1902—"Look Up" 434

November 6, 1902—Working with God 436

December 4, 1902—Unquestioning Faith 438

December 11, 1902—A Call to Service 440

January 1, 1903—In the Master's Service 442

January 22, 1903—"He That Gathereth Not with Me Scattereth Abroad" 444

January 29, 1903—Strength in Humility 446

February 12, 1903—Strength in Self-Sacrifice 449

February 19, 1903—Character-Building 452

March 5, 1903—Keeping the Heart 454

March 19, 1903—The Divine Teacher 458

March 26, 1903—Repentance a Gift of God 460

April 9, 1903—What We May Become 462

April 16, 1903—Our Great High Priest 463

April 23, 1903—God's Purpose Concerning Israel 466

May 14, 1903—Lessons from the Life of Daniel 2—Causes of the Babylonish Captivity 469

May 21, 1903—Lessons from the Life of Daniel 3—Early Training of Daniel and His Companions 472

June 4, 1903—Lessons from the Life of Daniel 4—Daniel's Temperance Principles—Part 1 475

June 25, 1903—Lessons from the Life of Daniel 5—Daniel's Temperance Principles—Part 2 478

July 9, 1903—Lessons from the Life of Daniel 6—The Reward of Temperance . 481

July 16, 1903—Lessons from the Life of Daniel 7—A Warfare Against Intemperance 484

August 6, 1903—Lessons from the Life of Daniel 8—Success in Education 487

August 20, 1903—Lessons From the Life of Daniel 9—Earnestness of Purpose 489

September 1, 1903—Lessons From the Life of Daniel 10—The Vision of the Great Image 492

September 8, 1903—Lessons From the Life of Daniel 11—The Interpretation of the Vision of the Great Image 495

September 22, 1903—Lessons From the Life of Daniel 12—The Moral Deterioration of the Nation 497

September 29, 1903—Lessons From the Life of Daniel 13—Obedience the Condition of God's Favor 500

November 24, 1903—Lessons From the Life of Daniel 15—True Wisdom 502

December 1, 1903—Lessons From the Life of Daniel 16—God's Prophetic Word 505

February 2, 1904—Lessons from the Life of Daniel 18—A Perversion of Truth 507

March 8, 1904—Lessons from the Life of Daniel 19—The Fiery Furnace—Part 1 510

March 29, 1904—Power of Song 512

April 12, 1904—Read and Heed 514

April 26, 1904—Lessons from the Life of Daniel—19—The Fiery Furnace—Part 2 515

July 12, 1904—The Life of Daniel—The Sabbath Test 518

October 11, 1904—The Power and Splendor of Babylon During Nebuchadnezzar's Reign 521

November 1, 1904—Nebuchadnezzar's Second Dream 523

November 1, 1904—Self-Denial Boxes 525

December 13, 1904—Nebuchadnezzar's Restoration 526

January 3, 1905—The Risen Saviour 528

March 28, 1905—Nebuchadnezzar's Humiliation 531

April 4, 1905—Lessons from the Life of Daniel—Self-exaltation 533

December 26, 1905—Unto You a Saviour 535

August 14, 1906—A Solemn Message to Our Youth 538

November 13, 1906—Jerusalem Destroyed by Titus 541

January 1, 1907—Privileges and Opportunities of the Youth—Written for the Young People's Day 544

August 20, 1907—Importance of Immediate Preparation for Service 548

September 10, 1907—Lessons in Economy and Self-Denial 549

September 24, 1907—Lessons from the Life of Daniel—A Warfare against Intemperance 552

October 29, 1907—With Full Purpose of Heart 555

November 12, 1907—With Full Purpose of Heart 559

December 31, 1907—"Them That Honor Me, I Will Honor" 561

February 11, 1908—New-Year Resolutions 563

March 3, 1908—A Preparation for Efficient Service 565

April 7, 1908—Knowing God 569

April 28, 1908—Wise Counsel to Youth 572

November 3, 1908—Suffer the Children to Come 574

April 27, 1909—The Fruit of Consecrated Service 578

May 25, 1909—Christ the Example of Children and Youth 581

August 17, 1909—Words to the Young 584

January 25, 1910—Decision of Character 586

January 17, 1911—Walk in the Light 589

July 18, 1911—An Appeal From Our Captain 592

November 21, 1911—Christ Our Pattern 594

April 23, 1912—Words to the Young 598

June 9, 1914—Following on to Know the Lord 602

March 24, 1898—Lessons From God's Handiwork

"The heavens declare the glory of God; and the firmament showeth his handiwork. Day unto day uttereth speech, and night unto night showeth knowledge. There is no speech nor language, where their voice is not heard. Their line is gone out through all the earth, and their words to the end of the world. In them hath he set a tabernacle for the sun, which is as a bridegroom coming out of his chamber, and rejoiceth as a strong man to run a race. His going forth is from the end of the heaven, and his circuit unto the ends of it: and there is nothing hid from the heat thereof."

The word of God and the things of nature around us are God's lesson book. God encourages us to contemplate his works in the natural world. He desires that we shall turn our minds from the study of the artificial to the natural. We shall understand this better as we lift up our eyes to the hills of God, and contemplate the works which his own hands have created. His hand has molded the hills, and balanced them in their position, that they shall not be moved except at his command. The wind, the sun, the rain, the snow, and the ice are all ministers to do his will.

By the Christian, God's love and benevolence can be seen in every gift from his hands. The beauties of nature are a theme for contemplation. In studying the natural loveliness surrounding us, the mind is carried up through nature to the Author of all that is lovely. All the works of God are speaking to our senses, magnifying his power, exalting his wisdom. Every created thing has in it charms which interest the child of God, and mold his taste to regard these precious evidences of God's love above the work of human skill.

In words of glowing fervor, the prophet magnifies God in his created works: "When I consider thy heavens, the work of thy fingers, the moon and the stars which thou hast ordained; what is man, that thou art mindful of him? and the son of man, that thou visitest him?" "O Lord our Lord, how excellent is thy name in all the earth! I will praise thee, O Lord, with my whole heart; I will show forth all thy marvelous works."

Those professed Christians who are constantly complaining, who seem to think happiness and a cheerful countenance a sin, have not the genuine attributes of religion. Those who look upon nature's beautiful scenery as they would upon a dead picture; who choose to look upon dead leaves rather than to gather the beautiful flowers; who take a mournful pleasure in all that is melancholy in the language spoken to them by the natural world; who see no beauty in valleys clothed in living green, and grand mountain heights clothed with verdure; who close their senses to the joyful voice that speaks to them in nature, and which is sweet and musical to the listening ear,--these are not in Christ. They are not walking in the light, but are gathering to themselves darkness and gloom, when they might just as well have the brightness and the blessing of the Sun of Righteousness arising in their hearts with healing in his beams.

God does not design that we shall take no pleasure in the things of his creation. He desires that we shall enjoy them. He has spread out before our senses the beauties of nature, and he watches with a Father's joy the delight of his children in the beautiful things around them.

While on earth, the Redeemer of the world sought to make his lessons of instruction plain and simple, that all might comprehend them; and can we be surprised that he should choose the open air as his sanctuary, that he should desire to be surrounded by the works of his creation? True, he taught in the synagogues, but the largest part of his work was done, the greatest number of his lessons were given, in the open air. He had special reasons for resorting to the groves and the seaside. He could there have a commanding view of the landscape, and make use of objects and scenes with which those in humble life were familiar. The things which his own hand had made he took as his lesson book. He saw in them more than finite minds could comprehend. The birds, caroling forth their songs without a care, the flowers of the valley glowing in their beauty, the lily that reposed in its purity on the bosom of the lake, the lofty trees, the cultivated land, the waving grain, the barren soil, the tree that bore no fruit, the everlasting hills, the bubbling stream, the setting sun, tinting and gilding the heavens,--all these he employed to impress his hearers with divine truth. He connected the work of God's finger in the heavens and upon the earth with the word of life. From these he drew his lessons of spiritual instruction. He would pluck the lilies, the flowers of the valley, and place them in the hands of the little children, as instructors to proclaim the truth of his word.

The root of the tree has a double office to fill. It is to hold fast by its tendrils to the earth, while it takes to itself the nourishment desired. Thus it is with the Christian.

When his union with Christ, the parent stock, is complete, when he feeds upon him, currents of spiritual strength are given to him. Can the leaves of such a branch wither?--Never! As long as the soul reaches toward Christ, there is little danger that he will wilt, and droop, and decay. The temptations that may come in like a tempest will not uproot him. The true Christian draws his motives of action from his deep love for his Redeemer. His affection for his Master is true and holy. And it is the cheerful, lovable Christian of whom Christ says, "Ye are my witnesses." Such a man is Christ's representative; for he reflects Christ in his daily life. It is when he recedes from the light, that he cannot diffuse its bright beams to others.

The Spirit of God is constantly impressing the mind to seek for those things which alone will give peace and rest,--the higher, holier joys of heaven. Our Saviour is constantly at work, through influences seen and unseen, to attract the minds of men from the unsatisfying pleasures of this life to the priceless treasure which may be theirs in the immortal future. The beauties of nature have a tongue that speaks to us without ceasing. The open heart can be impressed with the love and glory of God, as seen in the works of his hand. The listening ear can hear and understand the communications of God through the things of nature. There is a lesson in the sunbeam, and in the various objects of nature that God has presented to our view. The green fields, the lofty trees, the buds and flowers, the passing cloud, the falling rain, the babbling brook, the sun, moon, and stars in the heavens,--all invite our attention and meditation, and bid us become acquainted with him who made them all.

Mrs. E. G. White

March 31, 1898—The True Object of Education—No. 1

In the education and training of youth, the great object should be the development of character. Every individual should be fitted rightly to discharge the duties of the present life, and to enter at last upon the future, immortal life. Moral, intellectual, and physical culture must be combined in order to have well-developed, well-balanced men and women.

Education in book knowledge alone prepares the way for superficial, shallow thoughts. The neglect of some parts of the living machinery, while other parts are put to the tax, and wearied and overworked, makes many youth too weak to resist the temptation to evil practises. They have little power of self-control. The physical machinery being untaxed, the blood is called too liberally to the brain, and the nervous system is overworked. The brain is overworked, and Satan brings in his temptations to engage in forbidden pleasures, to "have a change," to "let off steam." Yielding to these temptations, they do wrong, injuring themselves, and doing mischief to others. This may be done only in sport, but some one must undo the mischief which they do under temptation. While studying authors and lessonbooks part of the time, students should study the human machinery with the same application, and at the same time use the physical organs in manual labor. Thus they answer the purpose of their Creator, and become useful, efficient men and women.

The student should place himself in school, if he can, through his own exertions, pay his way as he goes. He should study one year, and then work out for himself the problem of what constitutes true education. He should set himself to work. The learning heaped up by years of continued study is deleterious to spiritual interests. Let teachers be prepared to give good counsel to the student who enters school. Let them not advise him to give years exclusively to the study of books. Let the youth learn, and then impart to others the benefits he has received. If the student will humbly seek him, the Lord of heaven will open his understanding. The student should take time to review what he has gained in book knowledge; he should critically examine the advancement he has made in the schoolroom, and he should combine physical exercise with study. Thus he will acquire an education that will enable him to come out with solid principles, an all-round man.

Had teachers been learning the lessons the Lord would have them learn, there would not be a class of students whose bills must be settled by some one else, or they must leave college with a heavy debt hanging over them. Educators are not doing their work faithfully when they know a young man to be devoting years of his time to the study of books, not seeking to earn means to pay his own way, and yet do nothing in the matter. Every case should be investigated; every youth should be kindly inquired after, and his financial situation ascertained.

Many would be glad of the privilege of spending a short time in school, where they could be brought up on some points of study. There are those who would consider it an inestimable privilege to have the Bible opened to them in its pure, unadulterated simplicity; to be taught how to come close to hearts, and how, in simple, straightforward lines, to teach the truth so that it shall be clearly discerned.

One study to be put before the student as most valuable should be the exercise of his God-given reason in harmony with his physical powers. The right use of one's self is the most valuable lesson that can be learned. We are not to do brain work, and stop there, or make physical exertion, and stop there; we are to make the best use of the various parts that compose the human machinery,--brain, bone, muscle, head, and heart. No man is fit for the ministry who does not understand this.

The student who has neglected the training of the muscles proportionately with his mental powers should seek to obtain an all-round education. If he feels it beneath his dignity to take hold of the unlearned parts, and catch up the science of true education, he is unfitted to take hold of the work of educating youth. He need not think himself qualified to act as a teacher; for his very teaching will be superficial and one-sided. He does not understand that he lacks the very education that would make him a blessing, and would secure to him in the future, immortal life the benediction, "Well done, good and faithful servant."

Every student in our schools should begin his character-building upon the word of God. He is to study for time and for eternity. Paul's charge to Timothy was, "Study to show thyself approved unto God, a workman that needeth not to be ashamed, rightly dividing the word of truth." We cannot, in this day of peril, accept teachers merely because they have been in school two, three, four, or five years. The question is, With all their acquisition of knowledge, have they obtained a knowledge of what is truth? Have they searched for truth as for hidden treasure? or have they seized the surface rubbish in the place of pure truth, thoroughly winnowed? We cannot consent, at this period of time, to expose our youth to the chance of learning a mixture of truth and error. The youth who come from school without feeling the importance of making the word of God the first study, the main study, are not qualified to become teachers.

That course of study which is not dictated by the Holy Spirit, which does not embrace the high, holy principles of God's word, will open before the student a course unmarked by the approval of heaven. It will leave gaps, and mistakes, and misunderstandings all along the road he travels. Those who will not give themselves to a deep, earnest, prayerful study of the Scriptures will hold ideas contrary to the principles that should control the life.

Will parents who believe the truth, and who realize the importance of knowing the truth that is to make us wise unto salvation, trust their children to schools where error is believed and taught? Who will expose these precious souls to a conflict of changes, and place them where their highest interests are not made the first consideration?

If the Lord's will is done, students will not be encouraged to remain in schools continuously for years. This is the devising of man, not the plan of God. The student is not to feel that he must take a classical course before he can enter the ministry. A large number who have done this have disqualified themselves for the labor which it was essential for them to do. The long study of those books which should not be made study-books, unfits the youth for the work to be done in this important period of the world's history. These years of study cultivate habits and methods that cripple their usefulness. They have to unlearn many things which disqualify them for efficiency in any line of the work to be done for this time.

Mrs. E. G. White

April 7, 1898—The True Object of Education—No. 2

Students are to bear in mind that their life is a talent, to be highly appreciated and dedicated to the Lord. Those who attend school are to study the Book of books, and through prayer, and close, deep research, obtain a Bible education. They are to learn lessons in the school of Christ; they are to work in Christ's lines.

The right use of one's self includes the whole circle of obligations to one's self, to the world, and to God. Then use the physical powers proportionately with the mental powers. Every action derives its quality from the motive which prompts it, and if the motives are not high, and pure, and unselfish, the mind and character will never become well balanced. Those who come from their school life without having educated the muscles proportionately with the brain will seldom recover from the harm they received in their one-sided education. On the part of such there is seldom a deep, earnest purpose that leads to deep, earnest work. They are not fit to train other minds, because their own have never been trained. They are fitful in their movements. They cannot reason from cause to effect. They will speak when it would be eloquence to keep silence, and will be silent on those themes on which they should speak,--themes that should occupy the heart and mind and regulate the life.

The talents entrusted of God are a sacred treasure, and should be put to practical use. Useful work is a valuable education. If either this practical education or the study of books must be neglected, let it be the study of books, and let the student take up the real, practical duties of life. The youth who have been educated to consider the best plans for doing good at home will extend their work to the neighborhood, the church, and every line of missionary work.

God calls upon us all to render obedience to the principles he has revealed to us in the work appointed to Adam in Eden. There will be employment in Eden restored. Our dear young students who have not been trained at home by their parents, need to have an education that will counteract their home education. Until they learn the first principles of proper education, they cannot be trusted as teachers of the youth. They are to engage in a career that requires settled purposes, high principles, and holy aims. If they do not learn anew, they will bring into their religious life a superficial work which will disqualify them to teach the word of God. Their minds grasp at ideas that lead to error. Capricious fancies may for a time supply the place of truth; but the thoughts grasped have no foundation in truth. Their minds do not penetrate deep enough to see the outcome of assertions that will counterwork the work of God.

The study of Latin and Greek is of far less consequence to ourselves, to the world, and to God than the thorough study and use of the whole human machinery. It is a sin to study books to the neglect of the various branches of usefulness in practical life. Never can one who is ignorant of the house we live in have an all-round life.

Exercise should be taken, not in play and amusement merely to please self, but exercise that will teach the science of doing good. There is a science in the use of the hand. Students who think that education consists only in book study never make a right use of their hands. They should be taught to do the work that thousands of hands are never educated to do. The powers thus developed and cultivated can be most usefully employed. In the cultivation of the soil, in building houses, in studying and planning various methods of labor, the brain must be exercised, and students can apply themselves to much better purpose when a portion of their time is devoted to physical taxation, wearying the muscles. Nature will then give sweet repose.

Students, your life is God's property. He has entrusted it to you, that you may honor and glorify him. You are the Lord's; for he created you. You are his by redemption; for he gave his life for you. The only begotten Son of God paid the ransom for your deliverance from Satan; and for his sake you should appreciate every power, every organ, every sinew and muscle. Preserve every portion of the living machinery, that you may use it for God. Preserve it for him. Your health depends upon the right use of your physical organism. Do not misuse any portion of your God-given powers, physical, mental, or moral. All your habits are to be brought under the control of a mind that is itself under the control of God.

If young men and women would grow up to the full stature of Christ Jesus, they must treat themselves intelligently. Conscientiousness in methods of education is as essential as in the consideration of the doctrines of our faith. Unhealthful habits of every order--late hours at night, late hours in bed in the morning, rapid eating--are to be overcome. Masticate your food thoroughly. Let there be no hurried eating. Have your room well ventilated day and night, and perform useful physical labor. Tight-lacing is a sin, and will bring its sure results. The lungs, the liver, and the heart need all the room the Lord has provided for them. Your Creator understood how much room the heart and liver require in order to act their part in the human organism. Let not Satan tempt you to crowd the delicate organs, so that they shall be trammeled in their work. Do not, because the fashion of this degenerate world requires it, so crowd the life forces that they will have no freedom. Satan suggested all such fashions, that the human family might suffer the sure results of abusing God's handiwork.

All this must be a part of the education received in school; for we are God's property. The sacred temple of the body must be kept pure and uncontaminated, that God's Holy Spirit may dwell therein. We need to guard faithfully the Lord's property; for any abuse of our powers shortens the time that our lives could be used for the glory of God. Bear in mind that we must consecrate all--soul, body, and spirit--to God. All is his purchased possession, and must be used intelligently, to the end that we may preserve the talent of life. By properly using our powers to their fullest extent in the most useful employment, by keeping every organ in health, by so preserving every organ that mind, sinew, and muscle shall work harmoniously, we may do the most precious service for God.

Mrs. E. G. White

April 14, 1898—The Little Things—No. 1

The active service of God is directly connected with the ordinary duties of life, even its humblest occupations. We are to serve God just where he puts us. He is to place us individually, and not we ourselves. Perhaps service in the home life is the place we are to occupy for a time, if not always. Then a preparation for that work should be obtained, that we may do our best in service for the Lord.

The Lord is testing and proving us, to see what sort of timbers, or attributes, we are bringing into the character-building. If we are listless and indifferent, negligent and careless, in the small every-day duties, we shall never be fitted for any other service for God. He that is faithful in that which is least will be faithful also in much. He that is unfaithful in that which is least, would certainly repeat this unfaithfulness if placed in higher positions of trust and given larger responsibilities. Those who do their temporal business in a slack, shiftless manner, will be led to do business in more responsible places in the same way. The service of God will be done in a haphazard manner. But when there is order and exactness in the little things with which we have to do in ordinary life, what need for wonder that the same exactness is brought into the religious life?

The importance of little things is underrated, just because they are small; but the influence of the little things for good or for evil is great. They supply much of the actual discipline of life for every human being. They are part of the training of the soul in the sanctification of all our entrusted talents to God. Faithfulness in the little things in the line of duty makes the worker in God's service reflect more and more the likeness of Christ. Our Saviour is a Saviour for the perfection of the whole man. He is not the God of part of the being only. The grace of Christ works to the disciplining of the whole human fabric. He made all. He has redeemed all. He has made the mind, the strength, the body as well as the soul, partaker of the divine nature, and all is his purchased possession. He must be served with the whole mind, heart, soul, and strength. Then the Lord will be glorified in his saints, in even the common, temporal things, with which they are connected. "Holiness unto the Lord," will be the inscription placed upon them.

We would do well to consider the case of Elisha when chosen for his work. The prophet Elijah was about to close his earthly labors. Another was to be called to carry forward the work for that time. In his course of travel, Elijah was directed northward. How changed the scene before him now from that which the country had presented a little while before. Then the farming districts were unworked; the ground was parched; for neither dew nor rain had fallen for three years. Now everything seems to be springing up as if to redeem the time of famine and dearth. The plenteous rains had done more for the earth than for the hearts of humanity; the fields were better prepared for labor than were the hearts of apostate Israel.

Wherever Elijah looked, the land he saw was owned by one man,--a man who had not bowed the knee to Baal, whose heart had remained undivided in the service of God. Even during the captivity there were souls who had not gone into apostasy, and this family was included in the seven thousand who had not bowed the knee to Baal. The owner of the land was Shaphat. Busy activity was seen among the workers. While the flocks were enjoying the green pastures, the busy hands of his servants were sowing the seed for a harvest.

The attention of Elijah was attracted to Elisha, the son of Shaphat, who with the servants was plowing with twelve yoke of oxen. He was educator, director, and worker. Elisha did not live in the thickly populated cities. His father was a tiller of the soil, a farmer. Far from city and court dissipation, Elisha had received his education. He had been trained in habits of simplicity, of obedience to his parents and to God. Thus in quietude and contentment he was prepared to do the humble work of cultivating the soil. But though of a meek and quiet spirit, Elisha had no changeable character. Integrity and fidelity and the love and fear of God were his. He had the characteristics of a ruler, but with it all was the meekness of one who would serve. His mind had been exercised in the little things, to be faithful in whatsoever he should do; so that if God should call him to act more directly for him, he would be prepared to hear his voice.

The surroundings of Elisha's home were those of wealth; but he realized that in order to obtain an all-round education, he must be a constant worker in any work that needed to be done. He had not consented to be in any respect less informed than his father's servants. He had learned how to serve first, that he might know how to lead, instruct, and command.

Elisha waited contentedly, doing his work with fidelity. Day by day, through practical obedience and the divine grace in which he trusted, he obtained rectitude and strength of purpose. While doing all that he possibly could in co-operating with his father in the home firm, he was doing God's service. He was learning how to co-operate with God.

The youth should bear in mind that their physical strength, their mental qualifications, and their spiritual endowments, are to be devoted to service. These are never to be misapplied, never misused, never left to rust through inaction. Elisha increased in knowledge daily. Daily he prepared to do service in any way that opened before him. He served God in the little temporal duties. He grew in knowledge and in grace. And if the student today will develop reliability and soundness of principle in the things which are least, he will reveal that he has acquired adaptability to serve God in a higher capacity. He who feels that it is of no great consequence to serve in the lesser capacity will never be trusted of God to serve in the more honored position. He may present himself as fully competent to accomplish the duties of the higher position; but God looks deeper than the surface. A watcher is on his track, and after test and trial, there is written against him, "Thou art weighed in the balances, and art found wanting." That sentence in the courts of heaven decides for eternity the destiny of the human being.

Mrs. E. G. White (To be continued.)

April 21, 1898—The Little Things—No. 2

When the prophet saw Elisha with his servants plowing with twelve yoke of oxen, he came to the field of labor, and while passing by, he unfastened his mantle, and threw it upon the shoulders of Elisha. He then passed on as if that were the end of the matter. But he knew that Elisha understood the significance of the action; and he left him, without speaking a word, to decide whether he would accept or reject the call.

During the three years and a half of barrenness and famine, the family of Shaphat had become familiar with the mission of Elijah the prophet; and the Spirit of God impressed the heart of Elisha in regard to the meaning of this action. This was the signal that God had called him to be the successor of Elijah. He hastened after the prophet, and overtaking him, asked permission to take leave of his parents and bid farewell to his family.

The answer of Elijah was, "Go back again: for what have I done to thee?" This was not a repulse, but a test. If Elisha's heart clung to his home and its advantages, he was at liberty to remain there. But Elisha was prepared to hear the call of God. He had not been disorderly, running before the call had come; and when he was called, he showed that he would not hesitate nor draw back.

Had Elisha asked Elijah what was expected of him, what would be his work, he would have been answered, God knows; he will make it known to you. If you wait upon the Lord, he will answer your every question. You may come with me if you have evidence that God has called you; if not, forbear. Come not simply because I have called you. Know for yourself that God stands back of you, and that it is his voice you hear. If you can count everything but dross that you may win Christ, come.

In genuine faith there is a buoyancy, a steadfast principle, which neither time nor toil can weaken. "Even the youths shall faint and be weary, and the young men shall utterly fall: but they that wait upon the Lord shall renew their strength; they shall mount up with wings as eagles; they shall run, and not be weary; and they shall walk, and not faint."

The call of Elijah was similar to the commission of Christ to the young ruler. The ruler was commanded to leave all,--houses, lands, friends, riches, comforts, and ease,--and follow Jesus. How many have had and will have such tests! But with the call of Christ comes the question, Are we ready to advance? Are we willing? Shall we, like Moses, cheerfully deem the reproach of Christ greater riches than the treasures in Egypt?

The Lord will not accept half-hearted service. Those alone who love to do the will of God can do perfect service. Let not the heart that hears the gracious invitation of mercy, "Come; for all things are now ready," still question as to the outcome of the matter, saying, How much will I have to yield up? You are to have no arguments on this point. If we follow on to know the Lord, willingly, gladly, we shall know that "his going forth is prepared as the morning." If we have decided to obey Christ, we shall respond to his call, "If any man will come after me, let him deny himself, and take up his cross, and follow me."

Any work, however small it may appear, that is done for the Master with a thorough surrender of self, is as acceptable to him as the highest service. "Thus saith the Lord, Let not the wise man glory in his wisdom, neither let the mighty man glory in his might, let not the rich man glory in his riches: but let him that glorieth glory in this, that he understandeth and knoweth me, that I am the Lord which exercise loving-kindness, judgment, and righteousness, in the earth: for in these things I delight, saith the Lord."

Humble, willing service is before every one who claims to be a child of God. To every one the Lord has given his work. There is to be earnest, faithful waiting for the message from God, calling to his service. In prospect of the solemn event of the advent of Christ, there is to be no idle waiting with nothing to do. God's children are to prepare others for that great event. There is waiting and watching to be done, but this is to be combined with working. This will develop a harmonious Christian character. This will make the Christian an all-round man, perfect in Christ Jesus, "not slothful in business; fervent in spirit; serving the Lord."

The work of God is a perfect whole, because perfect in all its parts; and it is important that the worker for Christ shall take his Master with him in every department of labor. Whatever is done should be done with an exactness and despatch that will bear inspection. The heart should be in the work. Faithfulness in little things should characterize the life, true integrity should mark all the course of action. It is the conscientious attention to what the world calls little things that makes the great beauty and success of life. Little deeds of charity, little words of kindness, little acts of self-denial, a wise improvement of little opportunities, a diligent cultivation of little talents, make great men in God's sight. If these little things are faithfully attended to, if these graces are in you and abound, they will make you perfect in every good work.

Mrs. E. G. White

April 28, 1898—The Little Things—No. 3

Elisha immediately left all to begin his ministry. His leave-taking was not with mourning and bitter regrets. They made a feast in his home, in commemoration of the honor conferred upon one of the family. And what was the first work of Elisha?--It was to take up the little things, and do them with heartiness. He was the prophet's personal attendant. He is spoken of as pouring water on the hands of Elijah his master.

After Elisha had been some time in the service of the prophet, he was called to take his place in the first rank. No one in that time was to be greater than he. He had worked under Elijah as a learner, and the time came when the head manager was removed, and the one under him came to the front. And as Elijah was prepared to be translated, so Elisha was prepared to become his successor as a prophet.

"And it came to pass, when the Lord would take up Elijah into heaven by a whirlwind, that Elijah went with Elisha from Gilgal. And Elijah said unto Elisha, Tarry here, I pray thee; for the Lord hath sent me to Bethel. And Elisha said unto him, As the Lord liveth, and as thy soul liveth, I will not leave thee. So they went down to Bethel. And the sons of the prophets that were at Bethel came forth to Elisha, and said unto him, Knowest thou that the Lord will take away thy master from thy head today? And he said, Yea, I know it; hold ye your peace."

Unknown to Elijah, the tidings that he was to be translated had been made known to the disciples in the schools of the prophets, and in particular to Elisha. He therefore kept close beside Elijah.

Again Elijah said: "Elisha, tarry here, I pray thee; for the Lord hath sent me to Jericho. And he said, As the Lord liveth, and as thy soul liveth, I will not leave thee. So they came to Jericho. And the sons of the prophets that were at Jericho came to Elisha, and said unto him, Knowest thou that the Lord will take away thy master from thy head today? And he answered, Yea, I know it; hold ye your peace." Elijah said to him, "Tarry, I pray thee, here; for the Lord hath sent me to Jordan." Again were the words repeated, "As the Lord liveth, and as thy soul liveth, I will not leave thee."

There was a school of the prophets at Gilgal, and also at Bethel and at Jericho. Elijah wished to visit these important places before he was parted from them. His spirit was cheered as, by the direction of God, he was permitted to see the schools of the prophets and the work that was going on in those institutions,--an education which was to keep the wonderful works of God continually before the students, and which magnified the law of God, and make it honorable. The education was of that order which would preserve the souls of all who would be obedient to the law of God. While idolatry was prevailing to an alarming extent, Elijah could see the word of the Lord verified, "I have left me seven thousand in Israel, all the knees which... have not bowed unto Baal."

At every place where Elisha tarried with Elijah, he was given opportunity to separate from him. "Tarry here, I pray thee," said Elijah. Thus Elisha's faith was tried at every point. But by plowing in the field, Elisha had learned not to yield to discouragement. He had now set his hand to the plow in another work, and he would not fail nor be discouraged. Every time the invitation to turn back was given, he declared, "As the Lord liveth, and as thy soul liveth, I will not leave thee."

"And Elijah said unto him, Tarry, I pray thee, here; for the Lord hath sent me to Jordan. And he said, As the Lord liveth, and as thy soul liveth, I will not leave thee. And they two went on... And Elijah took his mantle, and wrapped it together, and smote the waters, and they were divided hither and thither, so that they two went over on dry ground."

"And it came to pass, when they were gone over, that Elijah said unto Elisha, Ask what I shall do for thee, before I be taken away from thee. And Elisha said, I pray thee, let a double portion of thy spirit be upon me. And he said, Thou has asked a hard thing: nevertheless, if thou see me when I am taken from thee, it shall be so unto thee; but if not, it shall not be so. And it came to pass, as they still went on, and talked, that, behold, there appeared a chariot of fire, and horses of fire, and parted them both asunder; and Elijah went up by a whirlwind into heaven. And Elisha saw it, and he cried, My father, my father, the chariot of Israel, and the horsemen thereof. And he saw him no more: and he took hold of his own clothes, and rent them in two pieces. He took up also the mantle of Elijah that fell from him, and ... smote the waters, and said, Where is the Lord God of Elijah? and when he also had smitten the waters, they parted hither and thither: and Elisha went over. And when the sons of the prophets which were to view at Jericho saw him, they said, The spirit of Elijah doth rest on Elisha. And they came to meet him, and bowed themselves to the ground before him."

Henceforth Elisha stood in the place of Elijah. He was called to the position of highest honor because he had been faithful over a few things. The question arose in his mind, Am I qualified for such a position? But he would not allow his mind to question. The greatest qualification for any man in a position of trust is to obey implicitly the word of the Lord. Elisha might exercise his reasoning ability on every other subject but the one that would admit of no reasoning. He was to obey the word of the Lord at all times and in all places. Elisha had put his hand to the plow, and he would not look back. He revealed his determination and firm reliance upon God.

This lesson is for us to study carefully. We are in no case to swerve from our allegiance. No duties that God presents before us should cause us to work at cross-purposes with him. The word of God is to be our counselor. It is only those who render perfect and thorough obedience to God that he will choose. Those who follow the Lord are to be firm and straightforward in obeying his directions. Any deviation to follow human devising or planning disqualifies them for being trustworthy. Even if they have to walk as did Enoch,--with God alone,--his children must separate from those who do not obey him, who show that they are not in vital connection with him. The Lord God is a host; and all who are in his service will realize the meaning of his words to Zerubbabel, "Not by might, nor by power, but by Spirit, saith the Lord of hosts."

The word of finite man is fallible. Human laws, that are supposed to take the place of the law of God, are not to be respected. Henceforth the nations are to be in a very uncertain state. Kings and rulers will be involved in greater perplexities than they have ever thought possible, and this because they are disobedient to the word of the Lord, and work entirely contrary to his principles. The question now comes home to all who have their Bibles, Are we prepared to follow the word of God? "If any man will come after me," says Christ, "let him deny himself, and take up his cross, and follow me." You cannot depend upon priests, rulers, human lawmakers; for, as in Christ's day, they teach for doctrines the commandments of men. They know not the Scriptures, nor the power of God. Man-made theories are placed above a plain "Thus saith the Lord." But the searching of the soul has come. Are we obedient to the law of God? Will every soul look up in faith, and answer to God, as did Elisha, "As the Lord liveth, ... I will not leave thee"? Whatever may come,--persecution, reproach, falsehood, or anything that shall arise,--I will not leave the source of my strength.

Mrs. E. G. White

May 5, 1898—Timothy

A noble, all-round manhood does not come by chance. It is the result of character-building in the early years of youth, a practise of the law of God in the home. The word of God must be studied, and this requires thought and prayerful research. While some passages are too plain to be misunderstood, others demand careful and patient study. Like the precious metal concealed in the hills and mountains, its gems of truth are to be searched out and stored in the mind. Only by a continual improvement of the intellectual as well as the moral powers, can we hope to answer the purpose of our Creator.

We may learn precious lessons in this respect from the life and character of Timothy. From a child, Timothy had known the Scriptures. Religion was the atmosphere of his home. The piety of his home life was not of a cheap order, but pure, sensible, and uncorrupted by false sentiments. Its moral influence was substantial, not fitful, not impulsive, not changeable. The word of God was the rule which guided Timothy. He received his instruction, line upon line, precept upon precept, here a little, and there a little. And the spiritual power of these lessons kept him pure in speech, and free from all corrupting sentiments. His home instructors co-operated with God in educating this young man to bear the burdens that were to come upon him at an early age.

Timothy was a mere youth when he was chosen by God as a teacher. But his principles had been so established by a correct education that he was fitted to be placed as a religious teacher, in connection with Paul, the great apostle to the Gentiles. And though young, he bore his great responsibilities with Christian meekness. He was faithful, steadfast, and true; and Paul made him his companion in labor and travel, that he might have the benefit of the apostle's experience in preaching the gospel and establishing churches.

Paul loved Timothy because Timothy loved God. The great apostle often drew him out, and questioned him in regard to Scripture history. He taught him the necessity of shunning every evil way, and told him that blessing would surely attend all who were faithful and true, giving them a noble manhood.

The lessons of the Bible have a moral and a religious influence upon the character as they are wrought into the practical life. Timothy learned and practised these lessons. He had no specially wonderful talents; but his work was valuable because he used his God-given abilities as consecrated gifts in the service of God. His intelligent knowledge of the truth and of experimental piety gave him distinction and influence. The Holy Spirit found in Timothy a mind that could be molded and fashioned to become a temple for the indwelling of the Holy Spirit, because he submitted to be molded.

The words of the apostle Paul just prior to his death, were: "Continue thou in the things which thou hast learned, and hast been assured of, knowing of whom thou hast learned them; and that from a child thou hast known the Holy Scriptures, which are able to make thee wise unto salvation through faith which is in Christ Jesus." "These things command and teach." And lest the churches should despise his youth, he wrote, "Let no man despise thy youth; but be thou an example of the believers, in word, in conversation, in charity, in spirit, in faith, in purity."

Paul could safely write this; for Timothy did not go forward in a self-sufficient spirit. He worked in connection with Paul, seeking his advice and instruction. He did not move from impulse. He exercised consideration and calm thought, inquiring at every step, "Is this the way of the Lord?"

"Till I come," Paul continued, "give attendance to reading, to exhortation, to doctrine. Neglect not the gift that is in thee, which was given thee by prophecy, with the laying on of the hands of the presbytery. Meditate upon these things; give thyself wholly to them; that thy profiting may appear to all. Take heed unto thyself, and unto the doctrine; continue in them: for in doing this thou shalt both save thyself, and them that hear thee."

The charge given to Timothy should be heeded in every household, and become an educating power in every family and in every school. He was enjoined, "Thou therefore, my son, be strong in the grace that is in Christ Jesus. And the things that thou hast heard of me among many witnesses, the same commit thou to faithful men, who shall be able to teach others also. Thou therefore endure hardness, as a good soldier of Jesus Christ." "Consider what I say; and the Lord give thee understanding in all things.... Study to show thyself approved unto God, a workman that needeth not to be ashamed, rightly dividing the word of truth."

In order that the youth may do this, there must be schools similar to the schools of the prophets to educate in the word of God, to "shun profane and vain babblings: for they will increase unto more ungodliness." This scripture is directly to the point. Those books which may contain some truth, but are intermingled with "vain babblings," should not be placed in the student's hands; for they are as seed sown in the human heart which, in time of temptation, will spring into life, and draw the minds of students into paths that lead away from God, away from truth.

"Their word," said Paul, "will eat as doth a canker: of whom is Hymenaeus and Philetus; who concerning the truth have erred, saying that the resurrection is past already; and overthrow the faith of some. Nevertheless the foundation of God standeth sure, having this seal, The Lord knoweth them that are his. And, Let every one that nameth the name of Christ depart from iniquity. But in a great house there are not only vessels of gold and of silver, but also of wood and of earth; and some to honor, and some to dishonor. If a man therefore purge himself from these, he shall be a vessel unto honor, sanctified, and meet for the Master's use, and prepared unto every good work. Flee also youthful lusts: but follow righteousness, faith, charity, peace, with them that call on the Lord out of a pure heart. But foolish and unlearned questions avoid, knowing that they do gender strifes. And the servant of the Lord must not strive; but be gentle unto all men, apt to teach, patient, in meekness instructing those that oppose themselves; if God peradventure will give them repentance to the acknowledging of the truth; and that they may recover themselves out of the snare of the devil, who are taken captive by him at his will."

This is the instruction and education which young men who enter schools should seek to obtain. These words come to every young man who purposes to enter the ministry, to all youth who shall engage in any part of the work. They need to listen to the word of God through the apostle Paul. That word is "profitable for doctrine, for reproof, for correction, for instruction in righteousness, that the man of God may be perfect, thoroughly furnished unto all good works." And what should this furnishing comprehend?--a knowledge of the Scriptures,--a book that our own experience teaches us should be the Book of all books for our schools.

The highest aim of our youth should not be to strain after something novel. There was none of this in the mind and work of Timothy. They should bear in mind that, in the hands of the enemy of all good, knowledge alone may be a power to destroy them. It was a very intellectual being, one who occupied a high position among the angelic throng, that finally became a rebel; and many a mind of superior intellectual attainments is now being led captive by his power. The youth should place themselves under the teaching of the Holy Scriptures, and weave them into their daily thoughts and practical life. Then they will possess the attributes classed as highest in the heavenly courts. They will hide themselves in God, and their lives will tell to his glory.

Mrs. E. G. White

May 12, 1898—The Fight of Faith

There are many precious promises on record for those who seek the Saviour early. Solomon says, "Remember now thy Creator in the days of thy youth, when the evil days come not, nor the years draw nigh, when thou shalt say, I have no pleasure in them." God declares, "I love them that love me, and those that seek me early shall find me." The Great Shepherd of Israel is still saying, "Suffer the little children to come unto me, and forbid them not: for of such is the kingdom of God."

Many of the youth have not a fixed principle to serve God. They sink under every cloud, and have no power of endurance. They do not grow in grace. They appear to keep the commandments of God, but they are not subject to the law of God, neither indeed can be. Their carnal hearts must be changed. They must see beauty in holiness: then they will pant after it as the hart panteth after the water-brooks; then they will love God and his law; then the yoke of Christ will be easy, and his burden light.

If your steps are ordered by the Lord, dear youth, you must not expect that your path will always be one of outward peace and prosperity. The path that leads to eternal day is not the easiest to travel, and at times it will seem dark and thorny. But you have the assurance that God's everlasting arms encircle you, to protect you from evil. He wants you to exercise earnest faith in him, and learn to trust him in the shadow as well as in the sunshine.

The follower of Christ must have faith abiding in the heart; for without this it is impossible to please God. Faith is the hand that takes hold of infinite help; it is the medium by which the renewed heart is made to beat in unison with the heart of Christ.

In her endeavors to reach her home, the eagle is often beaten down by the tempest to the narrow defiles of the mountains. The clouds, in black, angry masses sweep between her and the sunny heights where she secures her nest. For a while she seems bewildered, and dashes this way and that, beating her strong wings as if to sweep back the dense clouds. She awakens the doves of the mountains with her wild cry in her vain endeavors to find a way out of her prison. At last she dashes upward into the blackness, and gives a shrill scream of triumph as she emerges, a moment later, in the calm sunshine above. The darkness and tempest are all below her, and the light of heaven is shining about her. She reaches her loved home in the lofty crag, and is satisfied. It was through darkness that she reached the light. It cost her an effort to do this, but she is rewarded in gaining the object which she sought.

This is the only course we can pursue as followers of Christ. We must exercise that living faith which will penetrate the clouds that, like a thick wall, separate us from heaven's light. We have heights of faith to reach, where all is peace and joy in the Holy Spirit.

Have you ever watched a hawk in pursuit of a timid dove? Instinct has taught the dove that in order for the hawk to seize his prey, he must gain a loftier flight than his victim. So she rises higher and still higher in the blue dome of heaven, ever pursued by the hawk, which is seeking to obtain the advantage. But in vain. The dove is safe as long as she allows nothing to stop her in her flight, or draw her earthward; but let her once falter, and take a lower flight, and her watchful enemy will swoop down upon his victim. Again and again have we watched this scene with almost breathless interest, all our sympathies with the little dove. How sad we should have felt to see it fall a victim to the cruel hawk!

We have before us a warfare,--a lifelong conflict with Satan and his seductive temptations. The enemy will use every argument, every deception, to entangle the soul; and in order to win the crown of life, we must put forth earnest, persevering effort. We must not lay off the armor or leave the battle-field until we have gained the victory, and can triumph in our Redeemer. As long as we continue to keep our eyes fixed upon the Author and Finisher of our faith, we shall be safe. But our affections must be placed upon things above, not on things of the earth. By faith we must rise higher and still higher in the attainment of the graces of Christ. By daily contemplating his matchless charms, we must grow more and more into his glorious image. While we thus live in communion with Heaven, Satan will lay his nets for us in vain.

Conscious that the world lieth in wickedness, that he has constantly to battle with the enemy of God and man, and that in himself he does not possess power to purify the recesses of the heart, the humble follower of Christ will turn to the mighty Helper;

and unto him Christ is made wisdom, and righteousness, and sanctification, and redemption. To the praying soul, Jesus reveals himself as the One who hears and answers prayer,--the One who lifts up those that are cast down, and heals the broken in heart.

The young convert has everything to learn. He should meditate and pray much, that he may do thorough work in meeting God's standard of righteousness. "Honor thy father and thy mother," is part of that great standard; and through the apostle James, Christ declares, "Whosoever shall keep the whole law, and yet offend in one point, he is guilty of all." Yet how many youth who profess to be Christians are in the habit of speaking in a disrespectful manner to their parents! God has seen fit, dear youth, to entrust you to the care of your parents for them to train and discipline, and thus act their part in forming your characters for heaven. Yet it rests with you to say whether you will develop a Christian character.

Be entreated, then, to make an entire surrender of your soul to Christ. Take hold of his strength, follow his example, and you will have peace and rest and joy in him. Let every soul breathe the prayer that God will grant unto him according to the riches of his glory, to be strengthened with all might in the inner man, that Christ may dwell in the heart by faith, that he, being rooted and grounded in love, "may be able to comprehend with all saints what is the breadth, and length, and depth, and height; and to know the love of Christ, which passeth knowledge," being filled "with all the fulness of God."

Mrs. E. G. White

May 19, 1898—The Unseen Watcher—No. 1

"I saw in the visions of my head upon my bed," writes Daniel, "and, behold, a watcher and an holy one came down from heaven; he cried aloud, and said thus, Hew down the tree, and cut off his branches, shake off his leaves, and scatter his fruit: let the beasts get away from under it, and the fowls from his branches: nevertheless leave the stump of his roots in the earth, even with a band of iron and brass, in the tender grass of the field; and let it be wet with the dew of heaven, and let his portion be with the beasts in the grass of the earth: let his heart be changed from man's, and let a beast's heart be given unto him; and let seven times pass over him. This matter is by the decree of the watchers, and the demand by the word of the holy ones: to the intent that the living may know that the Most High ruleth in the kingdom of men, and giveth it to whomsoever he will."

Here we are shown that God holds even heathen kings subject to his will. He takes idolaters, and deals with them according to their evil ways and doings.

The same Watcher who came to Daniel was an uninvited guest at Belshazzar's sacrilegious feast. This monarch had everything to flatter his pride and indulge his passions. He was a great king, presiding over what was then the greatest kingdom on earth. His provinces were cultivated by captives, and his capital was enriched by the spoil of nations. He held the life and property of his subjects in his hand. To those who ministered to his pride and vanity, he was indulgent; they were his chosen favorites; but if at any moment they crossed his will, he was at once a cruel tyrant. His anger blazed forth against them without restraint.

Admitted to a share in kingly authority at fifteen years of age, Belshazzar gloried in his power, and lifted up his heart against the God of heaven. He despised the One who is above all rulers, the General of all the armies of heaven. "Belshazzar the king made a great feast to a thousand of his lords, and drank wine before the thousand." On this occasion there was music and dancing and wine-drinking. The profane orgies of royal mirth were attended by men of genius and education. Decorated women with their enchantments, were among the revelers.

Exalted by wine and blinded by delusion, the king himself took the lead in the riotous blasphemy. Reason no longer controlled him; his lower impulses and passions were in the ascendency. His kingdom was strong and apparently invincible, and he would show that he thought nothing too sacred for his hands to handle and profane. To show his contempt for sacred things, he desecrated the holy vessels taken from the temple of the Lord at its destruction.

A Watcher, who was unrecognized, but whose presence was a power of condemnation, looked on this scene of profanation. Soon the unseen and uninvited Guest made his presence felt. At the moment when the sacrilegious revelry was at its height, a bloodless hand came forth, and wrote words of doom on the wall of the banqueting hall. Burning words followed the movements of the hand. "Mene, Mene, Tekel, Upharsin," was written in letters of flame. Few were the characters traced by that hand on the wall facing the king, but they showed that the power of God was there.

Belshazzar was afraid. His conscience was awakened. The fear and suspicion that always follow the course of the guilty seized him. When God makes men fear, they can not hide the intensity of their terror. Alarm seized the great men of the kingdom. Their blasphemous disrespect of sacred things was changed in a moment. A frantic terror overcame all self-control.

Belshazzar had been given many opportunities for knowing and doing the will of God. He had seen his grandfather Nebuchadnezzar banished from the society of men. He had seen the intellect in which the proud monarch gloried taken away by the One who gave it. He had seen the king driven from his kingdom, and made the companion of the beasts of the field. But Belshazzar's love of amusement and self-glorification effaced the lessons he should never have forgotten; and he committed sins similar to those that brought signal judgments on Nebuchadnezzar. He wasted the opportunities graciously granted him, neglecting to use the opportunities within his reach for becoming acquainted with truth. "What must I do to be saved?" was a question that the great but foolish king passed by indifferently.

This is the danger of heedless, reckless youth today. The hand of God will awaken the sinner as it did Belshazzar, but with many it will be too late to repent.

The ruler of Babylon had riches and honor, and in his haughty self-indulgence he had lifted himself up against the God of heaven and earth. He had trusted in his own arm, not supposing that any would dare to say, "Why doest thou this?" But as the mysterious hand traced letters on the wall of his palace, Belshazzar was awed and silenced. In a moment he was completely shorn of his strength, and humbled as a child. He realized that he was at the mercy of One greater than himself. He had been making sport of sacred things. Now his conscience was awakened. He realized that he had had the privilege of knowing and doing the will of God. The history of his grandfather stood out as vividly before him as the writing on the wall.

In vain the king tried to read the burning letters. He had found a power too strong for him. He could not read the writing. "The king cried aloud to bring in the astrologers, the Chaldeans, and the soothsayers. And the king spake, and said to the wise men of Babylon, Whosoever shall read this writing, and show me the interpretation thereof, shall be clothed with scarlet, and have a chain of gold about his neck, and shall be the third ruler in the kingdom. Then came in all the king's wise men: but they could not read the writing, nor make known to the king the interpretation thereof." In vain the king offered honor and promotion. Heavenly wisdom can not be bought and sold. "Then was king Belshazzar greatly troubled, and his countenance was changed in him, and his lords were astonished."

Mrs. E. G. White

May 26, 1898—The Unseen Watcher—No. 2

There was in the palace a woman who was wiser than them all,--the queen of Belshazzar's grandfather. In this emergency she addressed the king in language that sent a ray of light into the darkness. "O king, live forever," she said; "let not thy thoughts trouble thee, nor let thy countenance be changed: there is a man in thy kingdom, in whom is the spirit of the holy gods; and in the days of thy father light and understanding and wisdom, like the wisdom of the gods, was found in him; whom the king Nebuchadnezzar thy father, the king, I say, thy father, made master of the magicians, astrologers, Chaldeans, and soothsayers: ... now let Daniel be called, and he will show the interpretation."

"Then was Daniel brought in before the king." Making an effort to brace himself, and to show his authority, Belshazzar said: "Art thou that Daniel, which art of the children of the captivity of Judah, whom the king my father brought out of Jewry? I have even heard of thee, that the spirit of the gods is in thee, and that light and understanding and excellent wisdom is found in thee.... Now if thou canst read the writing, and make known to me the interpretation thereof, thou shalt be clothed with scarlet, and have a chain of gold about thy neck, and shalt be the third ruler in the kingdom."

Daniel was not awed by the king's appearance, nor confused or intimidated by his words. "Let thy gifts be to thyself," he answered, "and give thy rewards to another; yet I will read the writing unto the king, and make known to him the interpretation. O thou king, the most high God gave Nebuchadnezzar thy father a kingdom, and majesty, and glory, and honor.... But when his heart was lifted up, and his mind hardened in pride, he was deposed from his kingly throne, and they took his glory from him.... And thou his son, O Belshazzar, hast not humbled thine heart, though thou knewest all this; but hast lifted up thyself against the Lord of heaven; and they have brought the vessels of his house before thee, and thou, and thy lords, thy wives, and thy concubines, have drunk in them; and thou hast praised the gods of silver, and gold, of brass, iron, wood, and stone, which see not, nor hear, nor know: and the God in whose hand thy breath is, and whose are all thy ways, hast thou not glorified."

"This is the writing that was written, Mene, Mene, Tekel, Upharsin. This is the interpretation of the thing: Mene; God hath numbered thy kingdom, and finished it. Tekel; Thou art weighed in the balances, and art found wanting. Peres; Thy kingdom is divided, and given to the Medes and Persians."

Daniel did not swerve from his duty. He held the king's sin before him, showing him the lessons he might have learned, but did not. Belshazzar had not heeded the events so significant to him. He had not read his grandfather's history correctly. The responsibility of knowing truth had been laid upon him, but the practical lessons he might have learned and acted upon had not been taken to heart; and his course of action brought the sure result.

This was the last feast of boasting held by the Chaldean king; for he who bears long with man's perversity had passed the irrevocable sentence. Belshazzar had greatly dishonored the One who had exalted him as king, and his probation was taken from him. While the king and his nobles were at the height of their revelry, the Persians turned the Euphrates out of its channel, and marched into the unguarded city. As Belshazzar and his lords were drinking from the sacred vessels of Jehovah, and praising their gods of silver and gold, Cyrus and his soldiers stood under the walls of the palace. "In that night," the record says, "was Belshazzar the king of the Chaldeans slain. And Darius the Median took the kingdom."

Could the curtain be rolled back before the youth who have never given their hearts to God, with others who are Christians in name, but who are unrenewed in heart and unsanctified in temper, they would see that God's eye is ever upon them, and they would feel as disturbed as did the king of Babylon. They would realize that in every place, at every hour in the day, there is a holy Watcher, who balances every account, whose eye takes in the whole situation, whether it is one of fidelity, or one of disloyalty and deception.

We are never alone. We have a Companion, whether we choose him or not. Remember, young men and young women, that wherever you are, whatever you are doing, God is there. To your every word and action you have a witness,--the holy, sin-hating God. Nothing that is said or done or thought can escape his infinite eye. Your words may not be heard by human ears, but they are heard by the Ruler of the universe. He reads the inward anger of the soul when the will is crossed. He hears the expression of profanity. In the deepest darkness and solitude he is there. No one can deceive God; none can escape from their accountability to him.

"O Lord, thou hast searched me, and known me," writes the psalmist. "Thou knowest my downsitting and mine uprising, thou understandest my thought afar off. Thou compassest my path and my lying down, and art acquainted with all my ways. For there is not a word in my tongue, but, lo, O Lord, thou knowest it altogether. Thou hast beset me behind and before, and laid thine hand upon me. Such knowledge is too wonderful for me; it is high; I can not attain unto it. Whither shall I go from thy Spirit? or whither shall I flee from thy presence? If I ascend up into heaven, thou art there: If I make my bed in hell, behold, thou art there. If I take the wings of the morning, and dwell in the uttermost parts of the sea; even there shall thy hand lead me, and thy right hand shall hold me. If I say, Surely the darkness shall cover me; even the night shall be light about me. Yea, the darkness hideth not from thee; but the night shineth as the day: the darkness and the light are both alike to thee."

Day by day the record of your words, your actions, and your influence, is being made in the books of heaven. This you must meet. "I saw the dead, small and great, stand before God; and the books were opened: and another book was opened, which is the book of life: and the dead were judged out of those things which were written in the books, according to their works.... And whosoever was not found written in the book of life was cast into the lake of fire."

I send you the note of warning to take heed. You are appointed to be "laborers together with God." This responsibility you may ignore; but your action in so doing will bring its sure result. God has given to each of you your work. He has given you faculties, means, light, and knowledge, and he holds you accountable for the way in which you use these powers. "We ought to give the more earnest heed to the things which we have heard, lest at any time we should let them slip. For if the word spoken by angels was steadfast, and every transgression and disobedience received a just recompense of reward; how shall we escape, if we neglect so great salvation; which at the first began to be spoken by the Lord, and was confirmed unto us by them that heard him?"

Mrs. E. G. White

June 2, 1898—The Second Adam

Christ is called the second Adam. In purity and holiness, connected with God and beloved by God, he began where the first Adam began. Willingly he passed over the ground where Adam fell, and redeemed Adam's failure.

But the first Adam was in every way more favorably situated than was Christ. The wonderful provision made for man in Eden was made by a God who loved him. Everything in nature was pure and undefiled. Fruits, flowers, and beautiful, lofty trees flourished in the garden of Eden. With every needed blessing, Adam and Eve were abundantly supplied. Not a shadow interposed between them and their Creator. They knew God as their beneficent Father, and in all things their will was conformed to the will of God. And God's character was reflected in the character of Adam. His glory was revealed in every object of nature. The invisible things of God were clearly seen, being understood by the things that were made, even his eternal power and Godhead.

But Satan came to the dwellers in Eden, and insinuated doubts of God's wisdom. He accused him, their Heavenly Father and Sovereign, of selfishness, because, to test their loyalty, he had prohibited them from eating of the tree of knowledge. "Hath God said, Ye shall not eat of every tree of the garden?" he said to Eve. "And the woman said, ... We may eat of the fruit of the trees of the garden: but of the fruit of the tree which is in the midst of the garden, God hath said, Ye shall not eat of it, neither shall ye touch it, lest ye die."

This was the smallest test that God could devise to prove the obedience of our first parents; but Eve fell under the temptation. Adam accepted the forbidden fruit from the hand of his wife; and by this act the flood-gates of woe were opened upon our world. Adam was endowed with a nature pure and sinless, but he fell because he listened to the suggestions of the enemy. His posterity became depraved; by one man's disobedience many were made sinners.

When Christ came, it was to a world disloyal to God--a world all seared and marred by the curse of rebellion. Since the fall, the arch-deceiver had carried on his work with intense vigor, until the curse of transgression had fallen heavily upon the earth. Men were corrupted by Satan's inventions. He had been leading them astray by his false representations of God's character. Claiming for himself the attributes of mercy, goodness, and truth, he had attributed his own character to God. These misrepresentations Christ knew he must meet in human nature, and prove to be false.

For this, he, the Commander of all heaven, one with God, clothed his divinity with humanity. He humbled himself, taking up his abode on the earth, that he might become acquainted with the temptations and trials wherewith man is beset. Before the heavenly universe he unfolded to men the great salvation that his righteousness would bring to all who accept it,--an inheritance among the saints and angels in the presence of God.

Christ was tempted by Satan in a hundredfold severer manner than was Adam, and under circumstances in every way more trying. The deceiver presented himself as an angel of light, but Christ withstood his temptations. He redeemed Adam's disgraceful fall, and saved the world.

With his human arm, Christ encircled the race, while with his divine arm, he grasped the throne of the Infinite, uniting finite man with the infinite God. He bridged the gulf that sin had made, and connected earth with heaven. In his human nature he maintained the purity of his divine character. He lived the law of God, and honored it in a world of transgression, revealing to the heavenly universe, to Satan, and to all the fallen sons and daughters of Adam, that through his grace, humanity can keep the law of God. He came to impart his own divine nature, his own image, to the repentant, believing soul.

There is hope for all who will come to Christ and receive him as their personal Saviour. The faith that lays hold upon Christ will work by love and purify the soul. "If our gospel be hid," Paul declares, "it is hid to them that are lost: in whom the god of this world hath blinded the minds of them which believe not, lest the light of the glorious gospel of Christ, who is the image of God, should shine unto them.... For God, who commanded the light to shine out of darkness, hath shined in our hearts, to give the light of the knowledge of the glory of God in the face of Jesus Christ."

Mrs. E. G. White

June 30, 1898—God's Word Our Study Book—No. 1

God calls for whole-souled consecration to his ways. Our highest powers are to be carefully cultivated. Our talents are lent us by God for use, not to be perverted or abused. They are to be improved by use, that they may do the work of God. Our time belongs to God. The moments are freighted with eternal consequences, and we have no right to squander them. When we use these gifts to the glory of God, he will increase them, that they may operate in a wider sphere. When the student fully realizes that it is Christ whom he is to honor; that Christ is to be his Guide, his Counselor, in everything he undertakes; that Christ alone can give fitness for work in any position; that it is Christ who restores the image of God in man,--when he understands that the very image, the character, of Christ is to be reflected in man, he will make every talent a power for good.

How much the student of nature can learn of God if, at the same time, he will become a student of the word! If, with the word of God in your heart, you go forth to break up and cultivate the soil, you will find your hearts softened and subdued by the Holy Spirit of God. The mind will be opened to the teachings of God in the natural world.

But the Bible is not studied as it should be; therefore the youth do not become wise in the Scriptures, and thoroughly furnished unto all good works. Light reading fascinates the mind, and makes the reading of God's word uninteresting. The Bible requires thought and prayerful research. It is not enough to skim over the surface. While some passages are too plain to be misunderstood, others demand careful and patient study. Like the precious metal concealed in the hills and mountains, its gems of truth are to be searched out, and stored in the mind for future use.

And when you search the Scriptures with an earnest desire to know the truth, God will breathe his Spirit into your heart, and impress your mind with the light of his word. The Bible is its own interpreter, one passage explaining another. By comparing scriptures referring to the same subject, you will see harmony and beauty of which you have never dreamed. There is no other book whose perusal strengthens and enlarges, elevates and ennobles, the mind as does the perusal of this Book of books.

The injunction of the word of God is, "Work out your own salvation with fear and trembling. For it is God which worketh in you both to will and to do of his good pleasure." God and the human being are to co-operate. Man is to work out that which God works in. The student of the word of God is to use the knowledge he has gained. He is to improve the opportunities that are thrown in his way. With a settled conviction of duty, he is to use his knowledge and influence in any channel, to the end that he may gain more by their use. He who would become an all-round man will find openings everywhere, and the privilege of being a learner will be his throughout his life.

It is not for you, students, to follow your own inclinations and pleasures and tastes. Study the life of Christ in this respect. Follow him from the manger to Calvary, and act as he acted. The great principles which he maintained, you are to maintain. Your standard is to be the character of him who was pure, holy, and undefiled. God would have you show respect for the principles of your teachers. He has made them his instruments, and you are to remember that the Lord is sending light to you through them. There is but little reverence in our world; and you, as students, are to act up to the highest standard of duty, in the fear and love of God.

It is a most difficult task to get away from old customs and established ideas, but the Lord would have everything that is false cut away from the life. The philosophy of common sense is of far more importance to the youth than the study of Greek and Latin. Too often the brain is used like the much-abused stomach; it receives a great amount of food which it can not take care of. The students think long periods of study to be all-sufficient for them, and after a few years are sent from school with their diplomas, as thoroughly educated men. But this is a farce. In these years of continued study a loss is sustained which but few realize. That which is crowded into the mind is of no advantage to the students. As a result, Satan comes in, and causes ideas of infidelity that they have received during their school education, to become a matter of great interest. A bewitching power holds the intellect and works it, until it becomes a curse instead of a blessing.

Mrs. E. G. White

July 7, 1898—God's Word Our Study Book—No. 2

Our students need lessons that they have not yet received. There must be no lowering of the standard as to what constitutes true education. It must be raised far above where it now stands. It is not men whom we are to exalt and worship; it is God, the only true and living God, to whom our worship and reverence are due. According to the teaching of the Scriptures, it dishonors God to address ministers as "reverend." No mortal has any right to attach this to his own name, or to the name of any other human being. It belongs only to God, to distinguish him from every other being. Those who lay claim to this title take to themselves God's holy honor. They have no right to the stolen word, whatever, their position may be. "Holy and reverend is his name." We dishonor God when we use this word where it does not belong.

"And the child grew, and waxed strong in spirit, filled with wisdom: and the grace of God was upon him." "And he went down with them, and came to Nazareth, and was subject unto them." "And Jesus increased in wisdom and stature, and in favor with God and man." Let the brightest example the world has yet seen be your example, rather than the greatest and most learned men of the age, who know not God, nor Jesus Christ whom he has sent. The Father and the Son alone are to be exalted.

The cross of Christ,--how many believe it to be what it is? How many bring it into their studies, and know its true significance? There could not be a Christian in our world without the cross of Christ. Then keep it before the schools as the foundation of all true education. Turn from the examples of the world, cease to extol the professedly great men; turn the mind from the glory of everything save the cross of Christ. Said Paul, "God forbid that I should glory, save in the cross of our Lord Jesus Christ." Let all, from the highest to the lowest, understand what it means to glory in the cross of Christ. That cross is to be bravely and manfully borne. Christ declares, "If any man will come after me, let him deny himself, and take up his cross, and follow me." And to all who will lift it, and bear it after Christ, the cross is a pledge of the crown of glory that can never fade away.

The most essential lessons for students to obtain are those that will point them to straight paths which lead, not to the world, but from the world, to the cross of Calvary.

Their studies should be of that character which will make them most successful in the service of God, and enable them to walk in the footsteps of Christ.

This is the highest science that we can learn,--the science of salvation. The cross of Calvary, rightly regarded, is true philosophy, pure and undefiled religion. It is eternal life to all who believe. By painstaking effort, line upon line, precept upon precept, here a little and there a little, it should be impressed upon the minds of students that the cross of Christ is just as efficacious now as in Paul's day, and should be as perfectly understood by them as it was by the great apostle, who could declare, "God forbid that I should glory, save in the cross of our Lord Jesus Christ, by whom the world is crucified unto me, and I unto the world."

Christ was crucified for fallen man. But to many who call themselves Christians this event is nothing. In practise they deny the cross of Christ. They know it not, they glory not in it. They admit that Christ died on the cross, but because there is a crucifixion for them to experience, they will not receive the lessons that lead to self-denial and self-sacrifice. They are Christians in name only. The central point of their faith is not a crucified and risen Saviour, who brings to all that receive him the privilege of being sons and daughters of God.

Students, study the Scriptures. Know that the only thing in which you can safely glory is that which will open to you the gates of the city of God. Learn from the word of God how to form characters fitted for the country you are seeking. Know that Christ is to be set forth among you, and that all that was lost in Adam the cross of Christ fully restores to every believing soul.

Then your testimony will be: "For me, Lord, thou wast fastened to the cross. Thy life was given for me, that I might have eternal life in the city of God. I will look to thee for my salvation. I will cleanse myself from all filthiness of the flesh and spirit, perfecting holiness through thy grace and in thy name. Thy blood alone can cleanse me from all sin. It speaks to me better things than that of Abel. Thy suffering becomes to me wisdom, and righteousness, and sanctification, and redemption. 'God forbid that I should glory, save in the cross of our Lord Jesus Christ, by whom the world is crucified unto me, and I unto the world.'"

Mrs. E. G. White

July 14, 1898—Be Ye Holy

The character of Christ is the standard which the Christian is to keep before him. His aim should be to possess those graces which were exemplified in the life of Christ in humanity; for only in the possession of these, can he honor his Redeemer, and render him the oblations of a pure heart.

The life practise of the believing child of God should exalt the gospel of Christ. It should testify to the power of the word upon the human life. Christ has said, "If ye love me, keep my commandments." And in his prayer to the Father for his followers, he said: "For their sakes I sanctify myself, that they also might be sanctified through the truth. Neither pray I for these alone, but for them also which shall believe on me through their word; that they all may be one; as thou, Father, art in me, and I in thee, that they also may be one in us: that the world may believe that thou hast sent me. And the glory which thou gavest me I have given them; that they may be one, even as we are one: I in them, and thou in me, that they may be made perfect in one; and that the world may know that thou hast sent me, and hast loved them, as thou hast loved me."

Christ would have the youth surrender themselves to him, with all that they possess. Our time, our character, our influence, belong to God, and should be given to do him service. Every hour of the day we should realize that the Lord is near, that he sees all we do, and hears every word we utter. "The eyes of the Lord are in every place, beholding the evil and the good." Says the psalmist, "There is not a word in my tongue, but, lo, O Lord, thou knowest it altogether."

Often the word has come to the youth, "Be sober-minded." It is upon this point that they most often fail. They do not show themselves men and women of common sense. They do not realize the peril they are in when not connected with God. The Lord calls upon them to deal honestly with themselves, to deal honestly with God. There must be no mingling of the sacred and the common in our conversation. Cheap, earthly, unchristian words may be represented as "strange fire," and with this God can have nothing to do. The loud, boisterous laugh is a denial of God in the soul; for it reveals that the truth is not ruling in the heart. All such professors have yet to be converted.

They are stumbling-blocks in the way which God has prepared at infinite cost. He would keep the path clear and plain, that no sinner may mistake it, or err because of the stumbling-blocks which unconverted professors place in the way by their unconsecrated, unholy lives. Let all lightness and trifling, all cheap conversation, be put away. By our vain words and unchristian example, we dishonor God, and imperil not only our own souls, but also the souls of those with whom we associate.

The example which Christ has given to the world forbids all levity and cheapness; and if the life is made fragrant by the grace of God, these elements will not appear. A genuine cheerfulness, an uplifting influence, will flow forth from all who love God and keep his commandments. And this carries with it a convincing, converting power. "Work out your own salvation with fear and trembling," says the apostle. Why with fear and trembling?--Lest you shall in any way misrepresent your holy faith by lightness, by trifling, by jesting or joking, and thus give others the impression that the truth which you profess has no sanctifying influence upon the character. This is the kind of fear and trembling with which we are to work out our salvation. "For," says the apostle, "It is God which worketh in you both to will and to do of his good pleasure."

Those who are easily overcome by a spirit of lightness and frivolity make manifest what they have treasured up in the soul temple. To them the word comes: "Gird up the loins of your mind, be sober, and hope to the end for the grace that is to be brought unto you at the revelation of Jesus Christ. As obedient children, not fashioning yourselves according to the former lusts in your ignorance. But as he which hath called you is holy, so be ye holy in all manner of conversation; because it is written, Be ye holy; for I am holy."

"And if ye call on the Father, who without respect of persons judgeth according to every man's work, pass the time of your sojourning here in fear," not in servility and uncertainty, but in a wholesome, godly fear. As Christians we are to "continue in prayer, and watch in the same with thanksgiving."

Paul enjoins us to "walk in wisdom toward them that are without, redeeming the time. Let your speech be alway with grace, seasoned with salt, that ye may know how ye ought to answer every man." "Do all things without murmurings and disputings: that ye may be blameless and harmless, the sons of God, without rebuke, in the midst of a crooked and perverse nation, among whom ye shine as lights in the world, holding forth the word of life." "Put on therefore, as the elect of God, holy and beloved, bowels of mercies, kindness, humbleness of mind, meekness, longsuffering; forbearing one another, and forgiving one another, if any man have a quarrel against any: even as Christ forgave you, so also do ye. And above all these things put on charity, which is the bond of perfectness."

For this work, reasons strong and convincing are urged. "Forasmuch as ye know that ye were not redeemed with corruptible things, as silver and gold, from your vain conversation received by tradition from your fathers; but with the precious blood of Christ, as of a lamb without blemish and without spot."

When we consider what is our relation to Christ, and what he is to us individually, our hearts will be softened and subdued. Beholding him, praying to him, we shall open our hearts to him, and become habitations of God through the Spirit. He will dwell in our hearts by faith. Then, turn whichever way we will, we shall behold his likeness. Our very thoughts will be brought into captivity to Jesus Christ. And as we contemplate him who loved us, and gave himself for us, his prayer to the Father for us will be answered.

Mrs. E. G. White

July 21, 1898—The Risen Saviour

The Sabbath is passed; and early in the morning of the first day of the week, while it is yet dark, Mary Magdalene is at the sepulcher. Other women are to meet her there, but Mary is the first at the tomb. Weeping, she draws near to the place where the body of Jesus had been laid, "and seeth the stone taken away from the sepulcher. Then she runneth, and cometh to Simon, Peter, and to the other disciple, whom Jesus loved, and saith unto them, They have taken away the Lord out of the sepulcher, and we know not where they have laid him. Peter therefore went forth, and that other disciple, and came to the sepulcher. And he stooping down, and looking in, saw the linen clothes lying; yet went he not in. Then cometh Simon Peter following him, and went into the sepulcher, and seeth the linen clothes lie, and the napkin that was about his head, not lying with the linen clothes, but wrapped together in a place by itself. Then went in also that other disciple, which came first to the sepulcher, and he saw, and believed. For as yet they knew not the scripture." "Thou wilt not leave my soul in hell; neither wilt thou suffer thine holy one to see corruption." "But God will redeem my soul from the power of the grave: for he shall receive me."

"Then the disciples went away again unto their own home. But Mary stood without at the sepulcher weeping: and as she wept, she stooped down, and looked into the sepulcher, and seeth two angels in white sitting, the one at the head, and the other at the feet, where the body of Jesus had lain. And they say unto her, Woman, why weepest thou? She said unto them, Because they have taken away my Lord, and I know not where they have laid him."

Feeling that she must find some one who will tell her what has been done with Jesus, Mary turns away even from the words of the angels. As she does so, another voice addresses her: "Woman, why weepest thou?" Through her tear-dimmed eyes, Mary sees one whom she supposes to be the gardener. "Sir," she says, "If thou have borne him hence, tell me where thou hast laid him, and I will take him away. Jesus saith unto her, Mary." At the familiar voice, she turns to him. She knows now that it is no stranger who speaks. Before her she sees the living Saviour. She springs toward him, as if to embrace his feet, saying, "Rabboni." But the Saviour raises his hand and says, "Touch me not; for I am not yet ascended to my Father: but go to my brethren, and say unto them, I ascend unto my Father, and your Father; and to my God, and your God."

There was no more weeping for Mary. Her heart was filled with rejoicing. She "came and told the disciples that she had seen the Lord, and that he had spoken these things unto her." "And they, when they had heard that he was alive, and had been seen of her, believed not." While Mary was absent, Jesus appeared to the women who had come to the sepulcher from another direction. These women had prepared sweet spices with which to anoint the body of their Lord. On the way to the sepulcher they had said, among themselves, "Who shall roll us away the stone from the door of the sepulcher?" When they reached the place, they saw that the stone had been rolled away. And entering into the sepulcher, they saw a young man sitting on the right side, clothed in a long white garment.

The women were greatly terrified, and bowed their faces to the earth; for the sight of the heavenly being was more than they could endure. The angel was compelled to hide his glory still more before he could converse with them. "And he saith unto them, Be not affrighted: Ye seek Jesus of Nazareth, which was crucified: he is risen; he is not here: behold the place where they laid him. But go your way, tell his disciples and Peter that he goeth before you into Galilee: there shall ye see him, as he said unto you."

As yet there had been no revelation of Christ to the eleven, and the women went to tell the disciples the wondrous news. "And as they went to tell the disciples, behold, Jesus met them, saying, All hail. And they came and held him by the feet, and worshiped him. Then said Jesus unto them, Be not afraid: go tell my brethren that they go into Galilee, and there shall they see me." Thus Christ made an appointment for a public meeting with his brethren in Galilee.

"It was Mary Magdalene, and Joanna, and Mary the Mother of James, and other women that were with them, which told these things unto the apostles. And their words seemed to them as idle tales, and they believed them not."

"Go your way," said the angel to the women; "tell his disciples and Peter that he goeth before you into Galilee." What a comforting message was thus given to Peter! The last look Jesus had given Peter was after the disciple's thrice-uttered denial. Peter was not forgotten by Christ, and this mention of his name signified to the repentant disciple that he was forgiven.

Said the angel: "Why seek ye the living among the dead? He is not here, but he is risen: remember how he spake unto you when he was yet in Galilee, saying, The Son of man must be delivered into the hands of sinful men, and be crucified, and the third day rise again."

The wonderful instruction that Christ had given his disciples was never to lose its force, but they had to be reminded of the lessons which he had repeatedly given them while he was yet with them.

"Remember," said the angel, "how he spake unto you when he was yet in Galilee, saying, The Son of man must be delivered into the hands of sinful men, and be crucified, and the third day rise again." The disciples were surprised that they had not thought of these things before. Why had his words been forgotten?

Christ had spoken to them in regard to his future. He had declared, "All ye shall be offended because of me this night: for it is written, I will smite the shepherd, and the sheep of the flock shall be scattered abroad." He had shown them "how that he must go unto Jerusalem, and suffer many things of the elders and chief priests, and scribes, and be killed." When going up to Jerusalem, he had taken the twelve apart by the way, and said to them: "Behold, we go up to Jerusalem; and the Son of man shall be betrayed unto the chief priests and unto the scribes, and they shall condemn him to death, and shall deliver him to the Gentiles to mock and to scourge, and to crucify him." If he had left the matter here, there would indeed have been cause for the disciples to be hopeless. But he added, "And be raised again the third day." "After I am risen again, I will go before you into Galilee."

Why, then, did the disciples look on the dark side, and feel so wholly discouraged? Had not Christ anticipated their disappointment? Had not given precious instruction? "Let not your heart be troubled," he had said; "ye believe in God, believe also in me. In my Father's house are many mansions; if it were not so, I would have told you. I go to prepare a place for you. And if I go and prepare a place for you, I will come again, and receive you unto myself; that where I am, there ye may be also ... Peace I leave with you, my peace I give unto you: not as the world giveth, give I unto you. Let not your heart be troubled, neither let it be afraid. Ye have heard how I said unto you, I go away, and come again unto you. If ye loved me, ye would rejoice, because I said, I go unto the Father: for my Father is greater than I. And now I have told you before it come to pass, that, when it is come to pass, ye might believe."

Christ had said everything encouraging that he could, in order that the faith of his disciples might not fail when he hung upon the cross. If, after his crucifixion and burial, in the place of giving way to their sorrow, the disciples had carefully reviewed what Christ had told them to prepare them for this time, they would not have been so wholly discouraged. They would have seen light amid the darkness.

Mrs. E. G. White

July 28, 1898—The Risen Saviour—Part 2

After the crucifixion of Christ, the priests and rulers did not feel the sense of victory which they had expected. They did not rejoice at their success in silencing the voice of the Great Teacher. They were afraid. Already his death was calling attention to his life and character. The priests were convicted that their attempts at revenge had failed; and they dreaded a dead Christ more, far more, than they had ever feared a living Christ.

At the time of the Passover, many had come from far-distant lands to see and hear Christ; and they were shocked at hearing of the work which had been done by the priests and rulers. Many had brought their sick and suffering to the temple; but when they applied to the priests and rulers for help and sympathy, they were sent empty away. The people were apparently determined to have the living Saviour with them again. But they were driven from the temple courts, and soldiers were stationed at its gates to keep back the crowds who came with their suffering ones demanding entrance.

On his last journey to Jerusalem, Jesus had spoken to his disciples saying, "Behold, we go up to Jerusalem; and the Son of man shall be betrayed unto the chief priests and unto the scribes, and they shall condemn him to death, and shall deliver him to the Gentiles to mock, and to scourge, and to crucify him: and the third day he shall rise again."

These words had come to the priests and rulers through Judas. When they had first heard them, they had mocked and ridiculed; but now, as they heard the clamor for Christ, the Healer,--he who had healed the sick and had raised Lazarus from the dead,--they were ill at ease. Had not Christ declared, "Destroy this temple, and in three days I will raise it up"? While the rulers had affected to regard these words as a mere boast, and had spoken of Christ as a deceiver, the rent veil of the temple, laying open to the gaze of all the sacred enclosure, had filled them with fears that were almost unendurable. Would Christ rise from the dead? What would he do if he should rise? Such were the questions that passed from lip to lip.

The murderers of Jesus did all that they possibly could to keep his body in the tomb. On the day that followed the day of the preparation, the chief priests and Pharisees went to Pilate, saying: "Sir, we remember that that deceiver said, while he was yet alive, After three days I will rise again. Command therefore that the sepulcher be made sure until the third day, lest his disciples come by night and steal him away, and say unto the people, He is risen from the dead: so the last error shall be worse than the first." "Ye have a watch," said Pilate; "go your way, make it as sure as ye can. So they went, and made the sepulcher sure, sealing the stone, and setting a watch."

Lest the prediction of Christ should come to pass, they affixed to the stone of the sepulcher the Roman seal, and stationed around it a guard of soldiers. But little did these murderers know how useless were their efforts to keep the body of Christ hidden in the tomb. The very precautions they had taken were designed by God to establish the facts of the resurrection. The greater the number of the soldiers around the tomb of Christ, the stronger would be the evidence of his resurrection.

Early on the morning of the resurrection, before any one had reached the sepulcher, there was a great earthquake. The mightiest angel from heaven, he who held the position from which Satan fell, received his commission from the Father; and, clothed with the panoply of heaven, he parted the darkness from his track. His face was like the lightning, and his garments white as snow. The Roman guard were keeping their weary watch when this angel came to the earth, and they were enabled to endure the sight; for they had a message to bear as witnesses of the resurrection of Christ.

The light of heaven encircled the tomb, and the whole heaven was lighted by the glory of the angel. The angel approached the grave, and rolling away the stone as if it had been a pebble, he sat upon it. Then his voice was heard, Son of God, come forth; thy Father calls thee; and Jesus came forth from the grave with the step of a mighty conqueror. There was a burst of triumph, for the heavenly family were waiting to receive him; and the mighty angel, followed by the army of heaven, bowed in adoration before him as he, the Monarch of heaven, proclaimed over the rent tomb of Joseph, "I am the resurrection, and the life." All united in the song, "Great and marvelous are thy works, Lord God Almighty; just and true are thy ways, thou King of saints.... Thou only art holy.... Thy judgments are made manifest." "Who for the joy that was set before him endured the cross, despising the shame."   Mrs. E. G. White

August 4, 1898—The Risen Saviour—Part 3

"I am the resurrection, and the life." He who had said, "I lay down my life, that I might take it again," came forth from the grave to life that was in himself. Humanity died: divinity did not die. In his divinity, Christ possessed the power to break the bonds of death. He declares that he has life in himself to quicken whom he will.

All created beings live by the will and power of God. They are recipients of the life of the Son of God. However able and talented, however large their capacities, they are replenished with life from the source of all life. He is the spring, the fountain, of life. Only he who alone hath immortality, dwelling in light and life, [could] say, "I have power to lay down my life, and I have power to take it again."

The words of Christ, "I am the resurrection, and the life," were distinctly heard by the Roman guard. The whole army of Satan heard them. And we understand them when we hear. Christ had come to give his life a ransom for many. As the Good Shepherd, he had laid down his life for the sheep. It was the righteousness of God to maintain his law by inflicting the penalty. This was the only way in which the law could be maintained, and pronounced holy, and just, and good. It was the only way by which sin could be made to appear exceeding sinful, and the honor and majesty of divine authority be maintained.

The law of God's government was to be magnified by the death of God's only begotten Son. Christ bore the guilt of the sins of the world. Our sufficiency is found only in the incarnation and death of the Son of God. He could suffer, because sustained by divinity. He could endure, because he was without one taint of disloyalty or sin. Christ triumphed in man's behalf in thus bearing the justice of punishment. He secured eternal life to men, while he exalted the law, and made it honorable.

Christ was invested with the right to give immortality. The life which he had laid down in humanity, he again took up and gave to humanity. "I am come," he says, "that they might have life, and that they might have it more abundantly." "Whoso eateth my flesh, and drinketh my blood, hath eternal life; and I will raise him up at the last day." "Whosoever drinketh of the water that I shall give him, shall never thirst; but the water that I shall give him shall be in him a well of water springing up into everlasting life."

All who are one with Christ through faith in him gain an experience which is life unto eternal life. "As the living Father hath sent me, and I live by the Father: so he that eateth me, even he shall live by me." He "dwelleth in me, and I in him." "I will raise him up at the last day." "Because I live, ye shall live also."

Christ became one with humanity, that humanity might become one in Spirit and life with him. By virtue of this union in obedience to the word of God, his life becomes their life. He says to the penitent, "I am the resurrection, and the life." Death is looked upon by Christ as sleep,--silence, darkness, sleep. He speaks of it as if it were of little moment. "Whosoever liveth and believeth in me," he says, "shall never die." "If a man keep my sayings, he shall never taste of death." "He shall never see death." And to the believing one, death is but a small matter. With him to die is but to sleep. "Them also which sleep in Jesus God will bring with him."

While the women were making known their message as witnesses of the risen Saviour, and while Jesus was preparing to reveal himself to a large number of his followers, another scene was taking place. The Roman guard had been enabled to view the mighty angel who sang the song of triumph at the birth of Christ, and hear the angels who now sang the song of redeeming love. At the wonderful scene which they were permitted to behold, they had fainted and become as dead men. When the heavenly train was hidden from their sight, they arose to their feet, and made their way to the gate of the garden as quickly as their tottering limbs would carry them. Staggering like blind or drunken men, their faces pale as the dead, they told those they met of the wonderful scenes they had witnessed. Messengers preceded them quickly to the chief priests and rulers, declaring, as best they could, the remarkable incidents that had taken place.

The guard were making their way first to Pilate, but the priests and rulers sent word for them to be brought into their presence. These hardened soldiers presented a strange appearance, as they bore testimony to the resurrection of Christ and also of the multitude whom he brought forth with him. They told the chief priests what they had seen at the sepulcher. They had not time to think or speak anything but the truth. But the rulers were displeased with the report. They knew that great publicity had been given to the trial of Christ, by holding it at the time of the Passover. They knew that the wonderful events which had taken place--the supernatural darkness, the mighty earthquake--could not be without effect, and they at once planned how they might deceive the people. The soldiers were bribed to report a falsehood; and the priests guaranteed that if the matter should come to Pilate's ears, as it most assuredly would, they would be responsible for the action of the soldiers. They bribed Pilate to silence, and by special messengers sent the report they had prepared to every part of the country.

Mrs. E. G. White

August 11, 1898—The Risen Saviour—Part 4

When Christ cried out while upon the cross, "It is finished," there was a mighty earthquake, that rent open the graves of many who had been faithful and loyal, bearing their testimony against every evil work, and magnifying the Lord of hosts. As the Life-giver came forth from the sepulcher, proclaiming. "I am the resurrection, and the life," he summoned these saints from the grave. When alive, they had borne their testimony unflinchingly for the truth; now, they were to be witnesses to him who had raised them from the dead. These, said Christ, are no longer the captives of Satan. I have redeemed them; I have brought them from the grave as the first-fruits of my power, to be with me where I am, nevermore to see death or experience sorrow.

During his ministry, Jesus raised the dead to life. He raised the son of the widow of Nain, the daughter of Jairus, and Lazarus; but these were not clothed with immortality. After they were raised, they continued to be subject to death. But those who came forth from the grave at Christ's resurrection were raised to everlasting life. They were the multitude of captives that ascended with him as trophies of his victory over death and the grave.

After his resurrection, Christ did not show himself to any save his followers; but testimony in regard to his resurrection was not wanting. Those who were raised with Christ "appeared unto many," declaring, Christ has risen from the dead, and we are risen with him. They bore testimony in the city to the fulfillment of the scripture, "Thy dead men shall live, together with my dead body shall they arise. Awake and sing, ye that dwell in dust: for thy dew is as the dew of herbs, and the earth shall cast out the dead." These saints contradicted the lie which the Roman guard had been hired to circulate,--that the disciples had come by night and stolen him away. This testimony could not be silenced.

Christ was the first-fruits of them that slept. It was to the glory of God that the Prince of life should be the first-fruits, the antitype of the wave-sheaf. "For whom he did foreknow, he also did predestinate to be conformed to the image of his Son, that he might be the first-born among many brethren." This very scene, the resurrection of Christ from the dead, had been celebrated in type by the Jews. When the first heads of grain ripened in the field, they were carefully gathered; and when the people went up to Jerusalem, these were presented to the Lord as a thank-offering. The people waved the ripened sheaf before God, acknowledging him as the Lord of the harvest. After this ceremony the sickle could be put to the wheat, and the harvest gathered.

So those who had been raised were to be presented to the universe as a pledge of the resurrection of all who believe in Christ as their personal Saviour. The same power that raised Christ from the dead will raise his church, and glorify it with Christ, as his bride, above all principalities, above all powers, above every name that is named, not only in this world, but also in the heavenly courts, the world above. The victory of the sleeping saints will be glorious on the morning of the resurrection. Satan's triumph will end, while Christ will triumph in glory and honor. The Life-giver will crown with immortality all who come forth from the grave.

The work of the Saviour on earth was finished. The time had come for him to return to his heavenly home. "And he led them [the disciples] out as far as to Bethany, and he lifted up his hands, and blessed them. And it came to pass, while he blessed them, he was parted from them, and carried up into heaven."

As Christ ascends while in the act of blessing his disciples, an army of angels encircle him as a cloud. Christ takes with him the multitude of captives. He will himself bring to the Father the first-fruits of them that slept, as an evidence that he is conqueror of death and the grave. At the portals of the city of God, an innumerable company of angels await his coming. As they approach, the escorting angels address the company at the gate in triumphant tones:

"Lift up your heads, O ye gates; And be ye lift up, ye everlasting doors; And the King of glory shall come in.' "Who is this King of glory?" the waiting angels inquire.

"The Lord strong and mighty, The Lord mighty in battle.

Lift up your heads, O ye gates; Even lift them up, ye everlasting doors; And the King of glory shall come in." Again the waiting angels ask, "Who is this King of glory?" and the escorting angels reply, in melodious strains: "The Lord of hosts, he is the King of glory." Then the portals of the city of God are opened wide, and the angelic throng sweep through.

There is the throne, and around it the rainbow of promise. There are seraphim and cherubim. The angels circle round him, but Christ waves them back. He enters into the presence of his Father. He points to his triumph in this antitype of himself,--the wave-sheaf,--those raised with him, the representatives of the captive dead who shall come forth from their graves when the trump shall sound. He approaches the Father; and if there is joy in heaven over one sinner that repents, if the Father rejoices over one with singing, let the imagination take in this scene. Christ says: Father, it is finished. I have done thy will, O my God. I have completed the work of redemption. If thy justice is satisfied, "I will that they also, whom thou hast given me, be with me where I am." And the voice of God is heard; justice is satisfied; Satan is vanquished. "Mercy and truth have met together; righteousness and peace have kissed each other." The arms of the Father encircle the Son, and his voice is heard, saying, "Let all the angels of God worship him."

Mrs. E. G. White

August 18, 1898—Prayer Our Stronghold

Amid the perils of these last days, the only safety of the youth lies in ever-increasing watchfulness and prayer. The youth who finds his joy in reading the word of God, and in the hour of prayer, will be constantly refreshed by drafts from the fountain of life. He will attain a height of moral excellence and a breadth of thought of which others can not conceive. Communion with God encourages good thoughts, noble aspirations, clear perceptions of truth, and lofty purposes of action. Those who thus connect themselves with God are acknowledged by him as his sons and daughters. They are constantly reaching higher and still higher, obtaining clearer views of God and of eternity, until the Lord makes them channels of light and wisdom to the world.

But prayer is not understood as it should be. Our prayers are not to inform God of something he does not know. The Lord is acquainted with the secrets of every soul. Our prayers need not be long and loud. God reads the hidden thought. We may pray in secret, and he who sees in secret will hear, and will reward us openly.

The prayers that are offered to God to tell him of all our wretchedness, when we do not feel wretched at all, are the prayers of hypocrisy. It is the contrite prayer that the Lord regards. "For thus saith the high and lofty One that inhabiteth eternity, whose name is Holy; I dwell in the high and holy place, with him also that is of a contrite and humble spirit, to revive the spirit of the humble, and to revive the heart of the contrite ones."

Prayer is not intended to work any change in God; it brings us into harmony with God. It does not take the place of duty. Prayer offered ever so often and ever so earnestly will never be accepted by God in the place of our tithe. Prayer will not pay our debts to God. The servants of Christ are to rely upon God as did Daniel in the courts of Babylon. Daniel knew the value of prayer, its aim, and its object; and the prayers which he and his three companions offered to God after being chosen by the king for the courts of Babylon, were answered.

There was another class of captives carried into Babylon. These the Lord permitted to be torn from their homes, and carried into a land of idolaters, because they were themselves continually going into idolatry. The Lord let them have all they desired of the idolatrous practises of Babylon. And the righteous with the unrighteous were taken away into a land where the name of Jehovah would not come to their ears; where songs of praise and thanksgiving to God would not be heard; where prophets with messages of warnings and reproof and counsel would be few and far between.

The youth have an example in Daniel, and if they are true to principle and to duty, they will be instructed as Daniel was. As the wisdom of the world viewed the matter, Daniel and his three companions had every advantage secured to them in the courts of Babylon, but it was here that their first great test was to come. Their principles were to come into collision with the regulations and appointments of the king.

"And the king appointed them a daily provision of the king's meat, and of the wine which he drank." Three years was this diet to last before their examination should take place, and then they were to be brought in before the king.

Daniel and his three companions did not take the position that because their food and drink were of the king's appointment, it was their duty to partake of it. They prayed over the matter, and studied the Scriptures. Their education had been of such a character that they felt even in their captivity that God was their dependence; and after carefully reasoning from cause to effect, "Daniel purposed in his heart that he would not defile himself with the portion of the king's meat, nor with the wine which he drank: therefore he requested of the prince of the eunuchs that he might not defile himself."

This request they did not prefer in a defiant spirit, but as if soliciting a great favor. The appearance of Daniel and his companions was like what every youth's should be. They were courteous, kind, respectful, possessing the grace of meekness and modesty. And the good behavior of these youth obtained favor for them. Of Daniel we read, "God had brought Daniel into favor and tender love with the prince of the eunuchs." And now as Daniel and his fellows were brought to the test, they placed themselves fully on the side of righteousness and truth. They did not move capriciously, but intelligently. They decided that as flesh-meat had not composed their diet in the past, it should not come into their diet in the future, and as wine had been prohibited to all who should engage in the service of God, they determined that they would not partake of it. The fate of the sons of Aaron had been presented before them, and they knew that the use of wine would confuse their senses, that the indulgence of appetite would becloud their powers of discernment. These particulars were placed on record in the history of the children of Israel as a warning to every youth to avoid all customs and practises and indulgences that would in any way dishonor God.

Daniel and his companions knew not what would be the result of their decision; they knew not but that it would cost them their lives; but they determined to keep the straight path of strict temperance even when in the courts of licentious Babylon. They rested their case in the hands of God, and the Lord co-operated with them. He took charge of these youth because they prayed to him, and sought his guidance in regard to the course they should pursue.

The strength acquired in prayer to God will prepare us for our daily duties. The temptations to which we are daily exposed make prayer a necessity. In order that we may be kept by the power of God through faith, the desires of the mind should be continually ascending in silent prayer. When we are surrounded by influences calculated to lead us away from God, our petitions for help and strength must be unwearied. Unless, this is so, we shall never be successful in breaking down pride and overcoming the power of temptation to sinful indulgences which keep us from the Saviour. The light of truth, sanctifying the life, will discover to the receiver the sinful passions of his heart which are striving for the mastery, and which make it necessary for him to stretch every nerve and exert all his powers to resist Satan that he may conquer through the merits of Christ.

Mrs. E. G. White

August 25, 1898—A Peculiar People

The Lord would have his people a separate and peculiar people. "For thou art an holy people unto the Lord thy God," he says; "the Lord thy God hath chosen thee to be a special people unto himself, above all people that are upon the face of the earth. The Lord did not set his love upon you, nor choose you, because ye were more in number than any people; for ye were the fewest of all people; but because the Lord loved you, and because he would keep the oath which he had sworn unto your fathers, hath the Lord brought you out with a mighty hand, and redeemed you out of the house of bondmen."

When man is created anew in Christ Jesus, he becomes a partaker of the divine nature. God unites him with divinity. He clothes him with the robe of Christ's righteousness. Man is enabled to discern the Savior, and by beholding him he is changed into the likeness of his character.

The conversation of those who are converted to God will not be the same as before their conversion. The words of the apostle Paul are: "Let your conversation be as it becometh the gospel of Christ: that whether I come and see you, or else be absent, I may hear of your affairs, that ye stand fast in one spirit, with one mind striving together for the faith of the gospel." "That we henceforth be no more children, tossed to and fro, and carried about with every wind of doctrine; ... but speaking the truth in love, may grow up into him in all things, which is the head, even Christ." "Grieve not the Holy Spirit of God, whereby ye are sealed unto the day of redemption. Let all bitterness, and wrath, and anger, and clamor, and evil-speaking, be put away from you, with all malice: and be ye kind one to another, tender-hearted, forgiving one another, even as God for Christ's sake hath forgiven you."

The law of God is the great standard of righteousness. This the apostle declares is holy, and just, and good. David says, "The law of the Lord is perfect, converting the soul." And Christ declares, "If ye love me, keep my commandments," "If ye abide in me, and my words abide in you, ye shall ask what ye will, and it shall be done unto you." "He that hath my commandments, and keepeth them, he it is that loveth me: and he that loveth me shall be loved of my Father, and I will love him, and will manifest myself to him." "If ye keep my commandments, ye shall abide in my love; even as I have kept my Father's commandments, and abide in his love."

The man who finds in his heart no resemblance to the great moral standard of righteousness, the word of God, has no Christ to confess. His language, his thoughts, are not in harmony with the Spirit of Christ. His profession of faith is a counterfeit. The soul must have the vivifying influence of the breath of life from Christ, in order to reveal that Christ is formed within, the hope of glory.

Those who are obedient to the will of God will not be miserable in this life. Hear again the words of Christ: "These things have I spoken unto you, that my joy might remain in you, and that your joy might be full." There is full assurance of hope in believing every word of Christ, in being united to him by living faith.

The Lord would have his people represent Christ, and show to the world his attractive character. We may have joy in the Lord if we will keep his commandments. If we indeed have our citizenship above, and a title to an immortal inheritance, an eternal substance, we have that faith which works by love and purifies the soul. If our citizenship is above, we are not called to take part in the strifes of the world. God says to his people: "Come out from among them, and be ye separate, ... and touch not the unclean thing; and I will receive you, and will be a Father unto you, and ye shall be my sons and daughters, saith the Lord Almighty." What more could we ask? We are members of the heavenly family, children of the heavenly King, heirs of God, and joint heirs with Christ. At this coming we shall have the crown of life that fadeth not away.

We are heaven-bound, and we should show the attractive part of our faith. We should not go as a crippled band of mourners, groaning and complaining all along the journey to our Father's house. Just before he left his disciples, Christ said to them: "Let not your heart be troubled: ye believe in God, believe also in me. In my Father's house are many mansions: if it were not so, I would have told you, I go to prepare a place for you. And if I go and prepare a place for you, I will come again, and receive you unto myself; that where I am, there ye may be also."

Mrs. E. G. White

September 1, 1898—Take Heed How You Hear

It is essential for the students of our schools to have a penetrating spirit in searching the word of God. You need, dear youth, to study most diligently, that you may understand the truths there revealed. You must bear in mind that your education is not a matter of merely human knowledge. Impressions must be made upon the mind and heart by the Spirit of God. The truth addresses itself to the heart and to the conscience. There must be a drawing nigh to the light of Christ, that you may catch his heavenly beams.

The truths for these times claim our especial attention; therefore take heed how you hear. You can not afford to be dull scholars in the study of the greatest and most important truths that have ever been presented to human understanding. The heart must be diligently guarded. When the precious opportunities presented to you in your school life end, you will be exposed to temptations from which you are now very largely excluded. Therefore a surface work in searching the Scriptures can be of no value to you.

Satan will put everything possible in operation to divert the mind, and occupy it with erring thoughts; but if your hearts are cleansed from all defilement, the word you hear will be mixed with faith. "Let us therefore fear, lest, a promise being left us of entering into his rest, any of you should seem to come short of it. For unto us was the gospel preached, as well as unto them: but the word preached did not profit them, not being mixed with faith in them that heard it." "Let us labor therefore to enter into that rest, lest any man fall after the same example of unbelief. For the word of God is quick, and powerful, and sharper than any two-edged sword, piercing even to the dividing asunder of soul and spirit, and of the joints and marrow, and is a discerner of the thoughts and intents of the heart. Neither is there any creature that is not manifest in his sight: but all things are naked and opened unto the eyes of him with whom we have to do. Seeing then that we have a great high priest, that is passed into the heavens, Jesus the Son of God, let us hold fast our profession. For we have not an high priest which can not be touched with the feeling of our infirmities; but was in all points tempted like as we are, yet without sin. Let us therefore come boldly unto the throne of grace, that we may obtain mercy, and find grace to help in time of need."

Students, you can not serve God, and yet retain your selfishness, your own ways, and your ambitious projects. Your ways must change, and God's ways must become your choice. You must fall upon the Rock and be broken, or the Rock will fall upon you, and grind you to powder. Self can not have the supremacy. You have been bought with a price. Will you search diligently the word of God, to see if you are indeed receiving Christ? "As many as received him, to them gave he power to become the sons of God, even to them that believe on his name." All who have this genuine faith will practise the works of Christ, will reveal his Spirit.

The Lord would have the students who attend our schools influenced by the truth that is kept before them. He would have them make a most diligent use of the light that shines from his word to them, and pursue no half-way course. Come out of self, away from self, and accept Jesus Christ. Be decided, be firm, be whole-hearted. Life and death are before you. Which will you choose? This matter calls for prompt and decided action. There should be no delay; for on this question, delays are dangerous.

"The law of the Lord is perfect, converting the soul." That law aims to convert mind and heart to correct principles of action. It will give reality to your works by making Christ your Redeemer, your stronghold. You will lay hold of his righteousness because he died to give you all the power and riches of his grace, that your practise might show your conversion. Believe in Jesus Christ as your complete Saviour. Change your way to God's way. Choose the new path, the narrow path of holiness, which will lead to perfect freedom in Christ. You may follow the Lamb whithersoever he goeth.

As line upon line and precept upon precept of the divine Word are opened before you, take heed how you hear. If the principles of our faith are accepted, new impressions will be made, new lines of work will be seen in our practise. If we give to the searching of the Scriptures a divided heart, we shall receive superficial impressions, which will quickly pass away. If we listen to the Word without giving it entrance to the heart, we shall be classed among the forgetful hearers. Only he remembers to do God's will who makes a decided confession of faith, showing to all that his faith is an active, working agency,--a faith that works by love and purifies the soul.

Students, take heed how you hear. The messages of God's word will not return to him void. They are to each a savor of life unto life or of death unto death. After hearing the word, we are no longer in the same position before God as before the light came. If we receive the light, and act upon it, we shall understand the scripture: "I know thy works: behold, I have set before thee an open door, and no man can shut it: for thou hast a little strength, and hast kept my word, and hast not denied my name."

There are those who will go forth from the place of opportunity and privilege, having heard to a purpose. Some eagerly gather up the precious gems of truth; and as they gather, their souls long for more. These will continually dig for the truth as for hidden treasure. They have anointed eyes to see, and sanctified ears to hear. They have not closed their eyes, lest they should see, nor their ears, lest they should hear. They have not barred the door of the heart, lest Jesus should find entrance. They have not stifled the conscience, nor prevented the work of the Holy Spirit upon the soul.

Now is the time when all should choose whom they will serve. You have been instructed abundantly in the truth: and if you now follow your own natural inclinations, it is because you reject light, and truth, and evidence. In refusing to be transformed and sanctified through the truth, you add to your past transgressions. After these opportunities and privileges, in having the truth kept before you day after day, after you have come in contact with truth and evidence and yet have made no change, your condemnation will stand written in the books of heaven. Your punishment will be just in proportion to the light you have slighted. How shall you escape if you neglect so great salvation? It would have been better for you to have been left in midnight darkness than to have had all the privileges and benefits you have received, and yet refuse to be obedient to the light given, refuse to be brought to the feet of Jesus to receive his pardon, and become witnesses for him.

Mrs. E. G. White

September 8, 1898—"And the Grace of God Was Upon Him"

"Unto us a child is born, unto us a son is given: and the government shall be upon his shoulder: and his name shall be called Wonderful, Counselor, The Mighty God, The Everlasting Father, The Prince of Peace." What is John's testimony concerning Christ?--"In the beginning was the Word, and the Word was with God, and the Word was God. The same was in the beginning with God. All things were made by him; and without him was not anything made that was made. In him was life; and that life was the light of men.... And the Word was made flesh, and dwelt among us, (and we beheld his glory, the glory as of the only begotten of the Father,) full of grace and truth."

"The Spirit of the Lord is upon me," Christ declared, "because he hath anointed me to preach the gospel to the poor; he hath sent me to heal the broken-hearted, to preach deliverance to the captives, and recovering of sight to the blind, to set at liberty them that are bruised, to preach the acceptable year of the Lord."

Christ wrought miracle after miracle when he was on this earth. In this work he showed what God can do for afflicted bodies and souls. This work he began when he was but a child. His whole being, pure and undefiled, was given to the Lord. Luke testifies of him, "And the child grew, and waxed strong in spirit, filled with wisdom: and the grace of God was upon him."

When Christ was twelve years old, he went with his parents to Jerusalem to attend the feast of the Passover, and on their return he was lost in the multitude. After Joseph and Mary had searched for him for three days, they found him in the court of the temple, "sitting in the midst of the doctors, both hearing them, and asking them questions. And all that heard him were astonished at his understanding and answers." He asked his questions with a grace that charmed these learned men. He was a perfect pattern for all youth. Ever he manifested deference and respect for age. The religion of Jesus will never lead any child to be rude and uncourteous.

When Joseph and Mary found Jesus, they were amazed, "and his mother said unto him, Son, why hast thou thus dealt with us? behold, thy father and I have sought thee sorrowing. And he said unto them, How is it that ye sought me?" Pointing heavenward, he continued, "Wist ye not that I must be about my Father's business?" As he spoke these words, divinity flashed through humanity. The light and glory of heaven illuminated his countenance. But "they understood not the saying which he spake unto them. And he went down with them, and came to Nazareth, and was subject unto them: but his mother kept all these sayings in her heart."

Christ did not enter upon his public ministry for eighteen years after this, but he was constantly ministering to others, improving every opportunity offered him. Even in his childhood he spoke words of comfort and tenderness to young and old. His mother could not but mark his words, his spirit, his willing obedience to all her requirements.

It is not correct to say, as many writers have said, that Christ was like all children. He was not like all children. Many children are misguided and mismanaged. But Joseph, and especially Mary, kept before them the remembrance of their child's divine Fatherhood. Jesus was instructed in accordance with the sacred character of his mission. His inclination to right was a constant gratification to his parents. The questions he asked them led them to study most earnestly the great elements of truth. His soul-stirring words about nature and the God of nature opened and enlightened their minds.

On the rocks and knolls about his home the eye of the Son of God often rested. He was familiar with the things of nature. He saw the sun in the heavens, the moon and the stars fulfiling their mission. With the voice of singing he welcomed the morning light. He listened to the lark caroling forth music to its God, and joined his voice with the voice of praise and thanksgiving. "Make a joyful noise unto God, all ye lands: sing forth the honor of his name: make his praise glorious. Say unto God, How terrible art thou in thy works! through the greatness of thy power shall thine enemies submit themselves unto thee. All the earth shall worship thee, and shall sing unto thee; they shall sing to thy name. Come and see the works of God: he is terrible in his doing toward the children of men." This psalm and portions of the sixty-eighth and seventy-second psalms were often sung by Christ. Thus in the most simple and unassuming way he taught others.

"And the child grew, and waxed strong in spirit, filled with wisdom: and the grace of God was upon him." He was an example of what all children may strive to be if parents will seek the Lord most earnestly, and if children will co-operate with their parents. In his words and actions he manifested tender sympathy for all. His companionship was as a healing, soothing balm to the disheartened and depressed.

No one, looking upon the childlike countenance, shining with animation, could say that Christ was just like other children. He was God in human flesh. When urged by his companions to do wrong, divinity flashed through humanity, and he refused decidedly. In a moment he distinguished between right and wrong, and placed sin in the light of God's commands, holding up the law as a mirror which reflected light upon wrong. It was this keen discrimination between right and wrong that often provoked Christ's brothers to anger. Yet his appeals and entreaties, and the sorrow expressed in his countenance, revealed such a tender, earnest love for them that they were ashamed of having tempted him to deviate from his strict sense of justice and loyalty.

From childhood to manhood, Christ taught that "the kingdom of God is not meat and drink; but righteousness, and peace, and joy in the Holy Ghost." He was the Truth. The Spirit of God was upon him. Why?--Because he did not by one act of disobedience separate himself from God. The grace of God was upon him, and he grew in favor with God and man. He lived a life of unceasing humiliation, and through it all his character was lovely. The peace of God was with him, and this peace was uninterrupted. In the sorrows of others he could always speak peace to the soul; for his peace was the result of supreme rectitude and loyalty, and was completely his own. None could give it; none could take it away.

After his ascension, Christ revealed himself to Paul. As Paul beheld the glory of the Saviour's countenance, it was more than he could endure. He was stricken to the earth, and as he lay thus, he heard a voice saying to him, "Saul, Saul, why persecutest thou me? And he said, Who art thou, Lord? And the Lord said, I am Jesus whom thou persecutest: it is hard for thee to kick against the pricks."

By this revelation Paul was converted. Afterward when asked by the Pharisees, Who is this deceiver, that you should leave your brethren to believe in him? the Spirit of God came upon Paul, and he testified of Christ. His face was illuminated, as if the subject of their conversation was before them in his great majesty, and he answered, in the language of Isaiah: "Who is this that cometh from Edom, with dyed garments from Bozrah? this that is glorious in his apparel, traveling in the greatness of his strength? I that speak in righteousness, mighty to save. Wherefore art thou red in thine apparel, and thy garments like him that treadeth in the winefat? I have trodden the winepress alone; and of the people there was none with me."

Mrs. E. G. White

September 15, 1898—Prayer Our Stronghold

Amid the perils of these last days, the only safety of the youth lies in ever-increasing watchfulness and prayer. The youth who finds his joy in reading the word of God and in the hour of prayer, will be constantly refreshed by drafts from the fount of life. He will attain a height of moral excellence and a breadth of thought that others can not conceive of. Communion with God encourages good thoughts, noble aspirations, clear perceptions of truth, and lofty purposes of action. Those who thus connect themselves with God are acknowledged by him as his sons and daughters. They are constantly reaching higher and still higher, obtaining clearer views of God and of eternity, until the Lord makes them channels of light and wisdom to the world.

But prayer is not understood as it should be. Our prayers are not to inform God of something he does not know. The Lord is acquainted with the secrets of every soul. Our prayers need not be long and loud. God reads the hidden thought. We may pray in secret, and he who sees in secret will hear, and will reward us openly.

The prayers that are offered to God to tell him of all our wretchedness, when we do not feel wretched at all, are the prayers of hypocrisy. It is the contrite prayer that the Lord regards. "For thus saith the high and lofty One that inhabiteth eternity, whose name is Holy; I dwell in the high and holy place, with him also that is of a contrite and humble spirit, to revive the spirit of the humble, and to revive the heart of the contrite ones."

Prayer is not intended to work any change in God; it brings us into harmony with God. It does not take the place of duty. Prayer offered ever so often and ever so earnestly will never be accepted by God in the place of our tithe. Prayer will not pay our debts to God. The servants of Christ are to rely upon God as did Daniel in the courts of Babylon. Daniel knew the value of prayer, its aim, and its object; and the prayers which he and his three companions offered to God after being chosen by the king for the courts of Babylon were answered.

There was another class of captives carried into Babylon. These the Lord permitted to be torn from their homes, and carried into a land of idolaters, because they were themselves continually going into idolatry. The Lord let them have all they desired of the idolatrous practises of Babylon. The righteous and the unrighteous were taken away into a land where the name of Jehovah would not come to their ears; where songs of praise and thanksgiving to God would not be heard; where prophets with messages of warning, and reproof, and counsel would be few and far between.

The youth have an example in Daniel; and if they are true to principle and duty, they will be instructed as he was. As the wisdom of the world viewed the matter, Daniel and his companions had every advantage secured to them in the courts of Babylon; but it was here that their first great test was to come; their principles were to come into collision with the regulations and appointments of the king.

"And the king appointed them a daily provision of the king's meat, and of the wine which he drank." Three years was this diet to last before their examination should take place, and then they were to be brought in before the king.

Daniel and his three companions did not take the position that because their food and drink were of the king's appointment, it was their duty to partake of it. They prayed over the matter, and studied the Scriptures. Their education had been of such a character that they felt, even in their captivity, that God was their dependence; and after carefully reasoning from cause to effect, "Daniel purposed in his heart that he would not defile himself with the portion of the king's meat, nor with the wine which he drank: therefore he requested of the prince of the eunuchs that he might not defile himself."

This request was not preferred in a defiant spirit, but as if soliciting a great favor. The appearance of Daniel and his companions was like what every youth's should be. They were courteous, kind, respectful, possessing the grace of meekness and modesty. And the good behavior of these youth obtained favor for them. Of Daniel we read, "God had brought Daniel into favor and tender love with the prince of the eunuchs."

And as Daniel and his fellows were brought to the test, they placed themselves fully on the side of righteousness and truth. They did not move capriciously, but intelligently. They decided that as flesh-meat had not composed their diet in the past, it should not come into their diet in the future; and as wine had been prohibited to all who should engage in the service of God, they determined that they would not partake of it. The fate of the sons of Aaron had been presented before them, and they knew that the use of wine would confuse their senses, that the indulgence of appetite would becloud their powers of discernment. These particulars were placed on record in the history of the children of Israel as a warning to every youth to avoid all customs and practises and indulgences that would in anyway dishonor God.

Daniel and his companions knew not what would be the result of their decision; they knew not but that it would cost them their lives; but they determined to keep the straight path of strict temperance when in the courts of licentious Babylon. They rested their case in the hands of God, and the Lord co-operated with them. He took charge of these youth because they prayed to him, and sought his guidance in regard to the course they should pursue.

The strength acquired in prayer to God will prepare us for our daily duties. The temptations to which we are daily exposed make prayer a necessity. In order that we may be kept by the power of God through faith, the desires of the mind should be continually ascending in silent prayer. When we are surrounded by influences of nature to lead us away from God, our petitions for health and strength must be unwearied. Unless this is so, we shall never be successful in breaking down pride, and overcoming the power of temptation to sinful indulgences which keep us from the Saviour. The light of truth, sanctifying the life, will discover to the receiver the sinful passions of his heart, which are striving for the mastery, and which make it necessary for him to stretch every nerve, and exert all his powers, to resist Satan, that he may conquer through the merits of Christ.

Mrs. E. G. White

September 22, 1898—"That I Should Bear Witness Unto the Truth"

The incarnation of Christ typified in the sacrificial service of Israel and symbolized in all their devotions, is a glorious mystery. In his only begotten Son, God was made manifest to the world. The Son of God laid aside his glory, and clothed himself with humanity. He became the meek and lowly Jesus. For the sake of sinful men, he became poor, that they through his poverty might be made rich.

Yet the men for whom he sacrificed so much, and for whom he labored so earnestly, did not recognize him. The enemy was at work upon human minds to keep light from the people of God. As Israel separated more and more from God, they failed to have a correct estimate of truth, and supplied its place with fanciful ideas and the imaginations of men. They doubted the mission of Christ, and although they had so long hoped and waited for him to come, they would not receive him when he did come.

The adversaries of Christ claimed to be just and holy men, but they regarded him with suspicion, because his teachings did not harmonize with their preconceived ideas. The good works which testified that Christ was the light of the world, they would allow to have no weight with them. He bore with him divine credentials; but their eyes were so blinded by prejudice that they could not discern the voice of the True Shepherd.

Christ was the living representative of the law. He knew that the Jews were eagerly watching him, hoping to find something which they might question and use to bring about his death as a false teacher; but he could look on that nation of witnesses, and say, "Which of you convinceth me of sin?" Christ stood in moral integrity, conscious of the authority and power that he had with the Father. He was on a level with the eternal throne. The glory of God fell directly upon him, and in the luster of his own greatness was reflected to the Father above.

The sin of the Jews was unbelief. The power of the destroyer had led Israel far astray. When they should have magnified God and talked of his goodness and power, they were found disbelieving and complaining. Every means which the deceiver could invent he used to sow in their hearts seeds of envy and discord, and of hatred against God. Thus when Christ came to the earth, Satan had brought in a religion for the Jews which pleased himself. The nation had departed from God, and another leader was guiding them.

And Satan pressed the advantage he had gained, and made the leaders of the Jewish nation his allies. Because in their blindness they could not understand the mysteries of the incarnation, because Christ did not praise and glorify them as most exalted in knowledge and piety, the priests and rulers were offended; and they determined to counteract his influence, and make of none effect his teachings. They followed him from place to place, that they might misconstrue and misstate his words. As they listened to the teachings of Christ, they were convinced that the power of God was with him, but they would not accept him as the Messiah. And they worked to prevent the people from accepting the light. "Do not be in haste to receive new things," they said; "there is danger of your being deceived. Can not you see that his teaching differs from that we have been giving you? Do not commit yourselves to these new doctrines. If this is the Christ, he will give you some remarkable evidence of his divine character." Thus these men, who might have been a power for good on God's side of the question, became a power for evil.

When Christ healed the paralytic, he said to him, "Be of good cheer; thy sins are forgiven thee." But the Pharisees, when they saw the miracle, and heard men praising God for the wonderful work, said within themselves, "Why doth this man thus speak blasphemies? who can forgive sins but God only?" But "Jesus knowing their thoughts said, Wherefore think ye evil in your hearts? For whether is easier, to say, Thy sins be forgiven thee; or to say, Arise, and walk? But that ye may know that the Son of man hath power on earth to forgive sins (then saith he to the sick of the palsy), Arise, take up thy bed, and go into thine house." Christ healed the man, both soul and body, showing that he had power to pardon sins, and bring peace and righteousness to the conscience-stricken soul.

Christ's conscious superiority, even as he descended step by step in the path of humiliation, gave his words an amazing power. What lessons of instruction he gave, and with what authority he rebuked the sins of men in high position. Truth was truth to him, and it never suffered in his hands; for he was the author of truth. "To this end," he says, "was I born, and for this cause came I into the world, that I should bear witness unto the truth."

But because men did not like to be told of their sins, because they did not wish to be reproved or corrected, they determined to resist him. Jesus saw that which those who were blinded by the enemy could not see. He tried to convince them that everything opposed to the principles he was teaching was a delusion and a falsehood. "Every one that is of the truth," he said, "heareth my voice." He was the embodiment of truth and holiness. He who had stood in the councils of God, who had dwelt in the innermost sanctuary of the Eternal, was speaking that whereof he knew. He was presenting truth of the highest order, revealing to men the mind of the Infinite. But the men who claimed to stand high in knowledge and spiritual understanding failed to comprehend his meaning; and that which had been evolved from eternity by the Father and Son, they in their ignorance stood as critics to condemn.

Christ crucified is ever drawing souls to him. On the other hand, Satan is drawing them away from Christ, that they may not walk in the light of his countenance, that they may not see Christ in his goodness and mercy, his infinite compassion and unsurpassed love. He intercepts himself by presenting the attractions of worldly inducements, that God in Christ may not be discerned. But Christ came that whosoever will believe in him may be saved. As a flower turns to the sun that its bright rays may aid in perfecting its beauty and symmetry, so should Christ's followers turn to the Sun of Righteousness, that heaven's light may shine upon them, perfecting their characters, and giving them a deep and abiding experience in the things of God. It is beyond our power to conceive the blessings that are brought within our reach through Christ, if we will but unite our human effort with divine grace.

There is an "eternal weight of glory" beyond. "Eye hath not seen nor ear heard, neither have entered into the heart of man, the things which God hath prepared for them that love him."

Mrs. E. G. White

October 13, 1898—"Search the Scriptures"—No. 1

It is of the highest importance that every human being endowed with reasoning powers should understand his relation to God. In our schools the work of redemption is not carefully studied. Many of the students have no real conception of what the plan of salvation means. God's word is pledged in our behalf. He who is touched with the feeling of our infirmities invites us: "Come unto me, all ye that labor and are heavy laden, and I will give you rest. Take my yoke upon you, and learn of me; for I am meek and lowly in heart: and ye shall find rest unto your souls. For my yoke is easy, and my burden is light.'

Students, you are safe only as, in perfect submission and obedience, you connect yourselves with Christ. The yoke is easy, for Christ carries the weight. As you lift the burden of the cross, it will become light; and that cross is to you a pledge of eternal life. It is the privilege of each to follow gladly after Christ, exclaiming at every step, "Thy gentleness hath made me great." But if we would travel heavenward, we must take the word of God as our lesson-book. In the words of inspiration we must read our lessons day by day.

The apostle Paul says: "Let this mind be in you, which was also in Christ Jesus: who, being in the form of God, thought it not robbery to be equal with God: but made himself of no reputation, and took upon him the form of a servant, and was made in the likeness of men: and being found in fashion as a man [as the representative of the human race], he humbled himself, and became obedient unto death, even the death of the cross. Wherefore God also hath highly exalted him, and given him a name which is above every name: that at the name of Jesus every knee should bow."

The humiliation of the man Christ Jesus is incomprehensible to the human mind; but his divinity and his existence before the world was formed can never be doubted by those who believe the word of God. The apostle Paul speaks of our Mediator, the only begotten Son of God, who in a state of glory was in the form of God, the Commander of all the heavenly hosts, and who, when he clothed his divinity with humanity, took upon him the form of a servant. Isaiah declares: "Unto us a child is born, unto us a son is given: and the government shall be upon his shoulder; and his name shall be called Wonderful, Counselor, The Mighty God, The Everlasting Father, The Prince of Peace. Of the increase of his government and peace there shall be no end, upon the throne of David, and upon his kingdom, to order it, and to establish it with judgment and with justice from henceforth even forever."

In consenting to become man, Christ manifested a humility that is the marvel of the heavenly intelligences. The act of consenting to be a man would be no humiliation were it not for the fact of Christ's exalted pre-existence. We must open our understanding to realize that Christ laid aside his royal robe, his kingly crown, his high command, and clothed his divinity with humanity, that he might meet man where he was, and bring to the human family moral power to become the sons and daughters of God. To redeem man, Christ became obedient unto death, even the death of the cross.

The humanity of the Son of God is everything to us. It is the golden chain that binds our souls to Christ, and through Christ to God. This is to be our study. Christ was a real man; he gave proof of his humility in becoming a man. Yet he was God in the flesh. When we approach this subject, we would do well to heed the words spoken by Christ to Moses at the burning bush, "Put off thy shoes from off thy feet, for the place whereon thou standest is holy ground." We should come to this study with the humility of a learner, with a contrite heart. And the study of the incarnation of Christ is a fruitful field, which will repay the searcher who digs deep for hidden truth.

The Bible is our guide in the safe paths that lead to eternal life. God has inspired men to write that which will present the truth to us, which will attract, and which, if practised, will enable the receiver to obtain moral power to rank among the most highly educated minds. The minds of all who make the word of God their study will enlarge. Far more than any other study, this is of a nature to increase the powers of comprehension, and endow every faculty with new vigor. It brings the mind in contact with broad, ennobling principles of truth. It brings us into close connection with all heaven, imparting wisdom, and knowledge, and understanding.

In dealing with commonplace productions, and feeding on the writings of uninspired men, the mind becomes dwarfed and cheapened. It is not brought into contact with deep, broad principles of eternal truth. The understanding unconsciously adapts itself to the comprehension of the things with which it is familiar; and in the consideration of these things the understanding is weakened, its powers contracted.

God designs that the Scriptures, the source of science that is above all human theory, shall be searched. He desires that man shall dig deep in the mines of truth, that he may gain the valuable treasure they contain. But too often human theories and wisdom are put in the place of the science of the Bible. Men engage in the work of remodeling God's purposes; they try to distinguish between the books of the Bible. Through their inventions they make the Scriptures testify to a lie.

God has not made the reception of the gospel to depend upon human reasoning. The gospel is adapted for spiritual food, to satisfy man's spiritual appetite. In every case it is just what man needs. Those who have felt it necessary to have the students in our schools study many authors are themselves the most ignorant on the great themes of the Bible. The teachers themselves need to take up the Book of all books, and learn from the Scriptures that the gospel has power to prove its own divinity to the humble, contrite mind.

The gospel is the power of God and the wisdom of God. The character of Christ on earth revealed divinity, and the gospel which he has given is to be the study of his human heritage in all their educational departments, until teachers, children, and youth shall discern in the only true and living God the object of their faith and love and adoration. The Word is to be respected and obeyed. That book which contains the record of Christ's life, his work, his doctrines, his sufferings, and final triumphs, is to be the source of our strength. We are granted the privileges of school life in this world that we may obtain a fitness for the higher life,--the highest grade in the highest school, where, under God, our studies will continue through the ceaseless ages of eternity.

Mrs. E. G. White

October 20, 1898—"Search the Scriptures"—No. 2

The word of God is the great educating book, and it is to be searched diligently,--not as we would read a book among many books,--but it must be to us the book that meets the wants of the soul. Had the word of God been regarded as it ever should be,--as the voice of God to men,--children, youth, and parents would have made it not only their study, but their teacher and their guide, "that in the ages to come he might show the exceeding riches of his grace in his kindness toward us through Christ Jesus." "For," says the apostle, "by grace are ye saved through faith; and that not of yourselves: it is the gift of God. Not of works, lest any man should boast. For we are his workmanship, created in Christ Jesus unto good works, which God hath before ordained that we should walk in them."

Satan is constantly at work to obscure the vital truths that are essential for the well-being of man, making indistinct and unimportant the obedience that must be rendered to the commandments of God. It is his desire to keep the world from learning of Christ. He plans to crowd the mind so full that men can give no time to consider what they are to do with the knowledge they gain, what is the quality of their studies, or whether they are of such a character as to give them an increased knowledge of God, and of Jesus Christ, whom he has sent.

By Satan's subtle working, the truth has been placed out of sight, and errors have been substituted that have led men to idolize falsehood instead of glorifying God. The saving truths essential for the health of the soul have been regarded as non-essential, because the world does not exalt them, while Satan's sophistries are deemed so important that men devote their worship to them, and work to make every other human being disregard those things that God has sanctified.

Thus it is with the Sabbath of the fourth commandment. God's law is regarded as of no consequence. The true Sabbath, given to man as a memorial of creation, has been taken from its rightful place as a sacred command of God, and, instead, a false sabbath has been exalted and worshiped. Living, testing principles have been lost, as stars are said to become extinct in the firmament of heaven. But a message, the third angel's message, has come to the world, to exalt the truth to its right position, that it may stand fast as God's testing truth for these last days. God's requirements are to be given to the world in all their original freshness and power.

The words of Isaiah are given us for our thoughtful study, "And they that shall be of thee shall build the old waste places: thou shalt raise up the foundations of many generations; and thou shalt be called, The repairer of the breach, The restorer of paths to dwell in. If thou turn away thy foot from the Sabbath, from doing thy pleasure on my holy day; and call the Sabbath a delight, the holy of the Lord, honorable; and shalt honor him, not doing thine own ways, nor finding thine own pleasure, nor speaking thine own words: then shalt thou delight thyself in the Lord; and I will cause thee to ride upon the high places of the earth, and feed thee with the heritage of Jacob thy father: for the mouth of the Lord hath spoken it."

This is the work to be done for fallen humanity. The old waste places are to be built up. We need now to learn from the great Teacher how to raise up the foundations of many generations, which have been left to decay. We need to learn how to repair the breach made in God's law, and to restore the paths to dwell in. We are to proclaim the third angel's message.

And how shall the work be carried forward? The apostle Paul says: "You, that were sometime alienated and enemies in your mind by wicked works, yet now hath he reconciled in the body of his flesh through death, to present you holy and unblameable and unreproveable in his sight: if ye continue in the faith grounded and settled, and be not moved away from the hope of the gospel, which ye have heard, and which was preached to every creature which is under heaven; whereof I Paul am made a minister; who now rejoice in my sufferings for you, and fill up that which is behind of the afflictions of Christ in my flesh for his body's sake, which is the church; whereof I am made a minister, according to the dispensation of God which is given to me for you, to fulfil the word of God; even the mystery which hath been hid from ages and from generations, but now is made manifest to his saints: to whom God would make known what is the riches of the glory of this mystery among the Gentiles; which is Christ in you, the hope of glory: whom we preach, warning every man, and teaching every man in all wisdom; that we may present every man perfect in Christ Jesus: whereunto I also labor, striving according to his working, which worketh in me mightily."

Then let our lessons be appropriate for the day in which we live, that we may be co-laborers with God. The work will go hard, but the message must be carried to the world. Men have made void the law of God through the masterly working of Satan. But Christ is on the field of action, working with those who are laboring for him, that truth may appear in its divine, unchangeable, and eternal character. The Holy Spirit is at work. Divine agencies are combining with the human to take the important truths from their worn-out setting, reframe them, and hang them in memory's halls, and call men to the obedience of God's commandments.

If the Bible had been made the book of study in the schools, what a different showing there would be in society today! It is for our present and our eternal good to inquire at every step, Is this the way of the Lord? Since the fall of Adam, it has been the fashion of the world to sin, and it is for our interest to know what sin is. John declares: "Whosoever committeth sin transgresseth also the law: for sin is the transgression of the law. And ye know that he was manifested to take away our sins; and in him is no sin." The information is plainly given that sin is the transgression of the law. We need to compare our characters with the law of God, the standard of character for all who would enter his kingdom, and become citizens of the heavenly country. Let the students in our schools study the Book that has been so universally neglected. Let them read it with prayerful, earnest interest, lest they fail to be doers of the word.

Mrs. E. G. White

October 27, 1898—"Search the Scriptures"—No. 3

A bare assent to the truth is not Bible religion. Men do not become Christians merely by having their names written in the church-books. This belief is proving fatal to thousands upon thousands. It does not displease Satan to have any number of names upon the church-books while the heart is not brought into unity with Christ: he can work through those who have the form of godliness without the spirit and power. There are many professed Christians whose hearts are incased in a self-righteous armor that the arrow of the Lord, barbed and true-aimed by angel hands, would fail to pierce. Man must seek God for himself; then the Holy Spirit will take the precious truth, far above the price of rubies, as it falls from the lips of Jesus, and convey it, a living power, to the obedient heart.

Age after age the curiosity of men has led them to seek for the tree of knowledge; and often they think they are plucking fruit most essential, when, like Solomon in his research, they find it altogether vanity and nothingness in comparison with the science of true holiness, which will open to them the gates of the city of God. The mass of books which have been thought essential for school education contains erroneous principles, which, if carried into practical life, will lead the students into false paths, away from consecration to God, away from that knowledge which will live through endless ages.

The one great matter that should demand our attention is higher education. As a worker, Christ did not allow his labors to be of a character merely to satisfy curiosity or to give such demonstrations of truth as to make doubt impossible. He came to open the treasures of heaven, that others might search and find. He designed that the Word should be received and searched as a new revelation.

Human ambition has been seeking for that kind of knowledge that will bring to men self-exaltation and supremacy. Thus Adam and Eve were worked upon by Satan until God's restraint was snapped asunder, and their education under the teacher of lies began, in order that they might have the knowledge which God had refused them,--a knowledge of the consequences of transgression. And since that time, the sons of men have had a practical knowledge of evil; but Christ came to the world to show them that he had planted for them the tree of life, the leaves of which are for the healing of the nations. He came to restore the moral image of God in man, to elevate and ennoble our mental powers, so that our efforts in this life might not be misdirected and lost; and it is of the greatest consequence that every student in our schools obtain that knowledge which will enable him to co-operate with God in the grand work of forming a character after the divine pattern.

The Lord Jesus came to strengthen every earnest seeker for truth, he came to reveal the Father. He allowed nothing to divert his mind from the great work of restoring the moral image of God in man. And we must see that the great and important work for us is to receive the divine likeness, to prepare a character for the future life. We must appropriate the heavenly truths to our special use in practical life. And we may carry with us all the treasure of knowledge that gives us a fitness for the life that measures with the life of God.

The knowledge of God is as high as the heaven, as broad as the earth; and most blessed of God will be those schools that study with earnest, prayerful hearts to know, "What must I do to be saved?" The answer is given, Study the Word, obey God, and you will be brought into subjection to Christ. Only those who read the Scriptures as the voice of God speaking to them are the true learners. They tremble at the word of God; for to them it is a living reality. They study, they search for the hidden treasure. They open the understanding and heart to receive, and they pray for heavenly grace, that they may obtain a preparation for the future, immortal life. As the heavenly torch is placed in his hand, man sees his own frailty, his infirmity, his hopelessness in looking to himself for righteousness. He sees that in himself there is nothing to recommend him to God. He prays for the Holy Spirit, the representative of Christ, to be his constant guide, to lead him into all truth; and he receives the fulfilment of the promise of Christ, "The Comforter, which is the Holy Ghost, whom the Father will send in my name, he shall teach you all things, and bring all things to your remembrance, whatsoever I have said unto you."

Under the inspiration of the Holy Spirit, Paul wrote: "Blessed be the God and Father of our Lord Jesus Christ, who hath blessed us with all spiritual blessings in heavenly places in Christ: according as he hath chosen us in him before the foundation of the world, that we should be holy and without blame before him in love: having predestinated us unto the adoption of children by Jesus Christ to himself, according to the good pleasure of his will, to the praise of the glory of his grace, wherein he hath made us accepted in the Beloved. In whom we have redemption through his blood, the forgiveness of sins, according to the riches of his grace; wherein he hath abounded toward us in all wisdom and prudence; having made known unto us the mystery of his will, according to his good pleasure which he hath purposed in himself: that in the dispensation of the fulness of times he might gather together in one all things in Christ, ... in whom ye also trusted, after that ye heard the word of truth, the gospel of your salvation: in whom also after that ye believed, ye were sealed with that Holy Spirit of promise, which is the earnest of our inheritance until the redemption of the purchased possession, unto the praise of his glory."

These words reveal the far-reaching power of true godliness. They enlarge the narrow confines of human scholarship, and present before the mind a far deeper knowledge to be obtained through vital connection with God. They bring every student who is a doer of the word into a broader field of knowledge, and secure to him a wealth of learning that is imperishable. All knowledge gained in this life of probation which will fit us to be companions of the saints in light is true education. It brings blessings to ourselves and others in this life, and will secure to us the future, immortal life, with all its imperishable riches.

Mrs. E. G. White

November 3, 1898—Thy Father Which Seeth in Secret Shall Reward Thee Openly

"Take heed that ye do not your alms before men, to be seen of them: otherwise ye have no reward of your Father which is in heaven. Therefore when thou doest thine alms, do not sound a trumpet before thee, as the hypocrites do in the synagogues and in the streets, that they may have glory of men. Verily I say unto you, They have their reward. But when thou doest alms, let not thy left hand know what thy right hand doeth: that thine alms may be in secret: and thy Father which seeth in secret himself shall reward thee openly."

It was the custom of the Jews to do their deeds of charity in a conspicuous manner. They performed their almsgiving in public; and before doing this, often a proclamation was made, heralding their generosity. Thus many gave large sums of money, in order to have their names extolled by men, and that they might be thought liberal and righteous.

When Christ gave his instruction in regard to almsgiving, there was in the crowd a pitiable object soliciting charity. One of the Pharisees, with great display, gave a small sum to the applicant, at the same time commending his own benevolence. The people looked on with admiration, and praised the apparently liberal act. But this man's character was not merciful. He did not pity the suffering and the needy. He had no experience in deeds of love. His object in giving was merely to rid himself of a troublesome applicant, and to call attention to his own benevolence.

Jesus read the motive of the giver. He saw that his act was altogether for the occasion, and this furnished a lesson for the heavenly Teacher. Christ laid bare the motives of the hypocrite. He showed that this act was a counterfeit of benevolence, and would weigh against the doer in the day of God. Turning to his disciples, he cautioned them against giving merely for the honor and praise they might thus receive. The motive was wrong. If they had no higher motive than this, they would have no higher reward. He showed that those who bestow their gifts that they may receive the praise of men, will have no reward in heaven. They have their reward in worldly honor and applause. They give that they may obtain this, and this is all they receive.

Frequently the gifts bestowed on the poor, only confirm them in indolent, reckless pauperism. Money is given, but not instruction. We do not bring ourselves to the task of employing and teaching the poor and ignorant, thus helping them to help themselves. Such aid is often the most useful that can be given.

Let us not disdain to touch the applicant. When Christ healed the sick, he laid his hands upon them; and we must come near to those whom we wish to help. Let us realize that, as Christ's, we have nothing of our own. Everything that we have has come from God. Let us therefore impart judiciously to those less favored.

From their abundance the great men of the world often give large sums of money to colleges and societies, that their names may be extolled; while close to their stately mansions the widow and the fatherless are destitute of food and clothing. Christ teaches that our gifts should be made quietly and unobtrusively, from a heart of pitying tenderness for the unfortunate and the suffering. We should give kindly words with our gifts. Hearts are drawn together by words of kindly sympathy and genuine sorrow for the sufferer. There was no virtue in the gift of the Pharisee. Through it no blessing came to the heart of the receiver. He had given because he desired to be praised for his benevolence.

Self-sacrifice is an essential element of true Christian character. In his life on earth, Jesus has given his followers an example of this. It was love for the souls of men that brought Christ from a world of purity; and he reached to the very depths of wretchedness and woe, in order that he might help the suffering and the perishing. And the servant of Christ must follow in the footsteps of his Master if he would reach to the perfection of this wonderful, glorious Pattern.

While Jesus was giving this instruction, the attention of the people was diverted by the loud voice of prayer. The Pharisee has been reproved by the close, practical teaching of Christ. He felt angry that his sins had been made so apparent, although no word had been directly addressed to him. Feeling condemned before the people, he made an effort to hide the deformity of his character under a pretense of piety and devotion.

"And when thou prayest," Jesus continued, "thou shalt not be as the hypocrites are: for they love to pray standing in the synagogues and in the corners of the streets, that they may be seen of men. Verily I say unto you, They have their reward."

There is an expressed humility, an external appearance, which is born of pride and self-exaltation. Often there are those who parade their humility before others, that they may hear their piety extolled. They seek to impress others with the greatness of their humility. But such men are deceived. In their efforts to prove themselves possessors of this desirable quality, they show that it is not theirs. Those who really possess this grace are ignorant of the fact.

Judging the Pharisee by his hypocritical prayer, many of that company believed him to be a humble, devoted man. But Christ shows such zeal and fervor to be no sign of righteousness. God does not regard such prayers. The approval of men is all the reward those who thus parade their devotion will receive.

When Christ taught the people, he did not devote the time to prayer. He did not enforce upon his hearers, as did the Pharisees, long, tedious ceremonies and prayers. He taught his disciples how to pray: "But thou, when thou prayest, enter into thy closet, and when thou hast shut thy door, pray to thy Father which is in secret; and thy Father which seeth in secret shall reward thee openly. But when ye pray, use not vain repetitions, as the heathen do: for they think that they shall be heard for their much speaking. Be not ye therefore like unto them: for your Father knoweth what things ye have need of, before ye ask him."

We would not discourage prayer; for there is far too little praying and watching thereunto; and there is still less praying with the spirit and the understanding also. Fervent and effectual prayer is always in place, and will never weary. It is impossible for the soul to flourish while prayer is neglected. Family or public prayer alone is not sufficient. In secret prayer the soul should be laid bare to the inspecting eye of God: here every motive should be criticized.

How precious is secret prayer--the soul communing with God! Secret prayer is to be heard only by the prayer-hearing God. No curious ear is to receive the burden of petitions. Calmly, yet fervently, the soul is to reach out after God; and sweet and abiding will be the influence emanating from him who sees in secret, whose ear is open to the prayer arising from the heart. He who in simple faith holds communion with God will gather to himself divine rays of light to strengthen and sustain him in the conflict with Satan.

Mrs. E. G. White

November 10, 1898—The First King of Israel—No. 1

In the experience of God's people, there are always times of test and trial; and God does not design that men, women, or youth shall be shielded from the liabilities which test the character. Satan will reveal his workings, and will supply every soul he tempts with his evil-surmising, his evil-speaking, and accusing of the brethren. From this condition of things the Lord can not possibly shield those who place themselves on the enemy's side; for God does not compel the human mind. He gives his bright beams of light to guide all who will walk in the rays shining from him. But if men disregard the path lighted by the heavenly beams, and choose the way suited to their own natural hearts, they will stumble on in darkness, not knowing at what they stumble.

The Lord passed by Saul, the chosen king of Israel, because, as king of Israel, he did not follow the Lord's requirements, but chose to follow his own plans and methods. The Lord had blessed Saul. He had chosen and converted him, and made him ruler over all Israel.

"Then Samuel took a vial of oil, and poured it upon his head, and kissed him, and said, Is it not because the Lord hath anointed thee to be captain over his inheritance? ... And the Spirit of the Lord will come upon thee, and thou shalt prophesy with them, and shalt be turned into another man. And let it be, when these signs are come unto thee, that thou do as occasion serve thee; for God is with thee. And thou shalt go down before me to Gilgal; and, behold, I will come down unto thee, to offer burnt-offerings, and to sacrifice sacrifices of peace-offerings: seven days shalt thou tarry, till I come to thee, and show thee what thou shalt do.

"And it was so, that when he had turned his back to go from Samuel, God gave him another heart: and all those signs came to pass that day. And when they came thither to the hill, behold, a company of prophets met him; and the Spirit of God came upon him, and he prophesied among them. And it came to pass, when all that knew him beforetime saw that, behold, he prophesied among the prophets, then the people said one to another, What is this that is come unto the son of Kish? Is Saul also among the prophets? ... And when he had made an end of prophesying, he came to the high place."

Saul was not left alone to battle with his old, natural tendencies. God gave him another heart. Through his servant he had declared: "The Spirit of the Lord will come upon thee, and thou shalt prophesy with them, and thou shalt be turned into another man. And let it be, when these signs are come unto thee, that thou do as occasion serve thee; for God is with thee." The Holy Spirit came upon Saul, and he prophesied. Thus, with a new heart, under the molding influence of the Spirit of God, he entered into the responsible position of king of Israel.

After the Lord gave Saul the signal victory over the Ammonites, the people said to Samuel: "Who is he that said, Shall Saul reign over us? bring the men, that we may put them to death. And Saul said, There shall not a man be put to death this day; for today the Lord hath wrought salvation in Israel." In this decision, Saul revealed that he had a changed heart. His old, natural temperament was transformed by the power of God, who had laid these responsibilities upon him.

The ways and display of the nations under the rule of earthly kings had attractions for the nation that God had chosen, and wrought among by his own infinite power; and Israel had desired a king to reign over them. "And Samuel called the people together unto the Lord to Mizpah; and said unto the children of Israel, Thus saith the Lord God of Israel, I brought up Israel out of Egypt, and delivered you out of the hand of the Egyptians, and out of the hand of all kingdoms, and of them that oppressed you: and ye have this day rejected your God, who himself saved you out of all your adversities and your tribulations; and ye have said unto him, Nay, but set a king over us. Now therefore present yourselves before the Lord by your tribes, and by your thousands."

Samuel had obeyed the word of the Lord, and had granted the people their request for a king. And now the servant of God said to them: "When ye saw that Nahash the king of the children of Ammon came against you, ye said unto me, Nay; but a king shall reign over us: when the Lord your God was your king. Now therefore behold the king whom ye have chosen, and whom ye have desired! and, behold, the Lord hath set a king over you."

The children of Israel had made a great mistake in setting up their own way against God's way; but the Lord did not abandon his people, he did not leave them to their own devices. He left them not in any deception in regard to their course of action; but he still made conditions with them. "If ye will fear the Lord," he said, "and serve him, and obey his voice, and not rebel against the commandment of the Lord, then shall both ye and also the king that reigneth over you continue following the Lord your God: but if ye will not obey the voice of the Lord, but rebel against the commandment of the Lord, then shall the hand of the Lord be against you, as it was against your fathers."

The Lord was working for the good of the people, and for his own glory, in permitting Israel to have the thing that they had determined upon. If they had humbled their hearts and repented, they could have turned to the Lord, every man in the nation. But they failed to show contrition. They did not go back from their wicked course in choosing a king and rejecting God's rule.

God then gave the children of Israel an evidence from heaven that they should not think it a light matter that they had rejected the administration of God, and chosen human authority in the place of the divine. "Now therefore stand," Samuel said, "and see this great thing, which the Lord will do before your eyes. Is it not wheat harvest today? I will call unto the Lord, and he shall send thunder and rain; that ye may perceive and see that your wickedness is great, which ye have done in the sight of the Lord, in asking you a king. So Samuel called unto the Lord; and the Lord sent thunder and rain that day: and all the people greatly feared the Lord and Samuel. And all the people said unto Samuel, Pray for thy servants unto the Lord thy God, that we die not: for we have added unto all our sins this evil, to ask us a king."

After the displeasure of God had been revealed, and the people had acknowledged their sins, Samuel encouraged them, saying: "Fear not: ye have done all this wickedness: yet turn not aside from following the Lord, but serve the Lord with all your heart; and turn ye not aside: for then should ye go after vain things, which can not profit nor deliver; for they are vain. For the Lord will not forsake his people for his great name's sake: because it hath pleased the Lord to make you his people. Moreover as for me, God forbid that I should sin against the Lord in ceasing to pray for you; but I will teach you the good and the right way: only fear the Lord, and serve him in truth with all your heart: for consider how great things he hath done for you. But if ye shall still do wickedly, ye shall be consumed, both ye and your king."

Mrs. E. G. White

November 17, 1898—The First King of Israel—No. 2—The Presumption of Saul

To prove them, the Lord brought Israel into strait places. The Philistines gathered themselves together to fight against the Israelites, "thirty thousand chariots, and six thousand horsemen, and people as the sand which is on the seashore in multitude: and they came up, and pitched in Michmash, eastward from Beth-aven. When the men of Israel saw that they were in a strait (for the people were distressed), then the people did hide themselves in caves, and in thickets, and in rocks, and in high places, and in pits. And some of the Hebrews went over Jordan to the land of Gad and Gilead. As for Saul, he was yet in Gilgal, and all the people followed him trembling."

The people realized their sin in choosing a king, and they dared not put their confidence in him as they had trusted in the Lord as their ruler and authority. The new king was not God, and they were learning the meaning of defeat, even before the battle had been entered upon.

Samuel had given directions to Saul: "Thou shalt go down before me to Gilgal; and, behold, I will come down unto thee, to offer burnt-offerings, and to sacrifice sacrifices of peace-offerings: seven days shalt thou tarry, till I come to thee, and show thee what thou shalt do." And Saul "tarried seven days, according to the set time that Samuel had appointed: but Samuel came not to Gilgal; and the people were scattered from him."

The Lord designed this as a test for Saul. As head of the nation, he must follow implicitly the counsels of God. Under all circumstances he must obey the orders given him through one who received his instruction from heaven. But appearances were discouraging, and Saul looked at these appearances, instead of looking to God, trusting in him, and waiting for Samuel. He became impatient, and took upon himself responsibilities which the Lord had not laid upon him. He attempted to do a work which he could not acceptably perform.

"And Saul said, Bring hither a burnt-offering to me, and peace-offerings. And he offered the burnt-offering."

When the Lord exalted Saul to be king of Israel, he did not invest him with the sacred office of the priesthood. But as Saul saw the people terrified at the immense armies of the enemy; as he saw them fleeing to the caves, and hiding among the thickets and rocks, climbing to the tops of mountains, and down into the pits, he took upon him this office.

This was Saul's time to act his faith, to show his respect for the special directions given. A few hours of waiting was the test that the Lord gave Saul; but Saul did not bow his knees and his heart before the Lord, and trust in the God of Israel. He did not manifest the faith of Gideon, and of the Hebrew generals whom God had appointed. In the place of becoming humble and self-distrustful, he grew passionate and presumptuous, and knowingly transgressed in assuming the office of priest. He could have offered humble prayer to God without the sacrifice; for the Lord will accept even the silent petition of a burdened heart; but instead of this, he forced himself into the priesthood.

As the king "made an end of offering the burnt-offering, behold, Samuel came; and Saul went out to meet him, that he might salute him. And Samuel said, What hast thou done? And Saul said, Because I saw that the people were scattered from me, and that thou camest not within the days appointed, and that the Philistines gathered themselves together at Michmash; therefore said I, The Philistines will come down now upon me to Gilgal, and I have not made supplication unto the Lord: I forced myself therefore, and offered a burnt-offering."

And Samuel declared: "Thou hast done foolishly: thou hast not kept the commandment of the Lord thy God, which he commanded thee: for now would the Lord have established thy kingdom upon Israel forever. But now thy kingdom shall not continue: the Lord hath sought him a man after his own heart, and the Lord hath commanded him to be captain over his people, because thou hast not kept that which the Lord commanded thee."

In detaining Samuel, it was the purpose of God that the heart of Saul should be revealed, that others might know what he would do in an emergency. It was a trying position in which to be placed, but Saul did not obey orders. He felt that it would make no difference who approached God, or in what way; and, full of energy and self-complacency, he put himself forward into the sacred office.

The Lord has his appointed agencies; and if these are not discerned and respected by those who are connected with his work, if men feel free to disregard God's requirements, they must not be kept in positions of trust. They would not listen to counsel, nor to the commands of God through his appointed agencies. Like Saul, they would rush into a work that was never appointed them, and the mistakes they would make in following their human judgment would place the Israel of God where their Leader could not reveal himself to them. Sacred things would become mingled with the common.

Saul did not bear the test. He showed just what he would do under the pressure of circumstances. The Lord saw that if Saul pursued such a course in an emergency, the people would follow his example, and thus no distinction would be made between the sacred and the common. By his example he would leave it open for the men of war to assume the priesthood on any occasion or in any emergency.

Therefore he declared to him, through Samuel: "Thy kingdom shall not continue: the Lord hath sought him a man after his own heart, and the Lord hath commanded him to be captain over his people, because thou hast not kept that which the Lord commanded thee."

Mrs. E. G. White

November 24, 1898—The First King of Israel—No. 3

After this severe rebuke, Samuel left Saul to pursue his own way and follow his own impulses; and Saul found that the work left for him to do he had left undone. He had not acted his part as a kingly general over armies. The Hebrews had depended upon the facilities of the Philistines for their instruments of war. The Philistines had been wiser than the Hebrews, and had worked diligently to prevent them from learning to make their own swords and spears. And when the crisis came, there was no smith found throughout all the land of Israel. "So it came to pass in the day of battle, that there was neither sword nor spear found in the hand of any of the people that were with Saul and Jonathan: but with Saul and with Jonathan his son was there found."

Thus Saul was left without special direction from the Lord, and he knew not what to do. He had but a small army, and this was incomplete and unorganized, many of his soldiers hiding away for fear. As he looked at the immense armies of the Philistines, he felt that he must trust to his own skill and aptitude for success.

In Jonathan, the son of Saul, the Lord saw a man of pure integrity,--one to whom he could draw nigh, and upon whose heart he could move.

"Now it came to pass upon a day, that Jonathan the son of Saul said unto the young man that bare his armor, Come, and let us go over to the Philistines' garrison, that is on the other side. But he told not his father. And Saul tarried in the uttermost part of Gibeah under a pomegranate-tree which is in Migron: and the people that were with him were about six hundred men.... And Jonathan said to the young man that bare his armor, Come, and let us go over unto the garrison of these uncircumcised: it may be that the Lord will work for us: for there is no restraint to the Lord to save by many or by few.

"And his armor-bearer said unto him, Do all that is in thine heart: turn thee; behold, I am with thee according to thy heart. Then said Jonathan, Behold, we will pass over unto these men, and we will discover ourselves to them. If they say thus unto us, Tarry until we come to you; then we will stand still in our place, and will not go up unto them. But if they say thus, Come up unto us; then we will go up: for the Lord hath delivered them into our hand: and this shall be a sign unto us."

These two men gave evidence that they were moving under the influence and command of a more than human general. To outward appearance, their venture was rash, and contrary to all military rules. But the action of Jonathan was not done in human rashness. He depended not on what he and his armor-bearer themselves could do; he was the instrument that God used in behalf of his people Israel. They made their plans, and rested their cause in the hands of God. If the armies of the Philistines challenged them, they would advance. If they said, Come, they would go forward. This was their sign, and the angels of God prospered them. They went forward, saying, "It may be that the Lord will work for us."

"And both of them discovered themselves unto the garrison of the Philistines: and the Philistines said, Behold, the Hebrews come forth out of the holes where they had hid themselves." Their enemies knew of the weakness of the armies of Israel, of their hiding in the holes and the secret places, and they taunted Jonathan and his armor-bearer for this cowardice. The men of the garrison said: "Come up to us, and we will show you a thing. And Jonathan said unto his armor-bearer, Come up after me: for the Lord hath delivered them into the hand of Israel."

Jonathan and his armor-bearer had asked a sign of the Lord; and the challenge had come, the sign was given. These two men placed their hope in God, and went forward.

It was no easy passage for the brave adventurers. They had hard climbing to reach the top. On the top of the precipice was the camp of the Philistines; the two armies were in sight of each other; but up the steep sides of this rocky eminence, Jonathan and his armor-bearer ventured, using hands and feet in their climb, and saying at each step, "The Lord hath delivered them into the hand of Israel."

It would have been an easy matter for the Philistines to kill these two brave, daring men; but it did not enter into their minds that these two solitary men had come up with any hostile intent. The wondering men above looked on, too surprised to take in their possible object. They regarded these men as deserters, and permitted them to come without harm.

"And they fell before Jonathan; and his armor-bearer slew after him. And that first slaughter, which Jonathan and his armor-bearer made, was about twenty men, within as it were an half acre of land, which a yoke of oxen might plow."

This daring work sent a panic through the camp. There lay the dead bodies of twenty men, and to the sight of the enemy there seemed hundreds of men prepared for war. The armies of heaven were revealed to the opposing host of the Philistines. "There was trembling in the host, in the field, and among all the people; the garrison, and the spoilers, they also trembled, and the earth quaked: so it was a very great trembling."

December 1, 1898—The First King of Israel—No. 4—The Final Test

During this time, Saul, in discontent and fear, had been sitting with his six hundred men under a pomegranate-tree. Now he said "unto the people that were with him, Number now, and see who is gone from us. And when they had numbered, behold, Jonathan and his armor-bearer were not there. And Saul said unto Ahiah, Bring hither the ark of God. For the ark of God was at that time with the children of Israel. And it came to pass, while Saul talked unto the priest, that the noise that was in the host of the Philistines went on and increased: and Saul said unto the priest, Withdraw thine hand. And Saul and all the people that were with him assembled themselves, and they came to the battle: and, behold, every man's sword was against his fellow, and there was a very great discomfiture."

When they came to the place of conflict, lo, they saw the men in the Philistine army fighting one another, and not discerning that they were fighting their own army. And there was a very great battle.

"Moreover the Hebrews that were with the Philistines before that time, which went up with them into the camp from the country round about, even they also turned to be with the Israelites that were with Saul and Jonathan. Likewise all the men of Israel which had hid themselves in Mount Ephraim, when they heard that the Philistines fled, even they also followed hard after them in battle. So the Lord saved Israel that day."

Saul now became very zealous, and gave command, saying, "Cursed be the man that eateth any food until evening, that I may be avenged on mine enemies. So none of the people tasted any food." This rash oath of Saul's was a human invention. It was not inspired of God, and God was displeased with it. Jonathan and his armor-bearer, who, through God, had wrought deliverance for Israel that day, had become weak through hunger. The people also were weary and hungry.

"And all they of the land came to a wood; and there was honey upon the ground." This honey was of God's own providing. He desired that the armies of Israel should partake of this food, and receive strength. But Saul, who was not under the direction of God, had interposed his rash oath, saying: "Cursed be the man that eateth any food until evening, that I may be avenged on mine enemies.... And all they of the land came to a wood; and there was honey upon the ground. And when the people were come into the wood, behold, the honey dropped; but no man put his hand to his mouth: for the people feared the oath."

Jonathan had not heard his father's charge to the people; and "he put forth the end of the rod that was in his hand, and dipped it in an honeycomb, and put his hand to his mouth; and his eyes were enlightened." His whole system was strengthened to do the work before him.

"Then answered one of the people, and said, Thy father straitly charged the people with an oath, saying, Cursed be the man that eateth any food this day.... Then said Jonathan, My father hath troubled the land: see, I pray you, how mine eyes have been enlightened, because I tasted a little of this honey. How much more, if haply the people had eaten freely today of the spoil of their enemies which they found? for had there not been now a much greater slaughter among the Philistines?"

After this lesson, another test was prepared for Saul. The time had come for the Lord to punish the Amalekites, and Samuel brought Saul the message that Amalek was to be utterly destroyed. God gave commandment unto Saul: "Now go and smite Amalek, and utterly destroy all that they have, and spare them not; but slay both man and woman, infant and suckling, ox and sheep, camel and ass."

But Saul did not do the work which the Lord had given him to do. He brought in his own human judgment against God's commandments. "And Saul gathered the people together, and numbered them in Telaim, two hundred thousand footmen, and ten thousand men of Judah. And Saul came to a city of Amalek, and laid wait in the valley. And Saul said unto the Kenites, Go, depart, get you down from among the Amalekites, lest I destroy you with them: for ye showed kindness to all the children of Israel, when they came up out of Egypt. So the Kenites departed from among the Amalekites. And Saul smote the Amalekites from Havilah until thou comest to Shur, that is over against Egypt. And he took Agag the king of the Amalekites alive, and utterly destroyed all the people with the edge of the sword. But Saul and the people spared Agag, and the best of the sheep, and of the oxen, and of the fatlings, and the lambs, and all that was good, and would not utterly destroy them: but everything that was vile and refuse, that they destroyed utterly."

God had commanded Saul to go and smite the Amalekites, and utterly destroy all their possessions; and he was watching his course to see if Saul could be trusted with his work as king of Israel. But Saul only partially obeyed the command; he destroyed the inferior cattle, but reserved the best, and spared the wicked king. And God said to Samuel, "It repenteth me that I have set up Saul to be king: for he is turned back from following me, and hath not performed my commandments."

This message grieved the prophet, and he cried unto the Lord all night. He saw that the people of Israel were to have their trial very soon after coming under the rule of a king. Samuel had concluded that because of Saul's stature and beauty of countenance, he would be in favor with God; but the displeasure of the Lord was kindled against Saul because of his lack of keen perception to distinguish between sacred and profane things, to recognize the requirements of God as supreme,--because, when tried, he showed that he did not properly estimate the word given through God's faithful servant.

The next day Saul met the prophet Samuel with flattery and self-congratulations. Said he, "Blessed be thou of the Lord: I have performed the commandment of the Lord." But the prophet immediately answered, "What meaneth then this bleating of the sheep in mine ears, and the lowing of the oxen which I hear?"

Saul was confused, and sought to shirk responsibility by answering: "They have brought them from the Amalekites: for the people spared the best of the sheep and of the oxen, to sacrifice unto the Lord thy God; and the rest we have utterly destroyed." Samuel reproved the king, reminding him of the explicit command of God to destroy all things belonging to Amalek. He pointed out his transgression, and declared that he had disobeyed the Lord. But Saul refused to acknowledge that he had done wrong; he again excused his sin by pleading that he had reserved the best cattle to sacrifice to the Lord.

The prophet was grieved to the heart by the persistency with which the king refused to see and confess his sin. He sorrowfully asked: "Hath the Lord as great delight in burnt-offerings and sacrifices, as in obeying the voice of the Lord? Behold, to obey is better than sacrifice, and to harken than the fat of rams. For rebellion is as the sin of witchcraft, and stubbornness is as iniquity and idolatry. Because thou hast rejected the word of the Lord, he hath also rejected thee from being king."

Mrs. E. G. White

December 8, 1898—The Higher Education

Education means much, very much, to every child and young person. To educate means to impart that knowledge that will enable the mind to grasp and contemplate those things that will be for the student's highest present and eternal good. The contemplation of the word of God will make us wise unto salvation; the knowledge of this word will insure our happiness, and our success in the perfection of Christian character.

All who in faith receive the word of God will be doers of that word. Their minds will be enlarged by a true knowledge, which Christ represents as eating the flesh and drinking the blood of the Son of God. And as they practise the truth, they hold forth the word of life to others. Thus they become an influence among influences, a savor of life unto life.

Christ said: "It is the spirit that quickeneth; the flesh profiteth nothing: the words that I speak unto you, they are spirit, and they are life." "He that eateth my flesh, and drinketh my blood, dwelleth in me, and I in him. As the living Father hath sent me, and I live by the Father: so he that eateth me, even he shall live by me. This is that bread which came down from heaven: not as your fathers did eat manna, and are dead: he that eateth of this bread shall live forever."

Satan will do everything he can to satisfy the appetite for food that does not pertain to the knowledge of the only true God, and Jesus Christ whom he has sent. Those who retain the grosser traits of character, who continue to reveal human defects in their words and disposition, bear testimony that they are not eating the flesh and drinking the blood of the Son of God. Christ says, "He that eateth my flesh, and drinketh my blood, dwelleth in me, and I in him."

The truest, the most exalted, knowledge is found in the word of God. In its simplicity there is eloquence. There are those who will grasp the words of the supposed great men of the world, and love to dwell upon their phraseology as something they need to esteem and value. You will hear men exalting human beings, extolling those who are called great by this world. In doing this, they lose sight of

Christ in the Word. He is not to them all and in all,--the first, the last, the best, in everything. These need to sit at the feet of Jesus, and learn of him whom to know aright is life eternal. In reading the word of God, in studying the meaning of that word, in bringing its principles into the heart and life, the youth may eat the flesh and drink the blood of the Son of God. Then the mind will be enlarged by a true, saving knowledge. The heart will be softened, subdued, refined, expanded. They will be partakers of the divine nature, and will become one with Christ. They will communicate their knowledge to others, that it may bless mankind.

The disciple John says: "Whosoever abideth in him sinneth not: whosoever sinneth hath not seen him, neither known him. Little children, let no man deceive you: he that doeth righteousness is righteous, even as he is righteous.... In this the children of God are manifest, and the children of the devil: whosoever doeth not righteousness is not of God, neither he that loveth not his brother. For this is the message that ye heard from the beginning, that we should love one another. Not as Cain, who was of that wicked one, and slew his brother. And wherefore slew he him? Because his own works were evil, and his brother's righteous."

Whatever our profession may be, it amounts to nothing if Christ is not revealed in the actions, in works of righteousness. "Whatsoever we ask, we receive of him (because we claim to keep God's commandments?--No), because we keep his commandments, and do those things that are pleasing in his sight. And this is his commandment, That we should believe on the name of his Son Jesus Christ, and love one another, as he gave us commandment. And he that keepeth his commandments dwelleth in him, and he in him. And hereby we know that he abideth in us, by the Spirit which he hath given us."

"Beloved, let us love one another: for love is of God; and every one that loveth is born of God, and knoweth God. He that loveth not knoweth not God; for God is love. In this was manifested the love of God toward us, because that God sent his only begotten Son into the world, that we might live through him. Herein is love, not that we loved God, but that he loved us, and sent his Son to be the propitiation for our sins. Beloved, if God so loved us, we ought also to love one another."

Christ is our personal Saviour; and if we are his disciples, our wrong-doing will cease, unrighteousness will come to an end. The strife to be first will no longer exist;

for Christ will be formed within, the hope of glory. Pure and undefiled religion will be seen in our lives.

"If we love one another, God dwelleth in us, and his love is perfected in us." This is the result of an experimental knowledge of Christ. The truth, admitted into the heart, will be seen in the sanctification of the receiver. There will be a continual growth in grace, a preparation to accomplish that work that God has appointed us; we shall answer the purpose for which we were redeemed.

There must be a continual work going forward in us. We are to gain a more intelligent knowledge of how to work. The individual worker will receive an education that will be of the highest value to himself personally, and will qualify him to reach and save his fellow beings.

When Christ called the disciples from their fishing-nets, he told them that they were to be fishers of men. They were to communicate the truth to others, casting their nets on the right side of the ship. By this Christ meant that they were to work in faith to save souls. And this work for individuals would, in the providence of God, lead them to work for communities. So God desires that the youth shall become skilful, thorough laborers wearing Christ's yoke, lifting his burdens. "We are laborers together with God," he says.

Children and youth should seek to advance in understanding, in mental acquirements. In spiritual as well as temporal things, their aim should be to work on the plan of addition. The apostle Peter says: "Giving all diligence, add to your faith virtue; and to virtue knowledge; and to knowledge temperance; and to temperance patience; and to patience godliness; and to godliness brotherly kindness; and to brotherly kindness charity. For if these things be in you, and abound, they make you that ye shall neither be barren nor unfruitful in the knowledge of our Lord Jesus Christ."

All these virtues are essential, and will develop in the character of the receiver the attributes of Christ. They will enlarge his knowledge of the spiritual graces, and he will desire to impart to others.

Selfishness will not harmonize with advancement in true education. True knowledge comes from God, and returns again to God. His children are to receive that they may give again. Those who, through the grace of God, have received intellect and spiritual benefits are, as they advance, to carry others with them to a higher excellence. And this work, done to promote the good of others, will have the co-operation of unseen agencies. As we faithfully continue the work, we shall have high aspirations for righteousness, holiness, and a perfect knowledge of God. We shall be complete in Christ in this life, and shall take our increased capabilities with us to the courts above, there to continue the higher education.

Mrs. E. G. White

December 15, 1898—Peter's Fall and Restoration—No. 1

The reason so many of Christ's professed disciples fall into grievous temptation is that they have not a correct knowledge of themselves. Here is where Peter was so thoroughly sifted by the enemy. If we could understand our own weakness, we should see so much to do for ourselves that we would humble our hearts under the mighty hand of God. Hanging our helpless souls upon Christ, we would supplement our ignorance with his wisdom, our weakness with his strength, our frailty with his enduring might.

Peter fell because he did not know his own frailty. He thought himself strong. He said: "Lord, I am ready to go with thee, both into prison, and to death." "I will lay down my life for thy sake." Jesus answered him, "I tell thee, Peter, the cock shall not crow this day, before that thou shalt thrice deny that thou knowest me." But Peter "spake the more vehemently, If I should die with thee, I will not deny thee in any wise."

Christ had said to Peter: "Simon, Simon, behold, Satan hath desired to have you, that he may sift you as wheat: but I have prayed for thee, that thy faith fail not: and when thou art converted, strengthen thy brethren."

Had Peter walked humbly with God, hiding self in Christ; had he earnestly looked for divine help; had he been less self-confident; had he received the Lord's instruction and practised it, he would have been watching unto prayer, working out his own salvation with fear and trembling. Had he closely examined himself, the Lord would have given him divine help, and there would have been no need of Satan's sifting. The enemy can not overcome the humble learner of Christ, the one who walks prayerfully before the Lord. Christ interposes himself as a shelter, a retreat, from the assaults of the wicked one. The promise is given, "When the enemy shall come in like a flood, the Spirit of the Lord shall lift up a standard against him." Peter was not intelligent in regard to his own defects of character. He did not see his need of the power and grace of Christ in order that he might know himself.

Satan was permitted to tempt the too confident Peter, as he had been permitted to tempt Job; but when that work was done, he had to retire. Had Satan been suffered to have his way, there would have been no hope for Peter. He would have made complete shipwreck of faith. But the enemy dare not go one hair's-breadth beyond his appointed sphere. There is no power in the whole satanic force that can disable the soul that trusts, in simple confidence, in the wisdom that comes from God.

Mark the course pursued by Peter. His fall was not instantaneous, but gradual. Step after step was taken, until the poor, sinful one denied his Lord with cursing and swearing. He denied the Man of Sorrows in his acquaintance with grief.

The crowing of the cock reminded Peter of the words of Christ, and, surprised and shocked, he turned and looked at his Master. At that moment, Christ looked at Peter, and beholding that grieved look, in which compassion and love for him were blended, Peter understood himself. With startling vividness his self-confident words flashed upon his minds: "Although all shall be offended, yet will not I." "I am ready to go with thee, both into prison, and to death." And yet he had denied his Lord with cursing and swearing!

But Peter was not left in hopelessness. The look that Christ had given him brought a ray of hope to the erring disciple. He read there the words, "Peter, I am sorry for you. Because you are sorry and repent, I forgive you." While Peter's soul was passing through such deep humiliation, through the awful struggle with satanic agencies, he remembered the words of Christ, "I have prayed for thee;" and they were to him a precious assurance.

The watch-care of Christ for Peter was the cause of his restoration. Satan could do nothing against the all-powerful intercession of Christ. And the prayer that Christ offered for Peter he offers in behalf of all who are humble and contrite in heart. He is our Advocate through the Holy Spirit. Before the Father he pleads the power and efficacy of his word. John declares: "If any man sin, we have an advocate with the Father, Jesus Christ the righteous."

In Peter's fall we have before us our own individual cases. Just as verily as did Peter, many of the professedly commandment-keeping people of God dishonor and bring reproach upon their best Friend,--the One who can save them to the uttermost. But the Lord would restore to himself all who have put him to shame by their unscriptural course of action.

Peter sinned against light and knowledge, and against great and exalted privileges. It was self-confidence that caused him to fail, and it is this same evil that is now working in human hearts. It may be our purpose to be right and to do right, but we shall most surely err unless we are constant learners in the school of Christ. Our only safety is in walking humbly with God.

Mrs. E. G. White

December 22, 1898—Peter's Fall and Restoration—No. 2

Peter never forgot the painful scene of his humiliation. He did not forget his denial of Christ, and think that, after all, it was not a very great sin. All was painfully real to the erring disciple. His sorrow for his sin was as intense as had been his denial. After his conversion, the old assertions were not made in the old spirit and manner.

No restoration can be complete unless it reaches to the very depth of the soul by the transforming power of the Holy Spirit. Under the Holy Spirit's influence, Peter stood before a congregation of thousands, and in holy boldness charged the wicked priests and rulers with the very sin of which he himself had been guilty. "Ye denied the Holy One and the Just," he said, "and desired a murderer to be granted unto you; and killed the Prince of life, whom God hath raised from the dead; whereof we are witnesses.... And now, brethren, I wot that through ignorance ye did it, as did also your rulers. But those things, which God before had showed by the mouth of all his prophets, that Christ should suffer, he hath so fulfilled." There was now no moral insensibility upon Peter. As Christ's witness, under the inspiration of the Spirit of God, he gave evidence of his divine restoration.

Three times after his resurrection, Christ tested Peter. "Simon, son of Jonas," he said, "lovest thou me more than these? He saith unto him, Yea, Lord; thou knowest that I love thee. He saith unto him, Feed my lambs. He saith to him again the second time, Simon, son of Jonas, lovest thou me? He saith unto him, Yea, Lord; thou knowest that I love thee. He saith unto him, Feed my sheep."

This heart-searching question was necessary in the case of Peter, and it is necessary in our case. The work of restoration can never be thorough unless the roots of evil are reached. Again and again the shoots have been clipped, while the root of bitterness has been left to spring up and defile many; but the very depth of the hidden evil must be reached, the moral senses must be judged, and judged again, in the light of the divine presence. The daily life will testify whether or not the work is genuine.

When, the third time, Christ said to Peter, "Lovest thou me?" the probe reached the soul center. Self-judged, Peter fell upon the Rock, saying, "Lord, thou knowest all things; thou knowest that I love thee."

This is the work before every soul who has dishonored God, and grieved the heart of Christ, by a denial of truth and righteousness. If the tempted soul endures the trying process, and self does not awake to life to feel hurt and abused under the test, that probing knife reveals that the soul is indeed dead to self, but alive unto God.

Some assert that if a soul stumbles and falls, he can never regain his position; but the case before us contradicts this. Before his denial, Christ said to Peter, "When thou art converted, strengthen thy brethren." In committing to his stewardship the souls for whom he had given his life, Christ gave to Peter the strongest evidence of his confidence in his restoration. And he was commissioned to feed not only the sheep, but the lambs,--a broader and more delicate work than had hitherto been appointed him. Not only was he to hold forth the word of life to others, but he was to be a shepherd of the flock.

"Verily, verily," said Christ, "when thou wast young, thou girdest thyself, and walkedst whither thou wouldest: but when thou shalt be old, thou shalt stretch forth thy hands, and another shall gird thee, and carry thee whither thou wouldest not. This spake he, signifying by what death he should glorify God. And when he had spoken this, he saith unto him, Follow me. Then Peter, turning about, seeth the disciple whom Jesus loved following.... Peter seeing him saith to Jesus, Lord, and what shall this man do? Jesus saith unto him, If I will that he tarry till I come, what is that to thee? follow thou me."

Peter was now humble enough to understand the words of Christ, and without further questioning, the once restless, boastful, self-confident disciple became subdued and contrite. He followed his Lord indeed,--the Lord he had denied. The thought that Christ had not denied and rejected him was to Peter a light and comfort and blessing. He felt that he could be crucified from choice, but it must be with his head downward. And he who was so close a partaker of Christ's sufferings will also be a partaker of his glory when he shall "sit upon the throne of his glory."

Christ is our tower of strength, and Satan can have no power over the soul who walks with God in humility of mind. The promise is, "Let him take hold of my strength, that he may make peace with me; and he shall make peace with me." In Christ there is perfect and complete help for every tempted soul. Dangers beset every path, but the whole universe of heaven is standing on guard that none may be tempted above that which he is able to bear. Some have strong traits of character, that will need to be constantly repressed. If kept under the control of the Spirit of God, these traits will be a blessing; but if not, they will prove a curse. If we lean to our own wisdom, our wisdom will prove to be foolishness. But if we will give ourselves unselfishly to the work, never swerving in the least from principle, the Lord will throw about us the everlasting arms, and will prove a mighty helper. If we will look to Jesus as the One in whom we may trust, he will never fail us in any emergency.

Mrs. E. G. White

December 29, 1898—One That Is Mighty

The sincere Christian may grieve as he sees the havoc that sin has wrought: but only in a limited sense can human beings understand Christ's sadness as he looks upon the sin that exists in the human heart; only in a limited sense can man sympathize with suffering humanity.

Christ alone was able to bear the afflictions of all the human family. "In all their affliction he was afflicted." He never bore disease in his own flesh; but he carried the sickness of others. When suffering humanity pressed about him, he who was in the health of perfect manhood was as one afflicted with them. With tenderest sympathy, he looked upon the suffering ones. He groaned in spirit as he saw the work of Satan revealed in all their woe, and he made every case of need and of sorrow his own. Numbers did not distract him; anguish did not overwhelm him. Though the pain of the sufferers thrilled through his whole being, yet with a power that never quailed, he cast out the evil spirits that possessed both mind and body.

The power of love was in all his healing. He identified himself with suffering humanity. Of the suffering multitudes who were brought to Christ it is said, "He healed them all."

When the poor, suffering paralytic was brought to the Saviour, Christ understood his condition perfectly. He knew that this wretched man had a disease of the soul far worse than bodily suffering. He knew that the greatest burden he had borne for months was on account of sin. The crowd of people around waited, in almost breathless silence, to see how Christ would treat this apparently hopeless case; and they were astonished to hear the words fall from his lips, "Son, be of good cheer; thy sins be forgiven thee."

These were the most precious words that could fall upon the ears of that sick sufferer; for the burden of sin had lain so heavily upon him that he could not find the least relief. Christ lifted the burden that had oppressed him: "Be of good cheer," I, your Saviour, came to forgive sins. How quickly the pallid countenance of the sufferer changes! Hope takes the place of dark despair, and peace and joy take the place of distressing doubt and gloom. The mind being restored to peace and happiness, the suffering body can now be reached.

Next comes from the divine lips the command: "Arise, take up thy bed, and go to thine house." In the effort to obey the will, those helpless, bloodless arms are quickened; a healthy current of blood flows through the veins; the leaden color of his flesh disappears, and the ruddy glow of health takes its place. The limbs, which for long years have refused to obey the will, are now quickened to life; and the healed paralytic grasps his bed, and walks through the crowd to his home.

Christ was health and strength in himself; and when sufferers were in his immediate presence, disease was always rebuked. It was for this reason that he did not go at once to Lazarus when the message came, "He whom thou lovest is sick." He could not witness suffering, and not bring relief. He could not look upon disease or death without combating the power of Satan. The death of Lazarus was permitted that, through his resurrection, the last and crowning evidence might be given to the Jews that Jesus was the Son of God.

Christ was strong to save the whole world. He wanted all. He could not endure the thought that one should be lost. He wept at the grave of Lazarus, that he could not save every one whom Satan's power had laid low in death. He had given himself a ransom for many, even all who would avail themselves of the privilege of coming back to their loyalty to God. John, pointing to him, had said, "Behold the Lamb of God, which taketh away the sin of the world."

And in all this conflict with the powers of evil, there was ever before Christ the darkened shadow into which he himself must enter. Ever before him was the price which he must pay for the ransom of these souls. As he witnessed the sufferings of the human race, he knew that he must bear a greater pain, mingled with mockery; that he must suffer the greatest humiliation. When he raised Lazarus from the dead, he knew that for that life he must pay the ransom on the cross of Calvary. Every rescue made was to cause him the deepest humiliation. He was to taste death for every man.

In his life on earth, Christ developed a perfect character, he rendered perfect obedience to his Father's commandments. In coming to the world in human form, in becoming subject to the law, in revealing to men that he bore their sickness, their sorrow, their guilt, he did not become a sinner. Before the Pharisees he could say,

"Which of you convinceth me of sin?" Not one stain of sin was found upon him. He stood before the world the spotless Lamb of God.

From the light of his exalted purity, the world's Redeemer could see that the maladies from which the human family were suffering were brought upon them by transgression of the law of God. Every case of suffering he could trace back to its source. In every case he read the sad and awful end of unrepenting sinners. He knew that he alone could rescue them from the pit into which they had fallen. He alone could place their feet in the right path; his perfection alone could avail for their imperfection. He alone could cover their nakedness with his spotless robe of righteousness.

Had all who claim to believe in Christ followed his example, what a different aspect would our world present today! This work has been neglected by the church; she has been remiss in following Christ in self-denial and self-sacrifice. She has not reached down to the depths of misery into which Satan has dragged those who have listened to his temptations; but we thank God that there is an opportunity to redeem the time, to bear the message of mercy to the highways and the hedges. The world's Redeemer is still the world's Restorer. Today Christ is feeling the woes of every sufferer. When the evil spirit rends the suffering frame, the Saviour feels its curse. When fever is burning up the life-current, he experiences the agony as if it were his own. And he is strong to deliver. Help has been laid on one that is mighty. He encircles man with his long human arm, while with his divine arm he lays hold of Omnipotence. He who created man knows just how to rid the human machinery of the clogs that have weakened the action of nerve, brain, bone, and muscle, and poisoned the life-current of the body. He knows how to speak the word, "Be whole," and bid the sufferer, "Go, and sin no more."

His last injunction to his followers, his representatives upon the earth, was to lay hands on the sick, that they might recover. When the Master shall come again, he will commend those who have visited the sick, and relieved the necessities of the afflicted.

Mrs. E. G. White

March 30, 1899—The Resurrection of Lazarus—Part 1

"Now a certain man was sick, named Lazarus, of Bethany, the town of Mary and her sister Martha. (It was that Mary which anointed the Lord with ointment, and wiped his feet with her hair, whose brother Lazarus was sick.)" Mary's act of anointing Jesus was the fruit of her faith in him as the Son of God, and in thus pointing her out, the inspired writer shows the value that Christ places on acts of loving service.

Christ had no home of his own. He was dependent on the hospitality of his friends and disciples. The home of the family at Bethany was one of the Saviour's homes. Here he could find rest and repose. Often when weary, thirsting for human fellowship, he had been glad to escape to this quiet home, away from the suspicion and jealousy of the angry Pharisees. Here he found a sincere welcome and pure, holy friendship. Here he could speak with simplicity and perfect freedom, knowing that his words would be understood and treasured. He was able here to accomplish the work for which he came to the earth.

When Christ gave his disciples their commission, and sent them forth in his name to preach the gospel, he told them that they were to accept the hospitality of the people. And he would have his people entertain his messengers. But there are persons, even among those who profess to believe the truth, who are great talkers. They do not wait to learn from the messengers God sends. They wish rather to instruct them. Often they interpret their own opinions to be the opinions of their guests. Thus they lose much. God's servants understand those with whom they have to deal, and they see that they can not do these constant talkers much good; for they can not hear aright.

Our Saviour appreciated a quiet home and interested listeners. He longed for human tenderness, courtesy, and affection. Those who received the heavenly instruction he was always ready to impart, were greatly blessed. John was one of his most attentive listeners, and thus he was enabled to be a doer of his words.

As the multitudes followed Christ through the open fields, he unfolded to them the beauties of the natural world. He opened the eyes of their understanding that they might see how the hand of God upholds the world. He called the attention of his hearers to the soft showers of rain and the bright sunshine, given alike to good and evil. In order to call out an appreciation of God's goodness and benevolence, Christ gave lessons which showed that the divine appreciation given an object is proportionate to the rank which that object holds in the scale of creation. He bade them consider the lilies, telling them that Solomon, the greatest king that ever wielded a scepter, was not, in all his glory, arrayed like one of the simple flowers of the field. God paints the flowers with colors that outvie the glory of Solomon. "Wherefore," said Christ, "if God so clothe the grass of the field, which today is, and tomorrow is cast into the oven, shall he not much more clothe you, O ye of little faith?" If the grass of the field receives divine care, how much more will our Heavenly Father care for us! We should seek to realize more fully the regard that God bestows on the human instrumentalities he has created.

But the multitudes were slow of hearing, and in the home at Bethany, Christ found rest from the weary conflict of public life. Here he opened to an appreciative audience the volume of Providence, showing that in this volume each one has a page, on which every particular of his history is traced. The human soul is never absent from the mind of God.

In these private interviews, Christ unfolded to his hearers that which he did not attempt to tell to the mixed multitude. He needed not to speak to his friends in parables. He opened to them the very heart of God, showing them the exactness of his love and care for his children, even in temporal things. God has made provision for every soul; for the human race is his spiritual offspring.

Such depth and breadth was there in what he said that all that the listeners could do was to be still, "and know that I am God." Who can measure the gifts of infinite love? "Eye hath not seen, nor ear heard, neither have entered into the heart of man, the things which God hath prepared for them that love him." Though sin has been accumulating for ages, God's love has never ceased to flow earthward. It was only restrained till a suitable channel was provided for it. Christ, the only begotten Son of God, left the royal courts and came to this world, and through him God poured forth the healing flood of his grace.

As Christ gave his wonderful lessons, Mary sat at his feet, a reverent and devoted listener. On one occasion, Martha, perplexed with the care of preparing the meal, went to Christ, saying: "Lord, dost thou not care that my sister hath left me to serve alone? bid her therefore that she help me." Jesus answered: "Martha, Martha, thou art careful and troubled about many things: but one thing is needful: and Mary hath chosen that good part, which shall not be taken away from her." She was storing her mind with the precious words falling from the Saviour's lips, which were more precious to her than earth's most costly jewels.

When Lazarus was taken sick, his sisters sent to Christ, saying, "Lord, behold, he whom thou lovest is sick." They saw the violence of the disease that had seized their brother, but they knew that Christ had shown himself able to heal all manner of diseases, and they thought that he would immediately respond to their message, and be with them as soon as he could reach Bethany.

Anxiously they waited for a word from Jesus. As long as the spark of life was yet alive in their brother, they prayed and watched for the Saviour to come. But the messenger returned without him. Yet he brought the message, "This sickness is not unto death," and they clung to the hope that Lazarus would live. Tenderly they tried to speak words of hope and encouragement to the almost unconscious sufferer. When Lazarus died, they were bitterly disappointed, but they felt the sustaining grace of Christ, and this kept them from reflecting any blame on the Saviour.

When the disciples gave Christ the message, he did not manifest the sorrow that they expected him to. They thought he received this sad news coldly. Looking up to them, he said, "This sickness is not unto death, but for the glory of God."

"Now Jesus loved Martha, and her sister, and Lazarus." The love that Christ felt for these friends was not alone a divine love. It was human as well as divine. He was an example of the highest type of humanity, and he was also the Saviour of the world. He could not be indifferent to the sufferings of the family whose hospitality he had so often shared, where he had rested and been refreshed as he had talked with his friends of heavenly things.

Mrs. E. G. White (To be continued.)

April 6, 1899—The Resurrection of Lazarus—Part 2

"When he had heard therefore that he was sick, he abode two days still in the same place where he was." This delay was a mystery to the disciples. What a comfort his presence would be to the family in the severe affliction through which they are passing, the disciples thought. Christ loves all the human family, but to some he is bound by peculiarly tender recollections. His heart was knit by a strong bond of affection to the family at Bethany; and knowing this, the disciples were surprised that he did not respond to the sad message, "He whom thou lovest is sick." Had Christ's love changed?--No, no! and had Mary and Martha thought it had, they would have misjudged that tender, pitiful heart of human and divine love. It was for them and for his disciples that he tarried where he was for two days apparently leaving the afflicted ones to bear their burden alone.

During this time Christ seemed to dismiss the message from his mind; for he did not speak of Lazarus. The disciples thought of John the Baptist, the forerunner of Jesus. At the time of his death, they had wondered why Jesus, with the power to perform wonderful miracles, had permitted John to languish in prison, and die a violent death. Possessing such power, why did not Christ save John's life? This question had often been asked by the Pharisees, who presented it as an unanswerable argument against Christ's claim to be the Son of God.

But Christ did not forget John. In the lonely prison he manifested himself to him, showing him that erelong he himself was to suffer a most shameful, ignominious death. Not only that, but he was to bear the penalty of the transgression of the law of God, not to give men liberty to continue in sin, but to take away their inclination to sin, that they might not desire to transgress. Those who receive Christ are obedient to his commands; for his mind is given to them. He imbues them with his spirit of obedience, and they return to their loyalty.

Christ's two days' delay after hearing that Lazarus was sick was not a neglect or a denial on his part. It was his purpose to remain where he was till the death of Lazarus took place, that he might give the people an evidence of his divinity, not by restoring a dying man, but by raising to life a man that had been buried.

This should be an encouragement to us. We are sometimes tempted to think that the promise, "Ask, and it shall be given you; seek, and ye shall find; knock, and it shall be opened unto you," is not fulfilled unless the answer comes immediately when the request is made. It is our privilege to ask for special blessings, and to believe that they will be given us. But if the blessings asked for are not immediately granted, we are not to think that our prayers are not heard. We shall receive, even if the answer is delayed for a time. In carrying out the plan of redemption, Christ sees enough in humanity to discourage him. But he does not become discouraged. In mercy and love he continues to offer us opportunities and privileges. So we are to rest in the Lord, and wait patiently for him. The answer to our prayers may not come as quickly as we desire, and it may not be just what we have asked; but he who knows what is for the highest good of his children will bestow a much greater good than we have asked, if we do not become faithless and discouraged.

After waiting for two days, Jesus said to his disciples, "Let us go into Judea again." The disciples were perplexed by these words. If Jesus were going to Judea, why had he waited two days? They could see nothing but danger in the course he was about to pursue. "Master," they said, "the Jews of late sought to stone thee; and goest thou thither again? Jesus answered, Are there not twelve hours in the day?" I am under the guidance of my Father, and as long as I do his will, my life is safe. My twelve hours of day are not yet ended. I have entered upon the last remnant of my day; but while any of this remains, I am safe.

"If any man walk in the day," he continued, "he stumbleth not, because he seeth the light of this world." He who does the will of God, who walks in the path that God has marked out, can not stumble and fall. The light of God's guiding Spirit gives him a clear perception of his duty, and leads him aright till the close of his work. "But if a man walk in the night, he stumbleth, because there is no light in him." He who walks in a path of his own choosing, where God has not called him, who ventures presumptuously into danger, doing that which the Lord has not bidden him do, will stumble, because he has compassed himself about with the sparks of his own kindling. For him day is turned into night; and wherever he may be, he is not secure.

"These things said he: and after that he saith unto them, Our friend Lazarus sleepeth; and I go, that I may awake him out of sleep." "Our friend Lazarus sleepeth!" How touching these words! How full of sympathy! In the thought of the peril their Master was about to incur by going to Jerusalem, the disciples had almost forgotten the bereaved family, at Bethany. But not so Christ. The disciples felt rebuked. They had been disappointed because Christ did not respond more promptly to the message. They had been tempted to think that he had not the tender love for Lazarus and his sisters that they had thought he had, or he would have hastened back with the messenger. But the words, "Our friend Lazarus sleepeth," awakened right feelings in their minds.

"Then said his disciples, Lord, if he sleep, he shall do well. Howbeit Jesus spake of his death: but they thought that he had spoken of taking rest in sleep." Christ represents death as being a sleep to his believing children. Their life is hid with Christ in God; and until the last trump shall sound, those who die will sleep in him.

"Then said Jesus unto them plainly, Lazarus is dead. And I am glad for your sakes that I was not there, to the intent ye may believe; nevertheless let us go unto him." Thomas could see nothing but death in store for his Master if he went to Judea; but he girded up his spirit, and said to the other disciples, "Let us also go, that we may die with him." He knew the hatred of the Jews toward Christ. It was their purpose to compass his death, but this purpose had not succeeded, because some of his allotted time still remained. During this time, Jesus had the guardianship of heavenly angels; and no bodily harm could come to him, even in the regions of Judea, where the rabbis were plotting how they might take him and put him to death.

"Lazarus is dead. And I am glad for your sakes that I was not there, to the intent ye may believe." The disciples marveled at these words. Did the Saviour by his own choice avoid the home of his suffering friends? What sorrow Mary and Martha would have felt, thought the disciples, could they have heard these words! Knowing the love that Jesus had for Mary and Martha, the disciples were unable to explain his words on this occasion.

Mrs. E. G. White

April 13, 1899—The Resurrection of Lazarus—Part 3

Apparently, Mary and Martha and the dying Lazarus were left alone; but they were not alone. Christ beheld the whole scene; and after the death of Lazarus, the bereaved sisters were upheld by his grace. Did not Jesus witness the sorrow of their rent hearts, as their brother wrestled with his strong foe, death? He saw it all, he felt every pang of anguish; and he said to his disciples, "Lazarus is dead."

Christ had not only the loved ones at Bethany to think of; he had the training of his disciples to consider. They were to be his representatives to the world, that the Father's blessing might include all. For their sake he permitted Lazarus to die. Had he restored him from illness to health, the miracle that is the most positive evidence of his divine character would not have been performed.

Had Christ been in the sick-room, Lazarus would not have died; for Satan would have had no power over him. In the presence of the Life-giver, death could not have aimed his dart at Lazarus. Therefore Christ remained away. To a certain extent he suffered the enemy to exercise his power. He permitted him to go a certain length, that by his own life-giving power he might drive back the conquered foe. He permitted Lazarus to pass under the dominion of death, and the suffering sisters saw their brother laid in the grave. Christ knew that as they looked on the face of their dead brother, their faith in their Redeemer would be severely tried. Thus he was pruning the branches, that they might bring forth more fruit. He knew that because of the struggle through which they were now passing, their faith would shine forth with far greater power. He suffered every pang of sorrow that they endured. He loved them no less because he tarried; but he knew that for them, for Lazarus, for himself, and for his disciples, a victory was to be gained. This crowning miracle was to give the seal to his mission and divinity.

"I am glad for your sakes that I was not there." Not then did the disciples grasp the full meaning of these words; but the Holy Spirit, which Christ was to send to them after his ascension, would bring to their remembrance every word that he had spoken, imprinting his lessons indelibly on their minds, that they might have no misconception of his love or of his human sympathy.

Christ delayed, that by raising Lazarus from the dead, he might give to his stubborn, unbelieving people an evidence that he was indeed "the resurrection, and the life." He was loath to give up all hope of the Jewish people. They were to him as the poor, wandering sheep of the house of Israel. His heart was breaking because of their impenitence. He knew that by their course of action they would bring upon themselves swift destruction. God would not avert the terrible retribution that was to come upon the Jewish nation because of the treatment of his Son. They were loading the cloud of indignation that was soon to burst upon them with uncontrollable fury, leaving them a scattered people, and a curse in the whole earth. But in his mercy, Christ purposed to give his deceived, deluded countrymen one more evidence that he was the Restorer, the One who alone could bring life and immortality to light through the gospel. This was to be an evidence that the priests could not misinterpret to destroy the faith of all whom they could influence. This was why Christ deferred going to Bethany.

As Christ and his disciples drew near Bethany, a messenger was sent to the sisters, with the tidings of his arrival. Christ did not at once enter the house, but remained in a quiet place by the wayside. Among the Jews great outward display was observed at the death of friends or relatives. The numerous ceremonies were carried through with great precision. This ceremonial was not in harmony with the spirit of Christ. He did not wish to meet the sisters in the scene of confusion. And among the mourners were relatives of the family, some of whom held high positions of responsibility in Jerusalem. Among these were some of Christ's bitterest enemies. Christ knew their purposes, and therefore he did not at once make himself known.

The message was given to Martha so quietly that the others in the room did not hear. Absorbed in her grief, Mary did not hear the words. Rising at once, Martha went out to meet her Lord; but thinking that she had gone to the place where Lazarus was buried, Mary sat still in her sorrow, making no outcry.

Martha hastened to meet Jesus, her heart agitated by conflicting emotions. In his expressive face she read the same tenderness and love that had always been there. Her confidence in him was unbroken; but she thought of her dearly loved brother, whom Jesus also had loved. Hope was not all dead in her heart; for at last Christ had come. With grief surging in her heart because he had not come before, yet with hope that even now he would do something to comfort them in their grief, she said: "Lord, if thou hadst been here, my brother had not died." Over and over again, amid the tumult made by the mourners, the sisters had repeated these words.

With human and divine pity, Jesus looked into her sorrowful, care-worn face. Truly the branch is pruned that it may bring forth more fruit. Martha had no inclination to recount the past: all is expressed by the pathetic words, "Lord, if thou hadst been here, my brother had not died." But looking into the face of love, she said, "But I know, that even now, whatsoever thou wilt ask of God, God will give it thee."

Christ's answer was not calculated to inspire faith in any immediate change. Carrying her thoughts forward to the general resurrection, he said, "Thy brother shall rise again." Martha understood him to mean just what he intended she should. "I know that he shall rise again in the resurrection at the last day," she answered. Jesus said: "I am the resurrection, and the life: he that believeth in me, though he were dead, yet shall he live." His death will not be eternal. "And whosoever liveth and believeth on me shall never die." The saints who are living when Christ comes, will be translated to heaven without seeing death. "Believest thou this?" Christ asked. Martha did not comprehend in all their significance the words spoken by Christ; but she responded, "Yea, Lord: I believe that thou art the Christ, the Son of God, which should come into the world."

"And when she had so said, she went her way, and called Mary her sister secretly, saying, The Master is come, and calleth for thee." She delivered her message as quietly as possible; for the priests and rulers were prepared to arrest Jesus when opportunity offered.

Mrs. E. G. White

April 20, 1899—The Resurrection of Lazarus—Part 4

The cries of the mourners prevented Martha's words from being heard. On hearing the message, Mary rose hastily, and with an eager look on her face, left the room. Thinking that she had gone to the grave to weep, the mourners followed her. When she reached the place where Jesus was waiting, she knelt at his feet, and said, with quivering lips, "Lord, if thou hadst been here, my brother had not died." The noise made by the mourners was painful to her; for she longed for a few quiet words alone with Jesus. But she knew of the envy and jealousy cherished in the hearts of some present against Christ, and she was restrained from fully expressing her grief.

"When Jesus therefore saw her weeping, and the Jews also weeping which came with her, he groaned in the spirit, and was troubled." He read the hearts of all assembled. He saw that with many, what was looked upon as a demonstration of grief, was only pretense. He knew that some in the company, now manifesting hypocritical sorrow, would erelong be planning the death, not only of the mighty miracle-worker, but of the one to be raised from the dead. There were tender hearts in the throng, but there were also hypocrites. These pretended to manifest grief, but their hearts were full of malignity. Christ could have stripped from them their robe of pretended sorrow; he could have revealed their real sentiments. But he restrained his righteous indignation. The words that he could in all truth have spoken, he did not speak, because of the loved one kneeling at his feet in sorrow, who truly believed in him.

"Where have ye laid him?" he asked. "They said unto him, Lord, come and see." Together they proceeded to the grave. It was a mournful scene. Lazarus had been much beloved, and his sisters wept for him with breaking hearts, while those who had been his friends mingled their tears with those of the bereaved sisters. In view of this human distress, and of the fact that the afflicted friends could mourn over the dead while the Saviour of the world stood by, who had power to raise from the dead, "Jesus wept." Though he was the Son of God, he had taken human nature upon him, and he was moved by human sorrow. His tender, pitiful heart is ever awakened to sympathy by suffering. He weeps with those who weep, and rejoices with those who rejoice.

But it was not only because of his human sympathy with Mary and Martha, that Jesus wept. There was in his tears a sorrow as high above human sorrow as the heavens are higher than the earth. Christ did not weep for Lazarus; for he was about to call him from the grave. He wept because those now united with Mary in mourning for Lazarus would soon plan the death of him who was the resurrection and the life. But how unable were the unbelieving Jews rightly to interpret his tears! Some, who could see nothing more than the outward circumstances of the scene before him as a cause for his grief, said, softly, "Behold how he loved him!" Others, seeking to drop the seed of unbelief in the hearts of those present, said, derisively, "Could not this man, which opened the eyes of the blind, have caused that even this man should not have died?" If it was in Christ's power to save Lazarus, why did he suffer him to die?

With prophetic eye Christ saw the enmity of the Pharisees and Sadducees. He knew that they were premeditating his death. He was the Son of the infinite God; and yet, a victim to Jewish hatred and infatuation, he was soon to be laid in the grave. In three days he was to rise, thus becoming for all "the resurrection and the life;" but the power to give men life was to be gained by passing through death. And at his death few save the disciples would weep over their disappointed hopes.

Mrs. E. G. White

April 27, 1899—The Resurrection of Lazarus—Part 5

By shedding Jesus' blood the Jewish people were about to divorce themselves from heaven. Christ knew that some of those now apparently so sympathetic would soon close against themselves the door of hope and the gates of the city of God. A scene was about to take place, in his humiliation and crucifixion, that would result in the destruction of Jerusalem, and at that time none would make lamentation for the dead. If the Jewish people had only appreciated the privileges and opportunities so mercifully granted them, the calamity about to fall upon them would have been averted. But in their prejudice they closed their eyes to all evidence.

Christ's pleadings and importunities over them had been the reproaches of unrequited love. "O Jerusalem, Jerusalem," he said, as from the Mount of Olives he beheld the city and wept over it, "thou that killest the prophets, and stonest them which are sent unto thee, how often would I have gathered thy children together, even as a hen gathereth her chickens under her wings, and ye would not!" You would not come to me, that you might have life.

Standing there, in the very shadow of the cross, despised and rejected by those to whom he had come to give life, Christ might appropriately have lifted up his voice, and said: "Seek ye the Lord while he may be found, call ye upon him while he is near: let the wicked forsake his way, and the unrighteous man his thoughts: and let him return unto the Lord, and he will have mercy upon him; and to our God; for he will abundantly pardon. For my thoughts are not your thoughts, neither are your ways my ways, saith the Lord. For as the heavens are higher than the earth, so are my ways higher than your ways, and my thoughts than your thoughts."

Christ was ever touched by human sorrow; but a far greater grief filled his soul as he thought of his unbelieving people. He saw that those who now refused to accept him would from that time erect around themselves walls of impenetrable darkness and unbelief, through which the light from heaven could not enter. The retribution that was coming upon Jerusalem was plainly portrayed before him. He saw Jerusalem besieged by the Roman legions. He knew that many now weeping for Lazarus would die in the siege of the city, and in their death there would be no hope. They would not rise again to receive life eternal, but to receive the second death.

It was not only because of the scene before him that Christ wept. The weight of the grief of ages was upon him. He saw the terrible effects of the transgression of the law of God. He saw that in the history of the world, beginning with the death of Abel, the conflict between good and evil had been unceasing. Looking down the years to come, he saw the suffering and sorrow, the tears and death, that were to be the lot of men. His heart was pierced with the pain of the human family of all ages and in all lands. The woes of the sinful race were heavy upon his soul; and the fountain of his tears was broken up, as he longed to relieve all their distress.

"Jesus therefore again groaning in himself cometh to the grave." Lazarus had been laid in a cave in a rock, and a massive stone had been placed before the entrance. "Take ye away the stone," Christ said. Thinking that he wished only to look upon the dead, Martha said, "Lord, by this time he stinketh: for he hath been dead four days." This statement, made before the raising of Lazarus, left no room for Christ's enemies to say that a deception had been practised. In the past the Pharisees had circulated false statements regarding the most wonderful manifestations of the power of God. Already Christ had raised to life the daughter of Jairus and the son of the widow of Nain. Of the first of these he had said, "The damsel is not dead, but sleepeth." The people knew that she was indeed dead; but as she had been sick for only a short time before her death, Christ's enemies, the Pharisees, in an effort to destroy the effect of the miracle, declared that the child had not been dead; that Jesus himself had said that she was only asleep. They tried to make it appear that Jesus could not cure diseases, that there was false play about his miracles. But in this case, if evidence could break stubborn hearts, decided reformation must surely be made. This miracle marked the Jews' most solemn period of responsibility. Here they decided their own destiny; for no stronger evidence could be given them.

Mrs. E. G. White

May 4, 1899—The Resurrection of Lazarus—Part 6

When the Lord is about to do a work, Satan moves upon some one to object. "Take ye away the stone." Christ said. As far as possible, prepare the way for my work. But Martha's positive and ambitious nature asserted itself. Thinking that he wished only to look upon the body of her brother, she said, Lord, the work of corruption had made this impossible. She thought that it would be terrible to reveal the decomposing body to the beholders. Thus she expressed her unbelief. She did not realize that Jesus had tarried for two days where he was when he received the message, permitting Lazarus to die, that he might manifest the greatness of his power by raising him, thus giving all who should witness the miracle an evidence that could not be excelled.

Christ reproved Martha for her unbelief, but his words were spoken with the utmost gentleness. "Said I not unto thee, that, if thou wouldest believe, thou shouldest see the glory of God?" Why should you doubt my power? You have my word. If you will believe, you shall see the glory of God. Skepticism and unbelief are not humility. Implicit belief in Christ's word is true humility, true self-surrender.

Christ's every word is full of meaning; his every lesson is important. Was not his word sufficient for Martha, even in her sorrow? Why did she reason in opposition to his requirements? Natural impossibilities can not prevent the work of the Omnipotent One. Christ would not be hindered in taking the prey from the enemy, and giving his disciples another trophy of victory. But the human heart is slow to understand Christ's words, and Martha's faith had not grasped the true meaning of his promise.

"Take ye away the stone." Christ could have commanded the stone to remove, and it would have obeyed his voice. He could have bidden the angels who were close at his side to do this. At his bidding, invisible hands would have removed the stone. But the stone was to be taken away by human hands. Thus Christ would show that humanity is to co-operate with divinity. What human power can do, divine power is not summoned to do. God does not dispense with man's aid. He strengthens him, co-operating with him as he uses the powers and capabilities given him.

The order was obeyed. The stone was rolled away. Everything was done openly and deliberately. All were given opportunity to see that no deception was being practised. There lay the body of Lazarus in its rock grave, cold and silent in death. The cries of the mourners were hushed. Surprised and expectant, the company stood around the sepulcher, waiting to see what next would happen.

Calmly Christ stands before the grave. No hurried movements are made. A sacred solemnity exerts its influence upon all present. Christ steps closer to the sepulcher. Lifting his eyes to heaven, he says, "Father, I thank thee that thou hast heard me." Not long before this, Christ's enemies had taken up stones to cast at him because he claimed to be the Son of God. They had accused him of blasphemy, of performing his miracles by the power of Satan, thus blaspheming God themselves. But here Christ claims God as his Father, and with perfect confidence declares that he is the Son of God.

In all that he did, Christ was co-operating with his Father. Ever he had been careful to have it understood that he did not work independently, but that it was by faith and prayer that he wrought his miracles. Christ desired all to know his relationship with his Father. "Father," he said, "I thank thee that thou hast heard me. And I know that thou hearest me always: but because of the people which stand by I said it, that they may believe that thou hast sent me." Here the disciples and the people were to be given the most convincing evidence in regard to the relationship existing between Christ and God.

"And when he had thus spoken, he cried with a loud voice, Lazarus, come forth." His voice, clear and penetrating, falls with solemn power on the people, and pierces the ear of the dead. As he speaks, divinity flashes through humanity. The people see in his face, which is lighted up by the glory of God, the assurance of his power. Every eye is fastened on the entrance to the cave. Every ear is quickened to hear each word. With intense and painful interest, all wait for the test of Christ's claim, the evidence that is to substantiate the fact that he is the Son of God, or to extinguish the hope forever.

There is a stir in the silent tomb. He who was dead stands at the door of the sepulcher. His movements are impeded by the graveclothes in which he was laid away, and Christ says to the astonished spectators, "Loose him, and let him go." Again they are shown that what human hands can do, divine power does not attempt to perform. The human worker is to co-operate with God. In God's order, humanity is to work for humanity. There is a work that God alone can do. He alone can heal the sick. But the physician can co-operate with him by supplying right conditions. God alone can restore the diseased frame, but if man fails to do his part, he has no right to expect God to do his part.

This miracle exerted a powerful influence. "Many of the Jews which came to Mary, and had seen the things which Jesus did, believed on him." They received Christ, and in them the words were fulfilled, "As many as received him, to them gave he power to become the sons of God." "But some of them went their ways to the Pharisees, and told them what things Jesus had done." They had just witnessed the most wonderful evidence ever given to men that Jesus was the Messiah; but in spite of this, they surrounded their souls with darkness so dense that the divine light could not reach their souls.

Mrs. E. G. White

May 11, 1899—The Resurrection of Lazarus—Part 7

By raising Lazarus, Christ gave unmistakable evidence that he was the Sent of God. However humble his birth and appearance might be, he was the mighty God, the everlasting Father, the Prince of Peace. Who can fathom his longing desire to save those who had no mercy for themselves? He longed to give these deluded, fanatical people, whose fathers he had led through the wilderness, an evidence of his divinity, a display of his power, that would lead them to accept him. But he knew that though, as the result of this miracle, many souls would afterward be added to the church, the hearts of others would be steeled against him and his work.

Looking over the past, Christ saw how, during the record of a thousand years, the Jews had abused their precious privileges. God had borne long with his erring people. In visible glory he had dwelt in the Shekinah of the mercy-seat. He had sent his Son to redeem them, but in a short time they were to show to the heavenly universe, to the worlds unfallen, that they had chosen Satan to be their leader, and were determined to cherish his attributes. Satan's best allies are those who will not come to the light, who stubbornly refuse all evidence; and the Jews had long been working in these lines. They would soon make the words of John the Baptist, "Ye generation of vipers," true in every sense. They would break every God-given command, thus demonstrating the truth of Christ's words: "Ye are of your father the devil, and the lusts of your father ye will do. He was a murderer from the beginning, and abode not in the truth, because there is no truth in him. When he speaketh a lie, he speaketh of his own: for he is a liar, and the father of it."

Bethany was so near Jerusalem that the news of the miracle was soon carried to the city, and in a few hours the Jewish rulers were in possession of the facts. A meeting of the Sanhedrin was at once called, to decide what should be done. The priests were convinced that the miracle had been wrought by the power of God. They were greatly impressed; for the Holy Spirit convicted them of the sins which they had committed against Christ. But they closed their hearts, lest the beams of the Sun of righteousness should shine into them. They stood behind an impregnable wall of unbelief. They were determined that they would never receive Jesus of Nazareth as the Messiah. Now that his influence had been strengthened by this wonderful miracle, their hatred was, if possible, increased. They were more than ever determined to put a stop to his work. No misinterpretation could be placed on this miracle. It was a work above criticism. They decided that Christ's work must be stopped; for already many of the Jews had received him.

Though not favorable to Christ, the Saducees had not been so full of malignity toward him as were the Pharisees. Their hatred had not been so bitter. But they were now thoroughly frightened. They did not believe in a resurrection of the dead. Producing so-called science, they reasoned that it would be an impossibility for a dead body to be brought to life. Thus they showed themselves to be ignorant of the Scriptures and of the power of God. But by a few words from Christ, their theory had been overthrown. Lazarus had passed under the control of death. For four days his body had lain in the grave, yet at a word from Christ he had risen to life, in the presence of many witnesses. But this miracle did not open the eyes of the Saducees; for they were blinded by prejudice. They could see no possibility of removing the impression made on the people by the miracle; for in no way could they prove it to be a deception. Thus far they had not encouraged the plan of putting Christ to death; but after the resurrection of Lazarus they decided that only by his death could his denunciations against them be stopped.

The Pharisees believed in the resurrection, and they could not but see that this miracle was an evidence that the Messiah was among them. But they had ever opposed Christ's work. From the first they had hated Christ because he did not exalt them and their boasted righteousness. Instead, he had said to his disciples and to others, "I say unto you, That except your righteousness shall exceed the righteousness of the scribes and Pharisees, ye shall in no case enter into the kingdom of heaven." In his sermon on the mount, Christ had defined the far-reaching principles of the law of God, and had shown that its requirements do not consist in outward show, but in holiness of heart and life. This Christ placed far above all outward observances. He outlined the qualities that all must possess who would win the approbation of God.

In his scathing denunciation of the labored theology of the Pharisees, Christ said, "In vain they do worship me, teaching for doctrines the commandments of men." They bound upon others heavy religious burdens, from which, however, they excused themselves. Christ laid bare their avarice; their ambitious, intriguing plans for the priesthood; their exclusiveness, which led them to build a wall of partition between priest and people.

Mrs. E. G. White

May 18, 1899—The Resurrection of Lazarus—Part 8

Christ had encouraged all, however sinful, to go directly to God as their merciful Father. Neither by precept nor example had he directed the people to the priesthood. But the idea of repenting and receiving forgiveness for their sins was not for a moment to be entertained by the priests. They would not admit that through unbelief they had placed themselves where the blessing of God could not come to them. When Christ had opened the eyes of the man born blind, they had striven with all sophistry to change the truth into a lie, declaring that the man was not born blind, that sight could not be given to eyes that had never seen. The man told them the simple truth; but they could not see, they could not believe, because they would not. So it was that the raising of Lazarus hardened their hearts; for they returned from evidence to cavil and disbelief.

In the meeting called in haste, Pharisees and Sadducees were more nearly united than ever before. Divided hitherto, they became one in their opposition to the Spirit of God, and in their determination to adhere to the cause of the Prince of darkness, who brought sin into the world, and death through sin. What a council this was! The men who had been placed in positions of responsibility did not make investigation to see if these wonderful works bore the divine impress. They did not stop to question whether they were fighting against God. In their bigotry and prejudice they did not bow before God in humble prayer, with the Scriptures in their hands, asking God to show them if, in their opposition to Jesus, they were warring against heaven. So far had they separated from God, that they did not cast one glance heavenward.

But the members of the council were not all agreed. The Sanhedrin was no longer a legal assembly, but existed only by tolerance. Some of its number questioned the wisdom of putting Christ to death. They feared that this would cause an insurrection among the people, causing the Romans to withhold further favors from the priesthood, and to take from them the power they now held by sufferance. The Sadducees were united in their hatred of Christ, yet they were inclined to be cautious in their movements, fearing that the Romans would deprive them of their high standing.

In this Sanhedrin, assembled to plan the death of Christ, the Witness was present who heard the boastful words of Nebuchadnezzar, who witnessed the idolatrous feast of Belshazzar, who was present when Christ in Nazareth announced himself to be the Anointed One. This Witness was now impressing the rulers with the sinfulness of the work they were doing. Events in the life of Jesus rose up before them with a distinctness that alarmed them. They remembered the scene in the temple, when Jesus, a child of twelve, stood before the grave, learned doctors of the law, asking them questions at which they wondered. The miracle just performed appealed to their hearts, impressing them that Jesus was none other than the Son of God. Perplexed and troubled, the rulers asked, "What do we?" There was a division in the council. Under the impression of the Holy Spirit, the Pharisees could not banish from their minds the conviction that they were fighting against God. In their true significance, the Old Testament Scriptures regarding Christ flashed before their minds.

While the council was at the height of its perplexity, Caiaphas arose. He was high priest that year, and among his family connections were Sadducees, proud, bold, reckless, full of ambition and cruelty, which characteristics they hid under a cloak of pretended righteousness. With an assumption of knowledge, the high priest said, "Ye know nothing at all, nor consider that it is expedient for us, that one man should die for the people, and that the whole nation perish not." Can you not see that if you wish to retain your position in the nation, Jesus must die?

Caiaphas showed them that after this miracle the followers of Jesus would likely rise in revolt. The Romans will then come, he said, and will close our temple and abolish our laws, destroying us as a nation. What is the life of this Galilean worth, in comparison with the life of the nation? Whether innocent or guilty, if he stands in the way of the nation's well-being, is it not doing God a service to remove him? Better that one man perish than that the whole nation be destroyed.

This false idea had been taken from heathenism. Among the heathen, the dim consciousness that one was to die for the human race had led to the offering of human sacrifices. So Caiaphas thought to save the guilty nation, not from transgression, but in transgression, that they might continue in sin. Thus he thought to silence the remonstrances of those who dared say that as yet nothing worthy of death had been found in Jesus.

Mrs. E. G. White

May 25, 1899—The Resurrection of Lazarus—Part 9

At this council Christ's enemies had been deeply convicted. The Holy Spirit had impressed their minds. But Satan strove to gain control over them. He urged upon their notice the grievances they had suffered on account of Christ. How little he had honored their righteousness! He had presented a righteousness far greater, which all must possess who would be children of God. Taking no notice of their forms and ceremonies, he had made the service of God so simple that sinners were encouraged to go directly to God, as to a merciful Father, and make their wants known to him. Thus, in their opinion, Christ had set aside the priesthood. He had refused to acknowledge the theology of the rabbinical schools. He had exposed the evil practises of the priests, and had irreparably hurt their influence. He had injured the effect of their maxims and traditions, declaring that though they strictly enforced the ritual law, they made the law of God void by their traditions. He had accused them of being ignorant of the Scriptures and of the power of God, denouncing them as hypocrites. This Satan now brought to their minds, persuading them that they had a quarrel against Jesus, which nothing but his death could end.

Satan told them that in order to save their authority, they must put Jesus to death. This counsel they followed. The fact that they might lose the power they then exercised was, they thought, sufficient reason for coming to some decision. With the exception of a few who dared not speak their minds, the Sanhedrin received the words of the high priest as the words of God. Relief came to the council; the discord ceased. They resolved to put Christ to death at the first favorable opportunity. In coming to this shameful decision they eased their minds with the fact that many guiltless lives had been sacrificed to save others.

The rulers were well pleased with themselves. They regarded themselves as patriots, who were seeking the nation's salvation. Thus they persuaded themselves that they would be doing God a service in apprehending Christ. They thought that by putting him to death they could avert danger and preserve their power. Every device possible was to be tried to find something whereby Christ could be represented as working against the Roman power. By putting spies on his track, who would profess to be honest inquirers after truth, they hoped to entrap him. Thus by their own course of action they demonstrated as true all that Jesus had said of their malignity.

This spirit had been worked out in the history of Daniel. His enemies, who hated the faithful statesman for his integrity, and who wished to remove him from their path, that they might rise to eminence, planned and intrigued long in order to find some way by which he might be condemned and put to death.

By deciding to murder the Son of God, the Jewish rulers forged the fetters that were to hold them in irrevocable bondage. They loaded the cloud of vengeance that was soon to break over them, leaving them divorced from God and a prey to their enemies. From the time of this decision, the protection of God was withdrawn from the Jewish nation. The restraint of his Holy Spirit was removed.

Christ's act in raising Lazarus was the crowning act of his life. What an influence for good it should have had upon all! But the hearts of the priests were hardened by it. Heaven's light was shining upon them; the evidence was strong enough to lead them out of the dark shadow in which the enemy had enveloped them. But the words were verified: "Though he had done so many miracles before them, yet they believed not on him.... Because that Esaias said again, He hath blinded their eyes, and hardened their heart; that they should not see with their eyes, nor understand with their heart, and be converted, and I should heal them."

God never hardens the heart in any other way than by giving great light. Heaven's favors slighted, turned from, rejected, because of a perverse will, harden the heart. So Pharaoh's heart was hardened. In order to accomplish his purpose, the Lord continued to give him greater and still greater manifestations of his power. But the king's first resistance made obedience to God more difficult. To refuse first, and then obey, is humiliating.

God did not actually make Pharaoh stubborn and unyielding. He continued to give him light, and the king's increasing stubbornness brought its sure result. By resisting the will of God, seeds of disobedience are sown, and a harvest of evil is reaped. One seed of unbelief generates another and a stronger seed. By submission to the will of God, seeds are sown that will produce a rich harvest of good. The seed that is sown is the seed reaped; for seed reproduces itself. "Whatsoever a man soweth, that shall he also reap." As responsible agents, all are deciding for themselves what their harvest shall be.

God never urges any one on in wickedness. He never leads man to become desperate in his rebellion. He will not that any should perish, but that all should be saved. But he forces no one to accept the light. If, after bearing long with man, God sees that he will not submit, he leaves him to work out his natural hatred. He gives him up to the worst of all tyrants,--self.

From those who will not see the light, who are determined to go on in the hardness of their hearts, God gradually withdraws the restraining power of his grace.

Today, as in the days when Christ worked his wonderful miracles, the truth of God is made known. Men have within themselves the evidence of its divinity. The Holy Spirit impresses their minds by the manifestation of divine power. If received, the light sent from God leads to freedom, life, and salvation. But if by resistance, preconceived opinions are strengthened, if the God-given blessing is not received, the light becomes darkness.

Mrs. E. G. White

June 8, 1899—Doers of the Word—Part 1

Christ attaches great importance to the doing of the word, as well as to the hearing of it. Among those who listened to his teachings were some who found it easy to hear, but who did not bring into their practical life the truths they heard. Christ sought to teach them that the divine word is not to be treated indifferently, but that all who hear it are to be doers of it.

By a parable Christ warned his hearers: "Not every one that saith unto me, Lord, Lord, shall enter into the kingdom of heaven; but he that doeth the will of my Father which is in heaven. Many will say to me in that day, Lord, Lord, have we not prophesied in thy name? and in thy name have cast out devils? and in thy name done many wonderful works? And then will I profess unto them, I never knew you: depart from me, ye that work iniquity.

"Therefore whosoever heareth these sayings of mine, and doeth them, I will liken him unto a wise man, which built his house upon a rock: and the rain descended, and the floods came, and the winds blew, and beat upon that house; and it fell not: for it was founded upon a rock. And every one that heareth these sayings of mine, and doeth them not, shall be likened unto a foolish man, which built his house upon the sand: and the rain descended, and the floods came, and the winds blew, and beat upon that house; and it fell: and great was the fall of it."

As Christ spoke these words, he was walking near the seacoast. About him were houses, some completed, others in the process of erection, apparently in most desirable positions. The disciples expressed their admiration of the wisdom of the men who had chosen such beautiful and desirable locations; but these houses were built upon the sand. Still another house was built high upon an eminence, which would require hard climbing to reach. This house was built upon the rock.

Passing on some distance, Christ and his followers saw the place where a house had formerly stood; but the ruins alone remained to tell the story. This house had been washed away by storm and tempest, while fierce winds had not prevailed against the building whose foundation was riveted to the solid rock.

Christ used this instance to impress his lesson. He pointed to the house built high upon the rock, and then to the broken framework and debris about them, and showed the sure result of building upon a sandy foundation. He sought to convince his disciples of the lack of wisdom revealed by the man who built his house so insecurely. "Every one that heareth these sayings of mine," he said, "and doeth them, I will liken him unto a wise man, which built his house upon a rock: and the rain descended, and the floods came, and the winds blew, and beat upon that house; and it fell not: for it was founded upon a rock. And every one that heareth these sayings of mine, and doeth them not, shall be likened unto a foolish man, which built his house upon the sand: and the rain descended, and the floods came, and the winds blew, and beat upon that house; and it fell: and great was the fall of it."

Christ likened him who obeys the word of God to the man whom the world had many times denounced as foolish for placing himself in a place apparently so inaccessible. The greatest Teacher the world ever knew looked beneath the foundation, and showed the necessity of building securely, on the rock. Then when rain and tempest sweep down upon the building, it is found secure.

In the illustration we as well as the disciples have a profitable lesson to learn. The house which was apparently so difficult of access, but which had stood unmoved amid storm and tempest, illustrates the spiritual life of those who build upon the sure foundation.

Mrs. E. G. White

June 15, 1899—Doers of the Word—Part 2

The sayings of Christ are truth, eternal truth. He has sent his message, and we must hear with ears of faith. All who hear the word are to be doers of the word. The Saviour seeks to impress our minds with the necessity of charity, love, that earnest prayer that will ascend to God from hearts that are sincere in their religious duties. "Seek ye first the kingdom of God, and his righteousness, and all these things shall be added unto you."

When Christ asked his disciples, "Whom say ye that I am?" Peter answered: "Thou art the Christ, the Son of the living God. And Jesus answered and said unto him, Blessed art thou, Simon Bar-jona: for flesh and blood hath not revealed it unto thee, but my Father which is in heaven. And I say also unto thee, That thou art Peter [which by interpretation means a stone], and upon this rock I will build my church; and the gates of hell shall not prevail against it."

The name Peter means a stone, but Christ did not refer to Peter as the rock. He spoke of a rock altogether stable and immovable. He referred to the words Peter had spoken: "Thou art the Christ, the Son of the living God;" and he said, "I say unto thee, ... upon this rock I will build my church; and the gates of hell shall not prevail against it." The Truth, the Life, the Light of the world, was to be the foundation of the Christian church.

In plain language Isaiah tells who is the stone upon which the church is built: "Thus saith the Lord God, Behold, I lay in Zion for a foundation a stone, a tried stone, a precious corner-stone, a sure foundation: he that believeth shall not make haste. Judgment also will I lay to the line, and righteousness to the plummet: and the hail shall sweep away the refuge of lies, and the waters shall overflow the hiding-place."

Peter afterward wrote: "To whom coming, as unto a living stone, disallowed indeed of men, but chosen of God, and precious, ye also, as lively stones, are built up a spiritual house, an holy priesthood, to offer up spiritual sacrifices, acceptable to God by Jesus Christ. Wherefore also it is contained in the scripture, Behold, I lay in Zion a chief corner-stone, elect, precious: and he that believeth on him shall not be confounded. Unto you therefore which believe he is precious: but unto them which be disobedient, the stone which the builders disallowed, the same is made the head of the corner, and a stone of stumbling, and a rock of offense, even to them which stumble at the word, being disobedient: whereunto also they were appointed."

Those who build upon Christ Jesus will be safe; but those who build according to the wisdom of worldly-wise men, will find their wisdom foolishness. The great questions for us to settle are, How are we building? What characters are we forming in this our probationary time? The corner-stone of right character is Jesus Christ. His word, if practised, is sufficient to develop harmonious characters in all who believe, and who fashion their lives in accordance with it. The life that is given to God will become most valuable. He says, "I will make a man more precious than gold; even a man than the golden wedge of Ophir."

"Ye are God's husbandry, ye are God's building," and you are under obligation to God to render him perfect service. You are in Christ's training-school. What do you propose to do with yourselves,--to be taught of God, or to take yourselves into your own keeping, and live in opposition to the plans of your Redeemer? Do you purpose to lay up treasure in this world, simply to expend upon your desires, and thus become unblessed of God in this life, and bankrupt for eternity?

"Ye are not your own; for ye are bought with a price." All the physical strength you have is Christ's. You live because he keeps you by his power. He made you for himself. He has a right to you, soul, body, and spirit. He has given you his plan for your life. It is to meet his requirements, that he may endow you with the gift of everlasting life. In order to become a member of the royal family, you must receive Christ by faith, believe in him as your personal Saviour, and take your place in his service. All your possessions are God's not to be trifled away, not to be used to gratify yourselves. You are to remember that the gold and silver, the houses and lands, bear the royal stamp, the signature of God. All are his property, to be used to glorify his name. You are to be his representatives, his faithful stewards, using his means to advance his work. God is greatly dishonored when his entrusted goods are used unfaithfully, and diverted to please the selfish heart.

God would have you draw wisdom from him; then you will be all-around Christians, reaching the highest perfection of usefulness in this life. By bringing every advantage God has given you into this work, your consecrated efforts will win souls for Christ. Set Christ ever before you. Recognize him as the first, the last, the best, in everything. Lay all the plans of your life before the One who died for you, that he might bring to you life and immortality. Remember that just the character-building you now make will determine your eternal salvation or your eternal ruin.

Mrs. E. G. White

June 22, 1899—God's Purpose Concerning the Youth of Today—Part 1

Grave responsibilities rest upon the youth. God expects much from the young men who live in this generation of increased light and knowledge. He expects them to impart this light and knowledge. He desires to use them in dispelling the error and superstition that cloud the minds of many. They are to discipline themselves by gathering up every jot and tittle of knowledge and experience. God holds them responsible for the opportunities and privileges given them. The work before them is waiting for their earnest effort, that it may be carried forward from point to point, as the time demands. If the youth will consecrate their minds and hearts to God's service, they will reach a high standard of efficiency and usefulness.

This is the standard that the Lord expects the youth to attain. To do less than this is to refuse to make the most of God-given opportunities. This will be looked upon as treason against God,--a failure to work for the good of humanity.

Those who strive to become laborers for God, who seek earnestly to acquire in order to impart, will constantly receive light from God, that they may be channels of communication. If, like Daniel, young men and young women will bring all their habits, appetites, and passions into conformity to the requirements of God, they will qualify themselves for higher work. They should put from their minds all that is cheap and frivolous. Nonsense and amusement-loving propensities should be discarded, as out of place in the life and experience of those who are living by faith on the Son of God, eating his flesh and drinking his blood. They should realize that though all the advantages of learning may be within their reach, they may yet fail of obtaining that education which will fit them for work in some part of the Lord's vineyard. They can not engage in God's service without the requisite qualifications of intelligent piety. If they give to pleasure and amusement the precious mind that should be strengthened by high and noble purposes, they degrade the powers that God has given them, and are guilty before him, because they fail to improve their talents by wise use. Their dwarfed spirituality is an offense to God. They taint and corrupt the minds of those with whom they associate. By their words and actions they encourage a careless inattention to sacred things. Not only do they imperil their own souls, but their example is detrimental to all with whom they come in contact. They are utterly incompetent to represent Christ. Servants of sin, careless, reckless, and foolish, they scatter away from him.

Those who are satisfied with low attainments fail of being workers together with God. To those who let the mind drift where it will drift if not guarded, Satan makes suggestions which so fill the mind that they are trained in his army to decoy other souls. They may make a profession of religion, they may have a form of godliness; but they are lovers of pleasure more than lovers of God. There are youth who have a certain kind of cleverness, which is acknowledged and admired by their associates, but their ability is not sanctified. It is not strengthened and solidified by the graces and trials of experience, and God can not use it to benefit humanity and glorify his name. Under the guise of godliness, their powers are being used to erect false standards, and the unconverted look to them as an excuse for their wrong course of action. Satan leads them to amuse their associates by their nonsense and so-called wit. Everything that they undertake is cheapening; for they are under the control of the tempter, who directs and fashions their characters, that they may do his work.

They have ability, but it is untrained; they have capacity, but it is unimproved. Talents have been given them; but they misuse and degrade them by folly, and drag others down to their own low level. Christ paid the ransom for their souls by self-denial, self-sacrifice, humiliation, by the shame and reproach he endured. This he did that he might rescue them from the bondage of sin, from the slavery of a master who cares for them only as he can use them to ruin souls. But they make the love of the Redeemer in their behalf of no avail to them, and he looks with sadness on their work.

Such youth meet with eternal loss. How will their fun and frolic appear to them in the day when every man shall receive from the Judge of all the earth according to the deeds done in the body? They have brought to the foundation wood, hay, and stubble, and all their life-work will perish. What a loss!

O, how much better is the condition of those who act their part in God's service, looking to Jesus for his approval, writing daily in their account-book their mistakes, their errors, their sorrows, the victories they have gained over temptation, their joy and peace in Christ! Such youth will not have to meet their life-record with shame and dismay.

Mrs. E. G. White

June 29, 1899—God's Purpose Concerning the Youth of Today—Part 2

To keep our souls in the love of God, requires strict self-discipline and watchfulness, mingled with earnest prayer. Every youth should seek to make all he possibly can of himself, that he may grow in grace, and in favor with God and man. His highest aspiration should be to give to others the treasures of science and knowledge that he has gained by following God's will. Thus his works will harmonize with the works of Christ. Those who do this are constantly in communication with the angels of light, who minister to those who shall be heirs of salvation.

God expects the youth to think soberly and intelligently of how those of past generations toiled and sacrificed to leave to future generations a heritage of light. The patriarchs and prophets and the disciples of Christ received impressions from the Great Teacher, and this light and knowledge they bequeathed to those who live in this age. The youth now have the privilege of improving all the treasures that have been acquired by past generations. The Lord expects these hereditary trusts to be gathered up as golden treasures, and imparted to others.

Paul wrote to Timothy: "Young men likewise exhort to be sober-minded, in all things showing thyself a pattern of good works: in doctrine showing uncorruptedness, gravity, sincerity, sound speech, that can not be condemned; that he that is of the contrary part may be ashamed, having no evil thing to say of you." "Let no man despise thy youth; but be thou an example of the believers, in word, in conversation, in charity, in spirit, in faith, in purity."

God calls for large-hearted, large-minded young men, who hear the word of God and obey it; who are not trifling, but deeply in earnest. "Wherefore he saith, Awake, thou that sleepest, and arise from the dead, and Christ shall give thee light. See that ye walk circumspectly, not as fools, but as wise, redeeming the time, because the days are evil. Wherefore be ye not unwise, but understanding what the will of the Lord is." "I have written unto you, young men, because ye are strong, and the word of God abideth in you, and ye have overcome the wicked one."

God calls for young men who are cultivated, sanctified, refined, ennobled, through the truth, which has not merely been assented to, but brought into the inmost recesses of the soul, sanctifying the entire man. Such youth will learn daily in the school of Christ. Jesus died for the world, and souls are perishing for want of the knowledge that he came to bring. Knowing this, will young men who have all the facilities for gaining an education, both in science and religion, stand back, careless, unconcerned, and indifferent, content to spend their blood-bought time and privileges in self-gratification?

The great work for this time has already begun, and is awaiting men who, with hearts subdued by grace, will carry it forward and upward, their ability refined and purified to do God's will, their lips touched with the holy fire which burns its way to the hearts of the people. Will youth merely look on at such a time as this, feeling no burden of responsibility? Shall the work be crippled in all its branches for want of men to teach the truth to others? Where are the laborers who will go forth, consecrating to God their time, their talents, and every jot of the ability they possess?

At this late hour shall the work of saving souls be retarded? Shall but little be done, when the curse of sin has grown to such proportions that already the Spirit of God, insulted, rejected, and abused, is being withdrawn from the earth? Just as fast as God's Spirit is taken away, Satan's cruel work will be done upon land and sea. Judgments by fire and flood will increase in fearfulness; for Satan claims his harvest of souls in the destruction.

Will young men now humble their hearts before God, and give themselves to his service? Will they not accept the holy trust, and become light-bearers to a world ready to be consumed by the wrath of an offended God? The use of intoxicating drink, which dethrones reason, and of tobacco, which clouds the brain and poisons the life-current, is increasing. Are our young men prepared to lift their voices in defense of temperance, and show its bearing upon Christianity? Will they engage in the holy war against appetite and lust? Our artificial civilization encourages evils which are destroying sound principles. The Lord is at the door. Where are the men who will go forth to the work, fully trusting in God, ready to do and to dare? God calls, "Son, go work today in my vineyard." If the young men of today will give themselves to God, he will make them heaven's chosen depositaries of truth, and will empower them to present before the people truth in contrast with error and superstition. May the Lord roll the burden on strong young men, who have his word abiding in them.

July 13, 1899—"Give Us This Day Our Daily Bread"

The prayer that Christ taught his disciples had a deeper meaning than we realize. The petition, "Give us this day our daily bread," means more than a request for temporal food. No one could receive temporal food, were it not for the One who gave his life for the life of the world; but the words, "Give us this day our daily bread," refer not only to temporal food, but to spiritual food, which brings everlasting life to the receiver. When we believe and receive Christ's word, we eat his flesh and drink his blood.

When tempted by Satan to alleviate his hunger by turning stones into bread, Christ met the temptation with the words, "It is written, Man shall not live by bread alone, but by every word that proceedeth out of the mouth of God."

On one occasion Christ told his disciples and the multitude which thronged him that they did not follow him because of the miracles that he did, but because they ate of the loaves, and were filled. "Labor not for the meat which perisheth," he said; be not over-anxious for temporal food, "but for that meat which endureth unto everlasting life, which the Son of man shall give unto you: for him hath God the Father sealed.... Verily, verily, I say unto you, Moses gave you not that bread from heaven; but my Father giveth you the true bread from heaven. For the bread of God is he which cometh down from heaven, and giveth life unto the world. Then said they unto him, Lord, evermore give us this bread." The One then speaking to them had in the wilderness given their fathers angels' food to eat. Oh, had they but known who was addressing them, how changed would have been their attitude toward him!

"I am the bread of life," Christ said; "he that cometh to me shall never hunger; and he that believeth on me shall never thirst.... This is the bread which cometh down from heaven, that a man may eat thereof, and not die. I am the living bread which came down from heaven: if any man eat of this bread, he shall live forever: and the bread that I will give is my flesh, which I will give for the life of the world.... Verily, verily, I say unto you, Except ye eat the flesh of the Son of man, and drink his blood, ye have no life in you.... He that eateth my flesh, and drinketh my blood, dwelleth in me, and I in him."

When man believes in Christ as his personal Saviour, he is eating the daily bread which has been purchased for him at an infinite cost. As by eating temporal food the physical system becomes strong, so by eating the flesh of the Son of God the spiritual nature is strengthened. God's word is life to all who appropriate it. He who partakes of Christ's flesh and blood is a partaker of the divine nature. He is a branch of the Living Vine. As in nature the branch receives nourishment by its connection with the parent stalk, so the believer receives his life from Christ. A vital, life-giving current flows from the Saviour to him.

Man fell through disobedience, severing his life from the life of God. Christ stooped to take humanity, that through him man might gain eternal life. In the guise of humanity, Christ defeated the purpose of the enemy. But Satan has interposed between the sinful human being and the living source of power, so that it is impossible for man, of himself, to appropriate the circulating element of the divine nature. Unless man has a vital connection with God, he will pervert every blessing he receives, and employ every gracious gift as a weapon against the bountiful bestower. It is only as human beings receive Christ, that God can bless them. Thus only can they be elevated and placed on vantage-ground.

Christ stands at the head of humanity as its substitute and surety, to represent God to man, and, through his power, to cause a stream of spiritual life to flow earthward. The Sun of Righteousness, he desires to shine into the chambers of the mind, purifying and elevating the soul, that he may abide therein, and control the affections and emotions, bringing the entire being into conformity to his will.

When the human being receives daily spiritual food from God, a blessed union is formed between earthly and heavenly intelligences. The believer is sustained by the life of Christ. Continually he receives blessings from the hand of God, and continually he imparts. "God, who is rich in mercy, for his great love wherewith he loved us, even when we were dead in sins, hath quickened us together with Christ, ... and hath raised us up together, and made us sit together in heavenly places in Christ Jesus: that in the ages to come he might show the exceeding riches of his grace in his kindness toward us through Christ Jesus."

By receiving Christ we are made partakers of this nature. We live in him, and are enriched by the highest, fullest blessedness. This means a life hid with Christ in God,--a life purified, exalted, devoted to the grandest, noblest purposes. This is indeed having eternal life. God himself is enthroned in the hearts of his people, who are his representatives. This great and unspeakable gift is offered to all. The Jews would have made it a national blessing, confining it to themselves, but the Saviour proclaimed the truth that the bread of life is not confined to time or place, nation or people, but is free to all.

Mrs. E. G. White

July 20, 1899—"Sacrificed For Us"

In the councils of heaven God said, "Let us make man in our image, after our likeness.... So God created man in his own image, in the image of God created he him." The Lord created man's moral faculties and his physical powers. All was a sinless transcript of himself. God endowed man with holy attributes, and placed him in a garden made expressly for him. Sin alone could ruin the beings created by the hand of the Almighty.

The malice that Satan bore to God led him to form the purpose of destroying the Creator's work. But no sooner was Satan, as he supposed, wholly successful in placing Adam on his side, to work in unison with the fallen angels, than God interposed to rescue him. He "so loved the world, that he gave his only begotten Son, that whosoever believeth in him should not perish, but have everlasting life." Thus he showed to the heavenly universe and to the fallen world the value he placed on man. Not one jot nor tittle of his law could be changed to meet man in his fallen condition, and save him from eternal death. But God could give up his Son, to vindicate the honor of his law, and rescue the beings he had created. So Christ took upon himself the work of redemption,--a work which it was impossible for angels to do. The Son of God was made an offering for sin.

The work of redemption is called a mystery, and it is indeed the mystery by which everlasting righteousness is brought to all who believe. In consequence of sin, the race was at enmity with God. At an infinite cost, and by a process mysterious to angels as well as to men, Christ assumed humanity. Hiding his divinity, laying aside his glory, he was born a babe in Bethlehem. In human flesh he lived the law of God, that he might condemn sin in the flesh, and witness to heavenly intelligences that the law was ordained to life, to insure the happiness, peace, and eternal good of all who obey. But the same infinite sacrifice that is life to those who believe, is a testimony of condemnation to the disobedient, speaking death and not life.

This is the mystery of godliness,--that he who was equal with the Father should clothe his divinity with humanity, and laying aside all the glory of his office, descend step after step in the path of humiliation, enduring severe and still more severe abasement. Sinless and undefiled, he stood in the judgment-hall to be tried, to have his case investigated and pronounced upon, by the very nation he had delivered from slavery. The Lord of glory was rejected and condemned, yea, spit upon. With contempt for what they regarded as his pretentious claims, men smote him in the face. These men will one day call upon the rocks and mountains to fall upon them, and hide them from the wrath of the Lamb.

Pilate pronounced Christ innocent, declaring that he found no fault in him. Yet to please the Jews, he commanded him to be beaten, and then delivered him up to suffer the cruel death of crucifixion. The Majesty of heaven was led as a lamb to the slaughter, and amid scoffs and jeers, ridicule and false accusation, he was nailed to the cross. The crowd, in whose hearts humanity seemed to be dead, sought to aggravate his sufferings by their revilings. But as a sheep before his shearers is dumb, he opened not his mouth. He was giving his life for the life of the world, that all who believed in him might gain immortality.

Sweat-drops of agony stand upon the Saviour's brow, while from his murderers are heard the words, "If thou be the Son of God, come down from the cross." He is about to speak. What will he say?--From his pale, quivering lips come the words, "Father, forgive them; for they know not what they do."

What an exhibition of divine love! Thus Christ proclaimed the good news of pardon, even to his murderers. On the cross he revealed the love of the unknown God. There is mercy for all. The most hardened sinner, if he repents, will be forgiven.

"Behold the Lamb of God, which taketh away the sin of the world." Why, then, do those professing to believe in him show a hardness of heart, a lack of pity and love, which crucifies him afresh, and puts him to open shame?

Had the people known God, they would not have thought they were doing him service by persecuting and putting to death the prophets. But they forgot their Creator; and waxing bold in their supposed superiority, they put to death him who alone was able to give them life.

Christ's heart was pierced by a far sharper pain than that caused by the nails driven into his hands and feet. He was bearing the sins of the whole world, enduring our punishment,--the wrath of God against transgression. His trial involved the fierce temptation of thinking that he was forsaken by God. His soul was tortured by the pressure of great darkness, lest he should swerve from his uprightness during the terrible ordeal. Unless there is a possibility of yielding, temptation is no temptation. Temptation is resisted when man is powerfully influenced to do a wrong action; and, knowing that he can do it, resists, by faith, with a firm hold upon divine power. This was the ordeal through which Christ passed. He could not have been tempted in all points as man is tempted, had there been no possibility of his failing. He was a free agent, placed on probation, as was Adam, and as is every man. In his closing hours, while hanging on the cross, he experienced to the fullest extent what man must experience when striving against sin. He realized how bad a man may become by yielding to sin. He realized the terrible consequence of the transgression of God's law; for the iniquity of the whole world was upon him.

Reason, lost in an unfathomable depth of wonder and amazement, would question the truthfulness of such a history; but faith accepts the inspired record. It is true, and it would be blasphemy to attempt a denial. By giving his only begotten Son to die on the cross, God has shown us the estimate he places on the human soul. All that the world admires, all that it calls precious, sinks into insignificance when placed in the balance with one soul; for a priceless ransom has been paid for that soul. All heaven was given in one gift.

Christ is the representative of God to man, and the representative of man to God. He came to this world as man's substitute and surety, and he is fully able to save all who repent and return to their allegiance. Because of his righteousness, he is able to place man on vantage-ground. Christ our Passover has been sacrificed for us. He gave his precious, sinless life to save guilty human beings from eternal ruin, that through faith in him they might stand guiltless before the throne of God. What return have we made for his great sacrifice?

Mrs. E. G. White

July 27, 1899—The Character that God Approves—Part 1

The youth need to be instructed, carefully and prayerfully, that they may build their characters upon the abiding foundation. The reason so many make grievous blunders is that they do not heed the teachings of experience. The counsel of parents and teachers is lost upon them, and they yield to the temptations of the enemy. God loves the youth. He sees in them great possibilities for good, if they will realize their need of Christ, and build upon the sure foundation. He also knows their trials. He knows that they will have to battle against the powers of darkness, that strive to gain control of the human mind; and he has opened the way by which young men and young women may become partakers of the divine nature. The good they may accomplish by uniting themselves to Christ they will never know until, as overcomers, they enter the kingdom of Christ.

Character does not come by chance. It is not determined by one outburst of temper, one step in the wrong direction. It is the repetition of the act that causes it to become habit, and molds the character either for good or for evil. Right characters can be formed only by persevering, untiring effort, by improving every entrusted talent and capability to the glory of God. Instead of doing this, many allow themselves to drift wherever impulse or circumstances may carry them. This is not because they are lacking in good material, but because they do not realize that in their youth God wants them to do their very best. If the youth today would stand as Daniel stood, they must put to the stretch every spiritual nerve and muscle. The Lord does not desire that they shall remain novices. He wishes them to reach the highest point of excellence. He desires them to reach the very highest round of the ladder, that they may step from it into the kingdom of God.

The youth who leave their homes, and are no longer under the watch-care of their parents, are to a large extent left to choose their own associates. They should remember that the eye of their Heavenly Father is upon them, and that he sees their every necessity, their every temptation. There are always to be found in schools some youth who, by their course of action, reveal that their minds are cast in an inferior mold. Through unwise training in childhood, they have developed one-sided characters; and as they have advanced in years, these defects have remained to mar their experience. By precept and example, these souls lead astray those who are weak in moral power.

Time is golden, dear youth. You must not imperil your souls by sowing wild oats. You can not afford to be careless in regard to the companions you choose. Dwell upon that which is noble in the characters of others, and these traits will become to you a moral power in resisting the evil and choosing the good. Set your mark high. Your parents and teachers, who love and fear God, may follow you with their prayers day and night, they may entreat and warn you; but all this will be in vain if you choose reckless associates. If you see no real danger, and think you can do right as well as wrong, just as you choose, you will not discern that the leaven of wickedness is insidiously tainting and corrupting your mind.

Christ was afflicted, insulted, abused; on the right hand and on the left he was assailed by temptation, yet he sinned not, but presented to God a perfect obedience, that was entirely satisfactory. By this he removed forever every semblance of excuse for disobedience. He came to show man how to obey, how to keep all the commandments. He lay hold of divine power, and this is the sinner's only hope. He gave his life that man might be a partaker of the divine nature, having escaped the corruption that is in the world through lust. "Behold the Lamb of God, which taketh away the sin of the world."

God has given the youth talents to improve for his glory; but many apply these gifts to unsanctified, unholy purposes. Many have abilities which, if cultivated, would yield a rich harvest of mental, moral, and physical acquirements. But they do not stop to consider. They do not count the cost of their course of action. They encourage a recklessness and folly that will not listen to counsel or reproof. This is a terrible mistake. Young men would be sober-minded if they realized that God's eye is upon them, that angels of God are watching the development of character, and weighing moral worth.

Mrs. E. G. White

August 3, 1899—The Character that God Approves—Part 2

I appeal to the youth. Consider your ways. Take time to think. Weigh your actions, and see what advantage it will be to you to serve the purposes of Satan, and do his pleasure. In doing this, you dishonor God, and grieve the dear Redeemer, who has paid the ransom for you by dying on the cross of Calvary. No power will be sufficient for you, compassed as you are by temptation, until Christ dwells in the heart by faith. Then you will make him your daily pattern, practising his virtues. You need to cherish that faith which works by love and purifies the soul. This faith will be revealed in your life when you make Christ your personal Saviour. As you cast your helpless soul on Christ, you will receive pardon for past transgression; and the truth, brought into the sanctuary of the soul, will transform the whole character.

No youth can withstand the temptations of Satan if the truth, with its purifying, uplifting power, is not abiding in the heart. Truth has a correcting influence upon the life. It is a divine sentinel, keeping watch in your souls, and rousing to action against Satan's assaults. Under the divine influence of truth, the mind will be strengthened, the intellect invigorated, and there will be a growing up in the knowledge of the only true God, and Jesus Christ, whom he has sent. Do not tarnish the truth by indulging in habits and practises that are inconsistent with its holy character, but hold it as a treasure of highest value.

If you would resist the temptations around you, you need to be sure that you are on the Lord's side, serving in the army of Prince Emmanuel. The Lord desires you to understand the position you occupy as sons and daughters of the Most High, children of the Heavenly King. He desires you to live in close connection with him. Cut away from everything frivolous.

Do not think you must indulge in this pleasure and in that. Determine that you will be on the Lord's side. If you will stand under the blood-stained banner of Prince Emmanuel, faithfully doing his service, you need never yield to temptation; for One stands by your side who is able to keep you from falling. Every youth is granted a probation, in which to form a character for the future, immortal life. Precious, golden moments these will be to you if you improve them according to the light God is permitting to shine upon you from his throne. While every grain of knowledge which parents and teachers are giving you should be carefully cherished, you are to bear in mind that there is a deeper teaching than any that human beings can give. Christ is the greatest Teacher the world has ever known. He must dwell in the heart by living faith. Then his Spirit will be through you a vitalizing power.

Will the youth turn their faces heavenward? Will they open the chambers of the mind to the Sun of Righteousness? Will they throw open the door of the heart, and welcome Jesus in? What beauty of character shone forth in the daily life of Christ! He is to be our pattern. There is a great work to be done in fashioning the character after the divine similitude. The grace of Christ must mold the entire being, and its triumph will not be complete until the heavenly universe shall witness habitual tenderness of feeling, Christlike love, and holy deeds in the deportment of the children of God.

Mrs. E. G. White

August 10, 1899—Marriages, Wise and Unwise

The Eden home of our first parents was prepared for them by God himself. When he had furnished it with everything that man could desire, he said: "Let us make man in our image, after our likeness: and let them have dominion over the fish of the sea, and over the fowl of the air, and over the cattle, and over all the earth, and over every creeping thing that creepeth upon the earth. So God created man in his own image, in the image of God created he him, male and female created he them."

We have here revealed to us the truth concerning the origin of man. These words prove how false is the invention of Satan, which has been reiterated by man, that the human race has been developed, stage by stage, from the lowest order of animals. This is one of the deceptions by which Satan seeks to lower in the eyes of man God's great work of creation.

God said, "Let us make man in our image." He gave to the work of his hands not only a form resembling his own, but a mind capable of comprehending divine things. His understanding, his memory, his imagination,--every faculty of man's mind,--reflected the image of God. In disposition and heart he was qualified to receive heavenly instruction. He possessed a right understanding, a true knowledge of his Creator, of himself, his duty, his obligations in respect to the law of God. His judgment was uncorrupted, unbiased, and disposed to obedience and affection, regulated according to reason and truth. He was capable of enjoying to the utmost capacity the good gifts of God. Everything upon which he looked was transporting to his senses; every sound was as music in his ears. Yet he was not placed beyond the reach of temptation. He stood as the representative of the human race,--a free moral agent.

The Lord was pleased with this last and noblest of all his creatures, and designed that he should be the perfect inhabitant of a perfect world. But it was not his purpose that man should live in solitude. He said: "It is not good that the man should be alone; I will make him a help meet for him." So God created Eve, and gave her to Adam as a companion.

Thus marriage was instituted. God himself united the holy pair; and this first marriage is an example of what all marriages should be. God gave the man one wife. Had he deemed it best for man to have more than one wife, he could as easily have given him two; but he sanctioned no such thing. Wherever polygamy is practised, it is against our Heavenly Father's wise arrangement. Under this practise the race degenerates, and all that makes married life elevated and ennobling is blasted.

Immature marriages are productive of a vast amount of the evils that exist today. Neither physical health nor mental vigor is promoted by a marriage that is entered on too early in life. Upon this subject altogether too little reason is exercised. Many youth act from impulse. This step, which affects them seriously for good or ill, to be a lifelong blessing or curse, is too often taken hastily, under the impulse of sentiment. Many will not listen to reason or instruction in the matter. They are unwilling to consider this subject from a Christian point of view.

The marriages formed by students at school are not right nor proper. Young boys and girls, unfitted in every way to bear life's responsibilities, do not guard their affections; and many who are too young to take care of themselves, too young to know their own minds, who have never been tested as to whether they can make home happy, and support themselves, assume the responsibilities of married life.

Many mothers have gone into the grave because the son or daughter, who heretofore had been respectful and obedient, would not be advised with reference to this important relation. The youth take this step regardless of the counsel of parents and friends, and heedless of the approval of God. His command, "Honor thy father and thy mother," is disregarded, and so his promise can not be fulfilled. His blessing can not rest upon those who pursue this course of reckless wilfulness. The minister of Christ may seek to warn them of their danger; but a bewitching power draws them away from the very ones who would do them good, and they determine to follow their own inclinations.

The world is full of misery and sin today in consequence of ill-assorted marriages. In many cases it takes only a few months for husband and wife to realize that their dispositions can never blend; and the result is that discord prevails in the home, where only the love and harmony of heaven should exist. By contention over trivial matters, a bitter spirit is cultivated. Open disagreements and bickering bring inexpressible misery into the home, and drive asunder those who should be united in the bonds of love. Thus thousands have sacrificed themselves, soul and body, by unwise marriages, and have gone down in the path of perdition.

It is a dangerous thing to form a worldly alliance. Satan well knows that the hour which witnesses the marriage of many young men and women closes the history of their religious experience and usefulness. For a time they may make an effort to live a Christian life, but all their strivings are made against a steady influence in the opposite direction. Once they felt it a privilege to speak of their joy and hope; but soon they become unwilling to make this a subject of conversation, knowing that the one with whom they have linked their destiny takes no interest in these things. Thus Satan insidiously weaves about them a web of skepticism, and faith in the precious truth dies out of the heart.

It is Satan's studied effort to secure the youth in sin; for then he is sure of the man. The enemy of souls is filled with intense hatred against every endeavor to influence the youth in the right direction. He hates everything that will give correct views of God and of Christ. His efforts are especially directed against those who are placed in a position favorable for receiving light from heaven; for he knows that any movement on their part to come into connection with God will give them power to resist his temptations. As an angel of light he comes to the youth with his specious devices, and too often succeeds in winning them, step by step, from the path of duty.

Young persons who are thrown into one another's society may make their association a blessing or a curse. They may edify, strengthen, and bless one another, improving in deportment, in disposition, in knowledge; or, by permitting themselves to become careless and unfaithful, they may exert only a demoralizing influence. The youth who finds joy and happiness in reading the word of God and in the hour of prayer, will be constantly refreshed by drafts from the fountain of life. He will attain a height of moral excellence and a breadth of thought that others can not conceive of. Communion with God encourages good thoughts, noble aspirations, clear perception of truth, and lofty purposes of action. Those who connect with God will be acknowledged by him as his sons and daughters. They will reach higher and still higher, obtaining clearer views of God and of eternity, until the Lord can make them channels of light and wisdom to the world.

Jesus will be the helper of all who will put their trust in him. Those who are connected with Christ have happiness at their command. They follow in the path where their Saviour leads, for his sake crucifying the flesh, with the affections and lusts. These persons build their hope upon Christ, and the storms of life are powerless to sweep them from the sure foundation.

Mrs. E. G. White

August 17, 1899—Self-culture

A character formed after the divine likeness is the only treasure that a man can take from this world to the next. I would urge the youth to regard every moment of time as golden. Do not waste it in indolence, do not spend it in folly, but use it in grasping higher treasures. Cultivate the thoughts and expand the soul by refusing to allow the mind to be filled with unimportant matters. Secure every advantage within your reach for strengthening the intellect. Do not rest satisfied with a low standard. Be not content until, by faithful endeavor, watchfulness, and earnest prayer, you have secured the wisdom that is from above. Thus you may gain an influence over other minds, which will enable you to lead them in the path of uprightness and holiness. This is your privilege.

Cherish every ray of light you can obtain by searching the word of God. Take up your God-given work today, and see how much good you can accomplish in the strength of Christ. Make God your counselor. Discipline and control the mental faculties. Self-control is a power which all may possess. It is gained by placing the will wholly on the side of God, taking the divine will for your will.

Christ remembered our nature in the requirements he made. He took our nature upon himself, and brought to man moral power to combine with human effort. He would conform us to his authority, that we may know his will. He can and will, if we submit to him, fill the chambers of the mind and the recesses of the soul with his Spirit. Then our will is in perfect harmony with the divine will. Our spirit may be so identified with his Spirit that in thought and aim we shall be one with him. Then Satan will no longer control us. Christ is our Leader, and his true followers like to keep in step with him. He speaks, and they obey his voice. His people are made willing in the day of his power.

The Lord's claims extend to our words and actions. Even the thoughts must be brought into captivity to Christ. Then the whole life is a witness for the right. God's true servants subordinate every act to the universal law of obedience. "Lord, what wilt thou have me to do?" is the inquiry of the soul. They keep their eyes directed heavenward, that they may be approved of God, workmen that need not to be ashamed. They maintain a watching, praying attitude. They remember the words, "Ye are not your own; for ye are bought with a price: therefore glorify God in your body, and in your spirit, which are God's." Thus Enoch walked with God, constantly realizing his accountability.

The intellectual, moral, and physical faculties are to be equally cultivated and improved, that we may reach the highest standard in the attainment of knowledge. Education is one-sided unless the whole of the human machinery is used. Those who are fitting themselves for ministers or teachers need to combine physical and mental labor. The intellect must not be allowed to become inactive. The mind must work, else it will become feeble, and will lose the power to think. It is not the length of time spent in acquiring an education that fits a man for a position of influence and responsibility. It is working with earnest effort to cultivate the talents, to wrestle with new problems. God has given us our reasoning powers for a high and holy purpose,--that we may grow in grace and in the knowledge of our Lord and Saviour Jesus Christ. Our faculties were given us to be improved, not to remain unused. He who knows of the goodness and mercy and love of Jesus Christ should make them known to his fellow men; for this knowledge is given to be imparted. The mental faculties are to be aroused to earnest activity. God designs that the youth shall consecrate all their gifts to their Creator. By a right use of their talents they may link themselves by a golden chain to the higher world. They may become partakers of the divine nature.

Daniel of sacred history was but a youth when with his friends he was taken captive to Babylon. But he stands before the heavenly universe, before the worlds unfallen, and before a rebellious world, as a bright example of what the grace of God can do for man. The Lord purposed what Daniel should do; and Daniel gave himself up, with all his energies, to carry out the plan of his Creator. It was not his choice to be exposed to the profligacy, the gluttony, and the spendthrift habits of that heathen nation. But he set his heart, while there, to serve the Lord. He co-operated with God. He stood under Christ's banner as a loyal subject of the heavenly King. As he educated himself to reach the highest standard, he carried with him the fragrance of Christ's righteousness. He was kind and submissive, he made friends with those who had charge over him; yet he would not swerve one inch from pure, true, righteous principles. He was willing to meet all the requirements of those who had rule over him, when he could do this consistently; but all the kings of the earth, all the nobles, all those in power, could not lead him to do one act that would mar his character. He was determined to be true to his God, and God calls him "a man greatly beloved."

To every human being, life should be a serious problem. The character formed in this world determines the destiny for eternity. The element of value in the life in this world will be of value in the world to come. Our future is determined by the way in which we now allow ourselves to be influenced. If we cherish hereditary and cultivated tendencies to wrong, indulging appetite and passion, we can never enter the kingdom of God. But if we strive to repress evil inclinations, if we are willing to be governed by the Spirit of Christ, we are transformed. We take Christ's yoke upon us, and learn his way. Thus we become strengthened, as were Joseph, Samuel, and Daniel. We show that we are God's husbandry, God's building, and that we are using only solid timbers in our character-building.

Mrs. E. G. White

August 24, 1899—"The Will of God Concerning You"

Through the apostle John, God sends the message to his people in these days: "I know thy works, that thou art neither cold not [nor] hot: I would thou wert cold or hot. So then, because thou art lukewarm, and neither cold nor hot, I will spew thee out of my mouth. Because thou sayest, I am rich, and increased with goods, and have need of nothing, and knowest not that thou art wretched, and miserable, and poor, and blind, and naked: I counsel thee to buy of me gold tried in the fire, that thou mayest be rich; and white raiment, that thou mayest be clothed, and that the shame of thy nakedness do not appear, and anoint thine eyes with eye-salve, that thou mayest see."

God's people are in danger of being separated from the Sun of Righteousness. "This is the will of God," the apostle says, "even your sanctification." This sanctification means perfect love, perfect obedience, entire conformity to the will of God. We are to be sanctified to him through obedience to the truth. Our conscience must be purged from dead works to serve the living God. If our lives are conformed to the life of Christ through the sanctification of mind, soul, and body, our example will have a powerful influence on the world. We are not perfect; but it is our privilege to cut away from the entanglement of self and sin, and go on unto perfection. "We all, with open face, beholding as in a glass the glory of the Lord, are changed into the same image from glory to glory, even as by the Spirit of the Lord." Great possibilities, high and holy attainments, are placed within the reach of all who have true faith. Shall we not anoint our eyes with eye-salve, that we may discern the wonderful things God has for us?

Paul's sanctification was a constant conflict with self. "I die daily," he said. Every day his will and his desires conflicted with duty and the will of God. But instead of following inclination, he did the will of God, however unpleasant and crucifying to his nature. If we would press forward to the mark of our high calling in Christ Jesus, we must show that we are emptied of all self, and supplied with the golden oil of grace. God is dealing with us through his providence. From eternity he has chosen us to be his obedient children. He gave his Son to die for us, that we might be sanctified through obedience to the truth, cleansed from all the littleness of self. Now he requires of us a personal work, a personal self-surrender. We are to be controlled by the Holy Spirit. God can be honored only when we who profess to believe in him are conformed to his image. We are to represent to the world the beauty of holiness, and we shall never enter the gates of the city of God until we perfect a Christlike character. If we, with trust in God, strive for sanctification, we shall receive it. Then, as witnesses for Christ, we may make known what the grace of God has wrought in us.

God is leading out a people to stand in perfect unity upon the platform of eternal truth. Christ gave himself for the world, that he might "purify unto himself a peculiar people, zealous of good works." This refining process is designed to purge his people from all unrighteousness and the spirit of discord and contention, that they may build up instead of tearing down, and consecrate their energies to the great work before them. God designs that his people shall come into the unity of the faith. In his prayer for his followers Christ said: "I pray not that thou shouldest take them out of the world, but that thou shouldest keep them from the evil. They are not of the world, even as I am not of the world. Sanctify them through thy truth: thy word is truth. As thou hast sent me into the world, even so have I also sent them into the world. And for their sakes I sanctify myself, that they also might be sanctified through the truth."

This touching and wonderful prayer reaches down the ages even to our day, for his words were: "Neither pray I for these alone, but for them also which shall believe on me through their word; that they all may be one; as thou, Father, art in me, and I in thee, that they also may be one in us: that the world may believe that thou hast sent me. And the glory which thou gavest me, I have given them, that they may be one, even as we are one: I in them, and thou in me, that they may be made perfect in one; and that the world may know that thou hast sent me, and hast loved them as thou hast loved me." With persevering earnestness we are to work out this prayer, pressing onward and upward, and reaching Christ's standard of holiness. We are laborers together with God, and we must work in harmony with one another and with him.

The Lord takes no pleasure in seeing us spiritually weak. "God, who commanded the light to shine out of darkness, hath shined in our hearts, to give the light of the knowledge of the glory of God in the face of Jesus Christ. But we have this treasure in earthen vessels, that the excellency of the power may be of God, and not of us." We who have named the name of Christ must awake from our indifferent, self-satisfied condition. God's people must have a fixed purpose. They will never be holy until they put all the energy of their being into the work of conforming to the will of God.

"This is the will of God concerning you, even your sanctification." Is it your will also? Your sins may be as mountains before you; but if you humble your heart and confess your sins, trusting in the merits of a crucified and risen Saviour, he will forgive, and will cleanse you from all unrighteousness. With intensity of desire, long after God, yea, pant after him, as the hart pants after the water-brooks. As your soul yearns after God, you will find more and still more of the unsearchable riches of his grace. As you contemplate these riches, you will come into possession of them, and reveal the merits of a Saviour's sacrifice, the protection of his righteousness, his inexpressible love, the fulness of his wisdom, and his power to present you before the Father without spot or wrinkle or any such thing. Those who accept of this salvation will bear the testimony: "We have redemption through his blood." "The law of the Spirit of life in Christ Jesus hath made us free from the law of sin and death." "We are more than conquerors through him that loved us."

Mrs. Ellen G. White

August 31, 1899—True Education

True education is to know and to do the will of God. This education is as lasting as eternity. The Bible is to be our text-book; for true religion is the foundation of all true education. Intellectual training can never safely be disconnected from religion; and with the study of books, manual training is to be combined, that the mind may be correctly balanced, and solidity be given to brain, bone, and muscle. This world is our preparatory school. The school and the college are necessary for the development of the mind and the formation of the character. But the cultivation of the intellect alone, apart from a moral and religious education, has a baleful influence. The man who neither loves nor fears God may reach dazzling heights in intellectual attainments, and yet use his acquired knowledge to war against his Maker. If men accept the Lord God of heaven as their teacher, will they not gain the best kind of knowledge, for this world as well as for the next? Mental strength comes alone from a knowledge of the laws that God has established in nature and in the human structure. We must be obedient to these laws, or our lives will be a failure.

Under the controlling influence of Christ, the human intellect can achieve wonderful things. The youth should be encouraged to reach the highest standard of intellectual acquirement. If the fear and knowledge of God are made first, there is no danger that the student will soar too high. The knowledge of God, the understanding of his will in his word, as far as human minds may grasp it, incorporated into the thoughts and woven into the character, will make efficient men and women. The study of the word of God will enable us to do his work intelligently and acceptably. The mind will be enriched, enlarged, and broadened. Those who thus constantly study the Word will go upward and forward toward the highest standard, because they are partakers of the divine nature.

Daniel was closely connected with the source of all wisdom, and this was to him more precious than the gold of Ophir. He kept his religious training on an equality with the advantages that were given him for becoming a wise and learned man. He used his entrusted capital aright. He was aroused by the situation in which he found himself in the king's court. He co-operated with God in the use of every power that had been given him, and we read: "As for these four children, God gave them knowledge and skill in all learning and wisdom: and Daniel had understanding in all visions and dreams." Daniel was connected with God, and the secrets of the Most High were opened to him; for God is with those that fear him. "And the king communed with them; and among them all was found none like Daniel, Hananiah, Mishael, and Azariah; therefore stood they before the king. And in all matters of wisdom and understanding, that the king inquired of them, he found them ten times better than all the magicians and astrologers that were in all his realm." Continual growth in religious wisdom and intelligence did not in any way disqualify these youth for the faithful discharge of the important duties assigned them in the kingdom of Babylon. God gave them his wisdom and knowledge for the perfecting of a thorough education.

Let children and youth be given true education. Teach them to give God their entire devotion; for they are wholly dependent on him in this life, and for the future, immortal life. The knowledge of truth is the nutrition that the soul needs, in order to be prepared to act as wise a part as did Daniel and his associates. Every time the conscience is violated, sin is committed, for which the wrong-doer must suffer the sure result. The penalty of sin is death. With persevering effort and patient forbearance, children must be taught that the fear of the Lord is the beginning of wisdom. When very young, they may be taught the statutes and commands of God. The thoughts and sentiments of his law are to be interwoven with their knowledge of the sciences. A true knowledge of the word of God is the only true scientific education.

We can not afford to separate spiritual from intellectual training. Well may parents dread intellectual greatness for their children unless it is balanced by a knowledge of God and his ways. It is of great importance that the youth take with them from school an intelligent love for God and his truth. This lies at the foundation of all true knowledge. We are in a world subject to disease and death. He who during his lifetime serves God faithfully has the assurance that he will come forth from the grave to a glorious immortality. Of such a one it may indeed be said, "It is well with his soul." In every school in our land the Lord God of Israel should be exalted, revered, and honored. In the place of unsanctified rivalry for earthly honor, the highest ambition of students should be to go forth strengthened, established missionaries for God, educators who can teach what they have learned.

Goodness alone is true greatness. With persevering faith, teachers are to hold to the infinite One, saying, as did Jacob, "I will not let thee go, except thou bless me." Education is not perfect unless the body, the mind, and the heart are equally educated. Students who go from school with this education will draw to Christ not only men and women, but children and youth. These need to learn to discipline self; to take up the duties nearest them; and then, however unpleasant the work may seem, to advance steadily. When they learn what constitutes them true children of God, a work will be done that Satan himself can not undo nor make of none effect. He who opens his heart to receive true education receives power from God to impart light to others.

Mrs. E. G. White

September 14, 1899—Teaching from Nature

Christ employed the things of nature to illustrate divine truth. He bade them speak that men might heed the voice of God. He used as object-lessons the flowers he had created and the things of the animal world. Under his teaching, nature utters her voice to declare the wonderful works of God, and to reprove man's unbelief and his forgetfulness of his constant dependence upon the Creator.

"Take no thought for your life," Christ said, "what ye shall eat, or what ye shall drink; nor yet for your body, what ye shall put on. Is not the life more than meat, and the body than raiment? Behold the fowls of the air: for they sow not, neither do they reap, nor gather into barns; yet your Heavenly Father feedeth them. Are ye not much better than they?" Consider the ravens. They neither sow nor reap; but they act the part God designed them to act, and he takes care of them. And will not that God who has given man all that he has, keep him in health and strength if he complies with the conditions by obedience to the laws of his being?

"Which of you by taking thought can add one cubit unto his stature?" Christ asked. "And why take ye thought for raiment? Consider the lilies of the field, how they grow; they toil not, neither do they spin: and yet I say unto you, That even Solomon in all his glory was not arrayed like one of these." Let the lily, beautifully tinted and gracefully formed by the great Master Artist, surpassing in its loveliness the artificial adorning of Solomon, teach us the lesson of simplicity and faith.

The lesson-book of nature is open to all. When men and women cease trying to counter-work the purposes of divinity, when they place themselves under the discipline of grace, they will see that they have a work to do in becoming conversant with plant and animal life. If less time were devoted to the preparation of elaborate meals for the gratification of appetite, and more in the contemplation of God's works in nature, men and women would be better fitted to serve their Creator.

God has entrusted human beings with talents. He has given men and women intellect, that they may study his dealings with them. All have the privilege of knowing the only true God, whom to know aright is life eternal. Shall we, then, follow our own inclinations, and indulge our inherited and cultivated tendencies to wrong, without reference to God's word? The birds of the air, guided by instinct, are obedient to the laws that govern their life; but the beings formed in God's image fail to honor him by obeying his laws. By disregarding the laws that govern the human organism, they disqualify themselves for serving God. God warns them to beware how they dishonor him by breaking the laws that govern their bodies; but habit is strong, and they will not heed.

The swallow and the crane observe the changes of the season. To find a suitable clime, they migrate from one country to another, as God designed they should. But men and women sacrifice life and health in seeking to gratify appetite. In their desire to accumulate earthly treasure, they forget the Giver of all their blessings. They abuse their health, and use their powers to carry out their unsanctified, ambitious projects. Their days are filled with pain of body and disquietude of mind because they are determined to follow wrong habits and practises. They sacrifice health, peace, happiness, to their ignorance.

The wise man addresses the indolent in these words: "Go to the ant, thou sluggard; consider her ways, and be wise: which having no guide, overseer, or ruler, provideth her meat in the summer, and gathereth her fruit in the harvest."

The habitations that the ants build for themselves show wonderful skill and perseverance. Only one little grain at a time can they handle, but by diligence and perseverance they accomplish wonders. Solomon points to their industry as a reproach to those who waste their hours in sinful idleness, or in practises that corrupt soul and body. The ant prepares for future seasons. Many who are gifted with reasoning powers entirely disregard this lesson, and fail entirely to prepare for the future life.

Stones have frequently been used as memorials of God's dealing with his people. Joshua, knowing that the time of his service as the visible leader of the children of Israel was about to end, gathered the people together, and caused them to renew their covenant with their Maker. Then he "wrote these words in the book of the law of God, and took a great stone, and set it up there under an oak, that was by the sanctuary of the Lord. And Joshua said unto all the people, Behold, this stone shall be a witness unto us; for it hath heard all the words of the Lord, which he spake unto us. It shall be therefore a witness unto you, lest ye deny your God."

None have an excuse for misusing their powers. Such misuse robs God of the service he demands. By creation and by redemption, man is the Lord's. The qualities with which he has been endowed show how high an estimate the Lord places on human beings. He has given every man his work. Every youth, every child, has a work to do in accordance with the Lord's revealed will. No one can waste his opportunities and privileges without robbing God. How can we ignore the responsibilities that rest upon us? The sun, the moon, the stars, the rocks, the flowing stream, the broad, restless ocean,--all teach lessons that we would do well to heed. Shall we not learn from God's great book of nature that he bestows his love, mercy, and grace on us every moment of our lives, that we, in turn, may serve him and our fellow men?

Mrs. E. G. White

September 21, 1899—An All-Powerful Saviour—Part 1

Christ took upon him the form of sinful man, clothing his divinity with humanity. But he was holy, even as God is holy. He was the sin-bearer, needing no atonement. Had he not been without spot or stain of sin, he could not have been the Saviour of mankind. One with God in purity and holiness, he was able to make a propitiation for the sins of the world.

Christ has declared our position. "He that followeth me," he says, "shall not walk in darkness, but shall have the light of life." He is the light of the world. Through him light shines amid moral darkness. He is the bright and morning star. He is the Sun of Righteousness, the brightness of the Father's glory. He is "the true Light, which lighteth every man that cometh into the world."

A physician, a healer, Christ came to restore the moral image of God. This is the covenant, the pledge, that if we come to him, renouncing our own ways and works, we shall receive the imputed righteousness of Christ. As man works out his own salvation, God works with him, to will and to do of his good pleasure. Those in whose hearts he abides are made all light in the Lord. The presence of the Saviour is apparent. Good and pleasant words reveal the Holy Spirit's influence. Sweetness of temper is manifested. There is no angry passion, no obstinacy, no evil-surmising. There is no hatred in the heart.

Faith is genuine only when it works by love and purifies the soul. Self must be crucified, else sin will remain to defile the whole being. The Cain-spirit must not be allowed to enter the heart; for the hatred it brings is next of kin to murder. Man can not enjoy divine blessings unless he shows love to God and to his neighbor. He has lost God's favor by sin, and can not be saved unless Christ takes away his sin. The moral image of God can not be restored in him while he cherishes his own image; for this means defilement. He must work diligently for the right, if he desires to see the restoration of the divine image.

Christ is a complete Saviour. It was a perfect sacrifice that he offered on Calvary's cross, that man might have a full and complete sanctification. Wonderful is the provision that he has made, yet many who claim to believe have only a nominal faith. Their profession does not convert them. They have not surrendered all to Christ. They have not opened the door of the heart to welcome him as a heavenly guest. They love themselves and their own ways, failing to realize that their ways, their words, and their characters are opposed to God. Such can never reach perfection unless they see themselves as they are. If the natural disposition is not changed, if it remains as it was before Christ spoke to them, they are lukewarm, neither cold nor hot. Christ says to them, "Because thou art lukewarm, and neither cold nor hot, I will spew thee out of my mouth." I can not plead in your behalf; for you have no desire for my glory.

Many professed Christians have never seen the Way, the Truth, and the Life. This is why there is so little genuine sanctification. One safeguard after another is removed from the sanctuary of the conscience. The failure to overcome, leaves the soul unguarded. Evil habits, unresisted, strengthen into chains of steel, binding the whole man.

Slipshod religion is a dangerous thing, in the home or in the church; and to educate the mind to look for defects in others unfits the soul for communion with God. This is the leaven of evil. The very act of looking for evil in others develops defects in those who look. These would be alarmed could they see the facts that are registered against them in the books of heaven. The man with the beam in his own eye thinks he has discovered a mote in his brother's eye. But the very discovery of the mote is the sign of the beam. Christ says to us: "Judge not, that ye be not judged. For with what judgment ye judge, ye shall be judged: and with what measure ye mete, it shall be measured to you again. And why beholdest thou the mote that is in thy brother's eye, but considerest not the beam that is in thine own eye? Or how wilt thou say to thy brother, Let me pull out the mote out of thine eye, and, behold, a beam is in thine own eye? Thou hypocrite, first cast out the beam out of thine own eye, and then shalt thou see clearly to cast out the mote out of thy brother's eye."

Mrs. E. G. White

September 28, 1899—An All-Powerful Saviour—Part 2

Shall we choose darkness rather than light because the light shows us our sins and reproves us? Shall we refuse to come to the light, lest our deeds shall be made manifest? When the truth controls the life, there is purity, freedom from sin. The glory, the fulness, the completeness, of the gospel plan is fulfilled in the life. The light of truth irradiates the soul-temple. The understanding takes hold of Christ. The light is not hated because it reproves and warns, but it is accepted and rejoiced in.

Christ declared, "I, if I be lifted up from the earth, will draw all men unto me." If man's will is submitted to the will of God, the man, though a sinner, will be drawn to Christ. He will realize something of the love manifested by God when he gave his Son to die on Calvary's cross, to bring life and immortality within the reach of men. The acceptance of the Saviour brings perfect peace, perfect love, perfect assurance. The beauty and fragrance of the Christ-life, revealed in the character, testifies that God has indeed sent his Son into the world. No other power could bring about so marked a change in a man's words, spirit, and actions.

Without Christ the heart of man is cold. But when one feels his need of the Sun of Righteousness; when he comes to Jesus, saying, Lord, I am sinful, unworthy, helpless; save me, or I perish, he is accepted in the Beloved, and his heart is warmed by the rays of divine love. By this sincere coming to Christ, he opens the door to him who has long been saying: "Behold, I stand at the door, and knock. If any man hear my voice, and open the door, I will come in to him, and will sup with him, and he with me." He is accepted, and he knows what it means to sit together in heavenly places in Christ Jesus. God says, Let there be light; and there is light. The soul possesses an abiding Christ, who is the light of life.

Christ humbles the proud heart by giving it a view of himself, his generosity, his great love. He desires to save us, soul, body, and spirit, by uniting us to himself. He desires us to behold his glory, as the glory of the only begotten of the Father. Then we can say, "Of his fulness have all we received, and grace for grace." He who shows that he appreciates the grace he receives, by imparting it to others, receives increased grace, in proportion to the grace he imparts. And he is so full of joy that he exclaims, "Thy gentleness hath made me great!"

The one great lesson all must learn--the poor sinner, dead in trespasses and sins, as well as the professed Christian, who has known the truth, but has clung to his unsanctified traits of character--is that God will save to the uttermost all who come to him. "Him that cometh to me," he says, I will in no wise cast out." The poor, the suffering, the sinful, may find in Christ all they need. As soon as they receive Jesus as a personal Saviour, the cries of distress and woe are changed to songs of praise and thanksgiving.

All may share Christ's grace if they will confess to the great sin-bearer, whose work it is to take away the sins of all who believe. You have the assurance that as you renounce your own righteousness, you will be clothed with his righteousness. Christ invites you, saying, "Let him take hold of my strength, that he may make peace with me; and he shall make peace with me." The door is opened to all. No one is turned away. God proffers to all a priceless treasure,--his peace,--a peace that the world can neither give nor take away. The everlasting gates of pearl will not open to those who come with the symbols of power, but they will open wide to the trembling touch of the meek and lowly. To be great in the kingdom of God is to be as a little child in simplicity and love. The Lord is able and willing to work in our behalf, and he will work if we come to him as children. He will lead us by the hand, upholding us that our feet shall not slip.

October 5, 1899—"We Have Seen His Star"—Part 1

"Now when Jesus was born in Bethlehem of Judea, in the days of Herod the king, behold, there came wise men from the east to Jerusalem, saying, Where is he that is born King of the Jews? for we have seen his star in the east, and are come to worship him."

These men were men of noble birth, learned in art and science. They were astrologers, and in the heavens they had seen the glory of God. But they had not a full knowledge of the Author of the wonders they studied. The magi of the East varied in honor and integrity, some sinking to a low level, and using their knowledge of science to impose on the credulity of others for their own selfish ends; while others refused thus to dishonor themselves and deceive the people. The latter class were noble men, who followed the indications of God's providence as revealed in the heavens and the earth.

It was not God's purpose that the light he had given to patriarchs and prophets should be confined to the Jewish nation. He designed that it should be carried to all parts of the earth. But the Israelites misinterpreted the command given them in regard to intermarrying with other nations. This command was given to guard God's people from idolatry. But they made it a wall of separation, a barrier to any communication with other nations. They regarded themselves as the only people whom God would acknowledge, and looked upon all others as despised by him. Thus they became narrow in their ideas; and while separating themselves from the heathen, they also separated themselves from God. By walking contrary to his requirements, they were building a wall of separation between themselves and God.

The children of Israel did not walk in the light given them by Him who had been their invisible leader through forty years of wilderness-wandering. Had they cherished the light and practised the gracious lessons given them by Christ, forming characters in accordance with the principles of truth, they would have retained God's favor. Great wisdom and knowledge would have been given them. God would have made them channels through which he could communicate truth, and by which he would have been made a praise in all the earth. Thus his wisdom and matchless love would have been sounded throughout the world.

God's people failed to carry out his purpose, but there were among them those who were faithful and loyal. In the providence of God, the Jews were scattered by captivity through all countries; and during these years of bondage, faith in God was kept alive by faithful witnesses. There were those who would not disregard the Sabbath of the Lord, who would not observe heathen festivals. These were persecuted, and many lost their lives, as God's people always have since the death of Abel. From the time of his expulsion from heaven, Satan has been working on these lines.

In various ways the light of truth was communicated to those in darkness. In Egypt, Joseph's example of unbending integrity witnessed for God; and the treatment he received shows that there were those in the kingdom who respected nobility of character, even when found in captives who were regarded as slaves. Loving and fearing God did not detract from the usefulness of God's servants; for God honored them and worked for them, so that they were enabled to be standard-bearers, carrying the banner of truth and knowledge through the dark places of the earth.

The history of Daniel and his three companions in Babylon is another instance of the way in which the Lord uses faithful men. They did not yield up their faith; but through all the temptations to which they were exposed, they preserved the knowledge of God. They made his honor prominent. They would not break his law to save themselves from being thought singular. When brought before kings and rulers to explain why they would not obey the laws of the land, they repeated the precepts and statutes of God, which they dared not transgress. And so wonderfully did God work in the kingdom of Babylon, that Nebuchadnezzar the king sent a proclamation throughout his dominion exalting the God of the Hebrews as one to be honored and revered above all heathen gods.

Thus through faithful witnesses the truth of God went to all parts of the earth. In every generation God manifested his power through those who held aloft the banner of truth, calling the attention of idol worshipers to the true and living God, the Creator of the world.

Because of a perverted knowledge of the system of sacrifices and offerings that God had established in Israel, the heathen offered sacrifices to idols. Many of these idolaters were as sincere in the performance of their religious service as were the

Israelites in theirs; and as the worshipers of the true God were brought face to face with these practises, light shone forth, and many noble and learned men listened eagerly to the truth in regard to the Messiah, and the true origin of sacrifices and offerings. Many believed, as they were told that these offerings symbolized the one great Sacrifice that was to be offered for the sins of the world.

Thus the knowledge of truth was imparted by the true Israelites to those living in idolatry. While they hung their harps upon the willows, bemoaning their captivity, light was shining in darkness, dispelling sophistry and superstition, and revealing the Saviour.

Mrs. E. G. White

October 12, 1899—"We Have Seen His Star"—Part 2

From various sources the magi of the East had learned of the expectation that One was to be born who should be King of the Jews. God was flashing his light upon those who were searching for truth; and while the priests and rulers of the Jewish nation, knowing not the time or manner of the Messiah's coming, though prophecy had plainly revealed this, were living in expectation of welcoming a king who would bring to their nation riches, honor, and power, there were those far less highly privileged, who were diligently searching for a knowledge of the great events that were to take place. Many were praying for light in regard to the Deliverer, who, they had been told, was to come as a warrior, subduing the world to himself by his power. Their faith in their religious customs did not satisfy the wants of the soul. They were hungering and thirsting for a knowledge of the God of whom they knew so little. They remembered the words spoken by Balaam when he was urged to curse Israel.

Balaam had a knowledge of the true God, and he claimed to be converted. But his education and experience in magic held a bewitching power over him; and when solicited by Balak to curse Israel, he was urged by his infatuation to do so. He longed to obtain riches and renown by cursing Israel, but the Lord told him he would not allow him to practise his incantations and sorceries against his people. And when Balaam rose up to do as the king of Moab had requested him to, his lips uttered words very different from the words the king hoped to hear spoken. "And Balak said unto Balaam, What hast thou done unto me? I took thee to curse mine enemies, and, behold, thou hast blessed them altogether."

In answer to the king's remonstrance, Balaam said: "Behold, I have received commandment to bless: and he hath blessed; and I can not reverse it. He hath not beheld iniquity in Jacob, neither hath he seen perverseness in Israel, the Lord his God is with him, and the shout of a king is among them. God brought them out of Egypt; he hath as it were the strength of a unicorn. Surely there is no enchantment against Jacob, neither is there any divination against Israel: according to this time it shall be said of Jacob and of Israel, What hath God wrought!"

Again the controlling power of God came upon Balaam, and once more he uttered words entirely contrary to his inclinations. As he saw Israel abiding in their tents according to their tribes, the veil of the future was removed, and he saw the prosperity that would attend them. He knew that One whom Satan and all his host could not overcome was standing in Israel's defense, and he exclaimed: "How goodly are thy tents, O Jacob, and thy tabernacles, O Israel! As the valleys they are spread forth, as gardens by the river's side, as the trees of lign aloes which the Lord hath planted, and as cedar-trees beside the waters.... I shall see him, but not now; I shall behold him, but not nigh: there shall come a Star out of Jacob, and a Scepter shall rise out of Israel, and shall smite the corners of Moab, and destroy all the children of Sheth."

These prophecies in regard to Christ's advent had been impressed upon minds from century to century. Devout men were waiting in anxious expectancy for a deliverer to appear. They were seeking earnestly for truth, praying for a clearer knowledge of the God whom as yet they but dimly comprehended. Truth was being revealed to them, it was sweeping away the dark clouds of idolatry; for God ever reveals himself to the humble seeker for light.

Mrs. E. G. White

October 19, 1899—"We Have Seen His Star"—Part 3

While the magi were studying the heavens, a luminous star, entirely new to them, made its appearance. As they stood gazing at it, they were impressed that it was the herald of some great event. They decided to investigate the matter, hoping that they would be rewarded by a knowledge of the promised Messiah. The Lord encouraged them to go forward; and as the pillar of cloud moved before the children of Israel through the wilderness, so the star guided the wise men as they journeyed toward Jerusalem. When they drew near Jerusalem, it no longer went before them, but was enshrouded in darkness. Entering Jerusalem, the magi made the eager inquiry, "Where is he that is born King of the Jews? for we have seen his star in the east, and are come to worship him." They knew that the Messiah had been born. The star that had guided them thus far was an outward evidence, and the Spirit of God was kindling ardent hopes in their hearts. They expected to see and worship the King.

The people of Jerusalem looked upon the magi with astonishment; for no one had seen anything peculiar in the heavens, no one had heard anything about the birth of the King. The very people over whom this King was to rule had not been favored with any special token; for they had no knowledge that anything unusual had taken place. The minds of the wise men were filled with astonishment. Could it be that in the city of Jerusalem, the people knew nothing of the birth of him who was to rule over Israel? Had they themselves read the prophecy incorrectly? The magi had thought to find all Jerusalem filled with anxious expectancy. As they related their experience, they were surprised at the jealousy shown by the scribes and Pharisees. Surely the Lord, whom they had been seeking, had suddenly come to his temple!

The tidings of the Messiah's birth reached the ears of Herod. He was startled. His jealousy was roused. Had One been born who had a better right than he to rule? Was he to be superseded? Why had he not heard of this wonderful event? Looking into the past, he reviewed the terrible conflicts through which he passed in order to gain the throne, and the murders he committed to secure his position. He has disposed of every rival in his way, and he determines that he will not rest until this new king, if there be one, is searched out and slain.

Herod was troubled by the tidings brought by the wise men, "and all Jerusalem with him." It was in harmony with Herod's jealous nature to be troubled over news of this character; but why should the leading men among the Jews be so perplexed and terrified? Had they studied and explained the Scriptures in vain? Why were they not intelligent in regard to this great event foretold by prophecy, which meant so much to them? They had traced down the chronology, and knew that this was the time when the Messiah should appear. Why, then, were they so alarmed? They had read the words: "Prepare ye the way of the Lord, make straight in the desert a highway for our God.... O Zion, that bringest good tidings, get thee up into the high mountain; O Jerusalem, that bringest good tidings, lift up thy voice with strength; lift it up, be not afraid; say unto the cities of Judah, Behold your God! Behold, the Lord God will come with strong hand, and his arm shall rule for him: behold, his reward is with him, and his work before him. He shall feed his flock like a shepherd: he shall gather the lambs with his arm, and carry them in his bosom." Why, then, were the priests and rulers, those in high position, so alarmed at the news of his coming?

The Jewish rulers were in ignorance of the coming of the Just One, because they had not been making ready for him. They had been separating from God by wicked works. The positions in the service of the priesthood were filled by men wholly unfitted for the work,--men who had not hesitated to stoop to falsehood and even murder to gain the coveted honor. They were not ready for Christ's coming. They had not heard the angel's message, "Behold, I bring you good tidings of great joy." They had not heard the song of the heavenly host, because they were estranged from God. Spiritual things are spiritually discerned. The Lord could not enlighten them; for so great was the darkness surrounding them that they would not have made a right use of the light.

The priests and rulers began to ask themselves what these things meant. The shepherds had borne witness regarding the visit of the angels; now men from the far East bore the tidings, "We have seen his star in the east, and are come to worship him." Men of another nation and faith were the first to herald the advent of the Messiah. If the report of the wise men were true, they, the rulers, stood in an unenviable position before their own people; for they had been passed by, while strangers were enlightened.

Herod was surprised that the Jewish rabbis--men looking upon themselves as favored above all other people--should apparently be in darkness, while those they termed heathen had received a sign from heaven that the King had been born. He was filled with perplexity. Why had the wise men made the long journey to Jerusalem with the inquiry, "Where is he that is born King of the Jews?" Had a king been born? Making an effort to appear gratified by the news, though his heart burned with jealousy at the mention of a rival, Herod gathered the chief priests and scribes together, and demanded of them where Christ should be born. "In Bethlehem of Judea," they answered; "for thus it is written by the prophet: And thou Bethlehem, in the land of Juda, art not the least among the princes of Juda; for out of thee shall come a Governor that shall rule my people Israel."

Calling the wise men to him, Herod "inquired of them diligently what time the star appeared. And he sent them to Bethlehem, and said, Go and search diligently for the young child; and when ye have found him, bring me word again, that I may come and worship him also. When they had heard the king, they departed, and, lo, the star, which they saw in the east, went before them, till it came and stood over where the young child was. When they saw the star, they rejoiced with exceeding great joy. And when they were come into the house, they saw the young child with Mary his mother, and fell down, and worshiped him: and when they had opened their treasures, they presented unto him gifts; gold, and frankincense, and myrrh. And being warned of God in a dream that they should not return to Herod, they departed into their own country another way."

Mrs. E. G. White

October 26, 1899—Against Principalities and Powers

God has need of workers who, as they labor with him, will comprehend the sacredness of the work, and the conflicts they must meet in order to carry it forward successfully,--workers who will not grow despondent as they see the arduous task before them. The Lord does not try to conceal from his people the stern conflicts they will meet in these last days. Instead, he shows the plan of battle; he points out the hazardous work to be done; he lifts his voice in warning, bidding men count the cost of their discipleship: but he encourages all to take up the weapons of their warfare; for the heavenly host will stand with them in the defense of truth and righteousness.

On every side God's people will meet the specious temptations of Satan. The enemy knows how desirable a place heaven is to every human being. He has a keen sense of what he has lost; and when he was cast out of heaven, he determined to use all the knowledge and power he possessed in warring against God, and taking from him the beings he had created. He knows that the work which Christ has purposed will be accomplished; he knows that the Scriptures will be fulfilled, and that a host that no man can number will encircle the throne where he so often stood as chorister, to sing songs of praise and adoration to God and the Lamb. And in accordance with his purpose, he is working to make of no effect the labors of Christ's followers.

Christ presents before his people their source of power and efficiency to meet the wiles of Satan, and his words of admonition are full of encouragement. "Be strong in the Lord," he says, "and in the power of his might. Put on the whole armor of God, that ye may be able to stand against the wiles of the devil. For we wrestle not against flesh and blood, but against principalities, against powers, against the rulers of the darkness of this world, against spiritual wickedness in high places. Wherefore take unto you the whole armor of God, that ye may be able to withstand in the evil day, and having done all, to stand. Stand therefore, having your loins girt about with truth, and having on the breastplate of righteousness; and your feet shod with the preparation of the gospel of peace; above all, taking the shield of faith, wherewith ye shall be able to quench all the fiery darts of the wicked. And take the helmet of salvation, and the sword of the Spirit, which is the word of God: praying always with all prayer and supplication in the Spirit, and watching thereunto with all perseverance and supplication for all saints."

Those who unshrinkingly stand in the forefront of the battle will feel the special attacks of the enemy; and realizing their need of help from God, they will flee to the stronghold for refuge. Perseverance, faith, and a perfect trust in God will insure success. In every stern conflict, feeble man will have strength to do the deeds of Omnipotence.

The mighty general of armies leads the hosts of heaven in defense of his people as verily as he led the armies of Israel at the taking of Jericho. Not one soul in all the hosts of Israel could boast of his strength to throw down the walls of that city. It was the Captain of the Lord's host who planned that battle, and his name alone could receive the glory. So the servants of Christ labor in the strength of their Master; and every victory they gain leads them, not to exalt self, but to lean more securely on the arm of God. Deep and fervent gratitude is awakened in their hearts, and they rejoice in tribulation. These willing servants are gaining experiences and forming characters that will do honor to the cause of God.

Writing to the church in Rome, Paul says: "We have peace with God through our Lord Jesus Christ: by whom also we have access by faith into this grace wherein we stand, and rejoice in hope of the glory of God. And not only so, but we glory in tribulations also, knowing that tribulation worketh patience, and patience, experience; and experience, hope: and hope maketh not ashamed; because the love of God is shed abroad in our hearts by the Holy Ghost which is given unto us." In Christ are hid all the treasures of wisdom and knowledge, and we are without excuse if we fail to avail ourselves of the provision made. Christ sacrificed everything in order to make it possible for man to gain heaven. Now it is for man to show what he will sacrifice for Christ's sake. Those who have any just sense of the magnitude of the plan of salvation, and of its cost, will never murmur that their sowing must be in tears, and that conflict and self-denial must be the Christian's portion. Why should we be unwilling to endure, to suffer, and to sacrifice, in order to secure an imperishable treasure,--a life that runs parallel with the life of God,--a crown of immortal glory, that fadeth not away?

When the follower of Christ meets with trial and perplexity, he is not to become discouraged. He is not to cast away his confidence if he does not realize all his expectations. When buffeted by the enemy, he should remember the Saviour's life of trial and discouragement. Heavenly beings ministered to Christ in his need, yet this did not make the Saviour's life one of freedom from conflict and temptation. He was in all points tempted like as we are, yet without sin. If his people will follow this example, they will be imbued with his Spirit, and heavenly angels will minister to them.

The temptations to which Christ was subjected were a terrible reality. As a free agent, he was placed on probation, with liberty to yield to Satan's temptations and work at cross-purposes with God. If this were not so, if it had not been possible for him to fall, he could not have been tempted in all points as the human family is tempted. The temptations of Christ, and his sufferings under them, were proportionate to his exalted, sinless character. But in every time of distress, Christ turned to his Father. He "resisted unto blood" in that hour when the fear of moral failure was as the fear of death. As he bowed in Gethsemane, in his soul agony, drops of blood fell from his pores, and moistened the sods of the earth. He prayed with strong crying and tears, and he was heard in that he feared. God strengthened him, as he will strengthen all who will humble themselves, and throw themselves, soul, body, and spirit, into the hands of a covenant-keeping God.

Upon the cross Christ knew, as no other can know, the awful power of Satan's temptations; and his heart was poured out in pity and forgiveness for the dying thief, who had been ensnared by the enemy.

"We wrestle not against flesh and blood, but against principalities, against powers, against the rulers of the darkness of this world, against spiritual wickedness in high places." But Christ has promised us "all power" for the conflict. "Lo, I am with you alway," he says, "even unto the end of the world." And the promise is "unto you, and to your children, and to all that are afar off, even as many as the Lord our God shall call." As we see the stubborn unbelief of men, and understand the risks that must be taken in the work, we must learn to listen to the voice of Jesus, "Be of good cheer; I have overcome the world." Yes, Christ is conqueror, and we can advance with him to victory. Because he lives, we shall live also.

Mrs. E. G. White

November 2, 1899—The Joy that is Set Before Us—Part 1

God asks the youth to serve him with consecrated minds. The call that he gave to the humble fishermen on the shores of Galilee he gives to each soul. "Follow me," he says, "and I will make you fishers of men."

The men of the world are ambitious for fame. They desire houses and lands and plenty of money, that they may be great according to the measure of the world. It is the height of their ambition to reach a place where they can look down with a sense of superiority upon those who are poor. These souls are building on the sand, and their house will fall suddenly. Superiority of position is not true greatness. That which does not increase the value of the soul is of no real value in itself.

The qualities which shine the brightest in the world have no place in the kingdom of God. Birth, position, wealth, and high-sounding titles find no special favor with him. Today, as when he walked among men, Christ passes these by, and accepts the men and women in the humble walks of life, who have his glory in view. The words he uttered on the mount are truth for all time. "Whosoever therefore shall break one of these least commandments, and shall teach men so, he shall be called the least in the kingdom of heaven: but whosoever shall do and teach them, the same shall be called great in the kingdom of heaven." Whatever his learning, his wealth and position, heaven estimates the transgressor as the least of all God's creatures; and the humble and obedient are regarded as of more value than the most exalted and wealthy and honored of earth.

Christ invites the youth to wear his yoke and lift his burdens. "Come unto me," he says "take my yoke upon you, and learn of me; for I am meek and lowly in heart: and ye shall find rest unto your souls. For my yoke is easy, and my burden is light." The reason we do so little in winning souls to Christ is that we have so little of Christ in us. The usefulness of the Christians will depend upon the measure of the grace he has received; and the measure of grace he receives will be proportionate to the use he makes of the blessings that God gives him.

You will have some estimate of your own worth when you become a laborer together with Christ, to fill the world with his righteousness. The Lord expects you to proclaim the message, "The kingdom of heaven is at hand." You are to work to bless those who have no sense of their need of a new heart, a new life and purpose. Some one must tell sinners of their great need; and those whom God has accepted as his sons and daughters must work as Christ worked. "If any man will come after me," the Saviour said, "let him deny himself, and take up his cross, and follow me." Those who heed this call will study the meekness and lowliness of Christ, and will join with him in his efforts to make the world better.

The commission Christ gave to the disciples he gives to all connected with him. We are to make any and every sacrifice for the joy of seeing souls saved. Whatever work is done in the name of Jesus to bless and elevate and restore human beings to the image of God, is as acceptable to the Lord as was the work of Moses or Joseph or Daniel. You who are the elect and chosen ones are to receive the divine commission to yoke up with Christ. You must never grow weary in well-doing. The highest honor that can be conferred upon human beings, be they young or old, rich or poor, is to be permitted to lift up the oppressed, comfort the feeble-minded, and support the weak. The world is full of suffering; go, heal the sick, pray for the hopeless, preach the gospel to the poor.

Mrs. E. G. White

November 9, 1899—The Joy That is Set Before Us—Part 2

The message of mercy that Christ brought from the Father to man was meant for the ears of the world: "I, if I be lifted up from the earth will draw all men unto me." Everlasting life has been purchased for man at an infinite cost. "God so loved the world, that he gave his only begotten Son, that whosoever believeth in him should not perish, but have everlasting life." Through this matchless gift, Christ encircles the world with an atmosphere of grace. All who choose to inhale this life-giving air will have eternal life.

That Christ should take human nature, and by a life of humiliation elevate man in the scale of moral worth with God; that he should carry his adopted nature to the throne of God, and there present his children to the Father, to have conferred upon them an honor exceeding that bestowed upon the angels,--this is love that melts the sinner's heart. It is too much for the human mind to grasp, that God, having gathered together all the riches of the universe, and laid open all the resources of his power, should place them in the hand of his Son, saying, All these I give to you for man. These are my gifts to him. Confer them upon him, that he may know that there is no love like mine, and that his eternal happiness consists in giving me his love in return. As the sinner contemplates this love, it broadens and deepens into infinitude, passing beyond his comprehension.

Co-laborers with God are to fill the space they occupy in the world with the love of Jesus. The world needs spiritual workers, who will plant the seeds of truth in every heart. Christ calls upon us to be "instant in prayer." By this he means that the heart is constantly to go out after God, while we watch for opportunities to do good to the souls that are ready to die.

"Seeing ye have purified your souls in obeying the truth through the Spirit unto unfeigned love of the brethren, see that ye love one another with a pure heart fervently." God has chosen you to salvation through sanctification of the spirit and belief of the truth. Therefore stand fast. Your hardest conflict will be in keeping the straight and narrow path that leads to eternal life. In order to do this, you must die daily. If you serve God faithfully, you will meet with prejudice and opposition; but do not become provoked when you suffer wrongfully. Do not retaliate. Hold fast your integrity in Jesus Christ. Set your face as a flint heavenward. Let others speak their own words, and pursue their own course of action; it is for you to press on in the meekness and lowliness of Christ. Do your work with steadfast purpose, with purity of heart, with all your might and strength, leaning on the arm of God. The true and exalted nature of your work you may never know. The value of your being you can measure only by the life given to save you.

The apostle gives us his experience and the experience of his fellow laborers in their work. "We are troubled on every side," he says; "yet not distressed; we are perplexed, but not in despair; persecuted, but not forsaken; cast down, but not destroyed; always bearing about in the body the dying of the Lord Jesus, that the life also of Jesus might be made manifest in our body." If we work the works of Christ, the mind will gather strength and firmness to resist the adversary of souls. The apostle says, "Think it not strange concerning the fiery trial which is to try you, as though some strange thing happened unto you." "Ye are in heaviness through manifold temptations: that the trial of your faith, being much more precious than of gold that perisheth, though it be tried with fire, might be found unto praise and honor and glory at the appearing of Jesus Christ." "Wherefore let them that suffer according to the will of God commit the keeping of their souls to him in well-doing, as unto a faithful Creator." "Humble yourselves therefore under the mighty hand of God, that he may exalt you in due time: casting all your care upon him; for he careth for you. Be sober, be vigilant; because your adversary the devil, as a roaring lion, walketh about, seeking whom he may devour: whom resist steadfast in the faith, knowing that the same afflictions are accomplished in your brethren that are in the world."

For every soul who is growing up into Christ there will be times of earnest and long-continued struggle; for the powers of darkness are determined to oppose the way of advance. But when we look to the cross of Christ for grace, we can not fail. The promise of the Redeemer is, "I will never leave thee nor forsake thee." "I am with you alway, even unto the end of the world."

Mrs. E. G. White

November 23, 1899—The Parable of the Talents—Part 1

It is not alone to the minister that God entrusts his talents. His goods are lent to every man as verily, as they are lent to the most exalted angel in the courts of heaven. To every man God has appointed his work, and the talents are given in proportion to the capabilities of the receiver. Every soul, in taking his position as a member of Christ's body, pledges himself to act faithfully his part as a steward of God; to work with the same prudence and wisdom in behalf of his Master that he would use if he were himself to be enriched by all that is gained.

By the parable of the talents, Christ teaches us the relation that man sustains to God. "The kingdom of heaven," he says, "is as a man traveling into a far country, who called his own servants, and delivered unto them his goods. And unto one he gave five talents, to another two, and to another one; and to every man according to his several ability; and straightway took his journey. Then he that had received the five talents went and traded with the same, and made them other five talents. And likewise he that had received two, he also gained other two. But he that had received one went and digged in the earth, and hid his lord's money.

"After a long time the lord of those servants cometh, and reckoneth with them." He sees the servant to whom he has entrusted five talents, and he asks him to give an account of his stewardship. The servant has been faithful; he has added five talents to the talents entrusted to him. He answers: "Lord, thou deliveredst unto me five talents: behold, I have gained beside them five talents more. His lord said unto him, Well done, thou good and faithful servant: thou hast been faithful over a few things, I will make thee ruler over many things: enter thou into the joy of thy lord."

The servant entrusted with two talents has also added to the capital lent him. "He also that had received two talents came and said, Lord, thou deliveredst unto me two talents: behold, I have gained two other talents beside them. His lord said unto him, Well done, good and faithful servant; thou hast been faithful over a few things, I will make thee ruler over many things: enter thou into the joy of thy lord."

Now the man to whom has been given the one talent is called to give an account. But he can only look with confusion upon the face of his lord; for he has followed the suggestions of the enemy. If he had been convinced that he could not use that one talent, he should have asked wisdom of God; but instead of this, he buried it in the earth. Now he comes to his lord with a falsehood on his lips. "I knew thee that thou art a hard man," he says, "reaping where thou hast not sown, and gathering where thou hast not strewed; and I was afraid, and went and hid thy talent in the earth: lo, there thou hast that is thine."

No man whose heart is converted can say such a thing as this; for it is impossible for the Lord to gather where he has not strewed. Heaven and earth are his property, and we can not bring to him anything that is not already his own.

"His lord answered and said unto him, Thou wicked and slothful servant, thou knewest that I reap where I sowed not, and gather where I have not strewed: thou oughtest therefore to have put my money to the exchangers, and then at my coming I should have received mine own with usury. Take therefore the talent from him, and give it unto him which hath ten talents. For unto every one that hath [improved his talents] shall be given, and he shall have abundance: but from him that hath not shall be taken away even that which he hath. And cast ye the unprofitable servant into outer darkness: there shall be weeping and gnashing of teeth."

The parable presents a truth which all should understand. God has not distributed his talents capriciously. To every man are given abilities which will fit him for the work he is called to do. To one are committed five talents; to another, two; to another, one: and each is accountable to God for his gifts. A time is coming when Christ will require his own with usury. He will say to each of his stewards, "Give an account of thy stewardship." Those who have hid their Lord's money in the earth, in worldly investments, instead of putting it out to the exchangers, to increase by use; and those who have squandered his money by expending it for needless things, instead of investing it in his cause, will receive the condemnation of the Master. Not only will they lose the talent lent them by God, but they will lose eternal life. The command will be given: "Take therefore the talent from him, ... and cast ye the unprofitable servant into outer darkness; there shall be weeping and gnashing of teeth." The faithful servant, who invests his talent in the cause of God, who uses his money to the glory of God, will receive the commendation, "Well done, thou good and faithful servant; ... enter thou into the joy of thy Lord." What will be this joy of the Lord?--It will be the joy of seeing souls saved in the kingdom of God. Those who are faithful stewards are partners with Christ, who, "for the joy that was set before him endured the cross, despising the shame, and is set down at the right hand of the throne of God."

Mrs. E. G. White

November 30, 1899—The Parable of the Talents—Part 2

God calls for missionaries. Those who know and love the truth should let their light shine to those who are in darkness. And in doing their appointed work, God will be to them wisdom and power. He will glorify himself by working with those who wholly follow him.

"If any man serve me," he says, "him will my Father honor." To every man God has given capabilities for work. To some he entrusts five talents, to others two, and to others only one; but he gives to every man according to his ability to use them. Are you who have named the name of Christ identifying yourself with him, and following his instruction? What are you doing with your Lord's entrusted capital? Your God-given advantages are to be carefully cherished, that you may do the best work in the Master's service.

Will you study the fourth chapter of Zechariah, and learn what the two olive branches mean? In this chapter the features of the work in which we are engaged are clearly set forth.

"And the angel that talked with me came again, and waked me, as a man that is wakened out of his sleep, and said unto me, What seest thou? And I said, I have looked, and behold a candlestick all of gold, with a bowl upon the top of it, and his seven lamps thereon, and seven pipes to the seven lamps, which are upon the top thereof: and two olive-trees by it, one upon the right side of the bowl, and the other upon the left side thereof. So I answered and spake to the angel that talked with me, saying, What are these, my lord? Then the angel that talked with me answered and said unto me, Knowest thou not what these be? And I said, No, my Lord. Then he answered and spake unto me, saying, This is the word of the Lord unto Zerubbabel, saying, Not by might, nor by power, but by my Spirit, saith the Lord of hosts."

We have no power nor efficiency in ourselves. The work must be done in the power of the Spirit of God. Zerubbabel could not understand this mystery; and as a little child, he confessed his ignorance, and placed himself as a learner. Then the word of the Lord came to him, "Not by might, nor by power, but by my Spirit, saith the Lord of Hosts." Man's weakness is no obstacle to the work God would have done; for he can save by many or by few.

"Then answered I, and said unto him, What are these two olive-trees upon the right side of the candlestick and upon the left side thereof? And I answered again, and said unto him, What be these two olive branches which through the two golden pipes empty the golden oil out of themselves? And he answered me and said, Knowest thou not what these be? And I said, No, my lord. Then said he, These are the two anointed ones, that stand by the Lord of the whole earth."

Great responsibilities rest upon those to whom the Lord has entrusted his goods. These gifts are to be cherished carefully. Our talents are not to be used to please and glorify self, but to honor him from whom the talents come. When our talents are appreciated and used, they will increase. The fulness of Christ awaits every receiver. Christ is waiting for us to ask him for the gift of the Holy Spirit. I may say, You will receive; but my word is not enough. You must take the words of Christ, and understand his willingness to bless and strengthen you, and give you the fulness of his riches. The more the precious treasures of grace are drawn upon, the more anxious shall we be for all to enjoy these riches. According to our capacity of understanding and appreciating them, will be our ability to impart. We are to draw from the inexhaustible source, and gladden starving souls by presenting to them the bread of life. We are to receive the holy oil from the heavenly messengers, and impart it to our fellow men.

Every youth should consider himself of value with God, because he has been entrusted with the richest gift that can be given. It is his privilege to be a living channel, through which God can communicate the treasures of his grace, the unsearchable riches of Christ.

Our sins may be as mountains before us, but if we humble our hearts in confession of them, trusting in the merits of a crucified and risen Saviour, we shall be forgiven, and shall be cleansed from all unrighteousness. The depth of a Saviour's love is revealed in our salvation. If we will accept this salvation, our testimony will be, "We have redemption through his blood." The law of the Spirit of life in Christ Jesus has made us free from the law of sin and death. We are more than conquerors through him that loved us, and gave himself for us.

It is here, right here in the world, that our talents are to be used. We are to lead souls to "the Lamb of God, which taketh away the sin of the world." It is our work, and should be our pleasure, to present in our lives the unsearchable riches of Christ. We may make daily progress in the path of holiness, and still find greater heights to be reached; but every stretch of the spiritual muscles, every tax on heart and brain, will bring to light the abundance of the supply of grace essential for us as we advance. The more we contemplate eternal things, the more we shall reveal the merits of a Saviour's sacrifice, the protection of his righteousness, the fulness of his wisdom, and his power to present us before the Father without spot, or wrinkle, or any such thing.

The words of the apostle to Timothy, "Take heed unto thyself, and unto the doctrine," may well be spoken to every church-member. The golden oil is the pure, unadulterated truth. When we receive and believe and practise the word, we shall be prepared for the great work that is waiting to be done, and we shall be fitted for the service we shall render to God through all eternity.

We are living amid the perils of the last days. There is need now of workers who will not fail nor be discouraged. We must be diligent in using the talents entrusted to us, that we may give back to God his own with usury.

Mrs. Ellen G. White

December 7, 1899—"Lord, Teach Us to Pray"

"And it came to pass, that, as he was praying in a certain place, when he ceased, one of his disciples said unto him, Lord, teach us to pray, as John also taught his disciples." Jesus answered them in the words of the Lord's prayer. "When ye pray," he said, "say, Our Father which art in heaven, Hallowed be thy name. Thy kingdom come. Thy will be done, as in heaven, so in earth. Give us day by day our daily bread. And forgive us our sins; for we also forgive every one that is indebted to us. And lead us not into temptation; but deliver us from evil."

Christ did not give us this prayer to repeat as a form. He gave it as an illustration of what our prayers should be,--simple, earnest, and comprehensive. "Our Father which art in heaven." The word "our" expresses a sense of human brotherhood; "father," that of childlike trust.

In ancient times there was usually associated with the name "father" all the affection and tenderness now centered in the word "mother." Affection and strength were combined; the exalted and stronger served the weaker. When we say, "Our Father," we worship God in truth. When we say, "Who art in heaven," we worship him in spirit. This petition carries the suppliant away from earth and human beings, to One who is unerring in judgment, compassionate, merciful, pure, and holy.

"Hallowed be thy name." Thus we give expression to our reverence for the divine nature. All true prayer will first recognize the presence of God, whose eye is open to all that his creatures do. The supplicant's first work is to honor God by giving expression to his reverence.

"Thy kingdom come. Thy will be done, as in heaven, so in earth." In heaven the will of God is perfectly carried out. Love to God makes his service a joy. On earth there are rebellion and variance. The disobedient and rebellious can not understandingly repeat the Lord's prayer. Their will has never been submitted to discipline; and until they are brought into conformity to the will of God, they can not intelligently pray that his will may be done in earth as it is in heaven. It should be the prayer of every true follower of Christ that God will subordinate everything in this world to his will.

Our temporal necessities are also to be the subject of our petitions. We are to call upon God for the very bread we eat. "Give us this day our daily bread," Christ said. But we are not to ask God for food, and then sit idly down, and do nothing. In order to supply our wants, our Heavenly Father puts work into our hands, that we may co-operate with him in answering our prayers.

"Forgive us our sins; for we also forgive every one that is indebted to us." We can not repeat this prayer from the heart, and dare be unforgiving; for we ask the Lord to forgive our trespasses against him as we forgive those who trespass against us. Very few realize the true import of this prayer. If those who are unforgiving comprehended the depth of its meaning, they would not dare repeat it, and ask God to deal with them as they deal with their fellow mortals.

Strength of character consists of two things--power of will and power of self-control. Many youth mistake strong, uncontrolled passion for strength of character; but the truth is that he who is mastered by his passions is a weak man. The real greatness and nobility of the man are measured by the power of the feelings that he subdues, not by the power of the feelings that subdue him. The strongest man is he who, while sensitive to abuse, will yet restrain passion, and forgive his enemies. Such men are true heroes.

"Lead us not into temptation." God sometimes allows Satan to tempt his children, that he may prove them. If they rely on their own strength, they will fail under the trial; but while they realize their inability to help themselves, and trust wholly in God, he will provide a way of escape for them. There are times when it is necessary for men to be exposed to dangers, and be placed amid corrupting influences, but a sense of their dependence on God will lead them to keep their hearts uplifted in prayer every hour for strength to resist and grace to overcome. The experience gained in these conflicts will fortify the soul to pass unscathed through more trying scenes.

Christ prayed to his Father in behalf of his followers: "I pray not that thou shouldest take them out of the world, but that thou shouldest keep them from the evil." Sin and pollution abound on every hand; and daily, hourly, the prayer should go forth from hearts that realize the dangers, "Deliver us from evil." The Christian who offers this prayer, realizing his weakness, makes the temptation of the enemy powerless.

"Men ought always to pray, and not to faint," Christ said. To every child of God the words of inspiration are spoken: "Continue in prayer, and watch in the same with thanksgiving." "The end of all things is at hand: be ye therefore sober, and watch unto prayer."

Mrs. E. G. White

December 21, 1899—"Tempted in All Points Like as We Are"—Part 1

As Christ's ministry was about to begin, he received baptism at the hands of John. Coming up out of the water, he bowed on the banks of the Jordan, and offered to the Father such a prayer as heaven had never before listened to. That prayer penetrated the shadow of Satan, which surrounded the Saviour, and cleaved its way to the throne of God. The heavens were opened, and a dove, in appearance like burnished gold, rested upon Jesus; and from the lips of the Infinite God were heard the words, "This is my beloved Son, in whom I am well pleased."

This visible answer to the prayer of God's Son is of deep significance to us. It assures us that humanity is accepted in Christ. The repenting cry of every sinner, the petition of every believing soul, will be heard, and the suppliant will receive grace and power. Christ has opened the way to the highest heavens for every bereaved heart. All may find rest and peace and assurance in sending their prayers to God in the name of his dear Son. As the heavens were open to Christ's prayer, so they will be opened to our prayers. The Holy Spirit will come to every son and daughter of Adam who looks to God for strength.

From the Jordan, Jesus was led into the wilderness of temptation. "And when he had fasted forty days and forty nights, he was afterward an hungered. And when the tempter came to him, he said, If thou be the Son of God, command that these stones be made bread."

Christ was suffering the keenest pangs of hunger, and this temptation was a severe one. But he must begin the work of redemption just where the ruin began. Adam had failed on the point of appetite, and Christ must conquer here. The power that rested upon him came directly from the Father, and he must not exercise it in his own behalf. With that long fast there was woven into his experience a strength and power that God alone could give. He met and resisted the enemy in the strength of a "Thus saith the Lord." "Man shall not live by bread alone," he said, "but by every word that proceedeth out of the mouth of God."

This strength it is the privilege of all the tempted ones of earth to have. Christ's experience is for our benefit. His example in overcoming appetite points out the way for those to overcome who would be his followers.

Christ was suffering as the members of the human family suffer under temptation; but it was not the will of God that he should exercise his divine power in his own behalf. Had he not stood as our representative, Christ's innocence would have exempted him from all this anguish; but it was because of his innocence that he felt so keenly the assaults of Satan. All the suffering that is the result of sin was poured into the bosom of the sinless Son of God. Satan was bruising the heel of Christ; but every pang endured by Christ, every grief, every disquietude, was fulfilling the great plan of man's redemption. Every blow inflicted by the enemy was rebounding on himself. Christ was bruising the serpent's head.

Satan had been defeated in the first temptation. He next took Christ to the pinnacle of the temple at Jerusalem, and asked him to prove his sonship to God by throwing himself down from the dizzy height. "If thou be the Son of God," he said, "cast thyself down: for it is written, He shall give his angels charge concerning thee: and in their hands they shall bear thee up, lest at any time thou dash thy foot against a stone." But to do this would be presumption on the part of Christ, and he would not yield. "It is written," he replied, "thou shalt not tempt the Lord thy God." Again the tempter was baffled. Christ was victor still.

Presumption is a common temptation, and when Satan assails men with this, he gains the victory almost every time. Those who claim to be enlisted in the warfare against evil frequently plunge without thought into temptation from which it would require a miracle to bring them forth unsullied. God's precious promises are not given to strengthen us in a presumptuous course, or to rely upon when we rush needlessly into danger. The Lord requires us to move with a humble dependence upon his guidance. "It is not in a man that walketh to direct his steps." In God is our prosperity and our life. Nothing can be done prosperously without his permission and his blessing. "Commit thy way unto the Lord; trust also in him; and he shall bring it to pass." As children of God, we are to maintain a consistent Christian character.

While you pray, dear youth, that you may not be led into temptation, remember that your work does not end with prayer. As far as possible you must answer your own prayers by resisting temptation. Ask Jesus to do for you that which you can not do for yourself. With God's word for our guide, and Jesus for our teacher, we need not be ignorant of God's requirements or of Satan's devices.

"Again, the devil taketh him up into an exceeding high mountain, and showeth him all the kingdoms of the world, and the glory of them; and saith unto him, All these things will I give thee, if thou wilt fall down and worship me." Then divinity flashed through humanity. "Get thee hence, Satan," Christ said; "for it is written, Thou shalt worship the Lord thy God, and him only shalt thou serve." Satan did not then present another temptation. He left the presence of Christ a conquered foe.

Mrs. E. G. White

December 28, 1899—"Tempted in All Points Like As We Are"—Part 2

Christ paid an infinite price to redeem the world. He sacrificed his honor, his riches, his glorious home in the royal courts, and endured the fierce assaults of Satan, that man might have strength to overcome as he overcame. The temptations that Satan brings to bear upon the human race are severe; but his test for the Son of God was a hundredfold more severe. It was not merely the gnawing pangs of hunger that made Christ's sufferings so intense; it was the guilt of the sins of the world, which pressed so heavily upon him. He who knew no sin was made sin for us. With this terrible weight of guilt upon him, he withstood the fearful test upon appetite; upon the love of the world and of honor; and upon pride of display, which leads to presumption. Christ endured these great temptations, overcoming in our behalf, and working out for us a righteous character.

Many who fall under temptation excuse themselves with the plea that Christ's divinity helped him overcome, and that man has not this power in his favor. But this is a mistake. Christ has brought divine power within the reach of all. The Son of God came to the earth because he saw that moral power in man is weak. He came to bring finite man in close connection with God. It is by combining divine power with his human strength that man becomes an overcomer.

When we are tempted to question whether Christ resisted temptation as a man, we must search the Scriptures for the truth. As the substitute and surety of the human race, Christ was placed in the same position toward the Father as is the sinner. Christ had the privilege of depending on the Father for strength, and so have we. Because he laid hold of the hand of infinite power, and held it fast, he overcame; and we are taught to do the same. He met every temptation with, "It is written;" and so must we. The one who resists evil in his strength can say, in the words of Inspiration: "The Lord God will help me: therefore shall I not be confounded: therefore have I set my face like a flint, and I know that I shall not be ashamed. He is near that justifieth me; who will contend with me? ... Behold, the Lord God will help me: who is he that shall condemn me?"

The language of Christ on many occasions shows that he was placed in the same position that we are. He had to walk by faith, as we walk by faith; and when temptations came to him with overwhelming power, he used the language that every child of earth must use. "The Son can do nothing of himself," Christ declared, "but what he seeth the Father do: for what things soever he doeth, these also doeth the Son likewise." "I can of mine own self do nothing: as I hear, I judge: and my judgment is just; because I seek not mine own will, but the will of the Father which hath sent me." "When ye have lifted up the Son of man, then shall ye know that I am he, and that I do nothing of myself; but as my Father hath taught me, I speak these things."

Christ has wrestled with the powers of darkness. He has trodden the road over which every son and daughter of Adam must pass. He knows how fierce is the conflict, and he gives us the gracious words of instruction and encouragement: "Who is among you that feareth the Lord, that obeyeth the voice of his servant, that walketh in darkness, and hath no light? let him trust in the name of the Lord, and stay upon his God."

This trust in God he contrasts with trust in self. "Behold, all ye that kindle a fire," he says, "that compass yourselves about with sparks: walk in the light of your fire, and in the sparks that ye have kindled. This shall ye have of mine hand; ye shall lie down in sorrow."

Christ is the Captain of our salvation. "It became him, for whom are all things, and by whom are all things, in bringing many sons unto glory, to make the Captain of their salvation perfect through sufferings." The suffering that poured in upon the Son of God is beyond anything that man will be called to endure; yet Christ overcame, and perfected a spotless character. By his suffering and resistance he made plain to man that perfection of character can be obtained and maintained by humanity.

When Satan fails to lead men into sin by the first two temptations, those of appetite and presumption, he besets them with the third, the love of the world; and in almost every case he leads them into apostasy by this means. It is the glory of this world that attracts and ensnares. But we have reason to thank God that the Captain of our salvation was made perfect through suffering, and came off conqueror in our behalf. Every son and daughter of Adam may have this divine strength. The promise of the Comforter has been given us. "He that believeth on me," said Jesus, "the works that I do shall he do also; and greater works than these shall he do; because I go unto my

Father." The power that came to Christ as a representative of the human race will come to every member of the human family who will make God his strength.

"We have a great high priest, which is passed into the heavens, Jesus the Son of God.... We have not an high priest which can not be touched with the feeling of our infirmities; but was in all points tempted like as we are, yet without sin. Let us therefore come boldly unto the throne of grace, that we may obtain mercy, and find grace to help in time of need." We may take courage, and believe that we shall overcome every imperfection of character. Our Redeemer has taken our nature, fought our battles, and in his name we shall conquer. Human nature may take hold of the strength of God, and be victorious.

Mrs. E. G. White

January 4, 1900—"Tempted in All Points Like as We Are"—Part 3

We have little idea of the strength that would be ours if we would connect with the source of all strength. We fall into sin again and again, and think it must always be so. We cling to our infirmities as if they were something to be proud of. Christ tells us that we must set our faces as a flint if we would overcome. He has borne our sins in his own body on the tree; and through the power he has given us, we may resist the world, the flesh, and the devil. Then let us not talk of our weakness and inefficiency, but of Christ and his strength. When we talk of Satan's strength, the enemy fastens his power more firmly upon us. When we talk of the power of the Mighty One, the enemy is driven back. As we draw near to God, he draws near to us.

Christ knows all about our trials and temptations; for he was tempted in all points like as we are, yet without sin. Before the heavenly universe he showed that men can keep the commandments of God, and perfect a Christian character. He poured out his petitions to the Father with strong crying and tears. He set his face as a flint to conquer. And he could say, "The prince of this world cometh, and hath nothing in me." In the life and character of Christ there was nothing that the enemy of souls could use to serve his evil purpose.

Many of us fail to improve our privileges. We make a few feeble efforts to do right, and then go back to our old life of sin. If we ever enter the kingdom of God, we must enter with perfect characters, not having spot, or wrinkle, or any such thing. Satan works with increased activity as we near the close of time. He lays his snares, unperceived by us, that he may take possession of our minds. In every way he tries to eclipse the glory of God from the soul. It rests with us to decide whether he shall control our hearts and minds; or whether we shall have a place in the new earth, a title to Abraham's farm.

The power of God, combined with human effort, has wrought out a glorious victory for us. Shall we not appreciate this? All the riches of heaven were given to us in Jesus. God would not have the confederacy of evil say that he could do more than he has done. The worlds that he had created, the angels in heaven, could testify that he could do no more. God has resources of power of which we as yet know nothing, and from these he will supply us in our time of need. But our effort is ever to combine with the divine. Our intellect, our perceptive powers, all the strength of our being, must be called into exercise. We must co-operate with God in this work of salvation. If we will rise to the emergency, and arm ourselves like men who wait for their Lord; if we will work to overcome every defect in our characters, God will give us increased light and strength and help.

Mrs. E. G. White

January 11, 1900—"Tempted in All Points Like as We Are"—Part 4

Christ bids you bring all of heaven you can into your life. Talk of the great reward that awaits the overcomer. Set your face as a flint heavenward, saying, as you advance, Hear what the Lord has wrought for me. Shall we not come up to the help of the Lord against the mighty? Shall we not work with all the power that God has given us to oppose the work of Satan? An eternal weight of glory awaits the overcomer. If we gain heaven, we gain everything. Shall we not put away sin, and let Christ abide in our hearts by faith? Not until we have the mind of Christ shall we be like him, and see him as he is. When the warfare is ended, and we have gained the crown of immortality, the harp of God, the palm branch of victory, and wear the white robe of Christ's righteousness, we shall say, Heaven is cheap enough.

By right of inheritance the universe belonged to Christ, but for this world he battled and fought; and by a terrible struggle he obtained the territory. When he yielded up his life on Calvary, he drew back into favor with God this world, which was lost. It is here that the saints of the Most High will reign. When the earth is cleansed by the purifying fires of God, those who have laid hold of the merits of Christ will dwell in the kingdom prepared for them. The disciple John writes: "I saw a new heaven and a new earth: for the first heaven and the first earth were passed away; and there was no more sea. And I John saw the holy city, New Jerusalem, coming down from God out of heaven, prepared as a bride adorned for her husband. And I heard a great voice out of heaven saying, Behold, the tabernacle of God is with men, and he will dwell with them, and they shall be his people, and God himself shall be with them, and be their God. And God shall wipe away all tears from their eyes; and there shall be no more death, neither sorrow, nor crying, neither shall there be any more pain: for the former things are passed away."

It is impossible for us to understand the depth of the ruin from which we have been rescued, only as we realize how deep the Son of God has reached to save us. We may estimate the love of Christ by the chain of mercy let down to lift us up. The disciple John could not find words to express the measureless love of God, and he calls us to "behold what manner of love the Father hath bestowed upon us, that we should be called the sons of God." We must accept the provisions of the gospel; we must be reconciled to God through obedience to his law, and faith in Christ. Through repentance, faith, and good works, we may perfect a Christian character; and through the merits of Christ we may claim the privileges of sons and daughters of God. The principles of divine truth, received and cherished in the heart, will carry us to a height of moral excellence that we have not dreamed it possible to reach. "It doth not yet appear what we shall be: but we know that, when he shall appear, we shall be like him; for we shall see him as he is. And every man that hath this hope in him purifieth himself, even as he is pure."

Mrs. E. G. White

February 1, 1900—Christ Before Pilate

"When the morning was come, all the chief priests and elders of the people took counsel against Jesus to put him to death: and when they had bound him, they led him away, and delivered him to Pontius Pilate the governor."

The priests and rulers were prepared to place themselves in a false position in order to sustain their charges against Christ. The Jews were bitter opponents of the Roman power, they hated Caesar's rule and supremacy; but to gain their end, they professed to be his loyal subjects. They had no conscience, no pure principles. When it was safe for them to be so, they were most tyrannical in their church requirements: when they aimed to bring about some purpose of cruelty, they exalted the power of Caesar. The world was gone after Christ, they declared, and all men would believe in him if he was permitted to live.

"They began to accuse him, saying, We found this fellow perverting the nation, and forbidding to give tribute to Caesar, saying that he himself is Christ a King."

These charges were wholly at variance with the appearance of Christ, and Pilate did not believe them. "He knew that for envy they had delivered him." To all their accusations Christ had answered nothing. "Then said Pilate unto him, Hearest thou not how many things they witness against thee? And he answered him to never a word, insomuch that the governor marveled greatly." The eloquent silence, the patience and serenity maintained by Jesus throughout the condemnation, had a different effect on the several actors. The same meekness and patience that spoke conviction to Pilate, excited satanic hatred in the hearts of the Jews.

"Art thou the king of the Jews?" Pilate asked. "Jesus answered him, Sayest thou this thing of thyself, or did others tell it thee of me? Pilate answered, Am I a Jew? Thine own nation and the chief priests have delivered thee unto me: what hast thou done? Jesus answered, My kingdom is not of this world; if my kingdom were of this world, then would my servants fight, that I should not be delivered to the Jews: but now is my kingdom not from hence. Pilate therefore said unto him, Art thou a king then? Jesus answered, Thou sayest that I am a king. To this end was I born, and for this cause came I into the world, that I should bear witness unto the truth. Every one that is of the truth heareth my voice. Pilate saith unto him, What is truth? And when he had said this, he went out again unto the Jews, and said unto them, I find in him no fault at all. But ye have a custom, that I should release unto you one at the Passover: will ye therefore that I release unto you the King of the Jews? Then cried they all again, saying, Not this man, but Barabbas. Now Barabbas was a robber.

"Then Pilate therefore took Jesus, and scourged him. And the soldiers platted a crown of thorns, and put it on his head, and they put on him a purple robe, and said, Hail, King of the Jews! and they smote him with their hands. Pilate therefore went forth again, and saith unto them, Behold, I bring him forth to you, that ye may know that I find no fault in him. Then came Jesus forth, wearing the crown of thorns, and the purple robe. And Pilate saith unto them. Behold the man! When the chief priests therefore and officers saw him, they cried out, saying, Crucify him, crucify him. Pilate saith unto them, Take ye him, and crucify him: for I find no fault in him. The Jews answered him, We have a law, and by our law he ought to die, because he made himself the Son of God.

"When Pilate therefore heard that saying, he was the more afraid." He went again into the judgment hall, and said to Jesus, "Whence art thou?" Jesus gave him no answer. "Then saith Pilate unto him, Speakest thou not unto me? knowest thou not that I have power to crucify thee, and have power to release thee? Jesus answered, Thou couldest have no power at all against me, except it were given thee from above: therefore he that delivered me unto thee hath the greater sin. And from thenceforth Pilate sought to release him."

"He that delivered me unto thee hath the greater sin." Christ here referred to Caiaphas, who, as high priest, represented the Jewish nation. Caiaphas knew the principles that controlled the Roman authorities. He had had light in the prophecies and in the written word, which testified of Christ; and according to his light, he would be judged.

The words of Christ filled Pilate with awe. He feared the results of his course of action. He had boasted of his power to crucify Christ or to release him, according to his view of the matter. But when he considered that this man was connected with the highest authority the world ever knew, he was afraid. He thought that he could on his own authority let Christ go forth uncondemned. But the Jews cried out, saying, "If thou let this man go, thou art not Caesar's friend: whosoever maketh himself a king speaketh against Caesar."

This threat increased the guilt of the Jewish nation before God. They were determined to accomplish their purpose. To gratify their envy, and get rid of Jesus, they placed themselves in a false position, professing loyalty to a ruler whom they hated. To have complaint of him go from the priests and rulers to Caesar was more than Pilate dared risk. To have them impeach his course of action might forfeit for him his place and authority. Therefore Pilate yielded up to the will of his enemies the One whom he had pronounced without fault. Christ was again scourged.

Again Pilate took his place on the judgment-seat. He had made his decision. In mockery he presented Jesus to them, saying, "Behold your King." But the mad cry was raised, "Crucify him, crucify him." In a voice that was heard far and near, Pilate asked, "Shall I crucify your King?" But the loud, ringing, awful cry came from profane, blasphemous lips, "We have no king but Caesar."

Though Pilate had given Christ over to the will of the infuriated mob, he was not willing to take upon himself the responsibility of his act. In an imposing manner he took water, and washed his hands before the people, saying, "I am innocent of the blood of this just person." Priests, scribes, and rulers answered, "His blood be on us and on our children."

What was Christ's grief to see the Jews fixing their own destiny beyond redemption! He alone could comprehend the significance of their rejection, betrayal, and condemnation of the Son of God. His last hope for the Jewish nation was gone. Nothing could avert her doom. By the representatives of the nation God was denied as their ruler. By worlds unfallen, by the whole heavenly universe, the blasphemous utterance was heard, "We have no king but Caesar." The God of heaven heard their choice. He had given them opportunity to repent, and they would not. Forty years afterward Jerusalem was destroyed, and the Roman power ruled over the people. Then they had no deliverer. They had no king but Caesar. Henceforth the Jewish nation, as a nation, was as a branch severed from the vine,--a dead, fruitless branch, to be gathered up and burned,--from land to land throughout the world, from century to century, dead,--dead in trespasses and sins,--without a Saviour!

Mrs. E. G. White

February 8, 1900—Christ Before Herod

From Pilate, Christ was hurried to the judgment hall of Herod. Herod had never met Jesus, but he had long desired to see him, and witness his marvelous power. As the Saviour was brought forth, the multitude surged and pressed about him. Herod commanded silence, for he wished to question Christ. He desired to have his curiosity gratified, and thought that Christ would do anything he asked, if he was given a prospect of release.

Herod ordered the fetters of Christ to be unloosed. He looked with curiosity into the serene face of the world's Redeemer, but he read there only innocence and noble purity. He was satisfied, as Pilate had been, that Christ had been brought there from motives of malice and envy. He urged Jesus to perform one of his wonderful miracles before him. At his command the decrepit and maimed were brought into the presence of Christ, and he was ordered to prove his claims by demonstrating his power before them. Men say that thou canst heal the sick, Herod said; I am anxious to see that thy wide-spread fame has not been belied. If thou canst work miracles for others, work them now; and it shall serve thee a good purpose.

But the Saviour stood before the king as one who neither saw nor heard. Herod felt that he was mocked. Again he commanded Jesus to work a miracle. Show us a sign, he said, that thou hast the power with which rumor hath accredited thee. He promised Christ that if he would perform a miracle in his presence, he would release him. But Christ preserved alike his silence and his godlike majesty. That ear that had ever been open to human woe had no room for Herod's words. Those eyes that had ever rested upon the sinner in pitying, forgiving love, had no look to bestow upon Herod. Those lips that had uttered the most impressive truths, that had ever pleaded in tones of tenderest entreaty, that had ever been ready to speak pardon to the most hardened sinner, were closed to him.

Some of Christ's accusers had seen with their own eyes the mighty works wrought by his power. Their ears had heard him command the grave to give up its dead. They had seen the grave obey his command, and fear seized them lest Christ should work a miracle and thus defeat their purposes. In great anxiety they raised their voices, declaring, He is a traitor, a blasphemer. He works his miracles through Beelzebub, the prince of the devils. He claims to be the Son of God, the king of Israel. The hall was one scene of confusion, some crying one thing, and some another.

Herod interpreted the silence of Christ as an insult to himself, a contempt for his power. Turning to him, he said: If you will not work a miracle, if you will give no proof of your claims, I will give you up to the soldiers and the people. They may succeed in making you speak. If you are an impostor, death at their hands is only what you merit; if you are the Son of God, save yourself.

No sooner were these words spoken than a rush was made for Christ. The Saviour was mocked, and dragged this way and that, Herod making suggestions as to how they could best humiliate him. And all this against a man who had been pronounced faultless. No accusation could be proved against him. He was the victim of the malice and jealousy of the people who had been the chosen of God.

Satan led the cruel mob in their abuse of the Saviour. It was his purpose to provoke him to retaliation, if possible, or to drive him to perform a miracle to release himself, and thus break up the plan of salvation. One stain upon his human life, one failure of his humanity to bear the terrible test, and the Lamb of God would have been an imperfect offering, and the redemption of man a failure. But he who by a command could bring the heavenly host to his aid, he who could have driven that mob in terror from his sight by one look of divinity, submitted to the coarsest insult and outrage with dignified composure. The crown of thorns encircling his brow was the symbol of his anointing as the great High Priest.

As Herod saw Jesus accepting all this indignity in silence, he was moved with a sudden fear that this was no common man before him. He was perplexed by the thought that his prisoner might be a god come down to the earth. He dared not ratify the condemnation of the Jews. He wished to relieve himself of the terrible responsibility, and so sent Jesus back to Pilate.

Mrs. E. G. White

February 15, 1900—"If Any of You Lack Wisdom, Let Him Ask of God"

True prayer, offered in faith, is a power to the petitioner. Prayer, whether offered in the public assembly, at the family altar, or in secret, places man directly in the presence of God. By constant prayer the youth may obtain principles so firm that the most powerful temptations will not draw them from their allegiance to God.

The child Samuel was surrounded with the most corrupting influences. He saw and heard things that grieved his soul. The sons of Eli, who ministered in holy office, were controlled by Satan. These men polluted the very atmosphere that surrounded them. Men and women were daily fascinated with sin and wrong; yet Samuel walked untainted. His robes of character were spotless. He had no fellowship with the sins that filled all Israel with fearful reports.

In God there is strength; in him there is power. If we would take hold of this strength and power, we must not cease our watchfulness and prayer for a moment. We are safe only when we feel our weakness, and cling with the grasp of faith to our mighty Deliverer.

The world's Redeemer spent much time in prayer. He loved the solitude of the mountain, where he could hold communion with his Father alone. We read: "And when he had sent the multitudes away, he went up into a mountain apart to pray: and when the evening was come, he was there alone." "And in the morning, rising up a great while before day, he went out, and departed into a solitary place, and there prayed." "He went out into a mountain to pray, and continued all night in prayer to God." If Jesus manifested so much earnestness, how much more need for us to wrestle with God, and say, "I will not let thee go, except thou bless me."

"Which of you shall have a friend," Christ said, "and shall go unto him at midnight, and say unto him, Friend, lend me three loaves; for a friend of mine in his journey is come to me, and I have nothing to set before him? And he from within shall answer and say, Trouble me not: the door is now shut, and my children are with me in bed; I can not rise and give thee. I say unto you, Though he will not rise and give him, because he is his friend, yet because of his importunity he will rise and give him as many as he needeth. And I say unto you, Ask, and it shall be given to you; seek, and ye shall find; knock, and it shall be opened unto you. For every one that asketh receiveth; and he that seeketh findeth; and to him that knocketh it shall be opened. If a son shall ask bread of any of you that is a father, will he give him a stone? or if he ask a fish, will he for a fish give him a serpent? or if he shall ask an egg, will he offer him a scorpion? If ye then, being evil, know how to give good gifts unto your children: how much more shall your Heavenly Father give the Holy Spirit to them that ask him?"

In the place of bearing your perplexities to a brother or a minister, take them to the Lord in prayer. Do not place the minister where God should be. The minister of Christ is like other men. True, he bears sacred responsibilities, but he is not infallible. He is compassed with infirmity, and needs grace and divine enlightenment. He needs the heavenly unction, in order to do his work with success. Those who know how to pray, who know what are the invitations of the gospel of Christ, show dishonor to God when they lay their burdens upon finite men. It is always right to counsel together; it is right to converse together; it is right to make the difficulties that present themselves in any enterprise plain before your brethren and your ministers. But do not depend upon man for wisdom. Seek God for the wisdom that comes from above. Ask your fellow laborers to pray with you; and the Lord will fulfill his word, "Where two or three are gathered together in my name, there am I in the midst."

The Lord does not say to us: If any man lack wisdom, let him go to his pastor or to his neighbor, and pray to him for help. Lay your burden on finite men, as weak as yourself, and seek their wisdom. He says: "If any of you lack wisdom, let him ask of God, that giveth to all men liberally, and upbraideth not; and it shall be given him. But let him ask in faith, nothing wavering. For he that wavereth is like a wave of the sea, driven with the wind and tossed. For let not that man think that he shall receive anything of the Lord."

The Lord invites us to ask of him. Shall we turn from God's wisdom, to ask of men? We can not obtain from men the help that comes alone from God, in whom is no variableness, neither shadow of turning. They may advise us to do what is best; but unless they receive their light from heaven, they can have no certain light to give us. The Lord is acquainted with our ignorance and darkness, and he bids us come to him, the source of all light and wisdom. "Come unto me," he says, "all ye that labor, and are heavy laden, and I will give you rest. Take my yoke upon you, and learn of me; for I am meek and lowly in heart: and ye shall find rest unto your souls. For my yoke is easy, and my burden is light."

Promises are estimated by the truth of the one who makes them. Many men make promises only to break them, to mock the heart that trusted in them. Those who lean upon such men lean upon broken reeds. But God is behind the promises he makes. He is ever mindful of his covenant, and his truth endures to all generations. "Blessed be the Lord, that hath given rest unto his people Israel, according to all that he promised: there hath not failed one word of all his good promise, which he promised by the hand of Moses his servant."

The gift of God's dear Son makes the promises ours of a surety. Christ clothed his divinity with humanity, and paid the ransom for man, and he desires that man shall rightly estimate the life thus provided. Man is to understand, by an experimental knowledge, the tender love of God for his creatures. God expressed his love in a wonderful way. He could not make man a partaker of the divine nature, until his only begotten Son, equal with the Father, should stoop to human nature, and reach man where he was. God did not withhold his Son. In Christ humanity touched humanity. In him man becomes a child of God, an heir to all the treasure of heaven.

The Lord is always the same. He keeps truth forever, and there is no unfaithfulness in him. We have confidence in our fellow men; then why are we so apt to distrust the promises of God? Christ declared that heaven and earth would pass away, but that not one word of God would fail. Why, then, do we not honor the Lord by believing his word, which is not yea and nay, but yea and amen in Christ Jesus? Why do we not come to our Heavenly Father as a little child comes to its earthly parent, and ask him for the things we need? Christ says: "If ye then, being evil, know how to give good gifts unto your children: how much more shall your Heavenly Father give the Holy Spirit to them that ask him?"

Let us not grieve the Spirit of God any more. Let us not show distrust of his word; for he alone is to be depended on. He is "the blessed and only Potentate, the King of kings, and Lord of lords." He has a mighty arm; strong is his hand, and high is his right hand. He is a mighty God, who is able to do exceeding abundantly above all we ask or think. He is wonderful in counsel, the only wise God. If he is for us, who can be against us? "Trust ye in the Lord forever: for in the Lord Jehovah is everlasting strength."

Mrs. E. G. White

February 22, 1900—The Saviour's Mission

The first gospel sermon was preached in Eden, when God said to the serpent, "I will put enmity between thee and the woman, and between thy seed and her seed; it shall bruise thy head, and thou shalt bruise his heel."

In Eden, Adam and Eve transgressed the law of God. God had forbidden them to eat of the tree of knowledge of good and evil. But instead of obeying the voice of God, they listened to the words of the tempter. "Hath God said, Ye shall not eat of every tree of the garden?" Satan asked. "And the woman said unto the serpent, We may eat of the fruit of the trees of the garden: but of the fruit of the tree which is in the midst of the garden, God hath said, Ye shall not eat of it, neither shall ye touch it, lest ye die. And the serpent said unto the woman, Ye shall not surely die: for God doth know that in the day ye eat thereof, then your eyes shall be opened, and ye shall be as gods, knowing good and evil.

"And when the woman saw that the tree was good for food, and that it was pleasant to the eyes, and a tree to be desired to make one wise, she took of the fruit thereof, and did eat, and gave also unto her husband with her; and he did eat."

The transgression of Adam plunged the human race in hopeless misery and despair. But God, in his wonderful, pitying love, did not leave men to perish. He could not change his law to meet man in his fallen condition, but he devised a plan whereby he might have hope. He gave his Son to bear the penalty of transgression.

Christ might have come to earth clothed with the glory of his Father. But he did not do this. He did not even take the form of an angel. "Verily," the apostle says, "he took not on him the nature of angels, but he took on him the seed of Abraham." Divinity took humanity, that humanity might touch humanity. With his human arm Christ encircled the race, while with his divine arm he grasped the throne of the infinite God. The world that was separated by sin from the continent of heaven, he drew back into favor with God.

Had Christ come in his former glory, humanity could not have endured the sight. When the angel Gabriel came to Daniel to give him skill and understanding, Daniel could not look upon him. The angel had to reveal himself as a man before he could speak with the prophet. Thus we see the wisdom of God in planning that Christ should come as a man.

Had Christ come as a mighty general of armies to break the yoke of oppression from the Jewish people, and restore to them their kingdom, the nation would have received him. But Christ did not come to rank with the rich and honored. He took his place among the lowly. Though he was rich, yet for our sake he became poor, that we through his poverty might be made rich. He was acquainted with the sorrows and temptations of childhood. He experienced the dangers and snares to which the youth are exposed.

The prophet Isaiah had declared: "He shall grow up before him as a tender plant, and as a root out of a dry ground: he hath no form nor comeliness; and when we shall see him, there is no beauty that we should desire him. He is despised and rejected of men; a man of sorrows, and acquainted with grief: ... he was despised, and we esteemed him not."

When Moses prayed to God, "Show me thy glory," the Lord said: "I will make all my goodness pass before thee.... And the Lord passed by before him, and proclaimed, The Lord, the Lord God, merciful and gracious, long-suffering, and abundant in goodness and truth, keeping mercy for thousands, forgiving iniquity and transgression and sin." These attributes are the attributes of God. But Satan had represented him to man as arbitrary, stern, and unforgiving. All the misery and suffering he had brought upon man, he charged to God. He declared that man could not keep the law, and that God was arbitrary and cruel in demanding of him something that he could not do.

Christ came to represent the Father, and to show in what tender relation we stand to him. He showed that humanity can keep the law. "I have kept my Father's commandments," he said. He came to take the prey out of the hands of the enemy. "He hath sent me to heal the broken-hearted," he said, "to preach deliverance to the captives, and recovering of sight to the blind, to set at liberty them that are bruised, to preach the acceptable year of the Lord."

Mrs. E. G. White

March 1, 1900—Justification by Faith—Part 1

Faith in Christ is the only condition upon which justification can be received; and the gift is bestowed only upon those who realize that they are sinners, and undeserving of mercy. The merits of the blood of Christ must be presented to the Father as the offering for the sins of men. When sinners seek God, and in repentance confess their sin, he pardons their transgressions, remits their punishment, and receives them into fellowship with himself, as if they had never transgressed. He imparts to them the righteousness of Christ.

The faith that accepts Christ as One who is able to save to the uttermost all who come unto God by him, means perfect belief and trust. To be intelligently convinced is not enough. The apostle James writes: "Thou believest that there is one God; thou doest well: the devils also believe, and tremble." Many there are who believe that Christ has died for the sins of the world, but they make no appropriation of this grand truth to their own souls. Their hearts are not enlisted in the service of God, their lives are not reformed. They are not sanctified by the truth they profess to believe. Not having the faith that works by love and purifies the soul, no genuine good appears in their lives. "Was not Abraham our father justified by works, when he had offered Isaac his son upon the altar?" asks the apostle. "Seest thou how faith wrought with his works, and by works was faith made perfect? And the scripture was fulfilled which saith, Abraham believed God, and it was imputed unto him for righteousness: and he was called the Friend of God."

The offering of Isaac was designed by God to prefigure the sacrifice of his Son. Isaac was a figure of the Son of God, who was offered a sacrifice for the sins of the world. God desired to impress upon Abraham the gospel of salvation to men, and in order to make the truth a reality, and to test his faith, he required Abraham to slay his darling Isaac. All the agony that Abraham endured during that dark and fearful trial was for the purpose of deeply impressing upon his understanding the plan of redemption for fallen man. He was made to understand in his own experience how great was the self-denial of the infinite God in giving his Son to rescue man from ruin.

To Abraham no mental torture could be equal to that which he endured in obeying the command to sacrifice his son. But he girds up his soul with firmness, ready for the work that God requires him to do. With a breaking heart and unnerved hand, he takes the fire, while Isaac inquires, "Behold the fire and the wood: but where is the lamb for the burnt-offering?" But oh, Abraham can not tell him now! Father and son build the altar, and the terrible moment comes for Abraham to make known to Isaac that which has agonized his soul during all that long journey,--that Isaac himself is the victim.

Isaac is not a lad; he is a full-grown young man. He could refuse to submit to his father's design, should he choose to do so; but he does not even seek to change his purpose. He submits. He believes in the love of his father, and that he would not make this terrible sacrifice if God had not bidden him do so. Isaac is bound by the trembling, loving hands of his pitying father, because God has said it. The son submits to the sacrifice because he believes in the integrity of his father. But when everything is ready, when the faith of the father and the submission of the son are fully tested, the angel of God stays the uplifted hand of Abraham, and tells him that it is enough. "Now I know that thou fearest God, seeing that thou has not withheld thy son, thine only son from me."

Mrs. E. G. White

March 8, 1900—Justification by Faith—Part 2

Abraham's great act of faith is recorded for our benefit. It teaches us the great lesson of confidence in the requirements of God, however close and cutting they may be; and it teaches children perfect obedience to their parents and to God. By Abraham's obedience we are taught that nothing is too precious for us to give to God.

But many do not know what self-denial and sacrifice for Christ's sake mean. Should God speak to them as he did to Abraham, saying, Sacrifice your possessions, your temporal benefits, that I have lent you, to advance my cause, they would be astonished, and think that God did not mean what he said. God knew to whom he spoke when he gave the command to Abraham. Abraham knew that One faithful and true had commanded,--One whose promises are unfailing. Had God commanded him to offer his gold, silver, or even his own life, he would have done so, knowing that he was only yielding to God his own. God requires no more of man than he in his infinite love has given.

The grief that Abraham endured during those three days of trial was imposed on him that he might learn the lesson of perfect faith and obedience, and that we might comprehend the self-denial of the Father in giving his Son to die for a guilty race. God surrendered his Son to the agonies of the crucifixion, that guilty man might live. Legions of angels witnessed Christ's sufferings; but they were not permitted to interpose as in the case of Isaac. No voice was heard to stay the sacrifice. God's dear Son was mocked, and derided, and tortured, till he bowed his head in death. What greater proof of his pity and love could the infinite God have given? "He that spared not his own Son, but delivered him up for us all, how shall he not with him also freely give us all things?"

The apostle Paul says: "If thou shalt confess with thy mouth the Lord Jesus, and shalt believe in thine heart that God hath raised him from the dead, thou shalt be saved. For with the heart man believeth unto righteousness; and with the mouth confession is made unto salvation. For the Scripture saith, Whosoever believeth on him shalt not be ashamed. For there is no difference between the Jew and the Greek: for the same Lord over all is rich unto all that call upon him."

God calls for faith in Christ as our atoning sacrifice. His blood is the only remedy for sin. For us he arose from the grave, and ascended to heaven to stand in the presence of God. He was delivered for our offenses, and raised again for our justification. When we take hold of his wonderful truth by faith, we shall say, with Paul, "We all, with open face beholding as in a glass the glory of the Lord, are changed into the same image from glory to glory, even as by the Spirit of the Lord." We behold the light of the glory of God in the face of Jesus Christ. Such a view of Christ irradiates with glory the word of God. It lays for our faith a foundation. It sets forth a hope to every believing soul. Well may we bow our souls before the majesty of this precious truth.

Mrs. E. G. White

March 22, 1900—Knowing God

We can not by searching find out God: but he has revealed himself in his Son, who is the brightness of the Father's glory, and the express image of his person. If we desire a knowledge of God, we must be Christlike. When Philip said to Christ, "Show us the Father, and it sufficeth us," the Saviour answered, "Have I been so long time with you, and yet hast thou not known me, Philip? he that hath seen me hath seen the Father; and how sayest thou then, Show us the Father?"

He who does not seek each day to be more Christlike can not know God. Living a pure life through faith in Christ as a personal Saviour will bring to the believer a clearer, higher conception of God. No man whose character is not Christlike can set forth God in a true light. He may preach Christ, but he does not show his hearers that Christ is an abiding guest in his heart.

"This do, and thou shalt live," Christ said to the lawyer who had answered his question with the words, "Thou shalt love the Lord thy God with all thy heart, and with all thy soul, and with all thy strength, and with all thy mind; and thy neighbor as thyself." Eternal life is the reward that will be given to all who obey the two great principles of God's law,--love to God and love to man. The first four commandments define and enjoin love to God; the last six, love to our fellow men. Obedience to these commands is the only evidence man can give that he possesses a genuine, saving knowledge of God. Love for God is demonstrated by love for those for whom Christ has died.

While enshrouded in the pillar of cloud, Christ gave directions regarding this love. Distinctly and clearly he laid down the principles of heaven as rules that his chosen people were to observe in their dealings one with another. These principles Christ lived out in his life of humanity. In his teaching he presented the motives that should govern the lives of his followers. "All ye are brethren," he said. Treat the purchase of my blood as I have given you an example.

God has manifested the most wonderful love for fallen man. He "so loved the world, that he gave his only begotten Son, that whosoever believeth in him should not perish, but have everlasting life." Those who partake of God's love through a reception of the truth will give evidence of this by making earnest, self-sacrificing efforts to give the message of God's love to others. Thus they become laborers together with Christ. Love for God and for one another unites them to Christ by golden links. Their life is bound up with his life in sanctified, elevated union. True sanctification unites believers to Christ and to one another in bonds of tender sympathy. This union causes rich currents of Christ's love to flow continually into the heart, and then flow forth again in love for others.

The qualities that it is essential for all to possess in order to know God are those that mark the completeness of Christ's character,--his love, his patience, his unselfishness. These attributes are cultivated by doing kind actions with a kindly heart. But Christ's requirements are not met by his people today. A strange deception is upon the people of God. Selfishness prevents the unity that should exist. True Christian love is rare in our churches. This shows that the members do not love God as they claim to. They give evidence that they need to be sanctified. It is the most fatal deception to suppose that a man can have faith unto life eternal without possessing Christlike love for his brethren.

He who loves God and his neighbor is filled with light and love. God is in him and all around him. There is no such thing as a loveless Christian; for "God is love," and "hereby we do know that we know him, if we keep his commandments. He that saith, I know him, and keepeth not his commandments, is a liar, and the truth is not in him. But whoso keepeth his word, in him verily is the love of God perfected: hereby know we that we are in him.... A new commandment I write unto you, which thing is true in him and in you: because the darkness is past, and the true light now shineth. He that saith he is in the light, and hateth his brother, is in darkness even until now. He that loveth his brother abideth in the light, and there is none occasion of stumbling in him. But he that hateth his brother is in darkness, and walketh in darkness, and knoweth not whither he goeth, because that darkness hath blinded his eyes."

Christ declared: "A new commandment I give unto you, That ye love one another; as I have loved you, that ye also love one another. By this shall all men know that ye are my disciples, if ye have love one to another." Christians will love those around them as precious souls for whom Christ died.

Mrs. E. G. White

March 29, 1900—John the Beloved—Part 1

The name of the disciple John is one of the few whose memory clusters round the earthly life of the Son of God. As John studied the life of Christ, he beheld as in a glass the glory of the Lord, and he became changed from glory to glory, from character to character, until he was like him whom he adored. He imitated the life in which he delighted. He knew the Saviour by an experimental knowledge; his Master's lessons were graven on his soul. When he testified of the Saviour's grace, his simple language was eloquent with the love that pervaded his whole being.

As a witness for Christ, John entered into no controversy, no wearisome contention. He declared what he knew, what he had seen and heard. When insult was put upon Christ, John felt it to the very depths of his being. Christ had humbled himself; he had taken man's nature; but few could see him as John saw him. For John the darkness had passed away. On him the true Light was shining.

It was John's deep love for Christ that led him always to desire to be close by his side; and this place was always given him. Jesus loves those who represent the Father, and John could talk of God's love as none of the other disciples could. He revealed to his fellow men that which he felt it to be his duty to reveal, representing in his character the character of God. The glory of the Lord was expressed in his face. The beauty of holiness, which had transformed him, shone with a Christlike radiance from his countenance.

The life and character of Christ stood out before the world in sharp contrast with the life and character of the professedly religious rulers of the nation. His life of purity condemned their life of selfishness and iniquity. And their jealousy and hatred of him were intense. "The world is gone after him," they declared, and they determined to rid themselves of him. At his trial they hired false witnesses to testify against him. When Barabbas was placed by the side of Christ, and Pilate asked, "Whom will ye that I release unto you, Barabbas? or Jesus, which is called Christ?" the mob, stirred to a pitch of frenzy by the priests and rulers, cried, "Not this man, but Barabbas." "What shall I do then with Jesus?" Pilate asked. And they answered, "Let him be crucified." The thief and murderer was released; while the Son of God, free from even the taint of sin, was condemned to die. Evil angels, under their leader, Satan, were the unseen agencies in this work. It was they who inspired the priests and rulers with the spirit of rebellion.

Christ was crucified; but he rose from the dead, appeared to his disciples, and ascended to heaven, escorted by myriads of heavenly beings. At the Father's throne he received the assurance that his sacrifice was accepted, and that the world that had been divorced from God by sin, was drawn across the gulf. Receiving Christ as a sin-pardoning Saviour, man might become an heir of God, and a joint heir with Christ; "for God so loved the world, that he gave his only begotten Son, that whosoever believeth in him should not perish, but have everlasting life."

John's testimony in regard to the life, crucifixion, resurrection, and ascension of Christ was clear and forcible. Out of the abundance of a heart overflowing with love for the Saviour he spoke, and no power could stay his words. With power he bore witness that Christ was a risen Saviour. "That which was from the beginning," he writes, "which we have heard, which we have seen with our eyes, which we have looked upon, and our hands have handled, of the Word of life: ... that which we have seen and heard declare we unto you, that ye also may have fellowship with us: and truly our fellowship is with the Father, and with his Son Jesus Christ."

If we study the epistles of John, we shall see why it was that this disciple could not be left in his old age to live in peace among his brethren. To please the Jews the Romans had crucified Christ, and they now sought still further to please them by placing John where his voice could not be heard by Jew or Gentile. Thinking to silence his voice, his enemies cast him into a caldron of boiling oil. But his testimony was not stayed. Like his Master, John patiently submitted to every attempt to put him to death; and the faithful servant was preserved as were the three worthies in the fiery furnace. As the words were spoken, "Thus perish all who believe in that deceiver, Jesus Christ of Nazareth," John declared: "My Master patiently submitted to all that Satan and his angels could devise to humiliate and torture him. He gave his life to save the world. He died that we might live. I am honored in being permitted to suffer for his sake. I am a weak, sinful man; Christ was holy, harmless, undefiled, separate from sin and sinners. He did no sin, neither was guile found in his mouth." These words of the disciple had an influence, and he was removed from the caldron by the very ones who had cast him in.

April 5, 1900—John the Beloved—Part 2

Again the enemies of the truth sought to silence the voice of the faithful witness, and John was banished to the Isle of Patmos. Here, they thought, he could no longer trouble Israel, or the wicked rulers of the world, and he must finally die from hardship and distress. But John made friends and converts even here.

To outward appearance the enemies of truth were triumphing, but God's hand was moving unseen in the darkness. God permitted his faithful servant to be placed where Christ could give him a more wonderful revelation of himself. He placed him where he could receive the most precious truth for the enlightenment of the churches. He placed him in solitude, that his ear and heart might be more fully sanctified to receive the truth. The Lord was preparing John to endure hatred and scorn for the sake of the word of God and the testimony of Jesus Christ. The man who exiled John was not released from responsibility in the matter. But he became the instrument in the hands of God to carry out his eternal purpose; and the very effort to extinguish light placed the truth in bold relief.

John was deprived of the society of his brethren, but no man could deprive him of the light and revelation of Christ. A great light was to shine from Christ to his servant. The Lord watched over his banished disciple, and gave him a wonderful revelation of himself. Richly favored was this beloved disciple. With the other disciples he had traveled with Jesus, learning of him and feasting on his words. His head had often rested on his Saviour's bosom. But he must see him also in Patmos. God and Christ and the heavenly host were John's companions on the lonely isle; and from them he received instruction that he imparted to those separated with him from the world. There he wrote out the visions and revelations he received from God, telling of the things that would take place in the closing scenes of this earth's history. When his voice could no longer witness to the truth, when he could no longer testify of the One he loved and served, the messages given to him on that rocky, barren coast were to go forth as a lamp that burneth. Every nation, kindred, tongue, and people would learn the sure purpose of the Lord, not concerning the Jewish nation merely, but concerning every nation upon the earth.

The Sabbath, which God had instituted in Eden, was as precious to John on the lonely isle as when he was with his companions in the cities and towns. The precious promises that Christ had given regarding this day he repeated and claimed as his own. It was the sign to him that God was his; for God had declared: "Verily my Sabbaths ye shall keep: for it is a sign between me and you throughout your generations; that ye may know that I am the Lord that doth sanctify you.... Wherefore the children of Israel shall keep the Sabbath, to observe the Sabbath throughout their generations, for a perpetual covenant. It is a sign between me and the children of Israel forever."

On the Sabbath day the risen Saviour made his presence known to John. "I was in the Spirit on the Lord's day," he writes, "and heard behind me a great voice, as of a trumpet, saying, I am Alpha and Omega, the first and the last: and, What thou seest, write in a book, and send to the seven churches.... And I turned to see the voice that spake with me. And being turned, I saw seven golden candlesticks; and in the midst of the seven candlesticks one like unto the Son of man, clothed with a garment down to the foot, and girt about the paps with a golden girdle.... And when I saw him, I fell at his feet as dead. And he laid his right hand upon me, saying unto me, Fear not; I am the first and the last: I am he that liveth, and was dead; and, behold, I am alive forevermore."

The persecution of John became a means of grace. Patmos was made resplendent with the glory of a risen Saviour. John had seen Christ in human form, with the marks of the nails, which will ever be his glory, in his hands and his feet. Now he was permitted again to behold his risen Lord, clothed with as much glory as a human being could behold, and live. What a Sabbath was that to the lonely exile, always precious in the sight of Christ, but now more than ever exalted! Never had he learned so much of Jesus. Never had he heard such exalted truth.

The appearance of Christ to John should be to all, believers and unbelievers, an evidence that we have a risen Christ. It should give living power to the church. At times dark clouds surround God's people. It seems as if oppression and persecution would extinguish them. But at such times the most instructive lessons are given. Christ often enters prisons, and reveals himself to his chosen ones. He is in the fire with them at the stake. As in the darkest night the stars shine the brightest, so the most brilliant beams of God's glory are revealed in the deepest gloom. The darker the sky, the more clear and impressive are the beams of the Sun of Righteousness, the risen Saviour.

Mrs. E. G. White

April 12, 1900—"A New Commandment"

"A new commandment I write unto you, which thing is true in him and in you: because the darkness is past, and the true light now shineth. He that saith he is in the light, and hateth his brother, is in darkness even until now. He that loveth his brother abideth in the light, and there is none occasion of stumbling in him."

Christ has specified the measure of the love we are to show for one another. "A new commandment I give unto you," he declared, "That ye love one another; as I have loved you, that ye also love one another." By this practical love, seen by the world, "shall all men know that ye are my disciples." When the softening, subduing influence of the Spirit of God rules the hearts of those who are connected with his service, they will honor him by keeping the new commandment,--new because Christ said, "As I have loved you, that ye also love one another." The disciples did not realize Christ's love for fallen man until they saw it expressed on the cross of Calvary,--until he rose from the dead, and proclaimed over the rent sepulcher of Joseph, "I am the resurrection and the life." The lessons that Christ gave in regard to this love are just as new to us, as far as practice is concerned, as they were to the disciples before his death and resurrection. When these lessons are brought into the practical life, when God's people love one another as he requires, there will be an entire change in their experience.

If we would be true lights in the world, we must manifest the loving, compassionate spirit of Christ. To love as Christ loved means that we must practice self-control. It means that we must show unselfishness at all times and in all places. It means that we must scatter round us kind words and pleasant looks. These cost the giver nothing, but they leave behind a precious fragrance. Their influence for good can not be estimated. Not only to the receiver, but to the giver, they are a blessing; for they react upon him. Genuine love is a precious attribute of heavenly origin, which increases in fragrance in proportion as it is dispensed to others.

But while we are ever to be kind and tender, no words should be spoken that will lead a wrongdoer to think that his way is not objectionable to God. This sympathy is earthly and deceiving. No license is given in the word of God for undue manifestation of affection, for sentimental pity. Wrongdoers need counsel and reproof, and they must sometimes be sharply rebuked.

God desires his children to remember that in order to glorify him, they must bestow their affection on those who need it most. None with whom we come in contact are to be neglected. No selfishness, in look, word, or deed, is to be manifested to our fellow beings, whatever their position, whether they be high or low, rich or poor. The love that gives kind words to only a few, while others are treated with coldness and indifference, is not love, but selfishness. It will not in any way work for the good of souls or the glory of God. We are not to confine our love to one or two objects.

Those who gather the sunshine of Christ's righteousness, and refuse to let it shine into the lives of others, will soon lose the sweet, bright rays of heavenly grace, selfishly reserved to be lavished upon a few. Those who possess large affections are responsible to God to bestow them, not merely on their friends,--this is selfishness, which has no place in the life of Christ,--but on all who need help. Self should not be allowed to gather to itself a select few, giving nothing to those who need help the most. Our love is not to be sealed up for special ones. Break the bottle, and the fragrance will fill the house.

There are many in the world who hide their soul-hunger. These would be greatly helped by a tender word or a kind remembrance. Coldness and hard-heartedness are not to be regarded as virtues. Those who cherish the attributes of Christ's character will never be cold, stern, and unapproachable in demeanor, confining their sympathies to a favored few. The souls of those who love Jesus will be surrounded with a pure, fragrant atmosphere. Like the Master, they will go about "doing good."

Christ's love is deep and full, flowing like an irrepressible stream to all who will accept it. In this heaven-born love there is no selfishness; and those in whose hearts it is an abiding principle will reveal it, not only to those they hold most dear, but to all with whom they come in contact. This love will lead us to make concessions, to perform deeds of kindness, to speak tender, true, encouraging words. It will lead us to bestow sympathy on those whose hearts are hungering for sympathy. The heavenly gifts that God has so richly and freely bestowed on us, we are in turn to bestow upon others.

"If there be therefore any consolation in Christ, if any comfort of love, ... fulfill ye my joy, that ye be likeminded, having the same love, being of one accord, of one mind. Let nothing be done through strife or vainglory; but in lowliness of mind let each esteem other better than themselves. Look not every man on his own things, but every man also on the things of others. Let this mind be in you which was also in Christ Jesus." "Be ye kind one to another, tender-hearted, forgiving one another, even as God for Christ's sake hath forgiven you."

Mrs. E. G. White

April 26, 1900—"Go Work Today in My Vineyard"

The Lord demands service of every soul. Those to whom the living oracles have been opened, who see the truth, and yield themselves, soul, body, and spirit, to God, will understand the words of the Saviour, "Go work today in my vineyard," to be a requirement, but not a compulsory one. God's will is made known in his word, and those who believe in Christ will be doers of his will.

The test of sincerity is not in words, but in deeds. Christ does not say to any man, "What say ye more than others?" but, "What do ye more than others?" Full of meaning are his words, "If ye know these things, happy are ye if ye do them." Words are of no worth unless they are spoken in sincerity and in truth. The talent of words is made of value when it is accompanied with appropriate deeds. It is of vital consequence to every soul to hear the word, and to be a doer of the word.

Good works do not purchase the love of God, but they reveal that we possess that love. By our words and our works we reveal to the world, to angels, and to men whether we believe in Christ as a personal Saviour. If we surrender our way and will to God, we shall not work for God's love; we shall obey the commandments of God because it is right to do this. The disciple John writes, "We love him, because he first loved us." The true spiritual life will be revealed in every soul who is doing service for Christ. Those who are alive to Christ are imbued with his Spirit, and they can not help working in his vineyard. They work the works of God. Let every soul think prayerfully, that he may act consistently.

When Adam and Eve transgressed the command of God, they could no longer cultivate their beautiful Eden home. They were shut out of the garden, to work among the thistles and brambles that Satan had sown. Satan told our first parents that by eating of the forbidden fruit they would have higher perceptions, and be like the angels in heaven. They believed and obeyed the words of the apostate, but they proved his words a lie. Henceforth they must work among the thorns and weeds brought by the curse.

Christ came to the world with the invitation, "Go work today in my vineyard." Satan will seek to allure by his temptations, but listen to my voice today. What blessings are here offered to every man, woman, and child! It is the privilege of all to say, "We are laborers together with God, ... God's husbandry, ... God's building."

Take heed to the living oracles, which give you the precious promise of becoming a partaker of the divine nature. If you will work on the plan of addition, God will work for you on the plan of multiplication. Therefore add to your faith virtue, to your virtue knowledge, to your knowledge temperance, to your temperance patience, to your patience godliness, to your godliness brotherly kindness, and to your brotherly kindness charity. "For if these things be in you, and abound, they make you that ye shall be neither barren nor unfruitful in the knowledge of our Lord Jesus Christ. But he that lacketh these things is blind, and can not see afar off, and hath forgotten that he was purged from his old sins. Wherefore the rather, brethren, give diligence to make your calling and election sure: for if ye do these things, ye shall never fall: for so an entrance shall be ministered unto you abundantly into the everlasting kingdom of our Lord and Saviour Jesus Christ."

If you cultivate faithfully the garden of your soul, you will not boast; for it is God that worketh in you. He is making you a laborer together with himself. Receive the grace and instruction of Christ, that you may impart to others a knowledge of how to cultivate the precious plants. Thus we may extend the Lord's vineyard. The Lord is watching for evidences of our faith and love and patience. He looks to see if we are using every spiritual advantage to become skillful workers before we enter the paradise of God, the Eden home from which Adam and Eve were excluded by transgression. It is ours to have that beautiful garden to cultivate under the supervision of God. Eden restored,--how beautiful it will be! how pleasant will be our employment! Then let us prove our industry by doing faithful work. Do not say, with the faithless sinner, "I will not," nor with the untrue son, "I go, sir," and go not; but at the call of Christ let us engage in sincere service.

God has claims upon us that we can evade only at eternal loss to ourselves. But in his service there is perfect freedom. Let us consider the life of Christ. Standing at the head of humanity, serving his Father, he is a pattern of what every youth should and may be. He was given to us to show us how to live the commandments of God. He counted no sacrifice too great, no toil too hard, in order to accomplish the work he came to do. At the age of twelve he said to his earthly parent, "Wist ye not that I must be about my Father's business?" He had heard the call, and taken up the work. At another time he said: "I must work the works of him that sent me, while it is day: the night cometh, when no man can work."

He only serves who acts up to the highest standard of obedience. Of Christ it is said, "Though he were a Son, yet learned he obedience by the things which he suffered." All who would be sons and daughters of God must prove themselves workers in the great firm with God and Christ and the heavenly angels. This is the test for every soul. Shall we prove our submission and obedience? Of those who faithfully serve him the Lord says, "They shall be mine ... in that day when I make up my jewels; and I will spare them, as a man spareth his own son that serveth him."

Mrs. E. G. White

May 3, 1900—The Student's Privileges and Responsibilities—Part 1

A great responsibility rests upon the youth who have the privileges of school life. They are given many precious opportunities. The word of God is opened before them day after day. They have the privilege of listening to the message that God sends, and of knowing what he requires of every human being. The youth who come to school determined to obtain instruction that will fit them for the higher grade, will have ministering angels to attend them at every step. The still, small voice will speak to them, saying, "This is the way; walk ye in it."

We read in the Word, "We are laborers together with God." If you could only realize that the God of heaven takes those who have been rebels against his government, and says to them, You may be laborers together with me, you would this day consecrate yourselves wholly to him. You may be in living connection with Jesus. You may be channels of light. Is it not wonderful that we can receive the rich current of grace from the Deity, and work in harmony with him? What does the Deity want with us--poor, weak, and feeble as we are? What can he do with us?--Everything, if we are willing to surrender all.

When God called me in my very childhood to work for him, I used to think, What can I do? God says, Do my bidding. This is all that any of us need do. I want to tell you what each of you, from the oldest to the youngest, can do: You can co-operate with God, with your teachers, and with one another. Are you prepared to co-operate with those who carry heavy burdens? If so, you will not drift along from day to day, just where your inclination leads you. You will not study how to please yourself. You will realize that you are responsible for the influence you exert.

At the very beginning of the school term it is your privilege to understand the meaning of the words, "We are laborers together with God; ye are God's husbandry." Think of it! He is seeking to work the mind, just as you work the land. He is trying to sow seed that will bear fruit to his glory. "Ye are God's building." But he does not build without any care for you. He says to each one: "Come unto me.... Take my yoke upon you, and learn of me; for I am meek and lowly in heart: and ye shall find rest unto your souls. For my yoke is easy, and my burden is light." Where do we find rest?--In meekness and lowliness. In submitting to God, as a dutiful child submits to his father.

The success of the school depends upon the consecration and sanctification of the students, upon the holy influence they feel bound under God to exert. There are your teachers. Instead of complaining of them for being strict, come into line with them. Let your teachers understand that you are working on their side. Draw with Christ. Take his yoke upon you, and learn of him, the meek and lowly One. You will never need to complain of your teachers' strictness if you will keep faithful watch over yourselves, guarding jealously the citadel of the heart. Ever remember the words: "What? know ye not that your body is the temple of the Holy Ghost which is in you, which ye have of God, and ye are not your own? For ye are bought with a price: therefore glorify God in your body, and in your spirit, which are God's." God longs to work in you, to will and to do of his good pleasure. Are you willing to submit to his working? The good we may accomplish by thus uniting with our Saviour we shall never know till, as overcomers, we enter the city of God.

Mrs. E. G. White

May 10, 1900—The Student's Privileges and Responsibilities—Part 2

We must put to the stretch every spiritual nerve and muscle if we would stand as Daniel stood. God spoke of Daniel as a man greatly beloved. Would we not rejoice if this could be said of us? Strive, then, to be like Daniel, affable, kind, and forbearing. Show your love for those who are striving to help you form right characters. Do all you can to help yourselves, that your intelligence may reach the highest point of excellence. God does not desire you to remain novices. He needs in his work everything that you can gain here in the lines of mental culture and clear discernment. He desires to have you reach the very highest round of the ladder, and then step off it into the kingdom of God.

The Lord desires you to understand the position you occupy as sons and daughters of the Most High, children of the heavenly King. He longs to have you live in close connection with him, so that your words may educate those around you. Cut away from everything frivolous. Do not think that you must indulge in this pleasure and that pleasure. Determine that you will be on the Lord's side from the beginning of the term till its close. If you will stand under the blood-stained banner of Prince Immanuel, faithfully doing his service, you will never yield to temptation; for One will stand by your side who is able to keep you from falling. But God can not do this work for you unless you give him all the powers of heart and mind. Angels are watching the development of character in the school. God is weighing moral worth. He longs to see every mind used aright. He has given you the precious talent of reason, and he calls upon you to use it in the right way. He desires you to feel that you can and will acquire greater and still greater strength.

Take heed to yourselves, lest you lead others astray. If by your course of action, others are turned aside from the right way, this is recorded against you in the books of heaven. We have one great object before us--the salvation of souls. Christ left the royal courts, and came to this earth in human flesh, to show us that we may co-operate with him to save souls. After he has made this great sacrifice for us, should we deem any sacrifice too great to keep our passions, our inherited and cultivated tendencies to wrong, under control?

We are living amid the perils of the last days, and we need to receive an education as missionaries. Let each student make up his mind that he will not stand in the army of the enemy. We are working for time and for eternity, and we expect to receive light and grace from the Lord. Strive to reach all that it is possible for you to reach with the blessing of God. When you have such a helper, when angels of God are watching your every movement, when all heaven is interested in your welfare, will you not do all in your power to help yourselves? Pray for yourselves. Take firm hold of the arm of divine power, determining, as did Daniel, not to swerve from any duty. Harness your habits. Put on the bit and bridle. Use all your intelligence in God's service.

"If ye then be risen with Christ," the apostle writes, "seek those things which are above, where Christ sitteth on the right hand of God. Set your affection on things above, not on things on the earth. For ye are dead, and your life is hid with Christ in God. When Christ, who is our life, shall appear, then shall ye also appear with him in glory.... And above all these things put on charity, which is the bond of perfectness. And let the peace of God rule in your hearts.... Let the word of Christ dwell in you richly in all wisdom; ... and whatsoever ye do in word or deed, do all in the name of the Lord Jesus, giving thanks to God and the Father by him."

\Mrs. E. G. White

May 17, 1900—"The Violent Take it by Force"—Part 1

"From the days of John the Baptist until now the kingdom of heaven suffereth violence, and the violent take it by force."

The preaching of John the Baptist created intense excitement. At the beginning of his ministry, religious interest was very low. Superstition, tradition, and fables had confused the minds of the people, and the right way was not understood. Zealous in securing worldly treasure and honor, men had forgotten God. John went forth to herald the Lord's anointed, and call men to repentance, saying: "Repent ye: for the kingdom of heaven is at hand. For this is he that was spoken of by the prophet Esaias, saying, The voice of one crying in the wilderness, Prepare ye the way of the Lord; make his paths straight." "Every valley shall be filled, and every mountain and hill shall be brought low; and the crooked shall be made straight, and the rough ways shall be made smooth; and all flesh shall see the salvation of God.... Now also the ax is laid unto the root of the trees: every tree therefore which bringeth not forth good fruit is hewn down, and cast into the fire."

The teaching of John aroused in the hearts of many a great desire to have a part in the blessings that Christ was to bring, and they received the truth. These saw the need of reform. They must not only seek to enter in at the strait gate; they must strive and agonize in order to have the blessings of the gospel. Nothing save a vehement desire, a determined will, a fixedness of purpose, could resist the moral darkness that covered the earth as the pall of death. In order to obtain the blessings that it was their privilege to have, they must work earnestly, they must deny self.

The work of John the Baptist represents the work for these times. His work, and the work of those who go forth in the spirit and power of Elijah to arouse the people from their apathy, are the same in many respects. Christ is to come the second time to judge the world in righteousness. The messengers of God who bear the last message of warning to be given to the world are to prepare the way for Christ's second advent as John prepared the way for his first advent. If the kingdom of heaven suffered violence in the days of John, it suffers violence now; today the blessings of the gospel must be secured in the same way. If form and ceremony were of no avail then, a form of godliness without the power can be of no avail now.

Two powers are at work. On the one side Satan is working with all his forces to counter-work the influence of the work of God; on the other hand God is working through his servants to call men to repentance. Which will prevail? Satan, knowing that his time is short, has come down with great power, and is working with all deceivableness of unrighteousness in them that perish. Every agent that he can employ he is using to prevent souls from coming to the light. The victories we gain over self and sin are gained at the expense of the enemy, and he will not let us enjoy the blessings of God without making determined efforts to resist us.

Mrs. E. G. White

May 24, 1900—"The Violent Take It by Force"—Part 2

There is need of earnest work, that we may have strength from God to resist the enemy when he shall come in like a flood. We must agonize in order to subdue self; for self-ease and self-indulgence are the most deceptive of sins, stupefying the conscience and blinding the understanding. Oh, that those who have heard the testing message would awake from their sleep, and no longer remain in careless indifference! We need the earnest desire of the importunate widow and the Syrophenician woman,--a determination that will not be repulsed.

Many, very many, are making a fatal mistake by failing to heed this lesson of God's providence. Peace and rest can be secured only by conflict. The powers of light and darkness are in array, and we must individually take a part in the struggle. Jacob wrestled all night with God before he gained the victory. As he pleaded with God in prayer, he felt a strong hand laid upon him; and thinking it to be the hand of an enemy, he put forth all his strength to resist him. He wrestled for hours, but gained nothing over his opponent, and he dared not relax his efforts for one moment, lest he should be overcome and lose his life. Thus the contest went on until the dawn of day, and neither had gained the victory. Then the stranger brought the conflict to a close. He touched the thigh of Jacob, and the wrestler's strength was paralyzed. It was not until then that Jacob learned who his opponent really was; and, falling crippled and weeping on his neck, he pleaded for his life.

The angel could easily have released himself from the grasp of Jacob, but he did not do this. "Let me go," he pleaded, "for the day breaketh." But the answer came from the suffering but determined Jacob, "I will not let thee go, except thou bless me." The suppliant's tears and prayers gained for him what he struggled in vain to obtain. "What is thy name?" the angel asked. "And he said, Jacob. And he said, Thy name shall no more be called Jacob, but Israel: for as a prince hast thou power with God and with men, and hast prevailed.... And he blessed him there."

Jacob was in fear and distress while he sought in his own strength to obtain the victory. He mistook the divine visitor for an enemy, and contended with him while he had any strength left. But when he cast himself upon the mercy of God, he found that instead of being in the hands of an enemy, he was encircled in the arms of infinite love. He saw God face to face, and his sins were pardoned.

"The kingdom of heaven suffereth violence, and the violent take it by force." This violence takes in the whole heart. To be double minded is to be unstable. Resolution, self-denial, and consecrated effort are required for the work of preparation. The understanding and the conscience may be united; but if the will is not set to work, we shall make a failure. Every faculty and feeling must be engaged. Ardor and earnest prayer must take the place of listlessness and indifference. Only by earnest, determined effort and faith in the merits of Christ can we overcome, and gain the kingdom of heaven. Our time for work is short. Christ is soon to come the second time. May God help those who have heard the warning message to remember that "the kingdom of heaven suffereth violence, and the violent take it by force."

Mrs. E. G. White

May 31, 1900—The Price of Our Redemption—Part 1

"And the chief priests and all the council sought for witness against Jesus to put him to death, and found none. For many bare false witness against him, but their witness agreed not together. And there arose certain, and bare false witness against him, saying, We heard him say, I will destroy this temple that is made with hands, and within three days I will build another made without hands. But neither so did their witness agree together. And the high priest stood up in the midst, and asked Jesus, saying, Answerest thou nothing? what is it which these witness against thee? But he held his peace, and answered nothing. Again the high priest asked him, and said unto him, Art thou the Christ, the Son of the Blessed?" "I adjure thee by the living God, that thou tell us whether thou be the Christ, the Son of God."

This appeal was made by the first magistrate of the nation--a man occupying the highest position in earthly courts. But Caiaphas was not accepted by God as the high priest. His fitness for this position ended with the garments that he wore. He was incapable and unworthy. His religion was a cloak that hid the deformities of a hard, cruel heart.

Christ knew that Caiaphas was unworthy to occupy the position he did. But knowing this, he responded to the high priest's appeal. He knew that he himself was appointed to his office by God, and there and then he might have glorified himself. He might have exercised a power that would have made his judges quail. But a body of flesh had been prepared for him. Being found in fashion as a man, he humbled himself. The true High Priest stood before the false high priest to be criticized and condemned.

To the charge of the high priest, Jesus said, "Thou hast said: nevertheless, I say unto you, Hereafter shall ye see the Son of man sitting on the right hand of power, and coming in the clouds of heaven." With dignity and assurance were these words spoken; for they fell from the lips of One whose spirit went with them. The only begotten Son of God was the speaker, and into the hearts of his hearers flashed the conviction, "Never man spake like this man."

Weighted with such great results, this was to Christ one of the most wonderful moments of his life. He realized that now all disguise must be swept away. The declaration that he was one with God had been made. He had openly proclaimed himself the Son of God, the One for whom the Jews had so long looked.

"Hereafter shall ye see the Son of man sitting on the right hand of power, and coming in the clouds of heaven." At that day Christ will be the Judge. Every secret thing will be set in the light of God's countenance. What a contrast there will then be between those who have refused Christ and those who have received him as a personal Saviour. Sinners will then see their sins without a shadow to veil or soften their hideousness. So woeful will be the sight, that they will desire to be hidden under the mountains or in the depths of the ocean, if only they may escape the wrath of the Lamb. But those whose life is hid with Christ in God can say: "I believe in him who was condemned at Pilate's bar, and given up to the priests and rulers to be crucified. Look not upon me, a sinner, but look upon my Advocate. There is nothing in me worthy of the love he manifested for me: but he gave his life for me. Behold me in Jesus. He became sin for me, that I might be made the righteousness of God in him."

The idea that there was to be a resurrection of the dead, when all would stand at the bar of God, to be rewarded according to their works, was not a pleasant thought to Caiaphas. He did not wish to think that in the future he would receive sentence according to his works. If there was to be no resurrection, he would flatter himself with the thought that he could securely keep his counsel. But if there was, what a revelation would be made of his dark deeds! There rose before his mind, as on a panorama, the scenes of the final Judgment. For a moment he saw the fearful spectacle of the graves giving up their dead, with secrets he had hoped were hidden forever. For a moment he felt as if he were standing before the eternal Judge, whose all-seeing eye was reading his soul, bringing to light mysteries supposed to be hidden with the dead.

But the scene passed from his vision. Christ's words cut him, a Sadducee, to the quick. He was maddened by satanic fury. Was this man, a prisoner before him, to be allowed to assail his most cherished theories? Rending his robe, that the people might see his horror, he demanded that without further preliminaries the prisoner be condemned for blasphemy. "He hath spoken blasphemy," he said: "what further need have we of witnesses? behold, now ye have heard his blasphemy. What think ye?" "And they all condemned him."

June 7, 1900—The Price of Our Redemption—Part 2

Conviction, mingled with passion, led Caiaphas to rend his robe. He was furious with himself for believing Christ's words; but instead of rending his heart under a deep sense of sin, he rent his priestly robe in determined resistance.

By this act, done to influence the judges to condemn Christ, Caiaphas condemned himself. By the law he was disqualified for the priest's work. A high priest was not to rend his garment. By the Levitical law this was prohibited under sentence of death. Among the Jews it was the general custom for the garments to be rent at the death of friends, but this custom the priests were not to observe. When Aaron lost two of his sons because they did not glorify God, he was forbidden to show sorrow by rending his garments. Moses said to him and to his sons, "Uncover not your heads, neither rend your clothes; lest ye die, and lest wrath come upon all the people."

Everything worn by the high priest was to be whole and without blemish. The pattern of the priestly robes was made known to Moses in the mount. Every article the high priest was to wear, and the way it should be made, were specified. These garments were consecrated to a most solemn purpose. By them was represented the character of the great antitype, Jesus Christ. They covered the priest with glory and beauty, and made the dignity of his office to appear. When clothed with them, the priest presented himself as a representative of Israel, showing by his garments the glory that Israel should reveal to the world as the chosen people of God. Nothing but perfection, in dress and attitude, in spirit and word, would be acceptable to God. He is holy; and his glory and perfection must be represented in the earthly service. nothing but perfection could properly represent the sacredness of the heavenly service. Finite man might rend his own heart by showing a contrite and humble spirit; but no rent must be made in the priestly robes.

The high priest who dared to appear in holy office, and engage in the service of the sanctuary, with a rent robe, was looked upon as having severed himself from God. By rending his garment, he cut himself off from being a representative character. He was no longer accepted by God as the officiating high priest. This course of action, as exhibited by Caiaphas, showed human passion, human imperfection. Caiaphas might truthfully have said of himself, "By our law I ought to die." He might have been arraigned before the Sanhedrin; for he had done the very thing the Lord had commanded should not be done.

By rending his garment, Caiaphas made of none effect the law of God, in order to follow the tradition of men. A man-made law provided that in case of blasphemy a priest might rend his garment in horror at the sin, and be blameless. Thus was the law of God made void by the laws of men.

Each action of the high priest was watched with interest by the people; and Caiaphas thought for effect to show his piety. And by displaying a horror that seemingly caused him to rend his beautiful garments, he gained a fanatical admiration from the people. But he was committing blasphemy. He was reviling the Son of God. Standing under the condemnation of God, he pronounced sentence against Christ as a blasphemer.

This pretended horror for sin has been acted out over and over again in the history of our world. And by exaggerated religious zeal and pretended piety, men will again deceive their fellow men.

The religion of those who crucified Christ was a pretense. The holy vestments of the priests covered hearts that were full of corruption, malignity, and crime. They interpreted gain to be godliness. Caiaphas was not a priest after the order of Melchisedec He never knew what it was to be obedient to God. He had the form of godliness, and this gave him the power to oppress. He acted toward Christ as a priestly judge, an officiating high priest, but he was not this by God's appointment. The priestly robes he rent in order to impress the people with his horror, covered a heart full of wickedness. Though clothed with a gorgeous dress, he was acting under the inspiration of Satan.

The rent garment ended Caiaphas's priesthood. By his own act he disqualified himself for the priestly office. After the condemnation of Christ he was unable to act without showing the most unreasonable passion. His tortured conscience scourged him, but he did not feel that sorrow which leads to repentance.

The act of Caiaphas in rending his garment was significant of the place that the Jewish nation would thereafter occupy toward God. The once favored people of God were separating themselves from him. Christ came to them with a message, but he was despised and rejected. As he stood on the crest of Olivet, he wept over Jerusalem, and lamented her fall. He foresaw the retribution which the deluded, disloyal nation could not, would not, see. The generation among whom he had worked the works of God he addressed as the most guilty, because of the great light they had had. "You have refused to listen to your Redeemer," he declared. "If thou art destroyed, O Jerusalem! thou alone wilt be responsible. Ye would not come unto me, that ye might have life. Ye would none of my counsel, ye despised all my reproof."

When upon the cross Christ cried out, "It is finished!" and the veil of the temple was rent in twain, the Holy Watcher declared that the Jewish people had rejected him who was the antitype of all their types, the substance of all their shadows. Well might Caiaphas rend his official robes, which signified that he claimed to be a representative of the great High Priest; for no longer had they any meaning for him or for the people.

Mrs. E. G. White

June 14, 1900—The Price of Our Redemption—Part 3

After condemning Jesus, the council of the Sanhedrin brought him to Pilate's judgment-hall, to have their sentence confirmed and executed. And there, though declaring, "I find no fault in him," Pilate gave the Saviour up to his accusers. He desired to deliver Jesus; but when he saw that he could not do this and retain his position, he chose, rather than lose worldly power, to sacrifice an innocent life. The priests "were instant with loud voices, requiring that he might be crucified." And "when Pilate saw that he could prevail nothing, but that rather a tumult was made, he took water, and washed his hands before the multitude, saying, I am innocent of the blood of this just person: see ye to it.... And when he had scourged Jesus, he delivered him to be crucified."

Christ was betrayed by Judas, and forsaken and denied by his disciples. He was scorned as a deceiver, and hunted down as one unfit for human sympathy. He was condemned by Pilate, and crowned with thorns. His hands and his feet were pierced with nails as he hung on the cross. Every step onward in the shameful scene was one of intense suffering.

Behold the Son of God suffering on the cross for three terrible hours of agony, enduring the penalty of transgression, in order that repentant, believing ones might have eternal life. And in the darkest hour, when the Saviour was enduring the greatest suffering that Satan could bring to torture his humanity, the Father hid from his Son his face of pity, comfort, and love. Twice, at the baptism and at the transfiguration, the voice of God had been heard proclaiming Christ as his Son. The third time, just before the betrayal, the Father had spoken, witnessing to his Son. But now the voice from heaven was silent. No testimony in the Saviour's favor was heard. Alone he suffered abuse and mockery.

In this trial Christ's heart broke. "My God, my God, why hast thou forsaken me?" he cried.

As the divine Sufferer hung upon the cross, angels gathered about him, and as they looked upon him, and heard his cry, they asked, with intense emotion, "Will not the

Lord Jehovah save him? Will not that soul-piercing cry of God's only begotten Son prevail?" Then were the words spoken: "The Lord hath sworn, and he will not repent. Father and Son are pledged to fulfill the terms of the everlasting covenant. God so loved the world, that he gave his only begotten Son, that whosoever believeth in him should not perish, but have everlasting life."

Christ was not alone in making his great sacrifice. It was the fulfilment of the covenant made between him and his Father before the foundation of the world was laid. With clasped hands they had entered into the solemn pledge that Christ would become the surety for the human race if they were overcome by Satan's sophistry.

After Adam fell, Jesus entered upon the work of redeeming man. In every part his sacrifice was perfect; for he could make a complete atonement for sin. Though he was one with God, yet he made himself of no reputation. He took upon him our nature. "Lo, I come," was his cheerful announcement of the clothing of his divinity with humanity, "to do thy will, O God!" He loved his church, and gave himself for it. "Therefore doth my Father love me," he said to the Pharisees, "because I lay down my life, that I might take it again."

"He saved others; himself he can not save," was the mocking taunt hurled at Christ during the agony of his death on the cross. At any moment he could have saved himself, and come down from the cross; but had he done this, the world would have been given over to the control of the great apostate. It was a marvel to the angels that Christ did not seal with death the lips of the scoffers. It was a marvel to them that he did not flash forth his righteous indignation upon the hardened, corrupt soldiers, as they mocked him, and fixed a crown of thorns on his head. But the Son of God knew that the greatest guilt belonged to the priests and rulers, the representatives of sacred trusts, which they were basely betraying. Pilate, Herod, the Roman soldiers, were ignorant of Jesus. They knew not that he was the sent of God. They thought by abusing him to please the priests and rulers. They had not the light so abundantly given to the Jewish nation. They were unacquainted with Old-Testament history. Had they known what the Jews knew, they would not have treated Jesus as cruelly as they did.

Mrs. E. G. White

June 21, 1900—The Price of Our Redemption—Part 4

Christ was not compelled to endure the cruel treatment inflicted upon him. He was not compelled to undertake the work of redemption,--to step down from his heavenly throne, and come to this earth to receive hatred, abuse, rejection, and a crown of thorns. The humiliation that he endured, he endured voluntarily, to save a world from eternal ruin. He might have continued to abide in the heavenly courts, clothed in garments of purest white, sitting as a prince at God's right hand. Voluntarily he offered himself, a willing sacrifice.

Not one of the angels could have become surety for the human race: their life is God's; they could not surrender it. The angels all wear the yoke of obedience. They are the appointed messengers of Him who is the commander of all heaven. But Christ is equal with God, infinite and omnipotent. He could pay the ransom for man's freedom. He is the eternal, self-existing Son, on whom no yoke had come; and when God asked, "Whom shall I send?" he could reply, "Here am I; send me." He could pledge himself to become man's surety; for he could say that which the highest angel could not say,--I have power over my own life, "power to lay it down, and ... power to take it again."

When Christ uttered the cry, "It is finished," he knew that the battle was won. As a moral conqueror, he planted his banner on the eternal heights. Was there not joy among the angels? Not a son nor a daughter of Adam but could now lay hold on the merits of the spotless Son of God, and say: "Christ has died for me. He is my Saviour. The blood that speaketh better things than that of Abel has been shed. The way into the holiest of all has been made manifest."

God bowed his head satisfied. Now justice and mercy could blend. Now he could be just, and yet the Justifier of all who should believe on Christ. He looked upon the victim expiring on the cross, and said, "It is finished. The human race shall have another trial." The redemption price was paid, and Satan fell like lightning from heaven.

The darkness rolled away from the Saviour and from the cross. Christ bowed his head and died. The compact between Father and Son was fully consummated. Christ had fulfilled his pledge. In death he was more than conqueror. His right hand and his glorious, holy arm had gotten him the victory.

When the loud cry, "It is finished," came from the lips of Christ, the priests were officiating in the temple. The lamb prefiguring Christ has been brought in to be slain. Clothed in his significant and beautiful dress, the priest stands with lifted knife, as did Abraham when about to slay his son. With intense interest the people look on. But the earth trembles and quakes; for the Lord himself draws near. With a rending noise the veil of the temple is torn from top to bottom by an unseen hand, throwing open to the gaze of the multitude a place once filled with the presence of God. In this place the Shekinah once dwelt. Here God had once manifested his glory above the mercy-seat. No one but the high priest ever lifted the veil separating this apartment from the rest of the tabernacle; and he entered in but once a year, to make atonement for the sins of the people. But lo! the veil is rent in twain. No longer is there any secrecy there.

All is terror and confusion. The priest is about to plunge his knife into the heart of the victim; but the knife drops from his hand, and the lamb, no longer fettered, escapes.

By the rending of the veil of the temple, God said, I can no longer reveal my presence in the most holy place. A new and living Way, before which there hangs no veil, is offered to all. No longer need sinful, sorrowing humanity await the coming of the high priest.

Type had met antitype in the death of God's Son. The Lamb of God had been offered as a sacrifice. It was as if a voice had said to the worshipers, "There is now an end to all sacrifices and offerings."

The crucifixion took place at the time of the Passover, and thousands beheld Christ's humiliation. Some look upon this publicity only as shame and defeat. But this God had appointed. The Saviour's work must be deep and thorough. Without shedding of blood there is no remission for sins. Christ must suffer the agony of a public death on the cross, that witness of it might be borne without the shadow of a doubt. It was God's purpose that publicity should be given to the whole transaction, point after point, scene after scene, one phase of the humiliation reaching into another.

June 28, 1900—The Price of Our Redemption—Part 5

At the time of the Passover the Jews and their adherents from far and near were drawn to the Hebrew capital; and it was in God's appointment that the crucifixion took place at this time. Universal interest must be attracted to the plan of redemption. Matters of eternal interest must now become the theme of conversation. The Old Testament must be searched as never before for the evidence of the work and character of the long-looked-for Messiah. Minds must be convicted, and led to ask, "Is not this the Christ?" God knew that every transaction in Christ's life--his trial, his condemnation, his crucifixion, and his resurrection--would become a matter of the deepest interest.

As Adam and Eve were banished from Eden for transgressing the law of God, so Christ was to suffer without the boundaries of the holy place. He died outside the camp, where felons and murderers were executed. There he trod the winepress alone, bearing the penalty that should have fallen on the sinner. How deep and full of significance are the words, "Christ hath redeemed us from the curse of the law, being made a curse for us." He went forth without the camp, thus showing that he gave his life not only for the Jewish nation, but for the whole world.

Look at the superscription above the cross. The Lord arranged it. Written in Hebrew, Greek, and Latin, it is a call for all, Jew and Gentile, bond and free, hopeless, helpless, and perishing, to come. Thus Christ declared to all nations, tongues, and peoples: "I have given my life for you. Look unto me, and be ye saved, all the ends of the earth."

As by his own choice Christ died in the presence of an assembled nation of worshipers, type met antitype. He is a true high priest; for after enduring humiliation, shame, and reproach, after being crucified and buried, he rose from the dead, triumphing over death.

When Christ died on the cross, Satan triumphed, but his triumph was short. The prophecy made in Eden was fulfilled, "I will put enmity between thee and the woman, and between thy seed and her seed; it shall bruise thy head, and thou shalt bruise his heel." Christ was nailed to the cross, but he gained the victory. The whole force of evil gathered itself together in an effort to destroy him who was the Light of the world, the Truth that makes men wise unto salvation. But no advantage was gained by this confederacy. With every advance move, Satan was bringing nearer his eternal ruin. Christ was indeed enduring the contradiction of sinners against himself. But every pang of suffering that he bore helped tear away the foundation of the enemy's kingdom. Satan bruised Christ's heel, but Christ bruised Satan's head. Through death the Saviour destroyed him that had the power of death. In the very act of grasping his prey, death was vanquished; for by dying, Christ brought to light life and immortality through the gospel. Never was the Son of God more beloved by his Father, by the heavenly family, and by the inhabitants of the unfallen worlds, than when he humbled himself to bear disgrace, humiliation, shame, and abuse. By becoming the sin-bearer, he lifted from the human race the curse of sin. In his own body he paid the penalty of that on which the power of Satan over humanity is founded--sin.

Not that sin might become righteousness, and transgression of the law a virtue, did Christ die. He died that sin might be made to appear exceeding sinful, the hateful thing that it is. By his death he became the possessor of the keys of hell and of death. Satan could no longer reign without a rival, and be reverenced as a god. Temples had been erected to him, and human sacrifices offered on his altars. But the emancipation papers of the race have been signed by the blood of the Son of God. A way has been opened for the message of hope and mercy to be carried to the ends of the earth. Now, whosoever will may take hold of God's strength, and make peace with him. The heathen are no longer to be wrapped in the darkness of superstition. The gloom is to disappear before the bright beams of the Sun of righteousness.

"Who is this that cometh from Edom, with dyed garments from Bozrah? this that is glorious in his apparel, traveling in the greatness of his strength? I that speak in righteousness, mighty to save. Wherefore art thou red in thine apparel, and thy garments like him that treadeth in the winefat? I have trodden the winepress alone, and of the people there was none with me." "Arise, shine; for thy light is come, and the glory of the Lord is risen upon thee. For, behold, the darkness shall cover the earth, and gross darkness the people: but the Lord shall arise upon thee, and his glory shall be seen upon thee. And the Gentiles shall come to thy light, and kings to the brightness of thy rising."

Mrs. E. G. White

July 12, 1900—Mary's Offering—Part 1

"Then Jesus six days before the Passover came to Bethany, where Lazarus was which had been dead, whom he raised from the dead. There they made him a supper; and Martha served; but Lazarus was one of them that sat at the table with him. Then took Mary a pound of ointment of spikenard, very costly, and anointed the feet of Jesus, and wiped his feet with her hair: and the house was filled with the odor of the ointment."

The feast at Simon's house brought together many of the Jews; for they knew that Christ was there. They came not only to see Jesus, but many were curious to see one who had been raised from the dead. They thought that Lazarus would have some wonderful experience to relate, and were surprised that he told them nothing. But Lazarus had nothing to tell. The pen of Inspiration has given light upon this subject: "The dead know not anything .... Their love, and their hatred, and their envy, is now perished." Lazarus had a wonderful testimony to bear, however, in regard to the work of Christ. He had been raised from the dead for this purpose. He was a living testimony to the divine power. With assurance and power he declared that Jesus was the Son of God.

Overwhelming evidence had been given to the Jewish leaders in regard to the divinity of Christ, but they had closed their hearts that no light might be admitted. The testimony of Lazarus was so clear and convincing that the priests could not resist it by argument. They could not deny it; for he who had been dead four days stood before them in the vigor of manhood, showing forth the praise of the great Restorer. They feared the effect of this miracle upon the people, "because that by reason of him, many of the Jews went away, and believe on Jesus." If Lazarus continued to bear his testimony, the number of Christ's followers would be greatly increased. They purposed to remove Lazarus secretly, and thus less publicity would be given to the death of Christ. They could bring no charge against Lazarus; but rather than admit evidence that could not denied, they plotted to kill him. The end, they argued, would justify the means. This men will always do when they separate themselves from God.

Unbelief takes possession of the mind; the heart is hardened, and no power can soften it.

At the feast the Saviour sat at the table with Simon, whom he had cured of a loathsome disease, on one side, and Lazarus, whom he had raised from the dead, on the other. Martha served at the table, but Mary was listening earnestly to every word that fell from the lips of Jesus. In his mercy Christ had pardoned Mary's sins, which had been many and grievous. Lazarus, her beloved brother, had been called from the grave, and restored to his family, by the power of the Saviour; and Mary's heart was filled with gratitude. She longed to do him honor. At great personal sacrifice she had purchased an alabaster box of precious ointment, with which to anoint the body of Jesus at his death. Now, taking the box in her hands, she quietly broke it, and poured the contents upon the head and feet of her Master.

Her movements might have passed unnoticed had not the ointment made its presence known by its rich fragrance, and published her act to all present. "When his disciples saw it, they had indignation, saying, To what purpose is this waste?" Judas was the first to make this suggestion, and others were ready to echo his words. Led by him, the disciples continued, "This ointment might have been sold for much, and given to the poor."

These words were the expression of a narrow mind. Judas wished to withhold this expensive favor from Christ, under pretense of helping the poor. He begrudged Christ the gift that he proposed to give to the poor. The world can judge of our knowledge and love of Jesus by the outward expression, the external testimony. Had the all-pervading love of Christ filled the hearts of the disciples, it would have been expressed in action. They would have shown that they recognized his supremacy, and knew him to be worthy the highest homage. But those who should have been first in these offices of love, were last; and Mary, who was considered the least, was first.

Jesus saw Mary shrink away abashed, expecting to hear reproof from the One she loved and worshiped. But instead of this she heard words of commendation. "Why trouble ye the woman?" Christ said, "for she hath wrought a good work upon me. For ye have the poor always with you; but me ye have not always. For in that she hath poured this ointment on my body, she did it for my burial. Verily I say unto you, Wheresoever this gospel shall be preached in the whole world, there shall also this, that this woman hath done, be told for a memorial of her." Her act is a prophetic anticipation of my death, and the record of it shall be repeated to the ends of the earth.

The look that Jesus cast upon the selfish Judas convinced him that the Master had penetrated his hypocrisy, and read his base, contemptible character. This was a more direct reproof than Judas had before received. He was provoked by it, and thus a door was opened through which Satan entered to control his thoughts. Instead of repenting, he planned revenge. Stung by the knowledge of his sin, and provoked to madness because his guilt was known, he rose from the table, and went to the palace of the high priest, where he found the council assembled. He was imbued with the spirit of Satan, and acted like one bereft of reason. The reward promised for the betrayal of his Master was thirty pieces of silver; and for a far less sum than the box of ointment cost he sold the Saviour.

In spirit and practice many resemble Judas. As long as there is silence in regard to the plague-spot in their character, no open enmity is seen; but when they are reproved, bitterness fills their hearts.

What a terrible action was this, both on the part of Judas and of the high priest! The rulers of Israel had been given the privilege of receiving their Saviour; but they refused the precious gift offered them in the tenderest spirit of constraining love. They refused the salvation that is of more value than gold, and bought their Lord for thirty pieces of silver!

The incident is full of instruction. The world's Redeemer was nearing the time when he was to give his life for a sinful world, yet how little even his disciples realized what was before them! Mary could not reason upon this subject; but by the Holy Spirit's power she saw in Jesus one who had come to seek and to save the souls that were ready to perish, and she was filled with a pure, holy love for him. The sentiment of her heart was, "What shall I render unto the Lord for all his benefits toward me?" The ointment, costly as it was, expressed but poorly Mary's love for the Saviour.

Christ delighted in Mary's earnest desire to do the will of her Lord. He accepted the wealth of pure affection that his disciples would not understand. The desire that Mary had to do this service was of more value to Christ than all the precious ointment in the world, because it expressed her appreciation of her Redeemer. It was the love of Christ that constrained her. The matchless excellency of the character of Christ filled her mind and heart, and the ointment was a symbol of the overflowing love of the giver. It was the outward demonstration of a love fed by heavenly springs until it overflowed.

Mrs. E. G. White

July 19, 1900—Mary's Offering—Part 2

The commendation of Christ after the condemnation of the disciples was of inexpressible value to Mary. Christ could appreciate the gift as the expression of Mary's love, and her heart was filled with peace and happiness.

The disciples did not take in the many lessons given in the Scriptures in regard to the faith that works by love and purifies the soul; and the work of Mary was just the lesson they needed to show them that to be more demonstrative in their appreciation of their Lord, would be wholly acceptable to him. He had been everything to them. They did not realize that soon they would be deprived of his presence, that soon they could offer him no token of their appreciation of his love. The loveliness of Christ, separated from the heavenly courts, living a life of humanity, was never understood nor appreciated by the disciples as it should have been. He was often grieved because they did not give him that which he should have received from them. He knew that if they were under the influence of the heavenly angels that accompanied him, they, too, would be inspired with zeal and true devotion, and with entire consecration to the mind and will of God. They would regard no offering of sufficient value to declare the heart's spiritual affection. Their after-knowledge helped them to realize how many things they might have done for Jesus, expressive of the love and gratitude of their hearts, while they were near him, enjoying his counsel. When Jesus was no longer with them, and they felt as sheep without a shepherd, there were many things they began to understand. They saw how they might have offered him attentions and shown him favor on many occasions. Oh, if they could have taken it all back--this censuring, this presenting the poor as more worthy of the gift than Christ! They felt his reproof keenly as they took from the cross the bruised body of their Lord.

The same lack is evident in our world today. But few appreciate all that Christ is to them. If they did, the great and beautiful love of Mary would be expressed--the anointing would be freely bestowed. The expensive ointment would not be called a waste.

Jesus approved of Mary's gift as a testimonial of her love for her Master, who was constantly working in behalf of others, doing good to the poor, and speaking words of comfort to the oppressed. Those who have caught the inspiration of the love that will exist in every heart in the family of the redeemed host, will enter into the joy of their Lord. The spirit of peace and heavenly joy will fill the hearts of those who can appreciate the heavenly Gift. Christ, the world's Redeemer, fills their hearts with love. By faith they are made one with Christ, and their hearts are drawn out to him. They live in Christ, and Christ in them. Nothing is too costly to give him. No self-denial, no self-sacrifice, is too great to be made for his sake.

The words spoken in indignation, "To what purpose is this waste?" brought vividly to the mind of Christ the greatest sacrifice ever made,--the one that could not be surpassed,--the gift of himself to be the propitiation for the sins of a lost world. His entire life had been one of self-denial and self-sacrifice. Declaring his mission in Galilee, he said: "The Spirit of the Lord is upon me, because he hath anointed me to preach the gospel to the poor; he hath sent me to heal the broken-hearted, to preach deliverance to the captives, and recovering of sight to the blind, to set at liberty them that are bruised, to preach the acceptable year of the Lord." The Lord would be so bountiful to his human family that it could be said of him that he could do no more. In the gift of Jesus to the world, he gave all heaven. His love is without a parallel. It did not stop short of anything. And having given us his only begotten Son, will he not with him also freely give us all things?

If left to be judged from a human point of view, such a sacrifice was a wanton waste; and well might the question be asked, Why does the Lord show such waste, such extravagance, in the multitude of his gifts? Well may the heavenly host look with amazement upon the human family, who cling to their rags of self-righteousness, and refuse to be clothed with the robe of Christ's righteousness,--refuse to be uplifted and enriched with the boundless love expressed in Christ. Well may they exclaim, Why is this great waste?

The supposed prodigality of Mary is an illustration of the method of God in the plan of salvation; grace and nature, related to each other, manifest the ennobling fullness of the source from which they flow. To human reason the whole plan of salvation is a waste of mercy. Self-denial and whole-hearted sacrifice meet us everywhere. But they are provided to accomplish the restoration of the moral image of God in man. The atonement for a lost world was to be full, abundant, and complete. Christ's offering was exceedingly abundant, reaching every soul that God had created. It could not be restricted nor measured so as not to exceed the number who would accept the great gift. All men are not saved; yet the plan of salvation is not a waste because it does not accomplish all that its liberality has provided for. There must be enough and to spare.

In the breaking of the alabaster box, in that the ointment filled the whole room with its fragrance, we have a representation of the sacrifice of Christ, which was to fill the whole world with the fragrance of infinite love. This action of Mary is never to lose its fragrance. This, which the disciples called waste, is repeating itself a thousand times to the susceptible hearts of others, telling ever the story of the abundant love of God for a fallen race.

Mrs. E. G. White

July 26, 1900—Our Words

Speech is one of the great gifts of God. It is the means by which the thoughts of the heart are communicated. It is with the tongue that we offer prayer and praise to God. With the tongue we convince and persuade. With the tongue we comfort and bless, soothing the bruised, wounded soul. With the tongue we may make known the wonders of the grace of God. With the tongue we may also utter perverse things, speaking words which sting like an adder.

The tongue is a little member, but the words it frames have great power. The Lord declares, "The tongue can no man tame." It has set nation against nation, and has caused battle and bloodshed. Words have kindled fires that have been hard to quench. They have also brought joy and gladness to many hearts. And when words are spoken because God says, "Speak unto them my words," they often cause sorrow unto repentance.

Of the unsanctified tongue the apostle James writes: "The tongue is a fire, a world of iniquity: so is the tongue among our members, that it defileth the whole body, and setteth on fire the course of nature; and it is set on fire of hell." Satan puts into the mind thoughts that the Christian should never utter. The scornful retort, the bitter, passionate utterance, the cruel, suspicious charge, are from him. How many words are spoken that do only harm to those who speak and those who hear! Hard words beat upon the heart, awaking to life its worst passions. Those who do evil with their tongues, who sow discord by selfish, jealous words, grieve the Holy Spirit; for they are working at cross purposes with God. They are working on lines marked out by the enemy of all good.

The inspired apostle, seeing the inclination to abuse the gift of speech, gives directions concerning its use. "Let no corrupt communication proceed out of your mouth," he says, "but that which is good to the use of edifying." The word "corrupt" means here any word that would make an impression detrimental to holy principles and undefiled religion, any communication that would obscure the view of Christ, and blot from the mind true sympathy and love. It includes impure hints, which, unless instantly resisted, lead to great sin. Upon every one is laid the work of barring the way against corrupt speech.

It is God's purpose that the glory of Christ shall appear in his children. In all his teaching, Christ presented pure principles. He did no sin, neither was guile found in his mouth. Constantly there flowed from his lips holy, ennobling truths. He spoke as never man spoke, with a pathos that touched the heart. He was filled with holy wrath as he saw the Jewish leaders teaching for doctrine the commandments of men, and he spoke to them with the authority of greatness. With terrible power he denounced all artful intrigue, all dishonest practices. He cleansed the temple from its pollution, as he desires to cleanse our hearts from everything bearing any resemblance to fraud. The truth never languished on his lips. With fearlessness he exposed the hypocrisy of priest and ruler, Pharisee and Sadducee. He entered into conversation with high and low, learned and unlearned. He encountered malice, misrepresentation, opposition, and falsehood, yet his whole life was without a flaw. He could say to his enemies, "Which of you convinceth me of sin?"

Guard well the talent of speech; for it is a mighty power for evil as well as for good. You can not be too careful of what you say; for the words you utter show what power is controlling the heart. If Christ rules there, your words will reveal the purity, beauty, and fragrance of a character molded and fashioned by his will. But if you are under the guidance of the enemy of all good, your words will echo his sentiments.

The great responsibility bound up in the use of the gift of speech is plainly made known by the word of God. "By thy words thou shalt be justified, and by thy words thou shalt be condemned," Christ declared. And the psalmist asks: "Lord, who shall abide in thy tabernacle? who shall dwell in thy holy hill? He that walketh uprightly, and worketh righteousness, and speaketh the truth in his heart. He that backbiteth not with his tongue, nor doeth evil to his neighbor, nor taketh up a reproach against his neighbor. In whose eyes a vile person is contemned, but he honoreth them that fear the Lord. He that sweareth to his own hurt, and changeth not. He that putteth not out his money to usury, nor taketh reward against the innocent. He that doeth these things shall never be moved."

"Keep thy tongue from evil, and thy lips from speaking guile." The wild beast of the forest may be tamed; "but the tongue can no man tame." Only through Christ can we gain the victory over the desire to speak hasty, unchristlike words. When, in his strength, we refuse to give utterance to Satan's suggestions, the plant of bitterness in our hearts withers and dies. The Holy Spirit can make the tongue a savor of life unto life.

Mrs. E. G. White

August 2, 1900—Our Influence

From every human being there goes forth an influence that either gathers with Christ or scatters from him. Our every action, our every word, exerts an influence either for good or for ill. This influence affects the eternal destiny of those with whom we associate. Influence and example, when viewed in the light of the cross and in their true relation to eternity, assume infinite importance. A word fitly spoken, an action rightly done, may save a soul from death. Day by day the example we set and the influence we exert are registered in the records going beforehand to judgment.

The child of God must never forget that he is only part of the whole. He is only a thread in the web of humanity. Everything he does makes an impression on his character, and influences others. The letters that are written sow the seeds either of tares or of wheat. Our thoughts, our words, the spirit in which we perform our daily duties,--all act their part in the formation of character.

The daily influence of purity and devotion, the observance of the courtesies of life, unbending integrity and steadfastness, will be to all around us a constant recommendation of our faith. But if those who profess the truth are light and trifling, reckless in their conversation and careless in their deportment, they deny Christ, and the world is made worse by their profession. With less of such advocacy the truth of God would stand higher in the estimation of unbelievers.

It is the duty of every Christian to show himself a true follower of Jesus, loving the truth for the truth's sake, hating every species of impurity, willingly denying self for Christ's sake. The poorest man in this world is rich as long as he preserves his integrity of character. The one who is victorious in life's battle is he who gives himself earnestly and unreservedly to God. The life of such a one is a constant confession of Christ. He who refuses to live for self-pleasing, who will not abate his efforts to live the truth, no matter what difficulties he may meet, walks the earth as a nobleman in his Master's sight. He is constantly doing and saying something to prepare himself and others for the future life. He has the mind of Christ, and in private and public life his light shines with clear, steady rays.

Judicious conversation exerts an influence which is a power for good. But often those who talk much do little deep, earnest thinking, little real work for the Master. Often they neglect those who have little to make life happy, in order to talk about what should be done for the needy and unfortunate. They think that by talking they can make up for their deficiency. They talk, but they fail to show by their actions that they are directed by the Spirit of God. To such the angels of God would say, Not words, but deeds. The daily life tells much more than any number of words. A uniform cheerfulness, tender kindness, Christian benevolence, patience and love, will melt away prejudice, and open the heart to the reception of the truth. It is the doers of the word who are justified before God.

God requires us to put ourselves into his hands without reserve, to obey his directions implicitly. When we take the Lord as our counselor, when we follow him, placing body, soul, and spirit under his control, we can work as Christ worked. Those who make Christ a personal Saviour, seeking him most earnestly in prayer, are enabled by his grace to live true, noble lives. They work in a way which Heaven approves. By unselfish actions they reveal the character of Christ. They realize that they can not afford to lose sight of Christ; for by so doing they give unbelievers an occasion to cast reproach upon the truth.

We are to be courteous to all men, tender-hearted, and sympathetic; for this was the character manifested by Christ when he was upon this earth. The more closely we are united to Christ, the more tender and affectionate we shall be in dealing with one another. The redemption of the fallen race was planned in order that man might be a partaker of the divine nature. When by the grace of Christ we become partakers of this nature, our influence on those around us will be a savor of life unto life. Looking unto Jesus, the author and finisher of our faith, we shall be a blessing to all with whom we come in contact.

Mrs. E. G. White

August 16, 1900—Seed-sowing

In his teaching, Christ called the attention of his hearers to the things of nature, the work of his own hands. He made the trees, the grass, the flowers, that they might teach us precious lessons. Nature was to him a great lesson-book, by which he sought to open the eyes of human beings to the love and power of God.

Nature is a lesson-book to which all, high and low, rich and poor, may have access; and from it the most helpful lessons may be learned. Ever in its varying seasons it repeats its lessons, that by its representations, man may grasp heavenly truth. The apparently commonplace things of earth are silent teachers, instructing us in purity, industry, economy, and patience.

The cultivation of the soil, the sowing of the seed, the care bestowed on the seed by the sower, represent different stages of Christ's work for the soul. First appears the blade, then the ear, then the full corn in the ear.

The man who sows seed apparently throws away that upon which he and his family depend for a living. But he is only giving up a present advantage for a much larger return. He throws the seed away that he may gather it again in an abundant harvest. By faith he may look forward to large returns.

In order for the seed to grow, it must have care; and when man has done his part, this is only the beginning. After man has prepared the soil, and planted the seed, showing care and thoughtfulness in the work, he must depend upon God, the great Husbandman, to send sunshine and showers to water the thirsty ground, and cause the seed to spring up and grow. The combined influence of the Lord's unseen agencies is necessary from the time the seed is buried in the ground till the harvest is gathered.

If we understood better the wonderful work of God in supplying his family on the earth with the necessities of life, we should know more of his power. He employs many unseen agencies to make the seed spring up and grow. It is his power that gives life to the seed. Without his power how could the harvest be perfected? Let man do his utmost, and he must still depend on the Creator, who understands just what is needed for the perfection of the fruit.

Christ taught his disciples to pray, "Give us this day our daily bread." God hears this prayer, and is constantly working to answer it. He makes his sun to shine on the just and on the unjust, and gives to all wind and rain, thunder and lightning. These are God's blessings, sent to purify the atmosphere from injurious, unhealthful agencies, which, if allowed to accumulate, would poison it, and destroy everything that breathes the breath of life.

Christ seeks to lead the mind from the natural seed cast into the ground to the gospel seed, the sowing of which will result in bringing man back to his loyalty. The Saviour came to this world to sow the seed of truth. Like a sower in the field, he scattered the seeds of truth in the hearts of men.

"He that received seed into the good ground is he that heareth the word, and understandeth it; which also beareth fruit, and bringeth forth, some an hundredfold, some sixty, some thirty." Shall the expectation of the sower of the seed be disappointed? God forbid! for it is for the present and future good of the receiver that the seed sown be received into good ground. When it is received in faith, it will spring up and bear fruit.

What does it mean to receive into the heart the good seed?--It means to receive the words of Christ. This is a remedy for sin. Some give the truth a partial reception, a half-sympathy, wishing at the same time they had never heard it. In such soil Satan sows his seed, and soon there is a growth of thorns, which chokes the good seed. But when the gospel seed is sown in soil that welcomes it, when it is incorporated with the life, direct and glorious results are seen,--results that testify to the infinite love of God and the transforming power of the gospel.

It means much to receive the good seed. In Luke we read, "That on the good ground are they, which in an honest and good heart, having heard the word, keep it, and bring forth fruit with patience." An honest heart is a heart, which, when the light shines into it, acknowledges that sin is the transgression of the law. "Take heed how ye hear," said the Great Teacher. What will it avail to spend the life in self-deception? When truth is received into the heart, the tares growing there are uprooted. The appeals of God to the conscience are no longer turned aside as of no consequence.

All who receive the word into good and honest hearts will bring forth fruit. In their hearts will spring up the precious fruits of the Spirit,--love, joy, peace, long-suffering, gentleness, goodness, faith, meekness, temperance.

Mrs. E. G. White

September 6, 1900—A Lesson From Daniel's Experience

God helps those who place themselves where they can be best qualified for his service. Divine power unites with the efforts of the earnest seeker for truth, giving him the fitness he needs for God's work. Daniel placed himself in right relation to God, and to his outward circumstances and opportunities. He was taken a captive to Babylon, and with others was placed under training to be prepared for a place in the king's court. His food and drink were appointed him; but we read that he determined not to defile himself with the king's meat, nor with the wine which he drank.

In taking this step, Daniel did not act rashly. He knew that by the time he was called to appear before the king, the advantage of healthful living would be apparent. Cause would be followed by effect. Daniel said to Melzar, who had been given charge of him and his companions: "Prove thy servants, I beseech thee, ten days; and let them give us pulse to eat and water to drink." Daniel knew that ten days would be time enough to prove the benefit of abstemiousness. "Then let our countenances be looked upon before thee, and the countenance of the children that eat of the portion of the king's meat: and as thou seest, deal with thy servants. So he consented to them in this matter, and proved them ten days. And at the end of ten days their countenances appeared fairer and fatter in flesh than all the children which did eat the portion of the king's meat."

Having done this, Daniel and his companions did still more. They did not choose as companions those who were agents of the prince of darkness. They did not go with a multitude to do evil. They secured Melzar as their friend, and there was no friction between him and them. They went to him for advice, and at the same time enlightened him by the wisdom of their deportment.

It was God's purpose that these youth should become channels of light to the kingdom of Babylon. Satan was determined to defeat this purpose. He worked upon the minds of the youth who had refused to be God's representatives, causing them to be jealous of Daniel and his companions. At Satan's suggestion they laid plans to entrap those who were making such steady, rapid advancement in knowledge. They tried to mislead and deceive the Hebrew youth, endeavoring by flattery to lead them into wrong. But they failed signally, because these youth had on the armor of light; they fastened themselves to the promise, "Let him take hold of my strength, that he may make peace with me; and he shall make peace with me."

Daniel and his friends knew that they must keep the eye single to the glory of God, seek wisdom and strength and grace from on high, and not allow themselves to be led, by smiles or frowns, to yield to the sophistry of Satan. They knew that no human power could be to them wisdom and righteousness and sanctification. Satan was trying to compass their destruction. Nothing but the wisdom and strength and firmness and heroism that God could give would enable them to maintain their position in the way of holiness. They knew that they were not yet fully acquainted with the character of Satan's enmity. They would have to watch unto prayer; for they were ignorant of the obstacles they would have to surmount. They knew that barriers would rise in their way, that embarrassment would surround them on every side.

They made a faithful study of the word of God, that they might know the divine will. By faith they believed that the One whom they served would communicate to them his will; and in answer to their faith God opened his will to them. The word of God was to them a light shining in a dark place. They made that word their text-book, looking upon it as the foundation upon which they must build character. They had only a part of the Old Testament. The youth of today have increased light. The Bible teaches the whole duty of men, women, and children.

Divine wisdom came to Daniel and his companions as they studied God's word. They knew that it was their authority, and that it demanded their obedience. The truth was to them of the highest importance; for it placed their duty before them in a clear light.

Satan often cast his shadow across their pathway, to obscure their view of divine light, and darken their faith and confidence in God. But they would not yield, and the Lord gave them wisdom and power to prevail with him in prayer. As they followed the course of study outlined for them in the courts of Babylon, they made it their aim to become statesmen who would never sacrifice principle in order to obtain advantages for themselves. They knew that they were in an enemy's country, under the power of the Babylonian king; and they were obedient in all things save where they were asked to sacrifice truth.

"Now at the end of the days that the king had said he should bring them in, then the prince of the eunuchs brought them in before Nebuchadnezzar. And the king communed with them; and among them all was found none like Daniel, Hananiah, Mishael, and Azariah: therefore stood they before the king. And in all matters of wisdom and understanding, that the king inquired of them, he found them ten times better than all the magicians and astrologers that were in all his realm."

He who gave wisdom and understanding to Daniel is willing to give wisdom and understanding to all who place themselves in the same relation to him that Daniel did. None need have a superficial education. Read how Paul enjoined on Timothy constancy and perseverance in the faithful performance of duty. "Thou therefore, my son," he wrote, "be strong in the grace that is in Christ Jesus.... Study to show thyself approved unto God, a workman that needeth not to be ashamed, rightly dividing the word of truth." Work for God with humility and earnestness, teaching truth from love to God and man. Untold good is accomplished by the faithful, humble Christian, who prays, and then lives his prayers.

Mrs. E. G. White

September 13, 1900—A Sin-pardoning Saviour—Part 1

Christ came to this world to reveal the Father, to give to mankind a true knowledge of God. He came to manifest the love of God. Without a knowledge of God, humanity would be eternally lost. Without divine help, men and women would sink lower and lower. Life and power must be imparted by him who made the world.

The promise made in Eden,--the seed of the woman shall bruise the serpent's head,--was the promise of the Son of God, through whose power alone could the counsel of God be fulfilled and the knowledge of God be imparted.

God made the promise to Abraham, "In thee shall all families of the earth be blessed." To Abraham was unfolded God's purpose for the redemption of the race. The Sun of righteousness shone upon him, and his darkness was scattered. Christ declared, "Your father Abraham rejoiced to see my day: and he saw it, and was glad."

Jacob declared: "The scepter shall not depart from Judah, nor a lawgiver from between his feet, until Shiloh come, and unto him shall the gathering of the people be."

To Moses God talked face to face, as a man talks with a friend. On him shone the light regarding the Saviour. He said to the people: "The Lord thy God will raise up unto thee a Prophet from the midst of thee, of thy brethren, like unto me; unto him shall ye hearken."

The sacrifices and offerings told their story of the coming Saviour, who was to be offered up for the sins of the world. They pointed forward to a better service than theirs, when God would be worshiped in spirit and truth and in the beauty of holiness.

In the Jewish service was typified the atonement demanded by the broken law. The victim, a lamb without spot or blemish, represented the world's Redeemer, who is so holy and so efficient that he can take away the sin of the world.

To David was given the promise that Christ should reign forever and ever, and that of his kingdom there should be no end.

The Hebrews lived in an attitude of expectancy, looking for the promised Messiah. Many died in faith, not having received the promises; but having seen them afar off, they believed and confessed that they were strangers and pilgrims on the earth.

God prepared the way for the coming of his Son by scattering the Old Testament Scriptures among heathen and idolaters. Divine power went with the Word. It carried with it the evidence of its power; for it bore the divine credentials.

Thus the way was prepared for the great Teacher. "But when the fullness of time was come, God sent forth his Son." Christ came to teach lessons that would echo and re-echo from generation to generation. The teaching of the rabbis consisted of a monotonous repetition of maxims and traditions. Christ spoke with an assurance that impressed his hearers. His whole being was charged with divine love. His heart was filled with sympathy for mental and physical distress, which he met wherever he went. He bore a living testimony that he came not to destroy life, but to save it. By look and word he drew men to himself. Sympathy and love flowed from him to the distressed and suffering. The beauty of his countenance and the loveliness of his character attracted the people. No sooner did they look upon his face, and hear his gracious words, than their hearts were filled with a warm glow of love.

The truth that had been given to patriarchs and prophets Christ rescued from the rubbish, and presented to the people in a way that made it seem like new truth. He also gave them many new truths, spoken on his own authority.

Mrs. E. G. White

September 20, 1900—A Sin-pardoning Saviour—Part 2

Christ's lessons reveal a high and holy purpose; but this purpose the blinded, bigoted Pharisees could not discern. Neither could they turn him from his appointed work. He announced in Nazareth: "The Spirit of the Lord is upon me, because he hath anointed me to preach the gospel to the poor; he hath sent me to heal the brokenhearted, to preach deliverance to the captives, and recovering of sight to the blind, to set at liberty them that are bruised, to preach the acceptable year of the Lord."

In spite of the opposition of the Jewish leaders, Christ went about doing good, healing the sick, and comforting the afflicted. He raised the ruler's daughter to life; "and the fame hereof went abroad into all that land. And when Jesus departed thence, two blind men followed him, crying, and saying, Thou Son of David, have mercy on us. And when he was come into the house, the blind men came to him: and Jesus saith unto them, Believe ye that I am able to do this? They said unto him, Yea, Lord. Then touched he their eyes, saying, According to your faith be it unto you. And their eyes were opened; and Jesus straitly charged them, saying, See that no man know it. But they, when they were departed, spread abroad his fame in all that country."

"As they went out, behold, they brought to him a dumb man possessed with a devil. And when the devil was cast out, the dumb spake: and the multitudes marveled, saying, It was never so seen in Israel."

The scribes and Pharisees had asked Christ to show them a sign. Christ had refused, saying that no sign should be given them. He wrought miracles that sent conviction to the hearts of the unprejudiced. As the people beheld these miracles, they expressed their wonder and amazement at the great power of God. The scribes and Pharisees saw that the people were convicted, and with lowering countenances they came to Christ and said: "Show us a sign; work a miracle for us." They did not make this request because they wished for evidence. They had rejected the greatest evidence that God could give, saying of Christ, "He casteth out devils through the prince of the devils." This was the sin against the Holy Ghost, which hath forgiveness neither in this world nor in the world which is to come.

Today Christ is inviting us, "Come unto me, ... and I will give you rest." He waits to raise to newness of life those who are dead in trespasses and sins. But he uses no compulsion. He employs no external force. We are left free to act as we choose. If we turn from disloyalty, and place ourselves under the banner of Christ, it is because that of our own free will we choose to do this.

The expulsion of sin is the act of the soul itself. In its great need the soul cries out for a power out of and above itself; and through the operation of the Holy Spirit the nobler powers of the mind are imbued with strength to break away from the bondage of sin.

When man surrenders to Christ, the mind is brought under the control of the law, but it is the royal law, which proclaims liberty to every captive. Only by becoming one with Christ can men be made free. Subjection to the will of Christ means restoration to perfect manhood. Sin can triumph only by enfeebling the mind and destroying the liberty of the soul.

Do you realize your sinfulness? Do you despise sin? Then remember that the righteousness of Christ is yours if you will grasp it. Can you not see what a strong foundation is placed beneath your feet when you accept Christ? God has accepted the offering of his Son as a complete atonement for the sins of the world.

Mrs. E. G. White

September 27, 1900—We Are His Witnesses—Part 1

For three years and a half the disciples of Christ were learning lessons from the greatest Teacher the world ever knew. As Christ's work of ministry drew to a close, and he knew that he would soon leave them to work without his personal presence, he sought to encourage and prepare them for this work. He knew also that they would meet with persecution and loss, and he would prepare them for these. "If the world hate you," he said, "ye know that it hated me before it hated you. If ye were of the world, the world would love his own: but because ye are not of the world, but I have chosen you out of the world, therefore the world hateth you. Remember the word that I said unto you, The servant is not greater than his lord. If they have persecuted me, they will also persecute you; if they have kept my saying, they will keep yours also. But all these things will they do unto you for my name's sake, because they know not him that sent me.... But when the Comforter is come, whom I will send unto you from the Father, even the Spirit of truth, which proceedeth from the Father, he shall testify of me: and ye also shall bear witness, because ye have been with me from the beginning."

Christ left a great work in the hands of his followers, but he left this promise with them: "Lo, I am with you alway, even unto the end of the world." In his prayer to the Father for them, he said: "I pray not that thou shouldest take them out of the world, but that thou shouldest keep them from the evil.... Sanctify them through thy truth; thy word is truth.... Neither pray I for these alone, but for them also which shall believe on me through their word." The lesson that Christ wished to impress indelibly on the minds of his followers was the importance of the agency of the Holy Spirit, and the field of usefulness that would open before them through the influence of this gift.

The parting interview of Christ with his disciples was an occasion of deepest interest. Clustering around him, a lonely company, expecting they knew not what, they were saddened as they realized that their beloved Master and Friend was soon to be separated from them. During the three years he had been with them, they had looked to him for guidance in all their difficulties, and for comfort in all their sorrows and disappointments, and they were greatly oppressed at thought of parting from him. Forebodings of evil filled their hearts, but the words of Christ were full of hope: "Let not your heart be troubled: ye believe in God, believe also in me. In my Father's house are many mansions: if it were not so, I would have told you. I go to prepare a place for you. And if I go and prepare a place for you, I will come again, and receive you unto myself; that where I am, there ye may be also." Christ's only thought was to offer consolation to his followers. He knew that in their coming trials their faith would be terribly shaken, and he appealed to them to believe in God as they had believed in him.

For forty days after his resurrection, Christ remained on earth, comforting his disciples, and opening to them the Scriptures. "Thus it is written," he said, "and thus it behooved Christ to suffer, and to rise from the dead the third day: and that repentance and remission of sins should be preached in his name among all nations, beginning at Jerusalem. And ye are witnesses of these things."

"And he led them out as far as to Bethany, and he lifted up his hands, and blessed them." As he stood on the mount of Olives, his hands outstretched in blessing, a cloud descended, and received him out of their sight. As the disciples watched to catch the last glimpse of their ascending Lord, two angels stood by them, who inquired: "Ye men of Galilee, why stand ye gazing up into heaven? this same Jesus, which is taken up from you into heaven, shall so come in like manner as ye have seen him go into heaven." Thus the disciples were encouraged with the promise that their Master would come again. They returned to Jerusalem with great joy, not because they had lost the companionship of their Lord, but because of the promise that he would come again. This was a precious thought to them in the trying future.

Mrs. E. G. White

October 4, 1900—We Are His Witnesses—Part 2

In their very first work, the disciples met with trial and persecution, even as Christ had forewarned them. As Peter and John went up to the temple at the hour of prayer, a lame man who was daily carried to the gate Beautiful to petition help from the worshipers who came thither, asked alms of them. "And Peter, fastening his eyes upon him with John, said, Look on us. And he gave heed unto them, expecting to receive something of them. Then Peter said, Silver and gold have I none; but such as I have give I thee: In the name of Jesus Christ of Nazareth rise up and walk. And he took him by the right hand, and lifted him up: and immediately his feet and ankle bones received strength. And he leaping up stood, and walked, and entered with them into the temple, walking, and leaping, and praising God. And all the people saw him walking and praising God: and they knew that it was he which sat for alms at the Beautiful gate of the temple: and they were filled with wonder and amazement at that which had happened unto him. And as the lame man which was healed held Peter and John, all the people ran together unto them in the porch that is called Solomon's, greatly wondering."

Then Peter and John preached Christ to the people, saying: "The God of Abraham, and of Isaac, and of Jacob, the God of our fathers, hath glorified his Son Jesus; whom ye delivered up, and denied him in the presence of Pilate, when he was determined to let him go. But ye denied the Holy One and the Just, and desired a murderer to be granted unto you; and killed the Prince of Life, whom God hath raised from the dead; whereof we are witnesses.... And as they spake unto the people, the priests, and the captain of the temple, and the Sadducees, came upon them, being grieved that they taught the people, and preached through Jesus the resurrection from the dead. And they laid hands on them, and put them in hold unto the next day."

The next day the disciples were brought before the high priest and elders and scribes, who demanded by what name or power they had healed the lame man. "Then Peter, filled with the Holy Ghost, said unto them, Ye rulers of the people, and elders of Israel, if we this day be examined of the good deed done to the impotent man, by what means he is made whole; be it known unto you all, and to all the people of Israel, that by the name of Jesus Christ of Nazareth, whom ye crucified, whom God raised from the dead, even by him doth this man stand here before you whole. This is the stone which was set at naught of you builders, which is become the head of the corner. Neither is there salvation in any other: for there is none other name under heaven given among men, whereby we must be saved.

"Now when they saw the boldness of Peter and John, and perceived that they were unlearned and ignorant men, they marveled; and they took knowledge of them, that they had been with Jesus. And beholding the man which was healed standing with them, they could say nothing against it. But when they had commanded them to go aside out of the council, they conferred among themselves, saying, What shall we do to these men? for that indeed a notable miracle hath been done by them is manifest to all them that dwell in Jerusalem; and we can not deny it. But that it spread no further among the people, let us straitly threaten them, that they speak henceforth to no man in this name. And they called them, and commanded them not to speak at all nor teach in the name of Jesus. But Peter and John answered and said unto them, Whether it be right in the sight of God to hearken unto you more than unto God, judge ye. For we can not but speak the things which we have seen and heard. So when they had further threatened them, they let them go, finding nothing how they might punish them, because of the people: for all men glorified God for that which was done."

Mrs. E. G. White

October 11, 1900—We Are His Witnesses—Part 3

The Lord continued to bless his followers as they bore their testimony. Believers were added to the church, the sick were healed, and wonderful works were wrought, "insomuch that they brought forth the sick into the streets, and laid them on beds and couches, that at the least the shadow of Peter passing by might overshadow some of them. There came also a multitude out of the cities round about unto Jerusalem, bringing sick folks, and them which were vexed with unclean spirits: and they were healed every one."

Here were light and evidence that none could gainsay. But did these signs have weight with the priests and rulers?--No; they were filled with indignation, and laid their hands on the apostles, and put them in the common prison. Satan was striving to make of none effect the work of Christ, to blot his name from the earth. But Heaven was determined to give evidence to the people that Jesus was the Son of God. An angel of the Lord was commissioned to go to the prison, and say to the disciples, "Go, stand and speak in the temple to the people all the words of this life."

Will the disciples obey the voice of God, or the voice of the men who have taken it upon themselves to close the door against knowledge and truth? "And when they heard that, they entered into the temple early in the morning, and taught. But the high priest came, and they that were with him, and called the council together, and all the senate of the children of Israel, and sent to the prison to have them brought. But when the officers came, and found them not in the prison, they returned, and told, saying, The prison truly found we shut with all safety, and the keepers standing without before the doors: but when we had opened, we found no man within. Now when the high priest and the captain of the temple and the chief priests heard these things, they doubted of them whereunto this would grow. Then came one and told them, saying, Behold, the men whom ye put in prison are standing in the temple, and teaching the people. Then went the captain with the officers, and brought them without violence: for they feared the people, lest they should have been stoned. And when they had brought them, they set them before the council; and the high priest asked them, saying, Did not we straitly command you that ye should not teach in this name? and, behold, ye have filled Jerusalem with your doctrine, and intend to bring this man's blood upon us."

Then the disciples told how the angel of God had released them from prison, and had bidden them go and preach Jesus to the people. "We ought to obey God rather than men," they said. These faithful witnesses had a testimony to bear; for light from heaven had flashed upon them. "The God of our fathers," they fearlessly declared, "raised up Jesus, whom ye slew and hanged on a tree. Him hath God exalted with his right hand to be a Prince and a Saviour, for to give repentance to Israel, and forgiveness of sins. And we are his witnesses of these things; and so is also the Holy Ghost, whom God hath given to them that obey him."

When these words were spoken, "they were cut to the heart." But was their spirit softened? Did they repent of their wicked rejection of the Son of God?--No; the same spirit that had prompted them to action against Christ still raged in them, to silence the voice of the apostles. "They took counsel to slay them." But there was one man in the council who recognized the voice of God in the word spoken to them. This man, Gamaliel, a doctor of the law, "commanded to put the apostles forth a little space." He well knew the elements he had to deal with. He knew that the murderers of Christ would hesitate at nothing, if only they might carry out their purposes. "Ye men of Israel," he said, "take heed to yourselves what ye intend to do as touching these men.... Refrain from these men, and let them alone: for if this counsel or this work be of men, it will come to naught: but if it be of God, ye can not overthrow it; lest haply ye be found even to fight against God.

"And to him they agreed: and when they had called the apostles, and beaten them, they commanded that they should not speak in the name of Jesus, and let them go. And they departed from the presence of the council, rejoicing that they were counted worthy to suffer shame for his name. And daily in the temple, and in every house, they ceased not to teach and preach Jesus Christ."

Paul and Silas were imprisoned because they proclaimed the truth that Christ had bidden them teach. Many stripes were laid upon them, and their feet were placed in the stocks. But they did not think of murmuring. They did not say, It does not pay to preach Christ. Instead, they sang praises to God, that they were counted worthy to suffer shame for his name. All heaven was interested in these men who were suffering for Christ's sake, and angels were sent to visit the prisoners. At their tread the prison doors were shaken open, and a bright light flooded the prison. The jailer awoke, and supposing the men to have escaped, was about to take his own life. But Paul cried out, "Do thyself no harm; for we are all here." Then the jailer hastened into the prison, to see what manner of men these were whom he had treated so severely; and casting himself before them, he asked their forgiveness. "Sirs, what must I do to be saved?" he asked. "And they said, Believe on the Lord Jesus Christ, and thou shalt be saved, and thy house. And they spake unto him the word of the Lord, and to all that were in his house."

The apostles did not wait until they were refreshed, and their wounds were dressed, before they began their work. This is not the spirit manifested by the natural heart; but Paul and Silas had the spirit of Christ, not the spirit of revenge. And the jailer "took them the same hour of the night, and washed their stripes; and was baptized, he and all his, straightway."

We have a work to do in presenting Christ. We need to talk of Christ, and the practical lessons he gave, until our hearts are warmed with the love of God. We should not make much of the trials and opposition we meet. It is true they may close the door of influence for a time, but it will open to us the wider after a little. The work for us to do is rightly to represent our faith in our life and character as well as in our words. By living faith we must cling to the promises of God.

Christ says of his people, "Ye are the light of the world." Let your light shine amid the moral darkness. You need the Spirit of Christ to dwell in your hearts by faith, if you would be prepared to teach men the way to heaven.

Mrs. E. G. White

October 18, 1900—Love Not the World

"Behold, what manner of love the Father hath bestowed upon us, that we should be called the sons of God; therefore the world knoweth us not, because it knew him not."

Christ's life on earth was the embodiment of purity and holiness. He was in the world, but not of the world. The world did not understand him. His life of self-sacrifice was to them a mystery. He lived a life apart from them. Had he united with them in eager pursuit for applause, for riches, for worldly honor, they would have known him; for he would have been of them.

Christ was the Light of the world, but the world knew him not; and because it knew him not, it knows not his followers. We can not follow Jesus, and keep the friendship of the world. True Christians will take Christ as their pattern, loving him with the whole heart, and serving him with the entire being.

"Ye can not serve God and mammon." "Know ye not that the friendship of the world is enmity with God? Whosoever therefore will be a friend of the world is the enemy of God." There must be an entire surrender on the part of the Christian, a complete forsaking and turning away from the things of the world. God's word declares, "If any man love the world, the love of the Father is not in him."

Christ has given us an example of how we should work. He did not come to this world to save the righteous: there were no righteous. He came to call sinners to repentance, to save those who felt their need of a Saviour. He identifies his interests with the interests of all who will receive his grace.

Christ labored to save men from delusion. To this end his servants must work. God has given to every man a measure of light, and he is to let this light shine forth to others. No Christian lives to himself. He who is devoted to self-serving is not learning of the divine Teacher, though he may profess to be a Christian.

Unless truth leads to right actions, it proves only the condemnation of the hearer. Truth is to be woven into the daily experience, controlling the life, making us pure, even as Christ is pure. We may know without doubt who are the true sons and daughters of God. And "every man that hath this hope in him purifieth himself, even as he is pure." As Christ is pure in his sphere, so man may be pure in his sphere.

Conformity to the world is decidedly forbidden in the word of God. Paul writes: "I beseech you therefore, brethren, by the mercies of God, that ye present your bodies a living sacrifice, holy, acceptable unto God, which is your reasonable service. And be not conformed to this world: but be ye transformed by the renewing of your mind."

The mighty power of the Holy Spirit is a cleaver which separates men from the world, and sends them forth as missionaries for God into the highways and byways of life, to seek and to save lost, perishing souls, to minister to the physical and spiritual needs of suffering humanity. Thus Christ worked, and he says to us, "Learn of me." "Love not the world, neither the things that are in the world.... For all that is in the world, the lust of the flesh, and the lust of the eyes, and the pride of life, is not of the Father, but is of the world."

We can either honor or deny Christ. His work was to reveal to the world the glorious perfection of God. This is also our work. We are not to shut ourselves away from the world to escape from it. Christ's prayer to God in behalf of his disciples was, "Not that thou shouldest take them out of the world, but that thou shouldest keep them from the evil." We have a work to do--the work of seeking for lost souls. If you are necessarily associated with worldlings, remember that Christ is to be honored as your companion, your leader, your wisdom and sanctification. He says, "I am at your right hand to help you." The child of God must not allow himself to be guided or governed by human wisdom; for this always leads from the path of self-denial and cross-bearing cast up for the ransomed of the Lord to walk in. The undivided affections must be given to God. It is for our eternal welfare to stand with him who is "the way, the truth, and the life." "Whosoever will come after me," Christ said, "let him deny himself, and take up his cross, and follow me."

John thought it an honor of infinite importance for men to be called the sons of God, to be acknowledged by the Creator of the universe as his children. In comparison with this, all other honor sinks into insignificance. If our names are even mentioned with favor by the great men of this earth, we think it a matter of sufficient importance to cherish, yes, and tell again and again, that others may see how we have been honored. But the lips that give us this supposed honor are only mortal. Dust they are, and to dust they must return. Our names may be uttered with joy by the lips of Christ. It is our privilege to be honored by him who is King over all kings. If we are faithful, the eternal God will claim us as his sons and daughters. Then is it any condescension on our part to receive Christ?

John holds up before us the infinite sacrifice made in our behalf, and points us to the infinite possibilities that lie before us. "Behold, what manner of love the Father hath bestowed upon us, that we should be called the sons of God." We may enter into this sacred relationship. No pen can describe the honor this will bring to us. Many act as if it were a great humiliation to accept Christ as their Saviour. But there is no true honor except that which comes through Christ. Our highest good is found in following his example. We meet with many failures because we do not realize this. If we lift the cross cheerfully, Christ will guide us by his counsel, and afterward receive us into glory. "It doth not yet appear what we shall be: but we know that when he shall appear, we shall be like him; for we shall see him as he is."

Mrs. E. G. White

October 25, 1900—Words to the Youth

"Remember now thy Creator in the days of thy youth, while the evil days come not, nor the years draw nigh, when thou shalt say, I have no pleasure in them."

Early piety insures to its possessor the full enjoyment of all that makes life happy, and will give him a right to the future, immortal life. Those who seek God early have the assurance that they shall find him. Those who wait until the span of life is almost ended before they seek God, lose a life of pure, elevated happiness,--happiness that never comes in the pursuit of the pleasures that this life affords. Those who have been long acquainted with God, who from their youth have drawn their happiness from the pure fountain of heaven, are prepared to enter the family of God.

Good and evil are set before the youth of today. They are left free to choose which they will. In yielding to Satan, they give up eternal happiness for pleasures which are vain and fleeting. That which he promises them they never obtain; for the path of sin is a path of sorrow.

The youth who fear God will make a conscientious use of their time. They will have firm reliance upon God, and will look to him for help when exposed to temptations which would lead them away from moral rectitude. Divine aid must combine with human effort, in order that the wily foe may be resisted. The youth who desire to become qualified for a life of usefulness must be able to resist temptation and battle against wrong. They must cultivate the mind, so that when they leave school, their time will not be spent in idleness. The heavens may be to them a study-book, from which they may learn lessons of intense interest. The moon and the stars may be their companions, speaking to them in the most eloquent language of the love of God.

God expects us to build characters in accordance with the pattern set before us. We are to lay brick by brick, adding grace to grace, finding our weak points, and correcting them in accordance with the directions given. When a crack is seen in the walls of a mansion, we know that something about the building is wrong. In our character-building, cracks are often seen. Unless these defects are remedied, the house will fall when the tempest of trial beats upon it.

In the work of character-building we need the help of the Holy Spirit. Then the building will grow in symmetrical proportions. "Ye are God's husbandry, ye are God's building." Keep looking to Jesus. Never seek for praise or self-glorification. Strive, by watchfulness and prayer, to build up a Christian character, perfect in all its parts. Remember that you are building for eternity. Be careful how you build. Day by day we need to realize the necessity of being converted. Do not stand on the line of demarcation, trying to balance between Christ and the world. Keep in the path cast up for the ransomed of the Lord. By beholding Jesus, you will become changed into his likeness. Your views will be enlarged. You will see the excellence of the truth as it is in Jesus. Your conceptions will be clearer. You will be imbued with the Spirit of God. You will not seek praise from men; you will exalt Christ, saying, "He must increase, but I must decrease."

We can not afford to lose eternal life because we are not willing to separate from the world. Self must be hidden in Christ. Our sight must be filled with a view of his perfection. We must stand wholly on the Lord's side, remembering the word, "We are laborers together with God." God desires us to learn in the school of Christ to be meek and lowly in heart. Self is to be crucified, with the affections and lusts. There is no second probation for fallen man. Heaven is not the place for overcoming defects in the character. God says to us now: "Work out your own salvation with fear and trembling. For it is God which worketh in you both to will and to do of his good pleasure." But let no one think that in his own strength he can leave off sinful practices and accustomed indulgences; and then, after he has made himself good, come to Jesus. Christ says, "Without me ye can do nothing." No man can, in his own strength, repent of and forsake his sin. It is God who leads him to repentance. All outward manifestations of repentance are vain unless God first works within. Then it is that man becomes a partaker of the divine nature. God and Christ work unitedly for the restoration of the divine image in man, furnishing him with power to distinguish between right and wrong.

Acting as our high priest and intercessor, Christ prepared and presented to God the sacrifice which paid the ransom for sin. It is Christ who draws the sinner to God, who constrains him to acknowledge the Father's goodness and love. To those who represent the Father as a frowning Judge, whose work it is to condemn and destroy, he says: "Ye know not what manner of spirit ye are of. For the Son of man is not come to destroy men's lives, but to save them."

Christ has manifested himself as the way, the truth, and the life. Earnestly and untiringly he seeks to save those who are lost. No one can return to the fold without the drawing of the Holy Spirit. Christ supplies all the opportunities and privileges: and unless the sinner responds to his overtures of mercy, laying hold of the promises, he can not be saved. With every power given him, he must respond to God's working. He must accept all the help offered. He must believe and obey. He must make the most of every opportunity, working diligently and conscientiously. As he works thus, he becomes a partner in the heavenly firm. Daily he grows in grace and in the knowledge of Christ.

Our success in perfecting Christian characters will be proportionate to the zeal and earnestness with which we seek for godliness. Every soul who enters the gates of the city of God will be like Jesus. Being good and doing good are indispensable to the perfection of character. No man lives to himself. All who gain the precious boon of immortality will follow the example of Christ, who went about doing good, who cheerfully gave up his life to ransom those ready to perish.

November 1, 1900—God's Care for His Children

Under the reign of Darius, Daniel was exalted to a position of great honor, because the king saw in him an "excellent spirit." But when the leading men of the kingdom saw Daniel thus favored, they became jealous of him, and soon envied and hated him. His course of unbending integrity was in marked contrast to their own lives. The more upright and righteous he was, the more they hated him. Long they sought to find something whereby he might be condemned. It angered them to think that they could lay nothing to his charge. But he was prime minister of the kingdom, and they knew they would have to prove any charge they brought against him.

Daniel's position was not an enviable one. He stood at the head of a dishonest, prevaricating, godless cabinet, whose members watched him with keen, jealous eyes, to find some flaw in his conduct. They kept spies on his track, to see if they could not in this way find something against him. Satan suggested to these men a plan whereby they might get rid of Daniel. Use his religion as a means of condemning him, the enemy said.

Daniel was a man of prayer. Three times a day he knelt before the Lord; and Satan told his enemies that his destruction must be compassed on this ground.

A large number of the princes and nobles were in the secret, but the king was kept in ignorance of their purpose, they went to him, and asked him, in honor of his kingly dignity, to pass a decree commanding that for thirty days no one in the kingdom should ask anything of any god save Darius.

"All the presidents of the kingdom, the governors, and the princes, the counselors, and the captains have consulted together," they said, "to establish a royal statute, and to make a firm decree, that whosoever shall ask a petition of any god or man for thirty days, save of thee, O king, he shall be cast into the den of lions. Now, O king, establish the decree, and sign the writing, that it be not changed, according to the law of the Medes and Persians, which altereth not."

The king's vanity was flattered. Not for a moment did he think that Daniel, his beloved and honored servant, would in any way be affected by the law. He signed the decree, and with it in their possession, the presidents and princes went forth from his presence, evil triumph depicted on their countenances. They deemed that the man they hated was now in their power.

Daniel heard of what had been done, but he made no protest. He could see the design of his enemies. He knew that they would watch closely his going out and his coming in, but he calmly attended to his duties, and at the hour of prayer he went to his chamber, and kneeling by the open window, with his face toward Jerusalem, he prayed to his God. From his youth he had been taught that in prayer his face should be turned toward the temple, where by faith he saw the revelation of Jehovah's glory.

Daniel prayed more fervently than was his wont, that He who understands the secret working of Satan and his agents would not leave his servant, but would care for him. He prayed for strength to endure the trial.

Some may ask, Why did not Daniel lift his soul to God in secret prayer? Would not the Lord, knowing the situation, have excused his servant from kneeling openly before him? Or why did he not kneel before God in some secret place, where his enemies could not see him?

Daniel knew that the God of Israel must be honored before the Babylonian nation. He knew that neither kings nor nobles had any right to come between him and his duty to his God. He must bravely maintain his religious principles before all men; for he was God's witness. Therefore he prayed as was his wont, as if no decree had been made.

"Then these men assembled, and found Daniel praying and making supplication before his God."

Eagerly they hastened to Darius, concealing their cruel joy under a cloak of regret that they were obliged to inform against Daniel. But they declared that by Daniel's act the king's position as sovereign of the land was endangered, and his authority despised. "That Daniel, which is of the children of the captivity of Judah, regardeth not thee, O king, nor the decree that thou hast signed, but maketh his petition three times a day."

"Then the king, when he heard these words, was sore displeased with himself."

Too late he understood the snare that had been laid for the destruction of his favorite servant. Sorely troubled, he tried in every way to rescue Daniel. Till the going down of the sun he labored to deliver him. But Daniel's accusers had managed the matter so well that there was no way of escape. "Know, O king," they said, "that the law of the Medes and Persians is, That no decree nor statute which the king establisheth may be changed."

Daniel was brought before the king and his princes to answer the accusation brought against him. He had opportunity to speak for himself, and he boldly acknowledged his belief in the living God, the maker of heaven and earth. He made a noble confession of faith, relating his experience from his first connection with the kingdom.

In his perplexity and distress, Darius said to Daniel, I have done all I can to save you. I can do no more. "Thy God, whom thou servest continually, he will deliver thee," he added, as he bade him a sorrowful farewell.

Daniel was cast into the den of lions. "And a stone was brought, and laid upon the mouth of the den; and the king sealed it with his own signet, and with the signet of his lords, that the purpose might not be changed concerning Daniel." Full of satanic exultation, Daniel's enemies returned to their homes. They drank freely of wine, and congratulated themselves on their success in putting out of the way one whom they could not bribe to forsake the path of integrity.

Not so did Darius pass the night. Daniel's testimony had made a deep impression on his mind. He had some knowledge of the dealing of God with the people of Israel, and Daniel's conduct sent home to his heart the conviction, that the God of the Hebrews was the true God. He was filled with remorse for having signed the decree brought to him. His conscience was awakened, and he passed a sleepless and troubled night. The chamber of royalty was one of sorrow and prayer. All music was hushed. All amusements were laid aside. No comforters were admitted.

During that sleepless night the king thought as he had never thought before. Early the next morning, hoping and yet despairing, condemning himself, and praying to him whom he began to recognize as the true God, Darius went to the lions' den, and cried aloud: "O Daniel, servant of the living God, is thy God, whom thou servest continually, able to deliver thee from the lions?"

With intense anxiety he waited for an answer, and unspeakable thankfulness filled his heart as a voice came up from below: "O king, live forever. My God hath sent his angel, and hath shut the lions' mouths, that they have not hurt me: forasmuch as before him innocency was found in me and also before thee, O king, have I done no hurt.

"Then was the king exceeding glad for him, and commanded that they should take Daniel up out of the den. So Daniel was taken up out of the den, and no manner of hurt was found upon him, because he believed in his God." And we read of him, "Daniel prospered in the reign of Darius, and in the reign of Cyrus the Persian."

Thus the Lord cared for his faithful servant, and thus will he care for all who put their trust in him. "The angel of the Lord encampeth round about them that fear him, and delivereth them."

Mrs. E. G. White

November 8, 1900—Ye Are Not Your Own

We sometimes hear the questions: Am I never to do as I please? Am I never to have my own way? Am I always to be restrained? Can I never act in accordance with my inclinations?

The less you follow natural inclinations, the better it will be for yourself and for others. The natural inclinations have been perverted, the natural powers misapplied. Satan has brought man into collision with God. He works continually to destroy the divine image in man. Therefore we must place a restraint on our words and actions.

When the grace of God takes possession of the heart, it is seen that the inherited and cultivated tendencies to wrong must be crucified. A new life, under new control, must begin in the soul. All that is done must be done to the glory of God. This work includes the outward as well as the inward man. The entire being, body, soul, and spirit, must be brought into subjection to God, to be used by him as an instrument of righteousness.

The natural man is not subject to the law of God; neither, indeed, of himself, can he be. But by faith he who has been renewed lives day by day the life of Christ. Day by day he shows that he realizes that he is God's property.

Body and soul belong to God. He gave his Son for the redemption of the world, and because of this, we have been granted a new lease of life, a probation in which to develop characters of perfect loyalty. God has redeemed us from the slavery of sin, and has made it possible for us to live regenerated, transformed lives of service.

God's stamp is upon us. He has bought us, and he desires us to remember that our physical, mental, and moral powers belong to him. Time and influence, reason, affection, and conscience,--all are God's, and are to be used only in harmony with his will. They are not to be used in accordance with the direction of the world; for the world is under a leader who is at enmity with God.

The flesh, in which the soul tabernacles, belongs to God. Every sinew, every muscle, is his. In no case are we by neglect or abuse to weaken a single organ. We are to co-operate with God by keeping the body in the very best possible condition of health, that it may be a temple where the Holy Ghost may abide, molding, according to the will of God, every physical and spiritual power.

The mind must be stored with pure principles. Truth must be graven on the tablets of the soul. The memory must be filled with the precious truths of the word. Then, like beautiful gems, these truths will flash out in the life.

The value that God places on the work of his hands, the love he has for his children, is revealed by the gift he made to redeem men. Adam fell under the dominion of Satan. He brought sin into the world, and death by sin. God gave his only begotten Son to save man. This he did that he might be just, and yet the justifier of all who accept Christ. Man sold himself to Satan, but Jesus bought back the race.

At an infinite cost to heaven we have been given a second probation. Then should not God be in all our thoughts? Should not his will control our actions?

You are not your own. Jesus has purchased you with his blood. Do not bury your talents in the earth. Use them for him. In whatever business you may be engaged, bring Jesus into it. If you find that you are losing your love for your Saviour, give up your business, and say, "Here I am, Saviour; what wilt thou have me to do?" He will receive you graciously, and love you freely. He will abundantly pardon; for he is merciful and long-suffering, not willing that any should perish. He is a loving Redeemer, whose pity survives the neglect and abuse of his mercy, the resistance of his claims.

We, and all that we have, belong to God. We should not regard it as a sacrifice to give him the affection of our hearts. The heart itself should be given to him as a willing offering.

Impressed with man's great obligation to God, Paul wrote: "I beseech you therefore, brethren, by the mercies of God, that ye present your bodies a living sacrifice, holy, acceptable unto God, which is your reasonable service." He urges a recognition of God's claims. "Know ye not," he asks, "that your body is the temple of the Holy Ghost which is in you, which ye have of God, and ye are not your own? For ye are bought with a price: therefore glorify God in your body, and in your spirit, which are God's."

Mrs. E. G. White

November 15, 1900—From Persecutor to Disciple—Part 1

Christ had suffered an ignominious death; and, in the most positive terms, the Sanhedrin had forbidden the disciples to preach the doctrines of Christianity. But every effort to put down the new religion seemed only to increase its strength, till it threatened to destroy the rites of the temple, and the customs which for generations had been followed by the Jewish nation.

Saul was aroused. He saw that decisive measures must be taken to suppress the new faith. A sensation had been created in Jerusalem by the death of Stephen. The persecution that followed drove the disciples abroad, and the priests and rulers hoped that by vigilant efforts and stern discipline the heresy might be suppressed.

In Damascus the new faith seemed to have acquired fresh life and energy. The work of suppression must be begun there, and Saul was selected for this work. "Breathing out threatenings and slaughter against the disciples of the Lord," he went to the high priest, "and desired of him letters to Damascus to the synagogues, that if he found any of this way, whether they were men or women, he might bring them bound up to Jerusalem."

As Saul journeyed, "suddenly there shined round about him a light from heaven." Frightened, bewildered, and blinded, he fell to the earth. As he fell, he heard a voice saying to him: "Saul, Saul, why persecutest thou me? And he said, Who, art thou, Lord? And the Lord said, I am Jesus whom thou persecutest: it is hard for thee to kick against the pricks."

A general slain in battle is a loss to his army, but his death gives no additional strength to the enemy. But when a man of integrity and sterling principle joins the opposing force, not only are his services lost, but those to whom he joins himself gain a decided advantage. Saul of Tarsus might easily have been struck dead by the Lord, as he was on his way to Damascus, and much force would have been withdrawn from the persecuting power. But his life was spared, and by the mighty power of God he was carried from the side of the enemy to the side of Christ.

Saul had talents that would have enabled him to serve in any position. He was courageous, independent, and persevering. His reasoning powers were of no ordinary value. By his withering sarcasm he could place an opponent in no enviable position. He was an eloquent speaker and a severe critic. A man of stern purpose and undaunted courage, he possessed the very qualifications needed in the Christian church.

After Paul's conversion, he spent some time in Damascus, showing his brethren there the genuineness of his experience. Then he went to Arabia. Returning to Jerusalem, he tried to join himself to the disciples, that he might be recognized as a follower of the Saviour. But they were all afraid of him, not believing that he was a disciple. So great had been his zeal in persecuting the church, that the believers thought his conversion only a pretense. It was difficult for them to believe that so bigoted a Pharisee, one who had done so much to destroy the church, could become a sincere follower of Jesus.

"But Barnabas took him, and brought him to the apostles, and declared unto them how he had seen the Lord in the way, and that he had spoken to him, and how he had preached boldly at Damascus in the name of Jesus. And he was with them coming in and going out at Jerusalem. And he spake boldly in the name of the Lord Jesus, and disputed against the Grecians: but they went about to slay him. Which when the brethren knew, they brought him down to Caesarea, and sent him forth to Tarsus."

In the past the labors of the apostles had been put forth wholly in Palestine. Round this place their hopes had clustered. They regarded the Jews as the covenant people of God. Paul was raised up by God to preach the gospel to the Gentiles. Of him God said to Ananias, "He is a chosen vessel unto me, to bear my name before the Gentiles, and kings, and the children of Israel." While Paul and Barnabas were laboring in Antioch, the Holy Spirit gave direction, "Separate unto Me Barnabas and Saul for the work whereunto I have called them. And when they had fasted and prayed, and laid their hands on them, they sent them away."

Paul went to Greece to proclaim as the Christ a Jew of lowly origin, brought up in a town proverbial for its wickedness, a man who had been rejected by his own nation, and crucified as a malefactor. How could Paul awaken an interest in this man?

The Greeks looked upon philosophy and science as the only road to true elevation and honor. They believed that there was need of elevating the race; but could Paul lead them to believe that the cross of Christ would do this? There is to us a sacredness about the cross of Calvary. The scenes and associations connected with it are hallowed. But when Paul preached the gospel in Corinth, the cross was regarded with the same feeling of repulsion as the gibbet of today. Any reference to a Saviour who had met his death on the cross would naturally meet with opposition.

Paul knew how his message would be regarded by the Greeks. "We preach Christ crucified," he said, "unto the Jews a stumbling-block, and unto the Greeks foolishness." In the estimation of the Greeks his words would be absurd folly. They would look upon Paul as weak-minded for endeavoring to show how the cross could have any connection with the elevation of the race or the salvation of men.

But the cross was to Paul the one object of interest in the world. He determined to know nothing among the Corinthians "save Jesus Christ, and him crucified." He presented the cross to them as the only means of salvation. He stood forth before them declaring: "The preaching of the cross is to them that perish foolishness; but unto us which are saved it is the power of God."

By Paul's labors in Corinth a church was established. Many were turned from the worship of idols.

Mrs. E. G. White

November 22, 1900—From Persecutor to Disciple—Part 2

On one occasion Paul said: "Ye know, from the first day that I came into Asia, after what manner I have been with you at all seasons, serving the Lord with all humility of mind, and with many tears, and temptations, which befell me by the lying in wait of the Jews: and how I kept back nothing that was profitable unto you, but have showed you, and have taught you publicly, and from house to house, testifying both to the Jews, and also to the Greeks, repentance toward God, and faith toward our Lord Jesus Christ. And now, behold, I go bound in the spirit unto Jerusalem, not knowing the things that shall befall me there: save that the Holy Ghost witnesseth in every city, saying that bonds and afflictions abide me. But none of these things move me, neither count I my life dear unto myself, so that I might finish my course with joy, and the ministry, which I have received of the Lord Jesus, to testify the gospel of the grace of God."

These words explain the secret of Paul's power and success. He kept back nothing that was profitable for the people. He preached Christ publicly, in the market-places and the synagogues. He taught from house to house, availing himself of the familiar intercourse of the home circle. He visited the sick and sorrowing, comforting the afflicted, and lifting up the oppressed. And in all that he said and did, he preached a crucified and risen Saviour.

Paul's great desire was to preach the gospel at Rome. In his letter to the church at that place he wrote: "For God is my witness, whom I serve with my spirit in the gospel of his Son, that without ceasing I make mention of you always in my prayers; making request, if by any means now at length I might have a prosperous journey by the will of God to come unto you. For I long to see you, that I may impart unto you some spiritual gift, to the end ye may be established; that is, that I may be comforted together with you by the mutual faith both of you and me."

It was not curiosity that made Paul desire to see the capital of the world. He had been assured in a vision that he would be permitted to bear witness for the Lord in Rome.

Paul went to Rome as a prisoner. As he approached the city, his brethren came out to meet him. In the eyes of the world he was a criminal worthy of death, but in the eyes of his fellow Christians he was worthy of special honor. He tells us what effect his bonds had upon them. "Many of the brethren in the Lord," he declares, "waxing confident by my bonds, are much more bold to speak the word without fear."

After Paul had been in Rome three days, he called the chief men of the Jews together, and explained why he had been brought to Rome as a prisoner. He stated that he had done nothing against the people or the customs of the fathers; and that after being examined before the Roman authorities, he would have been set at liberty, had it not been for the opposition of his countrymen.

Paul manifested true Christian forbearance. He had been falsely accused by his countrymen in Judea, and had been subjected by them to an unjust trial. He had endured the hardships and perils of the journey to Rome, and was now awaiting his trial before the emperor. Yet when he told his brethren in Rome about his imprisonment, he made no complaint. Not that I had aught to accuse my nation of, he said; I did not come to accuse any one. I have called you together to speak of the hope of Israel, for which I am held in bonds. Acts 28:30.

"And Paul dwelt two whole years in his own hired house, and received all that came in unto him, preaching the kingdom of God, and teaching those things which concern the Lord Jesus Christ, with all confidence, no man forbidding him."

Though kept a prisoner at Rome, Paul exerted a powerful influence. He was near the palace of the emperor, and he wrote to the Philippians: "I would ye should understand, brethren, that the things which happened unto me have fallen out rather unto the furtherance of the gospel; so that my bonds in Christ are manifest in all the palace, and in all other places." We know that converts were made in the court of the emperor; for in concluding his letter to the Philippians, Paul said, "All the saints salute you, chiefly they that are of Caesar's household."

For hundreds of years after Paul had laid off his armor, the papacy bore sway. Then Luther, an Augustine monk, brought up under the straitest rules of the papacy, went on a pilgrimage to Rome. He sought for salvation in the rites and ceremonies of a corrupt church. As he was performing an act of penance, slowly climbing on his knees up Pilate's staircase, the words of Paul to the Romans came with peculiar force to his darkened mind, arousing his senses and touching his heart. "The just shall live by faith," a voice seemed to say to him. That one sentence changed Luther's whole life, and brought about one of the greatest reformations the world has ever witnessed.

Mrs. E. G. White

December 6, 1900—In Meekness and Lowliness of Heart

God desires that meekness and gentleness, the distinguishing characteristics of Christ, shall be brought into the lives of his followers. The Saviour gives to all the invitation: "Come unto me, all ye that labor and are heavy laden, and I will give you rest. Take my yoke upon you, and learn of me; for I am meek and lowly in heart: and ye shall find rest unto your souls."

In self-love, self-exaltation, and pride there is great weakness; but in humility there is strength. True dignity is not maintained when we think most of self, but when God is in all our thoughts, and when our hearts are all aglow with love for our Redeemer and for our fellow men. In pride and separation from God we are constantly seeking to exalt self, and we forget that lowliness of mind is power. Christ's power lay, not in sharp words that would pierce the soul, but in his gentleness. This made him a conqueror of hearts. We are invited to learn of him who was meek and lowly in heart.

The life of Christ is to be our pattern. His life and work in the world are a sample of what our life and work should be. "I receive not honor of men," he said. In his service we need not expect ease of worldly honor; for the Majesty of heaven did not receive these things. "He was despised and rejected of men."

The light reflected from the cross of Calvary will humble every proud thought. Those who seek God with all the heart, and accept the great salvation offered them, will open the door of the heart of Jesus. They will cease to ascribe glory to themselves. They will not pride themselves on their acquirements, or take credit to themselves for their capabilities, but will regard all their talents as God's gifts, to be used to his glory. Every intellectual ability they will regard as precious only as it can be used in the service of Christ. "If any man be in Christ," the apostle says, "he is a new creature: old things are passed away; behold, all things are become new." Everything in life or character that is unlike Christ is put away. An indwelling Christ purifies the soul from selfishness and iniquity. A new life enters the dry, sapless branch, and it becomes fruit-bearing. Love, joy, peace, long-suffering, gentleness, goodness, patience, faith, meekness, are revealed in the life.

True greatness never has a tendency to exalt self. Truly great men are invariably humble. Those who have stored their minds with useful knowledge, and who possess genuine attainments and refinement, will be the most willing to admit their own weakness. They are not self-confident nor boastful; but in view of the higher attainments to which they might rise, they seem to themselves to have only begun the ascent.

The enemy of God and man takes advantage of the weak points in the characters of men and women. If men are inclined to self-esteem and self-exaltation, he makes a special effort in that direction. If one is puffed up with vain conceit, Satan says: I will set my agents to work to surround that man with temptations. I will make him believe that he is of great consequence. I will work his ruin by extolling him and seconding all his efforts. Thus I will lead him to trust to himself, and walk in the sparks of the fire of his own kindling. For a time the world is stirred with an apparently deep interest in the man whom Satan is seeking to deceive and ruin; but when he has separated himself from God, and the object of the enemy is accomplished, the world no longer interests itself in him. It has led him into difficulties, but it does not lead him out again, and Satan rejoices in the ruin of his soul.

Salvation has been brought within the reach of man at an infinite cost. It is the free gift of God. Nothing can be added to it, nothing can be taken from it. It is complete, perfect. Christ does not say to any one of us, You are complete in yourself, in your own talents, your trusted endowments; but he does say, "Ye are complete in him." "He that believeth on me hath everlasting life." Not the possessions of a man determine his character, but the heart purity, the steadfast purpose. The character built with good and noble deeds is a monument that the angelic hosts respect,--the character which, when life has closed, lives in the memory, perpetuated by the good deeds done for others.

The true Christian will not think of himself more highly than he ought to think. He will not be ambitious for worldly honor and esteem. A learner in the school of Christ, he will be gentle, distrustful of self. His life will be characterized by a Christlike simplicity. Luxury, ease, and wealth have no attractions for him; for he looks to the one who for his sake became a man of sorrows and acquainted with grief, who was wounded for his transgressions, bruised for his iniquities, and by whose stripes he is healed. It is "the hidden man of the heart, in that which is not corruptible, even the ornament of a meek and quiet spirit, which is in the sight of God of great price." The meek and quiet spirit will testify of itself in good works. This is that which distinguishes the people of God from worldlings. In their sympathy for others, their tenderness, their meekness and lowliness of heart, they reveal that they wear Christ's yoke, and are recipients of the gift of the Holy Spirit.

Mrs. E. G. White

December 13, 1900—The Burning Bush

Nearly two thousand years ago a voice of strange and mysterious import was heard from the throne of God: "Sacrifice and offering thou wouldst not, but a body hast thou prepared me: ... then said I, Lo, I come:" "in the volume of the book it is written of me, I delight to do thy will, O my God: yea, thy law is within my heart." Here is made the announcement that Christ is to visit our world, and become incarnate.

God ordained that his chosen church should be educated in regard to the coming of the Redeemer. Ways were appointed whereby the infinite sacrifice to be made for the redemption of man might be gradually revealed. Impressive symbols were employed to unfold the plan of God. Those who desired to look into these things might understand them.

This system is not to be passed over in our study of the revelation of truth. From the time when the promise was made in Eden, Christ was shadowed forth in types and symbols. The light gradually increased,--becoming more and more distinct until the fullness of the time came. Then the great Antitype, the originator of all the Jewish economy, appeared in our world. In Christ, type met antitype. The gloomy shadows were lightened by the appearance of him who was the full signification of all the symbols.

The burning bush, in which God appeared to Moses, revealed Christ. There is living truth in this spectacle. In mercy God was about to deliver his people from Egyptian bondage; and he appeared to Moses, telling him that he had been selected as the visible leader of God's people. Moses was chosen by the Lord as his representative to bear a message to Pharaoh. He must receive his commands directly from God: a most important responsibility had been placed upon him.

Moses had received a thorough education in the court of the king of Egypt. He was qualified to be the honored general of armies, and to engage in warfare with other nations. But although he was the king's recognized grandson, with a prospective kingdom before him, and although he had enjoyed the highest educational advantages that Egypt could offer, he was not qualified to engage directly in the work to which the Lord saw fit to call him; he was not fitted to take his place as the visible leader of a vast multitude, receiving from God instruction in regard to framing their laws, and laying the foundation of their economy in a system of types and symbols; he could not then lead the people of God through the rocky, barren desert into the land of promise. He must first receive an education from heaven.

He who sees the end from the beginning, watched over and guarded his servant. God transferred Moses from the courts of luxury, where his every wish was gratified, to a more private school. Here the Lord could commune with Moses, and so educate him that he would obtain a knowledge of the hardships, trials, and perils of the wilderness. He gave him sheep to care for, that he might become qualified to be the shepherd of God's people. God saw that the experience Moses would gain while minding sheep would qualify him to be the leader of his people; it would enable him to sympathize with those who had everything to learn. It was necessary to select for this position a man who was tender, patient, and sympathizing,--a man whose heart would ever be touched by human woe, as a shepherd is touched by the sufferings of the sheep and lambs of his flock.

God designed to make of Moses a channel through which he could communicate instruction to an undisciplined people, whose worship of God was mingled with idolatrous sentiments. From these sentiments this worship must be purified before they could be made the depositaries of truth, which was to be held in trust for future generations. During the forty years in which Moses was engaged in pastoral work, he was obtaining a knowledge of God. It was while he was following this lowly calling, that the Lord appeared to him in a flame of fire in the midst of a bush. Moses looked, "and behold, the bush burned with fire, and the bush was not consumed." This arrested his attention, and he said: "I will now turn aside, and see this great sight, why the bush is not burnt. And when the Lord saw that he turned aside to see, God called unto him out of the midst of the bush, and said, Moses, Moses. And he said, Here am I. And he said, Draw not nigh hither: put off thy shoes from off thy feet, for the place whereon thou standest is holy ground. Moreover he said, I am the God of thy father, the God of Abraham, the God of Isaac, and the God of Jacob. And Moses hid his face; for he was afraid to look upon God."

Let this lesson be carefully studied. Before God could talk with Moses, he educated him in the mountains, among the sheepfolds. Exiled from the courts of Egypt and from the temptations of city life, Moses held communion with God. For forty years

God tested and disciplined him, preparing him for his important work. For forty years Moses dwelt in the wilderness, receiving from God an education that made him a wise, tender, humble man. When this time was ended, his self-confidence was gone; he was meek and lowly, so divested of self that God could communicate to him his will in regard to the people he had chosen, and whom he designed to educate and discipline in their wilderness life, while he was preparing for them a home in the land of Canaan.

Mrs. E. G. White

December 20, 1900—Christ's Humiliation

It will baffle the keenest intellect to interpret the divine manifestation of the burning bush. It was not a dream; it was not a vision; it was a living reality,--something that Moses saw with his eyes. He heard the voice of God calling to him out of the bush, and he covered his face, realizing that he stood in the immediate presence of God. God was conversing with humanity. Never could Moses describe the impression made upon his mind by the sight he then saw, and by the sound of the voice that spoke to him; but this impression was never effaced. Heaven came very near to him as, with reverent awe, he listened to the words, "I am the God of thy father, the God of Abraham, the God of Isaac, and the God of Jacob." What wondrous condescension for God to leave the heavenly courts, and manifest himself to Moses, talking with him face to face, "as a man speaketh unto his friend."

This lesson contains instruction that is profitable for all. Here is revealed a symbol radiant with the glory of Christ, the Great Teacher. The symbol chosen for the representation of the Deity was not a cedar of Lebanon, but a lowly bush, that seemingly had no attractions. This enshrined the Infinite. The all-merciful God shrouded his glory in a most humble type, that Moses might look upon it, and live. God declared: "Thou canst not see my face: for there shall no man see me, and live." All the manifestations of God's glory have been shrouded, that man might behold it, and not be consumed. Veiled in a pillar of cloud by day, and a pillar of fire by night, God could honor finite man by communicating to him his will, and imparting to him his grace. God's glory must be subdued, and his majesty veiled, that the weak vision of finite man may look upon it.

This symbol, obscuring the manifestation of God's glory, foreshadowed Christ's appearance in our world, his divinity clothed with humanity. Surely in the eyes of the world Christ possessed no beauty that they should desire him, yet he was the incarnate God. This is the mystery of godliness. Human science, even though it be of the highest order, can not explain it. Men may think that they possess superior qualities, represented by the noble oak, or the stately cedar. Mark the humble birth of Christ, his condescending grace, his infinite humility, the depths to which he descended. He is the eternal Word. Yet he was made flesh, and dwelt among us.

Before Christ came in the likeness of men, he existed in the express image of his Father. He thought it not robbery to be equal with God. Nevertheless he voluntarily emptied himself, and took the form of a servant. He was the incarnate God, the light of heaven and earth. In him are hid all the treasures of wisdom and knowledge. Yet he was born in a stable, in Bethlehem of Judea. He was the son of Mary, supposed to be the son of Joseph, and he grew up as any other child. His earthly life was one of self-denial and self-sacrifice. "The foxes have holes," he said, "and the birds of the air have nests; but the Son of man hath not where to lay his head."

"We see Jesus," writes Paul, "who was made a little lower than the angels for the suffering of death, crowned with glory and honor; that he by the grace of God should taste death for every man." Thus will the testimony appear in clear lines in that day when all must hear the final decision of a righteous Judge, when every case will be decided, and every man rewarded according to his works. The loyal and believing children of God will then be separated from the children of the wicked one, as the sheep are divided from the goats. The righteous will be placed on the right hand of God, while the transgressors will be placed on his left hand.

Prophecy foretold that Christ was to appear as a root out of dry ground. "He hath no form nor comeliness," wrote Isaiah, "and when we shall see him, there is no beauty that we should desire him. He is despised and rejected of men; a man of sorrows, and acquainted with grief: and we hid as it were our faces from him; he was despised, and we esteemed him not." This chapter should be studied. It presents Christ as the Lamb of God. Those who are lifted up with pride, whose souls are filled with vanity, should look upon this picture of their Redeemer, and humble themselves in the dust. The entire chapter should be committed to memory. Its influence will subdue and humble the soul defiled by sin and uplifted by self-exaltation.

Think of Christ's humiliation. He took upon himself fallen, suffering human nature, degraded and defiled by sin. He took our sorrows, bearing our grief and shame. He endured all the temptations wherewith man is beset. He united humanity with divinity: a divine spirit dwelt in a temple of flesh. He united himself with the temple. "The Word was made flesh, and dwelt among us," because by so doing he could associate with the sinful, sorrowing sons and daughters of Adam.

The glory of Christ was veiled, that the majesty and beauty of his outward form might not become an object of attraction. In this is a lesson for all humanity. "Verily man at his best state is altogether vanity." Christ came with no outward display. Finding himself in fashion as a man, he humbled himself, showing that fallen man must ever walk humbly before God. Riches, worldly honor, human greatness, can never save a soul from death. "To this man will I look," declares the Lord, "even to him that is poor and of a contrite spirit, and trembleth at my word."

Mrs. E. G. White

December 27, 1900—Rejoice in the Lord

Christ says to his followers, "Ye are the light of the world." Then let your light shine forth in clear, steady rays, Do not wrap about you a cloud of darkness. Cease to suspect others. By good works represent the character of Christ. When you are tempted to yield to despondency, look to Jesus, and talk with him. Your Elder Brother will never make a mistake. He will judge righteously. He will guide you aright.

God is not pleased to see his children wrapped in gloom and sadness. His arm is mighty to save all who will lay hold on him. He desires us to be cheerful, but not trifling. He says to each one of us, "But as he which hath called you is holy, so be ye holy in all manner of conversation." God wants us to be happy. He desires to put a new song on our lips, even praise to our God. He wants us to believe that he forgives our sins, and takes away our unrighteousness. He wants us to make melody in our hearts to him.

The "hope set before us"--what is it?--The hope of eternal life. Nothing short of this will satisfy the Redeemer; and it is our part to lay hold of this hope by living faith in him. If we are partakers with him in his sufferings, we shall be partakers with him in the glory which will be his; for his merits have purchased forgiveness and immortality for every sinful, perishing soul. "This hope we have as an anchor of the soul, both sure and steadfast." Our trust in this hope, purchased for us by the atonement and intercession of Christ, is to keep us steadfast and unmovable in every hour of conflict. With such a hope as this before us, shall we allow Satan to cast his shadow across our pathway, to eclipse our view of the future?

Christ values human beings with a value that is beyond any human computation. Then let us encourage faith. Take your eyes off yourself. Faith and hope are not to be centered in self: they are to enter into that within the veil, whither our Forerunner is for us entered. Talk of the blessed hope and glorious appearing of our Lord and Saviour Jesus Christ. We are exposed to great moral danger; and if we trust in self, looking no higher, we shall make shipwreck of faith. Do not fail nor be discouraged. Hope is an anchor to the soul, both sure and steadfast when it enters into that within the veil. Thus the tempest-tossed soul becomes anchored in Christ. Amid the raging of temptation, he will neither be driven upon the rocks nor drawn into the whirlpool. His ship will outride the storm.

Close the door of the heart to distrust, and throw it open to the heavenly Guest. Put away all fretting and complaining; for these things are a snare of the devil. Let us make a pledge before God and the heavenly angels that we will not dishonor our Maker by cherishing darkness and unbelief, by speaking words of discouragement and mistrust. Let every word we utter, every line we write, be fraught with encouragement and unwavering faith. If we live faith, we shall talk faith. Think not that Jesus is the Saviour of your brother only. He is your personal Saviour. If you entertain this precious thought, you will beat back the clouds of despondency and gloom, and make melody to God in your soul. It is our privilege to triumph in God. It is our privilege to lead others to see that their only hope is in God, and to flee to him for refuge.

Every act of consecration to God brings joy; for as we appreciate the light he has given us, more and greater light will come. We must banish the spirit of complaining, and open the heart to the bright beams of the Sun of Righteousness. There is peace in perfect submission. Peace follows grace. They work in perfect harmony, and are multiplied in progression. When the hand of faith takes hold of the hand of Christ, the expression of the heart is: "Blessed be the God and Father of our Lord Jesus Christ, which according to his abundant mercy hath begotten us again unto a lively hope by the resurrection of Jesus Christ from the dead, to an inheritance incorruptible, and undefiled, and that fadeth not away."

Open the windows of the soul heavenward, and let the rays of the Sun of Righteousness in. Look on the bright side. Let the peace of God reign in your soul. Then you will have strength to bear all suffering, and you will rejoice that you have grace to endure. Praise the Lord; talk of his goodness; tell of his power. Sweeten the atmosphere that surrounds your soul. Do not dishonor God by words of fretfulness and repining. Praise, with heart and soul and voice, him who is the health of your countenance, your Saviour, and your God.

Mrs. E. G. White

January 3, 1901—Tempted in All Points

Christ offered himself as a willing sacrifice in our behalf. He stooped from his high place in heaven to rescue human beings from the slavery of sin. The Son of God gave up his honor and glory, and tasted the bitterness of death, that men might become partakers of the divine nature. He died that all might have an opportunity to choose God as their leader.

"When the fullness of the time was come, God sent forth his Son, ... to redeem them that were under the law, that we might receive the adoption of sons." The star of hope arose upon our world, and its brightness increased as our Saviour increased in wisdom and stature, and in favor with God and man.

In the wilderness Christ endured temptations that no human being can comprehend. Here he was brought face to face with Satan, the fallen angel, who tempted him with all his subtle power. The enemy began by disputing Christ's divinity. If you are the Son of God, he said, give me evidence that you are. Here you are in the wilderness, hungry, starving for food. You do not look like a sovereign. Give me evidence that you are what you claim to be. Command that these stones be made bread.

But the One whom Satan was trying to overcome was the Lord of heaven, and all the tempter's efforts were without avail. Though Jesus was physically weak from his long fast, he would not yield one inch to the wily foe. His will was anchored in the will of his Father. "It is written," came from his pale and quivering lips, as Satan told him to turn the stones into bread, "Man shall not live by bread alone, but by every word that proceedeth out of the mouth of God."

Satan then took Christ to the pinnacle of the temple, and challenged him to cast himself down, saying: "If thou be the Son of God, cast thyself down: for it is written, He shall give his angels charge concerning thee: and in their hands they shall bear thee up, lest at any time thou dash thy foot against a stone." Thus Satan tried to lead Christ to commit the sin of presumption. He reminded him that God had promised to protect him by angel ministration. But no temptation could induce the Saviour to accept the challenge. "It is written again," he said, "Thou shalt not tempt the Lord thy God." Christ's time to show his divine power had not yet come. He was fully aware of the glory he had with the Father before the world was. But then he willingly submitted to the divine will, and he was unchanged now. This was his time of trial and temptation; he must endure the test, however cruel it might be. But he knew that by suffering and sorrow and a cruel death he was to bruise the serpent's head. The giving of his life was to be the price of the world's redemption.

Satan next took Christ to the top of a high mountain, and there presented before him all the kingdoms of the world and the glory of them, saying: "All this power will I give thee, ... for that is delivered unto me; and to whomsoever I will I give it. If thou therefore wilt worship me, all shall be thine." Then it was that divinity flashed through humanity, and the fallen angels saw Christ glorified as he said, "Get thee behind me, Satan: for it is written, Thou shalt worship the Lord thy God, and him only shalt thou serve."

The victory was gained. Christ had redeemed Adam's disgraceful failure and fall, and had placed man on vantage-ground.

"Then the devil leaveth him, and, behold, angels came and ministered unto him." The angels had been watching the contest, but they could do nothing to relieve the Saviour until the last temptation had been resisted. The commander of heaven, Christ was accustomed to receive the attendance and adoration of angels; and at any time during his life on this earth he could have called to his Father for the help of angels. But no bribe, no temptation, could induce him to deviate from the path of God's appointment. Great cunning was shown by the tactics that Satan followed. He assailed Christ on the point of appetite. He appealed to his trust in God. He presented to him earth's most captivating scenes. But Christ failed not. He saw a world perishing in sin, and steadfastly and firmly he moved forward in the path of resistance. He had a world to rescue. He had come to seek and save that which was lost.

Christ passed over the ground where Adam fell, and overcame in our behalf. He endured every test that man will ever be called upon to endure. He met all the temptations that man will have to meet. He traveled over the path in which he calls us to walk. Every step Christ took was taken in dependence upon God, and upon not a single point did the enemy overcome him.

When God gave Jesus to our world, he gave all heaven. This gift has secured for us our adoption into God's family. The Father's promise is Yea and Amen in Christ Jesus. Never will he falsify. Never will he alter the thing that has gone out of his mouth. The clouds of uncertainty and unbelief rolled back as the Saviour cried out upon the cross, "It is finished." And today he who overcame the world, stands in the heavenly courts as our Advocate. He is touched with the feeling of our infirmities; for he was "in all points tempted like as we are, yet without sin." Mrs.

E. G. White

January 10, 1901—Rejoice in the Lord Alway

In this life we shall be tempted and tried. Friends may prove treacherous, enemies may be inspired by Satan to cause sadness. In these trials let us turn to the Strong for strength. There we shall find comfort, consolation, and tender sympathy.

Christ interposes between us and the difficulties that appear so formidable. The flame and the flood are behind him. Then lift him up, with voice and song, and let the melody of thanksgiving and praise ascend to heaven in your life service. Keep cheerful, full of faith and courage and hope. Elijah was subject to like passions as we are, yet the Lord was his strength. He prayed most earnestly, and the Lord heard his prayer. Let us, under all circumstances, preserve our confidence in Christ. He is to be everything to us,--the first, the last, the best in everything. Then let us educate our tongues to speak forth his praise, not only when we feel gladness and joy, but at all times.

Let us keep the heart full of God's precious promises, that we may speak words that will be a comfort and strength to others. Thus we may learn the language of the heavenly angels, who, if we are faithful, will be our companions through the eternal ages. Every day we should make advancement in gaining perfection of character, and this we shall certainly do if we press toward the mark of the prize of our high calling in Christ Jesus. Let us not talk of the great power of Satan, but of the great power of God. We are to speak even as Christ spoke, allowing no harsh, impatient words to fall from our lips. Thus we shall be a savor of life to all with whom we come in contact.

In every soul two powers are struggling earnestly for the victory. Unbelief marshals its forces, led by Satan, to cut us off from the source of our strength. Faith marshals its forces, led by Christ, the author and finisher of our faith. Hour by hour, in the sight of the heavenly universe the conflict goes forward. This is a hand-to-hand fight, and the great question is, Which shall obtain the mastery? This question each must decide for himself. In this warfare all must take a part, fighting on one side or the other. From the conflict there is no release.

Paul says to those who are fighting on the side of truth: "We wrestle not against flesh and blood, but against principalities, against powers, against the rulers of the darkness of this world, against spiritual wickedness in high places." We are urged to prepare for this conflict. "Be strong in the Lord, and in the power of his might. Put on the whole armor of God, that ye may be able to stand against the wiles of the devil." The warning is repeated, "Wherefore take unto you the whole armor of God, that ye may be able to withstand in the evil day, and having done all, to stand."

He who is mighty in counsel, to whom all power in heaven and earth has been given, will come to the help of those who trust in him. In the Scriptures we read that in certain places Christ could not do many mighty works, because of the unbelief existing there. It is of great importance that we have a faith that will not wait for the evidence of sight before it ventures to advance. "Through faith we understand that the worlds were framed by the word of God, so that things which are seen were not made of things which do appear. By faith Abel offered unto God a more excellent sacrifice than Cain, by which he obtained witness that he was righteous, God testifying of his gifts: and by it he being dead yet speaketh. By faith Enoch was translated that he should not see death; and was not found, because God had translated him: for before his translation he had this testimony, that he pleased God. But without faith it is impossible to please him: for he that cometh to God must believe that he is, and that he is a rewarder of them that diligently seek him."

Mrs. E. G. White

January 17, 1901—Faithful in That Which Is Least

"He that is faithful in that which is least is faithful also in much."

It is conscientious attention to what the world terms "little things" that makes life a success. Little deeds of charity, little acts of self-denial, speaking simple words of helpfulness, watching against little sins,--this is Christianity. A grateful acknowledgment of daily blessings, a wise improvement of daily opportunities, a diligent cultivation of intrusted talents,--this is what the Master calls for.

He who faithfully performs small duties will be prepared to answer the demands of larger responsibilities. The man who is kind and courteous in the daily life, who is generous and forbearing in his family, whose constant aim it is to make home happy, will be the first to deny self and make sacrifices when the Master calls.

We may be willing to give our property to the cause of God, but this will not count unless we give him also a heart of love and gratitude. Those who would be true missionaries in foreign fields must first be true missionaries in the home. Those who desire to work in the Master's vineyard must prepare themselves for this by a careful cultivation of the little piece of vineyard he has intrusted to their care.

As a man "thinketh in his heart, so is he." Many thoughts make up the unwritten history of a single day; and these thoughts have much to do with the formation of character. Our thoughts are to be strictly guarded; for one impure thought makes a deep impression on the soul. An evil thought leaves an evil impress on the mind. If the thoughts are pure and holy, the man is better for having cherished them. By them the spiritual pulse is quickened, and the power for doing good is increased. And as one drop of rain prepares the way for another in moistening the earth, so one good thought prepares the way for another.

The longest journey is performed by taking one step at a time. A succession of steps brings us to the end of the road. The longest chain is composed of separate links. If one of these links is faulty, the chain is worthless. Thus it is with character. A well-balanced character is formed by single acts well performed. One defect, cultivated instead of being overcome, makes the man imperfect, and closes against him the gate of the Holy City. He who enters heaven must have a character that is without spot or wrinkle or any such thing. Naught that defileth can ever enter there. In all the redeemed host not one defect will be seen.

God's work is perfect as a whole because it is perfect in every part, however minute. He fashions the tiny spear of grass with as much care as he would exercise in making a world. If we desire to be perfect, even as our Father in heaven is perfect, we must be faithful in doing little things. That which is worth doing at all, is worth doing well. Whatever your work may be, do it faithfully. Speak the truth in regard to the smallest matters. Each day do loving deeds and speak cheerful words. Scatter smiles along the pathway of life. As you work in this way, God will place his approval on you, and Christ will one day say to you, "Well done, thou good and faithful servant."

At the day of Judgment, those who have been faithful in their every-day life, who have been quick to see their work and do it, not thinking of praise or profit, will hear the words, "Come, ye blessed of my Father, inherit the kingdom prepared for you from the foundation of the world." Christ does not commend them for the eloquent orations they have made, the intellectual power they have displayed, or the liberal donations they have given. It is for doing little things which are generally overlooked that they are rewarded. "I was an hungered, and ye gave me meat," he says. "Inasmuch as ye have done it unto one of the least of these my brethren, ye have done it unto me."

Mrs. E. G. White

January 24, 1901—The Christian Pathway

To be a Christian means to possess the attributes of Christ's character, to have a heart imbued with love for God, to delight to honor God, to reach earnestly after heavenly attainments. It means to render to God grateful songs of praise from a heart swelling with gratitude, to appreciate all that has its origin in God and heaven. The Christian loves what God loves. A heart filled with Christian love is lifted far above the atmosphere of selfishness. It lives in a pure, bright, holy atmosphere. The love that God puts into the heart is a love dictated by holy impulses, sustained by a sense of duty, and cherished by a resolute will. In the soul where this love is cherished, virtue will grow like a tree in a well-cultivated garden.

To be a Christian means to possess the Christian graces, to bear fruit unto righteousness, even the fruits of the Spirit,--"love, joy, peace, long-suffering, gentleness, goodness, faith, meekness, temperance." To be a Christian means to practice religion in the home. Where is it more needed? Home influence, all-powerful for good, is such only as it is carefully cherished. It can not bear the blast of rudeness or neglect without receiving a wound which can with difficulty be healed.

The motives and tastes of the Christian are entirely opposite to those of the worldling. It is impossible to be in harmony with Christ and with the world at the same time. But among the people of God, the love of the world has been increasing to an alarming extent. We feel alarmed as we see so many who profess to accept Christ going on from day to day the same as before. Too often believers act in such a way that unbelievers have no cause to think that they are living any nearer Christ than they themselves. Their conversation is flippant, their actions are unlike Christ. Many who take upon themselves baptismal vows do not live these vows even for one day. They have not come out from the world. They do not know what it means to hold communion with God. We fear that many youth have stopped short of genuine conversion. By their actions they testify that they have no part with Christ,--that they are only pretenders.

"Ye shall know them by their fruits." A genuine change of heart carries its evidence with it. The life of the one who is truly converted is separate and distinct from the life of the worldling. Instead of being absorbed in worldly pleasure, the Christian hungers and thirsts for the bread of life and the water of salvation. He is more anxious to learn the way of the Lord, and to secure his favor, than to please himself or those who are not in harmony with God.

"Enter ye in at the strait gate.... Strait is the gate, and narrow is the way, which leadeth unto life, and few there be that find it." When Christ spoke these words, many of his hearers were convinced of his doctrine, but they needed to be aroused to greater earnestness in regard to their eternal welfare. They had come to the place where two roads met, the wrong one apparently the most attractive. They had good desires, but they were not wholly decided to serve God. They followed the Saviour "afar off." The world's Redeemer saw their peril, and sought to rouse them to a realization of their danger. He longed to see them making an entire surrender to God. It pained him to see them living in a state of indecision.

His voice was raised in earnest entreaty in their behalf. "Wide is the gate, and broad is the way, that leadeth to destruction," he said, "and many there be which go in thereat." This road is wide; and in it the pleasure-lovers and the proud will find abundant room. The selfish, the covetous, the hypocrite, the sons and daughters of levity, the unthankful and unholy, will find the broad road well suited to their taste.

To walk in the narrow road requires earnest, self-denying effort. It is because of the straitness of this way that so few find it. Many seek to enter, but fail because of lack of earnestness. And in the end they step into the broad road, failing to see that the narrow way has joys that would compensate for any trials.

Some who have entered the broad road hear God's voice calling to them, "Enter ye in at the strait gate," and make a decided stand, determined to proceed no farther in the broad road. Through repentance and faith in Christ they enter the strait gate. They realize that all self-indulgence must be given up, that pride must be humbled, and self crucified. They see that they must lay aside every weight, and the sin that so easily besets them. They must urge their way through every obstacle, denying self, lifting the cross, resisting temptation, grasping all the help that God has placed within their reach. In deed and in truth they must accept the Saviour. They must press their way along the narrow path of self-sacrifice; for it is the path of salvation. Although the voices of pleasure-lovers invite them to carelessness and selfish enjoyment, they must turn neither to the right hand nor to the left.

January 31, 1901—Idleness Is Sin—Part 1

Ministers and physicians should understand their own building, the body. They should learn how to use and develop their capabilities. They should see the need of learning how to use every part of the human machinery, how to give solidity to the muscles by employing them in taxing, useful labor. Young men who do not think deeply enough to take in the situation, who do not reason from cause to effect, will never succeed as physicians. The love of ease, and I may say, of physical laziness, unfits a man to be either a physician or a minister. Those who are preparing to enter the medical work or the ministry should train brain, bone, and muscle to do hard work; then they can do hard thinking.

For healthy young men, stern, severe exercise is strengthening to the whole system. And it is an essential preparation for the difficult work of the physician. Without such exercise the mind can not be kept in working order. It becomes inactive, unable to put forth the sharp, quick action that will give scope to its powers. Unless he changes, the youth with such a mind will never become what God designed he should be. He has established so many resting-places that his mind has become like a stagnant pool. The atmosphere surrounding him is charged with moral miasma.

Study the Lord's plan in regard to Adam. He was created pure, holy, and healthy; and he was given something to do. He was placed in the garden of Eden "to dress it and to keep it." He was not to be idle. He must work.

God has ordained that the beings he has created shall work. Upon this their happiness depends. Healthy young men and women have no need of cricket, ball-playing, or any kind of amusement just for the gratification of self, to pass away the time. There are useful things to be done by every one of God's created intelligences. Some one needs from you something that will help him. No one in the Lord's great domain of creation was made to be a drone. Our happiness increases, and our powers develop, as we engage in useful employment.

Action gives power. Entire harmony pervades the universe of God. All the heavenly beings are in constant activity, and the Lord Jesus, in his life-work, has given an example for every one. He went about "doing good." God has established the law of obedient action. Silent but ceaseless, the objects of his creation do their appointed work. The ocean is in constant motion. The springing grass, which today is, and tomorrow is cast into the oven, does its errand, clothing the field with beauty. The leaves are stirred to motion, and yet no hand is seen to touch them. The sun, moon, and stars are useful and glorious in fulfilling their mission.

At all times the machinery of the body continues its work. Day by day the heart throbs, doing its regular, appointed task, unceasingly forcing its crimson current to all parts of the body. Action, action, pervades the whole living machinery. And man, his mind and body created in God's own similitude, must be active in order to fill his appointed place. He is not to be idle. Idleness is sin.

There is true dignity in labor. Among the believers in Christ there was not one apostle who was exalted as was Paul by the revelation of the Saviour in his conversion. And Paul labored with his hands as a tent-maker. In the midst of his zeal in persecuting the Christians, Paul had been arrested by a voice and a great light from heaven. During his ministerial labors he had several visions, of which he spoke little. He saw and heard many things not lawful for a man to utter. That which was given him as a special revelation from God was not at all times dwelt upon when he spoke to the people. But the impression was ever with him, enabling him to give a correct representation of the Christian life and character. The impression made upon his mind by the revelation of Christ never lost its force. It influenced his estimation and delineation of Christian character.

The history of the apostle Paul is a constant testimony that manual labor can not be degrading, that it is not inconsistent with true elevation of character. Paul worked day and night to avoid being a burden to his brethren, and at times he supported his fellow workers, he himself suffering from hunger in order to relieve the necessities of others. His toil-worn hands, as he presented them before the people, bore testimony that he was not chargeable to any man for his support. They detracted nothing, he deemed, from the force of his pathetic appeals, sensible, intelligent, and eloquent beyond those of any other man who had acted a part in the Christian ministry.

In Acts 20:17-35 we see outlined the character of a Christian minister who faithfully performed his duty. He was an all-round minister. We do not think it is obligatory on all ministers to do in all respects as Paul did. Yet we say to all that Paul was a Christian gentleman of the highest type. His example shows that mechanical toil does not necessarily lessen the influence of any one, that working with the hands in any honorable employment should not make a man coarse and rough and discourteous.

Mrs. E. G. White

February 7, 1901—Idleness Is Sin—Part 2

In the life-insurance plan given us in the first chapter of second Peter, a work of addition is presented. As in our character-building we add grace to grace, the great Giver will work for us on the plan of multiplication. Grace and peace will be multiplied to us. The young man who is seeking a preparation for usefulness needs to lay the foundation himself, by acquiring, through hard, diligent labor, the means to prosecute his designs. If the young men around him have allowed their parents to carry the burden of their education, let him say, I will never do that. I will, by using my physical and mental powers combined, make of myself all that it is possible.

No man is excusable for being without financial ability. Of many a man it may be said, He is kind, amiable, generous, a good man, and a Christian, but he is not qualified to manage his own business. As far as the proper outlay of money is concerned, he is a mere child. He has not been educated by his parents to understand and practice the principles of self-support. Such a man is not fitted to become a minister or a physician. The churches everywhere are suffering through the neglect of parents to train their children to bear hard, stern responsibilities. Too often the wicked love to do nothing but use the mind takes possession of children and youth. Then the enemy takes control, and makes the mind his workshop, using in his service the ability needed in the family and in the church.

Many are destitute of the stern virtues required to build up the church. They are not capable of devising methods and plans of a healthy, solid character. They are deficient in the qualifications necessary to the prosperity of the church. It is this kind of education that needs to be changed to an education that is sound and sensible, in harmony with Bible principles.

Let your aspirations and your motives be pure. In every business transaction be rigidly honest. However you may be tempted, never deceive nor prevaricate. At times a natural impulse may tempt you to vary from the straightforward path of honesty, but do not yield to this impulse. If in any matter you make a statement as to what you will do, and afterward find that you have favored others to your own loss, do not vary one hair's breadth from principle. Carry out your agreement. By seeking to change your plans, you would show that you could not be depended on. And if you should draw back in small transactions, you would draw back in larger ones. Under such circumstances, some are tempted to deceive, saying that they were not understood. They did mean what they said, but lost the good impulse, and then wanted to draw back from their agreement, lest it prove a loss to them.

Let the youth set up well-defined landmarks, by which they may be governed in emergencies. When a crisis comes that demands active, well-developed physical powers, and a clear, strong, practical mind; when difficult work is to be done, where every stroke must tell, where perplexities will arise which can be met only by wisdom from on high, then the youth who have learned how to overcome difficulties can respond, to the call for workers, "Here am I; send me." Let the hearts of young men and women be as clear as crystal. Let not their thoughts be trivial, but sanctified by virtue and holiness. If their thoughts are made pure by the sanctification of the Spirit, their lives will be elevated and ennobled.

I repeat: It should be the fixed purpose of the youth to aim high in all their plans for their life-work. They should adopt for their government in all things the standard which God's word presents. This is the Christian's positive duty, and it should be also his positive pleasure. Cultivate respect for yourself because you are Christ's purchased possession. Success in the formation of rights habits, advancement in that which is noble and just, will give you an influence that all will appreciate and value. Live for something besides self. If your motives are pure and unselfish, if you are ever looking for work to do, if you are always on the alert to show kindly attentions and do courteous deeds, you are unconsciously building your own monument. This is the work God calls upon all children and youth to do. Do good, if you would be cherished in the memory of others. Live to be a blessing to all with whom you come in contact, wherever your lot may be cast. Let the children and youth awake to their opportunities. By kindness and love, by self-sacrificing deeds, let them write their names in the hearts of those with whom they associate.

Mrs. E. G. White

February 14, 1901—Ministering Spirits

God has recorded many narratives in his inspired word to teach us that the human family is the object of the special care of heavenly angels. Man is not left to become the sport of Satan's temptations. All heaven is actively engaged in the work of communicating light to the inhabitants of the world, that they may not be left without spiritual guidance. An eye that never slumbers nor sleeps is guarding the camp of Israel. Ten thousand times ten thousand, and thousands of thousands of angels are ministering to the needs of the children of men. Voices inspired by God are crying, This is the way, walk ye in it. If men will hear the voice of warning, if they will trust to God's guidance and not to finite judgment, they will be safe.

The experience of Paul shows that the Lord will open up ways before those who will put their trust in him. Paul was on his way to Damascus to persecute the believers in Christ. Full of zeal, he determined to take all, both men and women, and punish them with imprisonment and death. The record declares that he was "exceeding mad" against them. But the Commander of heaven beheld the suffering brought upon his church, and he made his voice heard to arrest the bold persecutor. As Paul journeyed, "suddenly there shined round about him a light from heaven: and he fell to the earth, and heard a voice saying unto him, Saul, Saul, why persecutest thou me? And he said, Who art thou, Lord? And the Lord said, I am Jesus whom thou persecutest."

Again, in the case of Cornelius we are taught that God is interested in every human being. Cornelius was following on to know the Lord, and this won for him the salvation of all his house. He "feared God with all his house," and "gave much alms to the people, and prayed to God alway. He saw in a vision, evidently about the ninth hour of the day an angel of God coming in to him, and saying unto him, Cornelius. And when he looked on him, he was afraid, and said, What is it, Lord? And he said unto him, Thy prayers and thine alms are come up for a memorial before God. And now send men to Joppa, and call for one Simon, whose surname is Peter: he lodgeth with one Simon a tanner, whose house is by the seaside: he shall tell thee what thou oughtest to do." The Lord knows every child of his by name. When we truly believe this, we shall have courage, faith, and patience to work out our own salvation with fear and trembling; for we shall know that it is God who worketh in us. With fear and trembling we shall co-operate with God.

Heavenly angels watch those who are seeking for enlightenment, and co-operate with those who try to win souls to Christ. This is shown in the experience of Philip and the Ethiopian.

A heavenly messenger was sent to Philip to show him his work for the Ethiopian. The evangelist was directed to "arise, and go toward the south unto the way that goeth down from Jerusalem unto Gaza, which is desert. And he arose and went: and, behold, a man of Ethiopia, a eunuch of great authority under Candace, queen of the Ethiopians, who had charge of all her treasure, and had come to Jerusalem for to worship, was returning, and sitting in his chariot read Esaias the prophet."

Angels of God were taking notice of this seeker for light. The Ethiopian could not understand the prophecy that he read: and the Spirit directed Philip to go and teach him, saying, "Go near, and join thyself to this chariot." This man of high authority was being drawn to the Saviour, and he did not resist the drawing. He did not make his position an excuse for refusing to accept the crucified One. The evangelist asked him: "Understandest thou what thou readest? And he said, How can I, except some man should guide me? And he desired Philip that he would come up and sit with him," and explain to him the word of God.

Today, as then, angels are leading and guiding those who will be led and guided. The angel sent to Philip could himself have done the work for the Ethiopian, but this was not God's way of working. As God's instruments, men must work for others.

When God pointed out to Philip his work, the disciple did not say, as many are saying today, God does not mean that. I will not be too confident, or I shall make a mistake. Philip that day learned a lesson of conformity to God's will that was worth everything to him. He learned that every soul is precious in the sight of God, and that angels will bring light to those who are in need of it. Through the ministration of angels, God sends light to his people, and through his people this light is to be given to the world. The Holy Spirit will guide and instruct men and women if they will show themselves willing to be guided, by placing themselves in a position where they can communicate the light received.

While angels from heaven are doing their work, evil angels are seeking to draw the mind to something else. Satan is interposing obstacles, so that the mind that would understand the word of God shall become confused. Thus he worked with Christ in the wilderness of temptation. Had Philip left the eunuch with his case hanging in the balance, he might never have accepted the Saviour. Evil angels were waiting for an opportunity to press in their falsehoods, and divert the Ethiopian from seeking after truth. The Lord's agencies must be wholly consecrated to his service, that they may be quick to understand their work. As wise stewards, they must take advantage of every circumstance to draw men to Christ.

Satan is ever on the alert to deceive and mislead. He is using every enchantment to allure men into the broad road of disobedience. Because evil agencies are striving to eclipse every ray of light, heavenly beings are appointed to do their work of ministry,--to guide, guard, and control those who shall be heirs of salvation. None need despair because of inherited tendencies to evil. When the Holy Spirit convicts of sin, the wrong-doer must repent, and confess and forsake the evil. Faithful sentinels are on guard, to direct souls in right paths.

February 21, 1901—Christ's Entry Into Jerusalem—Part 1

The time of Christ's entry into Jerusalem was the most lovely season of the year. The mount of Olives was carpeted with green, and the groves were beautiful with varied foliage. From the regions round about Jerusalem many people had come to the feast with an earnest desire to see Jesus. The crowning miracle of the Saviour, in raising Lazarus from the dead, had had a wonderful effect upon the people, and a large and enthusiastic multitude was drawn to the place where Jesus was tarrying.

The afternoon was half spent when Jesus sent his disciples to the village of Bethphage, saying: "Go into the village over against you, and straightway ye shall find an ass tied, and a colt with her: loose them, and bring them unto me. And if any man say ought unto you, ye shall say, The Lord hath need of them; and straightway he will send them."

This was the first time during his life of ministry that Christ had consented to ride, and the disciples interpreted this move to be an indication that he was about to assert his kingly power and authority, and take his position on David's throne.

Joyfully they executed the commission. They found the colt, and loosed him. "And certain of them that stood there said unto them, What do ye, loosing the colt? And they said unto them even as Jesus had commanded: and they let them go. And they brought the colt to Jesus, ... and he sat upon him."

As Jesus takes his seat upon the animal, the air becomes vocal with acclamations of praise and triumph. He is the object of universal homage. He bears no outward sign of royalty. He wears no dress of state, nor is he followed by a train of soldiers. But he is surrounded by a company wrought up to the highest pitch of excitement. They can not restrain the joyous feelings of expectancy that animate their hearts.

Many flatter themselves that the hour of Israel's emancipation is at hand. In imagination they see the Roman army dispersed, and driven from Jerusalem, and the Jewish nation once more free from the yoke of the oppressor. From lip to lip the question passes, "Will he at this time restore again the kingdom to Israel?" Many in the throng recall the word of the prophet: "Rejoice greatly, O daughter of Zion; shout,

O daughter of Jerusalem: behold, thy king cometh unto thee: he is just, and having salvation; lowly, and riding upon an ass." Each strives to excel the other in responding to the prophetic past. The shout echoes from mountain and valley, "Hosanna to the Son of David: Blessed is he that cometh in the name of the Lord; hosanna in the highest."

No mourning nor wailing is heard in that wonderful procession. No captives are to be seen in chains of humiliation. Those who have once been blind, but whose eyes have felt the healing touch of the Son of God, lead the way. They press close to the side of Jesus, while one whom he has raised from the dead leads the animal upon which he is seated. Those once deaf and dumb, with ears opened and tongues unloosed, help to swell the glad hosannas. Cripples, now with buoyant steps and grateful hearts, are most active in breaking down palm branches, and strewing them in his path, as their tribute of homage to the mighty healer.

The leper, who has listened to the dread words of the priest, "Unclean!" which shut him out from intercourse with his fellow men, is there. But the curse of the loathsome disease no longer contaminates those within touch of him. He has felt the compassionate touch of the Saviour, and has been cleansed by his power. Now he lays his untainted garment in the path of the Saviour, exclaiming, "O give thanks unto the Lord; for he is good: for his mercy endureth forever."

The healed demoniac is there, not now to have the words wrenched from his lips by satanic power, "Let us alone;" but "clothed, and in his right mind." He adds his testimony to that of others: "The Lord hath done great things for me, whereof I am glad."

The restored dead are there. Their tongues, once palsied by the power of Satan, take up the song of rejoicing, He hath brought the dead from their graves; I will open my lips in praise to him.

The widow and the orphan are there to tell of his wonderful works. Little children are inspired by the scene. There are present those who have been healed of their diseases, and brought back from the grave by the word of the Life-giver; and with palm branches and flowers these bestrew the path of the Redeemer.

Mrs. E. G. White

February 28, 1901 Christ's Entry Into Jerusalem—Part 2

On the crest of Olivet the procession pauses. Before them lies the city of Jerusalem, with its temple of pure white marble, which just now is gilded with glory by the rays of the setting sun. It is a picture of unsurpassed loveliness. Well might the people apply to this city the words of the prophet, "a crown of glory in the hand of the Lord, and a royal diadem in the hand of thy God." At the entrancing sight, the throng join with renewed fervor in their shouts of praise. Branches are stripped from the palm trees, and placed in the path of the Saviour, while hill and mountain give back the glad shouts of the joyous and triumphant multitude. Their eyes turn to Christ, to see how he is impressed by the scene; but lo, the Son of God is in tears.

The glad company can not understand the cause of the Saviour's sorrow; they do not know that the iniquities of Jerusalem are bringing her final calamities upon her. A mysterious awe falls upon the procession, and calms in a degree its enthusiasm.

As Christ's eyes rest upon the temple so soon to be desolated, he weeps. The Israel of God, to whom he has given every advantage, will soon reject their King and their God. In a few short hours the world's Redeemer will be taken by wicked hands and crucified. Not the Romans, not the Gentiles, but the people for whom he has done so much, are to be his murderers. Christ's prophetic eye takes in the future of Jerusalem, when the glory which God designed should rest upon this chosen nation would be removed, and the grace which bringeth salvation would no longer be heard in the city. This is the cause of the Saviour's sorrow. He weeps not for himself, but for those who have rejected his love and despised his mercy. The tender tears he sheds over Jerusalem are the tears of rejected love. In a voice of anguish and lamentation he cries: "O Jerusalem, Jerusalem, which killest the prophets, and stonest them that are sent unto thee; how often would I have gathered thy children together, as a hen doth gather her brood under her wings, and ye would not! Behold, your house is left unto you desolate: and verily I say unto you, Ye shall not see me, until the time come when ye shall say, Blessed is he that cometh in the name of the Lord."

Christ had come to the earth to reveal the principles of the kingdom of heaven. His character as Saviour and Life-giver had been demonstrated only a short time before at the grave of Lazarus but in their pride the Jews rejected him. To the Hebrew nation had been committed the oracles of God. They had been taught the commandments and statutes and judgments of the Lord. God designed that the faith of this people should be communicated to all other peoples on the face of the earth. How different would have been Christ's attitude, had the priests and rulers been true to the trust reposed in them! Had they done the work that God designed they should do, the glory of the Lord would have been revealed to the idolatrous nations.

"And when he was come into Jerusalem, all the city was moved, saying, Who is this? And the multitude said, This is Jesus the prophet of Nazareth of Galilee." A large number in that throng bear in their own bodies the evidence that divine power is among them, and each has his story to tell of the merciful works of Christ. The relation of these wonderful works only increases the fervor of their feelings. Disciples and people join together in the songs of praise.

"Who is this?" We ask Isaiah, and he answers: "Unto us a child is born, unto us a son is given: and the government shall be upon his shoulder: and his name shall be called Wonderful, Counselor, The mighty God, The everlasting Father, The Prince of Peace." John the Baptist tells us who he is: "Behold the Lamb of God," he says, "which taketh away the sin of the world." And the beloved disciple adds his testimony: "In the beginning was the Word, and the Word was with God, and the Word was God."

Mrs. E. G. White

March 21, 1901—"Show Us a Sign From Heaven"

The Pharisees also with the Sadducees came, and tempting desired him that he would show them a sign from heaven. He answered and said unto them, When it is evening, ye say, It will be fair weather: for the sky is red. And in the morning, It will be foul weather today: for the sky is red and lowering. O ye hypocrites, ye can discern the face of the sky; but can ye not discern the signs of the times?"

The sign they asked was a miracle,--some wonderful token in the heavens to gratify their curiosity. Signs were frequently given by the prophets; and if he were the Messiah, they argued, he would give some evidence to prove it. Those miracles which included only the relief of human necessities, the healing of the woes of mankind, had no particular interest for them; for they looked upon suffering and distress with hard-hearted, unsympathetic indifference. In relieving the oppressed and suffering, Christ cast a reproach upon them, not only for their careless indifference toward the poor, but because they were themselves the direct cause of much of the misery that existed.

Well had the prophet declared of this people: "Hear, O heavens, and give ear, O earth: for the Lord hath spoken, I have nourished and brought up children, and they have rebelled against me.... Israel doth not know, my people doth not consider. Ah sinful nation, a people laden with iniquity, a seed of evil-doers, children that are corrupters: they have forsaken the Lord, they have provoked the Holy One of Israel unto anger, they are gone away backward.... Every one loveth gifts, and followeth after rewards: they judge not the fatherless, neither doth the cause of the widow come unto them." "Judgment is turned away backward, and justice standeth afar off: for truth is fallen in the street, and equity can not enter. Yea, truth faileth; and he that departeth from evil maketh himself a prey."

Christ tried to present before the Pharisees their inconsistency. By certain indications in the heavens they professed themselves wise to foretell the weather. "When it is evening," he said, "ye say, It will be fair weather: for the sky is red. And in the morning, It will be foul weather today: for the sky is red and lowering. O ye hypocrites, ye can discern the face of the sky; but can ye not discern the signs of the times?" If these signs in the heavens are sufficient evidence on which to base your faith, why do you not believe the evidence given of my mission? The works that I do, they testify of me.

The relation of the Jewish nation to God has often been presented as a marriage relation,--God the husband, the nation the wife. Their separation from God by wicked works is called adultery. The Jews had been unfaithful to the covenant that God had made with them. Not only spiritually but literally they were transgressors of the law of God. Christ would work no miracle to satisfy the curiosity of the people. "A wicked and adulterous generation seeketh after a sign," he said, "and there shall no sign be given unto it, but the sign of the prophet Jonas."

It was not Christ's mission to exalt himself as an astrologer. His work was with sinful human beings, whom he came to save from hopeless woe and misery. The angel that foretold his birth declared, "Thou shalt call his name Jesus: for he shall save his people from their sins." And more than six hundred years before, he himself had declared: "The Spirit of the Lord God is upon me; because the Lord hath anointed me to preach good tidings unto the meek; he hath sent me to bind up the broken-hearted, to proclaim liberty to the captives, and the opening of the prison to them that are bound; to proclaim the acceptable year of the Lord, and the day of vengeance of our God; to comfort all that mourn; to appoint unto them that mourn in Zion, to give unto them beauty for ashes, the oil of joy for mourning, the garment of praise for the spirit of heaviness." This was his mission.

Even the wicked Herod could perceive the greatness of the works of Christ; but the scribes and Pharisees could not be convinced. The works which they could not explain away they charged to the agency of the devil. The Holy Spirit was sent down to bless this people, but they barred the door of their hearts against his influence. Christ well knew that however strong and uncontrovertible the evidence he might give them, they would not receive it. Therefore he kept steadily at the work which had been planned in the councils of heaven, healing the sick and relieving the oppressed. He knew that in this work he has giving ample proof of his mission to those who were honest in heart. His heart was grieved by their obstinacy and determined resistance of light and truth. "If I had not done among them the works which none other man did," he said, "they had not had sin: but now have they both seen and hated both me and my Father."

Christ was God manifest in the flesh; in him dwelt "all the fullness of the Godhead bodily." All this glory he longed to pour upon the world, but men refused to receive it. They were given evidence upon evidence; but they bound themselves up in their stubborn unbelief and prejudice. Therefore they were without excuse.

We are to learn a lesson from the sin of this people. Today there are many who have taken their position on the side of unbelief, as if it were a virtue, the sign of a great mind, to doubt. Because the works of God can not be explained by finite minds, Satan brings his sophistry to bear upon them, and entangles them in the meshes of unbelief. If these doubting ones would come into close connection with God, he would make his purposes clear to their understanding.

The position of those who resist light is thus set forth by the apostle Paul: "If our gospel be hid, it is hid to them that are lost: in whom the god of this world hath blinded the eyes of them which believe not, lest the light of the glorious gospel of Christ, who is the image of God, should shine unto them." The operation of the Spirit is foolishness to the unrenewed heart; but to those who are humble, teachable, honest, childlike, and who desire to know the will of the Father, his word is revealed as the power of God unto salvation.

Mrs. E. G. White

April 4, 1901—How to Meet Criticism

There are those who can not speak in favor of the very best of blessings without attaching a criticism, to cast a shadow of reproach. Let us be guarded. Let us refuse to allow the criticisms of any one to implant objections in our minds. Let us educate ourselves to praise that which is good when others criticise. Murmurers will always pick flaws, but let us not be saddened by the accusing element. Let us not look upon it as a virtue to make and suggest difficulties, which will harass and perplex. Keep the atmosphere surrounding the soul clear by dwelling upon the bright sunshine of heaven, which is always shining to make us happy. Let us bring all the pleasantness possible into our lives.

When others begin to question and criticise, let us be determined, either by silence or by turning the conversation into another channel, to cut off the words which would not be spoken in wisdom. We are to continue to wait upon the Lord, making every effort to keep the door of our lips, so that we shall not utter one word savoring of unbelief.

We are to walk by faith, practicing the very things we have asked the Lord to give us grace to do. Thus we work out our own salvation, trying to help and save those in trouble by faithful words and kind deeds. It is God who works in us, both to will and to do of his good pleasure. The finite and the infinite are to unite in accomplishing the work that needs to be done. God has pledged himself to supply us with strength, cheerfulness, pleasantness, and joyfulness in our Saviour. Abiding in him, the word that would cast a shadow over others is left unsaid.

Let us remember that every one has some dark spot in his experience; and let us do all we can to bring cheerfulness and hope into the lives of others. What a blessing this will be to them! In turn they will speak words of good cheer to others, to bring sunshine into their hearts. As we do this work, we shall be in a position to realize, that the Lord hears our prayers, because we work in harmony with them, fulfilling all the duty we owe to God and to ourselves. We shall go about our work in a thankful, prayerful frame of mind.

By faith we may claim the promise, "Ask, and it shall be given you; seek, and ye shall find." Yes, we shall find the answer to our prayers; for God will do exceeding abundantly above our highest expectation. What precious witness we shall then bear for God! What an honor we shall be to the truth of his word!

Doleful, discouraging words will do no good. When Christ abides in the heart, we shall not even repeat the false statements we hear. We shall not retaliate nor bring railing accusation against any, because this would wound our souls deeply, and make us forget our resting-place of confidence and peace in Christ.

The enemy leads those whose hearts are not stayed upon God to admit into their minds unpleasant and disagreeable thoughts. These they ponder over, and then pass along as food for other minds. But this is food of Satan's preparation, and impoverishes the soul.

With the sweet melody of song, in his childhood, youth, and manhood, Jesus corrected passionate, unadvised words and unbelieving, accusing utterances. When he was assailed by criticisers, his voice was raised in song: "Many, O Lord my God, are thy wonderful works, which thou hast done, and thy thoughts, which are to us ward: they can not be reckoned up in order unto thee: if I would declare and speak of them, they are more than can be numbered.... I delight to do thy will, O my God: yea, thy law is within my heart. I have preached righteousness in the great congregation: lo, I have not refrained my lips, O Lord, thou knowest. I have not hid thy righteousness within my heart; I have declared thy faithfulness and thy salvation: I have not concealed thy loving-kindness and thy truth from the great congregation. Withhold not thou thy tender mercies from me, O Lord; let thy loving-kindness and thy truth continually preserve me."

Mrs. E. G. White

April 11, 1901—In Gethsemane

When the passover supper was ended, Jesus left the upper chamber with his disciples, and together they crossed the brook Kedron. Sorrow and anguish pressed upon the heart of the Saviour, and with sadness he said to his disciples: "All ye shall be offended because of me this night; for it is written, I will smite the shepherd, and the sheep of the flock shall be scattered abroad." Peter, always foremost in speech, assured his Master of his fidelity. "Though all men shall be offended because of thee," he said, "yet will I never be offended. Jesus said unto him, Verily I say unto thee, That this night, before the cock crow, thou shalt deny me thrice. Peter said unto him. Though I should die with thee, yet will I not deny thee. Likewise also said all the disciples."

As Christ entered the garden of Gethsemane, he bade his disciples remain near the entrance, while he took Peter, James, and John with him a short distance. Then urging these three to watch and pray, he left them. The Saviour desired to be alone with God, that he might wrestle with him in prayer. The agony that pressed upon his soul was not for the physical suffering that he must endure. He was feeling the offensive character of the sin that he must bear. He must suffer the penalty of the broken law, and bear the Father's wrath.

A little distance from his disciples, Christ fell on his face and prayed. "O my Father," he cried, "if it be possible, let this cup pass from me: nevertheless not as I will, but as thou wilt."

In the deepening gloom that surrounded him, every stay seemed falling from Christ, and his soul reached out for human sympathy. At length, and pressed with an inexpressible weight of agony, he arose, and moved through the darkness to the place where he had left his three friends. But he found them sleeping. "What, could ye not watch with me one hour?" he asked.

At this most important time--the time when Jesus had made special request for them to watch with him--the disciples slept. Christ had taken them with him that they might be a strength to him, and that the events they should witness that night, and the instruction they should receive, might be indelibly imprinted on their memories. This was necessary in order that their faith might not fail, but be strengthened for the test just before them. But instead of watching with Christ, they fell asleep. Even the ardent Peter, who only a few hours before had declared that he would suffer, and, if need be, die for his Lord, was asleep when Jesus needed his sympathy and prayers.

With the words, "Watch and pray, that ye enter not into temptation," the lonely Sufferer turned again to his solitude and prayer. Again his voice was borne upon the sympathizing air: "O my Father, if this cup may not pass away from me, except I drink it, thy will be done. And he came and found them asleep again: for their eyes were heavy.

"And he left them, and went away again, and prayed the third time, saying the same words." The Saviour is alone in his sorrow. Jerusalem is in slumber; even the disciples in Gethsemane are sleeping. His form bowed to the earth, Jesus prays such a prayer as the angels have never before listened to. It is the voice of helpless suffering that speaks. "O my Father," he says, "if it be possible, let this cup pass from me." His heart seems bursting with agony, and from his pale brow fall drops of blood. The very life-current seems flowing from his bleeding heart.

The powers of darkness were encompassing the Son of God; for the destiny of a lost world hung in the balance. Satan was clothing him with the garments of sin. Christ had placed himself in the sinner's stead, and he felt that a great gulf separated him from his Father. It was a moment of soul-agony for the Son of God. It was the hour of the power of darkness. Shall he drink the cup? Shall he take upon his divine soul the guilt of a lost world, and consent to be numbered with the transgressors? It was here that the mysterious cup trembled in his hand. The billows of wrath were rolling over his head, but the woes of a lost world also rose before him; and he consented to the sacrifice. "Nevertheless," he said, "not my will, but thine, be done."

The Redeemer had poured out his soul with strong crying and tears unto Him who was able to save him from death; and he was heard. Even with Calvary before him, he had defeated the enemy, and his soul rested calmly in his Father's love.

Again Christ came to his disciples, and found them sleeping. "Sleep on now," he said. "and take your rest: behold, the hour is at hand, and the Son of man is betrayed into the hands of sinners. Rise, let us be going: behold, he is at hand that doth betray me."

Soon glaring torches were seen among the trees, and the heavy tramp of an approaching mob broke the stillness of the night. Helmeted soldiers, with glittering swords and flaming torches, drew up around the Son of God. As his eye rested on them, Christ inquired, "Whom seek ye? They answered him, Jesus of Nazareth. Jesus saith unto them, I am he." As they looked upon the blood-stained face of Christ, their physical strength failed them, and they fell as dead men to the ground. It was not Christ's suffering that unnerved them; for they were accustomed to the sight of human suffering. It was the voice of God speaking to them through Christ that melted their hearts in terror.

Seeing their foe fallen, the disciples took courage. "Simon Peter having a sword drew it, and smote the high priest's servant, and cut off his right ear.... Then said Jesus unto Peter, Put up thy sword into the sheath: the cup which my Father hath given me, shall I not drink it? Then the band and the captain and officers of the Jews took Jesus, and bound him, and led him away."

Mrs. E. G. White

April 25, 1901—After the Crucifixion

Christ was crucified. The Prince of life had been taken by wicked hands and slain. In his spotless purity he has been killed as a disturber of the peace. He was lying in Joseph's new tomb. Christ descended into the grave as our sin-bearer, opening a grave for the sins of all who will accept him as their personal Saviour.

The night following the crucifixion was the darkest night the church had ever known. But the redemption price for a fallen world had been paid; the sacrifice for sin had been offered. All heaven was triumphant.

At the setting of the sun on the evening of the preparation day, trumpets sounded, signifying that the Sabbath had begun. The next day the courts of the temple were filled with worshipers. The high priest for Golgotha was there, splendidly robed in his sacerdotal garments. White-turbaned priests, full of busy activity, were preparing to perform their duties. The ceremonies of the Passover moved on with the usual routine. But the imposing dress of the high priest covered a heart that needed the molding of the Spirit of God. The ostentatious and ceremonious rites of the Jewish religion were mingled with selfishness, fraud, discontent, and unholy passions. The priests had chosen Barabbas, and Barabbas they would have as long as life should last. They had cried out against Christ. "Crucify him, crucify him." "His blood be on us, and on our children." The blood they had invoked upon themselves would indeed rest upon them. The characters they had chosen would forever be their characters. By their lives they contradicted the meaning of their ceremonies. Jesus never spurned the true penitent, but he hated hypocrisy cloaked by a garment of religion.

Some of the worshipers of the temple were not at rest as the blood of bulls and goats was offered for the sin of Israel. They were not conscious that type had met antitype, that an infinite sacrifice had been made for the sin of the world. But never before had the ritual service been witnessed with such conflicting feelings. The musical instruments and the voices of the singers were as loud and clear as usual. But a sense of strangeness pervaded everything. One after another inquired about the strange event that had taken place. Hitherto the most holy place had always been sacredly guarded from intrusion. Only once a year had it been entered, and then by the high priest. But now horror was seen on all countenances; for this apartment was open to all eyes. At the very moment when Christ had expired, the heavy veil of tapestry, made of pure linen and beautifully wrought with gold and scarlet and purple, had been rent from top to bottom. The place where Jehovah had met with the priest, to communicate his glory, the place which had been God's sacred audience-chamber, lay open to every eye, no longer recognized by the Lord.

Many who at this time united in the services of the Passover, never took part in them again. Light was to shine into their hearts. The disciples were to communicate to them the knowledge that the Messiah had come.

According to their custom, the people brought their sick and suffering to the temple courts, inquiring, Who can tell us of Jesus of Nazareth, the Healer? Some had come from far to see and hear him who had healed the sick and raised the dead to life. With persistent earnestness they asked for him. They would not be turned away. But they were driven from the temple courts, and the people of Jerusalem could not fail to see the difference between this scene and the scenes of Christ's life.

On every side was heard the cry, "We want Christ, the Healer!" A world without a Christ was blackness and darkness, not only to the disciples, but to the sick and suffering, to the priests and rulers. The Jewish leaders and even the Roman authorities found it harder to deal with a dead Christ than with a living Christ.

The people learned that Jesus had been put to death. Inquiries were made regarding his death. The particulars of his trial were kept as private as possible, but during the time when he was in the grave, his name was on thousands of lips, and the report of his mock trial and of the cruelty of the priests and rulers was circulated everywhere.

By men of intellect the priests were called upon to explain the prophecies concerning the Messiah, and while trying to frame some falsehood in reply, the priests became like men insane. Upon many minds rested the conviction that the Scriptures had been fulfilled.

Entire justice was done in the atonement. In the place of the sinner, the spotless Son of God received the penalty, and the sinner goes free as long as he receives and holds Christ as his personal Saviour. Though guilty, he is looked upon as innocent. Christ fulfilled every requirement demanded by justice. God's character as a God of holiness, a God of goodness, compassion, and love combined, was revealed in his Son. In the cross of Christ, God gave the world a mighty pledge of his justice and love. "For if the blood of bulls and of goats, and the ashes of an heifer sprinkling the unclean, sanctifieth to the purifying of the flesh; how much more shall the blood of Christ, who through the eternal Spirit offered himself without spot to God, purge your conscience from dead works to serve the living God?"

When Christ bowed his head and died, he bore the pillars of Satan's kingdom with him to the earth. He vanquished Satan in the same nature over which in Eden Satan obtained the victory. The enemy was overcome by Christ in his human nature. The power of the Saviour's Godhead was hidden. He overcame in human nature, relying upon God for power. This is the privilege of all. In proportion to our faith will be our victory.

Mrs. E. G. White

May 2, 1901—The Lord Is Risen

The Jewish rulers had carried out their purpose of putting the Son of God to death, but they did not feel the sense of victory that they had thought they would after silencing the voice of the great Teacher. Even in the hour of their apparent triumph they were harassed with doubt as to what would next take place. They dreaded a dead Christ more, a great deal more, than a living Christ. They had a deep conviction that their revenge against Jesus for exposing their hypocrisy would not bring rest to their souls. They had heard the cry, "It is finished," "Father, into thy hands I commend my spirit." They had seen the rocks rent, and had felt the mighty earthquake, and they were restless and uneasy. The words spoken by Christ when he was under their cruel power recurred to their minds.

Not on any account would the priests have allowed Christ's body to hang on the cross during the Sabbath, for already the agitation caused by his death was giving publicity to his life and mission. When the people heard that the mighty Healer was dead, and that the sick and suffering had no one to relieve their distress, they applied to the priests and rulers for sympathy and relief. They were sent away empty; but apparently they were determined to have the living Christ among them again, and soldiers were stationed at the temple gates to keep back the multitude that came with their sick and dying, demanding entrance.

The world without a Christ made an impression that a living Christ could not have made. People came from far and near to see the one of whom the priests and rulers had declared, "The world is gone after him." The recital of the deeds done by the priests shocked the people. They would not have allowed Christ to be thus treated; for had he not shown compassion to their sick? Never had he turned one away with the harsh denunciations used by the Pharisees.

Christ had said to his disciples, "Behold, we go up to Jerusalem; and the Son of man shall be betrayed unto the chief priests and unto the scribes, and they shall condemn him to death, and shall deliver him to the Gentiles to mock, and to scourge, and to crucify him: and the third day he shall rise again." Overwhelmed with sorrow, the disciples did not see the hope and comfort in these words. By Judas they were repeated to the priests, and when they heard them, they mocked and ridiculed, speaking of Christ as a deceiver, a name that might appropriately have been applied to themselves. But now, when they heard the clamor for Jesus, the mighty Healer, who had cured the sick and raised the dead, they thought of his words, and remembered that he had said he would rise the third day, and they were horrified at the thought. Would he rise from the dead, and as judge arraign his accusers before his bar?

Death and the grave must hold him whom they had crucified. "Command therefore," they said to Pilate, "that the sepulcher be made sure unto the third day, lest his disciples come by night, and steal him away, and say unto the people, He is risen from the dead: so the last error shall be worse than the first." "Ye have a watch," said Pilate, "go your way, make it as sure as ye can." The priests gave directions to have a stone rolled before the opening of the tomb. Across this they placed cords, sealing them with the Roman seal. Soldiers were then stationed around the sepulcher, to prevent it from being tampered with. The priests did all they could to keep Christ's body where they had laid it. He was sealed as securely in his narrow tomb as if he were to stay there through all time.

So weak men counseled and planned to secure the body so hated by the Jewish dignitaries, and so precious to the disciples. Little did the murderers realize the uselessness of the efforts they were making to keep Christ in the tomb. By their actions Christ was glorified. The very efforts made to prevent Christ's resurrection are the most convincing proofs of his resurrection. The greater the number of soldiers placed around the tomb, the stronger would be the testimony borne in regard to his resurrection.

There was only one entrance to the tomb, and neither human fraud nor force could tamper with the stone that guarded the entrance. Here Jesus rested during the Sabbath. A strong guard of angels kept watch over the tomb, and had a hand been raised to remove the body, the flashing forth of their glory would have laid him who ventured powerless on the earth. He who died for the sins of the world was to remain in the tomb for the allotted time. He was in that stony prison house as a prisoner of divine justice, and he was responsible to the Judge of the universe. He was bearing the sins of the world, and his Father only could release him.

Christ had declared that he would be raised from the dead on the third day; and at the appointed time a mighty angel descended from heaven, parting the darkness from his track, and resting before the Saviour's tomb. "His countenance was like lightning, and his raiment white as snow: and for fear of him the keepers did shake, and became as dead men." Brave soldiers, who had never been afraid of human power, were now as captives taken without sword or spear. The face they looked upon was not the face of mortal warrior; it was the face of a heavenly messenger, sent to relieve the Son of God from the debt for which he had become responsible, and for which he had now made a full atonement. This heavenly visitant was the angel that on the plains of Bethlehem had proclaimed Christ's birth. The earth trembled at his approach, and as he rolled away the stone from Christ's grave, heaven seemed to come down to earth. The soldiers saw him removing the stone as he would a pebble, and heard him call, Son of God, thy Father saith, Come forth. They saw Jesus come from the grave as a mighty conqueror, and heard him proclaim, "I am the resurrection, and the life." The angel guards bowed low in adoration before the Redeemer as he came forth in majesty and glory, and welcomed him with songs of praise.

May 9, 1901—Sowing and Reaping

"Be not deceived; God is not mocked: for whatsoever a man soweth, that shall he also reap. For he that soweth to his flesh shall of the flesh reap corruption; but he that soweth to the Spirit shall of the Spirit reap life everlasting."

The choice we make in this life will be our choice through all eternity. We shall receive either eternal life or eternal death. There is no middle ground, no second probation. God calls upon us to overcome as Christ overcame, that we may sit down with the Saviour in his throne. He has provided us with abundant opportunities and privileges, making it possible for us to overcome. But in order to do this, there must be in our lives no petting of self. All selfishness must be cut out by the roots.

When a man accepts Christ, he promises to represent him in this world. To him the words are spoken, "Ye are God's husbandry, ye are God's building." "Work out your own salvation with fear and trembling. For it is God which worketh in you both to will and to do of his good pleasure." Those engaged in the work of character-building should educate themselves to acknowledge the workmanship of God. Have faith that you can use every intrusted capability to God's glory. He has not given us talents to hide away in a napkin. We are to impart as we receive. Thus we are sowing seed which will bring forth a harvest of joy.

When God gives many talents to one person, it is not that he shall exalt himself, as if he had not received these talents from God. He who depends on his own merits, placing great confidence in his knowledge and judgment, is not accepted by God. Only the faith that works by love and purifies the soul is acceptable to him. No amount of profession can take the place of honesty and fidelity.

Fraud in any line is a grievous sin in God's sight; for the goods we are handling belong to him; and if we would be pure and clean in his sight, we must use them to the glory of his name. The religion that carries in its hand the scant measure and the deceitful balance is an abomination in the sight of God. He who cherishes such a religion will be brought to confusion; for God is a jealous God.

God's law is the standard of character. To it we are required to conform, and by it we shall be judged in the last great day. In that day men will be dealt with according to the light they have received. The number of talents intrusted will determine the returns expected. The sinner's guilt will be measured by the opportunities and privileges which he failed to improve. He will not be punished merely for his own rejection of the offer of salvation. He will be called to account for the influence he has exerted in encouraging others in sin. He was given ability to use for the Lord. He was given opportunity to co-operate with the Redeemer. Had he been true and faithful, he would not only have won eternal life for himself, but would have drawn others to the kingdom.

Those who reject Christ place themselves on the side of the great apostate. Those who do not accept the offer of salvation show open contempt for the Saviour, and their conduct makes others more bold and defiant. The punishment of the sinner will be measured by the extent to which he has influenced others in impenitence. He refused to wear the yoke of restraint and obedience, to surrender all to God, and thus he placed himself on the side of the enemy of Christ. His refusal to wear the yoke of Christ himself, kept others from seeing their wrong.

Mrs. E. G. White

May 16, 1901—Character-Building

God gives us strength, reasoning power, time, in order that we may build characters on which he can place his stamp of approval. He desires each child of his to build a noble character, by the doing of pure, noble deeds, that in the end he may present a symmetrical structure, a fair temple, honored by man and God.

In our character-building we must build on Christ. He is the sure foundation,--a foundation which can never be moved. The tempest of temptation and trial can not move the building which is riveted to the Eternal Rock.

He who would grow into a beautiful building for the Lord must cultivate every power of the being. It is only by the right use of the talents that the character can develop harmoniously. Thus we bring to the foundation that which is represented in the Word as gold, silver, precious stones--material that will stand the test of God's purifying fires.

In our character-building Christ is our example. He placed himself at the head of the human race to show us how to live in a way that God can approve. He is the only one who has lived a perfect life, who has formed a pure, spotless character. He has shown us what it means to be a perfect human being. He has shown us what God is, and what we are to become,--godlike in character.

God does not ask us to carry forward the work of character-building in our own strength. We are not sufficient of ourselves to think anything of ourselves. The Holy Spirit is our efficiency in this work. When we think ourselves capable of molding our character aright, we deceive ourselves. Never can we in our own strength obtain the victory over temptation. But he who trusts in Christ, and submits to the guidance of his Spirit, will grow daily into the likeness of God. His growth will be proportionate to his dependence on the Spirit's help. Such a one in every time of difficulty will turn, and not in vain, to the One who has said. "Come unto me, ... and I will give you rest." On the one side is the all-wise, all-powerful God, infinite in wisdom, goodness, and compassion; on the other his frail, erring creatures, weak, sinful and absolutely helpless. God proposes to make them laborers together with him in the building of character, and all his mighty power is at their disposal as they co-operate with him.

It is one thing to assent to a truth, and another to practice it; one thing to admire the grace of Christ, and another to make that grace our own, reflecting in spirit and person the divine likeness. Many who profess to be children of God are a continual reproach to him because of their unconsecrated lives. They talk about sanctification and holiness. When there is a revival in the church, they mourn over their unchristian lives. They make many good resolutions, but they fail to carry them out. Their goodness is as lasting as the frost before the morning sun. Their words are many, but the Holy Spirit is not with them.

He who would build a strong, symmetrical character, who would be a well-balanced Christian, must begin at the foundation. He must crucify self. He must give all and do all for Christ; for the Redeemer accepts no divided service. Daily he must learn the meaning of self-surrender. He must study the word of God, getting its meaning, and seeking to carry out its precepts. Thus he may reach the highest standard of Christian excellence. There is no limit to the spiritual advancement we may make if we are partakers of the divine nature.

To be one with Christ, to build a character like his,--this is the high ideal set before us. Let us look earnestly at this ideal, and then strive to reach it. In the councils of love, provision was made to enable us to do this. We may be more than conquerors through him who has loved us. If at times we fail, let us not become discouraged, but try again, looking always to Jesus. Thus we shall become changed into his image.

The Christian has the mind that is in Christ. His hopes and aspirations are pure and noble; for he is growing up into Christ. In his daily life he reveals the fragrance of Christ's character. Day by day God works with him, perfecting stroke by stroke the character which is to stand in the day of final test.

Mrs. E. G. White

June 6, 1901—Unquestioning Obedience

In a vision of the night, in his home at Beersheba, when he was one hundred and twenty years old, Abraham received the startling command: "Take now thy son, thine only son Isaac, whom thou lovest, and get thee into the land of Moriah; and offer him there for a burnt-offering upon one of the mountains which I will tell thee of."

There was no more sleep for Abraham that night. The voice of God had spoken, and had been heard. Isaac, his only son, the son of promise, must be sacrificed.

God had promised Abraham that in his old age he should have a son, and this promise had been fulfilled. But now God says: "Take now thy son, ... and offer him there for a burnt-offering." God left Ishmael out of the question saying, "Thine only son Isaac."

Had Abraham been a selfish, cold-hearted man, absorbed in ambitious projects, with no affection for his son, he would not have felt so deeply this terrible summons; but he loved his son tenderly. It seemed like sacrificing his own life to give up Isaac.

As Abraham stepped out into the night, he seemed to hear the divine voice that called him out of Chaldea fifty years before, saying, "Look now toward heaven, and tell the stars, if thou be able to number them.... So shall thy seed be." Can it be the same voice that commands him to slay his son? He remembers the promise: "I will make thy seed as the dust of the earth: so that if a man can number the dust of the earth, then shall thy seed also be numbered." Is it not the voice of a stranger that commands him to offer his son as a sacrifice? Can God contradict himself? Would he cut off the only hope of the fulfillment of the promise?

But Abraham does not reason; he obeys. His only hope is that the God who can do all things will raise his son from the dead.

The knife was raised; but it did not fall. God spoke, saying, "It is enough." The faith of the father and the submission of the son had been fully tested. The Lord said, "Now I know that thou fearest God, seeing thou hast not withheld thy son, thine only son from me."

Abraham's test was the most severe that could come to a human being. Had he failed under it, he would never have been registered as the father of the faithful. Had he deviated from God's command, the world would have lost an inspiring example of unquestioning faith and obedience.

The lesson was given to shine down through the ages, that we may learn that there is nothing too precious to be given to God. It is when we look upon every gift as the Lord's, to be used in his service, that we secure the heavenly benediction. Give back to God your intrusted possession, and more will be intrusted to you. Keep your possessions to yourself, and you will receive no reward in this life, and will lose the reward of the life to come.

God tries his people today to test their faith and obedience. There are many who have never made an unreserved surrender of themselves to God. They have not a right idea of the infinite sacrifice made by God to save a ruined world. If God should speak to them as he did to Abraham, they would not be sufficiently acquainted with his voice to know that he was calling upon them to make a sacrifice, in order to test the depth of their love and the sincerity of their faith.

The plague spot of selfishness is as contagious as leprosy. Those who enter the heavenly courts must be purified from every vestige of this plague. Look at the world's Redeemer, and remember that as he sacrificed, so must we. He did a work so large and broad that it included the world. His was the ministry of love, yet he said, "The foxes have holes, and the birds of the air have nests; but the Son of man hath not where to lay his head."

The Lord has a great work for us to do, and he invites us to look to him, to trust in him, to walk with him, to talk with him. He invites us to make an unreserved surrender of all that we have and are to him, that when he shall call upon us to sacrifice for him, we may be ready and willing to obey. We shall enjoy the fullness of divine grace only as we give all to Christ. We shall know the meaning of true happiness only as we keep the fire burning on the altar of sacrifice. God will bequeath the most in the future to those who have done the most in the present. He chooses his helpers in accordance with their unselfish endeavor. Each day, under different circumstances, he tries us; and in each true-hearted endeavor he chooses his workers, not because they are perfect, but because they are willing to work unselfishly for him, and he sees that through connection with him they may gain perfection.

Mrs. E. G. White

June 13, 1901—Joshua's Last Words—Part 1

For several years the children of Israel had been in possession of the land of Canaan. The wars of conquest ended, Joshua had withdrawn to the peaceful retirement of his home at Timnath-serah.

"And it came to pass a long time after that the Lord had given rest unto Israel from all their enemies round about, that Joshua ... called for all Israel, and for their elders, and for their heads, and for their judges, and for their officers." The Lord had impressed his faithful servant to do as Moses had done before him,--to recapitulate the history of the people, and call to mind the terms which the Lord had made with them when he gave them his vineyard.

Several years had passed since the people had settled in their possessions, and already could be seen cropping out the same evils that had heretofore brought judgments upon Israel. As Joshua felt the infirmities of age stealing upon him, he was filled with anxiety for the future of his people. It was with more than a father's interest that he addressed them, as they gathered once more about him. "Ye have seen," he said, "all that the Lord your God hath done unto all these nations because of you; for the Lord your God is he that hath fought for you." Although the Canaanites had been subdued they still possessed a considerable portion of the land promised to Israel, and Joshua exhorted the people not to settle down at ease, and forget the Lord's commands utterly to dispossess these idolatrous nations.

The people in general were slow to complete the work of driving out the heathen. The tribes had dispersed to their possessions, and it was looked upon as a doubtful and difficult undertaking to renew the war. But Joshua declared: "The Lord your God, he shall expel them from before you, and drive them from out of your sight; and ye shall possess their land, as the Lord your God hath promised unto you. Be ye therefore very courageous to keep and to do all that is written in the book of the law of Moses, that ye turn not aside therefrom to the right hand or to the left."

Joshua appealed to the people themselves as witnesses that, so far as they had complied with the conditions, God had faithfully fulfilled his promises to them. "Ye know in all your hearts and in all your souls," he said, "that not one thing hath failed of all the good things which the Lord your God spake concerning you; all are come to pass unto you, and not one thing hath failed thereof." He declared that as the Lord had fulfilled his promises, so he would fulfill his threatenings. "It shall come to pass," he said, "that as all good things are come upon you, which the Lord your God promised you; so shall the Lord bring upon you all evil things.... When ye have transgressed the covenant of the Lord, ... then shall the anger of the Lord be kindled against you, and ye shall perish quickly from off the good land which he hath given unto you."

Satan deceives many with the plausible theory that since God's love for his people is so great, he will excuse sin in them; that while the threatenings of God's word are to serve a certain purpose in his moral government, they are never to be literally fulfilled. But in his dealings with his creatures, God has maintained the principles of righteousness by revealing sin in its true character,--by demonstrating that its sure result is misery and death. The unconditional pardon of sin never has been and never will be. Such pardon would show the abandonment of the principles of righteousness which are the very foundation of the government of God. It would fill the unfallen worlds with consternation. God has faithfully pointed out the results of sin, and if these warnings are not true, how can we be sure that his promises will be fulfilled? That so-called benevolence which would set aside justice, is not benevolence, but weakness. God is the Lifegiver. From the beginning, his laws were ordained to give life. But sin broke in upon the order that God had established, and discord followed. As long as sin exists, suffering and death are inevitable. It is only because the Redeemer has borne the curse of sin in our behalf, that man can hope to escape its dire results.

Mrs. E. G. White

June 20, 1901—Joshua's Last Words—Part 2

Once again before his death Joshua summoned the people before him. He knew that the infirmities of age were upon him, and that soon he must lay his responsibilities upon the representative men of the nation. Obedient to his summons, the tribes assembled at Shechem. No spot in the land possessed so many sacred associations. It carried their minds back to God's covenant with Abraham and Jacob, and recalled also their own solemn vows upon their entrance to Canaan. Here were the mountains Ebal and Gerizim, the silent witnesses of those vows which now, in the presence of their dying leader, they had assembled to renew. On every side were reminders of what God had wrought for them; how he had given them a land for which they did not labor, and cities which they built not, vineyards and olive-yards which they planted not.

By Joshua's direction the ark had been brought from Shiloh. The occasion was one of great solemnity, and this symbol of God's presence would deepen the impression which he wished to make upon the people. Earnestly and solemnly Joshua gave his last charge to those who would soon be left without his counsel. He reviewed once more the history of Israel, recounting the wonderful works of God, that all might have a sense of his love and mercy, and might serve him "in sincerity and truth." Briefly he mentioned the most important points of their history since leaving Egypt, reviving their faith by calling on them to remember that not one of God's promises had failed.

After presenting the goodness of God toward Israel, Joshua called upon the people, in the name of Jehovah, to choose whom they would serve. The worship of idols was still to some extent secretly practiced, and Joshua endeavored now to bring the people to a decision that they would banish this sin from Israel. "If it seem evil unto you to serve the Lord," he said, "choose ye this day whom ye will serve." Joshua desired to lead them to serve God, not by compulsion, but willingly. Love to God is the very foundation of religion. To engage in his service merely from the hope of reward or the fear of punishment, would avail nothing. Open apostasy would not be more offensive to God than hypocrisy and mere formal worship.

The aged leader urged the people to consider, in all its bearings, what he had set before them, and to decide if they really desired to live as did the idolatrous nations around them. If it seemed evil to them to serve Jehovah, the source of power, the fountain of blessing, let them that day choose whom they would serve,--"the gods which your fathers served," from whom Abraham was called out, "or the gods of the Amorites, in whose land ye dwell." These last words were a keen rebuke to Israel. The gods of the Amorites had not been able to protect their worshipers. Because of their abominable and debasing sins, that wicked nation had been destroyed, and the good land which they once possessed had been given to God's people. What folly for Israel to choose the deities for whose worship the Amorites had been destroyed. "As for me and my house," said Joshua, "we will serve the Lord." The holy zeal that inspired the leader's heart was communicated to the people. His appeal called forth the unhesitating response, "God forbid that we should forsake the Lord to serve other gods."

"Ye can not serve the Lord," Joshua said; "for he is a holy God; ... he will not forgive your transgressions nor your sins." Before there could be any permanent reformation, the people must be led to feel their utter inability, in themselves, to render obedience to God. They had broken his law; it condemned them as transgressors; and it provided no way of escape. While they trusted in their own strength and righteousness, it was impossible for them to secure the pardon of their sins; they could not meet the claims of God's perfect law, and it was in vain that they pledged themselves to serve God. It was only by faith in Christ that they could secure pardon of sin, and receive strength to obey God's law. They must cease to rely upon their own righteousness, they must turn from idolatry, and trust wholly in the merits of the promised Saviour, if they would be accepted by God.

To us today Christ says, "Without me ye can do nothing." He is stronger than the strongest human power. The weaker you know yourself to be, the more you should realize the necessity of leaning on the Great Teacher, and the stronger you may become in his strength. In your weakness he will perfect his strength. Sanctify the Lord God of hosts, and let him be your fear, and let him be your dread. Only trust him; and though weak, he will strengthen you; though faint, he will revive you; though wounded, he will heal you.

Men gain nothing by rushing on before the Lord. Many have thought their own endowments sufficient for an enterprise. So Moses thought when he slew the

Egyptian. But he was obliged to flee for his life to the desert. Here he kept sheep for forty years, until he learned to be a shepherd of men. He learned his lesson so perfectly that though the Lord revealed himself to him, and spoke with him face to face, as a man speaketh to a friend, he did not become lifted up. "Follow me," Jesus says. Do not run before me. Follow where my footsteps lead the way. Then you will not meet the armies of Satan alone. Let me go before you, and you will not be overcome by the enemy's planning.

Mrs. E. G. White

July 18, 1901—In the Wilderness With God

Obedient to the onward movement of the pillar of cloud, the children of Israel left Rephidim, and began their march to the desert of Sinai. They wound their way through narrow defiles, with high cliffs rising abruptly on either side. They climbed steep ascents, and descended into deep valleys.

With intense interest the Israelites watched the movements of the cloud, which was leading them over plains of desolation, broken by rugged mountains. Often the question arose in their minds, Where will this weary march end? Was God leading them through the wild passes of the wilderness to their destruction? Again and again, when passing through the mountain fastnesses, they came to a place where their way appeared to be entirely hedged in. Then a passage would open before them.

What a sight was this!--More than a million persons marching through the desert, led by day by a pillar of cloud, and guarded at night by a pillar of fire!

Thus God led his people. The wilderness was their school. Christ was their Instructor. He desired to teach them to depend on him in all the circumstances of life.

During all their march through the wilderness, the children of Israel were sustained by bread from heaven. The hoary-topped mountains, could they speak, would bear witness to the way in which the people were fed by the miraculous power of God. As the people lay in their tents, wrapped in slumber, bread from heaven fell quietly round the encampment.

At length the people came in their march to a long range of mountains, with one lofty peak towering above the rest. Here the pillar of cloud rested, overlooking the plain where the people were to encamp.

The encampment was placed in order. In harmony with God's direction, captains were appointed over different companies. The elders and judges chosen to relieve Moses of some of his many burdens, were given their work, that order and harmony might be preserved in the camp.

I would that those who today rebel against rules and regulations could realize that it is God's plan to have all things done with order and discipline.

In the morning, as the sun began to rise behind the ridge of eastern mountains, filling with light the dark gorges, it seemed as if golden beams of mercy from the throne of God were shining upon the weary, almost discouraged travelers.

The encampment was soon astir, and the busy activities of the day began. With anxious eyes the people looked upon the pillar of cloud resting over the mountain, wondering where next it would lead them. Around them lay a country strange and solemn. Immense piles of rugged rock, stretching upward into the heavens, looked like the ruins of a world. Frequently the people contrasted the verdant valleys of Egypt with these dark and cheerless ravines.

God had a purpose in leading his people to this place. He had gathered them to himself, apart from the world, that he might talk with them. In these mountain solitudes, where there was nothing to lead the mind away from the Creator, God was to give the people his law. Everything in this wild region tended to make the people feel their own nothingness, and the greatness of him who weigheth the mountains in scales, and the hills in a balance.

God has left these hoary sentinels to stand through all the ages as a memorial of the time when the Infinite held communication with mortal man, giving him the law which was to rule the nations of the world through all time.

God called Moses to come up into the mount, and Moses immediately obeyed. Placing his feet in steps made without hands, he ascended the mount, and entered the presence of God. Here the Lord told him that it was his design to take Israel into close connection with himself. They were to be his church, a nation governed and controlled by him.

For three days before the giving of the law, the people were encamped before the mount. They were given ample opportunity to review their past experiences, and to repent of their continual distrust and unbelief.

God commanded Moses to sanctify the people, to instruct them, to point out to them what God required. Much was included in this command, and great responsibility was laid upon Moses. Faithfully he was to point out to the people their past wrongs, and show them their need of humbling the heart before God.

The people were to spend their time in fasting and prayer. All outward impurity was to be put away, and their hearts were to be cleansed from all iniquity. Had there been one in that vast multitude who was defiling himself by the use of tobacco, he would have been required to cleanse himself from all filthiness. Had he failed to do this, he would have been slain by the bolts of God's wrath at the first revelation of his glory.

The children of Israel were to do all in their power to cleanse themselves from inward and outward defilement. This is the work God requires us to do if we would be brought into close communion with him. The battle with wrong habits and sinful indulgence will be long and severe, but it must be undertaken. Through Christ, victory is sure.

The divine presence of Christ could bring to the aid of the Israelites a power which, when combined with human effort, would sanctify them to God. So today this Presence can bring us power to consecrate ourselves wholly to God.

Many look upon the days of Israel as a time of darkness, when men were without Christ, without repentance and faith. Many hold the erroneous doctrine that the religion of the children of Israel consisted in forms and ceremonies, in which faith in Christ had no part. But men in that age were saved by Christ as verily as men are saved by him today. They were under a discipline of mercy, and had special privileges in their day, even as we have in ours. Christ was shadowed forth in the sacrifices and symbols, which were to last till type should reach antitype in his coming to our world. The Hebrews rejoiced in a Saviour to come. We rejoice in a Saviour who has come, and who is coming again.

Shrouded in the pillar of cloud, the world's Redeemer held communion with Israel. Let us not say, then, that they had not Christ. When the people thirsted in the wilderness, and gave themselves up to murmuring and complaint, Christ was to them what he is to us,--a Saviour full of tender compassion, the Mediator between them and God. After we have done our part to cleanse the soul-temple from the defilement of sin, Christ's blood avails for us, as it did for ancient Israel.

Mrs. E. G. White

July 25, 1901—With Power and Great Glory

Christ's second coming will be in marked contrast with his first coming. Then his glory was veiled with the garb of humanity. He came with no outward manifestation of glory. When he comes the second time, his divinity will not be concealed. He will come with his own glory and the glory of his Father. He will come as One equal with God, as his beloved Son, the Prince of heaven and earth. Instead of a crown of thorns, he will wear a crown of glory. Instead of a garment of humility, he will be clad in a garment of royalty. Upon his vesture will be written the name, "King of kings, and Lord of lords."

At his first coming, Christ was denied and rejected by men, and by them dragged as a criminal to Pilate's bar, where they charged him with blasphemy. He was scourged and crucified. Nails were driven through his hands and feet. For three hours he hung on the cross, while his enemies said, tauntingly: "He saved others; himself he can not save. If he be the King of Israel, let him now come down from the cross, and we will believe him. He trusted in God; let him deliver him now, if he will have him: for he said, I am the Son of God."

At his second coming, the scene is changed. He is acknowledged by all as the King of glory. At the name of Jesus every knee shall bow, and every tongue shall confess that Jesus is the Christ, the Lord of heaven and earth, to the glory of God the Father. The angels bow in adoration before him. His enemies see the mistake they have made, and every tongue confesses his divinity.

Christ's glory did not appear when he was upon this earth. He was then a man of sorrows and acquainted with grief. Men hid their faces from him. But he was following the path God had marked out for him. Still bearing humanity, he ascended to heaven, triumphant and victorious. He has taken the blood of his atonement into the holiest of all, sprinkled it upon the mercy-seat and his own garments, and blessed the people. Soon he will appear the second time to declare that there is no more sacrifice for sin. His believing ones have made their calling and their election sure. They come forth at the first resurrection, and by innumerable voices is sung the song: "Behold, the tabernacle of God is with men, and he will dwell with them, and they shall be his people, and God himself shall be with them, and be their God. And God shall wipe away all tears from their eyes; and there shall be no more death, neither sorrow, nor crying, neither shall there be any more pain: for the former things are passed away."

Christ is soon to come in the clouds of heaven, with power and great glory. Are we preparing to meet him in peace, to be among that number in whom, when he comes, he can be admired? "Beloved, now are we the sons of God, and it doth not yet appear what we shall be: but we know that, when he shall appear, we shall be like him; for we shall see him as he is."

Mrs. E. G. White

August 22, 1901—A Perfect Ideal

Christ is the ideal for all humanity. He has left a perfect example for childhood, youth, and manhood. He came to this earth, and passed through the different phases of human life. He talked and acted like other children and youth, except that he did no wrong. Sin found no place in his life. Ever he lived in an atmosphere of heavenly purity. From childhood to manhood he preserved unsullied his trust in God. The word says of him, "The child grew, and waxed strong in spirit, filled with wisdom." He "increased in wisdom and stature, and in favor with God and man."

In the sanctuary of the home, Jesus received his education, not merely from his parents, but from his Heavenly Father. As he grew older, God opened to him more and more of the great work before him. But notwithstanding his knowledge of this, he assumed no airs of superiority. Never did he by disrespect cause his parents pain or anxiety. He delighted to honor and obey them. Although he was not ignorant of his great mission, he consulted their wishes, and submitted to their authority.

Christ had been Commander of the heavenly host; but he did not because of this excuse himself from labor, allowing his parents to support him. While still quite young, he learned a trade, and faithfully discharged his daily duties, contributing to the support of the family.

Christ was the light and joy of the family circle. How many children and youth are seeking to be like him,--kind, thoughtful, and obedient? How many, by following his example, are making their characters attractive? Those who seek to do this will enjoy the favor of God and man.

There is a great difference between Christ and the youth of today. Many youth are restless and selfish, content to spend their days in idleness while their parents toil for them. They are disobedient, unthankful, and unholy. Whatever natural ability such youth may have, they are not increasing in wisdom and in favor with God and man.

The youth may think to find happiness by seeking their own pleasure; but true happiness will never be theirs while they pursue this course. The Saviour lived not to please himself. We read of him that he went about "doing good." He spent his life in loving service, comforting the sorrowing, ministering to the needy, lifting up the bowed down. He had no home in this world, only as the kindness of his friends provided one for him as a wayfarer. Yet it was heaven to be in his presence. Day by day he met trials and temptations, yet he did not fail nor become discouraged. He was surrounded with transgressors, yet he kept his Father's commandments. He was always patient and cheerful, and the afflicted hailed him as a messenger of life and peace and health. He saw the needs of men and women, children and youth, and to all he gave the invitation, "Come unto me, all ye that labor and are heavy laden, and I will give you rest: Take my yoke upon you, and learn of me; for I am meek and lowly in heart: and ye shall find rest unto your souls. For my yoke is easy, and my burden is light."

What a wonderful example Christ has left for us in his life-work. Who of his children are living, as he did, for the glory of God? He is the Light of the world; and the one who works successfully for the Master must kindle his taper from that divine life.

To his disciples Christ said: "Ye are the salt of the earth: but if the salt have lost his savor, wherewith shall it be salted? it is thenceforth good for nothing, but to be cast out, and to be trodden under foot of men." How careful, then, we should be to follow the example of Christ. Unless we do this, we are worthless--salt which has lost its savor.

Only by following Christ's example can we find true happiness. When he is accepted, the heart is subdued, and its purposes are changed.

Young friends, remember that in order to grow in favor with God and man, you must follow the example Christ has left you. He loves you. It was because of this that he came from heaven to show you how to live a pure, true life. He knows every trial and sorrow of childhood and youth. He was once just your age. The temptations and trials which come to you came also to him. The sorrows which come to you came to him. But he was never overcome by temptation. His life held nothing that was not pure and noble. He is your helper, your Redeemer.

Mrs. E. G. White

September 12, 1901—Conquering Temptation

"Let the peace of God rule in your hearts, ... and be ye thankful. Let the word of Christ dwell in you richly in all wisdom; teaching and admonishing one another in psalms and hymns and spiritual songs, singing with grace in your hearts to the Lord."

This was Christ's practice. He was often assailed by temptation, but in place of yielding or being provoked, he sang God's praises. With spiritual songs he stopped the fluent speech of those whom Satan was using to create strife. He sang with fervency and melody.

When those who love God are tempted, let them sing the praises of their Creator rather than speak words of accusing or faultfinding. The Lord will bless those who thus try to make peace. Trust in God. Be careful not to give the enemy any advantage by your unguarded words. Keep looking to Jesus. He is your strength. By steadfastly beholding him, you will be changed into the same likeness.

When the enemy tempts you to become discouraged, remember that Christ has said, "Let him take hold of my strength, that he may make peace with me; and he shall make peace with me." Draw nigh to God, and he will draw nigh to you. Then when the enemy comes in like a flood, the Spirit of the Lord will lift up for you a standard against him. Your part is to take hold of the strength that is as firm as the throne of God. Believe in God. Although you have trials, lose not your faith. Remember that Christ was tempted in all points like as you are. Remember that nothing in this world is so dear to God as his church. The Lord knows and loves those who are his.

"Stand therefore, having your loins girt about with truth, and having on the breastplate of righteousness; and your feet shod with the preparation of the gospel of peace; above all, taking the shield of faith, wherewith ye shall be able to quench all the fiery darts of the wicked. And take the helmet of salvation, and the sword of the Spirit, which is the word of God."

We must put on every piece of the armor, and then stand firm. The Lord has honored us by choosing us as his soldiers. Let us fight bravely for him, maintaining the right in every transaction. Rectitude in all things is essential to the welfare of the soul. As you strive for the victory over your own inclinations, he will help you by his Holy Spirit to be circumspect in every action, that you may give no occasion for the enemy to speak evil of the truth. Put on as your breastplate that divinely protected righteousness which it is the privilege of all to wear. This will protect your spiritual life.

Be so considerate, so tender, so compassionate, that the atmosphere surrounding you will be fragrant with heaven's blessing. Do not discourage yourself and others by talking of defects of character. Talk of the light of which heaven is full. Look away from the imperfections of others to the perfection of Christ. Praise wherever you can. Love God and those around you. Forget yourself.

Improve is the word I have for all. Use to a purpose the capabilities God has given you. Let the love of Christ lead you to strive for victory. You can, if you will do his will, reach the ideal which he has set before you. Let joy and love and the grace of Christ perfect your character. Let a willingness to obey make your path bright. Believe, and receive to impart. Without a murmur or complaint lift the cross. In the act of lifting it, you will find that it lifts you. You will find it alive with mercy, compassion, and pitying love.

Mrs. E. G. White

September 26, 1901—"A New Heart Also Will I Give You"

Then will I sprinkle clean water upon you, and ye shall be clean: from all your filthiness, and from all your idols, will I cleanse you. A new heart also will I give you, and a new spirit will I put within you: and I will take away the stony heart out of your flesh, and I will give you an heart of flesh."

Many who speak to others of the need of a new heart do not themselves know what is meant by these words. The youth especially stumble over this phrase, "a new heart." They do not know what it means. They look for a special change to take place in their feelings. This they term conversion. Over this error thousands have stumbled to ruin, not understanding the expression, "Ye must be born again."

Satan leads people to think that because they have felt a rapture of feeling, they are converted. But their experience does not change. Their actions are the same as before. Their lives show no good fruit. They pray often and long, and are constantly referring to the feelings they had at such and such a time. But they do not live the new life. They are deceived. Their experience goes no deeper than feeling. They build upon the sand, and when adverse winds come, their house is swept away.

Many poor souls are groping in darkness, looking for the feelings which others say they have had in their experience. They overlook the fact that the believer in Christ must work out his own salvation with fear and trembling. The convicted sinner has something to do. He must repent and show true faith.

When Jesus speaks of the new heart, he means the mind, the life, the whole being. To have a change of heart is to withdraw the affections from the world, and fasten them upon Christ. To have a new heart is to have a new mind, new purposes, new motives. What is the sign of a new heart?--A changed life. There is a daily, hourly dying to selfishness and pride.

Some make a great mistake by supposing that a high profession will compensate for real service. But a religion which is not practical is not genuine. True conversion makes us strictly honest in our dealings with our fellow men. It makes us faithful in our every-day work. Every sincere follower of Christ will show that the religion of the Bible qualifies him to use his talents in the Master's service.

"Not slothful in business." These words will be fulfilled in the life of every true Christian. Even though your work may seem to be a drudgery, you may ennoble it by the way in which you do it. Do it as unto the Lord. Do it cheerfully, and with heaven-born dignity. It is the noble principles which are brought into the work that make it wholly acceptable in the Lord's sight. True service links the lowliest of God's servants on earth with the highest of his servants in the courts above.

It means much to be a consistent Christian. It means to walk circumspectly before God, to press toward the mark of the prize of our high calling in Christ. It means to bear much fruit to the glory of him who gave his Son to die for us. As sons and daughters of God, Christians should strive to reach the high ideal set before them in the gospel. They should be content with nothing less than perfection; for Christ says, "Be ye therefore perfect, even as your Father which is in heaven is perfect."

Let us make God's holy word our study, bringing its holy principles into our lives. Let us walk before God in meekness and humility, daily correcting our faults. Let us not by selfish pride separate the soul from God. Cherish not a feeling of lofty supremacy, thinking yourself better than others. "Let him that thinketh he standeth take heed lest he fall." Peace and rest will come to you as you bring your will into subjection to the will of Christ. Then the love of Christ will rule in the heart, bringing into captivity to the Saviour the secret springs of action. The hasty, easily-roused temper will be soothed and subdued by the oil of Christ's grace. The sense of sins forgiven will bring that peace that passeth all understanding. There will be an earnest striving to overcome all that is opposed to Christian perfection. Variance will disappear. He who once found fault with those around him will see that far greater faults exist in his own character.

There are those who listen to the truth, and are convinced that they have been living in opposition to Christ. They are condemned, and they repent of their transgressions. Relying upon the merits of Christ, exercising true faith in him, they receive pardon for sin. As they cease to do evil and learn to do well, they grow in grace and in the knowledge of God. They see that they must sacrifice in order to separate from the world; and after counting the cost, they look upon all as loss if they may but win Christ. They have enlisted in Christ's army. The warfare is before them, and they enter it bravely and cheerfully, fighting against their natural inclinations and selfish desires, bringing the will into subjection to the will of Christ. Daily they seek the Lord for grace to obey him, and they are strengthened and helped. This is true conversion. In humble, grateful dependence he who has been given a new heart relies upon the help of Christ. He reveals in his life the fruit of righteousness. He once loved himself. Worldly pleasure was his delight. Now his idol is dethroned, and God reigns supreme. The sins he once loved he now hates. Firmly and resolutely he follows in the path of holiness.

Mrs. E. G. White

October 3, 1901—The True Shepherd

"My sheep hear my voice, and I know them, and they follow me: and I give unto them eternal life; and they shall never perish, neither shall any man pluck them out of my hand. My Father, which gave them me, is greater than all; and no man is able to pluck them out of my Father's hand."

Christ is the Good Shepherd. He leads the way, calling upon his sheep to follow him. Those who hear and obey his voice will follow his example in all things. Becoming acquainted with him, they will grow daily more and more like him. They will be meek and lowly, free from jealousy and envy.

Do we hear Christ's voice? Are we following him? It is of great importance that we know whether we are following the True Shepherd. In order to know this, we must search his word; for it is his voice speaking to us. "What saith the Scriptures?" is to be our watchword at every step. In God's word we may find an answer to every question. From it light shines upon our pathway, revealing the Good Shepherd as he goes before us.

Christ knew that man could not in his own strength overcome the enemy; so, laying aside his royal robe and kingly crown, he came to this earth to overcome in our behalf. He was tempted in all points like as we are, that he might know how to succor them that are tempted. He met and overcame Satan on every point. He has left us an example of perfect obedience. In his strength we can be more than conquerors. He is able to save to the uttermost all who come to God by him.

Christ is a conqueror, and those who follow him will be on the conquering side. There are precious victories before the Christian. He may be weak, but the Redeemer knows his need, and is able to strengthen him. Jesus knows that Satan is trying to get control of men and women, and he stands ready to help all who come to him for help. He is not willing that any should perish. He has made it possible for every tempted son and daughter of Adam, in every time of temptation, to gain a glorious victory. He has placed the power of heaven within the reach of his children.

God has done for us all that infinite love could suggest, and all he asks of us in return is obedience--conformity to his will. He has placed before us a standard of righteousness, which he desires us to reach. He calls upon us to return to our loyalty to him, that we may be admitted into the Eden-home from which Adam was banished by his disobedience. A young man came to Christ, asking him what he should do to inherit eternal life. The Saviour answered, "If thou wilt enter into life, keep the commandments." This is his answer to his followers for all time. Our duty is outlined in the commandments; and if we obey them, we shall gain eternal life. If we desire heaven and its joy, we must cease from transgression; for the law of God is the rule by which character is measured.

Satan works zealously to prevent us from forming characters which will meet God's approval. But they that are with us are more than all they that are against us. God sends heavenly angels to the side of his children to keep them from evil. If we have placed ourselves in his care, we may rest securely; for he has promised that no man shall pluck us out of his hand.

In the past many have suffered for the truth's sake. To them truth was dearer than all else, and they willingly gave up this present life for the life eternal. We shall be called upon to sacrifice for the truth's sake. Those who share in Christ's glory must share also in his suffering. But let us remember that in the home which the Saviour is preparing for us, there is no sorrow nor suffering. Of those who overcome it is written: "Therefore are they before the throne of God, and serve him day and night in his temple .... They shall hunger no more, neither thirst any more; neither shall the sun light on them, nor any heat. For the Lamb which is in the midst of the throne shall feed them, and shall lead them unto living fountains of waters: and God shall wipe away all tears from their eyes."

The royal command has gone forth, "Come out from among them, and be ye separate, ... and touch not the unclean thing; and I will receive you, and will be a Father unto you, and ye shall be my sons and daughters." What greater honor could be conferred on mortal man? When men are going to appear before an earthly monarch, how carefully they prepare to meet him! How carefully, then, should we prepare,--we who expect to meet the King of kings? If our preparation meets his approval, we shall dwell with him forever, clothed in the spotless robe of Christ's righteousness. Surely this is worth striving for. The free gift of eternal life is ours on one condition: "Blessed are they that do his commandments, that they may have right to the tree of life, and may enter in through the gates into the city." May God help you to live so that you may enter the holy city, is my prayer.

Mrs. E. G. White

November 21, 1901—Apostasy

"And Moses came and told the people all the words of the Lord, and all the judgments: and all the people answered with one voice, and said, All the words which the Lord hath said will we do.... And he took the book of the covenant, and read in the audience of the people: and they said, All that the Lord hath said will we do, and be obedient."

Thus did the children of Israel pledge themselves to obey the law which, amid awful manifestations of power, God had just spoken from Sinai.

When the law was proclaimed, Satan said: "Here is work for us. At the foot of Sinai, in the very presence of God, let us lead the people to break the law." God called Moses into the mount, and during his absence Satan worked among the people. He told them that Moses would not return, and suggested that they make a golden calf to worship.

The enemy obtained all that he wished. The people had entered into covenant relation with God. He had espoused them to himself, promising to make them a kingdom of priests if they would obey him. And they had promised to be obedient. But as soon as Moses left them, they treacherously revolted from their Leader. They changed the glory of God into the similitude of an ox. What a terrible sin! The heathen nations could boast of being true to their false gods; but Israel turned from the One who had done such marvelous things in their behalf, to a golden calf. "Up, make us gods, which shall go before us," they said to Aaron; "for as for this Moses, the man that brought us up out of the land of Egypt, we wot not what is become of him."

Aaron saw the fierce determination of the ringleaders, and instead of firmly suppressing the discontent, he weakly yielded. Had he stood firm to principle, God would have vindicated his cause. But his wavering made the instigators of evil yet more persistent. Aaron's history will ever be tarnished by his failure to stand bravely against wrong. By yielding, he sanctioned a great sin, made tenfold greater because the people were in the immediate presence of God and the holy angels.

"And all the people brake off their golden earrings which were in their ears, and brought them unto Aaron. And he received them at their hand, and fashioned it with a graving tool, after he had made it a molten calf: and they said, These be thy gods, O Israel, which brought thee up out of the land of Egypt."

God saw what was going on in the camp. He saw that the people, even while the divine glory still rested upon Sinai, had yielded to the temptations of Satan, and were plotting against the rule which they had promised to obey. He suffered the treason to rise to its height, that he might teach the evil of apostasy. Then he said to Moses, "Go, get thee down; for thy people, which thou broughtest out of the land of Egypt, have corrupted themselves: they have turned aside quickly out of the way which I commanded them: they have made them a molten calf, and have worshiped it, and have sacrificed thereunto.... I have seen this people, and, behold, it is a stiff-necked people: now therefore let me alone, that my wrath may wax hot against them, and that I may consume them: and I will make of thee a great nation."

Many men would have said: "It is the purpose of God. If he wishes to destroy Israel, I can not help it. They will be destroyed." Not so Moses. He loved his people better than himself, and in the very words, "Let me alone," he saw encouragement to hope that if God were earnestly importuned, he would spare the people. He resolved to intercede for them, and he chose the strongest argument he could find. He reminded the Lord of the wonderful work he had done in behalf of Israel. He entreated him not to forget how he had brought them forth out of the land of Egypt with great power and with a mighty hand. "Lord, what will the Egyptians say," he asked, "if you cut off those for whom you have done so much?"

All the nations of the earth had heard how mightily God had worked in delivering his chosen people from Egyptian bondage,--how, because of Pharaoh's resistance, his land had been desolated, and all the firstborn of the Egyptians had been slain. They had heard how the host of Pharaoh, pursuing the Israelites, had been drowned in the Red Sea, and a terrible fear had fallen upon them. They wondered what the God of Israel would do next in defense of his people. And now, if Israel should be blotted out, their enemies would triumph, and the name of God would be dishonored. The heathen would say, Instead of the Israelites being delivered so that they could worship their God, they were taken into the wilderness to be destroyed.

"Remember Abraham, Isaac, and Israel, thy servants," Moses said, "to whom thou swarest by thine own self, and saidst unto them, I will multiply your seed as the stars of heaven, and all this land that I have spoken of will I give unto your seed, and they shall inherit it forever.

"And the Lord repented of the evil which he thought to do unto his people." Nevertheless, sin must be punished. The people had broken the law, and it was time for God to work. He must show that he is the supreme Ruler, and that his commands must be obeyed.

Going down to the camp, Moses stood in the gate, and said, "Who is on the Lord's side? let him come unto me." Opportunity was given for all to take their stand against idolatry. Those who remained obstinate and defiant must bear the penalty of sin. To those who had taken their position on the Lord's side Moses said: "Thus saith the Lord God of Israel, Put every man his sword by his side, and go in and out from gate to gate throughout the camp, and slay every man his brother, and every man his companion, and every man his neighbor. And the children of Levi did according to the word of Moses; and there fell of the people that day about three thousand men."

Thus God showed the fearful result of bold, defiant sin. He commanded that the leaders of the treason should be slain. Thus he bore a public testimony against sin, so that in the future, when God's people condemned idolatry, and their enemies threw at them the taunt that they had themselves deserted God for a calf, they could answer, "It is true; but judgment fell upon the transgressors. God's government is unsullied; for swift punishment overtook those who rebelled against him."

Mrs. E. G. White

December 5, 1901—The Reward of Faithful Toil

Let the youth remember that the indolent forfeit the invaluable experience gained by a faithful performance of the daily duties of life. He who is indolent and willingly ignorant, places in his pathway that which will always be an obstruction. He refuses the culture that comes from honest toil. By failing to put forth a helping hand in behalf of humanity, he robs God. His career is very different from the career which God marked out for him; for to despise useful employment encourages the lower tastes, and effectually paralyzes the most useful energies of the being.

Not a few, but thousands, of human beings exist only to consume the benefits which God in his mercy bestows on them. They forget to bring the Lord gratitude offerings for the riches he has intrusted to them in giving them the fruit of the earth. They forget that God desires them, by trading wisely on the talents lent them, to be producers as well as consumers. If they had a realization of the work the Lord desires them to do as his helping hand, they would not feel it a privilege to shun all responsibility and be waited on.

Real happiness is found only in being good and doing good. The purest, highest enjoyment comes to those who faithfully fulfill their appointed duties. No honest work is degrading. It is ignoble sloth which leads human beings to look down on the simple, every-day duties of life. The refusal to perform these duties causes a mental and moral deficiency, which will one day be keenly felt. At some time in the life of the slothful his deformity will stand out clearly defined. Over his life-record is written the words, A consumer, but not a producer.

From all the vocations of life, useful spiritual lessons may be learned. Those who till the soil may, as they work, study the meaning of the words, "Ye are God's husbandry." In the human heart the seeds of truth are to be sown, that the life may bear the beautiful fruit of the Spirit. God's impress on the mind is to mold it into graceful symmetry. The crude energies, both physical and mental, are to be trained for the Master's service.

The youth who is studying for a physician has before him the very highest example, even the example of him who left heaven to live on this earth a man among men. To all Christ has given the work of ministry. He is the King of glory, yet he declared, "The Son of man came not to be ministered unto, but to minister." He is the Majesty of heaven, yet he willingly consented to come to this earth to do the work laid upon him by his Father. He has ennobled labor. That he might set us an example of industry, he worked with his hands at the carpenter's trade. From a very early age, he acted his part in sustaining the family. He realized that he was a part of the family firm, and willingly bore his share of the burdens.

Children and youth should take pleasure in making lighter the cares of father and mother, showing an unselfish interest in the home. As they cheerfully lift the burdens that fall to their share, they are receiving a training which will fit them for positions of trust and usefulness. Each year they are to make steady advancement, gradually but surely laying aside the inexperience of boyhood and girlhood for the experience of manhood and womanhood. In the faithful performance of the simple duties of the home, boys and girls lay the foundation for mental, moral, and spiritual excellence.

Remember, dear young friends, that each day, each hour, each moment, you are weaving the web of your own destiny. Each time the shuttle is thrown, there is drawn into the web a thread which either mars or beautifies the pattern. If you are careless and indolent, you spoil the life which God designed should be bright and beautiful. If you choose to follow your own inclinations, unchristlike habits will bind you with bands of steel. And as you walk away from Christ, your example will be followed by many who, because of your wrong course, will never enjoy the glories of heaven. But if you make brave efforts to overcome selfishness, allowing no opportunity to pass for helping those around you, the light of your example will guide others to the cross.

Mrs. E. G. White

January 16, 1902—A Call to Labor

"And I heard the voice of the Lord, saying, Whom shall I send, and who will go for us? Then said I, Here am I; send me."

The Lord calls upon young men to enter the harvest-field, and work diligently as harvest-hands. Let them go forth to trade on their talents. He who has called them to labor in the gospel will give them evidence that they are chosen vessels, and will give them words to speak.

One of the very best ways in which young men can obtain a fitness for the ministry is by entering the canvassing field. Let them go into towns and cities as canvassers for the books which contain the truth for this time. In this work they will find opportunity to speak the words of life. The seeds of truth they sow will spring up to bear fruit.

When young men take up the canvassing work filled with an intense longing to save their fellow men, they will see souls converted. From their work a harvest for the Lord will be reaped. Then let them go forth as missionaries to circulate present truth, praying constantly for increased light, and for the guidance of the Spirit, that they may know how to speak words in season to those that are weary. They should improve every opportunity for doing deeds of kindness, remembering that thus they are doing errands for the Lord.

They will be invited to take meals with the families they visit. Flesh-meat will be passed to them. As they refuse it, giving their reasons for so doing, they will, perhaps, have opportunity to present the principles of health reform. In their work they should always take some health books with them; for health reform is the right hand of the message.

The canvasser should speak modestly, and he should never engage in controversy. He should feel that he is on trial before the heavenly universe. "Behold, I send you forth as sheep in the midst of wolves." Christ said: "be ye therefore wise as serpents, and harmless as doves." You will meet many precious souls ripe for the harvest.

Learn, therefore, to speak modestly and discreetly. Show that you have been with Jesus, and have learned of him.

This is the rule we are to follow,--to be like him who went about doing good. Christ said, "If any man serve me, let him follow me." Study the life of the Saviour; and find out how he lived and worked. Strive each day to live his life. Wear his yoke, learn his meekness and lowliness, walking in the path that leads heavenward.

Follow on to know the Lord, and you will know that his going forth is prepared as the morning. Seek constantly to improve. Strive earnestly for identity with the Redeemer. Live for the saving of the souls for whom he gave his life. Try in every way to help those with whom you come in contact. Let your love for Christ lead you to say, "Thy word have I hid in mine heart, that I might not sin against thee." Let your life fulfill the words, "Thou through thy commandments hast made me wiser than mine enemies." Talk with your Elder Brother; he will complete your education, line upon line, precept upon precept. A close connection with him who offered himself as a sacrifice to save a perishing world, will make you an acceptable worker. When you can lay your hand on truth, and appropriate it, when you can say, "My Lord and my God!" grace and peace and joy in rich measure will be yours.

Mrs. E. G. White

January 23, 1902—The Fair Flowers of Promise

As we look at a beautiful garden, with its opening buds, let us remember that this is an expression of our Father's love. As we note the varied tints of the flowers and inhale their delicate fragrance, let us think of the words, "Consider the lilies of the field, how they grow; they toil not, neither do they spin: and yet I say unto you, That even Solomon in all his glory was not arrayed like one of these." God has given us the flowers to teach us lessons of trust. "Wherefore, if God so clothe the grass of the field, which today is, and tomorrow is cast into the oven, shall he not much more clothe you, O ye of little faith?" If the great Master Artist makes perfect and lovely that which is today, and tomorrow is cast into the oven, will he not care much more for the beings purchased by the blood of his only begotten Son?

We are pilgrims and strangers on this earth, looking for a city which hath foundations, whose builder and maker is God. The path in which we travel is narrow, and calls for self-denial and self-sacrifice. We meet with trial and conflict. But God has not left us to travel without help. Our pathway to the heavenly Canaan is bordered with the fair flowers of promise. They blossom all along the way, sending forth their rich fragrance, like the flowers in the gardens of this earth.

To blot the promises of God from the word would be like blotting the sun from the sky. There would then be nothing to gladden our experience. God has placed the promises in his word to lead us to have faith in him. In these promises he draws back the veil from eternity, giving us a glimpse of the far more exceeding and eternal weight of glory which awaits the overcomer. Let us, then, rest in God. Let us praise him for giving us such a glorious revelation of his purposes.

All along our pathway, God places the flowers of promise to brighten our journey. But many refuse to gather these flowers, choosing instead the thorns and thistles. At every step they weep and mourn, when they might rejoice in the Lord because he has made the road to heaven so pleasant.

As we look at the promises of God, we find comfort and hope and joy; for they speak to us the words of the Infinite One. Properly to appreciate these precious promises, we should study them carefully, examining them in detail. How much joy we might bring into life, how much goodness into the character, if we would but make these promises our own! As we journey in the upward way, let us talk of the blessings strewn along the path. As we think of the mansions Christ is preparing for us, we forget the petty annoyances which we meet day by day. We seem to breathe the atmosphere of the heavenly country to which we are journeying, and we are soothed and comforted.

Do not think to find happiness in selfish amusement. The flowers thus gathered soon wither and die. True happiness is found only in the Master's service. In him who is the Light of the world we shall find comfort and hope. Our happiness comes not from what is around us, but from what is within us; not from what we have, but from what we are.

It is our privilege to sing the songs of Zion now, to turn our eyes to the light, to bring hope into our own hearts and into the hearts of others. God wants us to gather his promises, that we may be strengthened and refreshed. Let us take our eyes from the curse, and fix them on the grace so abundantly provided for us. God is dishonored when we fret and worry. Thus we show that we are not trusting in him, but in ourselves.

This life will have much brightness for us if we will gather the flowers and leave the briers alone. Comfort, encouragement, and support have been provided for every circumstance and condition of life. No temptation comes to us that Christ has not withstood, no trial that he has not borne. He knows each one of us by name. When a burden is placed on us, he stands by, to lift the heaviest weight. He has given us precious promises to lighten every burden. He assures us that his grace is sufficient. Today we have his help. Tomorrow we may be placed in new circumstances of trial, but the promise stands fast, "As thy days, so shall thy strength be."

Let us rejoice in the love of God. Let us praise him who has made us such royal promises. Let these promises keep our hearts in perfect peace. Let us honor God by weaving more of Jesus and heaven into our lives. Jesus lives. His hand is guiding us. This present life is not the summer but the winter of the Christian, nevertheless he may constantly enjoy the sunbeams of Christ's righteousness. He may have in his heart the peace "which passeth all understanding," even the peace which Christ gives.

February 6, 1902—Faithfulness in Service

In his infinite mercy and love God has given us light from his word, and Christ says to us, "Freely ye have received, freely give." Let the light God has given you shine forth to those in darkness. As you do this, heavenly angels will be beside you, helping you win souls for Christ. The Master is saying to us: "Come to me. Right counsel and sound judgment belong to me. I have understanding and strength for you."

Dear young friends, remember that it is not necessary to be an ordained minister in order to serve the Lord. There are many ways of working for Christ. Human hands may never have been laid on you in ordination, but God can give you fitness for his service. He can work through you to the saving of souls. If, having learned in the school of Christ, you are meek and lowly in heart, he will give you words to speak for him. Ask, and receive the Holy Spirit. But remember that the Spirit is given only to those who are consecrated, who deny self, lifting the cross and following their Lord.

Do all in your power to gain perfection; but do not think that because you make mistakes, you are excluded from God's service. The Lord knows our frame; he remembers that we are dust. As you use faithfully the talents God has given you, you will gain knowledge that will make you dissatisfied with self. You will see the need of sifting away harmful habits, lest by a wrong example you injure others.

Work diligently, giving to others the truth so precious to you. Then when there are vacancies to be filled, you will hear the words, "Come up higher." You may be reluctant to respond; but move forward in faith, bringing into God's work a fresh, honest zeal.

The secret of winning souls can be learned only from the great Teacher. As the dew and the still showers fall gently on the withering plant, so our words are to fall gently and lovingly on the souls we are seeking to win. We are not to wait till opportunities come to us; we are to seek for them, keeping the heart uplifted in prayer that God may help us to speak the right word at the right time. When an opportunity presents itself, let no excuse lead you to neglect it; for its improvement may mean the salvation of a soul from death.

February 13, 1902—God's Purpose for the Youth

Wonderful are the possibilities before the youth who grasp the assurances of God's word. Scarcely can the human mind comprehend the spiritual attainments which can be reached by them as they become partakers of the divine nature. Daily correcting mistakes and gaining victories, they grow into wise, strong men and women in Christ.

The Lord says to every one of you, "My son, give me thine heart." He sees your disorders. He knows that your soul is diseased with sin, and he desires to say to you, "Thy sins are forgiven." The Great Physician has a remedy for every ill. He understands your case. Whatever may have been your errors, he knows how to deal with them. Will you not trust yourself to him?

Before you are two ways,--the broad road of self-indulgence and the narrow path of self-sacrifice. Into the broad road you can take selfishness, pride, love of the world; but those who walk in the narrow way must lay aside every weight, and the sin which doth so easily beset. Which road have you chosen,--the road which leads to everlasting death, or the road which leads to glory and immortality?

The Lord has given you your life as a sacred trust. Spend it for him. Visit the sick; comfort the poor and sorrowful, speaking to them of the compassionate Redeemer. This work will bring to you health of body and peace of mind. Your countenance will reflect the joy that comes as the reward of unselfish service. The price of Christlike love is beyond computation; it makes human beings like Him who lived not to please himself.

In the history of Timothy are found precious lessons. He was a mere lad when chosen by God as a teacher; but so fixed were his principles by a correct education that he was fitted for this important position. He bore his responsibilities with Christlike meekness. He was faithful, steadfast, and true, and Paul selected him to be his companion in labor and travel. Lest Timothy should meet with slights because of his youthfulness, Paul wrote to him, "Let no man despise thy youth." He could safely do this, because Timothy was not self-sufficient, but continually sought guidance.

There are many youth who move from impulse rather than from judgment. But Timothy inquired at every step, "Is this the way of the Lord?" He had no specially brilliant talents, but he consecrated all his abilities to the service of God, and this made his work valuable. The Lord found in him a mind that he could mold and fashion for the indwelling of the Holy Spirit.

God will use the youth today as he used Timothy, if they will submit to his guidance. It is your privilege to be God's missionaries. He calls upon you to work for your companions. Seek out those you know to be in danger, and in the love of Christ try to help them. How are they to know the Saviour unless they see his virtues in his followers?

Take time to ask yourself, What am I doing for the Master? Work for him while the day lasts; the night is coming, and then you will not be able to work. Do not seek some great undertaking. Do the work nearest you, be it ever so humble. "He that is faithful in that which is least is faithful also in much." At the close of each day review your record, noting where you have failed to improve the precious opportunities that have come to you. Ask the Lord to pardon your neglect, and seek for strength to act with greater fidelity on the morrow.

Many youth are ready to make excuses for not entering the service of Christ. "I do not profess to be a Christian," one says, "and those who make a profession are no more Christlike than I am. If I professed to be a Christian, I would certainly do the works of a Christian." To the self-deceived ones who speak thus, come the words, He that knoweth his Master's will, and doeth it not, "shall be beaten with many stripes." If you have a clear understanding of the duties of the Christian life, and yet refuse to accept Christ, choosing rather to make yourself a stumbling-block by pointing to the errors of others, great will be your punishment.

At the eleventh hour the Lord will call into his service many faithful workers. Self-sacrificing men and women will step into the places made vacant by apostasy and death. To young men and young women, as well as to those who are older, God will give power from above. With converted minds, converted hands, converted feet, and converted tongues, their lips touched with a living coal from the divine altar, they will go forth into the Master's service, moving steadily onward and upward, carrying the work forward to completion.

Mrs. E. G. White

February 27, 1902—The Blessing of Labor

One of the first laws of the being is that of action. Every organ of the body has its appointed work, upon the development of which depends its strength. The normal action of all the organs gives vigor and life; inaction brings decay and death.

God placed our first parents in Paradise, surrounding them with all that was useful and lovely. In their Eden home nothing was wanting that could minister to their comfort and happiness. And to Adam was given the work of caring for the garden. The Creator knew that Adam could not be happy without employment. The beauty of the garden delighted him, but this was not enough. He must have labor to call into exercise the wonderful organs of the body. Had happiness consisted in doing nothing, man, in his state of holy innocence, would have been left unemployed. But he who created man knew what would be for his happiness; and no sooner had he created him, than he gave him his appointed work. The promise of future glory, and the decree that man must toil for his daily bread, came from the same throne.

Today thousands are sick and dying who might get well if they would; but imagination keeps them sick. Self-made invalids, they think that to work would make them worse, when work is just what they need to make them well. Without labor, they can never improve. When the body is inactive, the blood flows sluggishly, and the muscles decrease in size and strength. Rising above their aches and pains, forgetting that they have aching backs, sides, and heads, they should engage in useful employment. Physical exercise, and a free use of air and sunlight,--blessings which heaven has abundantly bestowed on all,--would give life and strength to many an emaciated invalid.

When not actively engaged in preaching, the apostle Paul labored at his trade as tent-maker. Before he accepted Christianity, he had occupied a high position, and was not dependent upon his trade for support. But among the Jews it was customary to teach children a trade, however high the position they were expected to fill, that a reverse of circumstances might not leave them incapable of sustaining themselves. In accordance with this rule, Paul learned the tent-maker's trade; and when his means had been expended in advancing the cause of God and in his own support, Paul resorted to his trade in order to gain a livelihood. Although feeble in health, he labored during the day in serving the cause of Christ, and then toiled a large part of the night, and frequently all night, that he might provide for his own and others' necessities.

Work is a blessing, not a curse. Diligent labor keeps many, young and old, from the snares of him who "finds some mischief still for idle hands to do." Let no one be ashamed of work; for honest toil is ennobling. While the hands are engaged in the most common tasks, the mind may be filled with high and holy thoughts.

Drowsiness and indolence destroy godliness, and grieve the Spirit of God. A stagnant pool is offensive; but a pure, flowing stream spreads health and gladness over the land. No man or woman who is converted can be anything but a worker. There certainly is and ever will be employment in heaven. The redeemed will not live in a state of dreamy idleness. There remaineth a rest for the people of God,--rest which they will find in serving him to whom they owe all they have and are.

Mrs. E. G. White

March 6, 1902—What Shall It Profit?

Cares, riches, pleasures, all are used by Satan in playing the game of life for the human soul. The warning is given: "Love not the world, neither the things that are in the world. If any man love the world, the love of the Father is not in him. For all that is in the world, the lust of the flesh, the lust of the eyes, and the pride of life, is not of the Father, but is of the world." He who reads the hearts of men as an open book says: "Take heed to yourselves, lest at any time your hearts be overcharged with surfeiting, and drunkenness, and cares of this life." And the apostle Paul, writing by the Holy Spirit, says: "They that will be rich fall into temptation and a snare, and into many foolish and hurtful lusts, which drown men in destruction and perdition. For the love of money is the root of all evil: which while some coveted after, they have erred from the faith, and pierced themselves through with many sorrows."

"And when he was gone forth into the way, there came one running, and kneeled to him, and asked him, Good Master, what shall I do that I may inherit eternal life?"

Christ pointed him to the commandments, and the young man answered, "All these things have I kept from my youth up: what lack I yet?"

"Then Jesus beholding him, loved him, and said unto him, One thing thou lackest: go thy way, sell whatsoever thou hast, and give to the poor, and thou shalt have treasure in heaven; and come, take up the cross, and follow me."

"But when the young man heard that saying, he went away sorrowful: for he had great possessions." He chose his riches instead of Jesus. He wanted eternal life, but he would not receive into the soul that unselfish love which alone is life. With a sorrowful heart he turned away from Christ.

As the young man turned away, Jesus said to his disciples, "How hardly shall they that have riches enter into the kingdom of God!" These words astonished the disciples. They had been taught to look upon the rich as the favorites of heaven: worldly power and riches they themselves hoped to receive in the Messiah's kingdom; and now if the rich were to fail of entering the kingdom, what hope could there be for them?

"Jesus answereth again, and saith unto them, Children, how hard is it for them that trust in riches to enter into the kingdom of God! It is easier for a camel to go through the eye of a needle, than for a rich man to enter into the kingdom of God. And they were astonished out of measure, saying among themselves, Who then can be saved? And Jesus looking upon them saith, With men it is impossible, but not with God: for with God all things are possible."

My dear young friends, God knows what your besetting sin is just as surely as he knew the ruler's. His word to him is a message to you. You must decide between Christ and the world. If you choose Christ, you must deny self, take up the cross, and follow him. The Saviour says to you: Withdraw your love from earthly treasure. Follow me, and you shall have treasure in heaven--a "far more exceeding and eternal weight of glory."

Christ does not ask his children to follow where he has not led the way. He was rich, but for our sake he became poor. He left the heavenly courts, and came to this earth to share the poverty of the poor and the toil of the laborer. He said of himself, "Foxes have holes, and the birds of the air have nests; but the Son of man hath not where to lay his head."

God is testing and proving his children to see if he can trust them with eternal riches. Are you living for him? Have you placed all you have at his disposal? Are you day by day revealing the unselfishness of the Redeemer? Life is uncertain. One may count on years of worldly pleasure, but accident or disease may suddenly cut him off. Are you ready for death?

God asks you: "What shall it profit a man, if he shall gain the whole world, and lose his own soul? Or what shall a man give in exchange for his soul?" "Behold, I come quickly, and my reward is with me, to give every man according as his work shall be."

Mrs. E. G. White

March 20, 1902—Living for Christ

It is a solemn thing to live, because we are not our own, but the Lord's, bought with the blood of his only begotten Son. Think of the estimate God has placed on us! When we were ready to perish, he sent his Son to die for us, that we might have an opportunity to regain what has been lost by sin. "God so loved the world, that he gave his only begotten Son, that whosoever believeth in him should not perish, but have everlasting life." This infinite sacrifice connects us with God. Satan can not hold us if we will accept Christ as our hope, our life, our personal Saviour. The spotless, sinless Son of God has borne our sins in his own body on the cross, that we might live unto God. When we truly receive Christ, we live his life, not our own. Our highest aim is to do his will, and represent his character.

Christ bore our sins that we might live unto righteousness. We were as sheep going astray, but he came from the heavenly courts to bring us back to the fold.

He died to make it possible for us to keep the law. But all are left to make their choice for themselves. God forces no one to accept the advantages secured for him at an infinite cost.

A large number of God's subjects have taken their position under the banner of rebellion; but God has not treated them as they deserve. They have declared of Christ, "We will not have this man to reign over us;" but the Lords's hand of love is stretched out still. Men have become bondmen of Satan, but the Lord is entreating them to enlist in his army.

Christ lived on this earth the life he desires his disciples to live,--a life of unselfish service. Let his children remember that he has a work for each one of them to do. He has given them talents, which they are to hold and use for him. But do we appreciate the privilege thus placed within our reach for blessing those around us? Do we use our talents to the best advantage? Are not many of us asleep, doing nothing to save our fellow men? Is not the Bible, God's great text-book of education, superficially read, and therefore superficially understood and superficially practiced?

Time is fast passing. Let us remember that while life is ours, we are under the solemn responsibility of working for God. Let us throw aside our narrow, selfish plans, and do our very best to accomplish the work God desires to have accomplished. Let us give the invitation, "Ho, every one that thirsteth, come ye to the waters, and he that hath no money; come ye, buy, and eat; yea, come, buy wine and milk without money and without price." Let us think of the sacrifice Jesus made to obtain our redemption. Let us study how we can most intelligently work for him. We have been bought with a price; therefore let us do all in our power to glorify him who has purchased us. God calls upon us to go to those in error, and point them to the right way. It is not only the ordained ministers who are to do this work. Ministering angels will co-operate with all who will labor unselfishly for the Master.

Mrs. E. G. White

April 17, 1902—"How Much Owest Thou?"

This question is broad and deep. We may try our best to compute by addition and multiplication the debt we owe to our Creator, but we shall fall far short of making a correct estimate of the favors and blessings he has bestowed upon us.

I have been trying to enumerate some of the blessings we receive from God. Two or three times a day we sit down to a table spread with food to supply us with strength. This food is the Lord's. Those who eat three times a day are indebted to the Lord for one thousand and ninety-five meals in one year. But how few remember, when they partake of food, that they are sitting at the Lord's table! How few bring the poor to their homes to share their blessings! Many are afraid to share with the poor that which the Lord has given them. They think that thus they would be made poor, forgetting the words, "There is that scattereth, and yet increaseth; and there is that withholdeth more than is meet, but it tendeth to poverty."

Many who profess to be waiting for the coming of the Lord are absorbed in the things of this life. Many who are already wealthy think only of how they can obtain more wealth. They take little or no interest in the advancement of Christ's kingdom. Dollars and cents are more to them than the souls of men. These may have earthly treasure, but in the sight of God they are poorer than the poorest. They may have houses and land and money at their disposal, but every year their soul-poverty increases. The record in the courts-above shows them to be bankrupt. They may be adding to their earthly gain, but each day they are adding to their eternal loss.

A professed Christian once said, "I have been a Christian for many years, and it has cost me only twenty-five cents." Think you that this man could expect to be a partaker in the glory of Him who gave his life for sinners? Could he look for a seat beside the One who counted not his life dear unto himself, that he might rescue the perishing? This professed Christian has been "rich in good works" to the value of twenty-five cents! Such was his estimate of the worth of redemption.

His testimony called forth from the minister the well-deserved reproof, "The Lord have mercy on you, poor, stingy soul!" And to this we say, Amen.

God tests all men. To some he intrusts riches. This he does to see if they will use earthly riches in such a way that he can bestow on them the heavenly riches. To others he sends poverty and affliction, to lead them to turn to him in trusting confidence.

Many who endure the test of poverty and sickness fail when prosperity comes to them. While they feel that they are dependent on their Heavenly Father for all they have, they preserve their purity and simplicity. But when prosperity comes to them, and they accumulate riches, they forget the Giver. They lose their trust in God. Self-confident and self-sufficient, they look upon their prosperity as the result of their own wisdom and perseverance. They forget that as their money increases, God desires them to use it in doing good.

The world says, It is of more consequence to be rich than good. And many in the church have adopted this standard, and are acting accordingly. Men who can make money are applauded. The love of money is lowering the standard of Christianity.

God's Son was sold for money. Filled with covetousness, Judas betrayed him to the priests for thirty pieces of silver. Thus is illustrated the power of covetousness over the human heart. Today men sell truth and righteousness for worldly gain. Covetousness has taken its abode in the hearts of professing Christians. Those who have all for which heart can wish, live for self-gratification, while the poor lie at their gates, unnoticed and unhelped.

Money is a curse unless it is used in the Master's service. With our means and our influence we are to work for him. God forbid that we should live for self, devoting time and means to selfish interests. When Jesus comes in the clouds of heaven, he will then have no use for the money he has intrusted to us. It is now that we are to give it to him. He calls upon us to bring him our tithes and offerings now, and he promises, if we do this, to pour upon us such a blessing that there will not be room enough to receive it.

Shall we take him at his word? His claims upon us transcend every other claim. The first and best of all that we have belongs to him.

Mrs. E. G. White

May 1, 1902—The Hand That Never Lets Go

The sun shone brilliantly on the dazzling snow of one of the highest mountains of the Alps, as a traveler followed his guide along the narrow path. The Englishman reveled in the scenes of beauty through which he passed. He had confidence in his guide, and followed fearlessly in his footsteps, though the track was entirely new to him. Suddenly he hesitated; for the bold mountaineer stepped across a narrow but very deep chasm, and then, holding out his hand, asked the Englishman to take it, and step across. Still the traveler hesitated, but the guide encouraged him to obey, saying, reassuringly. "Take my hand; that hand never lets go."

Dear young friends, One greater than any human guide calls upon you to follow him over the heights of patience and self-sacrifice. The path is not an easy one. Christ says, "Strait is the gate, and narrow is the way, which leadeth unto life, and few there be that find it." In order to follow this path, we must lay aside every weight, and the sin which so easily besets us. Directly at the entrance of the path lies the cross of self-denial. This we must lift if we would follow the Saviour. We must rid ourselves of pride and selfishness. While weighed down by them, we can not scale the heights over which Christ bids us follow him.

All the way along, Satan has prepared pitfalls for the feet of the unwary. But following our Guide, we may walk with perfect security; for the path is consecrated by his footsteps. It may be steep and rugged, but he has traveled it; his feet have pressed down the thorns to make the way easier for us. Every burden we are called upon to bear, he himself has borne. Personal contact with him brings light and hope and power. Of those who follow him, he says, "They shall never perish, neither shall any man pluck them out of my hand." "I the Lord ... will hold thy right hand, saying unto thee, Fear not; I will help thee." More precious in the Saviour's sight than the whole world is the soul who gives himself to Jesus. Christ would have passed through the agony of Calvary that one soul might be saved in his kingdom. He will never abandon one for whom he has died. Unless his children choose to leave him, he will hold them fast.

Christ's true disciples follow him through sore conflicts, enduring self-denial and experiencing bitter disappointment; but this teaches them the guilt and woe of sin, and they are led to look upon it with abhorrence. Being partakers of Christ's sufferings, they are destined to be partakers of his glory. In holy vision the prophet saw the triumph of the people of God. He says: "I saw as it were a sea of glass mingled with fire: and them that had gotten the victory ... stand on the sea of glass, having the harps of God. And they sing the song of Moses the servant of God, and the song of the Lamb, saying, Great and marvelous are thy works, Lord God Almighty; just and true are thy ways, thou King of saints."

June 5, 1902—The Danger of Self-confidence

Every day the youth are exposed to the perils of self-confidence. The enemy knows how to work most effectually to cripple their usefulness. He tries to fill their minds with thoughts of themselves, of their knowledge, of what they are able to accomplish. And with many he succeeds. Filled with self-sufficiency, they make no effort to correct the objectionable traits of character that have been handed down to them as a birth-right. They feel that they need no cautions. They are constantly making mistakes, but when corrected, they show impatience. "Pride compasseth them about." They think that by their course they are raising themselves in the estimation of others, but how greatly they mistake! The self-conceited youth gains little respect. It is reticence and modesty that win respect.

It is the superficial thinker who deems himself wise. Men of solid worth and high attainments are generally most ready to admit the weakness of their own understanding. Humility is the constant attendant of true wisdom.

I entreat our youth to guard against boastfulness and conceit. When placed in positions of responsibility, how many persons of great natural ability have fallen, while in the same position men of less ability and less education have succeeded. The reason is that the former trusted in themselves, while the latter trusted in Him who is wonderful in counsel and mighty in power.

Before honor is humility. To fill a high place before men, Heaven chooses the worker, who, like John the Baptist, takes a lowly place before God. Simplicity, self-forgetfulness, self-distrust, are attributes that Heaven values. These are the characteristics of real greatness.

The youth have many difficult lessons to learn before they are prepared for usefulness. In order to be fitted to fill positions of trust, they must submit to the stern teaching of rebuff and disappointment. Days of suffering are necessary to teach wisdom.

For the self-confident there is a lesson in the history of the apostle Peter. In his early discipleship, Peter thought himself strong. When on the eve of betrayal, Christ forewarned his disciples, "All ye shall be offended because of me this night," Peter confidently declared, "Though all men shall be offended because of thee, yet will I never be offended." Peter did not know his own danger. Self-confidence misled him. He thought himself able to withstand temptation; but in a few short hours the test came, and with cursing and swearing he denied his Lord.

When the crowing of the cock reminded him of the words of Christ, surprised and shocked at what he had just done, he turned and looked at his Master. At this moment, Christ looked upon Peter; and beneath that grieved look, in which compassion and love were blended, Peter understood himself. He went out, and wept bitterly.

The evil that led to Peter's fall is proving the ruin of thousands today. There is nothing so offensive to God, or so dangerous to the soul, as pride and self-sufficiency.

The nearer we come to Jesus, and the more clearly we discern the purity of his character, the more clearly shall we see the exceeding sinfulness of sin, and the less shall we feel like exalting ourselves. Those whom Heaven recognizes as holy ones are the last to parade their own goodness. Men who have lived near to God, men who would sacrifice life itself rather than knowingly commit a wrong act, men whom God has honored with divine light and power, have confessed the sinfulness of their own nature. They have put no confidence in the flesh, have claimed no righteousness of their own, but have trusted wholly in the righteousness of Christ. So will it be with all who behold the Saviour.

Mrs. E. G. White

June 12, 1902—In Service for Christ

There can be no self-seeking in the life of him who follows the Saviour. The true Christian banishes all selfishness from his heart. How can he live for self as he thinks of Christ hanging on the cross, giving his life for the life of the world?

In your behalf Jesus died a death of shame. Are you willing to consecrate yourself to his service? to hold yourself ready to be or to do anything he may require? Are you willing to put self aside, and speak a word of warning to the companion you see yielding to Satan's temptations? Are you willing to sacrifice some of your plans for the sake of trying to lead him in safe paths?

Many youth are in peril who might be saved if Christians would manifest toward them a loving, unselfish interest. By faithful effort they might be led to Jesus. But how many professing Christians there are who are so absorbed in self that they make no effort to help those in need of their help. Terrible will be their remorse in the day of judgment, when their mistake will be plainly revealed. The Spirit of God was striving with the straying ones, striving to lead them home. But those who should have cooperated with God were occupied with their own plans, too busy to see the opportunity that he offered them to work with him. Thus the connection between heaven and earth was broken. Those upon whom God called for help did not respond.

Remember that when you accepted Christ as your Saviour, you entered into a solemn covenant to employ your powers in his service. Into this work you are to put earnest, whole-hearted effort. Christ will not accept divided service. It is expected of a steward that he be found faithful. You are to make all temporal matters subordinate to the work the Lord has placed in your hands. He will call for a strict account of the use you have made of his gifts. The true Christian works unselfishly and untiringly for the Master. He does not seek ease or self-gratification, but holds all, even life itself, subject to God's call. And to him are spoken the words, "He that loseth his life for my sake shall find it."

To the indolent, those who are doing nothing for God, comes the inquiry: Why stand ye here all the day idle? Is there nothing to be done in my vineyard? Are there no souls for you to help? Have you forgotten that the judgment is coming? Work while it is called today; the night cometh, in which no man can work.

You are God's light-bearer. He has placed in your hands a lamp that you are to keep trimmed and burning for him.

By all that has given us advantage over another,--be it education and refinement, nobility of character, Christian training, religious experience,-- we are in debt to those less favored; and, so far as lies in our power, we are to minister unto them. If we are strong, we are to stay up the hands of the weak. Angels of glory, that do always behold the face of the Father in heaven, make such their special charge. Angels are ever present where they are most needed, with those who have the hardest battle with self to fight, and whose surroundings are the most disagreeable. And in this ministry, Christ's true followers will co-operate.

Mrs. E. G. White

June 26, 1902—Onward and Upward

I wish I could portray the beauty of the Christian life. Beginning in the morning of life, controlled by the laws of nature and of God the Christian moves steadily onward and upward, daily drawing nearer his heavenly home, where await for him a crown of life, and a new name, "which no man knoweth saving him that receiveth it." Constantly he grows in happiness, in holiness, in usefulness. The progress of each year exceeds that of the past year.

God has given the youth a ladder to climb, a ladder that reaches from earth to heaven. Above this ladder is God, and on every round fall the bright beams of his glory. He is watching those who are climbing, ready, when the grasp relaxes, and the steps falter, to send help. Yes, tell it in words full of cheer, that no one who perseveringly climbs the ladder will fail of gaining an entrance into the heavenly city.

Satan presents many temptations to the youth. He is playing the game of life for their souls, and he leaves no means untried to allure and ruin them. But God does not leave them to fight unaided against the tempter. They have an all-powerful Helper. Stronger far than their foe is he who in this world and in human nature met and conquered Satan, resisting every temptation that comes to the youth today. He is their Elder Brother. He feels for them a deep and tender interest. He keeps over them a constant watch-care, and he rejoices when they try to please him. As they pray, he mingles with their prayers the incense of his righteousness, and offers them to God as a fragrant sacrifice. In his strength the youth can endure hardness as good soldiers of the cross. Strengthened with his might, they are enabled to reach the high ideal before them. The sacrifice made on Calvary is the pledge of their victory.

The church of God is made up of vessels large and small. The Lord does not ask for anything unreasonable. He does not expect the smaller vessels to hold the contents of the larger ones. He looks for returns according to what a man has, not according to what he has not. Do your best, and God will accept your efforts. Take up the duty lying nearest you, and perform it with fidelity, and your work will be wholly acceptable to the Master. Do not, in your desire to do something great, overlook the smaller tasks awaiting you.

Beware how you neglect secret prayer and a study of God's word. These are your weapons against him who is striving to hinder your progress heavenward. The first neglect of prayer and Bible study makes easier the second neglect. The first resistance to the Spirit's pleading prepares the way for the second resistance. Thus the heart is hardened, and the conscience seared.

On the other hand, every resistance of temptation makes resistance more easy. Every denial of self makes self-denial easier. Every victory gained prepares the way for a fresh victory. Each resistance of temptation, each self-denial, each triumph over sin, is a seed sown unto eternal life. Every unselfish action gives new strength to spirituality. No one can try to be like Christ without growing more noble and more true.

The Lord will recognize every effort you make to reach his ideal for you. When you make failures, when you are betrayed into sin, do not feel that you can not pray, that you are not worthy to come before the Lord. "My little children, these things write I unto you, that ye sin not. And if any man sin, we have an advocate with the Father, Jesus Christ the righteous." With outstretched arms he waits to welcome the prodigal. Go to him, and tell him about your mistakes and failures. Ask him to strengthen you for fresh endeavor. He will never disappoint you, never abuse your confidence.

Trial will come to you. Thus the Lord polishes the roughness from your character. Do not murmur. You make the trial harder by repining. Honor God by cheerful submission. Patiently endure the pressure. Even though a wrong is done you, keep the love of God in the heart. "Keep thy tongue from evil, and thy lips from speaking guile. Depart from evil, and do good; seek peace, and pursue it. The eyes of the Lord are over the righteous, and his ears are open unto their cry."

"Beware of desperate steps; the darkest day, Wait but tomorrow, will have passed away."

"In quietness and in confidence shall be your strength." Christ knows the strength of your temptations and the strength of your power to resist. His hand is always stretched out in pitying tenderness to every suffering child. To the tempted, discouraged one he says, Child for whom I suffered and died, can not you trust me? "As thy days, so shall thy strength be."

"Commit thy way unto the Lord; trust also in him, and he shall bring it to pass.... Rest in the Lord, and wait patiently for him." He will be to you as the shadow of a great rock in a weary land. He says, "Come unto me, ... and I will give you rest,"--rest that the world can neither give nor take away. Come unto me, and your heart will be filled with the peace that passes all understanding.

Words can not describe the peace and joy possessed by him who takes God at his word. Trials do not disturb him, slights do not vex him. Self is crucified. Day by day his duties may become more taxing, his temptations stronger, his trials more severe; but he does not falter; for he receives strength equal to his need.

Mrs. E. G. White

July 3, 1902—A Faithful Witness—Part 1

When Paul was summoned to appear before Nero for his trial, it was with the near prospect of certain death. The nature of the crime charged against him, and the prevailing animosity against Christians, left little ground for hope of a favorable issue.

It was the practise among the Greeks and Romans to allow an accused person an advocate, to present his case and to plead in his behalf. By force of argument, by impassioned eloquence, or by entreaties, prayers, and tears, the advocate would often secure a decision in favor of the prisoner; or failing in this, would lessen the severity of the sentence. But no man ventured to act as Paul's advocate; no friend was at hand even to preserve a record of the charges brought against him by his accusers, or of the arguments he urged in his own defense.

Paul before Nero--how striking the contrast! The height of earthly power, authority, and wealth, as well as the lowest depths of crime and iniquity, had been reached by the haughty monarch before whom the man of God was to answer for his faith. In power and greatness, Nero stood unrivaled. There was none to question his authority, none to resist his will. Kings laid their crowns at his feet. Powerful armies marched at his command. The ensigns of his navies betokened victory. His statue was set up in the halls of justice, and the decrees of senators and the decisions of judges were but the echo of his will. Millions of subjects bowed in obedience to his mandates. To incur his displeasure was to lose property, liberty, life. His frown was more to be dreaded than a pestilence.

Without money, without friends, without counsel, Paul had been brought forth from a dungeon to be tried for his life. His experience had been one of poverty, self-denial, and suffering. With a sensitive nature, that thirsted for love and sympathy, he had braved misrepresentation, reproach, and abuse. Shrinking with nervous dread from pain and peril, he had fearlessly endured both. Like his Master, he had been a homeless wanderer; he had lived and suffered for the truth's sake, seeking to bless humanity and to live the Christ-life. How could Nero, a capricious, passionate tyrant, appreciate the character and motives of this son of God?

Paul and Nero face to face!--the countenance of the monarch bearing the shameful record of the passions that raged within; the countenance of the prisoner telling the story of a heart at peace with God and man. The result of opposite systems of education stood that day contrasted,--a life of unbounded self-indulgence and a life of entire self-sacrifice. Here were the representatives of two theories of life,--all-absorbing selfishness, which counts nothing too valuable to be sacrificed for momentary gratification, and self-denying endurance, ready to give up life itself, if need be, for the good of others.

The Jews brought against Paul the old charge of sedition and heresy, while both Jews and Romans accused him of instigating the burning of the city. While these accusations were urged against him, Paul preserved unbroken serenity. The people and the judges looked upon him with surprise. They had been present at many trials, and had looked upon many a criminal; but never had they seen a man wear a look of such holy calmness as did the prisoner before them. The keen eyes of the judges, accustomed to read the countenances of prisoners, searched Paul's face in vain for some evidence of guilt.

When Paul was permitted to speak in his own behalf, all listened with eager interest to his words. Once more he had opportunity to uplift before a wondering multitude the banner of the cross. With more than human eloquence and power he presented the truths of the gospel. His words struck a chord that vibrated in the hearts of even the most hardened. Truth, clear and convincing, overthrew error. Light shown into the minds of many who afterward gladly followed its rays. The words spoken on this occasion were destined to shake nations. They were endowed with a power that would enable them to live through all time, influencing the hearts of men when he who uttered them would be silent in a martyr's grave.

As Paul gazed upon the throng before him,--Jews, Greeks, Romans, with strangers from many lands,--his soul was stirred with an intense desire for their salvation. He lost sight of the occasion, of the perils surrounding him, of the terrible fate that seemed so near. He saw only Jesus, the Intercessor, pleading before God in behalf of sinful men. He pointed his hearers to the sacrifice made for the fallen race. An infinite price had been paid for man's redemption. Provision had been made for him to share the throne of God. By angel messengers, earth was connected with heaven, and all the deeds of men, whether good or evil, were open to the eye of infinite Justice.

Thus pleads the advocate of truth. Faithful among the faithless, loyal among the disloyal, he stands as God's representative, and his voice is as a voice from heaven. There is no fear, no sadness, no discouragement, in word or look. Strong in a consciousness of innocence, clothed in the panoply of truth, he rejoices that he is a son of God. His words are as a shout of victory above the roar of battle. He declares that the cause to which he has devoted his life is the only cause that can never fail. Though he may perish for the truth's sake, the gospel will not perish. God lives, and his truth will triumph.

Paul's countenance beams with the light of heaven. Many who looked upon him "saw his face as it had been the face of an angel." Tears dimmed many eyes. The gospel found its way to the hearts of many who, but for Paul's witness, would never have been led to the Saviour.

Mrs. E. G. White

July 10, 1902—A Faithful Witness—Part 2

From the judgment-hall, Paul returned to his prison-house, knowing that he had gained for himself only a brief respite. He knew that his enemies would compass his death; but he was not afraid. His heart was full of courage, his eyes shone with heavenly brightness: by faith he beheld the glories of the unseen.

The apostle's speech had gained him many friends, and he was visited by persons of rank, who accounted his blessing of greater value than the favor of the emperor of the world. But there was one friend for whose sympathy and companionship he longed in those last trying days. That friend was Timothy, to whom he had committed the care of the church at Ephesus, and who had therefore been left behind when Paul made his last journey to Rome. The affection between Paul and Timothy began with Timothy's conversion; and the tie had strengthened as they had shared the hopes, the perils, and the toils of missionary life, till they seemed to be as one. The disparity in their age and the difference in their character made their love for each other more earnest. The ardent, zealous, indomitable spirit of Paul found repose and comfort in the mild, yielding, retiring disposition of Timothy. The faithful ministration and tender love of this tried companion had brightened many a dark hour in the apostle's life. All that Melancthon was to Luther, all that a son could be to a loved and honored father, the youthful Timothy was to the tried and lonely Paul.

And now, sitting alone in his gloomy cell, knowing that at a word or nod from Nero, his life may be sacrificed, Paul thinks of Timothy, and determines to send for him. Under the most favorable circumstances, several months must elapse before Timothy can reach Rome. Paul knows that his own life is uncertain, and that Timothy may arrive too late. He has important counsel for him; and while urging him to come without delay, he dictates the charge that he may not be spared to utter. His heart is filled with loving solicitude for his son in the gospel, and for the church under his care; and he seeks to impress Timothy with the importance of fidelity to his trust. "I charge thee therefore," he says, "before God, and the Lord Jesus Christ, who shall judge the quick and the dead at his appearing and his kingdom; Preach the word; be instant in season, out of season; reprove, rebuke, exhort with all long-suffering and doctrine.... Watch thou in all things, endure afflictions, do the work of an evangelist, make full proof of thy ministry."

Paul has almost finished his course, and he desires Timothy to take his place, guarding the churches from the fables and heresies with which Satan and his agents would endeavor to lead them from the truth. He admonishes him to shun temporal pursuits and entanglements, which would prevent him from giving himself wholly to God's work. He is to endure with cheerfulness the opposition, reproach, and persecution to which his faithfulness would expose him. He is to make full proof of his ministry, employing every means of doing good to his fellow men.

Never had Paul been ashamed to confess Christ before men. Under all circumstances he had fearlessly placed himself on the side of right. Firmly believing the principles of truth, he never shrank from declaring them. His life was an illustration of the truths he taught; and in this lay his power. To him the voice of duty was the voice of God. His soul was filled with a deep sense of his responsibility, and he lived in close and constant communion with God. He clung to the cross of Christ as the only guaranty of success. The love of the Saviour was the power that upheld him in his conflicts with himself and with the power of Satan, in his struggles against spiritual wickedness in high places, in his life-long labors as he pressed forward against the unfriendliness of the world and the burden of his own infirmities.

What the church needs today is an army of workers who, like Paul, have a deep experience in the things of God, and who are filled with an earnest desire to do his service. Cultivated, refined, sanctified men are needed; men who will not shun trial and responsibility; men who are burden-bearers; men who are brave and true; men in whose hearts Christ is formed, and who, with lips touched with holy fire, will preach the word to those who are starving for the bread of life. For the lack of such workers, the cause of God languishes, and fatal errors, like deadly poison, taint the morals and blight the hopes of a large part of the race.

As the faithful, toil-worn standard-bearers are offering up their lives for the truth's sake, who among the youth will come forward to take their place? Will our young men accept the holy trust at the hand of their fathers? Are they now preparing to fill the vacancies made by the death of the faithful? Will they heed God's call to service?

Mrs. E. G. White

July 24, 1902—Search the Scriptures

This is the word that comes to us from Christ. Had it been essential for us to search the Fathers, he would have told us to do so. But the Fathers do not all speak the same thing. Which of them should we chose as a guide? There is no need for us to trust to such uncertainty. We pass by the Fathers to learn of God out of his word. This is life eternal, to know God. O, how thankful we should be that the Bible is the inspired word of God! Holy men of old wrote this word as they were moved by the Spirit.

The commentaries written about the word do not all agree. God does not ask us to be guided by them. It is his word with which we have to deal. All can search this word for themselves, knowing that the teaching of this precious book is unchangeable. The opinions of human beings differ, but the Bible always says the same thing. The word of God is from everlasting to everlasting.

God did not leave his word to be preserved in the memory of men, and handed down from generation to generation by oral transmission and traditional unfolding. Had he done this, the word would gradually have been added to by men, and we should have been asked to receive the teachings of men. Let us thank God for his written word.

The Bible was not given for ministers and learned men only. The poor man needs it as much as the rich man, the unlearned as much as the learned. Every person, young and old alike, should read the Bible for himself. Do not depend on the minister to read it for you. The Bible is God's word to you. And Christ has made this word so plain that in reading it no one need stumble. Let the humble cottager read and understand the word given by the wisest Teacher the world has ever known; for among kings, governors, statesmen, and the world's most highly educated men, there is none greater than he.

"Search the Scriptures; for in them ye think ye have eternal life." To search means to look diligently for something which has been lost. Search for the hidden treasures in God's word. You can not afford to be without them. Study the difficult passages, comparing verse with verse, and you will find that scripture is the key which unlocks scripture. Those who prayerfully study the Bible go from each search wiser than they were before. Some of their difficulties have been solved; for the Holy Spirit has done the work spoken of in the fourteenth chapter of John: "The Comforter, which is the Holy Ghost, whom the Father will send in my name, he shall teach you all things, and bring all things to your remembrance, whatsoever I have said unto you."

Nothing worth having is obtained without earnest, persevering effort. In business, only those who have a will to do, see successful results. Without earnest toil we can not expect to obtain a knowledge of spiritual things. Those who obtain the jewels of truth must dig for them as a miner digs for the precious ore hidden in the earth. Those who work indifferently and half-heartedly will never succeed. Young and old should read the word of God; and not only should they read it, but they should study it with diligent earnestness, praying, believing, and searching. Thus they will find the hidden treasure; for the Lord will quicken their understanding.

In your study of the word, lay at the door of investigation your preconceived opinions and your hereditary and cultivated ideas. You will never reach the truth if you study the Scriptures to vindicate your own ideas. Leave these at the door, and with a contrite heart go in to hear what the Lord has to say to you. As the humble seeker for truth sits at Christ's feet, and learns of him, the word gives him understanding. To those who are too wise in their own conceit to study the Bible, Christ says, You must become meek and lowly in heart if you desire to become wise unto salvation.

Do not read the word in the light of former opinions; but with a mind free from prejudice, search it carefully and prayerfully. If, as you read, conviction comes, and you see that your cherished opinions are not in harmony with the word, do not try to make the word fit these opinions. Make your opinions fit the word. Do not allow what you have believed or practised in the past to control your understanding. Open the eyes of your mind to behold wondrous things out of the law. Find out what is written, and then plant your feet on the eternal Rock.

Our salvation depends upon our knowledge of God's will as it is contained in his word. Never cease asking and searching for truth. You need to know your duty. You need to know what you must do to be saved. And it is God's will that you shall know what he has said to you. But you must exercise faith. As you search the Scriptures, you must believe that God is, and that he rewards those who diligently seek him.

O search the Bible with a heart hungry for spiritual food! Dig into the word as a miner digs into the earth to find the veins of gold. Do not give up your search till you have learned your relation to God and his will concerning you.

Mrs. E. G. White

July 31, 1902—Found Wanting

The Saviour's denunciation of the fruitless fig tree is a warning to all who claim to be Christians, and yet remain in blind unbelief. Thus from age to age the Lord would teach the danger of rejecting light. Christ has worked for and invited all. He will enlighten all who will search the Scriptures candidly. Today he is knocking at the door of the heart. Shall he have to say of us, In vain do ye worship me, teaching for doctrine the commandments of men?

The words spoken to the fig tree are applicable to all whose lives, though pretentious, are fruitless. The tree may have every indication of prosperity, but the Lord takes not its luxuriant foliage as an evidence of fruitfulness. His search for the fruit which alone makes the tree of value is close and critical. How is it with us? Can we bear the search made by him who never makes a mistake, or do we bear only the leaves of profession? Profession is nothing if it is only a mask to spiritual barrenness.

When the Saviour appears in the clouds of heaven, no one will be given another opportunity to gain salvation. All will have made their decision. Before the close of this world's history those who are willing to accept evidence will have the dark veil removed from their minds. Hearts will be cleansed through accepting Christ during the time that the whole world is lighted with the glory of the angel who comes down from heaven.

The time is right upon us when every kind of deception will be practised. Christ says, "Beware of false prophets, which come to you in sheep's clothing." They speak fair words, but all the time they are watching to see how they can get gain for themselves. They are full of selfishness, and work at cross purposes with God. "Ye shall know them by their fruits," the Saviour declares. "A good tree can not bring forth evil fruit, neither can a corrupt tree bring forth good fruit." Nothing but repentance and faith can make an impure heart pure.

God weighs every man in the balances of the sanctuary. In one scale is placed his perfect, unchangeable law, demanding perfect obedience. If in the other there are years of forgetfulness, of rebellion, of self-pleasing, with no repentance, no confession, no effort to do right, God says, "Thou art weighed in the balances, and art found wanting."

Thus the deciding line is drawn. Claiming to be righteous without manifesting the fruits of true conversion, is utterly worthless. External forms, even though they be such as God has commanded, are of no value unless accompanied by an inward work of cleansing. Outward works alone will never make a man perfect before God. Nothing but repentance and faith can make an impure heart pure.

In the great day of judgment how will transgressors appear in their own sight as they are permitted to see the record of their life as they have chosen to make it, regardless of the law which through eternity will govern the universe? During their lifetime they utterly refused to be made better. The efforts put forth in their behalf were in vain. They knew the claims of God, but they refused to comply with the conditions laid down in his word. By their own choice they united with the enemy. The powers given them to use in God's service they used in the service of self. They made self their god, refusing to submit to any other control. They arrayed themselves on the side of the power of darkness, and encouraged others to do the same.

As they stand before the bar of God, this opens before them. A flash of light will come to all lost souls. Scene after scene will rise before them. They will see the power of the mystery of godliness, which in this life they despised and hated. They will see what they might have become through the power of Christ. They will understand the robbery they have practised toward God. They will see the good they might have done but did not do.

The picture can not be changed. Their cases are forever decided. They realized that they must perish with the one whose ways and works they have chosen, and in terror they cry to the rocks and mountains, "Fall on us, and hide us from the face of him that sitteth on the throne, and from the face of the Lamb: for the great day of his wrath is come, and who shall be able to stand?"

Mrs. E. G. White

August 21, 1902—Liberty in Christ

"Behold what manner of love the Father hath bestowed upon us, that we should be called the sons of God."

John can not find words to describe the great love that God has bestowed upon us. He can only call upon us to behold it. That God should consent to let his only begotten Son come to a world all seared and marred with the curse, to walk a man among men, and to suffer death by crucifixion,--does not this bear eloquent witness to the power of God's love?

God's love is as high as heaven and as broad as eternity. Why was it bestowed on us?--That we might be called his sons. "But," says the young man, "I am not ready to be a Christian. I have not yet sown my wild oats." I once spoke to a company of prisoners. One of their number was a young man who had just been graduated from college. During his school life he had studied hard, and he had planned to have a good time after his graduation. He came in contact with evil companions; a crime was committed; they were brought before the court; and this young man was imprisoned for seven years. A sad result of his sowing of wild oats!

Young man, are you one of those who believe in sowing wild oats? Remember that the harvest time is coming, and that as you have sown, so you will reap. No frost will blight the crop, no storm blast it, no cankerworm destroy it. You are sure of a bountiful yield. If you spend your time in idleness, in amusement, in self-gratification, you will reap a harvest of sorrow. When adversity comes, you will find that the service of Satan is indeed bitter.

As I was pleading with a young man to turn to the Saviour, he said: "I am not ready. This band of music would be broken up should I leave it. I am needed in this circle of society. And besides, I want my liberty." But he did not know of what he was talking. There is no liberty save that which has been brought to us by Christ. We can find in sin nothing but slavery. What was Adam after he had disobeyed?--A captive to sin, his dark future illuminated only by the promise of the Saviour to come.

Those who think that a surrender to Christ means loss of liberty are in bondage to the worst of all tyrants. Satan binds them in chains of darkness, and exults in their ruin. And yet they talk of liberty! Liberty to sin, when the wages of sin is death!

Christ gives us all the blessings we enjoy. The beautiful things of nature are the work of his hands. Every breath we draw is an evidence of what we owe to divine power. But where is our devotion, our love for God? Many who profess to serve him are Christians in name only.

God has done so much to make it possible for us to be free in Christ, free from the slavery of wrong habits and evil inclinations. Dear young friends, will you not strive to be free in Christ? You point to this and that professed Christian, saying, We have no confidence in them. If their lives are examples of Christianity, we want none of it. Look not at those around you. Look instead at the only perfect pattern, the man Christ Jesus. Beholding him, you will be changed into the same image.

Will you not try to show those with whom you come in contact the better way, even the way which leads to the city whose builder and maker is God? If you walk humbly with God, the Holy Spirit will be your efficiency. As you let your light shine in good works, those with whom you associate will see light in your light. Let not your light grow dim; for this is dangerous not only to your own soul, but to the souls of others. Keep your light burning brightly. Be cheerful, hopeful, and steadfast. Gather grace and strength, daily becoming more trustful and hopeful. Pray and watch and work, lest the day of the Lord come on you as a thief in the night. Duties and responsibilities will increase with success. Satan will try to divert your mind from Jesus. He will try to make you believe that you will not reap what you have sown. Listen not to him. Make God supreme. Hide self in Christ. Welcome the Saviour into the heart as a cherished guest. You can do nothing without him, but with him you can do "all things." He is the Mighty God, the Everlasting Father, the Prince of Peace. He is invincible, and those who work in his strength will be more than conquerors.

Mrs. E. G. White

September 11, 1902—Living Water

In the incident of the Samaritan woman at the well, is shown one of the Saviour's ways of winning souls. While the woman was extolling Jacob's well, Christ was speaking to her of the water of everlasting life. He who drinks of the water of Jacob's well "shall thirst again," he said, but he who drinks "of the water that I shall give him shall never thirst."

Instead of disparaging Jacob's well, Christ presented something better. "If thou knewest the gift of God," he said, "and who it is that saith to thee, Give me to drink; thou wouldst have asked of him, and he would have given thee living water." He turned the conversation to the treasure he had to bestow, which would satisfy the craving of mind and heart. He offered the woman something better than anything she possessed, even living water, the joy and hope of the gospel of his kingdom.

This is an illustration of the way in which we are to work. It is of little use for us to go to pleasure-lovers, theater-goers, drunkards, and gamblers, and scathingly rebuke them for their sins. We must offer them something better than that which they have, even "the peace of God, which passeth all understanding." We must make it as plain as possible to them that the law of God is binding upon all human beings, and that this law is a transcript of the divine character, an expression of that which the Creator wishes his children to become.

These poor souls are engaged in a wild chase after worldly pleasure and earthly riches. They have no knowledge of anything more desirable. But pleasure will not satisfy the soul. Show them how infinitely superior to the fleeting joys of the world is the imperishable glory of heaven. Seek to convince them of the freedom and hope and rest and peace to be found in the gospel.

God's people, young and old, are to lift up Jesus, who alone can satisfy the restless craving of the heart, and give repose to the mind. Wealth can not do this. Intoxicating drink can not do it. Worldly pleasure can not do it. Title, rank, learning, power,--all are worthless unless the name is enrolled in the Lamb's book of life.

In the prayer which Christ offered to his Father just before the crucifixion, he said, "This is life eternal, that they might know thee the only true God, and Jesus Christ, whom thou hast sent." Only the religion that comes from God will lead to God. "He that believeth on the Son hath everlasting life." There is in his heart a well of living water, the influence of which is felt by all with whom he associates.

To the weary and heavy laden Christ says, "Come unto me, ... and I will give you rest." Restless, craving, exhausted heart, think of the Saviour's words, "Whosoever drinketh of this water that I shall give him shall never thirst." Drink from the wells of worldly pleasure, and you will thirst again. Drink of the water of life, and you will be satisfied and refreshed; for it will be in you "a well of water springing up into everlasting life." Love and light and truth and life are found in the everlasting gospel. Come, ye who labor and are heavy laden, come to the living water. "Let him that is athirst come. And whosoever will, let him take the water of life freely."

Mrs. E. G. White

October 2, 1902—"It Is My Way"

Sometimes one who professes to be a follower of Christ is heard saying, "You must not be surprised if I am rough, if I speak bluntly, if I manifest temper: it is my way."

You ask us not to be surprised! Is not Heaven surprised at such manifestations, since the plan of salvation has been devised, since an infinite sacrifice has been made on Calvary's cross, that you might reflect the image of Jesus? Will "your way" enter heaven? Suppose some one comes up to the pearly gates, and says, "I know that I have been rude and unkind, and that it is my disposition to lie and steal; but I want an entrance to the heavenly mansions." Will such a disposition find entrance through the portals of the heavenly city?--No, no! only those who keep God's way will enter there.

The manifestation of natural and cultivated tendencies to wrong-doing can not be excused by the plea, "It is my way." Christians realize that in order to bring the principles of Christianity into the daily life, they need much of the grace of Christ.

The youth who co-operate with Christ will find that their way is full of errors needing to be corrected. Brought into the character-building, these errors are as rotten timbers. Let no one allow them to remain. Let no one plead for the privilege of clinging to his imperfections, excusing himself by saying, "It is my way." Those who please self, refusing to give up their way for Christ's way, will suffer the sure result. They will find themselves strengthless, Christless.

Are you striving to walk in the way of truth and righteousness? Then be not discouraged by temptation. True, you will be tempted; but remember that temptation is not sin; it is no indication of the Lord's displeasure. He suffers you to be tempted, but he measures the temptation by the power which he imparts to enable you to resist and overcome. It is in the time of temptation and trial that you are to measure the degree of your faith in God, and to estimate the stability of your Christian character.

Do not say, "It is impossible for me to overcome." Do not say, "It is my nature to do thus and so, and I can not do otherwise. I have inherited weaknesses that make me powerless before temptation." In your own strength you can not overcome, but help has been laid upon One that is mighty. Breathe the prayer, "Show me thy ways, O Lord; teach me thy paths." Then believe the promise, "The meek will he guide in judgment: and the meek will he teach his way." Yes, the Lord says, "I will instruct thee and teach thee in the way which thou shalt go: I will guide thee with mine eye."

In order to receive the virtue of the blood of Christ, even the forgiveness of your sins, you must consent to the conditions he imposes. "If any man will come after me," he says, "let him deny himself, and take up his cross, and follow me." Seeking pardon of sin from his cross, you will seek direction from his throne. Looking to and believing in Christ as your personal Saviour, is your only hope of salvation. Receiving Christ in all his completeness, you are in truth able to sing:

"I will follow thee, my Saviour, Wheresoe'er my lot may be. Where thou goest, I will follow; Yes, my Lord, I'll follow thee."

God has given his Holy Spirit as a power sufficient to subdue all your hereditary and cultivated tendencies to wrong-doing. By yielding the mind to the control of the Spirit, you will grow into the likeness of God's perfect character, and will become an instrumentality through which he can reveal his mercy, his goodness and his love.

Whatever may be your defects, the Holy Spirit will reveal them, and grace will be given you to overcome. Through the merits of the blood of Christ you may be a conqueror, yes, more than a conqueror. Will you who read these words resolve never again to excuse your defects of character by saying, "It is my way"? Let no one again declare, "I can not change my natural habits and tendencies." Let the truth be admitted into the soul, and it will work to sanctify the character.

Beholding Christ, we are changed through the power of the Holy Spirit. When this change takes place, the hands, the tongue, the feet, act in accord with the heart's spiritual advancement. Faith is a shining light, shining more and more unto the perfect day. We no longer plead for our will to be done, or for our old ways and habits to be left undisturbed. The converting power of God molds us after the divine similitude,--after the likeness of the One who is "the Way, the Truth, and the Life."

Mrs. E. G. White

October 9, 1902—What Shall We Read?

Education is but a preparation of the physical, intellectual, and spiritual powers for the best performance of all the duties of life. The powers of endurance, and the strength and activity of the brain, are lessened or increased by the way in which they are employed. The mind should be so disciplined that all its powers will be symmetrically developed.

Many youth are eager for books. They desire to read everything that they can obtain. Let them take heed what they read as well as what they hear. I have been instructed that they are in the greatest danger of being corrupted by improper reading. Satan has a thousand ways of unsettling the minds of youth. They can not safely be off guard for a moment. They must set a watch upon their minds, that they may not be allured by the enemy's temptations.

Satan knows that to a great degree the mind is affected by that upon which it feeds. He is seeking to lead both the youth and those of mature age to read story-books, tales, and other literature. The readers of such literature become unfitted for the duties lying before them. They live an unreal life, and have no desire to search the Scriptures, to feed upon the heavenly manna. The mind that needs strengthening is enfeebled, and loses its power to study the great truths that relate to the mission and work of Christ,--truths that would fortify the mind, awaken the imagination, and kindle a strong, earnest desire to overcome as Christ overcame.

Could a large share of the books published be consumed, a plague would be stayed that is doing a fearful work upon mind and heart. Love stories, frivolous and exciting tales, and even that class of books called religious novels,--books in which the author attaches to his story a moral lesson,--are a curse to the readers. Religious sentiments may be woven all through a story book, but, in most cases, Satan is but clothed in angel-robes, the more effectively to deceive and allure. None are so confirmed in right principles, none so secure from temptation, that they are safe in reading these stories.

The readers of fiction are indulging an evil that destroys spirituality, eclipsing the beauty of the sacred page. It creates an unhealthy excitement, fevers the imagination, unfits the mind for usefulness, weans the soul from prayer, and disqualifies it for any spiritual exercise.

God has endowed many of our youth with superior capabilities; but too often they have enervated their powers, confused and enfeebled their minds, so that for years they have made no growth in grace or in a knowledge of the reasons of our faith, because of their unwise choice of reading. Those who are looking for the Lord soon to come, looking for that wondrous change, when "this corruptible shall put on incorruption," should in this probationary time be standing upon a higher plane of action.

My dear young friends, question your own experience as to the influence of exciting stories. Can you, after such reading, open the Bible and read with interest the words of life? Do you not find the Book of God uninteresting? The charm of that love story is upon the mind, destroying its healthy tone, and making it impossible for you to fix the attention upon the important, solemn truths that concern your eternal welfare.

The nature of one's religious experience is revealed by the character of the books he chooses to read in his leisure moments. In order to have a healthy tone of mind and sound religious principles, the youth must live in communion with God through his word. Pointing out the way of salvation through Christ, the Bible is our guide to a higher, better life. It contains the most interesting and the most instructive history and biography that were ever written. Those whose imagination has not become perverted by the reading of fiction will find the Bible the most interesting of books.

Resolutely discard all trashy reading. It will not strengthen your spirituality, but will introduce into the mind sentiments that pervert the imagination, causing you to think less of Jesus and to dwell less upon his precious lessons. Keep the mind free from everything that would lead it in a wrong direction. Do not encumber it with trashy stories, which impart no strength to the mental powers. The thoughts are of the same character as the food provided for the mind.

The Bible is the book of books. If you love the word of God, searching it as you have opportunity, that you may come into possession of its rich treasures, and be thoroughly furnished unto all good works, then you may be assured that Jesus is drawing you to himself. But to read the Scripture in a casual way, without seeking to comprehend Christ's lesson that you may comply with his requirements, is not enough. There are treasures in the word of God that can be discovered only by sinking the shaft deep into the mine of truth.

The carnal mind rejects the truth; but the soul that is converted undergoes a marvelous change. The book that before was unattractive because it revealed truths which testified against the sinner, now becomes the food of the soul, the joy and consolation of the life. The Sun of righteousness illuminates the sacred pages, and the Holy Spirit speaks through them to the soul. To those who love Christ the Bible is as the garden of God. Its promises are as grateful to the heart as the fragrance of flowers is to the senses.

Let all who have cultivated a love for light reading, now turn their attention to the sure word of prophecy. Take your Bibles, and begin to study with fresh interest the sacred records of the Old and New Testaments. The oftener and more diligently you study the Bible, the more beautiful will it appear, and the less relish you will have for light reading. Bind this precious volume to your hearts. It will be to you a friend and guide.

Mrs. E. G. White

October 23, 1902—"Look Up"

Several years ago, while journeying from Christiania, Norway, to Goteborg, Sweden, I was favored with a sight of the most glorious sunset it was ever my privilege to behold. Language is inadequate to picture its beauty. The last beams of the setting sun, silver and gold, purple, amber, and crimson, shed their glories athwart the sky, growing brighter and brighter, rising higher and higher in the heavens, until it seemed that the gates of the city of God had been left ajar, and gleams of the inner glory were flashing through. For two hours the wondrous splendor continued to light up the cold northern sky,--a picture painted by the great Master Artist upon the shifting canvas of the heavens. Like the smile of God it seemed, above all earthly homes, above the rock-bound plains, the rugged mountains, the lonely forests, through which our journey lay.

Angels of mercy seemed whispering: "Look up! This glory is but a gleam of the light which flows from the throne of God. Live not for earth alone. Look up, and behold by faith the mansions of the heavenly home." This scene was to me as the bow of promise to Noah, enabling me to grasp the assurance of God's unfailing care, and to look forward to the haven of rest awaiting the faithful worker. Ever since that time I have felt that God granted us this token of his love for our encouragement. Never while memory lingers, can I forget that vision of beauty, and the comfort and peace it brought.

As God's children, it is our privilege ever to look up, keeping the eye of faith fixed on Christ. As we constantly keep him in view, the sunshine of his presence floods the chambers of the mind. The light of Christ in the soul-temple brings peace. The soul is stayed on God. All perplexities and anxieties are committed to Jesus. As we continue to behold him, his image becomes engraved on the heart, and is revealed in the daily life.

But if, after conversion, we allow worldliness to creep into the heart, if we cherish it as a welcome guest, there is an entire change. The view of Jesus is eclipsed. The vision of his purity, his goodness, his matchless love, is dimmed. Peace is gone. No longer is the soul committed to him in simple, perfect trust. The whole Christian life seems uncertain.

My dear young friends, ever keep Christ in view. Thus only can you keep the eye single to God's glory. Jesus is your light and life and peace and assurance forever. By beholding him you are changed from glory to glory--from character to character.

"If therefore thine eye be single, thy whole body shall be full of light. But if thine eye be evil, thy whole body shall be full of darkness." "Take heed therefore that the light which is in thee be not darkness. If thy whole body therefore be full of light, having no part dark, the whole shall be full of light, as when the bright shining of a candle doth give thee light." In Him is no darkness at all.

When the soul is illumined by God's Spirit, the whole character is elevated, the mental conceptions are enlarged, and the affections, no longer centered upon self, shine forth in good works to others, attracting them to the beauty and brightness of Christ's glory.

Mrs. E. G. White

November 6, 1902—Working with God

Multitudes are vainly seeking happiness in worldly amusements. They crave something which they do not have. They are spending their money for that which is not bread, and their labor for that which satisfieth not. The hungering, thirsting soul will continue to hunger and thirst as long as it partakes of these unsatisfying pleasures. O that every such one would listen to the voice of Jesus, "If any man thirst, let him come unto me, and drink." Those who drink of the living water will thirst no more for frivolous, exciting amusements. Christ, the well-spring of life, is the fountain of peace and happiness.

God bestows various talents and gifts upon men, not that they may lie useless, nor that they may be employed in amusements or selfish gratification, but that they may be a blessing to others by enabling men to do earnest, self-sacrificing missionary work. God grants man time for the purpose of promoting his glory. When this time is used in selfish pleasure and amusement, it is lost to all eternity.

The youth, as well as those of more advanced age, are accountable to God for their time, their influence, and their opportunities. They hold their destiny in their own hands. They may rise to the highest excellence, or they may sink to the lowest depth of depravity. Every person is a free moral agent, by his daily life deciding his future. What course, then, is it wisest for us, as rational beings, to pursue? Shall we live as candidates for eternal life, or shall we fail of fulfilling the great end of our creation?

In our character-building we must work in union with our Heavenly Father, our will conformed to his will. We are to work in union with him "who gave himself for us, that he might redeem us from all iniquity, and purify unto himself a peculiar people, zealous of good works." Then why should we doubt him? Let us not stop, my dear young friends, with a work half done. Let us not rest satisfied before we receive a new and sanctified nature, in which will appear the fruits of righteousness. Those who stop short of this are Christians only in name. We are to make diligent work for eternity. Helping one another, and walking in all humility, we shall receive grace for grace.

Let the youth magnify the name of the Lord for his great goodness, his loving mercy, his tender compassion. They can magnify his name by revealing his grace through a well-ordered life and a godly conversation. And as they do this, the disposition is sweetened; irritability passes away.

To every young man and young woman I would say: Come to Jesus just as you are. With humility and contrition express to him your penitence. Make a vigilant, earnest effort to serve him, and perseveringly keep up this effort. Cherish constantly the spirit of gentleness and kindness. Cultivate sympathy--not for yourself, but for others; "in all things showing thyself a pattern of good works: in doctrine showing uncorruptness, gravity, sincerity, sound speech, that can not be condemned; that he that is of the contrary part may be ashamed, having no evil thing to say of you."

"The Lord make you to increase and abound in love one toward another, and toward all men, even as we do toward you: to the end he may stablish your hearts unblameable in holiness before God, even our Father, at the coming of our Lord Jesus Christ with all his saints."

Mrs. E. G. White

December 4, 1902—Unquestioning Faith

In the city of Capernaum a nobleman's son lies sick unto death. In vain his father has tried to save him. A messenger comes with hurried steps to the mansion, and asks to see the nobleman. He tells him that he has just come from Jerusalem, and that there is in Galilee a prophet of God, declared by some to be the long-expected Messiah. His work has awakened an intense interest in the city of Jerusalem, the messenger says, and crowds follow him wherever he goes. It may be that he can heal the child.

As the nobleman listens, the expression of his countenance changes from despair to hope. Determined to leave no means untried to save his child's life, he decides to go himself to see this prophet. The hope born in his soul strengthens as he prepares for his journey. Before the day dawns, he is on his way to Cana of Galilee, where Jesus is supposed to have gone. The journey is long and the road rough, but nothing can deter the anxious father.

Finding Jesus, he beseeches him to come to Capernaum and heal his son. "Except ye see signs and wonders, ye will not believe," Jesus answers. To a certain extent, the nobleman did believe, else he would not have taken the long journey at that critical time. But Christ desired to increase his faith.

With heartbroken entreaty the father cries, "Sir, come down ere my child die." He fears that each passing moment will place his son beyond the power of the Healer. But his faith is yet imperfect. Desiring to lead him to perfect faith, the Saviour replies, "Go thy way; thy son liveth."

"And the man believed the word that Jesus had spoken unto him, and he went his way." Assured that the death he has dreaded will not come to his son, the nobleman does not ask any question, nor seek any explanation. He believes. Over and over again he repeats the words, "Thy son liveth."

And the power of the words of the Redeemer flashes like lightning from Cana to Capernaum, and the child is healed. The nobleman shows his faith by not insisting on the presence of Jesus, and immediately the power of Satan is rebuked. The dying boy feels the joy of restoration.

The watchers by the bedside mark with bated breath the conflict between life and death. And when in an instant the burning fever disappears, they are filled with amazement. Knowing the anxiety of the father, they go to greet him with the joyful tidings. He has only one question to ask, When did the child begin to mend? They tell him, and he is satisfied. He believed when he turned his face homeward; now his faith is crowned with assurance. A holy atmosphere surrounds him, and as he looks upon his son, healed of all disease, spiritual life sanctifies his soul. He is converted. With the simple faith of a little child he receives the great gift of the kingdom of heaven. The same power which restores the child to health, banishes unbelief from the father's heart.

What a witness Christ has in this nobleman! He had asked for the life of his son, not expecting to receive anything himself. But he realized that a great power had taken possession of his soul. He recognized Christ as the physician of the soul as well as the body. Overjoyed, filled with peace and gladness, he exclaimed, Today is salvation come to this house. Spiritual life, with all its transforming power, was breathed into his soul, and he proclaimed in Capernaum the wonderful power of the Saviour.

In our work for Christ, we need more of the unquestioning faith of the nobleman. "Faith is the substance of things hoped for, the evidence of things not seen." By faith we behold God in his promises, and are armed with stability. The Christian knows in whom he has believed. He does not only read the Bible; he experiences the power of its teaching. He has not only heard of Christ's righteousness; he has opened the windows of the soul to the light of the Sun of righteousness. He has a knowledge which can not be wrested from him. The one who trusts his Saviour implicitly finds the gates of heaven ajar and flooded with glory from the throne of God.

Mrs. E. G. White

December 11, 1902—A Call to Service

God calls for workers. His cause needs men who are self-made, who, placing themselves in his hands as humble learners, have proved themselves workers together with him. These are the men that are needed in the work today. Let those who have shown themselves to be men, move out and do what they can in the Master's service. Let them step into the ranks, and by patient, continuous effort prove their worth. It is in the water, not on land, that we learn to swim. Let them fill with fidelity the place to which they are called, that they may be qualified for still higher responsibilities. God gives all opportunity to perfect themselves in his service.

He who puts on the armor to war a good warfare will gain greater and still greater ability as he strives to perfect his knowledge of God, working in harmony with the plan that God has given for the perfect development of the physical, mental, and spiritual powers.

Young men and young women, gather a store of knowledge. Do not wait till some human examination pronounces you competent to work, but go out into the highways and hedges, and begin to work for God. Use wisely the knowledge that you have. Exercise your ability with faithfulness, generously imparting the light that God gives you. Study how best to give to others peace, and light, and truth, and the many other rich blessings of heaven. Constantly improve. Keep reaching higher and still higher. It is the ability to put to the tax the powers of mind and body, ever keeping in view eternal realities, that is of value now. Seek the Lord most earnestly, that you may become more and more refined, more spiritually cultured. Then you will have the very best diploma that any one can have,--the indorsement of God.

However large, however small, your talents, remember that what you have is yours only in trust. Thus God is testing and trying you, giving you opportunity to prove yourself true. To him you are indebted for all your capabilities. To him belong your powers of body, mind, and soul, and for him these powers are to be used. Your time, your influence, your capabilities, your skill,--all must be accounted for to him who gives all. He uses his gifts best who seeks by earnest endeavor to carry out the Lord's great plan for the uplifting of humanity, remembering always that he must be a learner as well as a teacher.

Mrs. E. G. White

January 1, 1903—In the Master's Service

There is a battle for all to fight, for the young as well as the old. In the warfare against evil, every one has a part. Dear young friends, when you accepted Christ as your Saviour, you enlisted in his army. You left the black banner of the prince of darkness to stand under the bloodstained banner of Prince Immanuel. Your highest aim now should be to show yourselves faithful soldiers.

The powers of darkness are arrayed against you. Satan desires to see you deserting your Leader. He would be greatly pleased to see you disappointing the One who has done so much for you. Do not yield to his temptations. Fight bravely against his suggestions. Remember that God and Christ and the heavenly angels are fighting with you. John says, "I write unto you, young men, because ye are strong, ... and ye have overcome the wicked one." Had not God given his children power to overcome, these words would not have been written. In the strength of the Redeemer, you can be more than conquerors.

The history of Daniel and his companions is an illustration of what all youth may become in the service of God. The king determined to have them trained as statesmen, and with other youth they were given food and wine from his table. But they knew that if they ate of the king's food, and drank his wine, their power to distinguish between right and wrong would be dulled. They would be unable to obtain the education necessary to make them successful Christian statesmen. They would not appreciate the knowledge God had to give. They determined to be true to principle, to eat and drink to God's glory.

God honored their loyalty. He gave them wisdom and understanding; and when at the end of the term of years allotted to study, the king examined them, he found them "ten times better than all the magicians and astrologers that were in all his realm."

It is your privilege--a privilege which many do not enjoy--to know what is meant by wholesome food,--food that will bring health to body and mind. Make right eating and right drinking a part of your religion. Thus you place yourselves where God can enable you to distinguish between right and wrong.

God has given every youth the talent of speech to be improved for him. This is a most important trust; for God declares, "By thy words thou shalt be justified, and by thy words thou shalt be condemned." Let your words be life-giving, pointing those around you to the Saviour. Let them bring sunshine instead of gloom, harmony instead of animosity. Say nothing that you would not be willing to say in the presence of Jesus and the angels. Utter no word that will stir up strife in another heart. However provoked you may feel, restrain the hasty word. If you are Christlike in speech and action, those who associate with you will be blessed by the association. Righteous words and deeds have a more powerful influence for good than all the sermons that can be preached.

Christ desires to use the youth in his service. He needs missionaries. The barren fields all over the world call to heaven for laborers. If the youth will give themselves to God, he will give them wisdom and knowledge, preparing them for service. If they will consecrate themselves to him, he will make them vessels unto honor, into which he can pour the precious oil of the Spirit, to be imparted to others. God's helping hand--this is what you may be if you will yield yourselves to his keeping. He will help you to make straight paths for your feet.

Dear young friends, God loves you. He wants you to be saved. He wants you to make a success of the life that he has given you. If you let your life slip from you in idle dreaming, if you bring to the foundation wood, hay, and stubble, you may through repentance be saved; but where is your treasure? All eternity will testify to your loss.

You are not alone in the warfare against wrong. Could the curtain be rolled back, you would see heavenly angels fighting with you. This they must do; it is their work to guard the youth. "Are they not all ministering spirits, sent forth to minister for them who shall be heirs of salvation?" Ten thousand times ten thousand and thousands of thousands of angels minister to the youth.

As you move forward step by step, adding to your faith virtue, and to virtue knowledge, God will be with you, and you will never fall. As you work on the plan of addition, Christ works for you on the plan of multiplication. He aids you as you strive for the crown of life. Strive lawfully, serving God with heart and mind and soul and strength. Then when Christ comes to gather his jewels to himself, he will welcome you with the words, "Come, ye blessed of my Father, inherit the kingdom prepared for you from the foundation of the world."

January 22, 1903—"He That Gathereth Not with Me Scattereth Abroad"

The gospel of Christ has little to fear from its open enemies. Its most dangerous foes are its pretended friends,--unconsecrated Christians, who profess to be serving Christ, while in their lives they deny him. Such drive many away from the Saviour.

Christ declares, "He that is not with me is against me; and he that gathereth not with me scattereth abroad." A man is either a Christian or a sinner, an honor or a dishonor to his Redeemer. The Saviour says again, "Ye are the salt of the earth: but if the salt have lost his savor, wherewith shall it be salted? it is henceforth good for nothing, but to be cast out, and to be trodden under foot of men." As salt that has lost its saving properties is of no value as a preservative, so Christians who have lost their Christlikeness can not exert a saving influence upon those with whom they come in contact day after day.

To be converted means just what it says. It means that selfishness is cast away, and that its place in the heart is filled with the love of Christ. Old things have passed away; all things have become new.

He who is a friend of Christ studies his word, and brings its principles into the daily life, making every thought, word, and deed subject to the control of the Holy Spirit. He realizes that his talents were lent to him to be used in unselfish service, and that every gift not thus employed is wasted.

The Christian life is a life rescued, a life taken from sin and given to Christ, a life consecrated to doing the will of God. Such a life is filled with love for God and man.

When we submit to God's way, the Lord Jesus guides our minds and fills our lips with assurance. We may be strong in the Lord and in the power of his might. Receiving Christ, we are clothed with power. No unrighteousness is seen in the life. We are able to speak words in season to those who know not the Saviour. Christ's presence in the heart is a vitalizing power, strengthening the whole being.

"Thou wilt keep him in perfect peace, whose mind is stayed on thee: because he trusteth in thee. Trust ye in the Lord forever; for in the Lord Jehovah is everlasting strength."

Mrs. E. G. White

January 29, 1903—Strength in Humility

Moses was chosen for a special work. Having been adopted by Pharaoh's daughter, he was greatly honored in the king's court. Every one was intensely desirous of exalting him. Pharaoh determined to make him his successor on the throne.

Moses was a man of intelligence. In the providence of God he was given opportunity to gain a fitness for a great work. He was thoroughly educated as a general. When he went out to meet the enemy, he was successful; and on his return from battle, his praises were sung by the whole army. Notwithstanding this, he constantly remembered that through him God purposed to deliver the children of Israel.

But although he was "learned in all the wisdom of the Egyptians," while in the service of Pharaoh the character of Moses received a mold that disqualified him for the wonderful work he was to do, making him weak where he should have been strong. This weakness was manifested when he visited his brethren, and "spied an Egyptian smiting an Hebrew." Taking the case in his own hands, he privately "slew the Egyptian, and hid him in the sand." He would not have done this had he not, during his training in the Egyptian army, received the impression that the Israelites were to be delivered by the sword.

In order to prepare Moses for his work as the general of Israel, God removed him from Pharaoh's court, and placed him in another school,--the school of self-denial and hardship. The leader of the Egyptian armies went into the mountains, to become a keeper of sheep. What a change in his life and employment! Looking at the experience from a human point of view, men would pronounce it a failure.

Forty years Moses spent in the solitude of the wilderness. Here he had opportunity for study, meditation, and prayer. From the book of nature open before him, he drew many useful lessons. Surrounded by the evidences of God's power, he was led to humble himself, and to exercise living faith in God, thus obtaining a preparation for the work before him. God designed that Moses should stand alone, leaning only upon the arm of divine power.

Several years ago I saw the results of a tempest that had just passed through a forest, sweeping down everything before it. The trees standing close together had been uprooted and leveled like grass before a scythe. But a few trees standing out alone had not been overturned. I inquired the reason of this, and was told that the tap-roots of the trees unmoved by the hurricane were firmly fastened deep in the earth. These trees had gained strength to withstand the storm, while those that had stood close together were swept down.

The lesson is for us. We should know for ourselves what it means to stand firmly for God, ever learning that which Providence designs to teach us. But too often we think as others think, and do as they do. We are influenced by the habits of our associates. When we depend on finite help to support us, we do not really know our weakness, and when the storm comes, we are overthrown. But when thrust out where we must stand alone, our faith fastens upon the only sure support--the infinite God.

When at last Moses was called to bear God's message to Pharaoh, Moses had reached the place in his experience where he had a humble estimate of himself. He felt incapable of doing the work, and he pleaded earnestly that he might not be required to bear this responsibility. Not until the Lord had convinced him that he was his chosen instrument to deliver Israel, did he consent to go. He cherished no self-exaltation. While tending his flock among the lonely mountains, he had learned humility--that precious lesson so important for us all.

The more diligently we learn meekness and lowliness in the school of Christ, the greater advancement we shall make in a preparation for God's service. We should never feel that we have learned everything worth knowing. Let none think they are ready for graduation. As long as we remain on this earth, there will be new lessons for us to learn. And throughout the ages of eternity we shall have something to learn in regard to the wonderful plan of redemption.

Lack of humility is one great cause of our weakness. Too often we attempt in our own strength to do something great. Christ says, "Without me ye can do nothing." "Take my yoke upon you, and learn of me." By wearing his yoke, we can be co-workers with him. Every morning we should inquire, "Lord, what wilt thou have me to do?" Thus we shall learn of Christ.

Not he who is pompous, boastful, and unbelieving, but the humble, faithful soul, is in God's sight accounted a man of power. In order that he may answer the prayers of his people, the Lord desires them to obtain a personal knowledge of Christ. The clearer their view of the Saviour's loveliness, the more humble will be their opinion of themselves. And the lower their estimate of self, the more distinct will be their view of the glory and majesty of God. When we begin to have a high opinion of ourselves, let us remember that for whatever we are or have in advance of our fellow men we are indebted wholly to the gift of God.

"Esteeming the reproach of Christ greater riches than the treasures in Egypt," Moses kept his eye fixed on "the recompense of the reward." Let us likewise keep our eyes fixed on the reward that God has promised, and walk in humility before him; for He who says, "Them that honor me I will honor," will crown his faithful children with eternal honor.

Mrs. E. G. White

February 12, 1903—Strength in Self-Sacrifice

In order that Moses might know how to be kind and tender toward his erring brethren, God taught him, through the hardships incident to the life of a shepherd, precious lessons of kindness and tenderness, patience and self-sacrifice. Years afterward, while leading the children of Israel to the promised land, he was often severely tried by the waywardness of his brethren, but at such times he pleaded with God to work for them.

When in their flight from Egypt the Israelites came to the Red Sea, and learned that the Egyptians were following them, it seemed to them as if they had been taken there to perish. They were in a position of great peril, the Red Sea on one hand and an impassable mountain on the other, and Pharaoh pursuing them; and they murmured against Moses, saying, "Because there were no graves in Egypt, hast thou taken us away to die in the wilderness?" The Lord had wrought wondrously in their behalf, but still their faith was small.

But Moses had learned to trust in God. In this emergency he looked in faith to his invisible Leader, and his cry was heard. God gave the command, "Speak unto the children of Israel, that they go forward."

As the people stepped into the sea, the waters rolled back, a path was made, and they walked through on dry land. As they went forward in the path that Providence had made for them, the pillar of cloud rose and grandly moved over their heads, descending between the two armies, following the Israelites instead of going before them, thus shielding them from the sight of the Egyptians.

"The Egyptians pursued, and went in after them to the midst of the sea, even all Pharaoh's horses, his chariots, and his horsemen. And it came to pass, that in the morning watch the Lord looked unto the host of the Egyptians through the pillar of fire and of the cloud, and troubled the host of the Egyptians."

The mysterious cloud changed to a pillar of fire before their astonished eyes. The thunders pealed, and the lightnings flashed. "The clouds poured out water; the skies sent out a sound: thine arrows also went abroad. The voice of thy thunder was in the heaven: the lightnings lightened the world: the earth trembled and shook."

The Egyptians were seized with confusion and dismay. Amid the wrath of the elements, in which they heard the voice of an angry God, they endeavored to retrace their steps, and flee to the shore they had quitted. But Moses stretched out his rod, and the piled-up waters, hissing, roaring, and eager for their prey, rushed together, and swallowed the Egyptian army in their black depths.

The faith that Moses had is the faith that Jesus desires us to have. When difficulties arise, let us have confidence in God. When it seems that we must meet impossibilities, let us pray. Like Moses, we may commune with the God of heaven as with a friend, trusting in him to work for us. Wherever we are, we may send silent petitions to him for counsel and strength. His ear is ever open to the cry of his needy children. "Man's necessity is God's opportunity."

After the children of Israel had listened to the giving of the ten commandments, they fell into idolatry. The Lord said to Moses, "Let me alone, ... that I may destroy them: and I will make of thee a great nation." But no; the man who in the wilderness had so often sought the lost sheep, the man who had braved storm and tempest rather than leave one sheep to perish, could not give up the people placed in his care.

Moses discerned ground for hope where appeared only discouragement and wrath. The words of God, "Let me alone," he understood not to forbid but to encourage intercession; to imply that nothing but his prayers could save Israel, but that if thus entreated, God would spare his people. He "besought the Lord his God, and said, Lord, why doth thy wrath wax hot against thy people, which thou hast brought forth out of the land of Egypt with great power, and with a mighty hand?" And his earnest intercession prevailed.

When in need, we should bear in mind our relation to the children of Israel. Their history has been recorded for our admonition. We are not to imitate their example of murmuring. "Our light affliction, which is but for a moment, worketh for us a far more exceeding and eternal weight of glory; while we look not at the things which are seen, but at the things which are not seen: for the things which are seen are temporal; but the things which are not seen are eternal."

Cleanse the soul-temple of its defilement, that Christ may come in and reign supreme. Consecrate to God your strength, your mind, all your abilities. Wherever he places you, however humble your position, work with fidelity. In order to know the power of true godliness, you must hide in Jesus, giving yourself to him without reserve. When you make an entire surrender, laying yourself on his altar as a living sacrifice, you will be accepted.

Not all the gold or silver of this earth can redeem one soul. Neither intellect nor education can win the immortal inheritance. Only as a free gift, received through entire surrender to God, can we gain eternal life.

In this world there is neither comfort nor happiness without Jesus. Let us acknowledge him as our Friend and Saviour. How can we fail of loving him who has first loved us? In him are matchless charms. O, may we all so live during this brief period of probationary time that we shall reign with him throughout the ceaseless ages of eternity!

Mrs. E. G. White

February 19, 1903—Character-Building

"Whosoever heareth these sayings of mine, and doeth them, I will liken him unto a wise man, which built his house upon a rock: and the rain descended, and the floods came, and the winds blew, and beat upon that house; and it fell not: for it was founded upon a rock. And every one that heareth these sayings of mine, and doeth them not, shall be likened unto a foolish man, which built his house upon the sand: and the rain descended, and the floods came, and the winds blew, and beat upon that house; and it fell: and great was the fall of it."

The formation of character is the work of a lifetime, and it is for eternity. If all could realize this, if they would awake to the thought that we are individually deciding our own destiny for eternal life or eternal ruin, what a change would take place! How differently would this probationary time be occupied and what different characters would fill our world!

In character-building it is of the greatest importance that we dig deep, removing all the rubbish, and building on the immovable, solid Rock, Christ Jesus. The foundation firmly laid, we need wisdom to know how to build. When Moses was about to erect the sanctuary in the wilderness, he was cautioned, "See ... that thou make all things according to the pattern showed to thee in the mount." In his law God has given us a pattern, and it is after this pattern that we are to build. The law is the great standard of righteousness. It represents the character of God, and is the test of our loyalty to his government.

Thoroughness is necessary to success in character-building. There must be an earnest desire to carry out the plans of the Master-builder. The timbers used must be solid; no careless, unreliable work can be accepted; it would ruin the building.

The whole being is to be put into this work. It demands strength and energy; there is no reserve to be wasted in unimportant matters. There must be determined human force put into the work, in co-operation with the divine Worker. There must be earnest, persevering effort to break away from the customs and maxims and associations of the world. Deep thought, earnest purpose, steadfast integrity, are essential.

There must be no idleness. Life is a sacred trust; and every moment should be wisely improved. Its results will be seen in eternity. God requires each one to do all the good possible. We are to make the most of the talents he has intrusted to our keeping. He has placed them in our hands to be used to his name's glory and in the interests of our fellow men.

The Lord has a precious reward in this life for those who keep his law. He says, "My son, forget not my law; but let thine heart keep my commandments: for length of days, and long life, and peace, shall they add to thee. Let not mercy and truth forsake thee; bind them about thy neck; write them upon the table of thine heart: so shalt thou find favor and good understanding in the sight of God and man."

But a better than earthly reward awaits those who, basing their work on the solid rock, have built up symmetrical characters, in accordance with the living word. For them is prepared "a city which hath foundations, whose builder and maker is God." Its streets are paved with gold. It is in the paradise of God, watered by the river of life, which proceeds from the throne. "In the midst of the street of it, and on either side of the river, was there the tree of life, which bare twelve manner of fruits, and yielded her fruit every month: and the leaves of the tree were for the healing of the nations."

Remember that you are building for eternity. See that your foundation is sure; then build firmly, and with persistent effort, but in gentleness, meekness, and love. So shall your house stand unshaken, not only when the storms of temptation come, but when the overwhelming flood of God's wrath shall sweep over the world. Then every house built upon the sand shall fall, and great shall be the fall of it; for the ruin is for eternity.

Mrs. E. G. White

March 5, 1903—Keeping the Heart

"Keep thy heart with all diligence; for out of it are the issues of life." Diligent heart-keeping is essential to a healthy growth in grace. The heart in its natural state is a habitation for unholy thoughts and sinful passions. When brought into subjection to Christ, it must be cleansed by the Spirit from all defilement. This can not be done without the consent of the individual.

When the soul has been cleansed, it is the duty of the Christian to keep it undefiled. Many seem to think that the religion of Christ does not call for the abandonment of daily sins, the breaking loose from habits which have held the soul in bondage. They renounce some things condemned by the conscience, but they fail to represent Christ in the daily life. They do not bring Christlikeness into the home. They do not show a thoughtful care in their choice of words. Too often, fretful, impatient words are spoken, words which stir the worst passions of the human heart. Such ones need the abiding presence of Christ in the soul. Only in his strength can they keep guard over the words and actions.

Pray without Ceasing

In the work of heart-keeping we must be instant in prayer, unwearied in petitioning the throne of grace for assistance. Those who take the name of Christian should come to God in earnestness and humility, pleading for help. The Saviour has told us to pray without ceasing. The Christian can not always be in the position of prayer, but his thoughts and desires can always be upward. Our self-confidence would vanish, did we talk less and pray more.

We give evidence of the sincerity of our prayers by the earnestness of our endeavors to answer them, to overcome the sins which strive for a place in the life. Our prayers will be ineffectual unless we continually strive to correct that which is wrong and unlovely in our lives. If we ask God to work for us, and then make no effort to conquer self, our prayers will rise no higher than our heads. God helps those who co-operate with him. We can obtain forgiveness only through the blood of Christ. His atoning sacrifice is all-powerful. But in the struggle for immortality we have a part to act. Christ will help those who pray and then watch unto prayer. He calls upon us to use every power he has given us in the warfare against sin. We can never be saved in inactivity and idleness. We might as well look for a harvest from seed which we have not sown, and for knowledge where we have not studied, as to expect salvation without making an effort. It is our part to wrestle against the evil tendencies of the natural heart.

The Results of Disobedience Certain

Contrast man's physical, mental, and moral feebleness with Adam's perfection before he transgressed God's law. Among the waving trees of paradise the holy pair stood in their sinless beauty before God, and the privilege of unrestrained intercourse with him was theirs. Adam was a noble being, with a powerful mind, a will in harmony with the will of God, and affections that centered upon heaven. He possessed a body heir to no disease, and a soul bearing the impress of Deity. But all this rich inheritance, the gift of his Maker, did not save him from the result of disobedience.

God did not spare Adam, though his sin may seem to us a small one. Neither will he spare us, if we continue to disregard his requirements. He divorced Israel from him because her people walked not in his ways. Never was a people more beloved. Never had a nation greater evidence of the divine favor. Yet only two of the adults who left Egypt entered the promised land. The rest died in the wilderness, having proved unworthy to enter Canaan. Pride and self-indulgence were their ruin.

Their history has been traced by the pen of inspiration, that by their experience we may take warning. It is written for our admonition, upon whom the ends of the world are come. God will call us to account if we retain wrong traits of character, refusing to call to our aid the power of the word, and in the name of Jesus correct our faults and subdue the passions of the natural heart. Many enthrone Satan in the heart, to triumph over Christ by the indulgence of evil inclinations. Sin reigns where Christ should reign. Those who thus continue to cherish sin can never be saved as they are. Unless they change, they will never enter heaven themselves, and they make very difficult the path of those who are trying to overcome. Their faulty, unconsecrated lives place them on the side of the power of darkness, while they are professedly on the side of Christ. Jesus makes them the objects of his tender solicitude and unwearied labor, until, notwithstanding all his efforts, they become fixed in sin. Then those over whom he has wept and yearned in love and compassion are left to pursue their own course. The Saviour turns from them, saying, sadly, They are joined to their idols; let them alone. God forbid that this should be said of us.

Every Man That Hath This Hope in Him

The sins of fretfulness, impatience, love of the world, are grievous in God's sight. Some who cherish these defects confess that they are doing wrong; but year after year passes, and finds them still in bondage to these sins. Each year the same acknowledgment is made, but no change appears in the life. They confess, but they do not repent. They do not realize how grievous their sins are in the sight of God. If they were really one with Christ, if his Spirit were dwelling in them, they would see the sinfulness of sin. Not only would they confess; but they would forsake that which God abhors.

Those who remain in transgression, who do not strive for self-control, are ignorant of God. However high their claims of godliness, their spirituality is weak, their faith small, their love imperfect, their hopes and experience are governed by circumstances. But those who resolutely try to obtain the victory over temptation, who promptly and decisively resist the attacks of Satan, will become rooted and grounded in the truth. Their experience will not be dwarfed and sickly, but will bear rich fruit to the glory of God.

"Beloved, now are we the sons of God, and it doth not yet appear what we shall be: but we know that, when he shall appear, we shall be like him; for we shall see him as he is. And every man that hath this hope in him purifieth himself, even as he is pure."

This is our work. It is not enough to profess to be a child of God. He who has in him this hope will purify himself from all defilement. But this is the work from which every day nine tenths of us excuse ourselves. We seem to think that it does not matter if we get angry now and then, if we cheat now and then, if we are selfish and uncourteous.

Dear young friends, let us not spare ourselves. Let us with self-renunciation lift the cross of Christ, and follow in his footsteps. Let us begin in earnest the work of reformation. Let us crucify the flesh. Unholy habits will clamor fiercely for the victory, but in the name and through the power of Jesus we may conquer them. To him who seeks daily to keep his heart with all diligence, to be a true child of God, the promise is sure, "In all these things we are more than conquerors through him that loved us. For I am persuaded that neither death, nor life, nor angels, nor principalities, nor powers, nor things present, nor things to come, nor height, nor depth, nor any other creature, shall be able to separate us from the love of God, which is in Christ Jesus our Lord."

Living the life of him who went about doing good, overcoming self-love and every other species of selfishness, fulfilling bravely and cheerfully our duty to God and to those around us,--this makes us more than conquerors. This prepares us to stand before the great white throne, free from spot or wrinkle or any such thing, having washed our robes of character and made them white in the blood of the Lamb.

Mrs. E. G. White

March 19, 1903—The Divine Teacher

For thousands of years, men had been in thraldom to a degenerating power. Satan had perverted their conceptions of God, and of the plan and work of salvation. He had brought their minds so fully under his control that every heavenly attribute had been well-nigh destroyed. Of himself, man had not one thought nor impulse of a spiritual nature. He could do nothing to save himself. Only as Christ should draw him, could he take one step in repentance or reform.

God saw that the world was destitute of true knowledge, and he sent Christ into the world to live the law, and thus represent him. "The Word was made flesh, and dwelt among us ... full of grace and truth." The Truth, the Life, and the Light of the world, was to find a place in the hearts of men. For this Christ clothed his divinity with humanity. This was the only means by which he could reach humanity. Christ became one with the human family. He spoke in the language of men. He ate with them at their tables. He bore with them their trials and poverty, and shared their toils. Thus he assured them of his complete identification with humanity.

It was necessary that he should do all this. Though he came in human form, his wonderful works and the mystery of his character inspired the people with awe, and tended to shut them away from him. But by himself coming in close contact and sympathy with man, Christ broke down the barriers.

In his teaching, Christ did not conform to the practises of the great men of the world, or of the rabbinical teachers. Their teaching made dark and intricate that which was plain. They made a show of possessing great knowledge, knowledge which the common people could not comprehend. But their wisdom was foolishness. Christ's knowledge was great, his wisdom deep; but it was without pretense. It found expression in words beautiful with the grace of simplicity, yet clothed with dignity and power.

Christ, the author of truth, did not disdain to present truths that were old and familiar. The great purpose of his mission was ever kept in view. When this purpose could be served by the repetition of familiar truths, he employed them. By unsanctified minds, many of these truths had been disconnected from their true position, and had been employed to strengthen error. Christ recovered and replaced them as links in the great chain of redemption.

Many precious gems of light had lost their luster; they were buried beneath a mass of tradition and superstition. As the author of truth, Christ was able to distinguish every precious gem. His hand removed the rubbish of false teaching, and recovered the lost treasures. He reset them in all their original freshness and beauty in the framework of the gospel, and commanded that they should stand fast forever.

In his teaching Christ reached the minds of men by the pathway of their familiar associations. He linked his lesson with their most hallowed recollections and their tenderest sympathies. His illustrations were drawn from the great book of nature and from the treasury of household ties and affections. The simple lily of the field in its freshness and beauty was presented to the people by the great Master artist. With the common duties of life he bound up the most precious treasures of divine truth. The regenerating power of his grace was represented by figures that all could comprehend. Thus he made truth and light a part of the daily appointments. Everything connected with the common routine of life was invested with a solemn dignity, and shown to be related to eternal interests.

Christ taught the people that all true knowledge is divine, and that, acted upon, it will lead heavenward. In all his teachings he suggested to his hearers a new train of thought, in harmony with the transforming principles of truth. By meeting the people where they were, he carried them with him to a higher plane of thought and life. Their hearts were prepared to receive the rays of light shining from the Light of the world.

Though Christ had taken upon himself human nature, yet his divinity flashed through humanity. In all his education and discipline his superiority was revealed. In their simplicity the lessons which fell from his lips possessed a power and attractiveness which none of the teachings of the world's great men could equal. "The common people heard him gladly," and the testimony borne to his teaching was, "Never man spake like this man."

Mrs. E. G. White

March 26, 1903—Repentance a Gift of God

Those who are saved in the kingdom of God will have nothing of which to boast. The praise and the glory will all belong to God, and to him it will all be given. Sometimes young people who really desire to be children of God, are putting their trust in something besides the blood of Christ. They have faith in what they themselves can do. "I have a great deal to do before I can come to Jesus," they say. "When I have done all that I can do, then I will go to him for help." They think that when they have done what they can do to save their souls, Jesus will supply what is lacking, giving the finishing touches to their salvation.

But no one can be strong in God until he acknowledges his helplessness, and comes to Christ as the only one who can save him from the power of sin.

In Egypt the Israelites were required to sprinkle the lintels of their doors with the blood of a slain lamb, that when the angel of death went through the land, he might pass over their homes. But if, instead of performing this simple act of faith, they had barricaded the doors, taking every precaution to keep the destroying angel out, their efforts would have been in vain; for they would have testified to their unbelief. The blood on the lintel was enough. It secured the life of the firstborn. So it is today. It is the blood of Christ that cleanses from sin. Without this, all effort to gain salvation is in vain.

It is the work of the sinner to accept Christ as his righteousness. Thus he is reconciled to God. Only through faith in Christ can the heart be made holy. Many think that repentance is a work which men must carry forward themselves before they can come to Christ. They think that they have something to do before they can find Christ a mediator in their behalf. It is true that there must be repentance before there is pardon; but the sinner must come to Christ before he can find repentance. It is the grace of Christ that strengthens and enlightens the soul, making repentance possible.

Peter has made this matter clear. He says of Christ, "Him hath God exalted with his right hand to be a Prince and a Saviour, for to give repentance to Israel, and forgiveness of sins." Repentance is as certainly the gift of Christ as is forgiveness. He whom God pardons he first makes penitent. Repentance can not be found without Christ. From him comes the grace of contrition, as well as the gift of pardon. Only through his atoning blood can either be obtained.

Mrs. E. G. White

April 9, 1903—What We May Become

Young people may reach God's ideal for them if they will take Christ as their helper. Make an unreserved surrender to God. To know that you are striving for eternal life, will strengthen and comfort you. Christ can give you power to overcome. By his help you can utterly destroy the root of selfishness.

Christ died that the life of man might be bound up with his life in the union of divinity and humanity. He came to our world and lived a divine-human life, in order that the lives of his children might be as harmonious as God designed them to be. The Saviour calls upon you to deny self, and take up the cross. Then nothing will prevent the development of the whole being. The daily experience will reveal healthy, harmonious action.

In the strength of the Redeemer you can work with wisdom and power to help some crooked life to be straight in God. What is there that Christ can not do? He is perfect in wisdom, in righteousness, in love. Do not shut yourselves up to yourselves, satisfied to pour out all your affection upon those nearest you. Seize every opportunity to contribute to the happiness of those around you, sharing with them your affection. Words of kindness, looks of sympathy, expressions of appreciation, would to many a struggling, lonely one be as a cup of cold water to a thirsty soul. A word of cheer, an act of kindness, would go far to lighten the burdens that are resting heavily upon weary shoulders. It is in unselfish ministry that true happiness is found. And every word and deed of such service is recorded in the books of heaven as done to Christ. "Inasmuch as ye have done it unto one of the least of these my brethren," he says, "ye have done it unto me."

Live in the sunshine of Christ's love. Then your influence will bless the world. Let the Spirit of Christ control you. Let the law of kindness be ever on your lips. Forbearance and unselfishness mark the words and deeds of those who are born again, to live the new life in Christ.

Mrs. E. G. White

April 16, 1903—Our Great High Priest

Through sin, man has been severed from the life of God. The soul is palsied through the machinations of Satan, the author of sin. Of himself man is incapable of realizing the sinfulness of sin, incapable of reaching the high standard of perfection. And were this standard placed within his reach, there is nothing in it that the natural heart should desire it. The bewitching power of Satan is upon man. All the ingenious subterfuges that the enemy can suggest are presented to prevent every good impulse. Every faculty given by God to man has been used by man as a weapon against the divine Benefactor. So, although God loves man, he can not safely impart to him the gifts and blessing he desires to bestow.

But it is God's purpose that man shall stand before him upright and noble; and God will not be defeated by Satan. He sent his Son to this world to bear the death penalty of man's transgression, and to show man how to live a sinless life. There is no other way in which man can be saved. "Without me," Christ says, "ye can do nothing." Through him, and him alone, can the natural heart be changed, the affections transformed, the affections set flowing heavenward. Christ alone can give life to the soul dead in trespasses and sins.

In heaven Satan was next to the Son of God. But he yielded to the desire for self-exaltation, and was expelled from the heavenly courts. He came to this earth, to exercise over man his debasing power. This power increased with the ages, but its evil was not recognized, and God could not arbitrarily condemn its author. Satan's work was a deadly peril to the universe, but for the security of the world and of the government of heaven, he must be allowed to develop his principles in their true light.

Christ came to this world to save men from death; and from the manger to the cross his way was disputed by Satan. The enemy filled the minds of the Jews with hatred against their Redeemer. He rested not until Christ hung on the cross.

But in carrying out his enmity toward Christ till he crucified him,--hung him on the cross of Calvary, with bruised body and broken heart,--Satan completely uprooted himself from the affections of the universe. Christ's death silenced forever the charge that with God self-denial was impossible. It was seen that God denied himself because of his love for mankind.

More than we could possibly endure Christ endured in our behalf. Sinless to the last, he died for us. Justice demanded not merely that sin be pardoned; the death penalty must be met. The Saviour has met this demand. His broken body, his gushing blood, satisfied the claims of the law. Thus he bridged the gulf made by sin between earth and heaven. He suffered in the flesh, that with his robe of righteousness he might cover the defenseless sinner.

To resist Satan's temptations is no easy task. It calls for a firm hold on God. Christ has met every temptation which Satan can bring against man. He is the Way, the Truth, and the Life. In his strength man can keep the law of God.

Christ was crucified, but in wondrous power and glory he rose from the tomb. He took in his grasp the world over which Satan claimed to preside, and restored the human race to favor with God. And at this glorious completion of his work, songs of triumph echoed and re-echoed through the unfallen worlds. Angel and archangel, cherubim and seraphim, joined in the chorus of victory.

Christ is able to save to the uttermost all who come to God by him. He ever liveth to make intercession for us. In earnest appeals the cross continually proffers to the sinner complete expiation. In loving invitation Christ lifts his voice, saying, "Whosoever will, let him take the water of life freely."

As you draw near the cross of Calvary, you see love that is without a parallel. As by faith you grasp the meaning of the sacrifice made on that cross, you see yourself a sinner, condemned by a broken law. This is repentance. As you come with humble heart, you find pardon; for Jesus stands before the Father, continually offering a sacrifice for the sins of the world. He is the minister of the true tabernacle, which the Lord pitched, and not man. The typical offerings of the Jewish tabernacle no longer possess any virtue. A daily and yearly atonement is no longer necessary. But because of the continual commission of sin, the atoning sacrifice of a heavenly Mediator is essential. Jesus, our great high priest, officiates for us in the presence of God, offering in our behalf his shed blood.

And as Christ intercedes for us, the Spirit works upon our hearts, drawing forth prayer and penitence, praise and thanksgiving. The gratitude which flows from human lips is the result of the Spirit striking the chords of the soul, awakening holy music.

The prayer and praise and confession of God's people ascend as sacrifices to the heavenly sanctuary. But they ascend not in spotless purity. Passing through the corrupt channels of humanity, they are so defiled that unless purified by the righteousness of the great High Priest, they are not acceptable by God. Christ gathers into the censer the prayers, the praise, and the sacrifices of his people, and with these he puts the merits of his spotless righteousness. Then, perfumed with the incense of Christ's propitiation, our prayers, wholly and entirely acceptable, rise before God, and gracious answers are returned.

Mrs. E. G. White

April 23, 1903—God's Purpose Concerning Israel

[The foregoing article is the first of a series by Sister White on the history and experiences of Daniel and his companions in Babylon. The articles are in the form of a connected narrative, and we are sure they will be of much interest to our young people.]

Every temporal and every spiritual advantage was given to the Jewish nation, the Lord's chosen people. God himself wrought for them, multiplying them in Egypt, delivering them from bondage, and leading them to the land of Canaan, their promised inheritance.

To the Jewish nation were committed the oracles of God, which were to be as a wall of protection round about them. As his chosen people, the Israelites were to show to the nations of the earth that the law of God's kingdom is holy and just and good. By obedience to this law they were to be brought under the control of their Creator and Redeemer, and made a pure, wise people, whose joy it would be to deal justly, to love mercy, and to walk humbly with their God.

Never were the Israelites to depart from the instruction given them by Christ from the pillar of cloud. God declared that if his people would live by the pure, unselfish principles of his law, and thus fulfill his purpose for them, he would honor them before all the world. "Observe and hear all these words which I command thee," he said, "that it may go well with thee, and with thy children after thee forever, when thou doest that which is good and right in the sight of the Lord thy God. When the Lord thy God shall cut off the nations from before thee, whither thou goest to possess them, and thou succeedest them, and dwellest in their land; take heed to thyself that thou be not snared by following them, after that they be destroyed from before thee; and that thou inquire not after their gods, saying, How did these nations serve their gods? ... for even their sons and their daughters they have burnt in the fire to their gods. What thing so ever I command you, observe to do it: thou shalt not add thereto, nor diminish from it."

"Ye shall therefore keep all my statutes, and all my judgments, and do them: that the land, whither I bring you to dwell therein, spew you not out. And ye shall not walk in the manners of the nation, which I cast out before you: for they committed all these things, and therefore I abhorred them. But I have said unto you, Ye shall inherit their land, and I will give it unto you to possess it, a land that floweth with milk and honey: I am the Lord your God, which have separated you from other people."

God specified also the sure result of a disregard for his commandments. "If ye will not harken unto me," he declared, "and will not do all these commandments, ... I also will do this unto you; I will ... set my face against you, and ye shall be slain before your enemies: they that hate you shall reign over you.... And I will make your cities waste, and bring your sanctuaries unto desolation, and I will not smell the savor of your sweet odors. And I will bring the land into desolation: and your enemies which dwell therein shall be astonished at it. And I will scatter you among the heathen, and will draw out a sword after you: and your land shall be desolate, and your cities waste.... And ye shall perish among the heathen, and the land of your enemies shall eat you up."

With these solemn warnings foretelling the results of disobedience, were given words of encouragement. God declared that even if his people should fail of fulfilling his purpose, he would not forsake them utterly. "If they shall confess their iniquity," he said, "and the iniquity of their fathers, with their trespass which they trespassed against me, and that also they have walked contrary unto me; and that I also have walked contrary unto them, and have brought them into the land of their enemies; if then their uncircumcised hearts be humbled, and they then accept of the punishment of their iniquity: then will I remember my covenant with Jacob, and also my covenant with Isaac, and also my covenant with Abraham will I remember; and I will remember the land.... When they be in the land of their enemies, I will not cast them away, neither will I abhor them; to destroy them utterly, and to break my covenant with them: for I am the Lord their God. But I will for their sakes remember the covenant of their ancestors, whom I brought forth out of the land of Egypt in the sight of the heathen, that I might be their God: I am the Lord."

These are some of the prophecies concerning Israel. The special advantages and privileges that God's chosen people enjoyed, made their responsibility greater than that of any other people. By holiness of life, by steadfast loyalty, by faithfulness in the payment of tithes and offerings, by cheerful, devoted service, they were to acknowledge God's sovereignty, and testify in word and deed that they were made better by the favors bestowed upon them. Thus they were to be a light to the surrounding nations, revealing to idolatrous peoples the true God and the glory of his character.

Mrs. E. G. White

May 14, 1903—Lessons from the Life of Daniel 2—Causes of the Babylonish Captivity

In the third year of the reign of Jehoiakim king of Judah came Nebuchadnezzar king of Babylon unto Jerusalem, and besieged it. And the Lord gave Jehoiakim king of Judah into his hand, with part of the vessels of the house of God: which he carried into the land of Shinar to the house of his god; and he brought the vessels into the treasure-house of his god."

We also read of other invasions by the Babylonians a few years afterward, the first of which was in the reign of Jehoiachin the son of Jehoiakim:

"Nebuchadnezzar king of Babylon came up against Jerusalem, and the city was besieged. And Nebuchadnezzar ... carried away all Jerusalem, and all the princes, and all the mighty men of valor, even ten thousand captives, and all the craftsmen and smiths: none remained, save the poorest sort of the people of the land. And he carried away Jehoiachin ... into captivity from Jerusalem to Babylon.

"The king of Babylon made Mattaniah his father's brother king in his stead, and changed his name to Zedekiah. Zedekiah was twenty and one years old when he began to reign, and he reigned eleven years in Jerusalem.... And he did that which was evil in the sight of the Lord, according to all that Jehoiakim had done. For through the anger of the Lord it came to pass in Jerusalem and Judah, until he had cast them out from his presence, that Zedekiah rebelled against the king of Babylon.

"And it came to pass in the ninth year of his reign, ... that Nebuchadnezzar king of Babylon came, he, and all his host, against Jerusalem, and pitched against it; and they built forts against it round about. And the city was besieged unto the eleventh year of king Zedekiah.... And the city was broken up, and all the men of war fled by night: ... and the king went the way toward the plain. And the army of the Chaldees pursued after the king, and overtook him in the plains of Jericho: and all his army were scattered from him. So they took the king, and ... carried him to Babylon."

"In ... the nineteenth year of king Nebuchadnezzar king of Babylon, came Nebuzar-adan, captain of the guard, a servant of the king of Babylon, unto Jerusalem: and he burnt the house of the Lord, and the king's house, and all the houses of Jerusalem, and every great man's house burnt he with fire. And all the army of the Chaldees, that were with the captain of the guard, brake down the walls of Jerusalem round about. Now the rest of the people that were left in the city, and the fugitives that fell away to the king of Babylon, with the remnant of the multitude, did Nebuzar-adan the captain of the guard carry away. But the captain of the guard left of the poor of the land to be vine-dressers and husbandmen.... So Judah was carried away out of their land."

The prophet Nehemiah presents the evil-doings of the Jewish nation as the cause of their calamities. After recounting the Lord's dealings with them, and their oft-repeated rebellion, he declares: "They were disobedient, and rebelled against thee, and cast thy law behind their backs, and slew thy prophets which testified against them to turn them to thee, and they wrought great provocations. Therefore thou deliveredst them into the hand of their enemies."

God made Zion his holy habitation, the joy of the whole earth. But notwithstanding his goodness to his chosen people, they forgot him, and wandered into idolatry. Before their dispersion, repeated warnings came to them; but "they refused to harken, and pulled away the shoulder, and stopped their ears, that they should not hear. Yea, they made their hearts as an adamant stone, lest they should hear the law, and the words which the Lord of hosts hath sent in his Spirit by the former prophets: therefore came a great wrath from the Lord of hosts."

If men refuse to receive the admonitions of the Lord, if they persist in walking contrary to his instruction, he can not deliver them from the sure consequences of their own course. If they place themselves in opposition to his purposes, and forsake the principles of heaven, he permits their enemies to humble them.

Through Huldah the prophetess, God declared concerning the unrepentant nation: "Because they have forsaken me, and have burned incense unto other gods, that they might provoke me to anger with all the works of their hands; therefore my wrath shall be kindled against" Jerusalem.

And what was the result?--"Therefore came a great wrath from the Lord of hosts. Therefore it is come to pass, that as he cried, and they would not hear; so they cried, and I would not hear, saith the Lord of hosts: but I scattered them with a whirlwind among all the nations whom they knew not. Thus the land was desolate after them, that no man passed through nor returned: for they laid the pleasant land desolate."

The children of Israel were taken captive to Babylon because they separated from God; they did not maintain his principles unadulterated with the sentiments of the nations around them. The people who should have been a light amid the surrounding darkness, disregarded the word of the Lord. They lived for themselves, and neglected to do the special work God had appointed them. And because of their failure to fulfil his purpose, he permitted them to be humbled by an idolatrous nation.

The Lord could not work for the prosperity of his people, he could not fulfil his covenant with them, while they were untrue to the principles he had given them to maintain, that they might be kept from the methods and practises of the nations that dishonored him. By their spirit and works the children of Israel misrepresented the righteousness of God's character, and the Lord allowed the Babylonians to take them captive. He left his people to their ways; and in the calamities that befell them the innocent suffered with the guilty.

Mrs. E. G. White

May 21, 1903—Lessons from the Life of Daniel 3—Early Training of Daniel and His Companions

Among the children of Israel who were taken as captives to Babylon at the beginning of the seventy years' captivity, were Christian patriots, young men who were as true as steel to principle, who would not be corrupted by selfishness, who would honor God at the loss of all things. Upon these loyal and true young men the Lord looked with great pleasure. They had to suffer with the guilty, but in the providence of God this captivity was the means of bringing them to the front. Their example of untarnished integrity, while captives in Babylon, shines with heavenly luster.

Among those who remained true to God after reaching the land of their captivity, the prophet Daniel and his three companions are illustrious examples of what even youth may become when united with the God of wisdom. A brief account of the life of these four Hebrews is left on record for the encouragement of those who are called upon to endure trial and temptation.

After his return from the conquest of the Israelites, King Nebuchadnezzar "spake unto Ashpenaz the master of his eunuchs, that he should bring certain of the children of Israel, and of the king's seed, and of the princes; children in whom was no blemish, but well favored, and skilful in all wisdom, and cunning in knowledge, and understanding science, and such as had ability in them to stand in the king's palace, and whom they might teach the learning and the tongue of the Chaldeans. And the king appointed them a daily provision of the king's meat, and of the wine which he drank: so nourishing them three years, that at the end thereof they might stand before the king. Now among these were of the children of Judah, Daniel, Hananiah, Mishael, and Azariah: unto whom the prince of the eunuchs gave names: for he gave unto Daniel the name of Belteshazzar; and to Hananiah, of Shadrach; and to Mishael, of Meshach; and to Azariah, of Abed-nego."

It was not their own pride or ambition that had brought these young men into the king's court, into companionship with those who neither knew nor feared the true God. They were captives in a strange land, placed there by Infinite Wisdom. Separated from home influences and sacred associations, they sought to acquit themselves creditably, for the honor of their downtrodden people, and for the glory of him whose servants they were. These youth had received a right education in early life, and now they honored the instructors of their childhood. With their habits of self-denial were united earnestness of purpose, diligence, and steadfastness.

The education which these four youth had received in Judea was not after the order of the worldly schools, but according to the purpose and plan of God. The school in which they were educated was not after the order of the schools existing before the destruction of the old world by a flood,--schools in which infidel sentiments prevailed, and in which nature was acknowledged and worshiped above the God of nature. These youth were brought up in homes where they were taught the fear of the Lord.

Daniel's parents trained him in his childhood to habits of strict temperance. They taught him that in every act he must conform to nature's laws; that his eating and drinking had a direct influence upon his physical, mental, and moral nature; that he was accountable to God for all his capabilities; and that by no unwise course should he dwarf or enfeeble his powers. As the result of this teaching, God's law was exalted in his mind and reverenced in his heart.

And such an early education was to Daniel and his three companions the means of their preservation. The lessons learned in their earliest years led them to determine to avoid being corrupted in the courts of Babylon. The truth was truth to them. Its principles were stamped upon their hearts. They understood that with the heart man believeth unto righteousness, and with the mouth confession is made unto salvation. The first and great commandment, "Thou shalt love the Lord thy God with all thy heart, and with all thy soul, and with all thy mind," was truth to them, and it must be obeyed.

In the schools established under God's direction, the fear of the Lord was the foundation of all true education. The knowledge of God had been handed down from generation to generation. In Abel, whom Cain killed, and afterward in Enoch, Seth, Methuselah, Noah, and many others, the Lord had faithful witnesses, just men, who kept his fear before their generation. Their memories were not feeble and treacherous. They had received the words of instruction from Adam, and these they repeated to their children and their children's children. Much important history and truth was expressed in song.

Daniel and his companions were familiar with the lives of Abel, Seth, Enoch, and Noah. They cherished the truths that had been passed down from generation to generation. The image of God was engraved upon the heart. When surrounded by an atmosphere of evil, these youth remained uncorrupted. No power or influence could sway them from the principles they had learned in early life by a study of God's word and works.

Young men and young women, study the history of Daniel and his companions. Their lives should inspire you with a determination to be true to God. You must be either loyal or disloyal to him. Christian integrity is strengthened by serving the Lord faithfully. Uplift the standard on which is inscribed, "The commandments of God, and the faith of Jesus." Make no compromise with evil. The line of demarcation between the obedient and the disobedient must be plain and distinct. Firmly determine to do the Lord's will at all times and in all places.

June 4, 1903—Lessons from the Life of Daniel 4—Daniel's Temperance Principles—Part 1

Daniel early gave promise of the remarkable ability developed in later years. He and his three companions who were selected to serve in the court of the king, were of princely birth, and are described as "children in whom was no blemish, but well favored, and skilful in all wisdom, and cunning in knowledge, and understanding science, and such as had ability in them." Perceiving the superior talents of these youthful captives, King Nebuchadnezzar determined to prepare them to fill important positions in his kingdom. That they might be fully qualified for their life at court, according to Oriental custom, they were to be taught the language of the Chaldeans, and to be subjected for three years to a thorough course of both physical and intellectual discipline.

The youth in this school of training were not only to be admitted to the royal palace, but it was provided that they should eat of the food, and drink of the wine, which came from the king's table. In all this the king thought that he was not only showing them great honor, but securing for them the best physical and mental development.

In the food provided for the king's table were swine's flesh and other meats which were pronounced unclean by the law given through Moses, and which the Hebrews had been expressly forbidden to eat. Here Daniel was brought to a severe test. Should he adhere to the divine teaching, offend the king, and probably lose not only his position but his life? or should he disregard the commandment of the Lord, and retain the favor of the king, thus securing great intellectual advantages and the most flattering worldly prospects?

Daniel could have argued that, dependent as he was on the king's favor, and subject to his power, there was no other course for him to pursue than to eat of the king's meat and to drink of his wine. But Daniel and his fellows counseled together. They considered how their physical and mental powers would be affected by the use of wine. The wine, they decided, was a snare. They were acquainted with the history of Nadab and Abihu, the record of whose intemperance had been preserved in the parchments of the Pentateuch. They knew that by the constant use of wine these men had become addicted to the liquor habit, and that they had confused their senses by drinking just before engaging in the sacred service of the sanctuary. In their brain-benumbed state, not being able to discern the difference between the sacred and the common, they had put common fire upon their censers, instead of the sacred fire of the Lord's kindling, and for this sin they had been struck dead.

A second consideration with these youthful captives was the fact that the king, before eating, always asked the blessing of his gods upon the food. A portion of the food, and also of the wine, from his table was set apart as an offering to the false gods whom he worshiped. According to the religious ideas of the day, this act consecrated the whole to the heathen gods. Daniel and his three brethren thought that even if they should not actually partake of the king's bounties, a mere pretense of eating the food or drinking the wine, where such idolatry was practised, would be a denial of their faith. To do this would indeed be to implicate themselves with heathenism, and to dishonor the principles of the law of God.

Daniel did not long hesitate. He decided to stand firm in his integrity, let the result be what it might. He "purposed in his heart that he would not defile himself with the portion of the king's meat, nor with the wine which he drank."

In this decision there was much involved. The Hebrew captives were regarded as slaves, but Daniel and his companions were particularly favored because of their apparent intelligence and their comeliness of person. In making their decision they did not act presumptuously, but revealed a firm love for truth and righteousness. They did not choose to be singular, but they must be, else they would ruin their own characters, set a wrong example for others, and dishonor God.

Among professed Christians today there are many who would decide that Daniel was too particular, and would pronounce him narrow and bigoted. They regard the matter of eating and drinking as of too little consequence to require such a decided choice,--one involving the probable sacrifice of every earthly advantage. But in the day of judgment those who reason thus will find that they turned from God's express requirements, and set up their own opinion as a standard of right and wrong. They will find that what seemed to them unimportant was not so regarded by God. His requirements should be sacredly obeyed. Those who accept and obey one of his precepts because it is convenient to do so, while they reject another because its observance would require a sacrifice, lower the standard of right, and by their example lead others to regard lightly his holy law. A "Thus saith the Lord" is to be our rule in all things.

Mrs. E. G. White

June 25, 1903—Lessons from the Life of Daniel 5—Daniel's Temperance Principles—Part 2

Daniel was subjected to temptations as severe as any that can assail the youth of today; yet he was true to the religious instruction received in early life. He was surrounded with influences calculated to subvert those who would vacillate between principle and inclination; yet the word of God presents him as a faultless character. Daniel dared not trust to his own moral power. Prayer was to him a necessity. He made God his strength, and in all the transactions of his life, the fear of the Lord was before him.

Daniel possessed the grace of genuine meekness. He was true, firm, and noble. He sought to live in peace with all, but wherever principle was involved, he was as unbending as the lofty cedar. In everything that did not come in collision with his allegiance to God, he was respectful and obedient to those who had authority over him; but he had so high a sense of the claims of God that the requirements of earthly rulers were held subordinate. By no selfish consideration could he be induced to swerve from his duty.

The character of Daniel is presented to the world as a striking example of what God's grace can make of men fallen by nature and corrupted by sin. The record of his noble, self-denying life is an encouragement to our common humanity. From it we may gather strength nobly to resist temptation, and firmly, and in the grace of meekness, to stand for the right under the severest trial.

Daniel might have found a plausible excuse to depart from his strictly temperate habits; but the approval of God was dearer to him than the favor of the most powerful earthly potentate,--dearer even than life itself. Having by his courteous conduct obtained favor with Melzar, the officer in charge of the Hebrew youth, Daniel made a request that they might not eat of the king's meat, or drink of his wine. Melzar feared that by complying with this request, he might incur the displeasure of the king; and thus endanger his own life. Like many at the present day, he thought that an abstemious diet would render these youth pale and sickly in appearance, and deficient in muscular strength, while the luxurious food from the king's table would make them ruddy and beautiful, and would promote physical and mental activity.

Daniel requested that the matter be decided by a ten days' trial, the Hebrew youth during this time being supplied with simple food, while their companions ate of the king's dainties. The request was granted, and Daniel felt assured that he had gained his case. Although but a youth, he had seen the injurious effects of wine and luxurious living upon physical and mental health.

At the end of the ten days the result was found to be quite the opposite of Melzar's expectations. Not only in personal appearance, but in physical activity and mental vigor, those who had been temperate in their habits showed a marked superiority over their companions who had indulged appetite. As a result of this trial, Daniel and his associates were permitted to continue their simple diet during the whole course of their training for the duties of the kingdom.

The Lord regarded with approval the firmness and self-denial of these Hebrew youth, and his blessing attended them. He "gave them knowledge and skill in all learning and wisdom: and Daniel had understanding in all visions and dreams." At the expiration of the three years of training, when their ability and acquirements were tested by the king, he "found none like Daniel, Hananiah, Mishael, and Azariah: therefore stood they before the king. And in all matters of wisdom and understanding, that the king inquired of them, he found them ten times better than all the magicians and astrologers that were in all his realm."

The life of Daniel is an inspired illustration of what constitutes a sanctified character. It presents a lesson for all, and especially for the young. A strict compliance with the requirements of God is beneficial to the health of the body and the mind. In order to reach the highest standard of moral and intellectual attainments, it is necessary to seek wisdom and strength from God, and to observe strict temperance in all the habits of life. In the experience of Daniel and his companions we have an instance of the triumph of principle over temptation to indulge the appetite. It shows us that through religious principle young men may triumph over the lusts of the flesh, and remain true to God's requirements, even though it costs them a great sacrifice.

What if Daniel and his companions had made a compromise with those heathen officers, and had yielded to the pressure of the occasion, by eating and drinking as was customary with the Babylonians? That single instance of departure from principle would have weakened their sense of right and their abhorrence of wrong. Indulgence of appetite would have involved the sacrifice of physical vigor, clearness of intellect, and spiritual power. One wrong step would probably have led to others, until, their connection with Heaven being severed, they would have been swept away by temptation.

God has said, "Them that honor me I will honor." While Daniel clung to his God with unwavering trust, the spirit of prophetic power came upon him. While he was instructed of man in the duties of court life, he was taught of God to read the mysteries of future ages, and to present to coming generations, through figures and similitudes, the wonderful things that would come to pass in the last days.

Mrs. E. G. White

July 9, 1903—Lessons from the Life of Daniel 6—The Reward of Temperance

During their three years of training, Daniel and his associates maintained their abstemious habits, their allegiance to God, and their constant dependence upon his power. When the time came for their abilities and acquirements to be tested by the king, they were examined with other candidates for the service of the kingdom. But "among them all was found none like Daniel, Hananiah, Mishael, and Azariah." Their keen apprehension, their choice and exact language, their extensive knowledge, testified to the unimpaired strength and vigor of their mental power. Therefore they stood before the king. "And in all matters of wisdom and understanding, that the king inquired of them, he found them ten times better than all the magicians and astrologers that were in all his realm."

God always honors the right. The most promising youths from all the lands subdued by the great conqueror had been gathered at Babylon, yet amid them all, the Hebrew captives were without a rival. The erect form, the firm, elastic step, the fair countenance, the undimmed senses, the untainted breadth,--all these were insignia of the nobility with which nature honors those who are obedient to her laws.

The lesson here presented is one that we would do well to ponder. A strict compliance with the Bible requirements will be a blessing both to body and soul. The fruit of the Spirit is not only love, joy, and peace, but temperance also. We are enjoined not to defile our bodies; for they are the temples of the Holy Spirit.

The Hebrew captives were men of like passions with ourselves. Amid the seductive influences of the luxurious courts of Babylon, they stood firm. The youth of today are surrounded with allurements to self-indulgence. Especially in our large cities, every form of sensual gratification is made easy and inviting. Those who, like Daniel, refuse to defile themselves, will reap the reward of temperate habits. With their greater physical stamina and increased power of endurance, they have a bank of deposit upon which to draw in case of emergency.

Right physical habits promote mental superiority. Intellectual power, physical stamina, and length of life depend upon immutable laws. Nature's God will not interfere to preserve men from the consequences of violating nature's requirements. He who strives for the mastery must be temperate in all things. Daniel's clearness of mind and firmness of purpose, his power in acquiring knowledge and in resisting temptation, were due in a great degree to the plainness of his diet, in connection with his life of prayer.

There is much sterling truth in the adage, "Every man is the architect of his own fortune." While parents are responsible for the stamp of character, as well as for the education and training, of their sons and daughters, it is still true that our position and usefulness in the world depend, to a great degree, upon our own course of action. Daniel and his companions enjoyed the benefits of correct training and education in early life, but these advantages alone would not have made them what they were. The time came when they must act for themselves,--when their future depended upon their own course. Then they decided to be true to the lessons given them in childhood. The fear of God, which is the beginning of wisdom, was the foundation of their greatness.

The history of Daniel and his youthful companions has been recorded on the pages of the inspired word, for the benefit of the youth of all succeeding ages. Through the record of their fidelity to the principles of temperance, God is speaking today to young men and young women, bidding them gather up the precious rays of light he has given on the subject of Christian temperance, and place themselves in right relation to the laws of health.

There is now need of men who, like Daniel, will do and dare. A pure heart and a strong, fearless hand, are wanted in the world today. God designed that man should be constantly improving, daily reaching a higher point in the scale of excellence. He will help us, if we seek to help ourselves. Our hope of happiness in two worlds depends upon our improvement in one. At every point we should be guarded against the first approach to intemperance.

Dear youth, God calls upon you to do a work which through his grace you can do. "Present your bodies a living sacrifice, holy, acceptable unto God, which is your reasonable service." Stand forth in your God-given manhood and womanhood. Show a purity of tastes, appetite and habits that bears comparison with Daniel's. God will reward you with calm nerves, a clear brain, an unimpaired judgment, keen perceptions. The youth of today whose principles are firm and unwavering, will be blessed with health of body, mind, and soul.

Mrs. E. G. White

July 16, 1903—Lessons from the Life of Daniel 7—A Warfare Against Intemperance

No young man or young woman could be more sorely tempted than were Daniel and his companions. To these four Hebrew youth were apportioned wine and meat from the king's table. But they chose to be temperate. They saw that perils were on every side, and that if they resisted temptation, they must make most decided efforts on their part, and trust the results with God. The youth who desire to stand as Daniel stood must exert their spiritual powers to the very utmost, co-operating with God, and trusting wholly in the strength that he has promised to all who come to him in humble obedience.

There is a constant warfare to be maintained between virtue and vice. The discordant elements of the one, and the pure principles of the other, are at work striving for the mastery. Satan is approaching every soul with some form of temptation on the point of indulgence of appetite. Intemperance is fearfully prevalent. Look where we will, we behold this evil fondly cherished. In spite of the efforts made to control it, intemperance is on the increase. We can not be too earnest in seeking to hinder its progress, to raise the fallen, and to shield the weak from temptation. With our feeble human hands we can do but little, but we have an unfailing Helper. We must not forget that the arm of Christ can reach to the very depths of human woe and degradation. He can give us help to conquer even the terrible demon of intemperance.

There is no class of persons capable of accomplishing more in the warfare against intemperance than are God-fearing youth. In this age the young men in our cities should unite as an army, firmly and decidedly to set themselves against every form of selfish, health-destroying indulgence. What a power they might be for good! How many they might save from becoming demoralized in the halls and gardens fitted up with music and other attractions to allure the youth! Intemperance and profanity and licentiousness are sisters. Let every God-fearing youth gird on the armor and press to the front. Put your names on every temperance pledge presented. Thus you lend your influence in favor of signing the pledge, and induce others to sign it. Let no weak excuse deter you from taking this step. Work for the good of your own souls and for good of others.

The young men and young women who claim to believe the truth for this time can please Jesus only by uniting in an effort to meet the evils that have, with seductive influence, crept in upon society. They should do all they can to stay the tide of intemperance now spreading with demoralizing power over the land. Realizing that intemperance has open, avowed supporters, those who honor God take their position firmly against this tide of evil by which both men and women are being swiftly carried to perdition.

The followers of Jesus will never be ashamed to practise temperance in all things. Then why should any young man blush with shame to refuse the wine-cup or the foaming mug of beer? A refusal to indulge perverted appetite is an honorable act. To sin is unmanly; to indulge in injurious habits of eating and drinking is weak, cowardly, debased; but to deny perverted appetite is strong, brave, noble. In the Babylonian court, Daniel was surrounded by allurements to sin, but by the help of Christ he maintained his integrity. He who can not resist temptation, when every facility for overcoming has been placed within his reach, is not registered in the books of heaven as a man.

Dare to be a Daniel. Dare to stand alone. Have courage to do the right. A cowardly and silent reserve before evil associates, while you listen to their devices, makes you one with them. "Come out from among them, and be ye separate, saith the Lord, and touch not the unclean thing; and I will receive you, and will be a Father unto you, and ye shall be my sons and daughters."

At all times and on all occasions it requires moral courage to adhere to the principles of strict temperance. We may expect that by following such a course we shall surprise those who do not totally abstain from all stimulants; but how are we to carry forward the work of reform if we conform to the injurious habits and practises of those with whom we associate?

The holy intelligences of heaven watch the conflict going on between the tempter and the tempted. If the tempted turn from temptation, and in the strength of Jesus conquer, angels rejoice; for Satan has lost in the conflict. In our behalf, Christ, when weakened and suffering on account of hunger, fought the battle against appetite, and conquered Satan. In the name and strength of Jesus every youth may conquer the enemy today on the point of perverted appetite. My dear young friends, advance step by step, until all your habits shall be in harmony with the laws of life and health. He who overcame in the wilderness of temptation declares: "To him that overcometh will I grant to sit with me in my throne, even as I also overcame, and am set down with my Father in his throne."

Mrs. E. G. White

August 6, 1903—Lessons from the Life of Daniel 8—Success in Education

For three years the promising young men whom Nebuchadnezzar, king of Babylon, selected to be trained for filling responsible positions, studied to acquire "the learning and the tongue of the Chaldeans." "At the end of the days ... appointed for bringing them in, ... the king communed with them; and among them all was found none like Daniel, Hananiah, Mishael, and Azariah: therefore stood they before the king."

True success in any line is not the result of chance, of accident, or of destiny; it is the outworking of God's providence, the reward of faith and discretion, of virtue and persevering labor. In acquiring the wisdom of the Babylonians, Daniel and his three companions were far more successful than their fellow students, but their learning did not come by chance; they obtained knowledge by the faithful use of their powers, under the guidance of the Holy Spirit.

These youth placed themselves in connection with the Source of all wisdom. They made the knowledge of God the foundation of their education. Other young men had the same advantages, but they did not, like the faithful Hebrew youth, bend all their energies to seek wisdom,--the knowledge of God as revealed in his word and works. They did not unite with these youth in searching the portion of the Old Testament then written, and making God's word their highest instructor.

In faith the Hebrew captives prayed for wisdom, and then lived out their own prayers. To this end they avoided everything that would weaken physical or mental power. At the same time, they improved every opportunity given them to become intelligent in all lines of learning. They sought to acquire knowledge for a purpose,--to honor and glorify God. They realized that in order to stand as representatives of true religion amid the false religions of heathenism, they must have clearness of intellect, and must perfect a Christian character.

These youth determined to secure a well-balanced education. They became skilled in secular as well as religious knowledge; but they studied science without being corrupted. While obtaining a knowledge of the sciences, they were studying, also, the highest science that mortals can study,--the science of salvation. They received light direct from the throne of heaven. The Lord himself was their educator. The golden links of the chain of heaven connected the finite with the Infinite. Constantly praying, conscientiously studying, keeping themselves in touch with the Unseen, they walked with God, as did Enoch.

The history of Daniel and his companions contains a lesson for us. Inspiration declares that "the fear of the Lord is the beginning of wisdom." Religious principle lies at the foundation of the highest education. If our youth are but balanced by principle, they may with safety improve the mental powers to the very highest extent, and may take all their attainments with them into the future life. There are many who might become mighty men, if, like these faithful Hebrews, they would learn of Christ, the world's greatest Teacher.

We would not prevent the youth from obtaining knowledge in literature, science, and art; but we would impress upon the minds of all the necessity of first obtaining a knowledge of God and of his will, that the influence of his Spirit may direct every advancement in educational lines.

Daniel placed himself in the channel of heavenly light, where he could commune with God in prayer. God co-operates with the human agencies who place themselves in this channel. Increased light is constantly shining from heaven upon those who seek for divine wisdom. Those who do not choose to place themselves in this channel meet with terrible loss. Students who exalt the sciences above the God of science, will be ignorant when they think themselves wise. Young men, young women, if you can not afford time to pray, can not give time for communion with God, for self-examination, and do not appreciate the wisdom that comes from God alone, all your learning will be defective, and your education will prove a hindrance instead of an advantage.

The lesson that the youth of today most need to learn, is the importance of seeking with all the heart to know God and to obey him implicitly. The science of the salvation of the human soul is the first lesson of life. Every line of literary or scientific knowledge is to be made secondary to this. To know God, and Jesus Christ whom he has sent, is life eternal.

Mrs. E. G. White

August 20, 1903—Lessons From the Life of Daniel 9—Earnestness of Purpose

We read that Daniel "purposed in his heart" that he would not eat of the luxuries of the king's table, nor drink of his wines. This purpose was not formed without due reflection and prayer, and when once his position was taken, he was not to be moved from it.

Daniel's companions, also, resolutely purposed to choose the real, the true, and the useful, rather than the momentary indulgence of appetite and pride. They resolved that their God-given talents should not be perverted and enfeebled by selfish indulgence. They reverenced their own manhood. They kept their eyes steadfastly fixed on the good they wished to accomplish. They determined to do all in their power to place themselves in right relation to God; and the Lord was not unmindful of their persevering, earnest effort.

When the four Hebrew youth were receiving an education for the king's court in Babylon, they did not feel that the blessing of the Lord was a substitute for the taxing effort required of them. They were diligent in study; for they discerned that through the grace of God their destiny depended upon their own will and action. They were to bring all their ability to the work; and by close, severe taxation of their powers, they were to make the most of their opportunities for study and labor.

While these youth were working out their own salvation, God was working in them to will and to do of his good pleasure. Here are revealed the conditions of success. To make God's grace our own, we must act our part. The Lord does not propose to perform for us either the willing or the doing. His grace is given to work in us to will and to do, but never as a substitute for our effort. Our souls are to be aroused to co-operate. The Holy Spirit works in us, that we may work out our own salvation. This is the practical lesson the Holy Spirit is striving to teach us. "It is God which worketh in you both to will and to do of his good pleasure."

The Lord will co-operate with all who earnestly strive to be faithful in his service, as he co-operated with Daniel and his three companions. Fine mental qualities and a high tone of moral character are not the result of accident. God gives opportunities;

success depends upon the use made of them. The openings of Providence must be quickly discerned and eagerly entered. There are many who might become mighty men, if, like Daniel, they would depend upon God for grace to be overcomers, and for strength and efficiency to do their work.

I address you, young men: Be faithful. Put heart into your work. Imitate none who are slothful, and who give divided service. Actions, often repeated, form habits, habits form character. Patiently perform the little duties of life. So long as you undervalue the importance of faithfulness in the little duties, your character-building will be unsatisfactory. In the sight of Omnipotence, every duty is important. The Lord has said, "He that is faithful in that which is least is faithful also in much." In the life of a true Christian there are no non-essentials.

Many who claim to be Christians are working at cross-purposes with God. Many are waiting for some great work to be brought to them. Daily they lose opportunities for showing their faithfulness to God; daily they fail of discharging with whole-heartedness the little duties of life, which seem to them uninteresting. While waiting for some great work in which they may exercise their supposedly great talents, and thus satisfy their ambitious longings, their life passes away.

My dear young friends, do the work that lies nearest at hand. Turn your attention to some humble line of effort within your reach. Put mind and heart into the doing of this work. Force your thoughts to act intelligently on the things that you can do at home. Thus you will be fitting yourself for greater usefulness. Remember that of King Hezekiah it is written: "In every work that he began, ... he did it with all his heart, and prospered."

The ability to fix the thoughts on the work in hand, is a great blessing. God-fearing youth should strive to discharge their duties with thoughtful consideration, keeping the thoughts in the right channel, and doing their best. They should recognize their present duties, and fulfil them without allowing the mind to wander. This kind of mental discipline will be helpful and beneficial throughout life. Those who learn to put thought into everything they undertake, however small the work may appear, will be of use in the world.

Dear youth, be earnest, be persevering. "Gird up the loins of your mind." Stand like Daniel, the faithful Hebrew, who purposed in his heart to be true to God. Do not disappoint your parents and friends. And there is Another to be remembered. Do not disappoint Him who so loved you that he gave his life to make it possible for you to be co-laborers with God.

The desire to honor God should be to us the most powerful of all motives. It should lead us to make every exertion to improve the privileges and opportunities provided for us, that we may understand how to use wisely the Lord's goods. It should lead us to keep brain, bone, muscle, and nerve in the most healthful condition, that our physical strength and mental clearness may make us faithful stewards. Selfish interest, if given room to act, dwarfs the mind, and hardens the heart; if allowed to control, it destroys moral power. Then disappointment comes. The selfish man has divorced himself from God, and sold himself to unworthy pursuits. He can not be happy; for he can not respect himself. He has lowered himself in his own estimation. He is a failure.

True success is given to men and women by the God who gave success to Daniel. He who read the heart of Daniel looked with pleasure upon his servant's purity of motive, his determination to honor the Lord. Those who in their life fulfil God's purpose, must put forth painstaking effort, applying themselves closely and earnestly to the accomplishment of whatever he gives them to do.

Dear reader, will you not determine to be as was Daniel,--a loyal, steadfast servant of the Lord of hosts? The God of Daniel works mightily in behalf of every one who seeks to know and to do his will. By the impartation of his Spirit he strengthens every true purpose, every noble resolution.

September 1, 1903—Lessons From the Life of Daniel 10—The Vision of the Great Image

In the same year that Daniel and his companions entered the service of the king of Babylon, events occurred that severely tested the integrity of these youthful Hebrews, and revealed to an idolatrous nation the power and faithfulness of the God of Israel.

While King Nebuchadnezzar was looking forward with anxious forebodings to the future, he had a remarkable dream, by which "his spirit was troubled, and his sleep broke from him." Although this vision of the night made a deep impression on his mind, he found it impossible to recall the particulars. He applied to his astrologers and magicians, and with promises of great wealth and honor commanded them to tell him his dream and its interpretation. But they said, "Tell thy servants the dream, and we will show the interpretation."

The Lord in his providence had a wise purpose in view in giving Nebuchadnezzar this dream, and then causing him to forget the particulars, but to retain the fearful impression made upon his mind. The Lord desired to expose the pretensions of the wise men of Babylon. The king knew that if they could tell the interpretation, they could tell the dream as well. Angered over their inability to relieve his mind, he threatened that they should all be slain, if, in a given time, the dream were not made known. "The thing is gone from me," he said to the Chaldeans; "if ye will not make known unto me the dream, with the interpretation thereof, ye shall be cut to pieces, and your houses shall be made a dunghill. But if ye show the dream, and the interpretation thereof, ye shall receive of me gifts and rewards and great honor: therefore show me the dream, and the interpretation thereof." Still the wise men returned the same answer, "Let the king tell his servants the dream, and we will show the interpretation of it."

Nebuchadnezzar began to see that the men whom he trusted to reveal mysteries by means of their boasted wisdom, failed him in his great perplexity, and he said: "I know of a certainty that ye would gain the time, because ye see the thing is gone from me. But if ye will not make known unto me the dream, there is but one decree for you:

for ye have prepared lying and corrupt words to speak before me, till the time be changed: therefore tell me the dream, and I shall know that ye can show me the interpretation thereof.

"The Chaldeans answered before the king, and said, There is not a man upon the earth that can show the king's matter: therefore there is no king, lord, nor ruler, that asked such things at any magician, or astrologer, or Chaldean. And it is a rare thing that the king requireth, and there is none other that can show it before the king, except the gods, whose dwelling is not with flesh.

"For this cause the king was angry and very furious, and commanded to destroy all the wise men of Babylon."

When the decree went forth that all the wise men of Babylon should be destroyed, Daniel and his fellows were sought for, and informed that in accordance with the king's command, they must be slain. "Then Daniel answered," not in a spirit of retaliation, but "with counsel and wisdom," "the captain of the king's guard," who "was gone forth to slay the wise men of Babylon." "Why," Daniel inquired, "is the decree so hasty from the king?" Taking his life in his hand, he ventured to enter the king's presence, and begged that time be granted, in order that he ight reveal to him the dream and its interpretation. To this request the monarch acceded.

"Then Daniel went to his house, and made the thing known to Hananiah, Mishael, and Azariah, his companions: that they would desire mercies of the God of heaven concerning this secret; that Daniel and his fellows should not perish with the rest of the wise men of Babylon." Together the Hebrew youth presented the matter before God, and sought for wisdom from the Source of light and knowledge. Although for a time they had lived in the king's court, surrounded with temptation, they had not forgotten their responsibility to God. They were strong in the consciousness that His providence had placed them where they were; that they were doing His work, and meeting the demands of duty. They had confidence toward God. In times past they had turned to Him for strength when in perplexity and danger, and He had been to them an ever-present help.

The servants of God did not plead with Him in vain. They had honored Him, and in their hour of trial He honored them. The Spirit of the Lord rested upon Daniel and his fellows, and the secret was revealed to Daniel in a night vision. He hastened to request an interview with the king.

The Jewish captive stood before the monarch of the most powerful empire that the sun ever shone upon. Notwithstanding his riches and glory, Nebuchadnezzar was in great distress of mind, but the youthful exile was calm and happy in his God. Then, if ever, was an opportunity for Daniel to exalt himself--to make prominent his own goodness and superior wisdom. But his first effort was to disclaim all honor for himself, and to exalt God as the Source of wisdom:

"The secret which the king hath demanded can not the wise men, the astrologers, the magicians, the soothsayers, show unto the king; but there is a God in heaven that revealeth secrets, and maketh known to the king Nebuchadnezzar what shall be in the latter days."

Daniel proceeded to relate the dream. "Thy dream," he declared, "and the visions of thy head upon thy bed, are these; As for thee, O king, thy thoughts came into thy mind upon thy bed, what should come to pass hereafter: and he that revealeth secrets maketh known to thee what shall come to pass. But as for me, this secret is not revealed to me for any wisdom that I have more than any living, but for their sakes that shall make known the interpretation to the king, and that thou mightest know the thoughts of thy heart.

"Thou, O king, sawest, and behold a great image. This great image, whose brightness was excellent, stood before thee; and the form thereof was terrible. This image's head was of fine gold, his breast and arms of silver, his belly and his thighs of brass, his legs of iron, his feet part of iron and part of clay. Thou sawest till that a stone was cut out without hands, which smote the image upon his feet that were of iron and clay and brake them to pieces. Then was the iron, the clay, the brass, the silver, and the gold, broken to pieces together, and became like the chaff of the summer threshing-floors; and the wind carried them away, that no place was found for them: and the stone that smote the image became a great mountain, and filled the whole earth."

Listening with solemn attention as every particular was reproduced, the king recognized this as the dream over which he had been so troubled; and he was prepared to receive with favor the interpretation.

Mrs. E. G. White

September 8, 1903—Lessons From the Life of Daniel 11—The Interpretation of the Vision of the Great Image

Having described the image that the king had seen, Daniel gave the interpretation, foretelling the remarkable events that were to take place in prophetic history:

"Thou, O king, art a king of kings: for the God of heaven hath given thee a kingdom, power, and strength, and glory. And wheresoever the children of men dwell, the beasts of the field and the fowls of the heaven hath he given into thine hand, and hath made thee ruler over them all. Thou art this head of gold.

"And after thee shall arise another kingdom inferior to thee, and another third kingdom of brass, which shall bear rule over all the earth.

"And the fourth kingdom shall be strong as iron: forasmuch as iron breaketh in pieces and subdueth all things: and as iron that breaketh all these, shall it break in pieces and bruise. And whereas thou sawest the feet and toes, part of potters' clay, and part of iron, the kingdom shall be divided; but there shall be in it of the strength of the iron, forasmuch as thou sawest the iron mixed with miry clay. And as the toes of the feet were part of iron, and part of clay, so the kingdom shall be partly strong, and partly broken. And whereas thou sawest iron mixed with miry clay, they shall mingle themselves with t

"And in the days of these kings shall the God of heaven set up a kingdom, which shall never be destroyed: and the kingdom shall not be left to other people, but it shall break in pieces and consume all these kingdoms, and it shall stand forever. Forasmuch as thou sawest that the stone was cut out of the mountain without hands, and that it brake in pieces the iron, the brass, the clay, the silver and the gold; the great God hath made known to the king what shall come to pass hereafter: and the dream is certain, and the interpretation thereof sure."

Nebuchadnezzar felt that he could accept this interpretation as a divine revelation; for to Daniel had been revealed every detail of the dream. The solemn truths conveyed by the interpretation of this vision of the night made a deep impression on the sovereign's mind, and in humility and awe he "fell upon his face, and worshiped," saying, "Of a truth it is, that your God is a God of gods, and a Lord of kings, and a revealer of secrets, seeing thou couldest reveal this secret."

Daniel's exposition of this dream resulted in the king's conferring honor and dignity upon him and his companions. "The king made Daniel a great man, and gave him many great gifts, and made him ruler over the whole province of Babylon, and chief of the governors over all the wise men of Babylon. Then Daniel requested of the king, and he set Shadrach, Meshach, and Abed-nego, over the affairs of the province of Babylon: but Daniel sat in the gate of the king." "The gate of the king" was a place where justice was dispensed. Daniel's three companions were made counselors, judges, and rulers in the land. These men were not puffed up with vanity, but they saw and rejoiced that God was recognized above all earthly potentates, and that his kingdom was extolled above all earthly kingdoms.

The Lord was working in the Babylonian kingdom, and communicating light to the four Hebrew youth, in order that he might represent his work before the idolatrous nation. He would reveal that he had power over the kingdoms of the world,--power to enthrone and to dethrone kings. The King over all kings was communicating great truths to the Babylonian monarch, and awakening in his mind a realization of his responsibility to God. Nebuchadnezzar saw clearly the difference between the wisdom of God and the wisdom of the most learned men of his kingdom.

The events of the future, reaching down to the end of time, were opened before the king of Babylon, in order that he might have light on this important subject. The record of the dream and its interpretation was traced by the prophetic pen, in order that the rulers of the kingdoms that should succeed Babylon might have the same light.

September 22, 1903—Lessons From the Life of Daniel 12—The Moral Deterioration of the Nation

"Righteousness exalteth a nation: but sin is a reproach to any people."

The image revealed to Nebuchadnezzar, while representing the deterioration of the kingdoms of the earth in power and glory, also fitly represents the deterioration of religion and morality among the people of these kingdoms. As nations forget God, in like proportion they become weak morally.

Babylon passed away because in her prosperity she forgot God, and ascribed the glory of her prosperity to human achievement.

The Medo-Persian kingdom was visited by the wrath of heaven because in this kingdom God's law was trampled under foot. The fear of the Lord found no place in the hearts of the people. The prevailing influences in Medo-Persia were wickedness, blasphemy, and corruption.

The kingdoms that followed were even more base and corrupt. They deteriorated because they cast off their allegiance to God. As they forgot him, they sank lower and still lower in the scale of moral value.

The vast empire of Rome crumbled to pieces, and from its ruins rose that mighty power, the Roman Catholic Church. This church boasts of her infallibility and her hereditary religion. But this religion is a horror to all who are acquainted with the secrets of the mystery of iniquity. The priests of this church maintain their ascendency by keeping the people in ignorance of God's will, as revealed in the Scriptures.

It is sin that is ruining nations today. Even many leaders in the religious world have not a good conscience toward God. Many of those who claim to be Protestants have not the faith in God's word that Luther had in the early days of the Reformation. They have left the old landmarks, and depend on ceremony and formal display to make up for their lack of the purity and piety, the meekness and lowliness, found in obedience to God.

There is no real standard of righteousness apart from God's law. By obedience to this law the intellect is strengthened, and the conscience is enlightened and made sensitive. The youth need to gain a clear understanding of God's law. They are not left to follow blindly the guidance of men. The great prophetic waymarks which God himself has set up show the path of obedience to be the only path that can be followed with certainty.

Those who love and obey the law of God will meet with trials and temptations; but if they hope and pray, and trust his word, they will be able to say, with Paul, "I am persuaded, that neither death, nor life, nor angels, nor principalities, nor powers, nor things present, nor things to come, nor height, nor depth, nor any other creature, shall be able to separate us from the love of God, which is in Christ Jesus our Lord."

My dear young friends, have you wholly given yourselves up to God, to do his will? Are you transformed by the grace of Christ? Some claim to be one with Christ, while their special work is to make void the law of God. Will you accept their assertions? How will you distinguish God's true servants from the false prophets that Christ said would arise to deceive many? There is only one test of character,--God's holy law.

We are living in a momentous period of this earth's history. The final conflict is just before us. We see the world corrupted under the inhabitants thereof. Satanic agencies have made the earth a stage for horrors that no language can describe. War and bloodshed are carried on by nations claiming to be Christian. A disregard for God's law has brought the sure result.

"We wrestle not against flesh and blood, but against principalities, against powers, against the rulers of the darkness of this world, against spiritual wickedness in high places. Wherefore take unto you the whole armor of God, that ye may be able to withstand in the evil day, and having done all, to stand." "Be strong in the Lord, and in the power of his might. Put on the whole armor of God, that ye may be able to stand against the wiles of the devil."

There will be a sharp conflict between those who are loyal to God and those who cast scorn upon his law. The church has joined hands with the world. Reverence for God's law has been subverted. The religious leaders have taught for doctrine the commandments of men. As it was in the days of Noah, so it is in this age. But shall the prevalence of disloyalty and transgression cause those who have reverenced God's law to have less respect for it, or to unite with the powers of earth in attempting to make it void?

The test comes to every one. There are only two sides. Dear young reader, on which side are you standing?

Mrs. E. G. White

September 29, 1903—Lessons From the Life of Daniel 13—Obedience the Condition of God's Favor

The strength of nations and of individuals is not found in the opportunities and facilities that appear to make them invincible; it is not found in their boasted greatness. That which alone can make them great or strong is the power of God. They themselves, by their attitude toward his purpose, decide their own destiny.

Human histories relate man's achievements, his victories in battle, his success in attaining worldly greatness. God's history describes man as heaven views him. In the divine records all his merit is seen to consist in his obedience to God's requirements. His disobedience is faithfully chronicled as meriting the punishment he will surely receive. In the light of eternity it will be seen that God deals with men in accordance with the momentous question of obedience or disobedience.

Hundreds of years before certain nations came upon the stage of action, the Omniscient One looked down the ages, and predicted through his servants the prophets the rise and fall of the universal kingdoms. The prophet Daniel, when interpreting to the king of Babylon the dream of the great image,--an image symbolic of the kingdoms of the world,--declared to Nebuchadnezzar that his kingdom should be superseded. His greatness and power in God's world would have their day, and a second kingdom would arise, which also would have its period of trial as to whether it would exalt the one Ruler, the only true God. Not doing this, its glory would fade away, and a third kingdom would occupy its place. Proved by obedience or disobedience, this also would pass away; and a fourth, strong as iron, would subdue the nations of the world. These predictions of the Infinite One, recorded on the prophetic page and traced on the pages of history, were given to demonstrate that God is the ruling power in the affairs of this world. He changes the times and the seasons, he removes kings and sets up kings, to fulfil his own purpose.

Under King Nebuchadnezzar, Babylon was the richest and most powerful kingdom on the earth. Its riches and splendor have been faintly portrayed by Inspiration. But it did not fulfil God's purpose; and when his time had come, this kingdom of pride and power, ruled by men of the highest intellect, was broken, shattered, helpless. Christ has declared, "Without me ye can do nothing." The illustrious statesmen of Babylon did not regard themselves as dependent on God. They thought that they had created all their grandeur and exaltation. But when God spoke, they were as the grass that withereth, and the flower of the grass that fadeth away. The word and will of God alone endure forever.

If these several kingdoms had kept the fear of the Lord always before them, they would have been given wisdom and power, which would have bound them together and kept them strong. But the rulers of the kingdoms of the world made God their strength only when harassed and perplexed. Failing to obtain help from their great men, they sought it from men like Daniel, men who they knew honored the living God and were honored by him. To these men they appealed to unravel for them the mysteries of Providence; for they had separated themselves so far from God by transgression that they could not understand his warnings. They were forced to appeal to those whose minds were illuminated by heavenly light, for an explanation of the mysteries they could not comprehend.

The voice of God, heard in past ages, is sounding down along the line, from century to century, through generations that have come upon the stage of action and passed away. Shall God speak, and his voice not be respected? What power mapped out all this history, that nations, one after another, should arise at the predicted time and fill their appointed place, unconsciously witnessing to the truth of that which they themselves knew not the meaning.

The centuries have their mission. Every moment has its work. Each is passing into eternity with its burden, Well done, thou good and faithful servant, or, Woe to the wicked and slothful servant. God is still dealing with earthly kingdoms. He is in the great cities. His eyes behold, his eyelids try, the doings of the children of men. We are not to say, God was, but, God is. He sees the very sparrow's fall, the leaf that falls from the tree, and the king who is dethroned. All are under the control of the Infinite One. Everything is changing. Cities and nations are being measured by the plummet in the hand of God. He never makes a mistake. He reads correctly. Everything earthly is unsettled, but the truth abides forever.

In the eyes of the world, those who serve God may appear weak. They may be apparently sinking beneath the billows, but with the next billow, they are seen rising nearer to their haven. I give unto them eternal life, saith our Lord, and none shall be able to pluck them out of my hand. Though kings shall be cast down, and nations removed, the souls that through faith link themselves with God's purpose shall abide forever. "They that be wise shall shine as the brightness of the firmament; and they that turn many to righteousness as the stars forever and forever."

Mrs. E. G. White

November 24, 1903—Lessons From the Life of Daniel 15—True Wisdom

The prophetic events related in Nebuchadnezzar's dream were of consequence to him, but the dream was taken from him in order that the wise men should not place upon it a false interpretation. The lessons taught by the dream were given by God for those who live in our day. The inability of the wise men to tell the dream is a representation of the limitations of the wise men of the present day, who, not having wisdom and discernment from the Most High, are unable to understand the prophecies. Although he may be learned in the world's lore, the man who is not listening to hear what the Lord says in his word, and who is not opening his heart to receive this word, that he may give it to others, is not a representative of the God of heaven. Not many great and learned men of the earth will gladly receive the truth unto eternal life, though to all of them the truth will be proclaimed.

Young men and young women may obtain the highest earthly education, and yet may be ignorant of the first principles that would make them subjects of the kingdom of God. Human learning can not qualify any one for the heavenly kingdom. The subjects of Christ's kingdom are not made thus by forms and ceremonies, or by long study of books. "This is life eternal, that they might know thee the only true God, and Jesus Christ, whom thou hast sent." The members of Christ's kingdom are members of his body, of which he himself is the head. They are the elect sons of God, "a royal priesthood, an holy nation, a peculiar people;" that they should show forth the praises of him who has called them out of darkness into his marvelous light.

The Old and the New Testament Scriptures need to be studied daily. The knowledge of God and the wisdom of God come to the student who is a constant learner of his ways and works. The Bible is to be our light, our educator. When the youth learn to believe that God sends the dew, the rain, and the sunshine from heaven, causing vegetation to flourish; when they realize that all blessings come from him, and that thanksgiving and praise are due to him, they will be led to acknowledge God in all their ways, and discharge with fidelity their duties day by day; God will be in all their thoughts. Then they can trust him for tomorrow, and avoid the anxious care that brings unhappiness into the lives of so many. "Seek ye first the kingdom of God, and his righteousness; and all these things shall be added unto you."

Many young men, in talking about science, are wise above that which is written; they seek to explain, by something that meets their finite comprehension, the ways and work of God; but it is all a miserable failure. True science and Inspiration are in perfect harmony. False science is something independent of God. It is pretentious ignorance.

One of the greatest evils that has attended the quest of knowledge, the investigation of science, is that those who engage in these researches too often lose sight of the divine character of pure and unadulterated religion. The worldly wise have attempted to explain, on scientific principles, the influence of the Spirit of God upon the heart. The least advance in this direction will lead the mind into the mazes of skepticism. The religion of the Bible is simply the mystery of godliness; no human mind can fully understand it, and it is utterly incomprehensible to the unregenerate heart.

The youth will not become weak-minded or inefficient by consecrating themselves to the service of God. To many, education means a knowledge of books; but "the fear of the Lord is the beginning of wisdom." The youngest child who loves and fears God is greater in his sight than the most talented and learned man who neglects the matter of personal salvation. The youth who consecrate their hearts and lives to God are placing themselves in connection with the Fountain of all wisdom and excellence.

If the youth will but learn of the heavenly Teacher, as Daniel did, they will know for themselves that the fear of the Lord is indeed the beginning of wisdom. Having thus laid a sure foundation, they may, like Daniel, turn every privilege and opportunity to the very best account, and may rise to any height in intellectual attainments. Consecrated to God, and having the protection of his grace and the quickening influence of his Holy Spirit, they will manifest deeper intellectual power than the mere worldling.

To learn science through the interpretation that men have placed on it, is to obtain a false education. To learn of God, and of Jesus Christ, whom he has sent, is to learn the science of the Bible. The pure in heart see God in every providence, in every phase of true education. They recognize the first approach of the light that radiates from God's throne. Communications from heaven are made to those who will catch the first gleams of spiritual knowledge.

The students in our schools are to regard the knowledge of God as above everything else. Only by searching the Scriptures can this knowledge be attained. "The preaching of the cross is to them that perish foolishness; but unto us which are saved it is the power of God. For it is written, I will destroy the wisdom of the wise, and will bring to nothing the understanding of the prudent.... The foolishness of God is wiser than men; and the weakness of God is stronger than men.... But of him are ye in Christ Jesus, who of God is made unto us wisdom, and righteousness, and sanctification, and redemption: that, according as it is written, He that glorieth, let him glory in the Lord."

Mrs. E. G. White

December 1, 1903—Lessons From the Life of Daniel 16—God's Prophetic Word

When Nebuchadnezzar's dream of the great image was revealed to Daniel in a night vision, his first act was to thank God for this revelation. "Blessed be the name of God forever and ever," he exclaimed; "for wisdom and might are his: and he changeth the times and the seasons: he removeth kings, and setteth up kings: he giveth wisdom unto the wise, and knowledge to them that know understanding: he revealeth the deep and secret things: he knoweth what is in the darkness, and the light dwelleth with him. I thank thee, and praise thee, O thou God of my fathers, who hast given me wisdom and might, and hast made known unto me now what we desired of thee: for thou hast now made known unto us the king's matter."

In past ages the Lord God of heaven revealed his secrets to his prophets. The present and the future are equally clear to him. The voice of God echoes down the ages, telling man what is to take place. Kings and princes take their places at their appointed time. They think they are carrying out their own purposes, but in reality they are fulfilling the word that God has spoken.

Paul declares that the records of God's dealings with mankind in the past "are written for our admonition, upon whom the ends of the world are come." Daniel's history is given us for our admonition. "The secret of the Lord is with them that fear him." Daniel's God still lives and reigns. He has not closed heaven against his people. As in the Jewish age, so in this age, God reveals his secrets to his servants the prophets.

The apostle Peter says: "We have also a more sure word of prophecy; whereunto ye do well that ye take heed, as unto a light that shineth in a dark place, until the day dawn, and the day-star arise in your hearts: knowing this first, that no prophecy of the Scripture is of any private interpretation. For the prophecy came not in old time by the will of man: but holy men of God spake as they were moved by the Holy Ghost."

The unbelieving and godless do not discern the importance of the signs of the times, foretold in the prophetic word. In ignorance they may refuse to accept the inspired record. But when professed Christians speak sneeringly of the ways and means employed by the great I AM to make his purposes known, they show themselves to be ignorant both of the Scriptures and of the power of God. The Creator knows just what elements he has to deal with in human nature. He knows what means to employ to obtain the desired results.

Man's word fails. He who makes the assertions of men his dependence, may well tremble; for he will some day be as a shipwrecked vessel. God's word is infallible, and endures forever. Christ declares, "Verily I say unto you, Till heaven and earth pass, one jot or one tittle shall in no wise pass from the law, till all be fulfilled." God's word will endure throughout the ceaseless ages of eternity.

February 2, 1904—Lessons from the Life of Daniel 18—A Perversion of Truth

The dream of the great image, by which were opened future events reaching to the end of time, was given to Nebuchadnezzar that he might understand the part he was to act in the world's history, and also the relation that his kingdom sustained to the kingdom of heaven. This wonderful dream caused a marked change in his ideas and opinions, and for a little time he was influenced by the fear of God; but his heart was not yet cleansed from its pride, its worldly ambition, its desire for self-exaltation.

The prophet Daniel described to King Nebuchadnezzar the rise and fall of the kingdoms that were to succeed Babylon; but the king did not cherish the conviction that came to his mind in regard to the fall of all earthly governments, and the greatness and power of Jehovah's kingdom. After the first impression wore away, he thought only of his own greatness, and studied how the dream might be turned to his own honor.

The words, "Thou art this head of gold," made the deepest impression upon Nebuchadnezzar's mind. Seeing this, the wise men who had been unable to tell his dream, proposed that he make an image similar to the one seen by him, and set it up where all might behold the head of gold, which was a representation of his kingdom.

This suggestion pleased the king. His pride was flattered by the thought that he could thus represent his greatness; and instead of merely reproducing the image seen in his dream, he determined to make an image that should excel the original. This image was not to deteriorate in value from the head to the feet, like the one he had been shown, but was to be composed throughout of the most precious metal. Thus the whole image would represent the greatness of Babylon; and he determined that by the splendor of this image the prophecy concerning the kingdoms which were to follow, should be effaced from his mind, and from the minds of others who had heard the dream and its interpretation.

God had spoken plainly in regard to the heavenly kingdom. "In the days of these kings," said Daniel, "shall the God of heaven set up a kingdom, which shall never be destroyed: and the kingdom shall not be left to other people, but it shall break in pieces and consume all these kingdoms, and it shall stand forever.... The dream is certain, and the interpretation thereof sure."

The king had acknowledged the power of God. saying: "Of a truth it is, that your God is a God of gods, ... and a revealer of secrets;" but notwithstanding this acknowledgment, the years of prosperity that followed filled his heart with pride, and he forgot God, resuming his idol-worship with increased zeal and bigotry, and cherishing the thought that the Babylonian kingdom would stand forever.

At the time when Nebuchadnezzar saw the vision of the great image, he had purposed to destroy the wise men, because he discerned their deceptions, and was convinced that they did not have the learning and power that they claimed to possess. Only by the intercession of Daniel had they been saved from a cruel and ignominious death. The king now united with these men in planning to dishonor the God of Daniel. The light that had been permitted to shine from heaven upon Nebuchadnezzar was used to serve his pride and self-exaltation. The wise men, in counsel with the king, concluded that Babylon was the kingdom which was to break in pieces all other kingdoms; and they endeavored to make an image that would represent Babylon as eternal, indestructible, all-powerful,--a kingdom that would stand forever.

From the treasures obtained in war, Nebuchadnezzar "made an image of gold, whose height was threescore cubits, and the breadth thereof six cubits: he set it up in the plain of Dura, in the province of Babylon." This image was placed in a conspicuous position, and a proclamation was issued that all should worship it.

Thus the grand lesson which God had given to the heathen through the vision of the great image, was misconstrued and misapplied. That which was designed by God to give to the world clear, distinct rays of light, Nebuchadnezzar turned from its purpose, making it minister to his pride and vanity. The prophetic illustration of God's glory was made to serve for the glorification of humanity. The symbol designed to unfold important events was used as a symbol that would hinder the spread of the knowledge that God desired the kingdoms of the world to receive. By the magnificence and beauty of his image, the king sought to make error appear more attractive, more powerful, than the truths that God had revealed.

Those who are willing to be taught, may learn a lesson from the conduct of the king of Babylon. As Satan sought to make God-given light serve his own purposes, by leading the king to work for his own glory instead of the glory of God, so the enemy works today to pervert truth in order to hinder God's purposes. Truth unmixed with error, is a power mighty to save; but if we allow the enemy to work through us; if, by means of the light given us, we seek to exalt self, even truth, perverted, may become a power for evil.

Mrs. E. G. White

March 8, 1904—Lessons from the Life of Daniel 19—The Fiery Furnace—Part 1

The golden image set up in the plain of Dura, an image ninety feet in height and nine in breadth, presented an imposing and majestic appearance. Nebuchadnezzar issued a proclamation, calling upon all the officers of the kingdom to assemble at the dedication of this image, and, at the sound of musical instruments, to bow down and worship it. Should any fail of doing this, they were immediately to be cast into the midst of a burning fiery furnace.

The appointed day came, and at the sound of the music the vast company that was assembled at the king's command, "fell down, and worshiped the golden image." "At that time certain Chaldeans came near, ... and said to the king Nebuchadnezzar, O king, live forever.... There are certain Jews whom thou hast set over the affairs of the province of Babylon, Shadrach, Meshach, and Abed-nego; these men, O king, have not regarded thee: they serve not thy gods, nor worship the golden image which thou hast set up."

Filled with rage, the king commanded that the men be brought before him. "Is it true," he inquired, "do ye not serve my gods, nor worship the golden image which I have set up?" Pointing to the angry furnace, he reminded them of the punishment that would be theirs if they refused to obey his will.

The king decided to give them a second trial. "If ye be ready," he said, "at what time ye hear the sound of the cornet, flute, harp, sackbut, psaltery, and dulcimer, and all kinds of music, ye fall down and worship the image which I have made; well; but if ye worship not, ye shall be cast the same hour into the midst of a burning fiery furnace." Then, with hand stretched upward in defiance, he asked, "And who is that God that shall deliver you out of my hands?"

In vain were the king's threats. He could not turn these noble men from their allegiance to the great Ruler of nations. From the history of their fathers, they had learned that disobedience to God results in dishonor, disaster, and death; that the fear of the Lord is not only the beginning of wisdom, but the foundation of all true prosperity. They knew that they owed to God every faculty they possessed; and while their hearts were full of generous sympathy toward all men, they had a lofty aspiration to prove themselves loyal to God.

When the king was troubled in regard to his dream, these men, with Daniel, had fasted and prayed, that they might understand the dream. The Lord had heard their cries, and he had given to Daniel wisdom to interpret the dream to the king. Thus their own lives and the lives of the astrologers and soothsayers had been saved. Now the very men who had escaped death through the mercy of God to his servants, had been the prime movers in securing the decree in regard to the worship of the golden image. But the three Hebrews made no mention of these things; they knew that a controversy with the king would only increase his fury.

Standing before the angry monarch, with the image in sight, and the sound of the entrancing music in their ears, these young men thought of the promise made to the prophet Isaiah more than one hundred years before: "Fear not: for I have redeemed thee, I have called thee by thy name; thou art mine. When thou passest through the waters, I will be with thee; when thou walkest through the fire, thou shalt not be burned, neither shall the flame kindle upon thee."

The answer of Shadrach, Meshach, and Abed-nego was respectful, but decided. Looking with calmness upon the fiery furnace and the idolatrous throng, they said: "O Nebuchadnezzar, we are not careful to answer thee in this matter. If it be so [if this be your decision], our God whom we serve will deliver us out of thine hand, O king." These Hebrew youth had unquestioning faith in God, and they were determined to honor him at any cost. Their faith strengthened with the declaration that God would be glorified by delivering them, and with a triumphant ring of trust in their voices, they added: "But if not, be it known unto thee, O king, that we will not serve thy gods, nor worship the golden image which thou hast set up."

Mrs. E. G. White

March 29, 1904—Power of Song

The melody of praise is the atmosphere of heaven; and when heaven comes in touch with the earth, there is music and song,--"thanksgiving, and the voice of melody."

Above the new-created earth, as it lay, fair and unblemished, under the smile of God, "the morning stars sang together, and all the sons of God shouted for joy." So human hearts, in sympathy with heaven, have responded to God's goodness in notes of praise. Many of the events of human history have been linked with sacred song.

The history of the songs of the Bible is full of suggestion as to the uses and benefits of music and song. Music is often perverted to serve purposes of evil, and it thus becomes one of the most alluring agencies of temptation. But, rightly employed, it is a precious gift of God, designed to uplift the thoughts to high and noble themes, to inspire and elevate the soul. As the children of Israel, journeying through the wilderness, cheered their way by the music of sacred song, so God bids his children today gladden their pilgrim life. There are few means more effective for fixing his word in the memory than repeating them in song. And such song has wonderful power. It has power to subdue rude and uncultivated natures; power to quicken thought and to awaken sympathy, to promote harmony of action, and to banish the gloom and foreboding that destroy courage and weaken effort.

It is one of the most effective means of impressing the heart with spiritual truth. How often to the soul hard-pressed and ready to despair, memory recalls some word of God's--the long-forgotten burden of a childhood song,--and temptations lose their power, and courage and gladness are imparted to other souls!

The value of song as a means of education should never be lost sight of. Let there be singing in the home, of songs that are sweet and pure, and there will be fewer words of censure, and more of cheerfulness and hope and joy. Let there be singing in the schools, and the pupils will be drawn closer to God, to their teachers, and to one another.

As a part of religious service, singing is as much an act of worship as is prayer. Indeed, many a song is prayer. If the child is taught to realize this, he will think more of the meaning of the words he sings, and will be more susceptible to their power.

As our Redeemer leads us to the threshold of the Infinite, flushed with the glory of God, we may catch the themes of praise and thanksgiving from the heavenly choir round about the throne; and as the echo of the angels' song is awakened in our earthly homes, hearts will be drawn closer to the heavenly singers. Heaven's communion begins on earth. We learn here its keynote.

Mrs. E. G. White

April 12, 1904—Read and Heed

The world is flooded with books that might better be consumed than circulated. Books upon Indian warfare and similar topics, published and circulated as a money-making scheme, might better never be read. The heart-sickening relation of crimes and atrocities has a bewitching power over many youth, exciting in them the desire to bring themselves into notice by the most wicked deeds. There are many works more strictly historical whose influence is little better. The enormities, the cruelties, the licentious practices, portrayed in these writings, have acted as leaven in many minds, leading to the commission of similar acts. Books that delineate the satanic practises of human beings are giving publicity to evil works. The horrible details of crime and misery need not to be lived over again, and none who believe the truth for this time should act a part in perpetuating their memory.

Love stories and frivolous, exciting tales constitute another class of books that is a curse to every reader. The author may attach a good moral, and all through his work may weave religious sentiments; yet in most cases Satan is but clothed in angel robes, the more effectually to deceive and allure. The mind is affected in a great degree by that upon which it feeds. The readers of frivolous, exciting tales become unfitted for the duties lying before them. They live an unreal life, and have no desire to search the Scriptures, to feed upon the heavenly manna. The mind is enfeebled, and loses its power to contemplate the great problems of duty and destiny.

I have been instructed that the youth are exposed to the greatest peril from improper reading. Satan is constantly leading both the young and those of mature age to be charmed with worthless stories. Could a large share of the books published be consumed, a plague would be stayed that is doing a fearful work in weakening the mind and corrupting the heart. None are so confirmed in right principles as to be secure from temptation. All this trashy reading should be resolutely discarded.

Mrs. E. G. White

April 26, 1904—Lessons from the Life of Daniel—19—The Fiery Furnace—Part 2

The proud monarch was surrounded by his great men, the officers of the government, and the army that had conquered nations; and all united in applauding him as having the wisdom and power of the gods. In the midst of this imposing display stood the three youthful Hebrews, steadily persisting in their refusal to obey the king's decree. They had been obedient to the laws of Babylon, so far as these did not conflict with the claims of God; but they would not be swayed a hair's breadth from the duty they owed to their Creator.

The king's wrath knew no bounds. In the very height of his power and glory, to be thus defied by the representatives of a despised and captive race was an insult which his proud spirit could not endure. He commanded that the furnace be heated seven times hotter than was its wont. And without delay the Hebrew exiles were cast in. So furious were the flames, that the men who cast the Hebrews in were burned to death.

Suddenly the countenance of the king paled with terror. He looked intently upon the glowing flames, and, turning to his lords, in tones of alarm inquired, "Did we not cast three men bound into the midst of the fire?" The answer was, "True, O king." His voice trembling with excitement, the monarch exclaimed, "Lo, I see four men loose, walking in the midst of the fire, and they have no hurt; and the form of the fourth is like the Son of God"!

When Christ manifests himself to the children of men, an unseen Power speaks to their souls. They realize that they are in the presence of the Infinite One. Before his majesty, kings and nobles tremble, and acknowledge the living God as above every earthly power. The Hebrew captives had told Nebuchadnezzar of Christ, the Redeemer that was to come, and from the description thus given, the king recognized the form of the fourth in the fiery furnace as the Son of God.

His own greatness and dignity forgotten, Nebuchadnezzar descended from his throne, and hastened to the furnace. With remorse and shame he cried, "Ye servants of the most high God, come forth." And they obeyed, before that vast multitude showing themselves unhurt, not even the smell of fire being upon their garments. True to duty, they had been proof against the flames. Only their fetters had been burned.

"Then Nebuchadnezzar spake, and said, Blessed be the God of Shadrach, Meshach, and Abed-nego, who hath sent his angel, and delivered his servants that trusted in him, and have changed the king's word, and yielded their bodies, that they might not serve nor worship any god, except their own God."

A change passed over the multitude. The great golden image, set up with such display, was forgotten. Men feared and trembled before the living God. The king published a decree that any one speaking against the God of the Hebrews should be put to death; "because there is no other god that can deliver after this sort."

True Christian principle does not stop to weigh consequences. It does not ask, What will people think of me if I do this? or, How will it affect my worldly prospects if I do that? With singleness of purpose, the children of God desire to know what he would have them do, that their works may glorify him. The Lord has made ample provision that the hearts and lives of his followers shall be controlled by divine grace, that they may be as burning and shining lights in the world.

These faithful Hebrews possessed great natural ability; they had enjoyed the highest intellectual culture, and now occupied positions of honor; but they did not forget God. Their powers were yielded to the sanctifying influence of his grace. By their steadfast integrity, they showed forth the praises of him who had called them out of darkness into his marvelous light. In their wonderful deliverance were displayed, before that vast assembly, the power and majesty of God. Jesus stood by their side in the fiery furnace, and the glory of his presence convinced the proud king of Babylon that it could be no other than the Son of God. The light of heaven had been shining forth from Daniel and his companions, until all their associates understood the faith that ennobled their lives and beautified their characters. By the deliverance of his faithful servants, the Lord declares that he will take his stand with the oppressed, and overthrow all earthly powers that would trample upon the authority of the God of heaven.

What a lesson is here given to the faint-hearted, the vacillating, the cowardly in the cause of God! What encouragement to those who will not be turned aside from duty by threats or peril! These faithful, steadfast characters exemplify sanctification, while they have no thought of claiming the high honor. The amount of good which may be accomplished by comparatively obscure but devoted Christians, can not be estimated until the life-records shall be made known, when the judgment shall sit, and the books shall be opened.

Christ identifies his interest with this class; he is not ashamed to call them brethren. There should be hundreds, where there is now one among us, so closely allied to God, their lives so closely conformed to his will, that they would be bright and shining lights, sanctified wholly, in body, soul, and spirit.

The conflict still goes on between the children of light and the children of darkness. Those who name the name of Christ should shake off the lethargy that enfeebles their efforts, and should fulfil the momentous responsibilities that devolve upon them. All who do this may expect the power of God to be revealed in them. The Son of God, the world's Redeemer, will be represented in their words and in their works, and God's name will be glorified.

Mrs. E. G. White

July 12, 1904—The Life of Daniel—The Sabbath Test

Daniel and his companions had a conscience void of offense toward God. But this was not preserved without a struggle. What a test was brought on the three associates of Daniel, when they were required to worship the great image set up by King Nebuchadnezzar in the plain of Dura!

The three Hebrews were called upon to confess Christ in the face of the burning fiery furnace. It cost them something to do this, for their lives were at stake. These youth, imbued with the Holy Spirit, declared to the whole kingdom of Babylon their faith,--that He whom they worshiped was the only true and living God. The demonstration of their faith on the plain of Dura was a most eloquent presentation of their principles.

The lessons we may learn from the loyalty of the Hebrew captives toward God and his law, have a direct and vital bearing upon our experience in these last days. We have a confession to make different from that which we have made; and we shall have to make it under trying circumstances. In order to impress idolaters with the power and greatness of the living God, we, as his servants, must reveal our own reverence for God. We must make it manifest that he is the only object of our adoration and worship, and that no consideration, not even the preservation of life, can induce us to make the least concession to idolatry.

The vainglory and oppression seen in the course pursued by the heathen king, Nebuchadnezzar, is being and will continue to be manifested in our day. History will repeat itself. In this age the test will be on the point of Sabbath observance. The heavenly universe behold men trampling upon the law of Jehovah, making the memorial of God, the sign between him and his commandment-keeping people, a thing of naught, something to be despised, while a rival sabbath is exalted as was the great golden image in the plain of Dura. Men claiming to be Christians will call upon the world to observe this spurious sabbath that they have made. All who refuse will be placed under oppressive laws. This is the mystery of iniquity, the devising of satanic agencies, carried into effect by the man of sin.

The people of God will enter into no controversy with the world over this matter. They will simply take God's Word for their guide, and maintain their allegiance to him whose commandments they keep. They will obey the words of Jehovah: "Verily my Sabbaths ye shall keep: for it is a sign between me and you throughout your generations; that ye may know that I am the Lord that doth sanctify you. Ye shall keep the Sabbath therefore ... for a perpetual covenant."

When the Sabbath becomes the special point of controversy throughout Christendom, the persistent refusal of a small minority to yield to the popular demand will make them objects of universal execration. It will be urged that the few who stand in opposition to an institution of the church and a law of the state, ought not to be tolerated; that it is better for them to suffer than for whole nations to be thrown into confusion and lawlessness. This argument will appear conclusive; and against those who hallow the Sabbath of the fourth commandment will finally be issued a decree, denouncing them as deserving of the severest punishment, and giving the people liberty, after a certain time, to put them to death. Romanism in the Old World, and apostate Protestantism in the New, will pursue a similar course toward those who honor all the divine precepts.

The season of distress and anguish before us will require a faith that can endure weariness, delay, and hunger,--a faith that will not faint, though severely tried. Those who now exercise but little faith are in the greatest danger of falling under the power of satanic delusions and the decree to compel conscience. And even if they endure the test, they will be plunged into deeper distress and anguish in the time of trouble, because they have not made it a habit to trust in God. The lessons of faith which they have neglected, they will be forced to learn under a terrible pressure of discouragement.

We should now acquaint ourselves with God by proving his promises. Angels record every prayer that is earnest and sincere. We should rather dispense with selfish gratifications than neglect communion with God. The deepest poverty, the greatest self-denial, with his approval, is better than riches, honors, ease, and friendship without it. We must take time to pray. The youth would not be seduced into sin if they would refuse to enter any path save that upon which they could ask God's blessing.

My dear young friends, if you are called to go through a fiery furnace for Christ's sake, Jesus will be by your side. To you he declares: "When thou passest through the waters, I will be with thee; and through the rivers, they shall not overflow thee; when thou walkest through the fire, thou shalt not be burned; neither shall the flame kindle upon thee."

The threats of men sink into insignificance beside the word of the living God. Be loyal and true, and the God who walked with the three Hebrew children in the fiery furnace, who manifested himself to John on the lonely island, will be with you. His abiding presence will comfort and sustain you, and you will realize the fulfilment of the promise, "If a man love me, he will keep my words: and my Father will love him, and we will come unto him, and make our abode with him."

Mrs. E. G. White

October 11, 1904—The Power and Splendor of Babylon During Nebuchadnezzar's Reign

Nebuchadnezzar was the greatest ruler of the age in which he lived. Ezekiel spoke of him as "a king of kings" and prophesied that God would allow him to complete the destruction of Jerusalem, and that because the inhabitants of "the renowned city" of Tyre would say against Jerusalem "Aha, she is broken that was the gates of the people: she is turned unto me: I shall be replenished, now she is laid waste," God would "bring upon Tyrus Nebuchadnezzar king of Babylon," "the terrible of the nations" who would make this place "in the midst of the seas" "a desolate city" that should be "built no more." The prophet further declared: "Nebuchadnezzar king of Babylon caused his army to serve a great service against Tyrus: ... yet he had no wages, nor his army; ... therefore thus saith the Lord God: ... I have given him the land of Egypt for his labor wherewith he served against it, because they wrought for me."

The capital of Nebuchadnezzar's world-empire is spoken of by Isaiah as "Babylon, the glory of kingdoms, the beauty of the Chaldee's excellency," "the golden city;" "the lady of the kingdoms" "that dwellest upon many waters, abundant in treasures;" and by Jeremiah as "the praise of the whole earth." Jeremiah also speaks of "the broad walls of Babylon ... and her high gates;" Isaiah, of her "gates of brass."

Habakkuk describes the Babylonians as "that bitter and hasty nation, ... terrible and dreadful.... Their horses also are swifter than leopards, and are more fierce than the evening wolves." Jeremiah writes in regard to "the "mighty men of Babylon."

Nebuchadnezzar was an instrument of God's judgments. "Thus saith the Lord: ... I have made the earth, the man and the beast that are upon the ground, by my great power and by my outstretched arm, and have given it unto whom it seemed meet unto me. And now have I given all these lands into the hand of Nebuchadnezzar the king of Babylon, my servant; and the beasts of the field have I given him also to serve him. And it shall come to pass, that the nation and kingdom which will not serve the same Nebuchadnezzar the king of Babylon, and that will not put their neck under the yoke of the king of Babylon, that nation will I punish, saith the Lord, with the sword, and with the famine, and with the pestilence, until I have consumed them by his hand.

Therefore harken not ye to your prophets, nor to your diviners, nor to your dreamers, nor to your enchanters, nor to your sorcerers, which speak unto you, saying, Ye shall not serve the king of Babylon: for they prophesy a lie unto you, to remove you far from your land; and that I should drive you out, and ye should perish. But the nations that bring their neck under the yoke of the king of Babylon, and serve him, those will I let remain still in their own land, saith the Lord; and they shall till it, and dwell therein."

The vision of the great image, in which Babylon was represented as the head of gold, was given Nebuchadnezzar in order that he might have a clear understanding in regard to the end of all things earthly, and also in regard to the setting up of God's everlasting kingdom. Although in the interpretation he was declared to be "a king of kings," this was because "the God of heaven" had given him "a kingdom, power, and strength, and glory." His kingdom was universal, extending "wheresoever the children of men dwell," yet it was to be followed by three other universal kingdoms, after which "the God of heaven" would "set up a kingdom," which should "never be destroyed."

In the providence of God, Nebuchadnezzar was given ample opportunity to ascribe to the Lord the glory for the splendor of his reign. And for a time after the vision of the great image, he acknowledged God as supreme. Falling back into idolatrous habits, he was again, by the miraculous deliverance of the three Hebrews from the fiery furnace, led to acknowledge that God's "kingdom is an everlasting kingdom, and his dominion is from generation to generation." But once more the king perverted the warnings God had given him, and turned aside from the path of humility to follow the imaginations of his naturally proud heart. Thinking that his kingdom should be more extensive and powerful than any that would follow, he made great additions to the city of Babylon, and gave himself up to a life of pleasure and self-glorification. Of this time he himself says: "I Nebuchadnezzar was at rest in mine house, and flourishing in my palace."

Mrs. E. G. White

November 1, 1904—Nebuchadnezzar's Second Dream

Because Nebuchadnezzar did not continue to walk in the light he had received from heaven, he lost the holy impressions that had been made upon his mind. But God, in his mercy, gave the king another dream, to save him, if possible, from appropriating to himself the glory that belonged to the Supreme Ruler.

The dream given at this time to the king of Babylon was a very striking one. In a vision of the night he saw a great tree growing in the midst of the earth, towering to the heavens, and its branches stretching to the ends of the earth. "The leaves thereof were fair, and the fruit thereof much, and in it was meat for all: the beasts of the field had shadow under it, and the fowls of the heaven dwelt in the boughs thereof, and all flesh was fed of it."

As the king gazed upon that lofty tree, he beheld "a Watcher," even "an Holy One,"--a divine Messenger, similar in appearance to the One who walked with the Hebrews in the fiery furnace. This heavenly Being approached the tree, and in a loud voice cried:

"Hew down the tree, and cut off his branches, shake off his leaves, and scatter his fruit; let the beasts get away from under it, and the fowls from his branches: nevertheless, leave the stump of his roots in the earth, even with a band of iron and brass, in the tender grass of the field; and let it be wet with the dew of heaven, and let his portion be with the beasts in the grass of the earth: let his heart be changed from man's, and let a beast's heart be given unto him; and let seven times pass over him. This matter is by the decree of the watchers, and the demand by the word of the holy ones: to the intent that the living may know that the Most High ruleth in the kingdom of men, and giveth it to whomsoever he will, and setteth up over it the basest of men."

The king was greatly troubled by this dream. It was evidently a prediction of adversity. He repeated it to the magicians, the Chaldeans, and the soothsayers; but although the dream was very explicit, none of the wise men would attempt to interpret it. Those who neither loved nor feared God could not understand the mysteries of the kingdom of heaven. They could not approach unto the throne of him who dwelleth in light unapproachable. To them the things of God must remain mysteries.

In this idolatrous nation testimony was again borne to the fact that only the servants of God can understand the mysteries of God. In the early days of the king's acquaintance with Daniel, he had found that this man was the only one who could relieve him from perplexity; and now, in this later period of his reign, the king remembers his faithful servant of old,--a servant esteemed because of his unswerving integrity and constant faithfulness. Nebuchadnezzar knew that Daniel's wisdom was unexcelled, and that neither he nor his three fellow captives ever compromised principle in order to secure position in the court, or even to preserve life itself. The skill of his wise men proving ineffectual, the king sent for Daniel to interpret the dream.

Mrs. E. G. White

November 1, 1904—Self-Denial Boxes

Mrs. E. G. White, in speaking to the General Conference Committee at College View, Nebraska, Sept. 20, 1904, said:

"As I have considered the poverty and needs of the Southern field, I have been greatly distressed. I have earnestly desired that some method might be devised by which the work for the colored people could be sustained. One night as I was praying for this needy field, a scene was presented to me, which I will describe.

"I saw a company of men working, and asked what they were doing. One of them replied, 'We are making little boxes to be placed in the home of every family that is willing to practise self-denial, and to send of its means to help the work among the colored people of the South. Such boxes will be a constant reminder of the needs of this destitute race, and the giving of money that is saved by economy and self-denial will be an excellent education for all members of the family.'

"I have written concerning these boxes and the self-denial they will encourage, and I now ask if you will not respect the light that God has given to his people. These boxes should be used more than they have been. And let no one ever by pen or voice hinder their circulation.

"Let every mother teach her children lessons in self-denial. O, how much money we waste on useless articles in the house, on ruffles and fancy dress, and on candies and other articles we do not need! Parents, teach your children that it is wrong to use God's money in self-gratification. Tell them of the poor colored people, and their needs, and encourage them to save their pennies wherever possible, to be used in missionary work. They will gain rich experiences through the practise of self-denial, and such lessons will often keep them from acquiring habits of intemperance.

"Let the work of these self-denial boxes be carried on more than it has yet been. And do not become weary of their use. We also ask you to give of your clothing such articles as you do not need."

December 13, 1904—Nebuchadnezzar's Restoration

For seven years Nebuchadnezzar, in his degradation, was an astonishment to all his subjects. For seven years he was humbled before the world, as a punishment for ascribing to himself the glory that belonged to God. At the end of this time his reason was restored to him. Through his terrible humiliation he was brought to see his own weakness, and to acknowledge the supremacy of God.

In the book of Daniel is given the king's public confession of his restoration. We read: "At the end of the days I Nebuchadnezzar lifted up mine eyes unto heaven, and mine understanding returned unto me, and I blessed the Most High, and I praised and honored him that liveth forever, whose dominion is an everlasting dominion, and his kingdom is from generation to generation: and all the inhabitants of the earth are reputed as nothing: and he doeth according to his will in the army of heaven, and among the inhabitants of the earth: and none can stay his hand, or say to him,. What doest thou? At the same time my reason returned unto me; and for the glory of my kingdom, mine honor and brightness returned unto me; and my counselors and my lords sought unto me; and I was established in my kingdom, and excellent majesty was added unto me."

The chastening that came upon the king of Babylon wrought reformation in his heart, and transformed him in character. He now understands God's purpose in humiliating him. In this chastisement he recognizes the divine hand. Before his humiliation he was tyrannical in his dealings with others, but now the fierce, overbearing monarch is changed into a wise and compassionate ruler. Before his humiliation he defied and blasphemed the God of heaven, but now he humbly acknowledges the power of the Most High, and earnestly seeks to promote the happiness of his subjects.

At last, under the rebuke of God, the king had learned the lesson which all kings and rulers need to learn,--that true greatness consists in goodness. He acknowledged Jehovah as the living God, saying: Come, all ye that fear God, and I will make known to you what he hath done for my soul. It is now my wish that all the people of my realm shall learn what I have learned, that the God whom they should worship is not a golden image, but he who made the heavens and the earth. "I Nebuchadnezzar praise and extol, and honor the King of heaven, all whose works are truth, and his ways judgment: and those that walk in pride he is able to abase."

Thus the king upon the Babylonian throne became a witness for God, giving his testimony, warm and eloquent, from a grateful heart that was partaking of the mercy and grace, the righteousness and peace, of the divine nature. God's design that the greatest kingdom of the world should show forth his praise, was now fulfilled.

The public proclamation in which Nebuchadnezzar acknowledged his guilt and the great mercy of God in his restoration, is the last act of his life as recorded in Sacred History.

Mrs. E. G. White

January 3, 1905—The Risen Saviour

"I am the resurrection, and the life." He who had said, "I lay down my life, that I might take it again," came forth from the grave to life that was in himself. Humanity died; divinity did not die. In his divinity, Christ possessed the power to break the bonds of death. He declares that he has life in himself to quicken whom he will.

All created beings live by the will and power of God. They are recipients of the life of the Son of God. However able and talented, however large their capacities, they are replenished with life from the source of all life. He is the spring, the fountain, of life. Only he who alone hath immortality, dwelling in light and life, [could] say, "I have power to lay down my life, and I have power to take it again."

The words of Christ, "I am the resurrection, and the life," were distinctly heard by the Roman guard. The whole army of Satan heard them. And we understand them when we hear. Christ had come to give his life a ransom for many. As the Good Shepherd, he had laid down his life for the sheep. It was the righteousness of God to maintain his law by inflicting the penalty. This was the only way in which the law could be maintained, and pronounced holy, and just, and good. It was the only way by which sin could be made to appear exceeding sinful, and the honor and majesty of divine authority be maintained.

The law of God's government was to be magnified by the death of God's only begotten Son. Christ bore the guilt of the sins of the world. Our sufficiency is found only in the incarnation and death of the Son of God. He could suffer, because sustained by divinity. He could endure, because he was without one taint of disloyalty or sin. Christ triumphed in man's behalf in thus bearing the justice of punishment. He secured eternal life to men, while he exalted the law, and made it honorable.

Christ was invested with the right to give immortality. The life which he had laid down in humanity, he again took up and gave to humanity. "I am come," he says, "that they might have life, and that they might have it more abundantly." Whoso eateth my flesh, and drinketh my blood, hath eternal life; and I will raise him up at the last day." "Whosoever drinketh of the water that I shall give him shall never thirst; but the water that I shall give him shall be in him a well of water springing up into everlasting life."

All who are one with Christ through faith in him gain an experience which is life unto eternal life. "As the living Father hath sent me, and I live by the Father: so he that eateth me, even he shall live by me." He "dwelleth in me, and I in him." "I will raise him up at the last day." "Because I live, ye shall live also."

Christ became one with humanity, that humanity might become one in spirit and life with him. By virtue of this union in obedience to the word of God, his life becomes their life. He says to the penitent, "I am the resurrection, and the life." Death is looked upon by Christ as sleep,--silence, darkness, sleep. He speaks of it as if it were of little moment. "Whosoever liveth and believeth in me," he says, "shall never die." "If a man keep my saying, he shall never taste of death." "He shall never see death." And to the believing one, death is but a small matter. With him to die is but to sleep. "Them also which sleep in Jesus God will bring with him."

While the women were making known their message as witnesses of the risen Saviour, and while Jesus was preparing to reveal himself to a large number of his followers, another scene was taking place. The Roman guard had been enabled to view the mighty angel who sang the song of triumph at the birth of Christ, and hear the angels who now sang the song of redeeming love. At the wonderful scene which they were permitted to behold, they had fainted and become as dead men. When the heavenly train was hidden from their sight, they arose to their feet, and made their way to the gate of the garden as quickly as their tottering limbs would carry them. Staggering like blind or drunken men, their faces pale as the dead, they told those they met of the wonderful scenes they had witnessed. Messengers preceded them quickly to the chief priests and rulers, declaring, as best they could, the remarkable incidents that had taken place.

The guard were making their way first to Pilate, but the priests and rulers sent word for them to be brought into their presence. These hardened soldiers presented a strange appearance, as they bore testimony to the resurrection of Christ, and also of the multitude whom he brought forth with him. They told the chief priests what they had seen at the sepulcher. They had not time to think or speak anything but the truth. But the rulers were displeased with the report. They knew that great publicity had been given to the trial of Christ, by holding it at the time of the Passover. They knew that the wonderful events which had taken place--the supernatural darkness, the mighty earthquake--could not be without effect, and they at once planned how they might deceive the people. The soldiers were bribed to report a falsehood; and the priests guaranteed that if the matter should come to Pilate's ears, as it most assuredly would, they would be responsible for the action of the soldiers. They bribed Pilate to silence, and by special messengers sent the report they had prepared to every part of the country.

Mrs. E. G. White

March 28, 1905—Nebuchadnezzar's Humiliation

For many months after Nebuchadnezzar's dream in regard to his humiliation, his position was unaltered. The judgment of God lingered. The king lost confidence in the dream, and regarded it as a delusion. More proud and haughty than ever, he jested at his former fears.

About a year after the king had received the divine warning, he was walking in his palace, and thinking with pride of his power as the ruler of the greatest universal kingdom, when he exclaimed, "Is not this great Babylon, that I have built for the house of the kingdom by the might of my power, and for the honor of my majesty?"

The proud boast had scarcely left his lips when a voice from heaven announced to him that God's appointed time of judgment had come. Upon his ears fell the mandate of the Almighty: "O king Nebuchadnezzar, to thee it is spoken; The kingdom is departed from thee. And they shall drive thee from men, and thy dwelling shall be with the beasts of the field: they shall make thee to eat grass as oxen, and seven times shall pass over thee, until thou know that the Most High ruleth in the kingdom of men, and giveth it to whomsoever he will."

In a moment Nebuchadnezzar's reason was taken away, and he was placed on a level with the beasts of the field. "He was driven from men, and did eat grass as oxen, and his body was wet with the dew of heaven, till his hairs were grown like eagles' feathers, and his nails like birds' claws."

As the beasts have no knowledge of God, and therefore do not acknowledge his sovereignty, so Nebuchadnezzar had been unmindful of God and his mercies. Prosperity and popularity had led him to feel independent of God, and to use for his own glory the talent of reason that God had entrusted to him. Messages of warning were sent to him, but he heeded them not. The heavenly Watcher took cognizance of the king's spirit and actions, and in a moment stripped the proud boaster of all that his Creator had given him.

Nebuchadnezzar did not profit by the warnings he received. Only through severest discipline did he learn the lesson that the Lord, and not man, is ruler, and that God's kingdom endures forever. Only after passing through long years of humiliation did the king of Babylon learn that it was not his scepter, but the scepter of him whose kingdom is everlasting, that held supreme sway over the affairs of the nations.

Man may lift himself up in pride and boast of his power, but in an instant God can bring him to nothingness. It is Satan's work to lead men to glorify themselves with their entrusted talents. Every man through whom God works will have to learn that the living, ever-present, ever-acting God is supreme, and has lent him talents to use,--an intellect to originate; a heart to be the seat of his throne; affections to flow out in blessing to all with whom he shall come in contact; a conscience through which the Holy Spirit can convict him of sin, of righteousness, and of judgment.

God is infinitely holy, and he hates every species of iniquity. He is great in power, and he will punish the mightiest with the most depraved. He first gives to transgressors oft-repeated warnings. If the heart is hardened, if it refuses to heed the warnings given, and to accept the means of salvation, God will make men feel that as he has exalted and favored them, so he has to do with their casting down. When God has forsaken those whom he has highly favored, no earthly power can avail. God is long-suffering, not willing that any should perish; but his forbearance has a limit, and when the boundary is passed, there is no second probation. His wrath will go forth, and he will destroy without remedy.

Mrs. E. G. White

April 4, 1905—Lessons from the Life of Daniel—Self-exaltation

From the record of Nebuchadnezzar's experience we may learn how the Lord regards the spirit of self-exaltation. Had the Babylonian king heeded God's warnings in regard to self-exaltation, the humiliation with which he was threatened might have been averted; but he went on with proud superiority, using the gifts of God as his own to exalt self, until he felt the humbling hand of the Almighty. Not until he had passed through seven years of shame and suffering, did the king learn that God is able to abase those who walk in pride and self-exaltation. Nebuchadnezzar's experience is a warning to all.

The Creator has given abundant evidence that his power is unlimited, that he can establish kingdoms, and overturn kingdoms. He upholds the world by the word of his power. He made the night, marshaling the shining stars in the firmament. He calls them all by name. The heavens declare the glory of God, and the firmament showeth his handiwork, showing man that this little world is but a jot in God's creation. Should every member of the human family refuse to acknowledge him, saying, There is no God, he would not want for subjects to proclaim his power.

The inhabitants of the unfallen worlds look with pity and reproach on man's pride and self-importance. The wealthy and the honored of the world are not the only ones who glorify self. Many who profess to revere God, talk of their wisdom and their might. They act as if God is under obligations to them, as if he can not carry on his work without their aid. Let such gaze into the starry heavens, and with admiration and awe study the marvelous works of God. Let them think of the wisdom he displays in maintaining perfect order in the vast universe, and of the little reason that man has to boast of his attainments.

All that man has--life, the means of existence, happiness, and other blessings unnumbered that come to him day by day--is from the Father above. Man is a debtor for all he proudly claims as his own. God gives his precious gifts, that they may be used in his service. Every particle of the glory of man's success belongs to God. It is his manifold wisdom that is displayed in the works of men, and to him belongs the praise.

Every moment the Lord's grace is exercised in behalf of human agencies. Unless the Lord keeps the heart, we are overcome by the enemy. It is Satan who perverts man's powers, and fills the heart with thoughts of self-exaltation. To fear the Lord in holiness, to walk before him in contrition and humility, is the only way to true exaltation, for nations and for individuals; while to walk boastingly and proudly, in presumptuousness and transgression, ends in speedy humiliation, defeat, and ruin.

Men may forget, men may deny their wrong course of action, but a record of it is kept in the book of remembrance, and in the great day of judgment, unless men repent and walk humbly before God, they will meet this dread record just as it stands. If they repent, and keep the fear of the Lord before them, their sins will be blotted out.

God is infinitely gracious. He waits for us to return to him by heart-humiliation, confession, and repentance. He will have mercy on all, and will save all who cherish contrition of soul. The renunciation of self-confidence prepares the way for true faith in God. The moment human beings renounce their selfishness, covetousness, and idolatry, that moment God becomes their all-sufficient Helper. In the infinite fulness of his grace he imparts, for time and for eternity, whatever is needed for the souls and bodies of those who believe.

O that those upon whom light has been shining in rich abundance, might become humble, faithful men and women! O that they would, like the king of Babylon, raise their voices in recognition of God, revealing that they have come to their senses, and that their heart of stone has been changed to a heart of flesh! Then they might form the cabinet of God, being made, in truth, guardians of sacred trusts.

Mrs. E. G. White

December 26, 1905—Unto You a Saviour

The King of glory stooped low to take humanity. Rude and forbidding were his earthly surroundings. His glory was veiled, that the majesty of his outward form might not become an object of attraction. He shunned all outward display. Riches, worldly honor, and human greatness can never save a soul from death; Jesus purposed that no attraction of an earthly nature should call men to his side. Only the beauty of heavenly truth must draw those who would follow him.

The angels had wondered at the glorious plan of redemption. They watched to see how the people of God would receive his Son, clothed in the garb of humanity. Angels came to the land of the chosen people. Other nations were dealing in fables, and worshiping false gods. To the land where the glory of God had been revealed, and the light of prophecy had shone, the angels came. They came unseen to Jerusalem, to the appointed expositors of the Sacred Oracles, and the ministers of God's house. Already the forerunner, John the Baptist, was born, his mission attested by miracle and prophecy. The tidings of his birth and the wonderful significance of his mission had been spread abroad. Yet Jerusalem was not preparing to welcome her Redeemer.

With amazement the heavenly messengers beheld the indifference of that people whom God had called to communicate to the world the light of sacred truth. The Jewish nation had been preserved as a witness that Christ was to be born of the seed of Abraham and of David's line; yet they knew not that his coming was now at hand. In the temple the morning and the evening sacrifice daily pointed to the Lamb of God; yet even here was no preparation to receive him. The priests and teachers of the nation knew not that the greatest event of the ages was about to take place. They rehearsed their meaningless prayers, and performed the rites of worship to be seen by men, but in their strife for riches and worldly honor they were not prepared for the revelation of the Messiah. The same indifference pervaded the land of Israel. Hearts, selfish and world-engrossed, were untouched by the joy that thrilled all heaven. Only a few were longing to behold the Unseen. To these heaven's embassy was sent.

Angels attend Joseph and Mary as they journey from their home in Nazareth to the city of David. But in the city of their royal line, they are unrecognized and unhonored. Weary and homeless, they traverse the entire length of the narrow street, from the gate of the city to the eastern extremity of the town, vainly seeking a resting-place for the night. There is no room for them at the crowded inn. In a rude building where the beasts are sheltered, they at last find refuge, and here the Redeemer of the world is born.

Men know it not, but the tidings fill heaven with rejoicing. With a deeper and more tender interest the holy beings from the world of light are drawn to earth. The whole world is brighter for his presence. Above the hills of Bethlehem are gathered an innumerable throng of angels. They wait the signal to declare the glad news to the world. Had the leaders in Israel been true to their trust, they might have shared the joy of heralding the birth of Jesus. But now they are passed by.

In the fields where the boy David had led his flock, shepherds were still keeping watch by night. Through the silent hours they talked together of the promised Saviour, and prayed for the coming of the King to David's throne. "And, lo, the angel of the Lord came upon them, and the glory of the Lord shone round about them: and they were sore afraid. And the angel said unto them, Fear not: for, behold, I bring you good tidings of great joy, which shall be to all people. For unto you is born this day in the city of David a Saviour, which is Christ the Lord." "Heaven is love." Wonder, O heavens! and be astonished, O earth!

At these words, visions of glory fill the minds of the listening shepherds. The Deliverer has come to Israel! Power, exaltation, triumph, are associated with his coming. But the angel must prepare them to recognize their Saviour in poverty and humiliation. "This shall be a sign unto you," he says, "ye shall find the babe wrapped in swaddling clothes, lying in a manger."

The heavenly messenger had quieted their fears. He had told them how to find Jesus. With tender regard for their human weakness, he had given them time to become accustomed to divine radiance. Then the joy and glory could no longer be hidden. The whole plain was lighted up with the bright shining of the hosts of God. Earth was hushed, and heaven stooped to listen to the song.--"Glory to God in the highest, And on earth peace, good will toward men."

O that today the human family could recognize that song! The declaration then made, the note then struck, will swell till the close of time, and resound to the ends of the earth. When the Sun of Righteousness shall arise, with healing in his wings, that song will be re-echoed by the voice of a great multitude, as the voice of many waters, saying, "Alleluia, for the Lord God omnipotent reigneth."

Mrs. E. G. White

August 14, 1906—A Solemn Message to Our Youth

In connection with the petition of Christ, "Sanctify them through thy truth: thy word is truth," I felt impelled by the Spirit of God to appeal to the youth to study the Word. Let every one covenant with God to study the Word. Dear youth, cease to read the magazines containing stories. Put away every novel. In the days of Paul, those who were converted at Ephesus burned their magical books. We would do well to clear our houses of all the story magazines and the publications containing ridiculous pictures--representations originated by satanic agencies. The youth can not afford to poison their minds with such things. "What is the chaff to the wheat?" Let every one who claims to be a follower of Christ read only that which is true and of eternal value.

We must prepare ourselves for most solemn duties. A world is to be saved. The work is advancing in a most marvelous manner in foreign lands; and even within the shadow of our doors there are many, many opportunities for communicating to others the saving truths of the third angel's message. Publications are to be distributed like the leaves of autumn. This is the message that has been coming to us from the Lord for many years. In view of the great work to be done, how can any one afford to waste precious time and God-given means in doing those things that are not for his best good or for the glory of God? The Scriptures are to be studied diligently and are to be made the man of our counsel. None can afford to neglect this source of strength and blessing.

While in Mountain View, I was instructed, as God's messenger, to appeal to the youth connected with our institutional work. This message is applicable to all young men and young women who claim to be Sabbath-keepers, and especially to those who are laboring in our institutions:

Dear youth, there is great need of your examining yourselves. Many perished in the fearful calamity at San Francisco. How many who were destroyed by that awful earthquake were prepared for death? How many who are still alive will be admonished? None of us can foretell where the next destructive earthquake may be permitted to come. Who are prepared? ...

Let none begin to believe that amusements are essential, and that a careless disregard of the Holy Spirit during hours of selfish pleasure, is to be looked upon as a light matter. God will not be mocked. Let every young man, every young woman, consider: "Am I prepared today for my life to close? Have I the heart preparation that fits me to do the work which the Lord has given me to do?"

Every youth should make God's Word his guide, and daily gather from the Word the instruction given. If some refuse to be guided by this instruction, they are sowing seeds that the enemy has placed in their hands, and they will not care to reap the harvest. In view of the abundant opportunity given every one to walk in the light of God's Word, is it not sad to think that some are choosing their own way of careless pleasure?

Every talent of influence is to be sacredly cherished and used for the purpose of gathering souls to Christ. Young men and young women should not think that their sports, their evening parties and musical entertainments, as usually conducted, are acceptable to Christ.

Light has been given me, again and again, that all our gatherings should be characterized by a decided religious influence. If our young people would assemble to read and understand the Scriptures, asking, "What shall I do that I may have eternal life?" and then place themselves unitedly upon the side of truth, the Lord Jesus would let his blessing come into their hearts.

O that every church-member, every worker in our institutions, might realize that this life is a school in which to prepare for examination by the God of heaven, with regard to purity, cleanness of thought, unselfishness of action! Every word and act, every thought, is recorded on the record books of heaven.

To all, old and young, the word of the Lord is: Let the truth of God be inwrought in mind and soul. Let your prayer be, "O Lord, preserve my soul, that I shall not dishonor thee." Let your prayers ascend to God, that he may sanctify the soul in thought, in word, in spirit, in every transaction. Plead with God that not one thread of selfishness shall be woven into the fabric of your character. Let the prayer be offered: "Sanctify my heart through the truth. Let thy angels keep my soul in strict integrity. Let my mind be impressed with the simple, searching maxims in thy Word, given to guide me in this life as a preparation for the future, eternal life."

It is through the power and prevalence of truth that we must be sanctified, and elevated to the true dignity of the standard set forth in the Word. The way of the Lord can be learned only through most careful obedience to his Word. Study the Word.

Mrs. E. G. White

November 13, 1906—Jerusalem Destroyed by Titus

For forty years after the doom of Jerusalem had been pronounced by Christ himself, the Lord delayed his judgments upon the city and the nation. Wonderful was the long-suffering of God toward the rejecters of his gospel and the murderers of his Son; but this long-suffering only confirmed the Jews in their stubborn impenitence.

Terrible were the calamities that fell upon Jerusalem when the siege was resumed by Titus. The city was besieged at the time of the Passover, when millions of Jews were assembled within its walls. Their stores of provision, which if carefully preserved would have supplied the inhabitants for years, had previously been destroyed through the jealousy and revenge of the contending factions, and now all the horrors of starvation were experienced. So fierce were the pangs of hunger, that men would gnaw the leather of their belts and sandals and the covering of their shields.

Natural affection seemed to have been destroyed. Husbands robbed their wives, and wives their husbands. Children would be seen snatching the food from the mouths of their aged parents. "The hands of the pitiful women have sodden their own children: they were their meat in the destruction of the daughter of my people."

The Roman leaders endeavored to strike terror to the Jews, and thus cause them to surrender. Those prisoners who resisted when taken were scourged, tortured, and crucified before the wall of the city. Hundreds were daily put to death in this manner, and the dreadful work continued until, along the valley of Jehoshaphat and at Calvary, crosses were erected in so great numbers that there was scarcely room to move among them.

Titus would willingly have put an end to the fearful scene, and thus have spared Jerusalem the full measure of her doom. He was filled with horror as he saw the bodies of the dead lying in heaps in the valleys. Like one entranced, he looked from the crest of Olivet upon the magnificent temple, and gave command that not one stone of it be touched. Before attempting to gain possession of this stronghold, he made an earnest appeal to the Jewish leaders not to force him to defile the sacred place with blood. If they would come forth and fight in any other place, no Roman should violate the sanctity of the temple. In vain were the efforts of Titus to save the temple; One greater than he had declared that not one stone was to be left upon another.

The blind obstinacy of the Jewish leaders, and the detestable crimes perpetrated within the besieged city, excited the horror and indignation of the Romans, and Titus at last decided to take the city by storm. He determined, however, that if possible, it should be saved from destruction. But his commands were disregarded. After he had retired to his tent at night, the Jews, sallying from the temple, attacked the soldiers without. In the struggle a firebrand was flung by a soldier through an opening in the porch, and immediately the cedar-lined chambers about the holy house were in a blaze. Titus rushed to the place, followed by his generals and legionaries, and commanded the soldiers to quench the flames. His words were unheeded. In their fury the soldiers hurled blazing brands into the chambers adjoining the temple, and then with their swords they slaughtered in great numbers those who had found shelter there. Blood flowed down the steps like water.

It was an appalling spectacle to the Roman; what was it to the Jew? The whole summit of the hill which commanded the city blazed like a volcano. One after another the buildings fell in, with a tremendous crash, and were swallowed up in the fiery abyss. The roofs of cedar were like sheets of flame; the gilded pinnacles shone like spikes of red light; the gate towers sent up tall columns of flame and smoke. The neighboring hills were lighted up; and dark groups of people were seen watching in horrible anxiety the progress of the destruction; the walls and heights of the upper city were crowded with faces, some pale with the agony of despair, others scowling unavailing vengeance. The shouts of the Roman soldiery as they ran to and fro, and the howlings of the insurgents who were perishing in the flames, mingled with the roaring of the conflagration and the thundering sound of the falling timbers. The echoes of the mountains replied or brought back the shrieks of the people on the heights; all along the walls resounded screams and wailings; men who were expiring with famine rallied their remaining strength to utter a cry of anguish and desolation. The number of the slain exceeded that of the slayers.

After the destruction of the temple, the whole city fell into the hands of the Romans. The leaders of the Jews forsook their impregnable towers, and Titus found them solitary. He gazed upon them in amazement, and declared that God had given them into his hands.

The horrible cruelties enacted in the destruction of Jerusalem are a demonstration of Satan's vindictive power over those who yield to his control. God does not stand toward the sinner as an executor of the sentence against transgression; but he leaves the rejecters of his mercy to themselves, to reap that which they have sown. The destruction of Jerusalem is a solemn warning to all who are trifling with the offers of divine grace, and resisting the pleadings of divine mercy.

Mrs. E. G. White

January 1, 1907—Privileges and Opportunities of the Youth—Written for the Young People's Day

"I have written unto you, young men, because ye are strong, and the word of God abideth in you, and ye have overcome the wicked one. Love not the world, neither the things that are in the world. If any man love the world, the love of the Father is not in him. For all that is in the world, the lust of the flesh, and the lust of the eyes, and the pride of life, is not of the Father, but is of the world. And the world passeth away, and the lust thereof; but he that doeth the will of God abideth forever."

This exhortation is addressed especially to the young. Their youth does not excuse them from responsibility. They are strong, and are not worn down with the cares and the weight of years; their affections are ardent, and if they withdraw them from the world, and place them upon Christ and heaven, doing the will of God, they will have a hope of the better life that is enduring, and will be crowned at last with glory, honor, and immortality.

It is an alarming fact that the love of the world predominates in the minds of the young as a class. Many conduct themselves as if the precious hours of probation, while mercy lingers, were one grand holiday, and they were placed in the world merely for their own amusement, to be gratified with a continual round of excitement. They find their pleasures in the world, and in the things of the world, and are strangers to the Father and the graces of his Spirit. Many are reckless in their conversation. They choose to forget that by their words they are to be justified or condemned. God is dishonored by the frivolity and the empty, vain talking and laughing that characterize the life of many of our youth.

I have seen Satan as a wily, vigilant foe, intent upon leading the youth to follow a course of action entirely contrary to that which God would approve. The enemy well knows that there is no class who can do as much good as young men and young women consecrated to God's service. He makes special efforts to lead them to find happiness in worldly amusements, and to justify themselves by endeavoring to show that these amusements are harmless, innocent, and even important for health. He presents the path of holiness as difficult, while the paths of worldly pleasure are strewn with flowers. In false and flattering colors, he arrays the world with its pleasures before the youth. But the pleasures of earth will soon come to an end, and that which is sown must also be reaped. Are personal attractions, ability, or talents too valuable to devote to God, the author of our being, him who watches over us every moment? Are our qualifications too precious to devote to God?

The youth often urge that they need something to enliven and divert the mind. The Christian's hope is just what is needed. Religion will prove to the believer a comforter, a sure guide to the Fountain of true happiness. The young should study the Word of God, giving themselves to meditation and prayer. They will find that their spare moments can not be better employed. Wisdom's "ways are ways of pleasantness, and all her paths are peace."

Titus exhorts the youth to sobriety: "Young men likewise exhort to be soberminded. In all things showing thyself a pattern of good works; in doctrine showing uncorruptness, gravity, sincerity, sound speech that can not be condemned; that he that is of the contrary part may be ashamed, having no evil thing to say of you."

I entreat the youth, for their souls' sake, to heed the exhortation of the apostle. All these gracious instructions, warnings, and reproofs will be either a savor of life unto life or of death unto death.

The young are naturally inclined to feel that not much responsibility, caretaking, or burden-bearing is expected of them. But upon every one rests the obligation to reach the Bible standard. The light that shines forth in privileges and opportunities, in the ministry of the word, in counsels, warnings, and reproofs, will perfect character, or will condemn the careless. This light is to be cherished by the young as well as by those who are older. Who will now take their stand for God, determined to give his service the first-place in their lives? Who will be burden-bearers?

"Remember now thy Creator in the days of thy youth." Jesus desires the service of those who have the dew of youth upon them. He wants them to be heirs of immortality. They may grow up into noble manhood and womanhood, notwithstanding the moral pollution that abounds, that corrupts so many of the youth at an early age. They may be free in Christ; the children of light, not of darkness. God calls upon every young man and young woman to renounce every evil habit, to be diligent in business, fervent in spirit, serving the Lord. They need not remain in indolence, making no effort to overcome wrong habits or to improve the conduct. The sincerity of their prayers will be proved by the vigor of the effort they make to obey God's commands. At every step they may renounce evil habits and associations, believing that the Lord, by the power of his Spirit, will give them strength to overcome.

Individual, constant, united efforts will be rewarded by success. Those who desire to do a great deal of good in our world must be willing to do it in God's way, by doing little things. He who wishes to reach the loftiest heights of achievement by doing something great and wonderful, will fail of doing anything.

Steady progress in a good work, the frequent repetition of one kind of faithful service, is of more value in God's sight than the doing of one great work, and wins for the youth a good report, giving character to their efforts. Those who are true and faithful to their divinely appointed duties, are not fitful, but steadfast in purpose, pressing their way through evil, as well as good, reports. They are instant in season and out of season.

The youth can do good in laboring to save souls. God holds them accountable for the use they make of the talents entrusted to them. Let those who claim to be sons and daughters of God aim at a high standard. Let them use every faculty God has given them.

The youth who are consecrated to God sway a mighty influence for good. Preachers or laymen advanced in years, can not have one half the influence for good upon the young that the youth, if devoted to God, can have upon their associates. They ought ever to remember that upon them rests the solemn responsibility of doing all they can to save their fellow mortals, even at a sacrifice of pleasure and natural desires. Their time, their means, their influence,--all that they have and are should be consecrated to God.

Those who have really tasted the sweets of redeeming love will not, can not, rest, until all with whom they associate are made acquainted with the plan of salvation. The young should inquire, "Lord, what wilt thou have me to do? How can I honor and glorify thy name upon the earth?"

Souls are perishing all around us, and what are you doing, my young friends, to win souls to Christ? O that you would use you[r] powers of mind in seeking to approach sinners, so that you might win even one soul to the path of righteousness! What a thought! One soul to praise God through eternity! One soul to enjoy happiness and eternal life! One gem in your crown, to shine forever and ever! But you may be able, by the grace of Christ, to win more than one from sin to holiness, and your reward will be great in the kingdom of heaven. Through the prophet Daniel the Lord declares that those who turn many to righteousness shall shine as the stars forever and ever.

Upon the youth there rests grave responsibilities. God expects much from the young men who live in this generation of increased light and knowledge. He desires to use them in dispelling the error and superstition that cloud the minds of many. They are to discipline themselves by gathering up every jot and tittle of knowledge and experience. God holds them responsible for the opportunities given them. The work before them is waiting for their earnest efforts, that it may be carried forward from point to point as the time demands. If the youth will consecrate mind and heart to the Lord's service, they may reach a high standard of efficiency and usefulness. This is the standard that the Lord expects the youth to attain. To do less than this is to refuse to make the most of God-given opportunities. This will be looked upon as treason against God,--a failure to work for the good of humanity.

What are you doing, dear youth, to make known to others how important it is to take the Word of God for a guide, to keep the commandments of Jehovah? Are you by precept and example declaring that it is only by obedience to the Word of God that men can be saved? If you will do what you can, you will be a blessing to others. As you labor according to the best of your ability, ways and opportunities will open before you to do more.

Upon us God has bestowed great and precious gifts. He has given us light and a knowledge of his will, so that we need not err or walk in darkness. To be weighed in the balances and found wanting in the day of final settlement and rewards will be a fearful thing, a mistake that can never be corrected. Shall the book of God be searched in vain for our names?

There is no happiness or safety except in the fear of the Lord. My dear young friends, morning and evening let your prayers go up from unfeigned lips that the Holy Spirit may take possession of your hearts and keep you from the seductive influences of the world. Work for Jesus; stand up for Jesus; and he will stand up for you in the day of God's judgment.

Mrs. E. G. White

August 20, 1907—Importance of Immediate Preparation for Service

Now, as never before, the great and wonderful work of this message is to be carried on. Our periodicals are to be distributed by men and women in all stations and walks in life. Young and old are to act a part. We have, as it were, been asleep regarding this matter. Let every one professing the name of Christ act a part in sending forth the message, "The end of all things is at hand, prepare to meet thy God." Our publications should go everywhere. The circulation of our periodicals should be greatly increased.

It is our duty now to employ every possible means to help in the proclamation of the truth. We are to work as we have never worked before. The Lord is coming very soon, and we are entering into scenes of calamity. Satanic agencies, though unseen, are working to destroy human life. Now is our time to work with vigilance. Our books and papers are to be brought to the notice of the people; the gospel of present truth is to be given to our cities without delay. We need to arouse to our duties.

Just now, when people are thinking seriously, literature on the meaning of the signs of the times, wisely circulated, will have a telling effect in behalf of the truth. God's judgments are abroad in the land. Now is our opportunity to make known the truth to them.

The Lord is soon coming. In fire, in flood and earthquake, he is warning the inhabitants of this earth of his soon approach. We have no time to lose. We must make more determined efforts to lead the people of the world to see that the time of judgment is near at hand. Carefully prepared literature on the significance of the scenes we are now witnessing is to be circulated everywhere.

O, if our people would feel as they should the responsibility resting upon them to give the last message of mercy to the world, what a wonderful work would be done! A thousand times more work for God might be accomplished if all his children would fully consecrate themselves to him, using their talents aright.

Mrs. E. G. White

September 10, 1907—Lessons in Economy and Self-Denial

Much might be said to the young people regarding their privilege to help the cause of God by learning lessons of economy and self-denial. Many think that they must indulge in this pleasure and that, and in order to do this, they accustom themselves to live up to the full extent of their income. God wants us to do better in this respect. We sin against ourselves when we are satisfied with enough to eat and drink and wear. God has something higher than this before us. When we are willing to put away our selfish desires, and give the powers of heart and mind to the work of the cause of God, heavenly agencies will co-operate with us, making us a blessing to humanity.

Even though he may be poor, the youth who is industrious and economical can save a little for the cause of God. When I was only twelve years old, I knew what it was to economize. With my sister I learned a trade, and although we would earn only twenty-five cents a day, from this sum we were able to save a little to give to missions. We saved little by little until we had thirty dollars. Then when the message of the Lord's soon coming came to us, with a call for men and means, we felt it a privilege to hand over the thirty dollars to father, asking him to invest it in tracts and pamphlets to send the message to those who were in darkness.

It is the duty of all who touch the work of God to learn economy in the use of time and money. Those who indulge in idleness reveal that they attach little importance to the glorious truths committed to us. They need to be educated in habits of industry, and to learn to work with an eye single to the glory of God.

Deny Self and Improve Talent

Those who have not good judgment in the use of time and money, should advise with those who have had experience. With the money that we had earned at our trade, my sister and I provided ourselves with clothes. We would hand our money to mother, saying, "Buy, so that after we have paid for our clothing, there will be something left to give for missionary work." And she would do this, thus encouraging in us a missionary spirit.

The giving that is the fruit of self-denial, is a wonderful help to the giver. It imparts an education that enables us more fully to comprehend the work of Him who went about doing good, relieving the suffering, and supplying the needs of the destitute. The Saviour lived not to please himself. In his life there was no trace of selfishness. Though in a world that he himself had created, he claimed no part of it as his home. "Foxes have holes, and the birds of the air have nests," he said; "but the Son of man hath not where to lay his head."

If we make the best use of our talents, the Spirit of God will continually lead us to greater efficiency. To the man who had faithfully traded with his talents the Lord said, "Well done, good and faithful servant; thou hast been faithful over a few things, I will make thee ruler over many things: enter thou into the joy of thy Lord." The one-talented man was also expected to do his best. Had he traded with his lord's goods, the Lord would have multiplied the talent.

To every man God has given his work, "according to his several ability." God has the measure of our ability, and knows just what to lay upon us. Of the one who is found faithful, the command is given, Entrust him with greater responsibility. If he proves faithful to that trust, the word is given again, Trust him with still more. Thus through the grace of Christ he grows to the full measure of a man in Christ Jesus.

Have you only one talent? Put it out to the exchangers, by wise investment increasing it to two. Do with your might what your hands find to do. Use your talent so wisely that it will fulfil its appointed mission. It will be worth everything to you to hear the words spoken to you at last, "Well done." But only to those who have done well, will the "Well done" be spoken.

No Time to Lose

Young men and women, you have no time to lose. Seek earnestly to bring solid timbers into your character building. We beseech you for Christ's sake to be faithful. Seek to redeem the time. Consecrate yourselves every day to the service of God, and you will find that you do not need many holidays to spend in idleness, nor much money to spend in self-gratification. Heaven is watching for those who are seeking to improve and to become molded to the likeness of Christ. When the human agent submits to Christ, the Holy Spirit will accomplish a great work for him.

Every true, self-sacrificing worker for God is willing to spend and be spent for the sake of others. Christ says, "He that loveth his life shall lose it; and he that hateth his life in this world shall keep it unto life eternal." By earnest, thoughtful efforts to help where help is needed, the true Christian shows his love for God and for his fellow beings. He may lose his life in service; but when Christ comes to gather his jewels to himself, he will find it again.

Ellen G. White.

September 24, 1907—Lessons from the Life of Daniel—A Warfare against Intemperance

No young man or woman could be more sorely tempted than were Daniel and his companions. To these four Hebrew youth were apportioned wine and meat from the king's table. But they chose to be temperate. They saw that perils were on every side, and that if they resisted temptation, they must make most decided efforts on their part, and trust the results with God. The youth who desire to stand as Daniel stood must exert their spiritual powers to the very utmost, cooperating with God, and trusting wholly in the strength that he has promised to all who come to him in humble obedience.

There is a constant warfare to be maintained between virtue and vice. The discordant elements of the one, and the pure principles of the other, are at work, striving for the mastery. Satan is approaching every soul with some form of temptation on the point of indulgence of appetite. Intemperance is fearfully prevalent. Look where we will, we behold this evil fondly cherished. In spite of the efforts made to control it, intemperance is on the increase. We can not be too earnest in seeking to hinder its progress, to raise the fallen, and to shield the weak from temptation. With our feeble human hands we can do but little, but we have an unfailing Helper. We must not forget that the arm of Christ can reach to the very depths of human woe and degradation. He can give us help to conquer even the terrible demon of intemperance.

Our Youth and Intemperance

There is no class of persons capable of accomplishing more in the warfare against intemperance than are God-fearing youth. In this age the young men in our cities should unite as an army, firmly and decidedly to set themselves against every form of selfish, health-destroying indulgence. What a power they might be for good! How many they might save from becoming demoralized in the halls and gardens fitted up with music and other attractions to allure the youth! Intemperance and profanity and licentiousness are sisters. Let every God-fearing youth gird on the armor and press to the front. Put your names on every temperance pledge presented. Thus you lend your influence in favor of signing the pledge, and induce others to sign it. Let no weak excuse deter you from taking this step. Work for the good of your own souls and for the good of others.

The young men and women who claim to believe the truth for this time can please Jesus only by uniting in an effort to meet the evils that have, with seductive influence, crept in upon society. They should do all they can to stay the tide of intemperance now spreading with demoralizing power over the land. Realizing that intemperance has open, avowed supporters, those who honor God take their position firmly against the tide of evil by which both men and women are being swiftly carried to perdition.

The followers of Jesus will never be ashamed to practise temperance in all things. Then why should any young man blush with shame to refuse the wine cup or the foaming mug of beer? A refusal to indulge perverted appetite is an honorable act. The sin is unmanly; to indulge in injurious habits of eating and drinking is weak, cowardly, debasing; but to deny perverted appetite is strong, brave, noble. In the Babylonian court, Daniel was surrounded by allurements to sin, but by the help of Christ he maintained his integrity. He who can not resist temptation, when every facility for overcoming has been placed within his reach, is not registered in the books of heaven as a man.

Dare to be a Daniel. Dare to stand alone. Have courage to do the right. A cowardly and silent reserve before evil associates, while you listen to their devices, makes you one with them. "Come out from among them, and be ye separate, saith the Lord, and touch not the unclean thing; and I will receive you, and will be a Father unto you, and ye shall be my sons and daughters."

Moral Courage Required

At all times and on all occasions it requires moral courage to adhere to the principles of strict temperance. We may expect that by following such a course we shall surprise those who do not totally abstain from all stimulants; but how are we to carry on the work of reform if we conform to the injurious habits and practises of those with whom we associate?

The holy intelligences of heaven watch the conflict going on between the tempter and the tempted. If the tempted turn from temptation, and in the strength of Jesus conquer, angels rejoice; for Satan has lost in the conflict. In our behalf, Christ, when weakened and suffering on account of hunger, fought the battle against appetite, and conquered Satan. In the name and strength of Jesus every youth may conquer the enemy today on the point of perverted appetite. My dear young friends, advance step by step, until all your habits shall be in harmony with the laws of life and health. He who overcame in the wilderness of temptation declares: "To him that overcometh will I grant to sit with me in my throne, even as I also overcame, and am set down with my Father in his throne."

Mrs. E. G. White

October 29, 1907—With Full Purpose of Heart

From age to age the heroes of faith have been marked by their fidelity to God; and they have been brought conspicuously before the world that their light might shine to those in darkness. Daniel and his three companions are illustrious examples of Christian heroism and devotion to principle. A brief account of the life of these four Hebrews is left on record for the encouragement of those who are brought into temptation and trial. From their experience in the court of Babylon, we may learn what God will do for those who serve him with full purpose of heart.

In the reign of Jehoiakim, Nebuchadnezzar besieged Jerusalem, and carried away "all the princes, and all the mighty men of valor, even ten thousand captives, and all the craftsmen and smiths: none remained, save the poorest sort of the people of the land."

After his return from the conquest of the Israelites, Nebuchadnezzar" spake unto Ashpenaz the master of his eunuchs, that he should bring certain of the children of Israel, and of the king's seed, and of the princes; children in whom was no blemish, but well favored, and skilful in all wisdom, and cunning in knowledge, and understanding science, and such as had ability in them to stand in the king's palace, and whom they might teach the learning and the tongue of the Chaldeans."

Among those chosen from the captives of Judah were Daniel, Hananiah, Mishael, and Azariah, "unto whom the prince of the eunuchs gave names: for he gave unto Daniel the name of Belteshazzar; and to Hananiah, of Shadrach; and to Mishael, of Meshach; and to Azariah, of Abed-nego." The Babylonian officer had an object in thus changing the names of the Hebrew youth. Anciently the name of a child stood for his character, and the names given to these children were characteristic of what it was expected they would become. They were young in years, and this change in their names it was believed would make an impression on their minds. In a little while, it was hoped, their former religion would be forgotten, and they would become in character and purpose like the Chaldean youth about them.

That they might be fully prepared for their life at court, according to Oriental custom, these youth were to be taught the learning of the Chaldeans, and for three years they were to be subjected to a thorough course of physical and intellectual discipline. They were not only to be admitted to the royal palace, but it was also provided that they should eat of the meat and drink of the wine that came from the king's table. They were appointed "a daily provision of the king's meat, and of the wine which he drank: so nourishing them three years, that at the end thereof they might stand before the king." In all this the king thought that he was showing them great honor, and was securing for them the best physical and mental development.

"But Daniel purposed in his heart that he would not defile himself with the portion of the king's meat, nor with the wine which he drank."

In purposing that he would not eat the food that the king had provided, Daniel did not desire to be singular; but he was determined to be true to God. As a true Hebrew, he could not eat the meat nor drink the wine. In the food provided for the king's table, were swine's flesh and other foods which were proclaimed unclean by the law given to Moses. Again, a portion of the food, and also of the wine, was set apart as an offering to the false gods of Babylon. According to the religious ideas of the day, this act consecrated the whole to the heathen gods. Daniel and his three brethren thought that if they should not actually partake of the king's bounty, a mere pretense of eating the food and drinking the wine, where such idolatry was practised, would be a denial of their faith. To do this would be to implicate themselves with heathenism, and to dishonor the law of God.

What They Might Have Thought

Daniel and his companions might have taken the position that because their food and drink was of the king's appointment, it was their duty to partake of it. But they did not do this. As they were brought to the test, they placed themselves fully on the side of truth and righteousness. By earnest prayer and study of the Scriptures, they were prepared to act intelligently in the matter. Flesh meat had not composed their diet in the past, and they determined that it should not come into their diet in the future. From the fate of the sons of Aaron, they knew that the use of wine would confuse their senses, that the indulgence of appetite would becloud their powers of discernment; and as wine had been prohibited to all who should engage in the service of God, they resolved that they would not partake of it. They would not defile themselves with the portion of the king's meat, nor with the wine which he drank.

The faithful youth knew not what would be the result of their decision; but though they realized that it might cost them their lives, they resolved to keep the path of strict temperance in the courts of the licentious city of Babylon.

Daniel and his companions are illustrations of what the young men of today can be. Earnest, whole-souled, these youth would be true to principle at any cost. During the early years of his captivity, Daniel was passing through an ordeal that was to familiarize him with courtly grandeur, with hypocrisy, and with paganism. A strange school indeed to fit him for a life of sobriety, industry, and faithfulness! And yet he lived uncorrupted by this atmosphere of evil.

What to Do with Temptation

To those who will do as these youth did,--close the door to temptation, deny appetite, and place themselves in right relation to God,--the Lord will manifest himself. It is the privilege of the youth today to have principles so firm that the most powerful temptations will not draw them from their allegiance. The company they keep, the principles they adopt, the habits they form, will settle the question of their usefulness in this life, and of their future eternal interests, with a certainty that is infallible.

There is also a lesson for us to learn in the demand the king of Babylon made for perfection in the youth who should stand in his courts. They must be without blemish, well favored, skilful in wisdom, cunning in knowledge, and understanding science. If an idolatrous king should demand such excellence in those who were to stand before him, should not those who have a knowledge of the true God reach perfection of character and capability in his service? Those who expect one day to stand before the throne of the God of gods and Lord of kings, should live each day in such a way that the approval of God can rest upon them. They should seek daily to remove the blemishes in character that lead to sin, and bring into their lives the perfection of character that all must reveal who have a part in the kingdom of heaven.

Character will always be tested. If Christ dwells in us, day by day and year by year, we shall grow into a noble heroism. This is our allotted task, but it can not be accomplished without help from Jesus, without resolute decision, unwavering purpose, continual watchfulness, and unceasing prayer. Each has a personal battle to fight; each must win his way through struggles and discouragements. Those who decline the struggle, lose the strength and joy of victory. No one, not even God, can make our characters noble or our lives useful unless we make the effort necessary on our part. We must put features of beauty into our lives. We must seek to expel the unlovely traits, while God works in us to will and to do of his good pleasure.

Ellen G. White.

November 12, 1907—With Full Purpose of Heart

To carry out his purpose not to defile himself with the king's food, Daniel made request of the prince of the eunuchs for a simpler diet. "Now God had brought Daniel into favor and tender love with the prince of the eunuchs." This officer saw in Daniel good traits of character. He saw that he was striving to be kind and helpful, that his words were respectful and courteous, and his manner possessed the grace of modesty and meekness. It was the good behavior of the youth that gained for him the favor and love of the prince.

But the prince of the eunuchs hesitated to grant the request of Daniel, fearing that such rigid abstinence as he proposed would cause the Hebrews to become less ruddy in health than those who ate of the king's dainties. He said to Daniel, "I fear my lord the king, who hath appointed your meat and your drink: for why should he see your faces worse liking than the children which are of your sort? then shall ye make me endanger my head to the king."

But it was not the luxuries of the king that would give to these youth a clear countenance and bright eye. It was the consciousness of having the approval of God. And Daniel knew that if he and his companions were permitted to adopt a simple diet, by the time they were called to appear before the king, the advantages of health reform would be apparent in their physical health.

Daniel pleaded for a ten days' trial. "Prove thy servants, I beseech thee, ten days," he said; "and let them give us pulse to eat, and water to drink. Then let our countenances be looked upon before thee, and the countenance of the children that eat of the portion of the king's meat: and as thou seest, deal with thy servants. So he consented to them in this matter, and proved them ten days."

When they preferred their request, the Hebrew youth knew the seriousness of their position, and by earnest prayer they braced themselves for duty and for trial. Severe criticism was passed upon them by their companions; they had to meet ridicule and abuse; but sneers could not weaken their piety. With watchfulness and prayer they guarded every avenue of temptation. They had learned the principles of true service. They were captives, lonely, and in peril; but they were in possession of a treasure of priceless worth,--unbending integrity. They feared to do wrong.

"And at the end of the ten days their countenances appeared fairer and fatter in flesh than all the children which did eat the portion of the king's meat. Thus Melzar took away the portion of their meat, and of the wine that they should drink; and gave them pulse." The simple pulse and water, which they at first requested, was thereafter the food of Daniel and his companions.

From the experience of these Hebrew children, we can learn the precious lesson that the Lord watches over those who place themselves in right relation to him and to his requirements. God regarded with approval the firmness and self-denial of these youth, and his blessing attended them. In Daniel and his companions we have an instance of the triumph of principles over temptation and indulgence of appetite. It shows us that through religious principles young men may triumph over the lusts of the flesh, and remain true to God's requirements, even though it costs them great sacrifice.

What young men and women need is Christian heroism. God's Word declares that he that ruleth his spirit is better than he that taketh a city. To rule the spirit means to keep self under discipline. The youth must not suppose that they can go on living careless and indulgent lives, seeking no preparation for the kingdom of God, and yet in time of trial be able to stand firm for the truth. They need to seek earnestly to bring into their lives the perfection that is seen in the life of the Saviour, so that when Christ shall come, they will be prepared to enter in through the gates into the city of God. God's abounding love and presence in the heart will give the power of self-control, and will mold and fashion the mind and character. The grace of Christ in the life will direct the aims and purposes and capabilities into channels that will give moral and spiritual power--power which the youth will not have to leave in this world, but which they can carry with them into the future life and retain through the eternal ages.

Mrs. E. G. White

December 31, 1907—"Them That Honor Me, I Will Honor"

"As for these four children, God gave them knowledge and skill in all learning and wisdom: and Daniel had understanding in all visions and dreams. Now at the end of the days that the king had said he should bring them in, then the prince of the eunuchs brought them in before Nebuchadnezzar. And the king communed with them; and among them all was found none like Daniel, Hananiah, Mishael, and Azariah: therefore stood they before the king. And in all matters of wisdom and understanding, that the king inquired of them, he found them ten times better than all the magicians and astrologers that were in all his realm."

God always honors the right. The most promising youth from all the lands subdued by the great conqueror had been gathered at Babylon; yet among them all, the Hebrew captives were without a rival. The erect form, the elastic step, the fair countenance, the undimmed senses, the untainted breath,--all were so many certificates of good habits, insignia of the nobility with which nature honors those who are obedient to her laws.

During the past three years the youthful Hebrews had been gaining other wisdom than the learning of the Chaldeans; God had been giving them a knowledge of himself. They had placed themselves in right relation to God, and he could trust them with a deep knowledge of eternal truths.

The habits and understanding of the youth who were not instructed by God were in accord with the knowledge that comes from idolatrous practises, and that leaves God out of its reckoning. Daniel and his companions, from the first of their experience in the king's court, were gaining a clearer comprehension, a sounder and more accurate judgment, than all the wise men of the kingdom of Babylon. They placed themselves where God could bless them. They followed rules of life that would give them strength of intellect and would gain for them the greatest possible benefit from the study of God's Word.

While faithful to his duties in the king's court, Daniel so faithfully maintained his loyalty to God, that God could honor him as his messenger to the Babylonian monarch. It was to Daniel that Nebuchadnezzar, unable to get help from his wise men, turned for an account of his forgotten dream, and an interpretation of it. Daniel and his companions sought the Lord, and to Daniel was revealed the dream and its meaning. And when he had related to the king the vision God had shown him, Nebuchadnezzar said, "Of a truth it is, that your God is a God of gods, and a Lord of kings, and a revealer of secrets, seeing thou couldst reveal this secret."

The history of Daniel and his companions has been recorded on the pages of the Inspired Word for the benefit of the youth in all succeeding ages. What men have done, men may do. If the youth will make the unreserved surrender of the will that Daniel made, God will help them as he helped Daniel. If they will appreciate the opportunities he gives for growing in understanding of him, he will give them wisdom and knowledge, and will fill their hearts with unselfishness. He will put into their minds thoughts that will inspire them with hope and courage as they seek to bring others under the sway of the Prince of Peace. They will have the co-operation of God and the angels. They will work out with carefulness the sum of their salvation, God working in them to will and to do of his good pleasure.

As Daniel studied the Word of God, his understanding became ever clearer; and as he comprehended its ennobling principles, he purposed in his heart to form a character that God could approve. He could not foresee the result of his determination to be true to God in the courts of Babylon; but he resolved that even at the loss of all things, he would preserve his integrity. And the Lord fulfilled to him the word that he has pledged, "Them that honor me I will honor."

There is wonderful encouragement in the story of Daniel for the youth who today are striving to gain knowledge. In his Word the Lord has left his children a divine instructor that will never disappoint those who seek its direction with a sincere heart. Its teachings will give a strength of character and mental development that no other book can impart. Let the student make the Word of God the chief book of study, giving all other branches of learning a secondary place. And as the heart is opened to the entrance of the Word, light from the throne of God will shine into the soul. The Word, cherished in the heart, will yield to the student a treasure of knowledge that is priceless. Its ennobling principles will stamp the character with honesty and truthfulness, temperance and integrity.

Mrs. E. G. White

February 11, 1908—New-Year Resolutions

Although in one sense the first day of a new year is no more to God than any other day, yet he often puts into the heart of his children at that time a desire to begin the new year with good resolves,--perhaps with plans to carry out some worthy enterprise,--and with purposes to depart from the wrongs of the old year, and to live the new year with new determinations.

In God's plan for his ancient people, he gave the command, "On the first day of the first month shalt thou set up the tabernacle." We have no tabernacle to set up as had the children of Israel, but we have a work of building to do, the importance of which all need to understand. "Ye are God's husbandry, ye are God's building," said the apostle. If we will work with God in the building of this tabernacle, establishing it firmly on the broad principles of heaven, then it can truly be said of us, "We are laborers together with God."

We are yet in the early part of the new year. Let this work of consecration and progression be begun without delay. Let this first part of the new year be given to the work of pruning away the branches of selfishness. Let the mind turn with clear discernment to the work of examining critically our individual course of action. It is not our privilege to measure the actions of others or criticize their failings. God has not made us the bearers of others' sins. It is with our own selves we have to do. The more thorough the work of repentance and reform in our own lives, the less we shall see to criticize in others.

We do wrong when we measure ourselves by the defects we see in others. God does not do so. He understands the circumstances of every life, and he measures the human being by the advantages that each one has had for perfecting a Christian character. He takes into consideration the opportunities the human agent has had for obtaining a knowledge of God and his truth.

He who has a true estimation of the law of God will not compare his character with the character of others, or be led into having a pharisaical opinion of himself. He will judge his life by the holy law of God. When a certain lawyer came to Christ with the question, "What shall I do to inherit eternal life?" Christ said to him, "What is written in the law? how readest thou? And he answering said, Thou shalt love the Lord thy God with all thy heart, and with all thy soul, and with all thy strength, and with all thy mind; and thy neighbor as thyself." The lawyer recognized the two great principles which underlie the law of God. Jesus said to him, "Thou hast answered right: this do, and thou shalt live."

It is for our own benefit and safety that God asks us to abandon the selfish and questionable projects, and make thorough work in cleansing the soul temple of sin. In his instruction to his disciples the Saviour shows how complete must be the work of eradication of evil. "If thy right eye offend thee," he declares, "pluck it out, and cast it from thee: for it is profitable for thee that one of thy members should perish, and not that thy whole body should be cast into hell. And if thy right hand offend thee, cut it off, and cast it from thee: for it is profitable for thee that one of thy members should perish, and not that thy whole body should be cast into hell."

The fourth chapter of Ephesians contains precious instruction for the children of God at this time. We are to make continual advancement in the perfecting of Christian character, that we may be no more "children, tossed to and fro, and carried about with every wind of doctrine, by the slight of men, and cunning craftiness, whereby they lie in wait to deceive; but speaking the truth in love, may grow up unto him in all things, which is the head, even Christ."

Mrs. E. G. White

March 3, 1908—A Preparation for Efficient Service

There are many lines in which the youth can find opportunity for helpful effort. As they organize into bands for Christian service, their co-operation will prove an assistance and encouragement. Parents and teachers, by taking an interest in the work of the young people, will be able to give them the benefit of their own larger experience, and can help to make their efforts effective for good.

In this closing work of the gospel there is a vast field to be occupied; and, more than ever before, the work is to enlist helpers from the common people. Both the youth and those older in years will be called from the field, from the vineyard, and from the workshop, and sent forth by the Master to give his message. Many of these may have had little opportunity for education; but Christ sees in them qualifications that will enable them to fulfil his purpose. If they put their hearts into the work, and continue to be learners, he will fit them to labor for him.

With such preparation as they can gain, thousands upon thousands of the youth and those older in years should be giving themselves to the work. Already many hearts are responding to the call of the Master Worker, and their numbers will increase.

All who engage in ministry are God's helping hand. There is no line of work in which it is possible for the youth to receive greater benefit. They are co-workers with the angels; rather, they are human agencies through whom the angels accomplish their mission. Angels speak through their voices, and work by their hands. And the human workers, cooperating with heavenly agencies, have the benefit of their education and experience. As a means of education, what "university course" can equal this? With such an army of workers as our youth, rightly trained, might furnish, how soon the message of a crucified, risen, and soon-coming Saviour might be carried to the world!

He who puts on the armor to war a good warfare will gain greater and still greater ability as he strives to perfect his knowledge of God, working in harmony with the plan God has laid down for the perfect development of the physical, mental, and spiritual powers.

Young men and young women, gather a stock of knowledge. Do not wait until some human examination pronounces you competent to work; but go out into the highways and hedges, and begin to work for God. Use wisely the knowledge you have. Exercise your ability with faithfulness, generously imparting the light that God gives you. Study how best to give to others light, and peace, and truth, and the many other rich blessings of heaven. Constantly improve. Keep reaching higher and still higher. It is the ability to put to the test the powers of mind and body, ever keeping eternal realities in view, that is of value now. Seek the Lord most earnestly, that you may become more and more refined, more spiritually cultured. Then you will have the very best diploma that any one can have,--the indorsement of God.

However large, however small, your talents, remember that what you have is yours only in trust. Thus God is testing you, giving you an opportunity to prove yourself true. To him you are indebted for all your capabilities. To him belong your powers of body, mind, and soul, and for him these powers are to be used. Your time, your influence, your capabilities, your skill,--all must be accounted for to him who gives all. He uses his gifts best who seeks by earnest endeavor to carry out the Lord's great plan for the uplifting of humanity, remembering always that he must be a learner, as well as a teacher.

Every church is in need of the controlling power of the Holy Spirit; and now is the time to pray for it. But in all God's work for man, he plans that man shall co-operate with him. To this end the Lord calls upon the church to have a higher piety, a more just sense of duty, a clearer realization of their obligations to their Creator. He calls upon them to be a pure, sanctified, working people. The Christian Help work is one means of bringing this about; for the Holy Spirit communicates with all who are doing God's service.

To those who have been engaged in this work, I would say, Continue to work with tact and ability. Combine medical missionary work with the proclamation of the third angel's message. A new element needs to be brought into the work. God's people must realize their great need, and take up the work that lies nearest them.

With those who engage in this work, speaking words in season and out of season, helping the needy, telling them of the wonderful love of Christ for them, the Saviour is always present, impressing the hearts of the poor and miserable and wretched. When the church accepts its God-given work, the promise is, "Thy light shall break forth as the morning, and thine health shall spring forth speedily: and thy righteousness shall go before thee; the glory of the Lord shall be thy rereward." Christ is our righteousness. He goes before us in this work, and the glory of the Lord follows.

The youth who aim to labor in the Master's vineyard must be as apprentices who are to learn a trade. They must learn to be useful in the work by doing errands for the Lord, improving opportunities for missionary labor anywhere and in any capacity. Thus they may give evidence that they possess tact and qualifications for the greatest work ever entrusted to men. They should be continually improving in mind, in manners, in speech, learning how to become successful laborers. They should cultivate tact and courtesy, and manifest the spirit of Christ. Onward and upward should be their constant endeavor.

He who is seeking to qualify himself for the sacred work of God, should be careful not to place himself on the enemy's ground, but should choose the society of those who will help him to obtain divine knowledge. So far as it is consistent, we should shun every influence that would tend to divert the mind from the work of God. Especially should those who are young in faith and experience beware that they do not in self-confidence place themselves in the way of temptation. Those who take hold of the work aright will feel the necessity of having Jesus with them at every step.

Be careful to maintain the elevated character of the missionary work. Let all connected with missions be constantly inquiring, "What am I? and what ought I to be and do?" Let all consider that they can not give to others what they do not possess themselves; therefore they should not settle down content with their natural ways and habits, seeking to make no change for the better. Paul says that he had not attained; but, he adds, "I press toward the mark." There must be constant reformation, unceasing advancement, if we would perfect a symmetrical character.

All who become efficient workers must give much time to prayer. The communication between God and the soul must be kept open, that the workers may recognize the voice of their Captain. The Bible should be diligently studied. The truth of God, like gold, is not always lying right on the surface; it is to be obtained only by earnest thought and study. This study will not only store the mind with most valuable knowledge, but will strengthen and expand the mental powers, and it will develop a true estimate of eternal things. Let the divine precepts be brought into the daily life; let the life be fashioned after God's great standard of righteousness, and the whole character will be strengthened and ennobled.

He who has appointed "to every man his work," according to his ability, will never let the faithful performance of duty go unrewarded. Every act of loyalty and faith will be crowned with special tokens of God's favor and approbation. To every worker is given the promise, "He that goeth forth and weepeth bearing precious seed, shall doubtless come again with rejoicing, bringing his sheaves with him."

Mrs. E. G. White

April 7, 1908—Knowing God

It is the privilege of the youth to have an education in the things of God. God loves them, and he will give to them a rich experience if they will deny self for Christ's sake, if they will depart from sin, and serve the Lord with full purpose of heart. By giving up worldly pleasure, by ceasing to serve self, and learning to serve the Lord, they can give to the world one of the most striking evidences that God is working through his church on the earth.

God is giving to the children and youth many opportunities of knowing his will, and of learning how to do that will. In the Sabbath-school, in the services of the church, through the study of his Word in the home and in the school, he is constantly providing ways by which they may learn what is his purpose for the youth who accept him. By an earnest study of the Word of God, dear youth, you may learn to distinguish between right and wrong, between him that serveth God and him that serveth him not. If you will put away your novel and romance, and with simplicity of heart search the Scriptures, the Lord will impress your mind with his truth, and will make you a blessing to others. You will see the converting power of God come into the church.

A faithful study of the story of Daniel and his three friends will teach the principles that underlie a strong, true character. These young men had first learned to serve God in their homes. They had there learned the meaning of true religion and what God would do for them if they remained loyal to him. When they were carried to the court of Babylon, they determined to yield up life itself rather than be untrue to God.

A severe test came to three of these youth when Nebuchadnezzar issued a proclamation, calling upon all the officers of the kingdom to assemble at the dedication of the great image, and at the sound of the musical instruments, to bow down and worship it. Should any fail of doing this, they were immediately to be cast into the midst of a burning fiery furnace. The worship of this image had been brought about by the wise men of Babylon in order to make the Hebrew youth join in their idolatrous worship. They were beautiful singers, and the Chaldean wanted them to forget their God, and accept the worship of the Babylonian idols.

The appointed day came, and at the sound of the music, the vast company that had assembled at the king's command "fell down and worshiped the golden image." But these faithful young men would not bow down.

When the men of Babylon saw that the youth would not join in the songs or bend the knee, they went to Nebuchadnezzar, saying, "O king, live forever.... There are certain Jews whom thou hast set over the affairs of the province of Babylon, Shadrach, Meshach, and Abed-nego: these men, O king, have not regarded thee: they serve not thy gods, nor worship the golden image which thou hast set up."

The king was filled with rage, and commanded that the men be brought before him. "Is it true," he inquired, "do not ye serve my gods, nor worship the golden image which I have set up?" Pointing to the fiery furnace, he reminded them of the punishment that would be theirs if they refused to obey his will.

The king decided to give them a second trial. "If ye be ready," he said, "that at what time ye hear the sound of the cornet, flute, harp, sackbut, psaltery, and dulcimer, and all kinds of music, ye fall down and worship the image which I have made, well: but if ye worship not, ye shall be cast the same hour into the midst of a burning fiery furnace." Then, with hand stretched upward in defiance, he asked, "And who is that God that shall deliver you out of my hands?"

The fearless youth replied, "O Nebuchadnezzar, we are not careful to answer thee in this matter. If it be so, our God whom we serve is able to deliver us from the burning fiery furnace, ... but if not, be it known unto thee, O king, that we will not serve thy gods, nor worship the golden image which thou hast set up."

In vain were the king's threats. He could not turn these noble men from their allegiance to the great Ruler of nations. When opportunity was again given them to yield to the king's decree, and at the sound of the music the great men and officers of the kingdom bowed in worship before the image, the three Hebrews stood erect; they would not dishonor God by engaging in idol worship. They had been obedient to the laws of Babylon so far as these did not conflict with the claims of God; but they would not be swayed a hair's breadth from the duty they owed their Creator.

Then the king commanded the furnace to be heated seven times hotter than it was wont to be heated; and when this was done, the three Hebrews were cast in. So furious were the flames, that the men who cast the Hebrews in were burned to death.

Suddenly the countenance of the king paled with terror. He looked intently into the glowing flames, and turning to his lords, in tones of alarm, he inquired, "Did not we cast three men bound into the midst of the fire?" The answer was, "True, O king." His voice trembling with excitement, the monarch exclaimed, "Lo, I see four men loose, walking in the midst of the fire, and they have no hurt; and the form of the fourth is like the Son of God."

Nebuchadnezzar knew enough of the true God through Daniel to know whose was the form of the fourth in the flames. With remorse and shame, the king cried, "Ye servants of the most high God, come forth." And as they obeyed and came forth, there was not even the smell of fire upon their garments.

God asks the youth of today to serve him with the same earnest purpose that these Hebrew youth revealed. He bids you make straight paths for your feet. He does not promise you that your Christian life will be free from trial; for the enemy will come in some form to every child of God. But in every trial you may claim the companionship of the Son of God. "Lo, I am with you alway," he declares, "even unto the end of the world." "When thou passest through the waters, I will be with thee; and through the rivers, they shall not overflow thee: when thou walkest through the fire, thou shalt not be burned; neither shall the flame kindle upon thee. For I am the Lord thy God, the holy One of Israel, thy Saviour."

Mrs. E. G. White

April 28, 1908—Wise Counsel to Youth

"I write unto you, young men," says the apostle, "because ye have overcome the wicked one." There is a work of overcoming to be done, and it is given to the youth to experience the joys of the overcomer. Into the life of every believing child of God is to be brought the work of resisting evil.

Take the promises of God, and claim them as your own. If you fail,--and you may; for older persons fail,--do not give up in discouragement, and say, The Lord has forsaken me. If you have done wrong, go to the one you have wronged, and confess your fault. Then go to the Lord, and ask his forgiveness. He will receive you; for he has promised. "if we confess our sins, he is faithful and just to forgive us our sins, and to cleanse us from all unrighteousness." "God so loved the world, that he gave his only begotten Son, that whosoever believeth in him should not perish, but have everlasting life." When Christ abides in your life, you may look to him to complete the work he has begun in you.

God will give wisdom and understanding and knowledge to the youth who seek him with sincerity of heart. He will help the student to be a power for good in the schoolroom, and outside the school to live so true a life that the world will take knowledge of him that he has been with Jesus and learned of him. He will enable the older members of the family to set a true example before the younger members, and will teach them how to seek together for perfection of character.

God wants us to be good and to do good. It is your privilege to learn of God, and then teach others what they must do to be saved. The voice is a wonderful talent. God wants you to improve this talent, that you may be a blessing to others. Learn to speak the kind and helpful and tender word. It is your privilege to break away from every form of wrong-doing. By putting away pride and selfishness and coming into right relation with God, you may begin to have heaven right here on earth. And in this work you will be laborers together with God.

Do not cease to pray. The Lord will hear the prayer of the contrite heart. Repeat the promise. "Ask, and it shall be given you; seek, and ye shall find; knock, and it shall be opened unto you." With this threefold promise God desires to impress your hearts with the assurance that if you will go to him in your need, he will surely help you. When you make an entire surrender to God, he will give you most precious thoughts, and heavenly angels will co-operate with you. The Spirit of God will give you words to speak that will touch hearts and help you to reach souls.

Satan has a great desire to ruin souls; Christ has a great desire to save them. "Come unto me all ye that labor and are heavy laden," he invites, "and I will give you rest. Take my yoke upon you, and learn of me; for I am meek and lowly in heart: and ye shall find rest unto your souls. For my yoke is easy, and my burden is light." This is a blessed invitation to lay all our perplexities at the feet of Jesus, and to rest in his love.

Take time to think of the pleasures that await those who are faithful. When this earthly pilgrimage is ended, you will have the Saviour's presence with you continually. He will lead you to behold the beautiful scenes of the earth made new. He will talk to you about the things most precious, and will teach you a fuller knowledge of his way. The education you gain in the things of God in this life will not end here. All that you gain you will take with you to the future life; and Christ, as your teacher, will continue the work of education through the eternal ages. And your love for him will broaden and deepen as you realize more fully all that his sacrifice has purchased for you.

Transgression has almost reached its limit. Confusion fills the world, and a great terror is soon to come upon human beings. The end is very near. God's people should be preparing for what is to break upon the world as an overwhelming surprise.

Our time is precious. We have but a few, very few, days of probation in which to make ready for the future, immortal life. We have no time to spend in haphazard movements. We should fear to skim the surface of the Word of God.

Mrs. E. G. White

November 3, 1908—Suffer the Children to Come

When the Saviour was on earth, he took little children in his arms, and blessed them. On one occasion the disciples would have sent these little ones away, but Jesus heard their words of rebuke, and he said to them, "Suffer the little children, and forbid them not, to come unto me: for of such is the kingdom of heaven."

In the children who were brought in contact with him, Jesus saw the men and women who should be the heirs of his grace and subjects of his kingdom, and some of whom would become martyrs for his sake. He knew that these children would listen to him, and accept him as their Redeemer far more readily than would grown-up people, many of whom were worldly wise and hard-hearted. In his teaching he came down to their level. He, the Majesty of heaven, did not disdain to answer their questions, and simplify his important lessons to meet their childish understanding. He planted in their minds the seeds of truth, which in after-years would spring up and bear fruit unto eternal life.

It is still true that children are most susceptible to the teachings of the gospel; their hearts are open to divine influences, and strong to retain the lessons received. The little children may be Christians, having an experience in accordance with their years.

It has been my privilege to see many of the young converted and baptized, some in their early childhood. In one church where I labored with my husband in our early experiences in the message, there were about fourteen children nearly of an age, who wished to be baptized. A father came to Elder White and said, "What are you going to do with these children? They say they are converted to God; but they are too young to be baptized." "No, indeed, they are not," my husband responded. "My wife can tell you a story of what a child can experience in spiritual things, if you care to hear." Then I related my own experience in conversion.

I was eleven years old when the light broke into my heart. I had pious parents, who in every way tried to make their children acquainted with their Heavenly Father. We sang the praises of God in our household. Every morning and evening we had family prayer. There were eight children in the family, and every opportunity was improved by our parents to lead us to give our hearts to Jesus.

I was not unmindful of the voice of prayer daily going up to God. These influences were working on my heart; and in my earlier years I had often sought for the peace that there is in Christ; but I could not seem to find the freedom that I desired. A terrible feeling of sadness and despair rested upon my heart. I did not think of anything that I had done to cause me to feel sad; but it seemed that I was not good enough ever to enter heaven. Such a thing seemed altogether too much for me to expect.

The mental anguish I passed through at this time was very great. I believed in an eternally burning hell; and as I thought of the wretched state of the sinner before God, I was in deep despair. I feared that I should be lost, and that I should live through eternity suffering a living death. But I learned better than this. I learned that I had a God who is altogether too merciful to perpetuate throughout eternity the lives of the beings whom he created for his glory, but who, instead of accepting the Saviour, had died unrepentant, unforgiven, and unsaved. I learned that the wicked shall be consumed as stubble, and that they shall be as ashes under our feet in the new earth; they shall be as though they had not been. There is no eternally burning hell; there are no living bodies suffering eternal torment.

But for a long time not one ray of light pierced the dark cloud of distress and despondency that was surrounding me. My sufferings were very great. Night after night, while my twin sister was sleeping, I would arise, and bow by the bedside before the Lord, and plead with him for mercy. All the words that I had any confidence to utter were, "Lord, have mercy." Such complete hopelessness would seize me that I would fall on my face with an agony of feeling that can not be described. Like the poor publican, I dared not so much as lift my eyes toward heaven.

Finally I had a dream which gave me a faint hope that I might be saved. Soon afterward I attended a prayer-meeting, and when others knelt to pray, I bowed with them tremblingly; and after two or three had prayed, I began to pray. Then the promises of God appeared to me like so many precious pearls that were to be received only by asking for them. As I prayed, the burden and agony of soul, that I had felt so long, left me, and the blessing of God came upon me like gentle dew, and I gave glory to God for what I felt. Everything was shut out from me but Jesus and glory, and I did not know what was going on around me. It seemed as if I was at the feet of Jesus, and that the light of his countenance was shining upon me in all its brightness.

Everything appeared glorious and new, and as if smiling and praising God. I seemed to be shut in with God. I was then willing to confess Jesus everywhere. The sacrifice that my Redeemer had made to save me from death and sin seemed very great. I could not dwell upon it without weeping. I experienced the peace of Christ, which the world could not give nor take away. Although I expected to live but a few months because of feeble health, my life was peaceful and happy. I clung in faith to the Lord, and he took control of me and healed me.

From this time I felt that I was the happiest being on the earth. I could see Jesus in everything. How I loved him! How precious he was to me! I felt that I must reveal his loveliness to my companions, and I began at once to work for the young.

I arranged meetings with my young friends, some of whom were considerably older than myself, and a few were married persons. A number of them were vain and thoughtless; my experience sounded to them like an idle tale, and they did not heed my entreaties. But I determined that my efforts should never cease till these dear souls, for whom I had so great an interest, yielded to God. Several entire nights were spent by me in earnest prayer for those for whom I was so earnestly laboring.

Some of these attended from curiosity to know what I had to say; others thought me beside myself to be so persistent in my efforts, especially when they felt no concern on their part. But at every one of our little meetings I continued to exhort, and to pray for one and then another, until every one had yielded to Jesus, acknowledging the merits of his pardoning love.

Night after night in my dreams I seemed to be laboring for the salvation of souls. At such times special cases were presented to my mind; these I afterward sought out and prayed with.

Some of our more formal brethren feared that I was too zealous for the conversion of souls; but time seemed to me so short that it behooved all who had a hope of blessed immortality, and looked for the soon coming of Christ, to labor without ceasing for those who were still in their sins and standing on the awful brink of ruin.

Though I was very young, I felt that it was my duty to continue my efforts for the salvation of precious souls, and to pray, and confess Christ at every opportunity. My entire being was offered to the service of my Master. Let come what would, I determined to please God, and live as one who expected the Lord to come and reward the faithful. I felt like a little child coming to God as to my father, and asking him what he would have me to do. Then as my duty was made plain to me, it was my greatest happiness to perform it. Peculiar trials sometimes beset me. Those older in experience than myself endeavored to hold me back, and cool the ardor of my faith; but with the smiles of Jesus brightening my life, and the love of God in my heart, I went on my way with a joyful spirit.

The children and youth who give themselves to God can do a similar work of service for him. It is your privilege to lead your companions and associates to Christ. You can not tell what an influence you may have with the young of your own age. You can give them an example, and the older ones can help the children who want to give their hearts to God. You can have little prayer-meetings. I remember how in my childhood I used to go a mile to attend a little prayer-meeting in a family, and then another day we would go to another, and then to still another family. In these little meetings we used to read the Bible, sing a hymn, pray, and then speak to one another, relating experiences, and telling how we could love and serve God.

I know that if we had such experiences now, we would have happier homes. We would see of the salvation of God, and the light of his countenance would shine upon us. Begin to say that you love the Lord, and that you will give yourselves to him. In doing this, you will begin to have new courage and faith to believe that your hearts are converted, that your souls are saved.

God can not make you good, unless you condescend to be good. You must condescend to be good, and then God will co-operate with you, and he will help you to do good, and to keep from sinful ways. Shall we not together, young and old, get ready for the kingdom of heaven? Before we can enter the gates of the city of God, we must have the spirit that the heavenly beings possess; and we can never have this spirit until we bow in humility before God and accept the cross of Christ. "Whosoever will come after me," the Saviour said, "let him deny himself, and take up his cross, and follow me."

Ellen G. White.

April 27, 1909—The Fruit of Consecrated Service

By consecrated, personal effort, the youth may accomplish a wonderful work for themselves and others. A faithful reflection of the light of truth in good works and helpful words will result in a continual growth in spiritual knowledge. The heart that is influenced by the love of God to labor for needy souls, will be filled with the sweetness of peace and satisfaction. And the Lord will use such youth to do a great and good work for others. Through them he will represent to the world the ineffaceable characteristics of the divine nature.

The Prince of heaven came to this world to live in human nature a perfect life, a life that would be an example for all human beings. He lived a life free from self-seeking, wholly given to the service of others. Christ came in humility. He was of lowly birth. He might have chosen the highest parentage; for he was the Prince of heaven; but he chose to come in poverty and humiliation. The Owner of the world, he had not where to lay his head. Unrecognized and unhonored, he walked in and out among the people for whom he had done so much. Of himself he said, "Foxes have holes, and the birds of the air have nests; but the Son of man hath not where to lay his head." And to his followers he says, "If any man will come after me, let him deny himself, and take up his cross, and follow me."

The blessings that we daily enjoy cost the life of the Son of God. Does it become us to live for self? I tell you, No. We must be Christlike. In word and deed we must reveal a deep and abiding love for others.

"The Word was made flesh, and dwelt among us, ... full of grace and truth.... And of his fulness have all we received, and grace for grace." All who become the sons and daughters of God are possessed of his nature. They are the objects of his love. They dwell in Christ as Christ dwells in God. Knowing the power of his grace, they are commissioned and qualified to bear the message of salvation to a sinful world, to make known his grace and truth. As they consecrate themselves wholly to God, the grace they impart will be continually renewed to them. Converted to the truth, imbued with the Holy Spirit, they are under the transforming influence of divine grace. The life of self-indulgence they once lived becomes changed to a life of service.

We may understand something of our responsibilities to God, but would that we all might be brought into right relation to him. God desires above everything else that we shall love him and keep his commandments, and be happy in his love. He has given us his precious Word that we might live by it. When Christ has done so much for us, should we not show our appreciation of his love? There is a world to be saved. Shall we sit down contentedly in our homes, enjoying the privileges of church fellowship, and yet feel no burden for those who know not the truth? We have a duty to do in helping these to understand the truth for this time. The work of the Lord is to be carried in meekness and lowliness of heart. As God's children we are to have a part in this work, taking him as our helper.

The angels of God are sent forth as ministering spirits to watch the interests of the churches, and to guard and help those souls who are in special need of help and strength. In this work of ministry, God desires to use all who are humble in spirit. But unless we are fitted for service by sanctification through the truth, we shall spoil the pattern that is to reveal to men and women about us the design of heaven. The Spirit must bear witness with our spirit that we are coworkers with Christ, and that we are acting as his messengers. Only as we become partakers of the divine nature can we show that we are bound for a better country, and are only pilgrims and strangers here. If we will take hold of the work of God intelligently, angels of God will be with us to teach us, to lead us, to bless us. Then our hearts will be filled with a satisfaction that we do not dream of while we are careless and indifferent.

We are to reveal our faith in our dress. The time and means that are often spent on outward adornment are in God's sight worse than wasted. The teachings of the gospel are to make us Christians in practise as well as in profession; the truth we hold is to sanctify the soul. Christ bids us seek not that outward adornment, but the adorning of a meek and quiet spirit, which is in the sight of God of great price. It is the spirit of Christ's righteousness that we so greatly need.

There is need that a reformation in many lines be seen among us. We need to let our influence be felt on the side of self-denial. If we really loved the truth, we would talk the truth; we would pray much, and study the Word of God with diligence. And this would make us living channels through which Christ could convey the message of his love and power to many hearts.

Let us not become aliens from the service of Christ. A work is marked out for us by a heavenly Father's hand. It is not a work of drudgery, but a work of joyful service, by which the soul may become ennobled and sanctified, the heart cleansed, the will made obedient, and the life an outflowing of the streams of heavenly beneficence and love. It is not an irksome service, but one that will link the soul with God. Though the walk in life may be the lowliest, it may be dignified by the presence of him who says, "I am with you alway;" "I will never leave thee, nor forsake thee," and be made blessed by the ministration of heavenly beings who are sent forth to minister to them who shall be heirs of salvation.

We need to study our Bibles, and learn daily lessons at the feet of Christ. The formation of character is an individual, personal work; and in this work of character building, it is the privilege of every youth in the midst of abounding iniquity, to make it manifest that he is humble in heart, that he is imbued with the Spirit of God.

Christ is watching to see what spirit we will bring into our service for him. If we realize this, we shall seek to be reconverted daily. Our influence will grow sweeter, and no trace of the spirit that Satan loves to exercise will be seen in our lives. The blessedness of true religion will be revealed in unselfish, compassionate labor for others.

Mrs. E. G. White

May 25, 1909—Christ the Example of Children and Youth

Jesus came to this world as its light. "In him was life; and the life was the light of men." He says of himself, "I am the light of the world: he that followeth me shall not walk in darkness, but shall have the light of life."

The example of Jesus is a light to the young, as well as to those of mature years; for his was a representative childhood and youth. From his earliest years his example was perfect. In both his physical and his spiritual nature he followed the divine order of growth illustrated by the plant, as he wishes all youth to do. Although he was the Majesty of heaven, the King of glory, he became a babe in Bethlehem, and for a time represented the helpless infant in its mother's care. In childhood he did the works of an obedient child. He spoke and acted with the wisdom of a child, and not of a man, honoring his parents, and carrying out their wishes in helpful ways, according to the ability of a child. But at each stage of his development he was perfect, with the simple, natural grace of a sinless life. The sacred record says of his childhood, "The child grew, and waxed strong in spirit, filled with wisdom: and the grace of God was upon him." And of his youth it is recorded, "Jesus increased in wisdom and stature, and in favor with God and man."

The life of Christ, from his earliest years, was a life of earnest activity. He lived not to please himself. He was the Son of the infinite God, yet he worked at the carpenter's trade with his father Joseph. His trade was significant. He had come into the world as the character builder, and as such all his work was perfect. Into all his secular labor he brought the same perfection as into the characters he was transforming by his divine power.

He is our pattern. By many children and youth, time is wasted that might be spent in carrying home burdens, and thus showing a loving interest in father and mother. The youth might take upon their strong young shoulders many responsibilities which some one must bear.

Jesus did not, like many youth, devote his time to amusement. He applied himself diligently to a study of the Scriptures; for he knew them to be full of precious instruction to all who will make them the man of their counsel. He was faithful in the discharge of his home duties; and the early morning hours, instead of being wasted in bed, often found him in a retired place, meditating and searching the Scriptures, and in prayer. Every prophecy concerning his work and mediation was familiar to him, especially those having reference to his humiliation, atonement, and intercession. In childhood and youth the object of his life was ever before him, an inducement for his undertaking the work in behalf of fallen man. He would sow seed which would prolong their days, and the gracious purpose of the Lord should prosper in his hands.

Jesus studied the Word until he became familiar with its sayings. Even in his childhood, he was skilful in their use. When his parents lost him in Jerusalem, he was found sitting among the wise men of the nation, both hearing them and asking them questions. He inquired as one who wished to learn; but in his questions there were gems of light that not only pleased his hearers, but flashed into the Scriptures concerning the Messiah a meaning which these teachers of the law had never before seen. "All that heard him were astonished at his understanding and answers."

When his mother said to him, "Son, why hast thou dealt thus with us? behold, thy father and I have sought thee sorrowing," he answered, "How is it that ye sought me? wist ye not that I must be about my Father's business?" And when they understood not his words, he pointed upward. Although a child, he was engaged in the work that he came to do. He was revealing God, showing the meaning of his word to those leaders in Israel, giving a new significance to their sacrifices and services.

There is here a lesson for all children and youth on the duty of honor and obedience to parents; for the record continues, "He went down with them, and came to Nazareth, and was subject unto them." From Jerusalem he returned home with them, and aided them in their life of toil. He hid in his own heart the mystery of his mission, waiting submissively for the appointed time for him to enter upon his work. For eighteen years after he had recognized that he was the Son of God, he acknowledged the tie that bound him to the home at Nazareth, and performed the duties of a son, a brother, a friend, and a citizen.

Jesus carried into his labor cheerfulness and tact. It requires much patience and spirituality to bring Bible religion into the home life and into the workshop, to bear the strain of worldly business, and yet keep the eye single to the glory of God. This is where Christ was a helper. He was never so full of worldly care as to have no time or thought for heavenly things. Often he expressed the gladness of his heart by singing psalms and heavenly songs. Often the dwellers in Nazareth heard his voice raised in praise and thanksgiving to God. He held communion with heaven in song; and as his companions complained of weariness from labor, they were cheered by the sweet melody from his lips. His praise seemed to banish the evil angels, and like incense, filled the place with fragrance. The minds of his hearers were carried away from their earthly exile, to the heavenly home.

Jesus was the fountain of healing mercy for the world; and through all those secluded years at Nazareth, his life flowed out in currents of sympathy and tenderness. The aged, the sorrowing, and the sin-burdened, the children at play in their innocent joy, the little creatures of the groves, the patient beasts of burden,--all were happier for his presence. He whose word of power upheld the worlds, would stoop to relieve a wounded bird. There was nothing beneath his notice, nothing to which he disdained to minister.

Thus as he grew in wisdom and stature, Jesus increased in favor with God and man. He drew the sympathy of all hearts by showing himself capable of sympathizing with all. The atmosphere of hope and courage that surrounded him made him a blessing in every home. And often in the synagogue on the Sabbath day he was called upon to read the lesson from the prophets, and the hearts of the hearers thrilled as a new light shone out from the familiar words of the sacred text.

Jesus is our example. There are many who dwell with interest upon the period of his public ministry, while they pass unnoticed the teachings of his early years. But it is in his home life that he is the pattern for all children and youth. The Saviour condescended to poverty, that he might teach how closely we in a humble lot may walk with God. He lived to please, honor, and glorify his Father in the common things of life. His work began in consecrating the lowly trade of the craftsmen who toil for their daily bread. He was doing God's service just as much when laboring at the carpenter's bench as when working miracles for the multitude. And every youth who follows Christ's example of faithfulness and obedience in his lowly home, may claim those words spoken of him by the Father through the Holy Spirit, "Behold my servant, whom I uphold; mine elect, in whom my soul delighteth."

Mrs. E. G. White

August 17, 1909—Words to the Young

"God, who commanded the light to shine out of darkness, hath shined in our hearts, to give the light of the knowledge of the glory of God in the face of Jesus Christ." He who believes in Christ becomes one with Christ, to show forth the glory of God; for God hath put a new song into his mouth, even praise unto the Lord. He daily desires to know more of Christ, that he may become more like him. He discerns spiritual things, and enjoys contemplation of Christ; and by beholding him, he is changed, imperceptibly to himself, into the image of Christ. He is after the Spirit, and understands the things of the Spirit. He does not place his dependence for acceptance with God upon what he can do, but relies wholly upon the merits of Christ's righteousness. Yet he knows that he can not be slothful and be a child of God. He searches the Scriptures that testify to him of Christ, that present before him the perfect Pattern.

The believer finds in the Word of God counsel and comfort; and in following the direction, he walks in the path of life. Precious truth is unfolded to his mind, and he receives it into the inner sanctuary of the soul. The attractions of the world become tame to him; for the glory and value of eternity are opened before him. He can say with the apostle, "Now we have received, not the spirit of the world, but the Spirit which is of God; that we might know the things that are freely given to us of God." How can any one persuade himself that the Word of God is but a cunningly devised fable? How can he imagine that the life vitally connected with Christ is uninteresting? O that all might count the cost, and conclude that the most profitable thing for any soul to do is to make his calling and election sure, that day by day he may stand on vantage-ground, looking unto Jesus, the author and finisher of his faith!

He who has a genuine experience in the things of God will not be indifferent to those who are in darkness, but will inquire, What would Jesus say to these poor, needy souls? He will seek to let his light shine forth. He will pray for wisdom, grace, and tact, that he may know how to speak a word in season to him who is weary. In place of engaging in trifling conversation, in jesting and joking, he will, as a faithful steward of the grace of God, make the most of his opportunity, and the seed sown will spring up and bear fruit unto life eternal. The treasure of truth is in his heart, and he brings forth good things. The well-spring of life is in his soul, and the living waters flow forth.

Young men and women, is this your experience? Are you growing up into Christ, your living head? Are you laborers together with God, bearing fruit unto his glory? If not, you are not children of God, for you have not the image and superscription of Christ. You have not a clear title to the heavenly inheritance, and should sickness and death come upon you while you are thus neglecting the salvation so richly provided for you, what record would the books of heaven present? Could you meet that record with joy?

The Lord has given to the youth abundant privileges whereby they may become laborers together with God. They are to be living witnesses for Christ. Their lives and characters should bear decided testimony concerning the riches of Christ; for they should represent the Master, and make manifest the power of the truth upon the soul. But O, how many in life and character show that they are not consecrated to the service of Christ! They live to please themselves. They do not strengthen the church by their efficient efforts, but are rather a burden than burden-bearers. The church is what its members make it, and if names only are added to its records, and there is in the members no zeal, no purity, no intelligence in spiritual things, the church does not have increased power. Those who remain stationary in their religious experience, who do not grow up into Christ, their living head, seeking for perfection of character, are dead weights upon the church. They do not follow Jesus, the light of the world, and therefore have no light to diffuse to those who are sitting in darkness, and the world is no better because of their profession of godliness. Without an accession of spiritual power with its members, the church will fail to meet the expectation of the heavenly intelligences.

O that the youth may consider the life of Christ, and copy the Pattern! If they will do this, they will not be like the foolish virgins, who had no oil in their vessels with their lamps; but they will be wise, having their lamps trimmed and burning, and the cause of truth will not retrograde, the church will not become sickly and ready to die, but its members will become spiritual, and be able to discern spiritual things.

Mrs. E. G. White

January 25, 1910—Decision of Character

Every youth needs to cultivate decision. A divided state of the will is a snare, and has been the cause of ruin to many.

In Bunyan's "Pilgrim's Progress" there is a character called Pliable. Youth, shun this character. Those represented by it are very accommodating but they are as a reed shaken by the wind. They possess no will power. Be firm, else you will find your house--your character--built upon a sandy foundation.

Those who would keep in the path cast up for the ransomed of the Lord, must not be swayed in matters of conscience. They must show moral decision, and must not be afraid of being thought singular.

Many there are who are changed by every current. They wait to hear what some one else thinks, and his opinion is often accepted as altogether true. They do not say to the Lord, "Lord, I can not make any decision until I know thy will." If these youth would lean wholly upon God, they would grow strong in his strength.

We are not to fashion ourselves by the world's criterion or after the world's type. "Dare to be a Daniel; dare to stand alone." Thus, as did Moses, you will endure as seeing him who is invisible. A cowardly and silent reserve before evil associates, makes you one with them.

Have courage to do the right. Possess an individuality of your own. If you would succeed in anything that is elevating and ennobling, you must cultivate firmness for the right.

Jesus has revealed to you your value by the price he has paid for your redemption. Your salvation has been purchased with agony and blood. You have everything in your favor. Everything has been done that God could do. In giving Jesus to be the propitiation for your sins, God gave you power to resist and to overcome evil.

You can be resolute if you will. It will require higher help than any human friend can give you, but that help is promised, if you yourself will consent to form new habits. This will require effort on your part, persistent effort; for if Satan sees you taking a step decidedly for Christ, he will employ every ingenious method to deceive and ruin you. But Christ has provided a refuge for the weak and tempted. His angels will help, shield, and guide every trusting soul.

You have within your reach more than finite possibilities. A man, as God applied the term, is a son of God. "Now are we the sons of God, and it doth not yet appear what we shall be: but we know that, when he shall appear, we shall be like him; for we shall see him as he is. And every man that hath this hope in him purifieth himself, even as he is pure." It is your privilege to turn away from that which is cheap and inferior, and rise to a high standard,--to be respected by men and beloved by God.

The religious work which the Lord gives to young men, and to men of all ages, shows his respect for them as his children. He gives them the work of self-government. He calls them to be sharers with him in the great work of redemption and uplifting. As a father takes his son into partnership in his business, so the Lord takes his children into partnership with himself. We are made laborers together with God. Jesus says, "As thou hast sent me into the world, even so have I also sent them into the world." Would you not rather choose to be a child of God than a servant of Satan and sin, having your name registered as an enemy of Christ?

Young men and women need more of the grace of Christ, that they may bring the principles of Christianity into the daily life. The preparation for Christ's coming is a preparation made through Christ for the exercise of our highest qualities. It is the privilege of every youth to make of his character a beautiful structure. But there is a positive need of keeping close to Jesus. He is our strength and efficiency and power. We can not depend on self for one moment.

Young men and young women, exercise your ability with faithfulness, generously imparting the light that God gives you. Study how best to give to others peace, and light, and truth, and the many rich blessings of heaven. Constantly improve. Keep reaching higher and still higher. It is the ability to put to the tax the powers of mind and body, ever keeping eternal realities in view, that is of value now. Seek the Lord most earnestly, that you may become more and more refined, more spiritually cultured.

However large, however small, your talents, remember that what you have is yours only in trust. Thus God is testing you, giving you opportunity to prove yourself true. To him you are indebted for all your capabilities. To him belong your powers of body, mind, and soul, and for him these powers are to be used. Your time, your influence, your capabilities, your skill,--all must be accounted for to him who gives all. He uses his gifts best who seeks by earnest endeavor to carry out the Lord's great plan for the uplifting of humanity.

Persevere in the work that you have begun, until you gain victory after victory. Educate yourselves for a purpose. Keep in view the highest standard that you may accomplish greater and still greater good, thus reflecting the glory of God.

January 17, 1911—Walk in the Light

The whole earth is to be lightened with the glory of God. But how difficult for some to see and acknowledge the light and be converted, that I, Christ says, should heal them! The atmosphere of selfishness, pride, formality, and self-righteousness surrounds their souls, and it is very difficult for them to discern light as light and appreciate it. Some walk away from the light into darkness, and how much greater is the darkness that enshrouds their souls because they have had the light! Refusing to walk in the light, they stumble at most precious things. Refusing to see the truth, they stumble and know not at what they stumble. The light that has been graciously given has not been appreciated and brought into practical life, and many are not doers of the word. Every true believer should have a realization of his solemn responsibility before God, to be a missionary seeking to save those that are lost. We should see armies of consecrated workers seeking to do, not their own will or pleasure, but the will of God. They should be laborers together with God. They should work, pray, and continually look unto Jesus, who is the author and finisher of their faith. Those who surrender wholly to God will put thought and prayer and earnest, consecrated tact into their labor.

Young men and young women, if you are true disciples of Christ, you will consecrate every talent, and be able to reach out for the unconverted, by ways and methods that will be effective. You will be active, working agencies for Christ. In every church there should be devoted workers. All should realize that they are to seek counsel of God, that by well-directed personal efforts they may save souls for whom Christ died. No sinner should come within the sphere of a Christian's influence and feel that his interest has not been enlisted on the side of Jesus, the Lamb of God, who takes away the sin of the world. Those who profess to believe the truth should walk in the light of the precious beams of the Sun of Righteousness.

Who of our youth will give themselves to God for the purpose of laboring for the salvation of their fellow youth? Who will put their talent out to the exchangers? Who will feel their sacred accountability and put to use every ability given them of God to win souls? Young men and young women, can not you form companies, and, as soldiers of Christ, enlist in the work, putting all your tact and skill and talent into the Master's service, that you may save souls from ruin? Let there be companies organized in every church to do this work. It is stated that when the householder left his servants, "he gave to every man his work." Not one was to be idle.

I appeal to both young and old, and ask, Is Jesus your personal Saviour? If you do not realize that he is yours, by all means make him yours. Then without delay teach others what you have experienced in the Christian life. Instead of being as frail reeds blowing in the wind, show yourselves as those who have root in themselves--that you believe and that you practise the truth, and its sanctifying power is upon your life and character. Then you will be walking in the light while you have the light. Will the young men and young women who really love Jesus organize themselves as workers, not only for those who profess to be Sabbath-keepers, but for those who are not of our faith; for there is no respect of persons with God? All souls are precious; they are the purchase of the blood of the Son of God.

Why has there been so little interest and soul burden for sinners? Many outside of the ranks of Sabbath-keepers, who have not had the light, give more promise of becoming children of God, joint heirs with Jesus, than do those who have had the light of truth, and who have not appreciated it, but have walked in the sparks of their own kindling. No one can labor successfully for souls without true, earnest, unselfish interest. Those who do so labor will see souls converted, and will themselves grow in grace and in the knowledge of our Lord and Saviour Jesus Christ. They will not have a dwarfed experience in the things of God. They will be learners in the school of Christ, and educators as well, making known to others the things which they have learned of Jesus.

Let the young men and young women determine to love God supremely and to do his commandments. Under circumstances the most trying, let them remain faithful to duty--especially in their attitude toward the principles of health reform. Instead of being half-hearted reformers, let them make a whole-hearted reformation, in all things practising chastity and temperance. Let none begin to reform, and then stop. Resolve to overcome the wicked one. True victory is gained only when the repentant sinner pledges himself to unconditional obedience to God,--only when he pledges himself to honor God in every word, every business transaction, every act of his life. Those who do this may be like the youth whom John addressed in the words: "I have written unto you, young men, because ye are strong, and the word of God abideth in you, and ye have overcome the wicked one." It is possible for every youth to gain spiritual strength. Those who endeavor to increase their strength will pass through severe struggles, which will test their sincerity of purpose; but by remaining faithful, they prove that their determination to do God's will is prompted by high and holy motives. In every sense of the word, such youth are able to be overcomers; for Christ overcame in their behalf. Having overcome, they are brought into alliance with divine, unfailing resources.

Young men, young women, you are a spectacle to the world, to angels, and to men. By your determined efforts to be true and righteous, laying your foundation secure in faith, you may be able to provoke the older and more experienced brethren and sisters to love and good works.

E. G. White

July 18, 1911—An Appeal From Our Captain

The work of all believers is to cooperate with Christ in seeking those who are lost. Christ has given this work to his followers, and the members of the church stand arraigned before God as unfaithful, unless they undertake this work disinterestedly and thoroughly. Many will urge that there are other duties that keep them from doing the work, and so excuse themselves from being missionaries for God.

"And they that be wise shall shine as the brightness of the firmament; and they that turn many to righteousness as the stars forever and ever." There are many Christian youth that can do a good work if they will learn lessons in the school of Christ from the great Teacher. Even though pastors, evangelists, and teachers should neglect the seeking of the lost, let not the children and youth neglect to be doers of the word. The lesson of Christ in this scripture is to be received and believed and acted upon in living faith. Let young men, and women, and children go to work in the name of Jesus. Let them unite together upon some plan and order of action. Can not you form a band of workers, and have set times to pray together and ask the Lord to give you his grace, and put forth united action? You should consult with men who love and fear God, who have experience in the work, that under the movings of the Spirit of God, you may form plans and develop methods by which you may work in earnest and for certain results. The Lord will help those who will use their God-entrusted capabilities to his name's glory.

As you labor for others, the divine power of the Spirit will work upon their souls; for they have been purchased by the blood of the only begotten Son of God. We can be successful in winning souls for whom Christ has died, only as we depend on the grace and power of God to do the work of convicting and converting the heart. While you are presenting to them the truth of God, unbelief and uncertainty will strive to hold the mind; but let the pledged word of God expel doubt from your hearts. Take God at his word, and work in faith. Satan will come with his suggestions to make you distrust the word of your Heavenly Father; but consider, "Whatsoever is not of faith is sin." Press your faith through the dark shadow of Satan, and lodge it upon the mercy-seat, and let not one doubt be entertained. This is the only way in which you will gain an experience, and find the evidence so essential for your peace and confidence. As your experience grows, you will have increased ardor of soul, and warmer love for the service of God, because you have oneness of purpose with Jesus Christ. Your sympathies are begotten of the Holy Spirit. You wear the yoke with Christ, and are laborers together with God.

Mrs. E. G. White

November 21, 1911—Christ Our Pattern

I have a deep interest in the youth, and I greatly desire to see them striving to perfect Christian characters, seeking by diligent study and earnest prayer to gain the training essential for acceptable service in the cause of God. I long to see them helping one another to reach a higher plane of Christian experience.

Christ came to teach the human family the way of salvation, and he made this way so plain that a little child can walk in it. He bids his disciples follow on to know the Lord; and as they daily follow his guidance, they learn that his going forth is prepared as the morning. You have watched the rising sun, and the gradual break of day over earth and sky. Little by little the dawn increases, till the sun appears; then the light grows constantly stronger and clearer until the full glory of noontide is reached. This is a beautiful illustration of what God desires to do for his children in perfecting their Christian experience. As we walk day by day in the light he sends us, in willing obedience to all his requirements, our experience grows and broadens until we reach the full stature of men and women in Christ Jesus.

The youth need to keep ever before them the course that Christ followed. At every step it was a course of overcoming. Christ did not come to the earth as a king, to rule the nations. He came as a humble man, to be tempted, and to overcome temptation, to follow on, as we must, to know the Lord. In the study of his life we shall learn how much God through him will do for his children. And we shall learn that, however great our trials may be, they can not exceed what Christ endured that we might know the way, the truth, and the life. By a life of conformity to his example, we are to show our appreciation of his sacrifice in our behalf.

The youth have been bought with an infinite price, even the blood of the Son of God. Consider the sacrifice of the Father in permitting his Son to make this sacrifice. Consider what Christ gave up when he left the courts of heaven and the royal throne to give his life a daily sacrifice for men. He suffered reproach and abuse. He bore all the insult and mockery that wicked men could heap upon him. And when his earthly ministry was accomplished, he suffered the death of the cross. Consider his sufferings on the cross,--the nails driven into his hands and feet, the derision and abuse from those he came to save, the hiding of his Father's face. But it was by all this that Christ made it possible for all who will to have the life that measures with the life of God.

We shall appreciate more fully all that God has made possible for us if we will study more faithfully what great things Heaven has already done. Our redemption cost too much for us to regard as a light thing the salvation which God's Word bids us work out in our experience. Never feel that you need not be particular about the course you pursue; for you can never enter heaven until you have learned what it means to represent the life of Christ, until you have learned the need of living in dependence upon him. The powers of darkness are constantly gaining victories over those who do not serve God with full purpose of heart; but all who will follow on day by day to practise the virtues of Christ will triumph grandly over evil.

Many of us need a clearer understanding of what it means to overcome by the blood of the Lamb and the word of our testimony. The word of our testimony means a great deal. It is borne before all the universe of heaven, and before the world. The soul who by word or act dishonors God, places himself on the losing side. Satanic agencies gain the advantage, and the world loses the power that soul might have exerted for the right had he honored God.

Each one will have trials to meet. Each one has the natural temperament to contend with; but this is to be brought into subjection to Christ. The Lord will help all who will do their best, walking humbly with him. Let us be encouraged by the thought that we have a Mighty Arm to lean upon, and that so long as we rely upon his strength, we can not dishonor him.

We are on trial now, but under every test let us make it manifest to all around us that we are on the Lord's side. I am so thankful that none need dishonor Christ! We may all win heaven; we may all be welcomed to the city of God by the Father and the Son; we may all wear the crown of immortality.

The Lord looks with deepest interest on each striving soul. He loves each one. Did he not, he never would have given his only begotten Son to die.

When Christ ascended to the Father, he did not leave his followers without help. The Holy Spirit, as his representative, and the heavenly angels, as ministering spirits, are sent forth to aid those who against great odds are fighting the good fight of faith. Ever remember that Jesus is your helper. No one understands so well as he your peculiarities of character. He is watching over you, and if you are willing to be guided by him, he will throw around you influences for good that will enable you to accomplish all his will for you.

In this life we are preparing for the future life. Soon there is to be a grand review, in which every soul who is seeking to perfect a Christian character must bear the test of God's searching questions: Have you set an example that others were safe in following? Have you watched for souls as those that must give an account? The heavenly host are interested in the youth; and they are intensely desirous that you will bear the test, and that to you will be spoken the words of approval, "Well done, good and faithful servant; ... enter thou into the joy of thy Lord."

Let the youth remember that here they are to build characters for eternity, and that God requires them to do their best. Let those older in experience watch over the younger ones; and when they see them tempted, take them aside, and pray with them and for them. The Lord would have us recognize the great sacrifice of Christ for us by showing an interest in the salvation of those he came to save. If the youth will seek Christ, he will make their efforts effectual.

"Let not your heart be troubled," the Savior says; "ye believe in God, believe also in me. In my Father's house are many mansions; if it were not so, I would have told you. I go to prepare a place for you. And if I go and prepare a place for you, I will come again, and receive you unto myself; that where I am, there ye may be also."

Christ is preparing a place for us. Shall we prepare a place for him, in our homes, in our school life, in our gatherings for worship? God help us to do this. "If ye love me," Christ declared, "keep my commandments. And I will pray the Father, and he shall give you another Comforter, that he may abide with you forever; even the Spirit of truth; whom the world can not receive, because it seeth him not, neither knoweth him: but ye know him; for he dwelleth with you, and shall be in you.... He that hath my commandments, and keepeth them, he it is that loveth me: and he that loveth me shall be loved of my Father, and I will love him, and will manifest myself unto him."

Many of us are too half-hearted. We give up under trial, and let discouragement sap our spiritual strength. Let us change this manner of service. When we serve God with the entire affections, we shall see the salvation of God in our own experience and in the experience of others. Christ lives to make intercession for us. He wants to set his seal upon us, and to fashion our characters after the divine pattern. He wants to take from us everything that would stand in the way of our reaching the standard of his Word. He wants us to believe in him, and to turn away from our sins. He calls us to reach perfection. We can fulfil his purpose for us only as we study his life and follow his example.

April 23, 1912—Words to the Young

In all his godlike deeds, the world's Redeemer declares, "I can of mine own self do nothing." "This commandment have I received of my Father." All I do is in fulfilment of the counsel and will of my Heavenly Father. The history of the daily earthly life of Jesus is the exact record of the fulfilment of the purposes of God toward man. His life and character were the unfolding or representation of the perfection of the character that man may attain by becoming a partaker of the divine nature, and overcoming the world through daily conflicts. Jesus assumed human nature that he might work with human nature, and bring fallen man across the gulf which transgression had made between God and his creatures.

The Lord of life and glory clothed his divinity with humanity to demonstrate to man that God through the gift of Christ would connect us with him. Without a connection with God no one can possibly be happy. Fallen man is to learn that our Heavenly Father can not be satisfied until his love embraces the repentant sinner, transformed through the merits of the spotless Lamb of God. The work of all the heavenly intelligences is to this end. Under the command of their General they are to work for the reclaiming of those who by transgression, have separated themselves from their Heavenly Father. A plan has been devised whereby the wondrous grace and love of Christ shall stand revealed to the world. In the infinite price paid by the Son of God to ransom man, the love of God is revealed. This glorious plan of redemption is ample in its provisions to save the whole world. Sinful and fallen man may be made complete in Jesus through the forgiveness of sin, and the imputed righteousness of Christ.

Jesus Christ laid hold on humanity, that with his human arm he might encircle the race, while with his divine arm he grasped the throne of the Infinite. He planted his cross midway between earth and heaven, and said, "I, if I be lifted up from the earth, will draw all men unto me." The cross was to be the center of attraction. It was to speak to all men, and draw them across the gulf that sin had made, to unite finite man with the infinite God. It is the power of the cross alone that can separate man from the strong confederacy of sin. Christ gave himself for the saving of the sinner. Those whose sins are forgiven, who love Jesus, will be united with him. They will bear the yoke of Christ. This yoke is not to hamper them, not to make their religious life one of unsatisfying toil. No; the yoke of Christ is to be the very means by which the Christian life is to become one of pleasure and joy. The Christian is to be joyful in contemplation of that which the Lord has done in giving his only begotten Son to die for the world, "that whosoever believeth in him should not perish, but have everlasting life."

Those who stand under the blood-stained banner of Prince Immanuel should be faithful soldiers in Christ's army. They should never be disloyal, never be untrue. Many of the young will volunteer to stand with Jesus, the Prince of life. But if they would continue to stand with him, they must constantly look unto Jesus, their Captain, for his orders. They can not be soldiers of Christ, and yet engage with the confederacy of Satan, and help on his side, for then they would be enemies of Christ. They would betray sacred trusts. They would form a link between Satan and the true soldiers, so that through these living agencies the enemy would be constantly working to steal away the hearts of Christ's soldiers.

I ask you, dear youth, who profess to be soldiers of Jesus Christ, what battles have you fought? what have been your engagements? When the Word of God has plainly revealed your work, have you refused to do it because it did not suit your inclination? Has the attraction of the world allured you from the service of Christ? Satan is employed in devising specious allurements; and by transgression in what seem little matters, he draws you away from Jesus. Then larger attractions are presented to seduce you fully from God. You may have your name upon the church books, and claim to be a child of God, yet your example, your influence, misrepresents the character of Christ, and you lead others away from him. There is no happiness, no peace or joy, to a professed believer whose whole soul is not enlisted in the work the Lord has given him to do. He is constantly bringing the world into the church, not by repentance and confession and surrender to God, but by surrendering more and more to the world, and engaging on Satan's side in the battle, rather than on Christ's side. I would appeal to the youth to cut the finest thread which binds you in practise and in spirit with the world. "Come out from among them, and be ye separate, saith the Lord, and touch not the unclean thing; and I will receive you, and will be a Father unto you, and ye shall be my sons and daughters, saith the Lord Almighty."

Will our youth heed this voice of invitation? How little do our young people realize the necessity of setting before their youthful associates a Christlike example in their life and character. Many of our youth understand the theory of the truth, but how few understand by experimental knowledge the practical bearing of the truth upon their every action. Where are youthful missionaries doing any work that represents itself to them in the great harvest-field? Where are those who are daily learners in the school of Christ? Let them never feel that they are prepared to graduate. Let them wait in the courts of the Lord, that they may be directed as to how to work in unison with the heavenly intelligences. Dear youth, I wish to speak decidedly to you because I want you to be saved. Lose no more time. You can not serve God and mammon. You may apparently be Christians, but when temptations come, when sorely tried, do you not generally yield?

The conflict in which you have to take an active part is found in your every-day life. Will you not in times of trial lay your desires by the side of the Written Word, and in earnest prayer seek Jesus for counsel? Many declare that it is certainly no harm to go to a concert and neglect the prayer-meeting, or absent themselves from meetings where God's servants are to declare a message from heaven. It is safe for you to be just where Christ has said he would be. Those who appreciate the words of Christ will not turn aside from the prayer-meeting, or from the meeting where the Lord's messenger has been sent to tell them concerning things of eternal interest. Jesus has said, "Where two or three are gathered together in my name, there am I in the midst of them." Can you afford to choose your pleasure and miss the blessing? It is indulgence in these things that has a telling influence not only on your own life and character, but upon the life and character of your associates. If all who profess to be followers of Christ would be so in deed and in truth, they would have the mind of Christ, and would work the works of God. They would resist temptation to indulge self, and would show that they do not enjoy the frivolous pleasure of the world more than the privilege of meeting with Christ in the social meeting. They would then have a decided influence upon others, and lead them to follow their example.

Actions speak louder than words, and those who are lovers of pleasure do not appreciate the rich blessings of being in the assembly of the people of God. They do not appreciate the privilege of influencing their associates to go with them, hoping that their hearts will be touched by the Spirit of the Lord. Who goes with them into these worldly gatherings? Jesus is not there to bless those assembled. But Satan will bring to the mind many things to crowd out matters of eternal interest. It is his opportunity to confuse the right by mixing it up with the wrong. Through attendance at worldly gatherings a taste is created for exciting amusements, and moral power is weakened. Those who love pleasure may keep up a form of godliness, but they have no vital connections with God. Their faith is dead, their zeal has departed. They feel no burden to speak a word in season to souls who are out of Christ, and to urge them to give their hearts to the Lord.

June 9, 1914—Following on to Know the Lord

[Remarks by Mrs. E. G. White, Sanitarium, church school picnic, June 15, 1913.]

I am glad to have the privilege of meeting with those that have gathered here today. I feel an earnest desire that every one of you shall be victorious in the struggle against evil. For many years I have been laboring for the salvation of souls. I began this work at a very early age, and all through my life the Lord has sustained me in telling old and young of the hope that we have in Christ.

I have always had an especial interest in the youth. I see before me today those whom I know God can use if they will put their dependence in him. Children, if you will be in earnest in serving God, you will be a help to all with whom you associate. There is nothing to be ashamed of in being a Christian. It is an honor to follow the Saviour. And it is by obeying the instructions that he has given that you are to be prepared to meet him when he comes. If you will ask God to help you to overcome what is un-Christlike in your dispositions, he will prepare you for entrance into heaven, where no sin can enter. Those who daily give the life to Jesus, and who follow on to know him, will be greatly blessed. Say, Christ gave his life for me, and I must give my life for him. If you give yourselves wholly to him, you will be conquerors in the warfare against sin. The Lord Jesus will be your helper, your support, your strength, if you will receive and obey him.

To the older ones who are present, I wish to say, Set before the younger ones an example that will help them to press forward in the upward way. Remember that your words and acts have an influence upon them for good or for evil. It is unworthy a Christian to neglect to make every effort in his power to help those for whom the Saviour gave his life. Christ died that we might live, and we want to be sure that we are trying to do his will. Then we shall be acceptable to him. Angels of God will be near to help us, and we shall realize the aid of a power above ourselves.

I have recently been studying what we older ones can do to make the best impression upon the minds of the youth. What can we do? Let us study the Word, and as we have opportunity, talk Bible truth. As you do this, you will find that your own mind and heart are becoming subdued. As you strive to overcome everything that is displeasing to God, angels of heaven will help you to exert a right influence upon those who are younger. You will not be left to stumble along in uncertainty, not knowing what you are doing. Power from above will be given you, to enable you to show to others that we have a living Saviour, a Redeemer who can forgive our transgressions.

You can help the younger ones. You can be a blessing to them, even to the very young. And when Christ shall come in the clouds of heaven, he will say: "You have followed on to know me. I acknowledge you as my servants." You will have light in the Lord, and the glory of the Lord will be your rearward.

To these students I would say, Do not think it is an amusing thing to take advantage of a fellow student, and to lead him astray. God wants you to be constantly reaching higher and still higher for attainments that will enable you to help others, to be an example to those around you. And as you do this, the Lord will surely let his blessing rest upon you. But do not go only halfway in your efforts to serve God. Do not feel that there is no need of being particular. From the oldest to the youngest, you do need to be particular to avoid evil, even the appearance of evil. It is possible for the youth to be such earnest Christians that through them the Lord will send the truth home to those who have never known him.

I was very young when I began to serve the Lord. I am now eighty-five years old. In my childhood affliction came to me, and I have been a sufferer all my life. But the Lord has been my strength to do his service, and I have been able to speak again and again to congregations numbering thousands of people. For a great many years I have been engaged in active labor, speaking to the people and writing out the instruction opened before me. At times sickness has come upon me, and then I would cast my helpless soul upon Jesus Christ, and say: "Thou knowest, Lord, that I have chosen thee as my Redeemer. Give me not only spiritual strength, but physical strength, that I may follow on to know thee." And the Lord has never forsaken me. Always he has been my helper, as he will be yours if you will trust in him. It is because I so greatly desire to work for the salvation of souls that I do not give up to infirmities. I am determined that as long as God permits me to live, I will proclaim the message of warning to the world. I want my voice to reach many more before I shall give up my labors. I expect to have trials, but I do not dread them. The Lord knows what I can bear, and he will give me strength to endure. He will sustain me in my weakness, enabling me to follow on, and to know that his going forth is prepared as the morning.

Students, be determined that you will follow on to know the Lord. Remember that angels are beside you. They see all your efforts against wrong. They understand all your difficulties; and if in meekness you will give up your own way for Christ's way, taking his yoke cheerfully, you will find that he will give you daily strength to overcome. As I see you all here, the thought comes to me, Shall I meet them in the kingdom of heaven? What a meeting that will be when the redeemed are gathered home, saved, eternally saved. They have fought the good fight. They have pressed the battle to the gates. They have done all in their power to help others to follow in the Saviour's footsteps.

I know that there are many here who are trying to overcome through the blood of the Lamb and the word of their testimony. I want to say to you, Jesus wants every one of you. He died that you and I might be among those who shall wear the crown of life. He wants you, from the oldest to the youngest, to place your influence on his side. He wants your help. I pray that those who today have listened to me will lay hold upon the hope set before them in the gospel. I pray that in the great day of Christ's coming, their voices will help to swell the song of joy and triumph that will be raised by the overcomers. I beg of you, dear youth, to link up with Jesus Christ. He died on Calvary's cross for you and for me, and in his strength we may overcome.

Follow on to know the Lord. If you will do this, you will win souls to Christ. Not only will your own soul be saved; the power that converts your soul will enable you to set an example that will win others to Christ. These older children can be an example to the younger ones, leading and guiding them aright, speaking a word in season to them. Thus you can be laborers together with God. I want to say to these boys, You can overcome evil--evil thoughts, evil desires--by the blood of the Lamb and the word of your testimony. We cannot afford to sin. It costs too much. May the Lord bless you all. We shall think of you and pray for you. I want to offer a word of prayer now.

[Praying] Heavenly Father, we come to thee just as we are, needy and dependent. And we ask thee, Lord, that the few words spoken here today may lead those who have heard to seek with all their hearts to overcome by the blood of the Lamb and the word of their testimony. Lord, wilt thou work by thy Spirit, and let the light of truth shine into human hearts, that souls may turn to thee, and repent and be converted, that we may meet them in the kingdom of glory. Amen.

Don't lead people to believe they can go there and take their sins right along. The characters must be changed here. We must learn to sing the songs of redemption here if we ever sing the song of redemption in heaven. Sing of His goodness. Talk of His power.

Other important books of Ellen G. White that will be available very soon:

All available on Amazon

(LARGE PRINT A4)

1. Lesson from the Life of Solomon.
2. Lessons from the life of Daniel.
3. Lessons from the life of Nehemiah.
4. An exhaustive commentary on the book of Daniel.
5. An exhaustive commentary on the book of Revelation.
6. Loma Linda Messages.
7. Manuscripts of Ellen G. White Series (1844-1915).
8. Letters of Ellen G. White Series (1844-1915).
9. 1888 Materials Volumes 1-4.
10. Country Living.
11. Healthful Living.
12. Christian Temperance and Bible Hygiene.
13. Testimony Treasures 3 Volumes in 1.
14. Spiritual Gifts 4 Volume in One Book.
15. The Kress Collection.
16. Paulson Collection.
17. Spalding and Magan Collection.
18. Signs of The Times 4 Volumes.
19. Sermons and Talks Two Volumes in One.
20. Review and Herald 6 Volumes.
21. Manuscript Releases 21 Volumes.
22. Battle Creek Letters

AND MORE WILL COMING!!!!

*If you want to purchase at wholesale, the minimum are 50 books and you can contact us by email: kalhelministries21@gmail.com

Other important books from the message of 1888 available in english:

1. In Search of the Cross, Author: Robert J. Wieland.
2. Introduction to the 1888 message, Author: Robert J. Wieland.
3. 1888 Re-examined, Authors: Robert J. Wieland y Donald K. Short.
4. The Knocking at the Door, Author: Robert J. Wieland.
5. 10 Big Truths About The Gospel, Author: Robert J. Wieland.
6. Our Glorious Future, Author: Robert J. Wieland.
7. Modern Revivals, Author: Robert J. Wieland.
8. The Word was made Flesh, Author: Ralph Larson.
9. Proclaim his Power, Author: Ralph Larson.
10. The Gospel in the Book of Galatians, Author: E. J. Waggoner.
11. Letters to Romans, Author: E. J. Waggoner.
12. Everlasting Covenant, Author: E. J. Waggoner.
13. Christ and his Righteousness, Author: E. J. Waggoner.
14. 1888 Materials; Volumes 1-4 in english, Author: Elena G. de White.
15. The Consecrated Way to Christian Perfection, Author: A. T. Jones.
16. The Third Angel's Message; 3 Volúmenes, Author: A. T. Jones.
17. Lessons on Faith, Authors: A. T. Jones y E. J. Waggoner.
18. What every Adventist should know about 1888, Arnold V. Wallenkampf.
19. The Sanctuary and its Service, M. L. Andreasen.

AND MORE WILL COMING!!!!

*If you want to purchase at wholesale, the minimum are 50 books and you can contact us by email: kalhelministries21@gmail.com